CLIVE Rowland
MOUNTAIN SPORTS

Quality equipment and
advice for skiing,
camping, backpacking,
snowboarding, rock
and ice climbing
expeditions, skate
boarding,
mountaineering and
hillwalking

9/11 BRIDGE STREET,
INVERNESS.
TEL. 01463 238746

89 GRAMPIAN ROAD,
AVIEMORE.
TEL. 01479 810239

OLD MAN OF STOER
PHOTOGRAPH - EDDIE WEIR

Summit Meeting: Camera call on the top of Ben Nevis for those who attended the Christmas 1978 Meet at the CIC Hut. Back: Gordon McKenzie, Neil Quinn, Gerry Peet, Colin Stead, Doug Lang, Stuart Smith, Chris Gilmore, Andrew Walker and Dave Dawson. Front: Ken Crocket, Ian Fulton and Bob Richardson. *Photo Ken Crocket.*

THE SCOTTISH MOUNTAINEERING CLUB JOURNAL

| Vol. XXXVI | 1998 | No. 189 |

A SIGN OF THE TIMES

By Mike Jacob

OCCASIONALLY, I feel the strength of memories and the necessity to try and turn them into words. So, I've come to write this. The memories, like the boulders at the edge of the river, are softened and cloaked by the delicate green mosses and lichens of time and are jumbled up in no particular order – they are of wet heather and glistening rock and mist swirling on the steep, craggy hillside opposite and the tinkling, gurgling of the water at my feet. That is how it should be, for the place of which I write was created in no ordered way by the forces of Nature, by glacier and river and wind and ice, into one of those magical cradles that, I suppose, we all recognise, have, somewhere.

Now, the irony; that perfect place, created by random events, was subjected to the arranging forces of machinery, the stultifying design of man, and was thus destroyed, reduced by the unfeeling to inanimate objects for the unseeing. It had been the sort of place for the scattering of ashes in the wind, for the freeing of the spirit in such a place would have been entirely appropriate.

I can close my eyes, even as I sit in a warm room distanced in all dimensions from events, and see it all and the image is so strong that I can sense the smells, hear the wind, feel the cold and hunch my shoulders against the billowing cloud of sleet sweeping relentlessly down the glen on a biting easterly. I found the place by accident and was drawn back time after time. It wasn't far to walk but it might have been miles for, once there, it was a place of solitude.

I first went to Torridon as one of a group of inexperienced students and knew little of the realities of Winter's harsh wee traps, but, for all that, we had the power of youth. The southern flanks of Liathach seemed to overhang Glen Cottage so we scratched around the western end and, in an impossible wind, got as far as Mullach an Rathain but could manage no further. I had no crampons in those penniless and novice days. It was this occasion, and another day in the Mamores when we skarted around on hard névé getting nowhere whilst spiked demigods skipped round the summits, that induced me to spend my book grant on a pair of crampons from Rodney Street. I remember, now, why we tried from the west - it was because the wind was screaming in from that direction, so, of course, we had our backs to it. When we got to the cairn and clawed our way over the icy stones, I looked out behind me. The clouds parted and, like a sledge-hammer blow in the chest, I saw for the first time a pattern of sea-lochs and islands and distant peaks and not the blue sparkle of summer but the hard steel blue-grey of North Atlantic convoys.

> *But pleasures are like poppies spread –*
> *You seize the flow'r, its bloom is shed;*
> *Or like the snow falls in the river –*
> *A moment white – then melts forever.*
> **Robert Burns.**

The clouds raced in and the vision was gone but, in that instant, I had glimpsed Tir na n-Og.

I went back. Went to rock-climb the Northern Pinnacles and abseiled off ice-glazed rocks in a blizzard, whooping and sliding the tension away as we stumbled down. We got lost in the mist in Coire Liath Mhor looking for the 'easy' way and half-heartedly attempted a cleft drooling with ice before retreating over avalanching slabs. Retreat again after the first two pitches of a then unclimbed Central Buttress on Beinn Eighe in deep powder; thankfully, our start had been too late in the day, perhaps a subconscious ploy. These events did not count as failures for they were full of laughter. The winter traverse of Liathach, when it finally came, was worth the waiting years. The cold, the adrenalin pumping at the sight of the Patagonian-like Fasarinen and, near the end, out of the upwelling clouds, floated two, three golden eagles a wing's span away.

One summer, while Glasgow basked in a heatwave, I fulfilled a long-held dream and sailed a boat into Loch Torridon and anchored behind the island at Shieldaig. The rain and midges didn't matter for once; we had a cosy cabin warmed by a driftwood fire, good music, food and wine.

October was a regular visiting time. There was a wood-panelled room, another cosy fire, and a library of old books. Winter's chill was in the air and it always seemed to rain. The bracken was turning brown and there were few people about. Just to walk around the glens, with the mist down, although not giving the warm thrill of touching summer rock or the pressure of a winter's climb, seemed to reflect the season. Matching this autumnal atmosphere I discovered the technique of standing still. You stand there and gradually become part of the landscape and you see things that you would otherwise miss, like otters and reflections and fleeting hues of colour. This standing business is only incidental, by the way, for it's part of fly-fishing for those small sea-trout called finnock or herling.

A long, long time ago.
And yet if you are often on a hill
and know the places in the rocks and trees
where fairies and wise folk still love to play,
a moment comes when all the world grows still
and seems to wait for something, and the day
forgets that you are there.
Geoffrey Winthrop Young.

That is how I discovered the Abhain Thraill.

In spate, and especially high up between rock walls, the river is a roaring, spraying, foaming torrent of quite spectacular power. Even the feeder ditches that drain the heathery moor can be difficult to cross. When the water level started to fall, with much stealth, I would creep around the big, mossy boulders and search the back-eddies and glides with a couple of flashy wet-flies. I was captivated by the place and, resting the rod in the bog myrtle, became part of it.

Occasionally, if the conditions were right, I would take some of those pink-fleshed silver fish home for supper. One afternoon, as the hail drummed the back of my hood, there was an almighty pull on the line and a huge commotion in the water. I almost fell in. Line raced off the reel and then I saw a great shape leap out of the water - a salmon! It landed back with a shimmering splash and the line went slack. Try as I might, I could not get it to take one of the flies again. In keeping with the place, however, and in the fading light, we were both free to go. I never saw anyone else there.

Then, one year, I went back again. Something had happened. There was a sign near the road - 'Private Fishing' - and a car park. The little sheep path had been bulldozed into a Land-Rover track and, with increasing dismay, I discovered that the wildness had gone. Huge machines had piled those boulders, white bellies up, like so many bloated carcasses, at the side of the river which now resembled, in places, a canal imported from the English midlands. It had been done to 'improve' the fishing where such a thing is judged by numbers caught and entered in the hotel catch-book.

Angry and saddened, I later found some comfort in the wood-panelled room, in the words of William Henry Davies, to the same old question, echoed by Iain Smart* - Must it always end like this?

No time to see, in broad daylight
Streams full of stars, like skies at night.

When I originally wrote this, I wasn't sure how I wanted it to end, so it remained filed away, unfinished. I had been going to sound off about the destruction of wild places, afforestation and the like, but it was out of place. Then, last October, I went back, after a gap of several years. It was raining in Galloway, raining in Inverness and raining in Torridon. The hills were streaked with blazes of white fury as water cascaded down. A friend and I made the walk.

The feet of many sheep had rolled rocks down the eroding slopes onto the car-park and the river, thundering in swollen rage, would have none of artificial constraints and was returning to its old course.

Not there yet but it's fighting back and, to help, I threw the Private Fishing sign in the river and watched as the water spat it joyfully in the air and swept it towards the sea.

*An encounter with Gramsci. SMCJ No. 182. pp. 593 - 596, 1991.

FULFILMENT

Here, where the evening deer
Come down to drink,
I quietly wait for kindly fate
To help me think
Of some eternal magic.

No need. It happens,
For long legged bards
Dip into vocabularies
Of clear and rippling waters,
Then fill the early night
With odes and sonnets of peace.

Once rested,
They bound for another horizon
To antler a poem on the page
Of gently gathering dusk

George Philip.

CRACKERS

By Andy Nisbet

'CLIMB an overhanging crack with crackers,' said my new guidebook. What's a cracker? said me, the beginner rock-climber, and how do I climb it without even knowing what one is? But it was still irritating although Ventricle had the awesome grade of VS, and I would never be trying it. A week later at the end of a Glenmore Lodge beginners' course, there was still a weekend before work, so Alfie and I dragged half our fellow course members up to Coire an Lochain and Western Route. Now it was 'still technically Severe' despite 'employing combined tactics', and we didn't employ any, partly because we didn't know how. And Ventricle was only a grade harder; but what was a cracker?

Twelve years later I still didn't know what a cracker was, but I knew the winter Coire an Lochain had an awful lot of corners and not many routes, though Ventricle was last on the list. Colin and I had just climbed Auricle in an hour-and-a-half, so it was only lunchtime. 'How about Ventricle?' he said. 'You're crackers,' said me, and went home for tea.

Colin and I had arranged to climb together that winter (on the dole) and had been training through the autumn; we even climbed Insect Groove on the Aberdeen coast very quietly and without a single crampon scratch. Three weeks later it was Tough-guy, but December's short days and Lochnagar's deep powder soon brought darkness and we missed out the last pitch. Christmas brought Brian up for a few days and Colin away for a couple. Somewhat unaware of the competitive spirit, since I would always try equally to pass the crux on to either of them, I was naive not to realise that repeating Tough-guy with Brian on Boxing Day, in order to complete the summer route, was like lighting the touchpaper. I had arranged to climb with Colin the next day and as I struggled to find a line through the overhangs, having refused to concede to the dark for a second time, I struggled to find a solution involving Brian.

I solved it after the overhangs by a late evening phone call to Sandy. Returning to Aberdeen at midnight and leaving for Coire an Lochain at 4am left my resistance weakened against the unstoppable force towards Ventricle. But I would second anything, I said. It was a bitterly cold day so while we stopped for a brew in Jean's Hut, Colin warmed up by doing one-arm pull-ups with his winter sack on. This feat of strength, however, failed to intimidate Brian from joining us on Ventricle. The same could not be said for the three-hour wait at the bottom in wind and spindrift while Colin led the first pitch, so Brian somewhat sniffily said they might as well do that Auricle thing, even if it was only Grade IV.

In the meantime, I had been belaying Colin. The cliff was extremely wintry, deeply frosted and verglassed underneath; whether in or out of condition I'm not sure, but certainly unfriendly. The initial crack was brutal but Colin disposed of it by relentless power, then a traverse along a ledge and another hard wall to a niche. Through the wind I tried to suggest that the summer route was on the right but the overhanging groove had been keyed in. A peg was placed at head-height and the power switched on. Three one-arm pull-ups till the thin mantelshelf at the top spat him down to a thump on the ledge and a bounce into steep ground below. Despite my anxiety, firstly, that he might have hurt himself and, secondly, that the route wouldn't go, the aggression above merely increased and the groove succumbed with three one-arm pull-ups and an extra grunt. So now the frozen object at ground level had to climb.

The first wall was very tiring torquing up a wide and verglassed crack, then removing the last runner and a reach out right for good turf. Then the realisation that the body would be dangling down a blank overhanging wall and a lock-off would be required to reach for the next ledge. Possibly ability, and certainly willpower, was lacking, and the next runner was 10ft off to the right. So I retreated to the crack, where a failed attempt to regain strength forced a direct try. But the wall above bulged too much. A strangled brain hung on for ages trying to find a solution before, certainly in terms of energy supplies, gravity made the question irrelevant and I swung out into space inelegantly back behind the start. Now the brain received a little more warm blood and insisted on the only solution as starting up a groove away to the left (now Ventriloquist) and traversing to the top of the wall. The solution worked despite the loss of nervous energy due to the runner being 40ft sideways and the ground 20ft below. Now warmed up, I reached the groove. There were no placements and no footholds. I would have said impossible except I'd just seen it done, twice! I would have given up except for the irresistible force from above. My feet didn't touch the rock either and I landed below an even bigger and sillier groove. There was no worry about agreeing to carry on; the outcome was obvious and I didn't need to worry about seconding it.

Wrong again. Soon Colin was somewhere out behind my head and I was huddled at the bottom of the groove to escape from the wind. I couldn't see much; my neck doesn't bend that far. The groove was packed with snow but it fell out into mid air as I tried to make myself as small as possible to escape the weather and reality. Eventually, the axes were clipped and a high Friend and long sling allowed an escape to be made. Slow progress continued as the weather deteriorated and the spindrift started to penetrate even the back of my groove. The awful moment was approaching when I'd be expected to defy mid air. To my amazement, I found I could back-and-foot the groove, nearly as much outwards as upwards, until I could reach the sling and swarm over the top.

The bewilderment helped me up the next groove into twilight and, as the light faded, my determination surfaced from the depths. I'd climbed the overhanging groove; I still couldn't believe it was possible, but I was here. Admittedly, below a plumb-vertical smooth-walled corner plastered with snow and in the dark, but I had made it! And I certainly wasn't going to climb these grooves again on a future attempt. So no way were we abbing off. This bravado was fortunately reinforced by a perfect axe crack which miraculously appeared out of the deep frost, only waning 6ft below the top when holds and strength disappeared simultaneously. A weird thread allowed axes to be clipped and holds uncovered, before recovering enough strength to reach on to the powdery ledge above, crossing fingers for the 50/50 chance that the placements were good and the feet would hold. Which they did.

We were now on a huge ledge below a big wall and wide crack, looking even bigger and wider in the blizzard now on the go. But no way was I climbing those grooves again, so it was, hopefully, out right as the only possibility. And there was a chimney full of blocks and powder. 'I should put in a runner, but I'm too tired to dig for one,' I rationalised. So I was on the top, in the middle of the night, and the grooves were history. When the new grading system appeared; I suggested 9 for the bottom groove. On reflection, I should have said 10. And Colin wanted to grade the route IV because it was short!

I would never have to go back to those grooves. With only one snag; Brian wouldn't forget! Thirteen years later he still hadn't forgotten, and I had run out of other suggestions. I really didn't want to relive the nightmare but I'd been persuading him for 10 years to go somewhere else. And now I couldn't. It wasn't even very snowy, but that was no good either. So here we were, sacks dumped to look and see if there was enough snow on it. At first it looked a bit odd, ledges piled up with snow but vertical walls have no ledges, so a bit bare. But the grooves were full of ice, not very thick but well smeared, and even the walls below the ledges were smeared. You had to be at the right angle to see the light reflected off the ice, or you had to start to climb, when it became immediately obvious. So we did both.

The initial crack was again mean and icy; your lead, Brian. So he just reached over the ledge from the extra metre of snow in the gully and pulled up on the hard névé. Thirteen years' of fear was over in 30 seconds; how silly. Conditions were great; how often in the Cairngorms do you get snow-ice on the ledges? Soon Brian reached the dreaded groove. He poked his head in out of curiosity. 'Impossible,' he said, and turned his attention to the obvious crack of the summer route; so deeply covered with frost before that Colin hadn't seen it. But it wasn't that simple; the crack was good but the footholds were rounded breaks, and when the crack ran out, the footholds were still rounded breaks. At least there was some ice for placements but when that broke you were off, or at least Brian was. But it was sensible, so when he got up second time round, so did I. And the overhanging groove above, well I knew the trick. But could I free it? The memories were still too strong, and Brian was fired up. So he bridged it, and later I back-and-footed it, and both went free. But it's still an amazing groove. Now Brian hates losing his momentum, and that's what belaying does, so he just kept going and freed it all. The top corner was initially very icy, front pointing even, and no runners, so quite scary. We'd already climbed the wide crack on a winter ascent of Daddy Longlegs, and fortunately, the final pitch of Daddy Longlegs was bare of winter, so I could volunteer to lead the last pitch again. And we were up by lunchtime. I'm not telling you what he suggested for the afternoon; it might all start over again.

THE PRESIDENT'S MEAT

By Colin Stead

IT WAS up to CIC again for the meet, on the sole good weekend weather forecast this stormy winter. The morning did dawn clear, blue and windless, but our exit was as dilatory as ever, so that the hill was swarming with folk as we puffed up Observatory Gully, looking for inspiration. There was much loose snow in places. Bob Carchrie was well ensconced on Observatory Buttress as we contemplated the buttress opposite, on the flank of Tower Ridge. It looked steep and was hanging with green ice in its upper section. We'd give it a go.

Starting a wee way up the gully, it looked like a system of ledges led out right to the edge with a line of grooves and the icefall. I offered to do the first pitch and with no demur from himself, I set off. It was reasonable climbing to the target ledge which was blocked some way along by a large flake. It seemed to have a flimsy top which I was convinced was loose. Passing the flake seemed problematical, and after a few tries, I lassooed its top with Doug's long sling for a runner and tried again. No matter how I tried, I ended in a layback position quite unable to get any placements to pull out right. I did not fancy the ascent of the flake itself, but it seemed the only way. The crack on its left had a good placement and with its aid, I got a foot on a high, right rock hold. Another heave and I seized the top of the flake, clutched it to me and swung right – no thoughts now about it being loose as I landed on a higher ledge.

There was a horizontal ledge going right with a holdless and steep wall above. However, there were some footholds below and an incipient crack at the junction of the ledge and wall, so I pretended to torque my picks in the crack and shuffled right. After 5m, I got frightened and tapped in the tip of a Leeper for some mental assistance and moved right again to a hold below a bulge, above which easier ground led to a steep wall. I was now close to the edge up which we hoped to find a way.

The problem was simple and common. There were good placements above the bulge and smooth bare rock below on which no crampon purchase could be got. I heaved and dangled from those placements *ad nauseam* to no avail. I wondered about outflanking the bulge on the right – out of the frying pan . . . An invisible English voice below shouted: 'That looks incredible – does that route have a name?' I guess it must have looked good in profile. Doug's answer was inaudible and I returned to my contemplation. A couple of neurons got together. There was a dribble of ice high up on the right edge of the bulge that was a few centimetres thick, so I cut a foothold, leaned out on my picks and just managed to get a crampon point on and pulled. The crampon point scythed through and I dangled again. More sculpturing of the ice, same result. This went on for quite a while before a crampon point caught and I was over, wondering why it had taken so long.

Easier ground led to a corner where I expected the sanctuary of a belay, but my excavations were fruitless and I had to descend a bit and go up and left to a ledge where I eventually found a nut placement and some equanimity. Taking in the rope was a problem as I had taken a zigzag line and the yellow rope seemed to be jamming. I couldn't hear what Doug was saying, but everyone else on the mountain apparently could and it was not complimentary. Eventually, my partner appeared. 'You must be mad,' was all he said as he stormed past into the corner and out of sight. He was obviously so angry that there was to be no argument about leading the next pitch.

I settled down and watched the icicles dripping and the clouds swirl in as the un-forecast mank came in. Now began the most incredible sound show. There were grunts and groans and gasps as if he was having the orgasm to end all orgasms, all interspersed with 'I'm coming off', or, 'I think I can make it', and hammering noises and lumps of ice coming down. This invisible show was somewhat alarming as I hung on to the rope and kept telling myself I had a good belay. The rope edged out slowly and after about 15m paused again. Then some hammering and an announcement that he could bring me up to his peg belay. This was worrying, but being brought up on the writings of Marshall, I remembered the account of Gardyloo Buttress and pointed out that there was 30m of rope left and reinforced the point by asking if he would abseil from it. That shut him up and some slight progress resumed. A long time later, the rope trickled out and there was a euphoric shout as he gained the icefall and ran the rope out.

When I reached the orgasmic corner, I was amazed at the difference in its appearance. All the ice had peeled off from its left wall leaving a bare, wet, wall of rock. A poor placement on the right and a little rock wrinkle allowed a step up and a good left placement above. Trouble was, Doug had got a drive-in part way into the corner and it was not for unscrewing. I gyrated on my wrinkle, hanging on my left hand as I cut the wretched thing out. A lurch on to another tiny hold and I could regain ice in a groove. I don't remember much about the next bit until I landed on my knees on the proposed belay ledge. The peg came out easily.

The route then led right round a bulge to the icefall. The light was going, the visibility not helped by the mist which was coming and going. The ice of the bulge had also largely peeled off, being of that very brittle nature like toughened glass. As I flailed about, it suddenly came to me that there would be nowhere for my picks unless I stopped. The problem was to get my body round the bulge to reach the good ice so tantalisingly close on the right. I shuffled my feet a bit right while my body leaned left. The only placement on the bulge was to rest the pick of my right axe on the broken edge of a bit of ice, a couple of centimetres thick at waist height. I shuffled my gut carefully a little right, now left pick to join the right and lean a little. Look for a right placement – oh shit, there isn't one! Lean the pick again on another broken edge, shuffle a little more, change hands and the right tool reaches the good ice and it's easy to Doug's belay in the gloom.

We discussed the rest of the route, pack it in or continue up the east face of the Little Tower as originally intended – carry on. I raced up the easing ice to the ledge of East Wall route and hunted in the powder for a belay or a runner – nothing. I moved right until a voice round the corner belonging to a very late party on Tower Ridge showed I was too far right. That's one way to avoid the queues, start at dusk! I moved back left, abandoning my search for protection and went up a left-sloping groove. A call from below about rope. I see a possible belay 5m above, but I can't reach it, so I carry on and guess we must be moving together and then I find a belay. Doug passes and climbs into a dead end and has to climb down from a high runner and traverse right to gain the top of the Little Tower. I decline to go for the runner and have to untie one rope and then we are at the top. He accuses me of being bad tempered. I plead tiredness.

Should we go up or down? Down would be many abseils and we are hardly likely to find all the gear in place as we did last year. Up it is and then along the Eastern Traverse. As we descended by torchlight, we could see the late party silhouetted across the Gap. We are bothered about the snow, but I had seen parties coming down from the top of Tower Scoop while on the first belay, so we thought it would be OK and so it proved.

We were knackered when we reached the hut and as we sat unwinding and steaming in the extension, that prince of hut custodians brought us home-made soup. The prospect of fillet steak and wine was appealing, but tragedy had struck. Doug had left his steak in Godfroy's refrigerator (i.e. the gap between the window and the shutter) and it seemed that some fox *(Canis vulpis)* or perhaps *Homo sapiens vulpis* had made off with it. John Peden had seen a fox on the Friday night and there were plenty of the other variety around. Steam was coming out of the President's ears. A tantrum was imminent. I thrust some wine into his near teetotal hand and a promise of half my steak alleviated a very serious situation and so the day ended.

A DAY ON THE HILL

By Rob Milne

IN THE corner of my eye, I caught something unusual and glanced up. 'Graeme!' I shouted, 'what are you doing?' He seemed to have turned almost face out from the wall, 60ft above me, and appeared to be moon-walking on a vertical, blank wall, one ice axe in a snowy crack. He shouted down something like: 'This is what James Bond would do here.' In spite of the difficulty of climbing, he was obviously relaxed. Babbling like a happy baby, he turned back towards the wall, 10 points on each crampon showing, gingerly stretched up and slotted his axe pick in the narrow crack. The section of wall he was climbing looked impossible from my belay in the Left Branch of Y Gully. He had just ascended the obvious, but irregular crack line just left of the arête left of Grumbling Grooves high in Coire an Lochain. He was heading left across the blank wall to a thinner crack that led to a belay ledge. From below, the just-off vertical slab looked smooth and hostile. We had debated whether he would be able to change cracks before the right one got too wide to climb. We needn't have stressed ourselves, the wall had several one-inch wide flat ledges and the crack held the pick of the axe tighter than a frightened climber ever could. Although the climbing was strenuous, Graeme Ettle was prancing about like a ballet dancer.

I turned back to the climbers who had just soloed up the gully to below me and said: 'See, I told you it would be impressive!' Moments before, when Graeme was still in the wide crack, they had arrived, curious to see what was going down (or up). 'Wow! That looks wild' one of them prompted. With a smile, I replied: 'Hang about, he's going to cross the blank bit next.' They still hadn't believed me when Graeme probed gently with his tool, found a perfect slot and started to pretend he was James Bond.

They must have thought we were either cheeky or nuts! We were only fulfilling our primary purpose for the day, to have fun. As a by-product, we intended to explore this section of the wall. The previous summer, Graeme had noticed the wide crack and shallow chimney combination from the top of Ewen's Buttress. Using binoculars he confirmed that there was enough turf and little ledges to get from a wide flared crack to the plateau. Not only was the line stunning, but it was one of the only white mixed routes among the buttresses that were as black as our attitude to the poor winter weather so far.

Hanging straight-armed and leaning back from the wall, Graeme slotted a Friend and a stopper in the crack. On steep mixed routes, I normally take as much weight on my feet as possible. But Graeme had developed a new style. Such was the confidence in his strength and tool placements, that he would almost hang by one arm to place gear. 'Brilliant crack.' 'Excellent rock,' he called down. 'Superb,' he shouted as he locked off his left tool below his shoulder and reached high for a bit of turf. He leaned out again and walked his front points up the less than inch-wide ripples that ran across the wall. Twack, his left tool locked on to the turfy ledge. 'I'll just get some more gear before I pull on to the belay ledge,' he calmly sang out.

It was hard to believe that the pitch not only looked very hard, but also was close to a technical grade of 7. Graeme had danced up it with more grace than he shows on a disco floor. This was partly because the thin sections of crack seemed to be made for axe picks, while the intervening wide sections of the crack seemed made for protection. But the real reason was that we were having fun with our mates. To our right, two friends were ascending Grumbling Grooves. Graeme was trying to race the leader to see who could get to the next belay first. The couple doing the Left Branch of Y Gully were friendly enough, and the guy leading was feeling chuffed as he worked his way up. I could detect the trepidation in his voice when he started the pitch. But as he did each technical section and found more gear his calls back down to Stella increased with confidence. I had asked him once not to make sudden noisy movements, since I couldn't tell if that was him above me or whether Graeme was starting to fall. He understood the tone in my voice and laughed back.

Earlier in the morning, we were so engaged in conversation with three other friends that we had hardly noticed the walk in. As we wandered through wee tufts of heather sticking out of the light layer of snow, we laughed at how some climbers were so sad and desperate that they did mixed routes when they weren't in winter nick. The desperation had come from a few consecutive dreadful winters. We were all keen to get routes done, but in Scotland only ethical ascents should count. It was hard not to have a healthy respect for the rough crags protected by the fierce winter weather. That respect has to extend to climbing. We agreed that style was more important than a tick. Patience was vital.

As we picked our way through the boulder field, our focus turned to speculation about the possible impact if some of the top level, and very strong, rock climbers took up mixed climbing seriously. Almost all of the climbers currently climbing at the leading edge of mixed routes only lead E3 or E4. 'Luckily,' I said, 'they seem to get cold and miserable and head back to the warm indoor walls.' Stork, an E5+ climber currently checking out mixed climbing, countered that his ultra strong fingers didn't really help. 'Mixed climbing is a sport for mountaineers,' he declared. Although it is an interesting thought that could lead to a major advance in mixed standards, we couldn't take it seriously. We slagged each other off, good rock climbers and experienced mixed climbers alike. About the time we were trying to decide whether we were heroes for enduring the miseries of mixed climbing or fools for not heading for sun-drenched rock climbing in Spain, we arrived at the kitting-up boulder.

The short-term need to find a route in winter nick stopped our speculation about the long-term future. The snow girdling the coire was dotted with climbers. With the first blue-skied weekend in weeks; it seemed everyone was out to get a route. We chatted with each group of climbers we passed. Some we knew, some we didn't. We wished each party well, helping one group to find the start of their chosen route, lamenting with another pair how someone had climbed the out-of-condition bare rock of Fallout Corner the day before. Mixed climbing is usually a solitary activity, but these social days are nice.

'I'm safe,' Graeme shouted down.

My turn. I was looking forward to the pitch and keen to get started. Perhaps this is why my crampon slipped from the first placement and noisily skittered down the rock. 'Hey, don't damage the rock', Graeme shouted down with a smirk. 'I know, I know,' I replied, referring to the long debate about crampons marking the rock. At least this line wasn't even a summer rock route.

Although the main crack was on the right, Graeme had put some small wires in a thin crack in the middle of the wall and then tip-toed across on a small ledge. He had even made it look easy. Balanced on my front points, it looked a long way across! I fiddled with my tools for a few minutes, trying to work out the sequence. I finally hooked my right tool about chest level, and using it alone, I stepped out on to a two-inch ledge. Twisting the shaft slightly to hold myself against the wall, I slotted the left tool in above the first. I faced almost sideways and moved my toes backwards as far along the ledge as I could. Trusting my left tool, I leaned way right and slotted the pick in the other crack. It was a wide spread, but the picks were so secure, it was like holding fixed slings.

Placing my front points over a small flake to stop me from barn-dooring, I released my left tool, pulled up and hooked it high in the crack. 'Yeehaw,' I shouted, 'great Placements!' 'Piece of piss,' Graeme encouraged. I was feeling strong and confident, so I hung by one arm with my front points on tiny ledges to remove the protection. Soon I felt strangely unstable. My right foot was going like a sewing machine. After many years of winter climbing, I thought my calves would never get tired. Now my cockiness had caught up with me. I hooked a tool on a small square ledge and turned my foot. It still took half-a-minute for my calf to settle down.

Upward I hooked. Balancing on a tiny ledge and with a rope from above, I just placed my axe on a square ledge and pulled. 'Cheat,' Graeme shouted, 'I never get to do that when I am leading.' I didn't bother to tell him that although it was working, I didn't feel very secure. Not wanting to embarrass myself by falling off, I worked harder for a good next placement and took extra care in placing my feet.

As I worked the next Friend out of its hole, I was puzzled to hear Graeme shout: 'Well done, that looked good.' I realised he was talking to the lad leading the Left Branch of Y Gully straight across from us. It was only his second season and in these lean conditions it wasn't easy. 'Yes,' the lad shouted, feeling really chuffed at the top of a tricky step. 'Do you think that is harder than normal?' he asked Graeme. 'Definitely,' he responded encouragingly. Although the lad was climbing several grades below us, his personal achievement was probably bigger and we were happy to share in the resulting excitement.

Moving up on to the next ledge, I put a hand up to stroke one of my oldest and rarest pieces of gear. 'Cheat,' Graeme shouted again. 'This is only the second time I have seen this bong used in the 25 years I have owned it. I wanted to see how solid it was,' I partly lied. In the wide crack, Graeme had placed both a big Friend and my seldom-used antique bong. I had bought it when I was a mere child, just learning to climb (pegs were still in use in those days). It was nice to see such an old relic in use. Having satisfied myself that it was solid and that I was solidly on the small ledge, I leaned against the wall, almost in balance and whacked it out. It was solid!

Once I had removed the bong, huge Friend and a solid peg, reluctantly I had to leave the security of the small ledge and my foot wedged in the wide crack. On the one hand, I thought the moves ahead looked worryingly hard. On the other hand, this was wonderful climbing. Solid pick hooks, small foot ledges, unknown terrain; finding elegant climbing moves on a stage of fine red granite. I was keen to see what it would be like - the Risk versus Reward ratio had the potential to be very high. At first, I couldn't even see the thin crack. I leaned left and put my front points on another one-inch wide ledge. Gently shifting my weight on to my precariously perched points, I could finally see the crack. Slip. In went the pick of my axe. 'Awesome, dude!' I exclaimed to Graeme. Before I had even thought about it, I was turned sideways and adjusting my feet, just as Graeme had earlier. With a solid tool placement, it was easy to rearrange my body position while holding with only one arm. I slotted the other axe higher in the crack and delicately moved my front points on to higher ledges. Making the moves was like doing a pleasant dance routine, elegant, delicate, a bit of finesse. All the best aspects of mixed climbing.

The way I had set my feet, I couldn't reach high enough for the turf as had Graeme. Feeling cocky, I just placed the tip of the pick on a small ledge and held my hand very still. One wiggle and I would be off. But what the hell, it was fun to push it a bit. A short step to another thin seam and I could reach the turf. A couple more quick and exact placements and I was already pulling the last nut before the belay ledge. After shivering on the belay for a hour, it was nice to be warm again. Imagine my surprise to be actually sweating. Although the moves had been secure, they were strenuous. Oh well, it should keep me warm for longer at the belay, I thought, as I grabbed the edge of a flake with my left hand and laybacked on to the 10-inch-wide belay ledge.

Once clipped to the belay, I started effusing about how great the pitch had been. 'The first hooks were great – the lean to the right crack was really far – my foot kept sewing machining – the bong was cool – the move into the thin crack was really fun.' But Graeme's mood was very sombre. While I had been climbing, he had been looking at the next pitch. And it didn't look easy. He chatted bravely as he re-racked the gear, but his concern regarding the next pitch was almost oppressive. Between the lines, I could hear him thinking: 'This looks great. I want to do this. The flared crack looks awkward. If there isn't gear in that icy crack, I'm in trouble. The last section of the headwall looks like vertical ice, but no gear.' Although his gloves were wet, I was sure his palms were sweaty. But Graeme knew that this type of exploration was a primary reason he climbed. A bit of fear of the unknown added excitement. He had also been climbing like a machine lately. Fear and concern led to focus and up he went.

The climbing wasn't hard, but icy. The ice was a mixed blessing. In the back of the flared crack was perfect névé, ideal for the axes. But the ice also covered the thin crack that Graeme depended on for gear. With one foot in the névé and the points of the other on a small nick in the rock, he spent ages chopping the ice from the crack, looking for a placement. The climbing was now very different. The cracks on the first pitch were full of soft snow and easily cleaned. Now a layer of ice covered everything. Fun technical climbing had been replaced by serious considered movements. 'That one's not too bad,' he reported from 10ft up. 'That's pretty shite,' was the summary from 25ft up. 'These aren't very good' was the summary of 15 minutes of chopping and fiddling about. At this stage, I couldn't watch any more. Not because I was worried, but because the constant snow-clearing and chopping resulting in a sustained bombardment of my position. I put the sack back on and leaned as far out of the line of fire as the anchors would let me. I could hear Stella climbing across the branch of Y gully, but could only rarely sneak a peek at what she was doing. We were all in our own little worlds, dreading what would come next, but sure happiness was less than an hour away.

When I did get a break from the bombardment, I started to glance up quickly and estimate how far Graeme would go if he fell. He was now working up the vertical headwall, clearing six inches of foamy snow from the ice. He had passed the point where he would stop above me. If all the bad nuts ripped, he would now stop far enough below me that I would have trouble seeing the shock in his eyes. As I kept my head down I tried to determine if I would have enough rope to lower him to the gully. I wasn't really serious about these perverse thoughts. Both of us were confident in his ability to find good placements and keep a level head. However, the jokes and shouting had stopped; the climbing took full concentration.

Occasionally, I could see helmeted heads on the plateau. At one point, Graeme was shouting 'Hello' to our friends. They shouted encouragement back. As if he was on a stage, a crowd was gathering to watch the show. The line looked impressive and steep, if not crazy. Graeme realised the implications of an audience. If he fell, he might get hurt, but he would definitely get really embarrassed. He later told me that he felt secure all the way, but didn't want to look a fool in front of so many friends. I was just glad he was careful, whatever the reason.

As he neared the top, I could hear him talking again. Some friends had come over to wait for him on top. The bombardment stopped, the rope made a sudden short jump and I heard a shout. Bracing for a fall, I heard a happy 'Yo.' He was there and dancing a wee jig in front of his mates. We were up and home free.

He chatted excitedly with them as I cleared the anchors. Winter climbing is often solitary and cold, but on a few rare times each year the weather is good and you can share the fun with your mates. And now it was all fun again. The risk and fear had passed. The exploration was done. It was just a small matter of me seconding the pitch.

After all of Graeme's chopping, the climbing was easy. I kept shouting up that he was a wimp for whimpering and taking so long, as I just hooked my picks in the placements he had chopped out. The risk had been eliminated and I could enjoy the delicate placements. Seconding can be wonderful at times.

As we walked down, we chatted constantly and reminisced about the climb. 'Remember the move up into the crack? - What did you do where it got wide? - Wasn't the bong neat? - The névé in the flared crack was good, wasn't it? - What was all this stuff about James Bond? - The guy on Left Branch did pretty well . . .' We babbled for an hour like young children coming out of the circus for the first time. Such had been the excitement during the climb that between us, we could still visualise almost every move and remember what we felt. Fond memories of the hill start with good climbs and good mates. We had had a superb day. But of course it was superb - it was a day on the hill.

(The first ascent of Stage Fright VI,7, Coire an Lochain, Cairngorms.)

Graeme Ettle on the first ascent of 'Stagefright', Coire an Lochain, Cairngorm. Photo: Rob Milne.

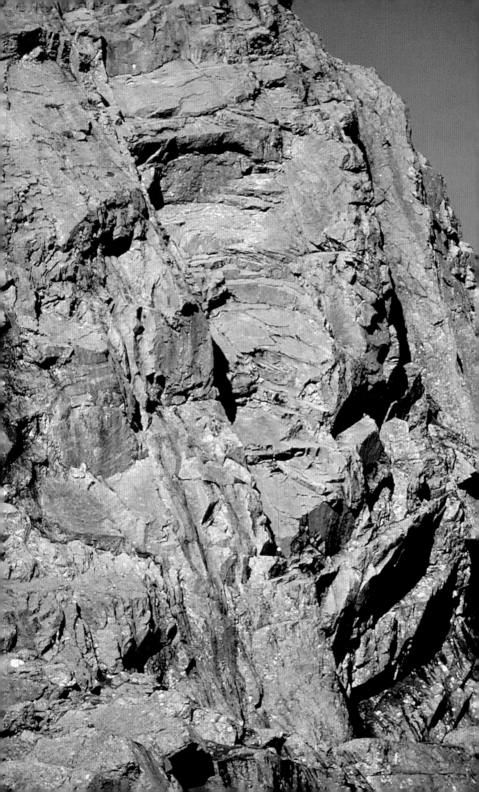

IN THE HALL OF THE MOUNTAIN KING

By Adam Kassyk

THE mountains slept. An uneasy calm lay on the land, as if an unseen power had withdrawn for a few moments, and silence prevailed. Thin, high clouds drained the watery moon of its light, which cast pale shadows in the snow. Two figures surveyed such a scene at one in the morning at Aberarder, and settled down to some sleep. We walked into Coire Ardair early that morning, our spirits buoyed by energy and optimism, as the dawn light touched the hillside with colour and warmth. The day was calm and clear, the snow seemed good, and we felt well prepared for whatever trials the mountain gods might hold in store for us. The vast amphitheatre of Creag Meagaidh was still and quiet, and ours were the only footprints in the snow. The mountain was heavily snowbound, and my partner, Keith Anderson, readily agreed that we should try 1959 Face Route on Pinnacle Buttress. The first obstacle proved to be simply getting established on the face. A full 60m of climbing on snow the consistency of cold porridge and ice like crusted sugar gained the sanctuary of a firm snow slope, and what turned out to be the promised land above. At one point we were both climbing together with only one runner interrupting the otherwise untrammelled downward sweep of the rope, and thus we both endured and passed the first trial. The promised land was indeed paradise gained, with good snow, and dizzying balconies, ramps and grooves, leading ever outwards above endless volumes of clean blue space. The early tension of the climb was replaced with a satisfying rhythm of positive movement.

Farther on, due to a lack of stances and a desire to press on, we both moved together with one or two runners on the rope. I was completing the passage of a steep icy groove, in the lead, when I was struck by a sudden and powerful gust of wind. I tensed immediately, arching like a coiled spring to place the maximum weight on the spikes of my feet and hands. The pressure plucked and pulled at my resisting body, then subsided in parallel with my own anxiety at this unwelcome difficulty and danger. As soon as the coast was clear, I hastened upwards to find a safe anchor, but cautiously, keeping a lookout for a further attack from our unseen enemy. I had now gained open snowfields, separated by short walls and steps, and I felt fully exposed to the potential violence of the wind. The day had been calm earlier, and we were both mentally unprepared for the unpleasant task of fighting the wind as well as the difficulties of the climb.

I tied myself to a little rocky outcrop, an island of hopeful security in a sea of open, unprotected snow fields, and glanced searchingly at the

Bill Stephenson and Rob Raynard on 'King Kong', Carn Dearg Buttress, Ben Nevis. Photo: Niall Ritchie.

mountainside, the sky and the distant horizon. The wind tugged at me a little, but for a while seemed content just to threaten. Then I heard, and felt, a sound. It swelled from a whisper to a thundering volume, like a jet engine going into reverse thrust from close by, surging with superhuman force across the gothic walls above, and I shuddered deeper into my jacket and my skin crawled with fear until the wind spent its power and drew away into the rocks to replenish its violence. We had been sounded a warning, the terms of combat had been changed. We were now firmly on the defensive, committed to fighting a superior force which had declared its aggression in uncompromising terms. Our isolation and vulnerability was emphasised when I saw two tiny figures crossing the corrie slopes far, far below, two mortal comrades sharing this arena, and the only other signs of human life we saw in the entire day.

We drew close to the upper fortress. From a deep chasm in the soaring walls of this gothic Gormenghast fell a cascade of ice - the second trial. An unusually serious atmosphere had now settled on our enterprise, as we fought to dodge and duck against the attacks of the storm, to find security for the rope, and to gain precious upward progress. The minutes ticked past and turned into hours. I found myself in the lead, on vertical ice, nerves and muscles stretched, but at last reassured and secured by the grip of steel and knotted cord. At this point our adversary, finding me thus exposed, released another hurricane blast to try to tear me from the wall of ice and hurl me into the void. My body felt like a spring being stretched to the point of breaking, as I tensed into a quivering arc and channelled all my energy into my feet and my hands to increase the grip of steel claws against the force of the wind. The tension reached a climax, hung in the balance for a moment, then drained as I too breathed out and relaxed. A few more moves and the trial was over.

I cowered in a shallow recess in the wall of the gully, looking out and down as Keith climbed up, the snow slope forming a brief foreground to the acres of space beyond. I felt dwarfed, frightened, and an increasing need to hide from the elemental forces which ruled in this mountain kingdom. A small flame of optimism flickered, because surely we were over the greatest difficulty now, but the increasing seriousness of the situation seemed to tip the balance against us still. Keith emerged from the depths, and continued up the gully. I sensed the light draining away from the colossal grey walls of the Pinnacle, still some 500ft above us. The sense of scale was overwhelming. My eyes were drawn up the length of the rope, unsecured by any belays, to where Keith was struggling to fix a peg. A gust of wind sucked at the rope, and pulled it like a bowstring into a taut curve impossibly far out from the rock face, forcibly drawing my line of sight to the awesome space surrounding us. A large block tumbled slowly past, the remains of Keith's attempts to secure the rope to a peg, and my stomach churned as the rock shot out over the icefall below in a practical reminder of our exposure.

The climbing was easier now, but the intensity and violence of the wind increased to compensate. Now even the simple act of climbing was a great struggle. Increasing amounts of strength and time were required to fight the aerial demon and merely remain attached to the mountain. Upward progress was only snatched during moments of respite. Battle was now engaged in earnest; what had been mere warning shots below, or an occasional ambush in a moment of weakness, was now all-out war. Trial by combat, and the stakes were steadily increasing. The slack rope billowed out into space above me as a constant reminder of the limits of our own adhesion to the solid earth. Above another ice pitch, where Keith had dislodged the loose block, we weighed the need for speed against the need for security. The light was failing, and there was a great temptation to hurry, but I truly feared the storm. One pitch farther on, as Keith climbed, I found I was constantly being blown off my feet onto the belay. It was impossible to manage the rope, and stay standing at the same time – both hands were needed to maintain an upright position against the battering of the storm. The wind was inexorably picking away at our defences, reducing our basic capacity to climb, to protect ourselves, to do anything. Then the evil demon twisted the slack into a huge and contorted tangle. This knot was bewitched and given a capricious mind of its own, and it danced wildly around me, mocking my presumption. I realised I had no hope of untangling it. I tried to dismantle my belay, and realised with a sense of shocked surprise that it would be impossible to take off my gloves, and the simple act of removing a peg was also quite beyond me. My horizon of activity had suddenly reduced to the simple act of hanging on, and the virtual inability to do anything else. The storm blasts of the wind were now succeeding each other so rapidly that the impact was almost continuous. My thoughts narrowed to a focus on one single necessity – if we don't get out of here quickly, we won't get out of here at all.

I abandoned the peg and set off like a crab emerging from its hole into open water surrounded by predators, following the frenzied rope which performed a manic dance in front of me. There was no way of communicating with Keith, nearly a full rope length above me in the gathering gloom. Progress was a matter of hanging on to the axes for dear life until the vicious assault slackened then gaining a few feet and as secure a position as possible before the next onslaught. With each attack all reserves of energy and determination were summoned to the defences as the holocaust pulled, plucked, pummelled, tore, battered and smashed at our punily resisting bodies. Then the violence would subside and gasping for breath we would recover our energies briefly in preparation for the next assault. The clock was ticking and human reserves could not indefinitely match this superhuman force.

At this point the tumbling dice of chance intervened in the grossly unequal struggle. The upper gully of our climb cut the edge of the broad snowfield at the top of Easy Gully. And the storm was blowing from the east. These two strokes of fortune tipped the scales just sufficiently in our favour - descent without the need to exit on to the plateau, and the impact of the wind was blowing us up the mountain, rather than off it. Unfortunately, Keith did not know about the first of these factors, and was continuing to climb upwards, onto rather steep and precarious ground. This presented something of a dilemma. Tugging hard on the rope would merely assist the wind in dislodging him, while tugging gently would not be noticed. Tentatively, with the rope at full stretch, I started to climb sideways, praying that he would get the message quickly. So it was that two tiny figures, joined yet separated by a tightly stretched, crazily-knotted umbilical cord, started the long and arduous traverse across the snowfield. As each blast of the wind struck, we paused with arms and legs splayed in a position of maximum stability, pressed flat against the snow, and clung on grimly. I could see Keith high above me, making a descending traverse on unpleasantly steep terrain, a small, spidery shape at the other end of the rope, totally isolated from me. Progress was painfully, desperately slow, and we were acutely aware of the huge drop below the snowfield, gnawing hungrily at our heels, in league with the wind to profit from our demise.

We inched our way across the snowfield, like two flies trying to escape from a gigantic spider's web. With every glance across at the Post Face, our objective seemed no nearer, and the mental tension was as great as the physical effort. At last the traverse started descending slightly and the odds swung a little farther in our favour. The shallow recess of Easy Gully seemed like a breakwater against the fury of the elements, and we gained its meagre shelter with profound relief. The speed of our descent improved from intermittent crawling to continuous progress. Below the Post Face, though the wind was still strong enough to knock us over, we could stand upright for the first time in hours. We made straight for the cave under the boulder by the lochan. I have never experienced such an intensity of relief and relaxation as when I stretched out full length on the floor of the cave, resting every muscle, joint and tendon, and wrapped in a secure mental blanket of peace and tranquillity. The third trial was over – and not one I would wish to undergo again.

We were very tempted to stop there, in our tiny oasis of shelter from this wild world of wind, snow and mayhem, hidden from the enemy who withers human strength and drains the spirit. But we knew that the more insidious threats of cold and hunger were also waiting, and our immediate relief would be replaced by a long, slow, shivering discomfort. Maybe that would have been the better option, because as we emerged into the storm once again we found that our trials were not yet over.

Staggering through deep drifts over the boulders, now facing directly into the full blast of a vicious easterly blizzard, we were seduced by the easier going of flat ground, until twice I fell through the snow into the lochan. A curious weightless sensation, then the creeping chill of icy fingers round my knees, followed by a cursing, frightened struggle to escape. I was well aware of the potential seriousness of the situation, and the increasing threat of hypothermia.

The enemy, cheated once of his prey, now marshalled his forces in a sustained offensive to prevent our escape. It was impossible to face into the stinging snow particles borne like missiles on the teeth of the storm, and the effort of making progress against the constant onslaught of the easterly wind drained our strength still further. The path was completely obliterated, and we stumbled across rough ground and snow drifts with wearied resignation. A compass bearing was necessary to find the way in the whiteout, and I counted paces, as much for concrete evidence of the progress we were making, as for navigational advantage. Thus two hunched figures battled on, leaning into the vicious blasts of the wind, along ground that obstinately refused to turn downhill. The mental strain, of coping with the knowledge that this struggle would go on for at least another hour, seemed as great as the actual physical effort. The stumbling, lurching, leaden-booted paces slowly ticked past, adding up to hundreds of metres, then to kilometres, and then we reached the first trees at the bend in the glen, and felt a pronounced release of tension with the knowledge that our escape was assured.

The ordeal was still not over when we reached the car. The long miles to the A9 and over Drumochter served to drain every last drop of nervous energy and concentration, staring with aching eyes and numb brain at a uniform grey landscape through a vortex of swirling white shapes dancing towards the windscreen, crawling at a painfully slow 5 or 10 miles an hour and trying to keep the car on the road and avoid falling into a coma at the same time. All for the promise of a warm bed and blissful sleep at the end of the journey. The things we do to go climbing.

THE HORSE AND THE BULL

By Bob Duncan

THE summer of 1976 was glorious all over Britain so, with impeccable planning, we went to the Alps, a filthy nomadic existence, chased from mountain range to mountain range by huge electrical storms. On the Torre Venezia, the Rosengartenspitze, various Sella Towers, the Cengalo and others whose names I have forgotten, our activities, usually as we approached the summit, were illuminated by brilliant blue-white flashes, accompanied by deafening, echoing crashes and bangs as the air was torn apart feet from us, or so it seemed. Particularly galling was the fact that only I of the party seemed to appreciate the danger posed by this dramatic backdrop, yet despite squatting in the approved manner whenever we stopped on exposed ridges or summits, guess who had the closest shave? The others floated around like they were at a summer fête, ooohing, and aaahing, prodding buzzing ironware and remarking on my rapidity of movement, especially in descent. It got to the stage that, heading for the Cima della Madonna, I hurled myself off a via ferrata rather than face another certain encounter with the flame-grill.

Then, in late summer, we returned to a scorched Britain, sunshine and – joy – no storms. We worked our way up north through *Hard Rock,* ending up on the Ben. Ian, having heard how good Torro was, in his contrary way went for King Kong with John, but Keith and I were happy to take the obvious option. While we had heard that each of Torro's pitches had been climbed without aid, we didn't know of anyone who had actually done a completely free ascent, so we were very pleased with ourselves when we managed it without a great deal of trouble. (Hubris got its just desserts the day after, on The Bat, but that's another story.) Over the years afterwards I remembered the immaculate rock and the airy positions, while the growing reputation of the route for quality reassured me I wasn't being misled by the rosy tint of retrospection. While often speaking of repeating it, typically, I never quite got round to it.

Then 1996 arrived. Despite a promising enough start, my big ideas for the year had foundered on the rocks of shoulder injury, the breakers of employment demands and, most deadly of all, the shifting sandbars of a congenital chronic indolence. My regular partner, Graeme Johnson, was having no better a time of it, although to be fair he had more excuse. Nature has been unkind to Graeme in its distribution of physical gifts, especially when it comes to climbing. Suffice to say that many have remarked on his resemblance to Mr Ed, 'The Talking Horse' (and not only when they see him climb).

I had said to Johnson often enough that he should do Torro. Now, on a glorious July morning we were headed for the Ben and, since I wasn't in shape to try those routes I still had ambitions for (ever the optimist), it seemed like the perfect opportunity. Graeme agreed that I could lead the pitches I had seconded before, so it would be sort of new to me, and anyway how much would I remember after 20 years? We parked the car and set off across the golf course under a cloudless sky.

The walk up was easier than I expected, perhaps because I'm more familiar with it in winter, in the dark and under a huge pack. Also, for once I was concentrating on my walking technique, deliberately keeping as long a stride as was comfortable and resisting the urge to increase my pace, while making polished and expert use of my Telescopic Walking Pole (for some reason, a source of amusement and indeed embarrassment to my partner). In this way I gradually wore down a pair who had set off in front of me at the dam, obviously all-out to stay ahead, but who were clearly unfamiliar with advanced walking skills. They scuttled off to the side under the pretext of going for a drink.

I never read specialist walking magazines, but I imagine pages devoted to skills and techniques, the walker's equivalent of the jam, crimp, pinch and slap. 'Next week – the three-quarter semi-stride and when to use it.' That's the way things are going. Every pastime is developing its own jargon, literature and specialist accoutrements, even when, basically, there's nothing to it. Darts, for example. What the hell can you say about darts? Something to keep you occupied in the pub when you've run out of conversation (in Johnson's case, about one point five seconds, about as long as it takes him to say: 'Mine's a pint'), but Peter Purves left Blue Peter to become an expert on the subject – now there's a challenge – and what is more, I've seen whole shops dedicated to darts. (OK, one, and it went belly-up in a couple of months, so maybe there is hope after all.) But I digress.

I reached the CIC without stopping and headed back right and up across the slope towards the base of Carn Dearg, pausing at a burn for a drink. Here I waited until Johnson had stopped and just taken off his pack, before casually throwing on my own and striding away again, as you do.

As I approached the foot of the cliff I could see lots of pale, semi-naked bodies milling about at the base of Centurion and anxiously watched to see if any headed towards Torro, but none did and I dropped my sack on the top of a large boulder directly below the first pitch, before going for a short walk.

Carn Dearg is constructed in such a way which, to the climber, makes it almost an erotic experience to gaze on its overlapping slabs, overhung walls and swooping, knife-cut grooves, to touch the compact, finely textured roughness of the beautiful grey andesite. Today the rock was almost white in the glare of the sun and hot to the touch, any moistness confined to the shadows. Grooves and walls leapt skywards. I hopped among the boulders in a delight of anticipation.

The group below Centurion, meanwhile, was busily engaged in the production of white noise. Bodies were dotted around the lower parts of Centurion and King Kong, while others half-queued for their turn to climb. Overseeing the events, or at least dominating them vocally, was a familiar figure, the shrinking violet otherwise known as the CIC custodian. While possessing a presence as dominating as the previous incumbents, the new custodian is (at least for the present) rather less terrifying, the embittering experience of the post not yet having exerted a noticeable effect, although it is surely only a matter of time.

I was surprised to see him there. Not known for his fondness for rock-climbing, he normally sticks to parachuting, golf and suchlike during the summer months. Closer inspection makes the reason for this clear. Adding all his digits together results in barely enough to pick your nose with, the result of extensive winter climbing epics. I began to suspect why so many were gathered with him, suspicions confirmed when I asked his intentions. 'King Kong,' he said, while I tried not to look surprised. Later in the year I examined the CIC route book, reading the laconic entry: 'King Kong. R. Clothier and Guest.' Anyone seeking an explanation for the complicated rope manoeuvres and sea-shanties which (allegedly) punctuated the ascent will be none the wiser for reading these economical few words.

Johnson, meanwhile, had arrived, all teeth and sweat. His sunglasses and sun hat with neck protector gave him an uncanny resemblance to a beach donkey.

After an interminable delay while various creams and lotions were applied, sandwiches eaten, bodily functions indulged and every other excuse for not actually climbing exhausted, I was allowed to set off up the first pitch. A crack led to a groove which steepened up for a few feet, before leaning back to a bit off the vertical. I vaguely remembered finding it quite strenuous, and so was pleased when I was able to hang extravagantly off the steepest part and comfortably place a runner. The moves kept coming at a reasonable, but interesting standard, until I found myself standing on a little pinnacle looking up at a few feet of rather more demanding climbing. Just before I launched out, I spotted a huge flake to the right which led back into the groove above where it eased back a bit. The groove was one of my lasting memories of the route, clean-cut and immaculate. At its top I belayed and brought up Johnson.

He led off, a bit hesitantly I thought, but I bit my tongue. I would save the encouragement for when it was needed. Eventually, he arrived at the top of a little groove where I knew he would be at the right edge of a slab, across which he had to make a descending traverse. He fiddled around, down, up, down. Up.

'Ye just go down across the slab, with yer feet at the lip,' I called helpfully.

No reply. 'Huh,' I thought, 'miserable git.' Then he disappeared from view, one of the ropes dropping and forming a dramatic arc in space below the slab, its upper end indicating progress as my partner made his way across. Climbing continued in fits and starts. Meanwhile, I had been joined by the first of a party of three Englishmen, who brought his mates up climbing together Alpine-style, a few feet apart. I started to get more twitchy about our rate of progress.

When it was my turn it was harder than I recalled getting to the edge of the slab, but there, right where I wanted it, was a lovely big peg with an eye big enough to thread a backrope through. The slab was dramatic but easy enough and at its far end I made a rising traverse over the void to Johnson, uncomfortably squatting in a little eyrie. 'Eh, Ah think the belay's up a wee bit, but Ah wasn't sure . . . so Ah stopped here,' he said, apologetically.

Sure enough, a couple of moves up and I landed in a spacious alcove between overhangs. I directed a withering stare back at the crestfallen Johnson. The route continued out up and right, and so did I – or at least tried to. Descending after not finding the holds I was certain must be lurking not far away, I very nearly came off. Giving thanks to the tremendous position (it having prevented anyone witnessing my close shave), I went up again and this time nearly lost a hand as it fell into a huge jug. The route continued out right, on a slab sandwiched between overhangs, directly above the lower pitches and in a brilliant position. I had entirely forgotten this pitch from before and could only think I must have been worried about leading the overhang above. I was really enjoying myself, and continued up to a little stance on the traverse line of The Bullroar.

Johnson joined me in reasonable time, although now and again he would pause for no apparent reason. 'Just up there,' or 'Aye, that's the line,' or 'Ah went left at that point,' I would say, by way of encouragement, but he said nothing in reply. When he reached me he looked up at the overlap above, the crux of the route, then silently started taking gear off my belt.

'It's not nearly as bad as it looks,' I said. 'Ah can't remember the details but Ah do remember finding it quite straightforward.'

Johnson grunted but looked strangely unreassured and kept removing all the spare gear at my waist.

I had also been watching the progress of a pair on The Bullroar. The leader was now approaching us across the slab, his last runner a long way behind him. He didn't seem exactly uncomfortable, but had a minor case of that rather sloppy footwork I always find disturbing. You know, throw your foot out, maybe pedal a bit until it sticks, but keep it moving on the hold, in a strange, spastic sort of way as you transfer your weight, concentrating all the while on looking anywhere except where to put your feet. 'They'll look after themselves' is the unspoken assumption. Advanced cases of this condition can be observed regularly at indoor climbing walls. Sufferers are invariably incredibly enthusiastic and incredibly useless. (I am told I display similar tendencies myself under stress.)

As Johnson prepared to leave, the team following us piled up on the slab below. Meanwhile, the man on The Bullroar reached across and got his hands on the holds below my belay ledge, and I relaxed. He had looked vaguely uncomfortable and I was very aware of the enormous pendulum he would take if he came off. 'Ye can get a runner in here,' I said, indicating the crack behind me, but he ignored me and fiddled something into a lower crack. As he pulled his rope up to clip the runner his right foot, which he had carelessly thrown sideways onto a little nubbin and forgotten about, reminded him of its existence as it shot off its hold. For one glorious, thrilling moment I thought he was going to follow it and describe a monster arc in between the overhangs, preferably head-first, but he was just too low for me to give him a discreet little shove with my foot and, unfortunately, his remaining point and a half of contact proved just enough. After clipping into his runner with some urgency he headed away, continuing his traverse, feet still flailing. The rest of us pulled faces. Finally, Johnson started off up, not at all cheered by the close shave he had just witnessed, (but then I've always thought he lacked the killer instinct).

After he left I was joined at the stance by the guy who had led the first pitch. We waited as Johnson slowly inched the rope out, pausing frequently to look up at the overhang, before apparently remembering why he was there and making another move, or maybe taking just another look at the overhang.

Despite my calm and agreeable nature, I could feel the irritation level rising. Here we were, two Scots on a Scottish route, climbing more slowly than three Englishmen. Johnson had climbed harder stuff than this with his hands tied behind his back. What was the problem?

'Where does it go here?' The tenor of his voice told me that, incredibly, Johnson thought he might be off route. The overlap meanwhile, firmly remained directly above him, neon signs flashing 'This way.'

'Just up there a wee bit, then on to the upper slab to the overlap, Ah dunno, just follow the holds.' This advice strangely didn't seem to help much and he moved up hesitantly, taking what seemed like an age. From time to time I would offer encouragement. 'Whut's the problem, ye're on the easy bit', 'Ah think ye'll find that hold's big enough to bivouac on', 'Ah was hoping ti get off this while Ah still had some teeth,' and other words carefully considered to nourish a positive mental attitude in my hesitant partner, but to depressingly little effect. Finally, he reached the overhang. Here an extended session of moving up and down, fiddling in runners, fiddling out runners, then fiddling them in again, resulted in a skirt of quickdraws dangling from the overhang. I could see it droop perceptibly under the weight of ironmongery. Then, before you could say: 'Well, that took ye a bloody age, ye useless sack o' bones,' he was up and clipping into a 0 RP, the only thing he had left. I climbed up in a high dudgeon, slowly relaxing as the enjoyment of the position and the feeling of movement helped me back into a better mood, ostentatiously casual for the benefit of any onlookers.

The next couple of pitches climbed deteriorating ground to a belay below the upper crux on Centurion. Someone carrying an enormous sack was completely failing to make any progress on this – despite liberal assistance from the rope – to his leader above. I wondered how long he had been on the route. The sack was big enough to carry food and equipment for a week, and at the current rate of progress might just see him to the top. I wondered if he was military. The gear and the build reminded me of something from Bravo Two Zero. I wisely resisted the temptation to hurl abuse. Eventually, with an extra hard pull from the rope he got to a hold big enough for even him to heave up on, and the pitch was free for me to set off. It was a return to interesting climbing and led to a belay on the upper slab where Torro headed back left.

By this time Johnson, the crux long behind him, was climbing at a rate significantly faster than mould growth and before I knew it he was setting off on the last pitch. He stepped off the lower end of a tapering slab into a steep groove just out of my line of vision, lit the blue touchpaper and reappeared seconds later at the top of the crag. I remembered being pleased getting to the top of this all those years ago, slightly cramped, but recalled nothing of the climbing. In the event it was a steep corner-groove and I chose a horizontal layback, declining the option of bridging holds to the right. Then I was on the ledge beside Johnson and it was all over. A brilliant route, every bit as good as I remembered it.

As I passed the CIC hut on the way down I turned and looked back up into Coire na Ciste. The slopes around the hut were dappled where long fingers of shadow ran down from the crenellations of the Castle and Castle Ridge as the summer sun dipped to the north-west behind the mountain, with the hut itself bathed in the late afternoon light. For once, the foreground view caught my eye rather than the huge cliffs which normally dominated the scene from this point, the lighting lending a texture to the slopes I had never seen before and, I pondered ruefully, at my current levels of activity might well never see again. And on this cheery thought I turned my face to the north and set off down after the stumbling, ungainly and sun-reddened figure of Johnson.

Much later, a few days after an intemperate outburst at what I considered another display of depressing incompetence from Johnson (given I knew of what he was capable), this time on a wintry Cobbler, my name apparently came up in a carload bound for Alien Rock, during a heated rant on the unpleasantness of climbing with certain people. My informant revelled in telling me how Johnson, his homely face disfigured by bulging blood vessels, spluttered his denunciation messily through tombstone teeth. 'See that miserable, torn-faced, ignorant wee rat Duncan, he thinks ye're just there to hold his ropes – he never lets ye enjoy yerself, it's all go, go, go. Ah kept stopping to savour the climbing on Torro and all Ah got was an earful of abuse. Bastard!'

UNDISCOVERED SCOTLAND

By John Mackenzie

I SUSPECT it all depends where you live; if for instance, you are stuck in North Rona then new routes are an essential if you still desire to rock climb. However, if living in the megalopolises of the Midlands then, unless you are an E6 leader, any new route has to be an unusual occasion. Fortunately, Scotland, particularly the North-west, has still untapped sources of hidden enjoyment, spirited away in unlikely or remote areas that mainly tempt the cogniscenti or the local.

It is a fact that climbers are either sheep or goats; you are either an inveterate guide book ticker of graded lists (where an easy E3 has more kudos than a hard E2), or you are drawn to the unknown where anything is possible; a classic route or a classic disappointment being but end poles of the likely spectrum.

It is still (just) possible to find not merely new routes but sizeable new crags. Of course, the modern concept of a 'crag' has been considerably reduced in size since the early pioneers found the Triple Buttress of Beinn Eighe virgin, but that has to be expected. Inland, the opportunities are perhaps fewer than on the sandstone sea cliffs in the far north, but that too is not exactly unexpected. With all the little bumps of rock scattered around northern Scotland, sometimes they can form into surprisingly big crags that might have been known about, even talked about openly, but never actually investigated.

Bob, the keenest 63-year-old still to be found in these parts, summed it all up. 'Never, ever, dismiss a crag from a distance.'

Go hillwalking, potter around on those dampish days, search funny little nooks and crannies and be insatiably curious; walk up to that "little" crag and find out its true scale. If you find something in excess of 150ft., then jump for joy, for that is quite reasonable find by today's standards. Study maps – which are actually pretty inaccurate at the scale we need – look at geological notes, get a "feel" for the surrounding countryside and, almost certainly, there will be something worth climbing.

So much for the preliminaries; this is not a boring old "how-to" article but a pleasing reminiscence of recent finds. As I said, Bob is keen and since he and Fay are also hillwalkers then it is not unknown for the phone to ring at about 10pm on a Sunday evening. To give a somewhat shortened and sanitised version of such a discovery the little conversation below is not too far out bar the expletives.

Bob. 'I think I have discovered a new crag, you will go absolutely ape when you see it, your eyes will be out on stalks, you'll be frothing at the mouth and God, you should see the lines, and . . .'

Me. 'Oh, aye, well where is it then and does it look climbable?'

Bob. ' . . . it is, seriously, bloody amazing; huge great crack lines and corners, at least 200ft. high on average and really steep Torridonian sandstone. It makes Stone Valley (another new crag) seem really piddly.

Me. 'It's not *that* crag is it – you know the one you can see from the opposite side of the bay, the one which Kev and Graham have talked about?'

Bob. 'It is – I went down as far as I could and it really grows from that amazing slab-and-groove sequence to vertical walls of perfect-looking clean sandstone, not the grotty stuff you often find high up in the hills.'

Me. 'When can we go, the forecast for this week looks good – warm and reasonably dry. But how about the walk-in, it's *miles?*'

Bob. 'I have made inquiries, we have a boat for this Wednesday.'

Me. 'Stuff the office, I'll delegate . . .'

Now, that's keen! To cut the misery short, the crag in question is the one "everyone" has talked about opposite the bay from Ardmair, the vertical edge that can be seen but reveals practically nothing. The approach is either by boat or by an hour and a half's walk from the friendly environs of Blughasary, the estate which welcomes visitors with such signs as No Parking, Stalking in progress, Private – Keep Out. This is all augmented by barbed wire, padlocked gates and miles of fence. Fortunately, not at all typical of the usual West Highland estate. For a first defence in reaching this crag, it's a pretty effective one.

The next line of defence is the old posties' track which follows the crest of the coastal cliffs below Ben More Coigeach towards Polbain. It is not exactly easy to follow and requires a certain faith in what is beyond. For all that, it is pleasant enough in dry weather with a great outlook to the west and south. Conversely, the "easy" sea approach depends on how well you know someone with a boat and if you know where to land, which was far from obvious on our first of many sorties.

Dreadnaught.

The aluminium-hulled, flattish-bottomed, ex-assault vessel heads straight across the bay in about 10 minutes. The vertical edge, of indeterminate size from the far shore, now grows. Small dots can be seen as fully grown Scots pines clinging to perilous ledges. The cliff rears in vertical format out of the sea and turns a corner to the left. We chug on a bit more and then that intriguing edge shows why Bob was frothing and foaming.

The vertical edge reveals a long red wall stretching gradually uphill, seamed with corners and cracks and an overhanging gully complete with chockstone

Me. 'Jings, are you sure it's virgin?'

Bob. (Manically pointing with insane gleam in eye). 'Yup, and it looks so clean that we'll do everything "on sight".'

Me. That's the line (a superb shallow corner arcing up the wall to the left of the vertical edge, ending in an impending wall). Let's go for that.'

We landed that time, and indeed every subsequent time, at a tiny inlet with a small waterfall foaming down its left side. We leapt ashore on to a boulder then scrambled up the bed of the stream to find knee-high heather running up steeply to the crag. We executed a vertiginous traverse above the lower cliffs to reach the base of our chosen line, the heather dropping alarmingly to the edge which simply keeled over out of sight to the waves below.

From here the stature of the cliff was more apparent and our proposed line began to the left of a curious flange, to reveal three short, clean walls leading to the base of the long and seemingly wet corner. The overhanging wall above looked blankish and I think we must have been a trifle optimistic to assume that "on sight, every time" would be possible. The three short walls, though looking harder, were no more than 4b on perfect clean sandstone. A fine stance bottomed the corner, which initially looked merely steep as compared to gently overhanging with two major bulges.

The right-angled corner gave a wonderful pitch of "classical stemming"; starting up a rather off-putting vertical section of pale whitish yellow sandstone which was more akin to that of Harrison's Rocks. Fortunately, this soon reverted back to the simply splendid solid stuff above. It was sufficiently awkward over the bulges, but also a reasonably protected feature that, at least for most routes, made blank sections more perceived than real. However, it was wet, but the rock's perfect friction negated this to the point of a mild inconvenience. It had a hardish exit, if I remember correctly, and the stance was perched below a grim-looking overhang of the yellow sandstone with the sea directly below.

Pitch three was the crux, the overhang being harder, bigger and more reachy for rounded holds than either of us liked. It led beyond the overhang to a gangway that in turn took us up a crack which sported both holds and protection where neither should have existed according to the usual laws of Torridonian sandstone. This feature ended at a cave which could have made a superb stance, but instead easier climbing led out right to where a belay could be taken with a view of what was above.

Invariably, caves in this crag are made out of a brown sandstone with innumerable frets and filigrees of fragile stone that form interstices between the frets. Such rock we called "chocolate", for reasons that should be obvious. Above was a fine little corner that led, without difficulty, to the top of the crag. Thus was born *Dreadnaught,* a worthy

E3 5c that despite a rather brutish crux gave nothing but elegance for its entire 250ft.

A second route that day climbed an equally fine corner system near the top left end of the crag, again with a fierce-looking overhang that barred all possible exits. Expecting a fight, the beautifully neat traverse under and to its right belied logical appearances, while the exit up an overhanging crack was the crux at HVS 5a. Again, well-protected and much, much easier than we initially thought. It had given 130ft of splendid quality and though we called it *Buccaneer,* a suitably nautical yet piratical name, it was, in fact, the second ascent of the route Graham Little and Kev Howett climbed in 1995 and named *The Great Escape* – a name totally appropriate for the moves under and around the top overhangs.

We had, it subsequently turned out, been fortunate. Terrible midges had driven off the intrepid duo of Kevin and Graham, thus denying them the opportunity of spying the true size and extent of the crag. This information naturally came at a much later date when we tried to piece together any early history of the crag, not an easy job and still possibly incomplete. Unless routes are written up, they will get lost within the seas of myth that surround such areas.

Keelhaul.

The longest route on the crag was obviously a sea-level ascent straight up the right wall of the crag's seeming "edge". Abandoned by the boat at low tide in our little bay, we descended right and down to the beach boulders, climbed a steep but easy chimney, traversed a grass ledge and descended back to sea level. Crawling through an amazing slot or tunnel cut right through the rock, pushing gear ahead of us, we then crossed an overhung and impending bay of some size, the base, in fact, of the corner of *Dreadnaught* 100ft. above. Another little sea-level traverse on small holds took us to the tiny wave-washed platform at the foot of where we wanted to be. Convoluted it might be, but even this approach was fully in keeping with the ambience of the cliff.

Climbing up honeycombed rock to a cave then moving up right to an exposed edge, resulted in a lonely pitch that seemed miles from any contact. It finished up three typically rounded mantels, quite unprotected in this case, but no more than 4c. An impressive stance on crumbly rock below a narrow chimney bordered an overhanging red and yellow wall of no great soundness, or at least so it looked to us. I think the true scale and atmosphere of the place was at last sinking in. We felt as much explorers as climbers and wisely took the tight chimney rather than a tempting, but bald-looking wall to its right. A very long wandering pitch of around 140ft. led us up shorter corners on increasingly good rock and in a less intimidating position. All this ended below the finest part of this seaward face, sound sandstone, whistle-clean and a choice of tempting groove and corner lines.

The central line, a deep corner groove, was chosen, and two excellent pitches resulted on rock that never went above 4c, was full in the sun and well protected; indeed what more could we possibly have wanted on a day like this? After all, it does not have to be E something-or-other to be thoroughly enjoyable. So, despite wanderings lower down, the top pitches made up for what had turned out to be a 400ft. route at an easier grade than we were anticipating.

Apart from the nasty overhang on *Dreadnaught,* nothing had been quite what it had appeared, the rock flattered and cajoled the climber, we had been seduced and now were quite laid back regarding future difficulties. This happy state of affairs did not last. The ascent of the overhanging cracks left of *Dreadnaught* which resulted in two fine pitches was not without incident.

Expecting (despite the obviously overhanging rock) the cracks to be more reasonable than they appeared we chose a line midway between the start of *Dreadnaught* and the overhanging groove to the right of the gully. Since this groove had again given two surprising pitches of 4c, contrary to what could have been in store, there was every confidence that the cracks to the right again would be a fine morning's route to be followed by something more leisurely in the afternoon. The first pitch, overhanging at its start, was tricky but good, taking in the best climbing at 5b, initially pulling on colossal jugs to a thin landing on a sloping shelf, followed by a traverse right to some interesting thin cracks that provided some 5b climbing to the halfway ledge.

As we shuffled left along the ledge, the straight crack-line above suddenly seemed a rather different ball game. In fact, the crack more than made up for our cavalier attitude. It was sharply overhanging, wide, rounded at the edges, had no rests and gear could only be placed in position from a "barn-door" style layback. The 'Och it will be all right' dismissal of lower down was now a classic sandstone nightmare of desperate laybacks, barn-doors into space and wilting everything. How on earth do you grade something like that? Fortunately, the remainder of the pitch was merely vertical and full of wonderful holds that led out right to the edge of all things; all the position you could want without the difficulty.

A rather nasty but easier (E2 5c) crack was the splendid corner line to the left of the overhanging gully. This gave three pitches of very varied contrast in style and rock. At least it looked hard and off-width in places, so optically we were now more prepared. Armed with colossal nuts, huge hexes that hung around one's neck like so many albatrosses, and a double rack of large Friends, it was, forsooth, difficult to leave the ground.

An initial, scrappy pitch led up a short, wet chimney then heather-bashed to the foot of the main corner. This began with a very free right-angled vertical section on the pale yellow rock that in this case enhanced the climbing rather than detracted from it. Wide 5a bridging, with protection from one of the "albatross" nuts, took us to a free slab stance below the depressingly overhanging off-width crack above. At least it was a corner, so it should provide more purchase than a blank wall. Armed with the massive nuts and Friends that flailed like a thresher on high octane, all the stories you ever heard about wild bridging, arm bars, knee-and-foot jams suddenly came true. The huge nuts simply rolled down the back of the sandy crack until they caught on a hidden protuberance of unseen quality while the Friends became enemies and if it wasn't for a hidden nub for a foot I think we would still be there now. As it was, the emergence onto a fine flat stance was akin to that of a cork from a bottle, with a pair of grovelling climbers licking their various wounds.

The crack above had now deepened into a fine chimney, almost cavernous in appearance. Easy at first, it provided a little resistance near the end where exposed and not brilliantly-protected climbing *à cheval* up the edge led to a final wall which in turn gave a pleasing and delicate slab to finish. In all, it was about 230ft. of climbing that varied from utter graunch to fancy footwork with, most importantly, the rock being not so powdery as first feared. Certainly, memories of the well-named *Keelhaul* will linger.

Pure Gold.

Other routes came and went but we had avoided a fierce-looking wall that lay to the right of the corners where we had climbed our supposed *Buccaneer* and its companions. A heather rake led to this wall and, once there, it was the classic proof that nothing should be dismissed until noses are rubbed up to it. Between 100ft. and 140ft. high it was bounded on the right by a fierce flanged crack that warned of more terrible struggles and upside-down moves, but turned out to be a hardish VS. Turning the wall to its left, its appearance could not be more enticing – solid red rock of immaculate quality and devoid of vegetation, tippled into sinuous curves and half-hidden suggestions of a promise of holds. It was difficult to gauge grades when so little information was released, only upward progress would tell.

Perhaps appropriately, the first foray took the wall up its centre. At 80° it was less steep than most of the climbing farther right, but the rough, rounded rock would require a more subtle approach. In the story so far I have deliberately avoided mentioning who led what and when, as it was, in truth, a joint effort. However, this was different in that it was very much a leader's route, one long pitch up into the blankness with absolutely nothing except faith in what had gone before.

Bob, fired up if a trifle nervous, launched over a starting bulge and committed himself to what lay above. I don't really know who was feeling the more apprehensive. Had we at last bitten off more than we could chew? His progress, despite my forebodings, was steady. He began to rave about the quality and the hidden edges that, to me, simply did not exist.

After some time, he topped out, obviously more than happy and eager for me to appreciate what was evidently something rather special. The result was a truly superb El, just about 5b and following a hidden series of agreeable surprises; holds that were invisible from just below turned out to be good and the position, friction and sheer quality of the climbing could not be bettered on the crag, despite it being only one pitch long. Definitely one of those surprising pitches that, in effect, sum up all that rock climbing should be about, a touchstone in more ways than one.

Though somewhat poorer in quality, the nearby black streak that poured down the sandstone to the right of Bob's *Pure Gold* was too good to miss. This was my turn at the imponderable face and, as if to reassure, the moves up the initial overhang were exceptionally well endowed with holds. Naturally, it could not last. The holds and protection ran out more or less simultaneously and I was faced with a series of 5c moves at the point farthest from rather marginal protection 15ft. below. The rock, of course, was flawlessly perfect, the friction good, but what holds existed formed exiguous scoops of a horribly-sloping nature and the climbing, if it was going to be done at all, was best done quickly. Which it was, somewhat heart in mouth, but oh! what rock, sun, position, flaky failure or fall would be entirely my own fault but as it was, the executed sequence went smoothly and arrived at holds and protection in abundance, as if the crag had merely held its breath for a while before resuming its normal indulgence. Easier climbing lay above, still good, but the memories are of those halting, serious, positions where a fall was unthinkable.

The impending corner well to the right of this "immaculate" wall "went" too, despite teasing us with visions of overhangs and rounded cracks. *Hit and Run* gave two pitches of relative ease at El, cutting through the blank walls on either side. The start had been reached by an exposed traverse across heather shelves that led to a nicely-positioned eyrie below the corner with a sizeable drop below. The slightly overhanging corner, complete with the usual bulges, provided a crux that gave wide strenuous bridging, a hoot of an overhang at the top and an exposed stance. This was followed by a ridiculously easy traverse right above this roof, a section that from below looked overhanging and blank, but led to huge pocket holds and so to the top. Though perhaps it epitomised the climbing here, it was the day we did it that was memorable. Faultless blue skies, no wind, a late October day with sun angling down huge shafts that illuminated Isle Martin and then the Outer Isles as the day wore on.

Climbing is not about tick lists really, or grades, though it can be of endless amusement to compare someone else's opinion of a route with one's own. To me, it's about places like this and the afterglow of memories, sometimes good and sometimes bad. Of course, we could have ended up with a cliff of the "usual" sandstone, tons of vertical rubbish swathed in clinging vegetation and not something more akin to gritstone at its best. In fact I had looked at the pinnacle and walls a mile back along the coast towards Blughasary, but was repulsed by the sight of crumbling crannies, tottering spires and maroon-coloured walls of disintegrating tot, as the Camus Mor cliffs so easily could have been, but were, thank God, not.

We went to other places too, exploration up on Breabag with moveable handholds of quartzite, lonely, remote and far from humankind, to the almost roadside at Stone Valley with Blyth, Graeme and Ian, filling in the gaps which turned out to be wider than had been previously thought. Later on, as the weather turned cold and the days short, we re-appraised the walls left of the road beyond the cliffs of Ardmair and found the excellent *Steel Spider* on Morning Crag, a nice complement to the routes on the nearby Evening Wall, strenuously overhanging but revealing hidden surprises, all pleasant, *en route*. But it was Camus Mor that really inspired, a hidden gem that, like so much in this area, needed a hands-on approach which repaid the effort of discovering it a hundredfold. As if any advice were needed, if in doubt, just go and look; you have nothing to lose but your prejudices.

Apologia

While in no way wishing to deny any, or all of the nefarious deeds described in the above article, I do, however, wish to plead NOT GUILTY to the literary effluvia flowing from his pen. It is his and his alone.

From the article members will picture me as some sort of crumbly on speed. 'Manically pointing with insane gleam in eye.' I was brought up to believe that it was rude to point. The gleam – sun on the specs! I have never used the word Yup. I am not a cowboy. As to the frothing at the mouth, this is more likely to be a case of senile dribble.

In defence of the article, I would like to say that John has rather understated the many hours of pure pleasure that the Camus Mor cliffs gave us. That we could have all this, to ourselves, in this day and age is just a wonder. Perhaps a reward for the frustrations of being faithful enough to seek our climbing in Scotland. May I wish you all that I wish myself – warm sun, dry rock, and a gentle breeze.

Bob Brown.

EDGE OF EMOTION

By Colwyn Jones

@%&!...(expletive deleted.) There was a white sling above me. Someone had climbed the route before. But why leave a sling at the top of the first pitch except to abseil? I made the last moves to the stance and smiled as I looked closer. It was bleached white where exposed, but deep in the rock it was green. We had used it to retreat back down on to the snow six months earlier. Perhaps the sun does shine in Scotland after all!

Knowing UV light and nylon don't mix, I threaded a new sling, clipped them both and shouted: 'Safe.' My long-suffering second answered that she was cold and didn't really want to climb. To be honest, I could see why. The wind was picking up and the watery sun shining through the trees when we had awoken was long gone. The first pitch was a series of tenuous, sloping grooves which, despite my attentions with an ice axe, were still rather vegetated. She had calmly watched my slow progress to the foot of the wall then the explosion of activity after the two solid nut placements were found. The struggle to stand upright on the sloping footholds, followed by the ignominious retreat to turn the bulging wall on the left. That had been six months ago and I was impressed by the density of crampon scratches I now found. Today I had rested pathetically on a tight rope determined to get over the bulge, before submitting to the final humiliation of pulling up on the gear.

I knew her comment was born of long, cold waiting, more rhetoric than protest. I took the ropes in and shouted that she could safely turn the wall on the left protected by the yellow rope. Experience had taught me compromise and while hanging like a baby in a spacewalker I had unclipped the yellow rope allowing her to follow along the Grade 4/5 mixed pitch we had torqued and struggled up earlier in the year. As always she climbed gracefully, easily and fluently and was warmer, if no happier, on the stance.

Yo-yoing down to collect the gear, I still couldn't get over the bulge without pulling on gear. 'What do you expect with that big sack on,' was the curt response to my confession of failure. But it was no rebuke, she had carefully, and thoughtfully, handed me the excuse I would need later when explaining the use of 'points of aid', to the lads.

We had been here before. Last time we had abseiled back down Crampoff Corner, a Grade 3 winter climb, but now the beautiful edge soared away above us. This was why I had returned. Six months earlier, unable to summon enough courage to continue my *à cheval* progress 20ft above my last runner, I had retreated. Now I relished the exposure, pulling on the edge and smearing on the slab. The moss was dry and easily brushed off. There was also plenty of gear now, but it had to be arranged so one rope protected a slide down the slab, the other a fall over the edge into Crampoff Corner. I had reached my last high point where the edge suddenly rears up. By standing on a slot where I'd placed a big hex, which might stop me going over the edge, I reached up, looking for rugosities on the slab to my left. Above, the moss was thick and overgrown where I'd unsuccessfully tried to get an ice-axe pick to stick in it. Finally, I unearthed some knobbles on the slab and standing on one, straightened up and was able to reach over the worst of the moss. 'Leave it for the next guy,' I thought.

From here the edge was exposed and perfect. The protection was good and I moved confidently up to a roomy, sheltered stance with a convenient spike belay, where the skulls, bones and feathers of small birds showed peregrine falcons had been there before me.

Ann climbed steadily up the edge and after some hesitation passed the steepening and was soon pulling her gloves back on next to me. She still hadn't forgiven me for making her climb in the cold, but didn't try to extinguish the twinkle in my eye.

The next short pitch followed the edge to easy ground and that was that, a fine route I thought. We moved up and were stopped by another slab. I moved left to bridge into a corner, which was perhaps the fifth pitch of Turfinator (Grade 2) we had climbed a year earlier. From there you just bridged up as far as you could. Stopping to excavate a nut placement or push a Friend into the slots which appeared in the side of the corner. An easy pitch but in keeping with the route.

At the block belay at the top I had spied another slab off to the left. This would be the final pitch of what was turning into a classic. From the foot of the slab I started up a left trending, thin groove to a shallow, vertical crack. After a few moves I became increasingly aware that the nut placement I had just excavated was now at least 10m below me. I made another thin and tenuous move up the increasingly vegetated crack. It was here I stopped and started wishing there was a peg. If this had been the Alps there would be a lovely solid peg nearby. I also knew if I found one then ours would not be a first ascent, but suddenly, I didn't care.

It was then that my watchful second pointed out a small edge on my right which I hadn't seen. I could undercling it and quickly stuffed a No. 2 Friend into the gap. Above, there was a six-inch-wide ramp going right but that was still two tricky moves above me. I checked the Friend and noted that the under cling moved slightly. I got a nut in higher up the crack but it was just as poor. Nothing else for it so I just continued up and after a couple of fraught moves was on the ramp. Halfway up the ramp, and by now 20m above my last decent bit of gear, I found the crack I had been praying for. A Friend slipped in, followed by a big wire just for good measure. The slab seemed to gently exhale, relax and sit back a few degrees. At the top of the ramp it was left again to a small, vertical overlap and after pulling a few holds off, but placing some reasonable gear, I manteled onto the summit plateau howling in wild delight. The wind blasted over the top of the slab and after finding a couple of unsatisfactory nut placements, I quickly brought my second up.

She was smiling now!

(Edge of Emotion, Ann's Buttress, Coire nan Gall, Carn Liath. 165m, HVS 5a (2 points of aid). First Ascent 28/9/97, C. Jones, A. MacDonald)

WHILE ROME BURNED

By Andrew Fraser

HOPES, aspirations, dreams. All of us have a tick list, climbers perhaps more than most. I would bet that your average climber's hit list probably includes a fair share of recognised 'classic' routes, well-kent faces whose invitations stare from the climbing glossies. No doubt it will also include a bit of peer pressure, routes to steal a march on, or merely keep up with the pack. After all, a well chosen route can, with the right amount of ingenuity and subterfuge, inflict enough psychological damage to keep your reputation intact for that little bit longer, à la Patey. So far it's all nice and logical.

On the other hand, there are parts of some tick lists which deny easy categorisation, sane or otherwise. Raeburn's Gully on Dumyat in the Ochils for example, a foul, vegetated, conglomerate but otherwise irresistible chimney [1]. One of my own secret (till now) peccadilloes has been Beta Route on the Orion Face in summer. The mere thought of installing a fishing garden gnome in the middle of this Big Bad Ben obscurity fills me with unaccountable glee. The only things that have stopped me have been the weight of the gnome and the fact that no-one would join me.

The reason that these routes stick out like sore thumbs is that they probably reveal the character of the climber. On the one hand, you have the likes of Don Whillans whose uncompromising and direct routes reflected his personality, a veritable Clint Eastwood of spaghetti climbing. At the opposite end of the spectrum are 'obscure ways traced by even more obscure men' [2]. Beta Route with the gnome would obviously fall into that category. In fact, I have a nagging doubt that most of my new routes would fall into that category. Not by any fault of the routes of course, but by deviousness or fatal obscurity of the character producing them.

All this goes some way to explain why the Nose of Sgurr an Fhidhleir in Coigach was in pole position on the grid for nearly 15 years. An early picture in Poucher's *Scottish Peaks* initially inspired, as did the chance encounter one misty day on Queensberry with an old chap who had been involved in one of the early debacles on the route (they got halfway up then unroped, each climber wandering about on those decomposing grass terraces in search of an escape, each managing eventually to get down safely – the thought doesn't bear thinking about). Later, a first visit to Coigach and the sight of that shark's fin of the Nose, incongruous even among the weirdos of Coigach and Assynt, was enough to hook me. Add to that the facts that I knew of no-one who had done the route, that its grade was uncertain (old Scottish V.S.), and that the route description included the following glittering lures:

'The climax to a series of attempts spread over the last century, and a milestone in the development of climbing in the North-west Highlands.'

'The difficulties are prolonged and serious. Dry conditions are recommended though a cross-wind on the exposed upper section could be intimidating, [3] or:–

'The first 500ft. consists of a cluster of sandstone slabs interspersed by grass and black moss-filled grooves. Above that for another 1000ft. rears a stone Leviathan, broad at the base and gradually tapering and steepening to a great prow, overhanging at the top. A *Titanic;* it is like looking at the massive bow of a ship advancing on you as you row frantically out of the way.' [4].

The years passed by and for a number of reasons my date with the Great White Whale remained distant. It wasn't that I avoided Coigach, quite the contrary in fact. The Achnahaird campsite and the Fuaran bar became regular haunts. Stac Pollaidh was plundered for a number of new routes, obscure or devious. The Reiff sea-cliffs were discovered by us (though the Journal a few months later revealed that every man and his dog had already climbed there).

No, the reason was Dickson. I could forgive the Fuaran epics which he dragged me into, even the 1p.m. barbecued breakfasts when alpine starts had been promised (resulting in most of our routes on the Stac being climbed in near darkness). He was a master at disparaging the best laid Fhidhleir plans, and of scaring likely candidates. Hard men were subjected to his bar room tales of vertical grass, Patagonian winds, the sunbathing potential of Reiff and other ploys. By the time he had finished the route had a large sign on it, beloved of ancient cartographers 'Here Be Dragons'. Worse, he had a repertoire of (admittedly true) tales about my exploits on turf, loose rock, etc. My sanity in proposing such a deadly heap of choss was obviously in question. And so it went on, for years.

Enter Kevin and Ann, relative initiates to the climbing game. A September weekend at Achnahaird, two days on Stac Pollaidh, the Fhidhleir still soaking after a summer of rain. Hardly even worth Dickson's while to flex his bar room skills on the Fhidhleir. He thought that I had forgotten, but obsessions aren't like that. Ask Captain Ahab (or the whale for that matter).

And so a glorious third day; Kevin and myself heading for Cul Beag, while Ann and Mephistopheles went to Reiff. A short day, though I toyed with the idea of taking the corporate dinner with us, just in case they got back earlier and got too peckish. Still, female company demands a certain amount of decorum and surely Ann would stop him from eating the lot. Dinner stayed in the tent.

Cul Beag's crags didn't really look up to much, and it would be an awful hassle to turn the car on that single track road. It would also be a shame to waste such a day on something minor. With such twisted logic the choice was obvious, a wee look at the Fhidhleir. After all, if time was short or if it was wet we could surely find something on the rubbish tip of Beinn an Eoin.

There is a quote that the only thing worse than not achieving your life's ambition is to achieve it. Underneath the Nose, eating a late lunch, that maxim seemed unlikely to apply. The Nose was much steeper than I had imagined. It was also somewhat wet, although the wettest part, a waterfall corner high on the face, was obviously off route. In short, it had all the attraction of a long starved Jabberwocky, drooling at the prospect of dinner. Nor did the time, now 3 o'clock, lend much encouragement.

On the other hand, I finally had a willing accomplice. It might be another 15 years till I had another, particularly if Dickson got his hands on them. Anyway, the nature of such obsessions is that they are oblivious to rational arguments and logic. They draw you, like water to a sponge (not a bad analogy as it turned out), Captain Ahab to the Fiddler.

The route, for those unfamiliar with it, goes up some miles of grooves to arrive at the Pale Slabs. These lead, with increasing difficulty, to the final nose. Above that, the rock gives up any pretence and the turf takes over, fortunately at an easier angle.

After 15 years I had expected to be disappointed. Not a bit of it. As a counter argument to Dickson I had always argued that as the lower pitches had been climbed in the primeval twilight of climbing history, then they must be piss-easy. A perfectly sound argument – when drunk! Fat chance, the rock was wet, the grass greasy and the climbing surprisingly engrossing. Pitch after 4b pitch followed one another up the grooves to arrive on the tilted grass beneath the first slab. With no belay in sight I continued up the steepening grass, decomposing steps of wet, slimy, unprotected mud. I reflected that it was perfect terrain for hobnailers and Norfolk jackets, not to mention the odd few pints of 'Mummery's Blood'.

Having effectively bypassed the first Pale Slab, it was time for the second one, climbed from the 'Hansom', a luxurious ledge and the perfect spot for a bivi if ever I saw one. Number Two slab provided 4c moves on soaking wet sandstone, not one of my specialities. Unusually, I got up, to land on another fine ledge beneath the crux, 5a slab.

All this had taken some time, entirely due to the inclement conditions and nothing whatsoever with the fact that my climbing has been referred to as 'The Abominable Slowman'. However, even Kevin was beginning to doubt my sanity and was indicating the need for speed in the face of approaching darkness. Fortunately, I had a trump card in knowing that there would be a full moon to shine directly onto the face, and with not a cloud in the sky, moonlight was a certainty.

The crux slab was strangely dry. Above, I remembered John Mackenzie's article where they had been led too far right into the Homeric epic of the Tower Finish. So I went leftwards, some lovely climbing on fine, sound rock, the sort of stuff that flatters your climbing abilities. Given the state of my climbing abilities that meant that it couldn't possibly be the real 5a finish and I was off route. My peregrinations had also led me over the steepest part of the face, making for an unattractive abseil option in the now near complete darkness [5]. I belayed in a wet corner, a miniature Niagara bearing an uncanny resemblance to the off route corner that we had viewed from the start. Kevin followed, somehow getting up the 5a slab in the dark, no questions asked about his means.

A waterfall presented an unattractive option in which to await the rapidly rising moon, so I set off up the corner. In the pitch dark I felt the crack widths and estimated Friends accordingly. These provided for healthy aid till the crack ran out.

A few moves leftwards, then blind groping eventually found turf and the sanctuary of a sloping grass ledge. As I brought up Kevin the moon rose and bathed the face in a superb, climbing-friendly light.

In the moonlight I could see three alternatives. To the right was the easiest angle, up slabs with invisible protection. To the left was an overhanging crack which could probably be aided. Above was an indeterminate line, worth closer inspection. All was in control.

Ten minutes later Kevin was on the ledge and the moon had completely disappeared under a wall of cloud. Darkness. A classic Fhidhleir joke! I tried of course. I got 15ft. up the middle line before it became obvious that we could see nothing and that I had no idea what ropes were clipped to what, or even whether I was belayed. The risk factor had become unacceptable and I retreated to await any reappearance of the moon.

The grass ledge was sloping and wet, but spectacularly scenic. Beneath, the crag heeled over 800ft. of space, Lochan Tuath perfectly framed by the precipices of Beinn an Eoin. In 20 years of climbing there are certain views or places which stand out, idylls to be enjoyed when faced with some particularly tedious bit of the office day. This was certainly one of those occasions. Mind you, we did have eight hours of moonless night in which to enjoy it (and they say that you can't have enough of a good thing!)

A sense of farce prevailed. Kevin was Sylvester Stallone in the just released *Cliffhanger,* regaling me for two hours with its unfeasible and unbelievable plot. I reflected that it was only slightly less improbable than a bivi in a whale. As bivis go it wasn't that uncomfortable. The cold was at the just shivering level which prohibits any sleep (Kevin's version of this was that he couldn't get any sleep for my snoring).

Kevin was, of course, somewhat concerned that Ann would not know his fate. I was also concerned – my reputation depended on Dickson adhering to the unwritten rule that the rescue should not be called out till the next morning (or alternatively that he would give them Simon Steer's name rather than mine). I reflected that it would have been a bad idea to have taken their dinner with us.

They were also concerned, but Dickson, on seeing the car parked at the Fhidhleir lay-by and surmising the late hour, had concluded that, like Pinocchio and Geppetto, we had been swallowed by the great whale. If only he had warned Kevin about (a) the Fiddler and (b) me.

Six a.m. and a murky dawn. Cold, creaking joints and their owner try to psych-up to the uncertain desperates lying above. Last night's 15ft. is climbed to reveal a grass stairway, cleaving easily through steep ground for 25ft. to exit through an arch. Above, only easy scrambling remained. An even bigger Fhidhleir joke! A bit like the whale giving Captain Ahab his leg back and saying: 'Have a nice day.'

Seven a.m. on top of the hill and things seem just as surreal, clanking about in rock boots and hardware while Achiltibuie slumbers. Beneath, we rendezvous with Dickson, rescue team still asleep and reputation intact. He was right of course, the route was everything that he had claimed, even in his most drunken excesses. But, so was I, it had fully lived up to expectations. And as for Kevin, well he enjoyed the experience so much that one year to the day he and Ann got benighted on the Romsdalhorn (he claims accidentally – it was raining at the time).

My one regret; if we had started the Phantom Fiddler (1000ft. Scottish V.S.) at eight a.m. that morning – now that would have made a tale!

References and Notes:

1. The current Editor resisted this 'route' with consummate ease.

2. An untraceable quote, too savage for a Patey and thus probably a Campbellism.

3. *SMC District Guide to the Northern Highlands.* Tom Strang. 1975.

4. *A Short Walk With Cemni-Kaze.* John Mackenzie. *SMCJ* 1980, pp. 26-32.

5. It appears that we unwittingly followed the line taken by Patey and Taylor on the second ascent in 1964. See *SMCJ* 1970, page 297.

SCOTTISH HILL-NAMES – THE ENGLISH CONNECTION

By Peter Drummond

HAVERS. Surely no? Norse and Irish connections (*SMCJs* 1996, 1997), aye . . . but the auld enemy? Actually, yah.

Most hill-names in the south-east of Scotland, from the Tay to the Tweed estuaries, have names that are Scots: this language was initially known as Inglis, for the simple reason that it was brought into the area by Anglian settlers from what is now England, from the 7th century on. It is a cousin rather than a son of what we now call English, since both Scots and English are descendants of the old dialects of Anglo-Saxon. The Angles coming into Scotland spoke the Northumbrian dialect, one branch of what became Old English, and that's why there are hill-words found both north and south of the Border, with a common linguistic ancestry – in the Anglo-Saxons' early English.

More than 200 years ago a local book on Tweeddale [1] noted some of these hill-words or elements – though not very elegantly, thus:

'Hills are variously named according to their magnitude: as Law, Pen, Kipp, Coom, Dod, Craig, Fell, Top, Drum, Tor, Watch, Rig, Edge, Know, Knock, Mount, Kaim, Bank, Hope, Head, Cleugh-head, Gare, Scarf, Height, Shank, Brae, Kneis, Muir, Green, etc.'

Almost 30 elements made up his list, including one or two errors (a hope is a valley, a green is not a hill), but omitting significant names like Cairn or Pike, and Seat or Side. He was probably wrong too in ascribing the difference to magnitude – shape may be equally significant. However, most Englishmen of his day, living 40 miles south and well beyond the national border would have recognised most of these words: but for fellow-Scotsmen living a similar distance north-west in the Gaelic fringes, they would have been a foreign tongue. Many of these words have English roots, as we will see. But first there is a problem of the biggest 'tree' in the 'wood' that he describes, so to speak: Armstrong has missed out the biggest English contribution to hill-names, in Tweeddale and elsewhere – the word, Hill itself.

Consider for a moment the words Hill and Mountain, widely used, often interchangeably. It is generally accepted that a mountain is higher than a hill, and for instance, the SMC Tables class Munros and Corbetts as mountains while Donalds are defined as hills. None of the Munros are Hills, and only 2% of the Corbetts (and, for instance, Corryhabbie Hill used to be called Cathadh – snowdrift before anglicisation), and 5% of the Grahams are Hills.

---

[1] Capt. M. J. Armstrong. Parish of Innerleithen, 1775.

But height is not the main distinction. Both Mountain and Hill can be used in the plural form to name an upland range – the Cairngorm Mountains or the Pentland Hills for instance. But whereas Hill is often the surname of an *individual* Hill – Black Hill, for example – Mountain never is so used in Scotland, and indeed very rarely is in the English-speaking world – with the intriguing exception being Ireland of the Gaeltacht. [2] (The Mount element in names like Mount Keen is an corruption or anglicisation of the Gaelic monadh.) And the reason for this is essentially linguistic, for while 'mountain' is a latecomer into English from French (where it is also a group word rarely applied to individual hill-names [3]), 'hill' is one of the oldest English words, deep-rooted in the language, and available to name heights with when that process took place. 'Hill' was used in written works from c.1000 AD, while 'Mountain' first appeared in c.1200 AD.

English is a Germanic language, and is believed to originate from immigrants from the Frisian area of the Netherlands. The Oxford English Dictionary data on the origin of the word 'hill' reads: 'Old English hyll = Old Frisian hel, Lower German hull, Middle Dutch hille, hil, hul . . . from the Indo-European base [-word] also of Latin coilis'.

A formidable pedigree there for hill as a founder-member of the language, and not surprising it was used from early on in place-names across southern and eastern England, and swept strongly into south-east Scotland with English speakers from the 7th century on. But it seems it did not shake off its origins as a relatively low hill, and it will be clear from map study that the hills called Hill are not the highest even in the south-east. For instance, in the Donald's Tables [4] of southern hills, although 23% of them are surnamed Hill, the highest is 13th in the old list (11th in the new).

Now it might be objected that Hill, in spite of its pedigree, had forced itself on older Gaelic names and produced a bastard or mongrel set. Examples of this can be found: the fate of Cathadh now Corryhabbie Hill mentioned above; King's Seat Hill in the Ochils, formerly Inner Cairn [5] or Pyket Stane in the Borders, now Pykestone Hill [1 – op cit]; and several examples of a hill-hill tautology where Hill is tacked onto a pre-existing Gaelic or Scots hill-name element to produce, for example, Binn Hill or Dod Hill. Also in this class of ersatz hill-names are the ubiquitous Hill of X names found in north-east Scotland and Shetland (e.g. – Hill of Fare or Hill of Cat): they are almost certainly full or partial translations of older Gaelic names (e.g. Meall na Faire or Cnoc a'Chait), or in the case of

---

[2] There are 92 mountains – e.g., Brandon Mountain – among Ireland's 453 Marilyns, as listed In TACit Press *The Hewitts and Marilyns of Ireland,* E. Clements 1997.
[3] Although the word means mountain, and is used in the plural to denote high ranges such as the Alps, as an Individual name montagne is often used in France for small hills – e.g. La Montagne, near Auxerre, 227m – especially in Brittany.
[4] Either the New Donalds in TACit's *The Grahams and New Donalds* , or In the SMC's *Munro's Tables, and other tables of lower hills.*
[5] Angus Watson. *The Ochils: Place-names, History, Traditions,* 1997.

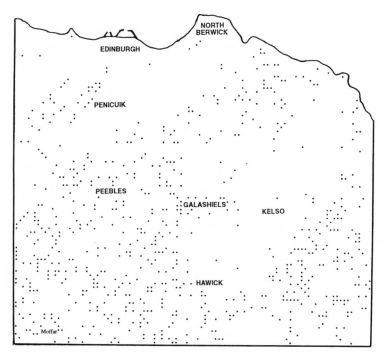

A distribution of hills containing the name-element Hill, in an area of south-east Scotland.

Shetland, marks of the influence of incoming Scots speakers [6]. But in the south-east heartland of Scots this Hill of X type is rare, and very few names there are in the tautological category either. Some figures: I counted all hills named on the 1:50000 OS maps in an area of south-east Scotland of 10,000 sq km [7]. There are 1787 hills named (not including farm names), of which 43% are surnamed Hill, and only 30 or so of these 775 Hills could be considered clear tautologies (such as Cairn Hill). (See map 1.)

So Hill must be considered a vibrant hill-name element, of impeccable old English ancestry, used in its own right to refer to relatively lower eminences: it is no coincidence that, being near the valleys, many of them are named after farms, or hopes, or the like. And although it is indeed found in the high heartlands of the Scottish Border hills, it is more common round the fringes and in the foothills of higher ground.

---

[6] Professor W. F. H. Nicolaisen *Scottish Place-Names* 1976. He examines names like Burn of X, Water of X, Bridge of X, to come to his conclusions: Hill of X as in the same mould. See pp 57-64 in his book.

[7] OS grid area NT, stretching from the Lothians to Moffat and the Merse, on OS sheets 66, 67, 73, 74, 79, 80 and parts of 72, 75, 78 and 81.

Topographical terms of Southern Scotland.

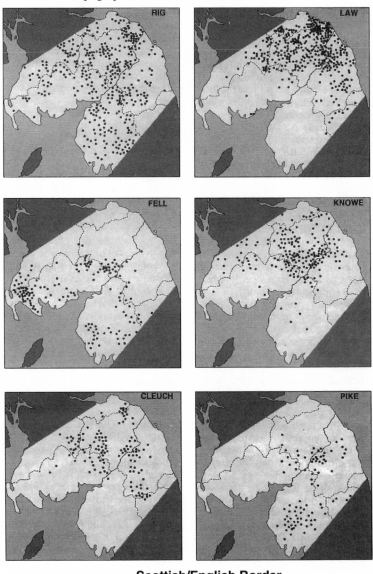

——— Scottish/English Border.
.... Region or County Border

Maps reproduced by kind permission of the Royal Scottish Geographical Society: published in the Scottish Geographical Magazine 1990 (see footnote 9).

But the one great irony for this quintessentially English word is that it is almost totally absent from the highest ground in England, the Lakeland Fells: in the new FRCC guide, listing the highest 244 fells [8], only two are surnamed Hill (the celebrated Loadpot Hill and Wether Hill) and they are well down the height league table. This underlines the importance of the linguistic factor, for Lakeland is a bastion of Norse names. But for the word Hill, used by English-speakers worldwide as the standard term for high ground, it is clearly a prophet without honour in its own hilly heartland.

Having taken to the Hills for a while, let us return to the other elements identified by our 18th century writer. Virtually all of them are found on both sides of the Border [9] (See map 2). Some of them come from the Norse connection, in particular Fell (from Norse fjell [10] which flowered in the English Lakes and possibly, simultaneously, in Galloway: Dod, Edge and Rig may also have come from this source. Some have Celtic roots like Pen, Cairn and Craig (appearing as Crag south of the Border), from the Britons who were replaced in south Scotland by the Gaels – these elements are widespread in upland Wales, where the Britons took final refuge. But two at least have fairly deep Anglo-Saxon roots – Law and Knowe [11].

Law springs from an Old English word Maw, meaning a tumulus (burial mound) in southern England, or a hill farther north, the transition of meaning taking place on its northward march somewhere in the north Midlands: in Northumberland, many hills called Law are small and rounded, resembling tumuli [12]. The same pattern can be found north of the Border in the Merse, the gently rolling lowland along the lower Tweed: no hills are high enough here to be named on the map, but instead there are dozens of farmhouses built on top of the gentle swellings, and whose names end in -law, obviously taking on the earlier hill-name. But both south and north of the Border, the name was then applied to higher, wilder hills – respectively. For instance, Bolt's Law at 540m near Consett, and

[6] Professor W. F. H. Nicolaisen *Scottish Place—Names* 1976. He examines names like Burn of X, Water of X, Bridge of X, to come to his conclusions: Hill of X as in the same mould. See pp 57-64 in his book.

[7] OS grid area NT, stretching from the Lothians to Moffat and the Merse, on OS sheets 66, 67, 73, 74, 79, 80 and parts of 72, 75, 78 and 81.

[8] J. Parker and T. Pickles *The Lakeland Fells,* FRCC. Ernest Press 1996.

[9] *Scottish Geographical Magazine* Vol. 106 (1990), pp 108-112 – I. M. Matley *Topographic terms of Southern Scotland: their distribution and significance.*

[10] *SMCJ* Vol. 36 (1996) pp 50-53, *Scottish Hill-Names – the Scandinavian Connection,* Peter Drummond,

[11] Other Scots hill-names are dealt with in more detail in chapter 7 (Kips and Laws) of *Scottish Hill and Mountain Names,* Peter Drummond, SMT 1992.

[12] Margaret Gelling, *Place-names in the Landscape,* 1984.

oor ain Broad Law at 840m, second-highest Donald. It has gone on to be one of the great success stories, in Scotland spreading to the Sidlaws, the Ochils, the Renfrew Heights, far beyond its Borders heartland. In the 10,000 sq km sample referred to previously, it is second only to Hill with 303 specimens (17%), and showing strongly in the Moorfoots and Lammermuirs.

What does Law signify? Two 19th century writers had little doubt: the 1808 *Etymological Dictionary of the Scottish Language* describes a law as 'a rounded hill, generally of a somewhat conical shape and conspicuous among others'. While James Hogg, the Ettrick Shepherd, described them 20 years later as 'the common green dumpling-looking hills [13] Perhaps he knew of the hill called Pudding Law near Yetholm. Agreement on shape in these two definitions, certainly, but there are Laws which break the rules, so to speak. Broad Law – originally called Broad Law of Hairstane – has a plateau top which Armstrong says 'might admit of a circuit horse-race of two miles without the smallest inequality of surface'. The many Laws in the Moorfoot-Lammermuir area are in keeping with the gentle swelling profiles of land there. Traprain Law, that volcanic plug injected into East Lothian fields, is precipitous rather than 'green and grassy', while The Law seen from Tillicoultry is perfectly conical but not rounded. Law, it would seem, is a hill-element big enough to be used for a variety of hill-shapes and -sizes, somewhat like Beinn is able to do in the Highlands.

Finally a look at the Knowes. Another element with a fine Old English pedigree from knoll (earlier cnoll) – first appearing in written work in c.880 AD – from Germanic cnol meaning a knob or hillock, it is easy to imagine how the soft ending 'll' dropped off in common usage. In the Scottish Borders it took root and developed into a more sizeable hill, just as Law and Hill have done, but not quite so successfully. In numerical terms, Knowes make up 8% of the sample area, making it fourth commonest after Hill, Law and Rig: in height term, there is only one Donald (SMC Tables), albeit a high one, Fifescar Knowe. In early English, knoll was initially used for rounded summits rather than whole hills. If you look at an OS map you will notice that most knowes are subsidiary tops, or ends of spurs above a valley, rather than separate peaks – like Peter Pan, they have never quite grown up.

---

[13] Both quoted in the *Scottish National Dictionary* under the entry for Law.

BIG GREY MAN – THE EVIDENCE

By Jack Hastie

THE appearance of the 3rd edition of Affleck Gray's book, *Big Grey Man of Ben Macdhui,* in 1994 and the publication of Rennie McOwen's *Magic Mountains* in 1996 make it opportune to review the evidence for the haunting of Ben Macdhui.

The legend first captured the headlines with a dramatic announcement on November 28, 1925 by Norman Collie, Professor of Organic Chemistry at University College London.

Collie was a scientist, a Fellow of the Royal Society and a past president of the Alpine Club; a pioneering mountaineer of his time, with experience in the Himalayas, Alps and Rockies. At the Annual Dinner of the Cairngorm Club that year he announced for the first time in public that, more than 35 years earlier, he had had a terrifying experience while climbing alone on Ben Macdhui in mist and snow.

He was coming down from the cairn when he began to think he heard sounds other than merely the noise of his own footsteps in the snow. For every few steps he took he heard a big crunch, and then another crunch as if someone was walking after him but taking steps three or four times the length of his own.

The Professor was seized with a blind terror and rushed down the mountain for several miles into the safety of Rothiemurchus Forest.

About 12 years later, Collie said, he told his story to Dr A. M. Kellas, lecturer in Chemistry at Middlesex Hospital Medical School and a veteran Himalayan explorer who subsequently died during a reconnaissance of Everest in 1921. Kellas told Collie that he too had had a weird experience on top of the mountain around midnight. He had seen a giant figure which had been invisible to his brother, who was also present, come up out of the Lairig Ghru and wander round the summit cairn. What had surprised him most was the size of the figure which he estimated at about 10ft. tall.

Collie's story is reported in the *Press and Journal,* Aberdeen of November 30, 1925, and the *Cairngorm Club Journal* of July, 1926. These reports are identical and appear to be verbatim transcripts of what Collie said at the time. Other versions exist.

Shortly after Collie's death in 1942, E. C. C. Baly, in *Obituaries of Fellows of the Royal Society,* quoted him as stating that he heard the footsteps as he was approaching the summit cairn. He stopped and retraced his steps, expecting to meet another climber but encountered no-one. When he started for the summit again the steps followed him again till he reached the cairn. Here he stopped, but the steps continued, coming nearer and nearer until they came right up to him. At this point Collie fled. Baly was a former student and assistant of Collie at University College and climbed with him in the Lofoten Islands in 1904. His account gives every impression of being a verbatim report of what Collie actually told him. However, it is not what Collie said at the Cairngorm Club dinner in 1925. There is no record of when the Baly version originated, but it was not published till 1945 and appears to be a late elaboration.

The mountaineering historian Ronald W. Clark repeats Baly's account in *Mountaineering in Britain* (1957) and in *Scotland's Magazine* of November 1961. In the latter he claimed that Collie had told his story much earlier at the turn of the century in New Zealand, that it was published there and that that was how Kellas came to hear of it.

Clark is certainly wrong about this; it contradicts what Collie himself said and it is known that he did not visit New Zealand till the 1930s. Another misconception is that he saw something. This arises from a phrase used by Seton Gordon in 1948: after mentioning the legend of the big grey figure he writes: 'Collie encountered this spectre.' The context, however, makes it clear that he did not imply that Collie actually saw anything.

A letter written by W. G. Robertson to the *Press and Journal* in December 1925, and citing as its authority Kellas's brother, gives a different version of the Kellas experience. In this, both brothers saw the figure coming towards them from the summit cairn in the late afternoon. Like Collie they experienced intense fear and, under the impression that the figure was following them, fled to lower ground.

Collie and Kellas were both extremely strong witnesses, being not only experienced climbers but academics of distinction. On the other hand, both events were made public only long after they had taken place; Kellas's experience dates from around 1900, Collie's from the late 1880s. Kellas, and his brother, were both dead when their stories were published. Moreover, it is clear from Baly's account that Collie subsequently embellished his tale.

It has been suggested that Collie made his story up because he had been asked, at short notice, to address the Cairngorm Club dinner. McOwen states that Collie had 'a mild reputation as a prankster'. However, Gray gives an entirely different impression of the man as 'of extreme reticence', 'sardonic and dry as dust, he did not suffer fools gladly' and 'utterly sincere', and it seems a long shot to suggest that the inspiration for his tale was the requirement that he make an after-dinner speech. According both to Baly and to his recent biographer, Christine Mill, he was something of a mystic, who believed, among other things, in the Loch Ness Monster.

The revelations of the experiences of Collie and Kellas, popularised the legend. Their accounts became a magnet which attracted reports of unusual experiences from all over the central and western Cairngorms.

There is, however, some evidence that even before Collie's speech, tales of something unusual on the top of Ben Macdhui were in circulation.

An article in the *Cairngorm Club Journal* of 1921 refers to a rumour that a giant spectral figure had been seen at various times during the previous five years walking about on the tops of the mountains. More significantly, the article states that the figure had a name - Ferlie Mor. This is an Anglicisation of the Gaelic 'Fear Liath Mor' - Big Grey Man - and the use of Gaelic implies that the legend goes back to the time when that language, then extinct in the area, was still spoken. George Duncan, an Edinburgh lawyer, had an unusual experience in 1914 in Glen Lui, to the south of Macdhui. He saw a tall figure, who reminded him of the Devil, surrounded by smoke on the hillside.

Duncan's experience was reported by a companion in 1916 and is the only concrete instance of a phenomenon recorded before 1925. Not only is it different in detail from later reports, but it did not take place on Ben Macdhui but on the lower slopes of an obscure hill called Meall an Lundain on the opposite side of Glen Derry.

Seton Gordon, writing in 1948, carries the story further back. He reports in *Highways and Byways of the Central Highlands* that the late Marquis of Ailsa had heard tales of the Big Grey Man on Speyside at the close of the 19th century.

John Hill Burton, in *The Cairngorm Mountains* (1854) mentions a legend of a giant shadowy figure called the Fahm and in 1813, in a poem *Glen Avin,* James Hogg also mentions the Fahm, although he has it appearing on Cairn Gorm, not Ben Macdhui.

It was presumably to this figure that the Gaelic name Fear Liath Mor, Big Grey Man, was given although the Gaelic phrase is not recorded before this century. The origin of the legend seems to be the phenomenon known as the Brocken Spectre, first reported from the Harz Mountains in Germany in 1780. This is nothing more sinister than the gigantic shadow of a climber thrown by the sun on to a bank of mist, and a sighting was reported on Macdhui by Sir Thomas Lauder in the *Edinburgh New Philosophical Journal* in 1831.

A less well known tradition is of a monster called the Fahm. This was a giant mole the size of a large dog which secreted a substance which made the grass on Ben Macdhui poisonous to horses. This legend is mentioned by Dr George Keith in *A General View of Aberdeenshire* (1811) and again in a poem written in 1847, after which it seems to have been forgotten.

The source of this story is an entry in the first *Statistical Account of*

Scotland for the parish of Kirkmichael, in Banffshire, which includes Loch Avon and the northern approaches to Macdhui. The account was written by the Rev. John Grant and dates from the 1790s.

Grant writes: 'It is asserted by the country people that there is a small quadruped which they call famh. In summer mornings it issues from its lurking places emitting a kind of glutinous matter fatal to horses if they happen to eat the grass upon which it has been deposited.

'It is somewhat larger than a mole, of a brownish colour, with a large head disproportionate to the body. From this deformed appearance and its noxious quality the word seems to have been transformed to denote a monster, a cruel mischievous person who, in the Gaelic language is usually called famh-fhear.'

In modern Gaelic *famh* means a mole and *fanhair* a giant and the legend of the large headed poisonous monster may have arisen from a misunderstanding by Grant of the meaning of the Gaelic words.

Presumably, it was from the *Statistical Account* that Hogg got the term *fahm,* a word which does not exist in Gaelic.

This story and reports of the Brocken Spectre apparently became confused because Hogg and Burton both mention the *Fahm* when referring to the giant, grey figure.

The post-Collie material dates mainly from the 1940s; nothing of significance quoted by Gray is later than 1948. The evidence is difficult to analyse because it is so diverse. It ranges in space from Coylumbridge and Glen Einich to the head of Loch Avon, in content from giant figures through footsteps, voices, bells and music to vague sensations of a 'presence', and in emotional association from the diabolical to the saintly.

The core experience, however, is of a giant figure and/or footsteps accompanied by a sense of terror on or near the summit of Ben Macdhui. No report should be admitted as evidence in support of this unless:

1. A natural explanation can be ruled out.
2. A phenomenon of an obviously different nature is not being described.
3. The encounter took place on or near Ben Macdhui.

For example, the reports of the sounds of music, voices or bells are almost certainly attributable to the effects of wind, water or rockfall. The present author has heard a sustained musical note when sleeping under the Shelter Stone on a windy night, and more than once the sound of girls' laughing voices when approaching a waterfall.

In 1972 an ornithologist who had left a tape recorder running near the summit to record bird song, was surprised, on playing the tape, to hear the sound of a cough. No approaching footsteps were recorded and the tape recorder had been in full view of the observer all the time. But then ravens and ptarmigan don't make audible footsteps, though they do make other eerie noises, and ptarmigan are very difficult to see against a background of boulders.

Some of the reported occurrences clearly refer to something entirely different from the core experience. Sir Hugh Rankine recalled that while in the Lairig Ghru with his wife in 1948 he had met a robed, oriental gentleman who addressed him in Sanskrit. Being a Buddhist Sir Hugh immediately recognised him as a Bodhisattva - a kind of saint - and replied in Urdu. Heavenly music played about them for about 10 minutes and then the saint vanished. If Sir Hugh really did enjoy such an experience he had an encounter of a quite different nature from Collie or Kellas and his experience can throw no light on theirs.

Joan Grant, a professional writer of historical fantasy who was convinced of her own psychic powers, had a panic attack while walking in Rothiemurchus in 1928. She fled in terror from something she could not see but which she sensed to be four-legged and whose hooves she could hear. At the time she was seven miles away from the mountain near Coylumbridge and her experience was certainly not the same as those of Collie or Kellas.

Tom Crowley heard footsteps and saw a grey figure in the early 1920s but he did not report it till long after the event; in any case he was on the western slopes of Braeriach at the time. The point is that it is not legitimate to cite any kind of unusual experience anywhere between Speyside and Deeside as evidence of the Big Grey Man.

Otherwise why not include the Bodach Lamh Dheirg, a giant figure in Highland dress whose hand drips blood and who haunts Glenmore east of Loch Morlich, about the same distance from the summit of Ben Macdhui as Duncan's experience in Glen Lui, or the ghostly washerwoman of Loch Alvie - only two miles beyond where Joan Grant had her panic attack - whose appearance means death to the beholder and who is closer in spirit to the Collie/Kellas experience than Rankine's Bodhisattva?

The quality of the core evidence cited by Gray is pretty shaky. Alexander Tewnion thought he heard footsteps and saw a giant figure in the mist when he was retreating from the summit into Coire Etchachan in 1943 but he subsequently came to believe that it had all been a trick of the mist.

Syd Scroggie, then a soldier on a training course in mountain warfare, was sitting by the Shelter Stone one evening in 1942 when he saw a tall figure cross the burns that flow into Loch Avon and disappear into the night. Scroggie followed the figure but found no footprints; shouted but heard no reply. He thinks to this day that he may have seen the Big Grey Man, but admits that it could have been a Norwegian soldier in training or a German agent.

Peter Densham, an aeroplane rescue worker, while alone on the hill in mist in 1945, was impelled by the sound of crunching footsteps to run in blind panic almost over the top of Lurcher's Crag into the Lairig Ghru. On another occasion when accompanied by his climbing companion, Richard Frere, they carried on an enjoyable conversation with an invisible third party. Strangely, when questioned later about this event, Frere could not recall it.

Frere did, however, tell of another friend who, on a brilliant moonlit night saw an enormous brown figure, 20ft. tall, 'swaggering' downhill from the summit. When the moon cast the creature's shadow on him he felt 'like a hunted animal'. Unfortunately, Frere did not feel able to reveal his friend's identity.

Gray repeats stories told by Alastair Borthwick and Wendy Wood of footsteps following a climber in snow on open ground. In both cases the climber was followed by giant crunching footsteps like those which followed Collie, and both experienced a similar fear. Gray himself quotes two possible explanations of this. A Mr Usher tells of an instance when on the summit of Macdhui he heard footsteps which turned out to be those of ski mountaineers in Coire Etchachan, two miles away and about 1500ft. below. Usher makes the point that in certain places and under certain conditions sounds can travel surprising distances.

Dr Adam Watson, of Aberdeen University's Institute of Ecology, suggests that under certain snow conditions a walker's footsteps will cause cracking in the snow under his feet and that the noise of this will follow his own footsteps but will not be in time with them. Collie's experience, as he described it in 1925, but not in Baly's account, can possibly be explained in this way.

That of Kellas's, in the version in which he alone saw the giant figure cannot be explained in terms of the Brocken Spectre since it is said to have occurred at midnight.

The Robertson version, in which two observers saw only one figure has been cited as proof that what they saw cannot have been their shadow on the mist.

This argument is invalid. When two or more people see the Brocken Spectre each sees only his own shadow, unless they are standing less than 10 yards apart. Sir Thomas Lauder quotes an example of this when in 1831 a party of three descending Ben Macdhui, about 50 yards apart, each saw his own shadow on the mist although those of the other two were invisible to him. When they came together and stood as close as possible each could see all three shadows, his own distinctly and those of the other two faintly. The effect has been frequently observed since. The reason is that a partially transparent volume of mist does not behave reflectively like an opaque surface such as a wall, and that two observers apparently looking at the same spot will actually see light reflected from different surfaces. It is therefore possible that Kellas and his brother each saw his own shadow without realising that they were not observing identical phenomena.

Since the late 1940s reports of the Grey Man have dried up. There has been nothing more sinister than that cough on the summit of the mountain. Today the ascent of Ben Macdhui is a trade route. Instructors at the Scottish Sports Council centre at Glenmore Lodge routinely take trainee mountain leaders up it in all weathers and nothing untoward has been encountered for the last 40 years. Syd Scroggie says the Big Grey Man 'seems to have gone into recession'.

However, there are still persistent reports of the sound of footsteps on the lower slopes of the mountain which cannot be explained in the way suggested by Watson.

According to Gray, in 1940 MacDonald Robertson heard footsteps crunching around outside while lying under the Shelter Stone. Catherene Allan heard something similar when lying in a sleeping bag near the head of Loch Avon.

McOwen quotes three cases when similar noises were heard by David Trainer in Corrour Bothy in the mid 1970s; Brian Cullimore in the Hutchison Hut in Coire Etchachan in 1986, and Tom Gilchrist in the Sinclair Memorial Hut.

In none of the five cases were those who heard the steps moving about at the time and in four they were in an enclosed shelter and heard them outside.

Borthwick tells a story of another friend who heard footsteps following him across not snow, but scree.

Usher's explanation might possibly account for this experience but the other five all happened at night when it was unlikely that other climbers would be on the move.

In the face of so many diverse reports and in the context that similar tales are told of mountains outside the Cairngorms, such as An Teallach, Sgurr Dearg (in the Cuillins), Mayar, Schiehallion and Ben Ime, perhaps all that can be said is that some people have felt, or for some reason have wanted it to be believed they had felt either a sense of evil or of good in the mountains. Some accounts are emotionally neutral, Syd Scroggie's for example. Collie and Kellas set the fashion for evil and terror and this was followed by Crowley, Grant and Wood.

Rankine encountered the sublime. Densham and Frere told both kinds of tale – but then their stories are the most professionally told of the lot!

FAILURE

By Donald M. Orr

BLUSTERY, snow-laden winds in early March allowed him to forego the dubious pleasures of the North and spend a casual Sunday alone on the Renfrewshire-Ayrshire border. Not on the ragged, heathery tops of the West Renfrew Heights but over on the high, sad moorland country that sweeps eastwards to Strathaven, the Aven Water and the long valley of the Clyde. Edged on the west by the trench of the Barrhead Gap, the area undulates below the 1000ft. contour and is pocked extensively by dams and small lochs that held the dull colour of the sky and caught and reflected its occasional brilliance.

He skirted through the meagre dusting of powder snow by the crags he had often used as a summer starter. Rediscovering, in the light evenings, the tendon twanging limits of chalked fingers and the less-than-adhesive properties of rubber on whinstone. Beyond the old quarry the upland fields dipped and rose under a thicker blanket towards the rounded, forested hill that was his target. Silently, pondering his way up the slope, he paused periodically to draw a deeper breath and take in a familiar view.

He stood on the grassy summit gazing north to the white escarpments of the Kilpatrick and Campsie Hills. Snow clouds smothered the humped top of Dumgoyne as his eyes scanned some unseen distance. Failure now haunted him where before it had driven him on.

He had found it easy to establish a reputation as a mountaineer. All it seemed to amount to was a collection of tops, ticked summits, underlined routes and a large pile of trashed gear.

What had fired him was essentially failure. What they had raved about together were the disasters, wash outs, epic retreats, because, he realised eventually, that was when he felt really tested. When they were off route on a strange crag, a few degrees out in the cloudy fastness of some unfrequented wilderness, or when the ice suddenly went rotten in a slushy spring gully, he felt the zest and burn within him of increased vulnerability that doubled the intensity of the experience and promoted the telling of the tale to saga status.

He focused again, briefly watching the light change in the grey distance, before he faded back into his internal dialogue. It struck him that success had only confirmed his abilities while the failures had stretched the limits, taken him out of himself and allowed a re-assessment of what his potential might be.

He started to move downhill under a lowering sky. It had, however, been easy to walk away from the successes: the effects of failure remained for a long time and the varieties could be as intricate as some of the routes he had followed. As he ducked under the branch of a larch tree that overhung the path his eyes connected with the frosted whinstone flakes that surfaced the trail. Their whitened forms resembled limestone fragments and triggered an initial wave of dizziness to lap inside his head. He gulped at the cold air but none seemed to enter his lungs and he sagged slowly on to the snow and leant wearily against the base of the larch. He recognised in his shifted perspective that the colour of the stones intensified an aura of menace still lingering in his memory.

No amount of training could have primed him for the sensations that he would experience. The Red Cross instructors had been thorough but they had not told him how he would taste the Austrian's last cigarette as he tried to force his frightened breath inside another man. Nor could they tell him of the smell of perfume that rose up from 'the casualty', left by his wife as she kissed and kissed and kissed him, desperately trying to force love and life back into her husband before he slipped away forever. In the delirious, dizzying pressure of reality, anxious sweat dripped from his face on to the older man's, splashing and deepening the darkening skin as he worked, panting in the humidity, trying to drive his breath past a stranger's purple lips. In a frantic spiral of desperation he tried to ignore the actualities before him for the promised joy of imagined recovery.

Mouth to mouth with a strange, overweight man, he never heard the helicopter, only a clatter of white stones as a paramedic and two nurses ran down the path. He was on the point of collapsing himself when they took over. Watching the medic give an adrenaline injection, and the nurses continue trying to revive their countryman, he sat on the path exhausted and bleeding and regarding in a dazed, apologetic manner the couple comforting the dead man's wife.

He was not sure how long they had been working on him but at some point, perhaps when he saw the bluish stain creep out across his chest, he realised the Austrian was dead and that there was no chance of reviving him. The medical team stopped their efforts and started to straighten out the body. The weeping woman was led away and a group that had materialised from a nearby hut assisted with the corpse. He remained sitting by the path stunned, disturbed and empty. Drained by the physical effort involved and shocked by the sudden turn of events that had turned his part in the drama into a very ill-defined role. The doctor turned and spoke quietly and politely in German which was lost on him. The nurses smiled and shrugged which said it all.

Later that night in the hut he was aware of the eyes watching him as he sat alone at the rough table awaiting his evening meal. He saw wonder and awe, recognised fear in those around him and once or twice glimpsed that look of envy on a face that saw status in one who had touched the dead.

He found himself picking at his food, listening to the gutteral blur of German surrounding him, at once glad yet anxious that he did not speak their language. The need to forget was being tormented by the desire to explain what he had done, how he had tried. He was now beyond his emotional margin, off route on a testing wall of unknown and unconsidered mental stress. He ordered a whisky, and another. By his third he felt he could have summarised to someone that it felt like a long, long runout with no protection. He wondered if they were watching him drinking, adding it up themselves and coming to some smug conclusion. He rose abruptly and left the dining room and went up to the small chamber under the eaves where he was sure no one else would wish to share the facilities.

A blackness tinged with green and pain was his only awareness. The blackness was pain and existed all around him. He could not understand the pain, could compute no reason for the greenish blackness. The pain made him move his head and his eyes opened. Slowly, these simple events and sights started the mechanism that tripped consciousness into being. Through his shattered senses the strange moss-covered rocks and the saplings around him only heightened his discomfort and uncertainty. The pain, now localised in his face, eased, and he propped himself up on his arms. The moss had been scraped off the rocks beneath him and bright red blood stains had soaked into the soft lichens making dark whorls within minute worlds, a miniature landscape drenched in blood. His temperature rose suddenly and dramatically, sending beads of sweat out across his forehead. Little trickles gathered in his hair as he continued staring at the ground wondering where and why?

'Okay, I'm okay,' he said quietly to himself in reassuring tones.

He pushed himself upright into a seated position and groaned as he lent his still-rucsacked back against a boulder. Running his tongue along his top lip he found a rounded hole on the inside where his bottom teeth had gone through. His hand found cuts on his chin and on the bridge of his nose but apart from these a blow to his left knee and some skinned knuckles were the only injuries he had sustained.

Looking up plunged his mind once more into swirling disorder as he failed to see the path or any other feature he recognised. He remembered navigating off the Wasen Spitz in low cloud and coming out of a drizzling mist to join the old track by the side of the Spullersee. He had followed a small path into a scented birch wood that cloaked the lower slopes of the mountain and remembered bending under a larch branch and feeling giddy.

This strange, moss-covered, boulder-strewn little valley filled with ash saplings was totally unknown to him. A sensation of fear penetrated the disorientation that filled his mind as he sat regaining his strength and composure. Struggling to his feet he tottered forward supporting himself with the branches. Yesterday's images trickled, then burst into his mind.

'I'm sorry! Oh Jesus, I'm sorry.' He closed his eyes and slid down the tree to his knees. Grief and fear, shock and dejection took their toll and he knelt moaning and crying, trying to atone with his tears and his misery. Eventually, at some point, he rose and stumbled off following the slope downward. Later, he was not aware that his feet had found the path and the sight of the evening lights of Klosterle a little way below him registered only vaguely on his mind.

It had been decided that a short holiday would be a good idea and he had agreed to all the gentle, clichéd argument knowing that his nerves were in rather a ragged state. Unable to concentrate, sleeping badly, seeing his family and friends through a confusion of guilt, he still somehow bore the weight of responsibility for other lives in another country.

Amy drove the long road down the length of Argyll to Kintyre while he sat softly beside her recognising in her unaccustomed role his weakness and convalescence.

While he had never visited this part of the country before he regarded it listlessly as if the landscape were simply being viewed on a screen. He felt no interest or attachment to the land. He was not moving with it, only passing through it.

Turning off the main road on to the estate track plunged them into a new set of sensations. The estate was densely wooded and flooded with the noise of wind in the trees and the rush of tumbling water from the peat-stained torrent that drained the valley. They drove slowly over the wooden bridges, crept through tunnels in the forest and spied the house across a rough, uncut meadow of lilac grasses. The building occupied a raised site above a bend in the river and backed into a bank of impenetrable vegetation that swept down the east side of the narrow glen. He took to the house immediately and from its main window the prospect of the steep, wooded slopes across the stream filled him with a sense of security that eased his mind and instilled a calmness for the first time in weeks.

The next morning was still and damp. Heavy overnight rains had washed the air and freshened his attitude. The seemingly vertical forest across the now raging river was still draped in mist and low cloud, creating the washed effect of a Chinese landscape painting. Into this oriental water colour he walked and explored, with growing enthusiasm, for the rest of the day.

In the evening he took the children down to the beach. While they played along the shoreline he built a fire, farther back, on the grey pebbles that flanked the bay. Gently coaxing up the flames and their comforting warmth he was caught suddenly in a soft sadness that swept over him like the smoke from the embers. He could find no echoed childhood memory or cross reference from recent events that might have been triggered by the fire and quietly relaxed into the mood, calmly watching the sticks glow and flare through tear-filled eyes. Clearing himself and coughing away the emotion he looked out over the still, grey reach of the sound to the great, whale-backed mass of Arran. At this distance the mountains appeared rounded, the peaks a faint detail and the famous airy ridges a mere suggestion of tone and line that reminded him of McCulloch's brushwork. He stared at the view recalling the walks and climbs he had enjoyed there and the incidents that had filled the days. Through the last of his snuffles he realised that nothing was wrong. In fact, everything, for the moment, was quite all right.

The weather throughout May had slowly improved to near perfection and he had gradually built up his confidence revisiting many of the local crags with old friends.

Successive weekends in Glen Coe and Ardgour and the prospect of a break with the family in the Lake District had primed him to the point of quiet enthusiasm. As he walked down from his office towards Central Station on a June evening he was delighted with the thought of having just secured a house on Colonsay for the summer, a venture the family had decided on and he endorsed. He acknowledged that a dull shadow still lingered from the past but the potential of the gloomy reverie was broken as he met some colleagues under the portico of the station and the conversation turned to business and Saturday's sporting fixtures as they headed for their suburban trains.

She was quite happy, for once, to see him thinking about rock climbing. They had talked over the event many times, reasoning out his feelings of inadequacy and incompetence and she now felt that it was a process of time before he rationalised his emotions and dissolved the feeling of total failure that he equated with the notion of no return, no second chance. Lying in the sun she looked out over the top of her book, past the children playing on the low tide sands, to where he was perched, bouldering on the rounded scoop of a sea cliff. She was aware that climbing demanded all his concentration and that in the precision of his next move there was no room for distraction. A good therapy for the big lump. Her eyes followed him as he moved on to a prow of sandstone and she considered how like dancing his movements were as his fingers took the weight and feet skipped out across pebble pocked conglomerate to weathered holds above a rash of barnacles.

Around the seaward edge of the arête came the tang of verdant obstacles and he wondered whether to traverse above the weed and kelp or follow the crackline in the wall overhead. A score of oystercatchers flighted a path over the summer tidefall, trilling their way across the beach and down the golden hoop of the bay fringed, below him, by the smoothed dross of stone that made a kind of rounded sea scree. He paused on a good hold to watch them pass and shake out the fatigue from his arm and chalky fingers then moved round the arête and into a hidden niche at the foot of an open corner. Squatting in the sheltered sunshine he viewed the dull smudge of the Ross of Mull nestling out on the western rim. He had not visited Iona for many years but the persistent and enduring nature of the site, its capacity to absorb the worst from history and offer a continuing solidity to the present, seemed to mesh with the recent conversations he had had with Amy. The distant island became personalised in his thoughts. They were both burdened with the weight of history and hindsight but he was not sure if their durability was despite or because of it.

The little squadron flew again between him and Amy sitting reading. He was aware she was watching him with that head-to-one-side aspect that always intimated she was thinking seriously. He thought of the balance of their lives together – still together after so many years. An image fixed in his mind of her on the trip to Coigach they had made before they were married. He remembered that specific day when the ragged ridge of Suilven lay like a blade against the wind, slashing cloud remnants apart that were combing over the serrations of Stac Pollaidh. Somewhere there he had found and grasped the handhold in her heart.

A soft sadness blew over the sea to envelope him, enhancing his sense of the immensity of the landscape, his small span within it and the finite nature of its range. He could feel for them all, sense the thrills and shocks that composed the rhythms of athletes out on the dun expanses of thin holds, the charged panoramas of the striders of alpine snow ridges, the eternal peace shrouding the smashed and shivered, locked in the blue tombs of frozen, tumbled rivers, and the cathedral quiet for those resting at life's last belay. Their life lines were route lines which mirrored the arêtes and edges of the ranges which contracted and echoed in the scores and scars that cramponed boots had gifted or nails donated in the rain, before they all ascended to the stars, and took to the hills again.

He glanced again towards Iona, grinning to himself.

AGAG'S GROOVE

By Hamish Brown

CUTTING the rope was simply an improbable ploy of the fiction hacks. The forensic boys would be on to that one at once. 'Climb when you're ready,' he yelled down to his invisible partner on January Jigsaw. 'Climbing,' came the billowy response, as Betty began to pick her way up the neat holds. Rannoch Wall would make anyone want to climb. She just wished she'd got Allan to take her years ago. She liked it when Norrie was there too. He was so much more gentle than her husband. But she'd have to be careful - ca canny - in case Allan thought there was anything going between them. Which there wasn't, 'mair's the pity', she muttered as she lifted a runner off a pink porphyry spike. 'Keep your mind on whit you're daein,' she told herself.

Allan and Norrie were partners in a garden ornament business. 'Selling garden gnomes' as Betty taunted him on their last screaming match. 'And whit's wrang wi' garden gnomes?' Allan had responded. 'Oh, naethin. It's jist you become mair an mair like them: Dopey, Sleepy, Grumpy.'

'Shut up then, Snow White,' he'd yelled and stomped out to slam the door and set the plates on the dresser quivering.

His anger was the worse because he knew she was hitting too damn close to the mark. They were overdrawn and in trouble and he'd no desire for Betty to discover that or, more importantly, her stuck-up father who was so correct and proper in everything; like ensuring Allan had taken out a good life policy before they married. (Betty, of course, was already covered, had been since birth.) 'Don't want my little lily left in the lurch, what?', he'd admonished in that smug voice of his.

The last straw had come with the patio Allan and Norrie had agreed to do for the colonel. At the last moment he'd wriggled out from his commitment and they'd been left with the materials, some of which were already looking tatty or rusting. They'd threatened the colonel for breach of contract but he pointed out there was no contract, he'd signed nothing and they'd get nothing, except a big bill for the costs. The bugger was probably right too. They gave up on that one. They were pretty well giving up full stop.

The odd Sundays when they could escape claustrophobic Helensburgh and head for the Coe were treasured respites from the pressures of failure. Allan and Norrie had come together through climbing and it had seemed a good idea, three years ago, to set up their own business. '70% of households in Scotland have gardens which are actually looked after,' he'd quoted. 'Man, there's the market.'

Somehow it didn't quite work. People who'd sink 25 quid for a fancy conifer or a weeping cherry grudged parting with even a tenner for some concrete eye-catcher. 'No taste, folks,' Norrie complained. Allan thought it was probably the opposite. Too many effing people had better taste than to want garden rubbish. Betty's father had creased himself when he'd set eyes on the first Seven Dwarfs set they'd stocked. He did not like his father-in-law; nor his daughter if it came to that.

He'd first suggested she came along on a climbing trip with the gloating hope of scaring the shit out of her but she'd taken to it. Liked it! And she was such a cocksure little bitch she never even noticed how she rubbed Allan's nose in it with her new enthusiasm. Betty's beloved father had - naturally - raised hell about her climbing. It was far too dangerous. Allan's efforts at explaining that Betty always had a rope on and couldn't fall, not seriously, never got through. 'You might fall,' he'd remonstrate. Allan thought: 'The way things are goin I'm mair like tae jump.'

'What's that you're muttering?'

'Nethin. Nethin. It's quite safe . . .'

But explaining that the old man was more at risk every time he stepped into his Rover had not gone down well. He tried again. 'If I'm leading I've got protection on. Besides, Norrie's usually seconding.'

'Well, he's probably more reliable.'

'Thanks.'

He kept very quiet about the fact that on a few recent occasions Betty had led routes. Norrie had had a job keeping a straight face while Allan and Betty argued over that. 'Your old man'll kill me!'

'Only if I kill masel,' she countered. 'And who's going to tell? You? Norrie?'

She reckoned she could lead January Jigsaw, or Agag's Groove. Rannoch Wall's exposure was exhilarating rather than scary. It was that verticality that first put the idea of mischief into Allan's head. If she peeled it would be easy to cut through the taut nylon. You could say a sharp edge cut it - except the experts could tell it was a knife cut. There must be some way though. Alas, Allan's preoccupation led to another row on the drive home, which started with Betty's shot across his bows: 'Right talkative tonight aren't we?', and only eased off when they ate their chip suppers in the lay-by before home. Actually laying hand on money enough to save their business as well as being rid of Betty seemed a really brilliant idea. But how?

Then, bit by bit, it came to him. Just a straight slip would do. At the top of the climb. There would be no evidence with that. Or would there? Betty's father could well be suspicious and if there was any probing, sufficient motive would be discovered. Men had murdered for a lot less. Maybe he could do something to the car next time she took it off by herself, her next 'Keep Fit' night? But that's all movie stuff too. He hadn't a clue how to go about it, never mind the time needed. The climbing accident would be best. Maybe encourage her to solo something and con her about the grade. Hope she'd fall. He'd not even be present - no suspicions then. She was too turned on for that though, she knew just how well she did climb and she'd want to read the description anyway. Oh shit! There had to be a way. If only he could fix it so he wasn't there. Nobody would make any dangerous background checking then.

The answer came to him in the owl hours of night. He'd get Norrie to do it. Take her up something. Agag's would do. Promise it was to study the line carefully so she could lead it the following weekend - except there wouldn't be one. When she unroped at the top it would only take a wee shove. People were often careless at the top of a climb. Accidents had happened like that before and never any alarm bells ringing. Great!

Except Norrie's eyebrows vanished into his fringe at the very idea. Sure, he knew they weren't exactly a happy family but that's no reason to actually kill the wife. And by proxy. Use him! 'You think I'm effin mad?'

'No, just aboot tae gang bankrupt,' Allan sneered. 'Wi the insurance money we're aff the hook. Betty's nethin tae me.'

'Well, I like her.'

'Merry her then!'

They argued blue murder every moment they had in private. Norrie simply wasn't the type to do such a thing but neither was he the type to relish the prospect of bankruptcy. A direct threat from the bank had him sick and sweaty with fear. He couldn't even despair at the thought that there was no way out. There was. He looked at the letter in his hands as they sat at the table in the corner of a shed in the yard that served as office and, without lifting the tired eyes, he squeezed out the words Allan longed for: 'I'll dae it'.

'Good lad,' Allan yelled, and came round to thump him on the back. He turned away without looking and nearly knocked over the figure of a winged Mercury that they'd been forced to bring inside. A prim lady of known determination had sworn next time when she came to collect her concrete bunnies, she was going to drape a towel round the statue to hide its immodesty. With luck, Allan thought, the old witch would never collect her bunnies. Once they'd got the insurance money they'd be away, at least he would be.

'Onythin just tae be shot o' this lot,' Norrie sighed.

'Exactly,' Allan giggled, to earn a glare, 'But I'll be killin twa burds wi the ane stane: the failed business and the failed wife, baith the gither'. It was a pity they couldn't do Betty's father as well but then, they'd have no call to see the old man ever again once the proprieties had been attended to.

With the ploy determined Allan even became quite pleasant to his wife which simply drew the response: 'It's no like you. You're efter summit ah bet.' Allan just stopped himself from crowing, 'Hoo much dae you bet?'

He knew and inwardly purred like a cat watching a dinner party and sure of a saucer of cream at the end.

They carried off the ploy quite effectively. The plan was that three of them would do Agag's together, then the following Sunday Betty could lead Norrie up it, that way placating the old man who objected to husband and wife ropes, even though they had no kids or dependants. But the second weekend would never be.

Allan, as planned, carefully 'forgot' his rock boots so dropped the others off at Jacksonville while he rushed on up to the Fort to rent another pair from Nevisport. He'd be back to join them after Agag's. Betty was quite happy with this and Norrie, licking his lips, nodded agreement.

He, poor lad, tried not to think what he was going to do as they wended up to the Buachaille through the heather. In some ways he was lucky being so feckless. He couldn't think deeply. It was as if the worn path through the cloying heather was a track on which he was set like a controlled toy train. It was all so routine and familiar. They hardly even talked as they put on their rock boots and harnesses and checked all the clobber. Norrie led off - surprising himself at his calm, but it was the set gracefulness of long practice. He was so programmed that he just shut out what he must do at the top of the climb.

He sat on the big ledge to bring Betty up. Norrie could feel the red rock warm on his back. His feet hung out over space. There was a solitary blaeberry on the ledge and he popped it into his mouth. 'Climb when you're ready.'

'Climbing.'

He watched her picking her way up, hands moving gently, fondling the rock, then gripping while she arched out and up on to the next foothold. She climbed steadily and well. Betty wasn't a bad soul really. It was just Allan riled her so. Ach, life had got everything the wrong way round he felt. And to escape its toils and coils he was going to commit murder. They'd never used the word in going over the details. It was 'an accident' always. But the doing of it was his responsibility even if Allan often reminded him they would both be equal beneficiaries.

'It wouldna bother me,' Allan had boasted. Norrie thought: 'No, it wouldn't; you're a richt bastard.'

The pitches were climbed steadily. The very routine of climbing is one of its comforts. You get lost in it and everyday cares drop away beyond the horizon. Norrie reached the top, pulled in some slack and went straight to the belay. He'd done Agag's three times before and didn't forget moves or such details. It was the finest V. Diff in Scotland. Classic.

'Climb when you're ready.'

'Climbing.' Came Betty's echo.

Norrie grimly muttered 'Falling' to himself and then switched off the nasty near future to concentrate on taking in the rope. Betty let her eyes sweep over the Moor, with the threads of roads laid on its sequined serge and the cocked hat of Schiehallion away in the east, then turned to the kindly rock. Aye, she could lead this no bother. She went up the last pitch and pulled over the top onto Crowberry Ridge.

As she did so, Norrie stood up, throwing the colourful coils of rope off his legs and began undoing the belay. Betty unclipped the rope from her harness and began untying the knot. She turned, as one always does, to look down the sheer 300ft route just climbed. It was Norrie's moment.

'Betty.' She turned her head to see his outstretched arm. 'Would you like a sweety?' There were two or three in his palm and she chose a mint. This was all part of their routine too. 'Ta.'

They sat in silence (but for a plane high overhead and the occasional rattle of a mint on teeth) and Betty thought happily ahead to the next weekend. Apart from bloody Allan, life was pretty good. Norrie was thinking of Allan too, imagining him coming back from the Fort, the intended hours' late, not to find flashing lights and the bustle of police and mountain rescue but an irate wife and a silent partner sitting at the car park. They would be ruined. And so what? He just couldn't do it.

He reached out a tentative hand and laid it briefly on Betty's shoulder so she turned to look at him. He gave her a smile that held a hundred secrets in it. Betty smiled back. She put out her tongue with the mint on it like a little girl might have done. They laughed.

Allan, having seen them set off, had gunned the car along the straight to Alltnafeidh and on for the Coe, his voice roaring out a song. They were saved! What a sucker Norrie was, being persuaded like that. Allan just hoped he could be the person who broke the news to the old man: the shock would be as good as sticking a knife in him. The bastard had even set this up with all his talk a few years back about having adequate life insurance. Well, the insurance would certainly save some lives, and the detestable business.

It did too, though he never knew how - not in the way he'd planned.

He swept round the bend at the Study just as a dithery old couple pulled in to see the falls. This distracted him so that he momentarily took his eyes off the road and was slow in reacting to a bulky, long HGV grinding up the glen. All he could do was swerve. The barrier bounced him back and he was exhaling a Whew! when the tail of the lorry smashed in the corner of the windscreen and removed half his head in a single stroke.

Betty's father was more smug than ever when the insurance cheque came through. And his little lily blossomed. Maybe it was as well however, that a year later, he did not see her solo Agag's Groove while her fiáncé, Norrie, looked on. While they were climbing on the Buachaille he was hoeing the rose bed he'd planted round the statue of the winged Mercury which Norrie had sold to him.

TWO'S COMPANY

By P. J. Biggar

ALLAN was poking the potatoes, and I was relaxing by the fire, when a figure burst into the room. The candle flames guttered wildly and snowflakes eddied into the corners.

'Jesus what a fright.'

'Sorry. Didn't mean to startle you-like.' The figure was male, tall. The rucksack and ropes he carried were plastered with snow. He still had his head torch on, and all I could see of his face were gleaming white teeth. He lowered his sack and sank on to the rough wooden bench.

'God, were we glad to see that light.'

'We?'

'Christ, I was forgetting.' He stood up and hurried outside. Allan and I exchanged glances,

"Just our luck, eh?'

'You don't get peace for long, Mick, not bloody anywhere.'

'Not nowadays.'

Presently, the young man returned with another snow-covered figure, a woman. He helped her off with her sack.

'Anyone else out there?' Allan's voice came from the window. 'No, there's just us two.'

'Good, then I'll bring the candle to the fire.' Allan resumed his seat. I sat on the bench by the table, leaving the chair by the fire vacant. The woman sat down hesitantly.

'Weren't you sitting here?'

'That's okay, I'm cooking.'

'Thanks.' Her damp clothing started to steam. She leant forward, pale with exhaustion, shivering, stretching out her hands to the fire. Presently, she unzipped her fashionable, purple, fleece jacket and shook out her long hair; it was red, but what shade I couldn't tell in the poor light.

'You've had a rough walk.'

'It was dreadful.' She covered her face with her hands, and for a moment I thought she was going to give way to tears.

'Would you two like some tea? The water's just boiled.' Allan's gruff tones jerked her back. 'Have you got mugs?' The young man fumbled in the packs.

She sniffed the steam from her bright yellow mug. 'This isn't just tea is it?'

'Aye, well, *you* were lucky, you looked all in.' Allan chuckled grimly, amused at his own meanness. I picked up my flask and gestured to the young man.

'That's okay, mate, I've got some in the bag. I'll get it later.'

'Where did you walk from?'

'The far end of the loch, it's a bloody long way.'

'Best part of eight miles.'

'It wouldn't have been so bad in the daylight, but we'd a long drive first.' Her accent was much farther south. 'We came from London.'

'You're not a Londoner though?' Allan looked at the young man.

'No mate, Birkenhead originally-like, but I work in London now.'

'We couldn't get off work until late Friday,' the woman explained. 'Even with getting up at four we didn't make Edinburgh until this afternoon.'

'You must be keen.' Allan's tone was poised between admiration and irony. 'Oh we are mate, dead keen, aren't we Val?'

'Oh sure.' Her tone was different. Perhaps she was just exhausted. She was staring moodily into the fire. I let my eyes rest on her face for a few moments. Surely, she was much older than him? He was mid-20s at most. She had a lithe figure to go with her good looks, but I'd have said 35 and she might have been more. The young man didn't seem to notice the way she spoke.

'Down home y'know, I read books all the time 'bout the climbing up here, Glencoe, Nevis, the 'Gorms and that. It's really frustrating-like not bein' able to get up here very often. You get all the gear, and you know just what you want to go for, and then you don't get the time off work. And then sometimes, when you do get here, there's no snow to be seen an' you could tear your hair out, honest. They say it's Global Warming, but all I know is it's bloody infuriating.' We knew what he meant; we'd been young too. 'Anyway,' he said, half apologetically, 'what've you guys been doing?'

'We did the Ridge today,' Allan told him.

'Never. Great. That's top of our list isn't it Val?'

'So you say.'

'Aye well, we were only too pleased to get back down. The wind got up this afternoon and it was very tricky finding the way off. It's a long route, You need good conditions. 'We were lucky.'

'Yeah the Ridge. There's a picture in that book by old Whatsisname, remember Val? The sun all glinting on the snow. And you can see the pinnacles reflected in the water . . .'

'It wasn't anything like that today . . .'

'And there's this bloke dressed in red just getting to the top, You can see the rope trailing back over the snow . . .'

'. . .and it'll be worse now with all this fresh snow,' I added.

'The sun's just settin' behind the hills and everything's glowing-like. Yeah, the Ridge, it'll be great . . . Sorry guys, I got a bit carried away there, what were you saying?'

'Oh nothing,' said Allan, 'forget it. How's that meat doing, Mick? These tatties have been ready for a while.'

Last thing before turning in, Allan and I were outside in the shelter of the gable. The wind had dropped a little and it was no longer snowing, but no stars were visible.

Allan rinsed his mouth and spat. 'She's old enough to be his mother.'

'Isn't that a bit harsh? She is a good bit older I'll grant you . . .'

'A toy boy.'

'Aye, but she's fond of him.'

'She's doubtless fond of a bit of him.'

'You're too cynical.'

'I know. I'm getting old. But just our luck, eh? A pair of half-wits from the South! It just ruins the atmosphere.'

'They're a bit worrying, aren't they?'

'Are they?'

'You know perfectly well you tried to warn him off the Ridge.'

'A waste of breath.'

'She was listening.'

'What's the use of that?'

Deep in the night I was still awake. I don't sleep well before climbing. I don't sleep well the night after a long route either. Allan says he's the same. But I try not to let it bother me. I just lie there quietly and rest, and maybe I'll drop off at last for a couple of hours.

'Billy.' I heard Val's urgent whisper 'Billy, are you awake?'

Yeah, just. What's the matter?'

'Billy, I'm not sure about this Ridge thing.'

'Ah you'll be fine, love, you'll see.'

'No, but Billy I'm serious. I feel exhausted as it is.'

'You'll be all right girl, trust me!'

'You know I trust you.'

'Well then?'

'Couldn't you *hear?* They were trying to warn us.'

'Ah, they're gettin' a bit old and cautious like.'

'They're experienced.'

'Look! Just trust me will yer? You'll be okay.'

'For God's sake stop saying that.' There was silence for a few moments. I think she might have been crying. I heard a rustle as if he had put his arm round her.

'There are times,' I heard her hiss, 'when I wish I'd never answered that bloody ad.' He chuckled softly and no more was said.

So that was how this unlikely relationship had come about. The papers were full of them. Drowsily, I wondered what his ad. had said . . .

> Young man GSOH into mountain-
> eering and pubs seeks mature wo-
> man for fun times and maybe more . . .?

And why had she answered it? Divorced? Deserted? Looking for something different? Perhaps in the beginning she hadn't wanted much: a bit of company, some fun, but after a while liking set in, and after that . . .

An alarm woke me while it was still dark. I heard her groan. Billy shot out of his bag and made for the door. I couldn't hear any wind. In a few seconds he was back.

'C'mon Val girl. It's a great day. There's no wind and the sun's just gettin' up.' She groaned again and rolled over. A match spurted and I heard him fumbling with their stove; the gas canister was low and he cursed impatiently.

Allan's estimate of the weather was more cautious. 'It's not so bad now, right enough. The wind's away and there's a gleam of sun, but there's a big bank of cloud out to the West.'

When I'd finished the mug of tea he brought me, I got out reluctantly and went to sniff the air myself. Even as I watched, the cloud was moving in and strangling the faint rays of sunlight. A herd of deer moved slowly across the hillside, leaving deep tracks. I looked up at the snow-laden branches of the old rowan tree by the door; tiny drops of water were starting to form and trickle down the grey bark, leaving black trails. I turned back towards the smell of frying bacon.

Billy was hurrying about, making preparations. In between humming snatches of song, he laughed uproariously at his own jokes. Val sat at the table, trying to force down a plate of some cold, modern cereal. She looked even older in the morning light, but there was a kind of defiance in her expression. I took to her. Allan was quietly attending to the frying pan.

I got some porridge, refilled my mug and sat down.

'How do you feel this morning?'

'Not too bad thanks.' She smiled bravely. 'I was really exhausted when we got here last night.'

'You looked very tired. Did you get some sleep?'

'Yes, I got off eventually. I hope we didn't disturb you? We talked for a while.'

'Oh that's okay, I never sleep well after climbing.'

'I'm sorry.'

Billy was zipping expensive gaiters around new-looking plastic boots. 'You 'bout ready Val?'

'Give me a moment, love, I haven't finished my tea.'

'Are you heading for the Ridge, then?' Allan's voice came from the window.

'Oh yeah.'

'The weather doesn't look too promising to me.'

'It's a lot better than yesterday.'

'There's a lot of cloud coming in.'

'And the temperature's rising,' I put in. 'With all this fresh snow, you could have problems.' He wasn't really listening. I looked across at Val. She was pale but resigned. Perhaps she thought the weather would break before they got on to the climb, or that she could talk him out of it when she got him on her own. She pushed the remains of the cereal away and finished her tea. I made one last effort.

'Allan and I were thinking of having a short day on the lower crag,' I said. 'The ice should still be thick there, and the routes don't have much snow above them.' Val knew what I was trying to do, and she smiled. Our eyes met. Billy was already outside; we could hear him stamping impatiently.

'It's all right,' she said. 'I'd better humour him.' She spoke as if he was a wayward child. The door banged shut and the sound of the Primus was suddenly loud.

'We tried,' I said. 'Pointless, wasn't it?'

The lower crag, which wasn't so far from the bothy, gave us a good, short day's entertainment. Water was starting to run behind the ice, but we found a pleasant chimney system with a safe, rocky finish. As we stowed the gear at the top, the wind was starting to rise again. We hadn't seen the sun since early morning.

'What d'you think? Will they have pushed it?'

'He's daft enough.'

'She's got some sense.'

'Aye,' said Allan, 'but the worst mistake she ever made was answering that advert.'

'You heard them too?'

'Couldn't help it.'

All the way back, the wind was rising. Cloud obliterated the tops. As we crossed the last burn it began to rain. Surely, the others would have abandoned their climb early in the day as conditions worsened? But when the cottage came in sight there was no smoke from the chimney. The place was empty and exactly as we'd left it. I made tea while Allan lit the fire.

After supper the waiting began in earnest. We put a candle in the window; there was nothing more we could do. Outside, the south-westerly was rising to a gale. Wet snow slid from the roof, making us startle uneasily. Allan immersed himself in *Pride and Prejudice*. I skimmed through the log book. We had taken nine hours on the Ridge; the longest time I could find recently, was 11, and that had been a party of four. Val and Billy had now been out for 13 hours. Several times we thought we heard cries and went outside, but each time, when we extinguished our lights, the darkness was unbroken. On the last occasion it was nearly midnight,

'What's the plan then?' Allan's tone was fatalistic. 'It's pointless going up there now.'

'Of course.'

'First light, one of us should go out for help and the other up to the corrie, I suppose?'

Pausing as I toiled up the long slope in the early morning chill, I looked back, Far beyond the loch I could see a tiny, black figure nearing the top of a rise, Allan had gone by torchlight, well before dawn; he was going well. The wind had dropped again in the early hours and the sky had cleared.

'Stupid! Stupid!' Silence threw the words back. If only they'd been content to wait for a day and a night. Here was a perfect day for climbing. Sharp frost had turned the melting snow to crisp snow-ice; even the lower snowfields bore my weight.

Sweat soaking my back, I hurried on, though in truth I didn't know why I was hurrying. Billy and Val had now been out for more than 25 hours. It came to me how easily I used their names. They were almost complete strangers. We had exchanged a few hundred words and overheard a conversation in the night. We had made assumptions about them. They would have discussed us too. Little currents of warmth and cold had been created:

'He's a toy-boy . . .'

'See that Allan, what a grumpy old sod . . .'

'Mick's nice.'

'He fancies you.'

'Don't be silly . . .'

The ground grew steeper below the lip of the corrie where the half-iced burn flowed down the rocks. I paused to put on crampons.

As the Ridge came into view, I got Allan's binoculars out and scanned every foot. Nothing. Any steps would have been removed by the high wind and thaw. I paid particular attention to the long, hanging funnel which led through steep rocks to the final slopes. To gain this you had to come out on the flank of the Ridge. I'd been very relieved to get it behind me two days before. Below, slabs fell in unbroken waves to a short wall rising from the scree. With masses of fresh snow lying in the funnel, and yesterday's thaw, it was an obvious place for trouble. Sure enough, there were dirty brown marks on the slabs, and beyond the frozen lochan I thought I could see the tell-tale features of an avalanche cone.

And I was right. Piled high on the steep screes and craglets above the lochan, the snout rose in a darker, lumpy mass, merging with the purer white of the surrounding slopes. I clambered forlornly upwards over the debris. There was almost no chance of anyone being alive in this, but what else could I do? I needed to find something, an axe, a helmet, a glove . . .

I don't know how long I stumbled and lurched forwards and backwards, prodding and poking, perhaps an hour, maybe longer. I couldn't find a thing. At length I felt so weary that I sank down on a large lump of debris and sat with my head between my hands and my eyes closed.

Why? They were only taking innocent recreation. They weren't high on drugs. They hadn't robbed a train. The question, of course, was foolish. I knew that perfectly well. Providence was not a net for fools to fall into when they took bad decisions. They'd had a choice. Nobody compelled them to attempt the Ridge. Hadn't we tried all we knew to dissuade them? What had happened to them was entirely a result of their being where they should never have been at the time. Today it would have been safe, yesterday it wasn't. They were warned, they went, they suffered the consequences. It was rough on the woman, though. She seemed a gentle person; I'd liked her. She'd been looking for something and she'd found him. Having found him, she didn't want to lose him. Her choice was not so freely made.

'A bit too harsh . . .' I muttered aloud and opened my eyes. I must have been gazing vacantly at them for several seconds before I realised what I was seeing, a few fine red hairs lifting in the cold breeze not a yard from my feet.

'Oh God!' Frantic, gentle, scrapings uncover her face, white but un-marked except for a ragged cut on the chin. No helmet. Torn off? Face is cold, no sign of life. Fingers on neck, is that a pulse? Imagination! Feel! Feel! Wishful thinking. No. It's there. It's ever so faint. Her chest is constricted. If only I can free it she might breathe better. Breathe. Idiot. Check her airways. Fingers crudely probe her mouth. No clots, no mess. Her tongue is where it should be, and it's warm, warm.

I chip at the block of compacted snow pressing on Val's chest. It won't come. Her arms are pinned back under the surface. Something else is constricting her. Then a chunk comes free and I see what: the ropes, running taught from her harness which has ridden up, they go deep into the heart of the avalanche. Cut. Cut. Bag. Knife. I slice them off. He doesn't need them now.

Fingers on neck again. Where's that pulse? Still there? Just? But is she breathing? Her lips are going blue. Christ. I've never done this before, only read about it. I take a deep, shuddering breath – is it 14 times a minute? I clamp my lips on hers and pinch her nose shut, then blow ever so gently. Her chest rises. I look at my watch . . .

AN EDWARDIAN SCRAMBLER

By Peter Warburton

THIS is written in appreciation of Arthur L. Bagley who was active on British hills from the 1890s to the 1920s and was the author of *Walks and Scrambles in the Highlands* (1914); *Holiday Scrambles in North Wales* (1920); *Holiday Rambles in the English Lake District* (1925).

To describe him as unjustifiably neglected is tempting, but it raises the question of personal judgment. 'Little known' is neutral and uncontentious: his books, only the third of which ran to a second edition (1936) have long been out of print. Although the format of mostly short chapters devoted to single expeditions should commend him to anthologists, he seems to have escaped their notice. His works are not even listed in other writers' bibliographies partly, perhaps, because many of them did not consider him a suitable role model.

If the name is familiar to a few, it will probably be because he turns up, unexpectedly, yet entirely appropriately, as Rev. A. R. G. Burn's correspondent and adviser (*Burn on the Hill,* by Elizabeth Allan, Bidean Books, 1995). Mrs Allan quotes letters from Bagley which Burn had kept between the pages of his surviving diaries of the period 1915-27. There does not appear to have ever been any thought of their joining forces on the hill – Bagley, though a strong walker, would not have been able to match the remarkably fast pace maintained by Burn (1887-1972), who was about 30 years his junior. In the Lake District volume, Burn is the Scottish mountaineering friend who spent a week at Wasdale Head without climbing Scafell Pike and then compounded the offence by conceding that it was quite a good hill and that there were 'several in Scotland inferior to it'. Bagley too, was very much his own man. Not once does he mention either Sir Hugh or Munros, evidently quite untouched by Burn's consuming ambitions on that subject. Again, although he admired E. A. Baker (1869-1941), the friend he first met by chance on Cairn Toul, his own comments on the powers of Highland proprietors and their misuse are mild and good humoured compared with Baker's views which, even when formally phrased for publication, were pretty fierce by the standards of the day. Baker appears, anonymously, as 'No. 5', the energetic leader of the party in Bagley's idiosyncratic account of an Easter weekend on Snowdon and the Glyders. Thirteen years later Baker published his version, in which the unnamed Bagley appears as 'the malingerer' (Chapter VIII of *The British Highlands with Rope and Rucksack,* Witherby, 1933, reprint EP, 1973).

Ben Cruachan was Bagley's first mountain, with the single exception of Snowdon, where he had been some years earlier on a very bad day and 'had then come to the conclusion that the game was not worth the candle'.

Starting from Taynuilt, he took the 8.42a.m. train to Loch Awe station and traversed the main ridge, coming down to the road at Bridge of Awe through a wilderness of boulders followed by a terrible time floundering in bog. It was the only day in a fortnight's holiday on which there was no rain and while he was sitting on the western summit it had been clear enough for him to see a man had appeared on the eastern peak: 'I waved my stick at him and drank his health in my last remaining drop of whisky.' He was back at his hotel at 6p.m. What he described as his conversion to the elect was complete and from then the hills absorbed all his leisure time, first as a hillwalker, later as a solo climber to Moderate and Difficult standard. The date was Monday, September 21, year irritatingly unstated. Reference to a perpetual calendar leaves 1891 as possible, but 1896 as the more likely. In an aside in the Lakes volume he lets slip the fact that he was nearly 40 years old at the time.

Bagley's books contain neither prefaces nor introductions and the texts are very sparing of autobiographical material. He was usually alone on the hill but on one outing to Cader Idris his companion of the day took the photograph that appears in the Welsh volume. It shows a solid middle-aged figure of medium height, slightly overfilling a Norfolk jacket. He was a businessman from the English Midlands, an archetypal bachelor living in lodgings. He had a fortnight's holiday a year, nearly always taken in Scotland in May-June or September-October. Christmas, Easter, Whitsuntide and many short weekends were spent in North Wales or the Lakes. So much, and little more emerges.

Some of the Scottish chapters had first appeared in the *Cairngorm Club Journal,* the *Climbers' Club Journal* and *The Field,* and this degree of fame must have been helpful in finding a publisher. Skeffington & Sons accepted the Highland volume but 1914 was hardly an auspicious launch year and it was far from being a best seller. Bagley commented ruefully on the slowness of sales in a letter to Burn, Skeffington still had copies on hand when they published the Welsh volume in 1920 and in an effort to clear their remaining stock (price 3s 6d, postage 4d) they were moved to quote the *Western Morning News:* 'A more readable record among the mountains, valleys and lochs of Scotland has probably never been published.'

One of the fascinations of the books for present day readers is the then-and-now aspect, the contrasts between the things that have changed over the past 100 years and those which have remained the same. Keepers fall into the second category. Bagley's route to Slioch was a clockwise circuit leaving the Loch Maree shore path about a mile beyond the mouth of Glen Bianasdale and finishing down that glen. Near the beginning of the ascent, at the keeper's cottage of Smiorsair, he was spotted and intercepted. 'I gave him my card and after a few minutes' chat proceeded on my way, my life having been spared this time.' Smiorsair holds no such threat today. Miss Pochin Mould passed that way in 1947 or 48. 'Beside the sparkling cascade is a little house built in warm red Torridon sandstone. But the house is roofless, and no-one but the half-wild goats, who peer at you over the rocks inhabit the ruins of Smiorsair.' (*Roads from the Isles* by D. D. C. Pochin Mould, Oliver & Boyd, 1950). The presentation of the card is a nice touch. It is amusing (well, slightly) to speculate on what effect it might have had on encounters 70 or 80 years later – how, for example, would that purple tweeded blackguard, with matching complexion and vocabulary who tried to order the writer off Beinn a' Bhuird, have reacted, or the politely suspicious Glen Feshie keeper who interpreted the carrying of binoculars as evidence of criminal intent?

Bagley expresses mild indignation after an encounter in Glen Torridon. He had been caught in a heavy storm on Liathach and was tramping back along the road to Kinlochewe, soaked to the skin, when, 'I was stopped by a keeper who asked whether I had been on the hills, and upon my admitting the soft impeachment, demanded my name and address. Surely, it is coming it a little strong when a peaceful pedestrian is stopped on the King's highway by the myrmidons of Scottish landlordism'.

Kinlochewe was one of Bagley's favourite haunts. He climbed the usual hills but also reports a low-level outing to Glen Tulacha which few will have undertaken. 'The glorified tea-kettle which does duty as lake steamer on Loch Maree' was not due to call at Letterewe, but the captain readily agreed to land Bagley, the only passenger. While he was trying to decide whether the path ran through the garden or the barn, the housekeeper emerged. However, all went well. The laird was not in residence and she was glad to talk, at length, to anybody. 'She said the path through the barn was the right one: it seemed a curious idea to put a barn on a public path, but it is the sort of thing they do up here'. The path down Glen Tulacha marked on the map was absent on the ground and the whole way down the glen to Loch Fada was, and no doubt still is, unremitting bog. Hopes of firmer going along the shore of Loch Fada proved illusory and there was further disappointment when he reached Claonadh, a mile along the loch, where one suspects that he had entertained hopes of refreshment. 'I found only four bare walls, and not much even of them, of what had once been a cottage. A grassy patch, a tiny oasis in the boggy desert around was the only sign that human life had existed here'. It is a long march from Claonadh via the Heights of Kinlochewe to the hotel and the weather had been poor all day, but Bagley describes it as a most delightful walk.

The glorified tea-kettle was the *SS Mabel* (tonnage 30, horsepower 35), the smallest boat in David MacBrayne's fleet. It had been put on Loch Maree in about 1882 to offer travellers an alternative to the coach for part of the journey between the railway at Achnasheen and the coast at Poolewe or Gairloch but the emphasis soon shifted and the service – June-September only – was advertised as one stage of an all-day round trip from Gairloch to Kinlochewe by coach and steamer. By the early 1920s the steamer service only attracts passing mention as a thing of the past. There appears to have been a concerted effort in the 1870s and 1880s to develop the tourist potential of the district. Sir Kenneth Mackenzie of Flowerdale had the Gairloch Hotel built in 1872-73 (more than 60 beds can be made up; bathing machines etc. etc.) and extensions were soon put in hand (1894 – accommodation for nearly 200 sleepers; billiard room; English service is held in the drawing room during the season etc.) Sir Kenneth was also responsible for the building of the Loch Maree Hotel in the early 1870s. Queen Victoria's patronage in 1877 has remained a selling point. At Gairloch a golf links was later added to the attractions and there was even one at Kinlochewe which has not survived.

All these developments would have passed Bagley by. In his Scottish writing he restricted himself to the matter in hand, being the route and the circumstances of the climb or the walk. There is an occasional ill-informed aside on the meaning of place-names but nothing whatever of the usual stock in trade of clan warfare, supernatural events or the pipes. He had neither camera nor, best of all, dog. There is a doctorate to be collected on The Dog as Literary Padding with particular reference to authors' failure to realise that the silent majority find their pets a bore.

It seems wholly unreasonable today, but climbers of the period – Munro, Robertson and Burn among others – assumed that they could rely on the provision of meals and often overnight accommodation by keepers and shepherds in the smallest and most remote of cottages. Bagley was in this respect far less guilty than most of his contemporaries. He responded gratefully to the hospitality and persisted long enough to prevail upon his hosts to accept some payment. The account of a June walk from the Glen Affric Hotel to the Glen Shiel Inn illustrates the kindness and unsolicited hospitality a stranger might receive. As he reached Loch Beinn a' Mheadhoin, Bagley was overtaken by a keeper on a bicycle who offered to carry his rucksack as far as Affric Lodge, where it was not handed over until he had been given lunch. At Alltbeithe, now a Youth Hostel, but occupied by keepers until the 1930s, he was given 'a copious tea in a very comfortable room'. In heavy rain he passed Camban (then the highest occupied house in Ross-shire, described as derelict as early as 1932, but renovated as an open bothy by the MBA as a memorial to Philip Tranter (1939-66).) At Glenlicht Cottage (now in use as a club hut) he was invited in for a rest and given tea and eggs. He reached the road at 10.30p.m. and 'from there it was plain sailing for about two-and-a-half miles to the Shiel Inn'. He adds his regret that 'this old fashioned hotel has lately been suppressed'. It was shut down by the proprietor in 1907 and extended to make a shooting lodge: Baker is more vehement on the subject.

After two days confined by atrocious weather to the Inn, he continued to Kyle Rhea. There were language difficulties at the inn on the mainland side and his tea there was expensive, so he crossed the ferry to see what the inn on the Skye side was like. The verdict was no better and he walked on to Broadford – another hard day. Both these inns too are long closed.

Bagley's usual walking clothes were a Norfolk suit i.e. jacket, waistcoat and breeches worn over a flannel shirt. He also used puttees and in the Cader Idris photo is wearing a nondescript hat. This ensemble would be as weatherproof as the garb the average hill walker was wearing until, say, 1950. In other words he got very wet quite often, and expected to. Items variously described as a thin Mackintosh cape, a Burberry cape and an Inverness cape were found to be a net disadvantage on the hill but were sometimes worn on the road. The appearance of a heavily-laden traveller apparently walking for pleasure could surprise older people in remoter parts and he was once taken for a pedlar by an old lady who, whatever he said, replied that she had no money to buy anything from him. On day outings he took sandwiches in his pocket but nothing to drink except a little whisky. The lack of a Thermos or water bottle led to hardship in dry country but he ruled them out of consideration to avoid having to carry a rucksack. He dutifully carried a compass, but found little use for it. First Aid equipment consisted of a tin of zinc ointment and space was always found for maps.

Camping or sleeping rough were evidently not regarded as possibilities, but accommodation rarely provided problems. It was only on Skye that difficulties arose. Neither Sligachan nor Elgol were satisfactory bases for the southern Cuillin and, like so many since, he failed, during his first few visits, to find a bed in Glen Brittle. The novel solution he devised was to book accommodation on the island of Soay. There was one sailing a week from Oban that stood off the island in the small hours of Wednesday, but since this did not suit his itinerary he arranged for his Soay host to pick him up one evening from the Skye coast opposite the island. Bagley left Broadford on foot at 9.30a.m., reaching Camasunary at 2.30p.m. He had brought no food in the expectation, based on previous experience, of getting a meal there. Indeed, it has been his intention to book a night's accommodation for the return journey so that he could use the farm as a starting point for Blaven. Unfortunately, he met with a cool reception: they were no longer catering for tourists. It required all his powers of persuasion to coax a way past the front door 'on the distinct understanding that I was to have my lunch and then clear out'. Bagley sounds uncharacteristically peevish and the reader instinctively sides with the woman of the house, only to be disarmed by his subsequent troubles with a lost puttee, missing stepping stones at both river crossings, an arduous shoreline circuit of Loch na Cuilce and a trackless route across the shoulder of Gars-bheinn. It was not until 8.30p.m., an hour after the appointed time, that he arrived at the approximate rendezvous. Throughout the account the reader has the feeling that Soay is going to be a poor substitute for Glen Brittle, and so it turned out.

The transition from Victorian walker to Edwardian scrambler began at the deep end. The account of his first expedition on Skye is a splendid example of how not to make a first approach to the Cuillin, a fact of which he became keenly aware as the morning progressed.

The typically precise opening sentence: 'On Monday morning I left the hotel at 8.50 for Sgurr nan Gillean via the Pinnacles.' The climb is described as nothing more than rough walking until the top of the third pinnacle. 'Then I did rather wonder whether I should ever leave it alive...Retreat was not to be thought of, yet I could not see how I was to descend...As a matter of rock climbing...I had not even got nails in my boots for I was then so ignorant of the very ABC of rock-climbing, that I did not know that nails were necessary...The orthodox route is on the left, but I did not know that then and when I went to the left I did not like the look of it at all.' So he descends to the right, easily enough at first until faced with a situation vividly familiar to generations of us incompetents. 'The difficulty was that I could not see the lower part of the gully, or even if it had a lower part at all; also, and particularly, that though it was easy enough to drop down the smooth holdless rock into the gully it would apparently be impossible to climb up again in case I could not proceed down the gully... it was madness to descend any place which I could not reascend if necessary. Yet what was I to do? . . . I sat there for 10 minutes debating the question, then suddenly let myself go and the thing was done. Fortunately, the gully descended with sweet reasonableness to the col between the pinnacles.' There were no further alarms and he reached the summit at 2.20p.m. ('which of course is a preposterous time from Sligachan, even for a novice') and returned via the West Ridge, the Bhasteir corrie and 'across the moor to the fleshpots of Sligachan'.

Bagley, like any other visitor from the distant south was anxious not to waste any part of his fortnight's holiday. He was knowledgeable about timetables, maps and accommodation possibilities, booked some of his beds in advance, knew what he wanted to do each year and had fall back plans to make the best of bad weather. In short, he was well organised, yet in the Pinnacles adventure he appears remarkably ill-informed and naive for someone in his mid-40s. Part of the reason was the scarcity of published material on anything beyond the popular routes on popular hills as described in such places as the mountain section of Baddeley's guides. Bagley, at the time something of a loner, shows no awareness of the early editions of the *SMCJ*. In the Pinnacles chapter he writes: 'The beneficent stream of mountain literature which of late has gushed forth from Keswick and elsewhere had not then begun to flow and I had not understood what lay before me.'

After that first visit Skye became an essential part of each annual holiday. Welsh weekends were used to improve his rockwork. Self taught on Tryfan would sum it up. He was soon disregarding the Easies in favour of Moderates and selected Difficults and had become proficient enough at these levels to introduce a young nephew to Welsh climbing. The later Skye episodes reflect increasing confidence. Clach Glas – Blaven from Elgol provided some awkward moments: 'To tell the truth it, (Clach Glas) is hardly a suitable place for a solitary climber' and the 11 hours it took on an autumn day meant an unwelcome after-dark return. The Basteir Tooth on the other hand presented few problems. Having, on earlier visits, eliminated the chimney routes on the Coire a' Bhasteir side and Naismith's as all beyond his ability, he appears to have sailed up Collie's route: 'It was rather a longer climb than I had expected, but there was no real difficulty and on the way I found a few bilberries which made a most welcome extra plat to the otherwise dry lunch which I consumed in solitary state on top of the Tooth.'

From the Tooth to Bhasteir summit gave more cause for thought at the crux but: 'I picked out the least offensive route and in two or three minutes, after a strenuous heave and struggle was sprawling on top of the wall.'

By the time he tackles the Cioch he is aware of the several feasible variations on Collie's original route, the one he used, and acknowledges the help of Ashley P. Abraham's *Rock Climbing in Skye* (Longmans, 1907). Nevertheless, he came close to disaster when one foot jammed in the crack. 'I tried to wriggle it out, but could not move it. I could not see the boot, nor get down to it with a hand and for a few awful moments I thought that I was chained to that abominable slab for the remainder of my life, which in the circumstances would not be unduly prolonged.' An attempt to reach down with a knife to cut the lace and release the foot fails but, 'after some few minutes' struggling and wriggling I managed to extricate the boot and a fine object lesson against solitary climbing was lost.' He finished with an experimental ascent of the East Gully. From Sron na Ciche summit he 'sauntered slowly homewards, taking it very easily and stopping to rest occasionally.

Bagley's one notable recorded failure in the Highlands was the Inaccessible Pinnacle, which he had particularly wanted to climb. On what must have been at least his sixth visit to Skye and so probably about his 25th hill day there, he was on Sgurr Dearg for the first time. It was a day of very strong wind from which the West Ridge of the Inaccessible Pinnacle would have offered some protection, but the prospect of the first 15 or 20 feet of that climb 'quite choked me off' and, the wind having risen to gale force, he reluctantly gave up any thought of an ascent by the easier East Ridge. Instead, he continued along the main ridge to Sgurr na Banachdich. This change of plan is the origin of one of the most telling sentences in the book. On Banachdich summit he finds two men. 'I think this is the only time that I have ever met a human being on the Coolins.'

WHO WAS GARRICK OF GARRICK'S SHELF?

By Fraser Gold

GARRICK'S SHELF on the north side of Crowberry Ridge is a name which seems to have stuck, and originates from an article by J. Allan Garrick in the 1924 Journal, Vol. 17 pp 1-10, describing his climb there in May 1923 with D. Biggart, although the route had earlier been climbed by Wilding and Piggot. He and Biggart had pioneered a route on the south buttress of Creag Tharsuinn, Arrochar, in April 1921 which gave 300ft. of continuous climbing. (SMC Journal Vol 16 p 90 and Vol 17 pp 190-193). [1] These references appear to be virtually Garrick's only public utterances in print, yet he was widely and highly talented.

Born in Sunderland in 1894, his family background was in shipping, and his own training was in engineering. He joined the Fell and Rock Climbing Club in 1915, and remained a member until 1939, attending many meets with the club in the years following the Great War. In 1920 he was appointed to the Royal Technical College (now University of Strathclyde), and retired from there in 1960 as Senior Lecturer in the Department of Heat Engineering, being in charge of the drawing section.

Glasgow-based, he joined the SMC at the same time, attending New Year meets at Killin and Blair Atholl, and getting out into the Scottish hills with friends or alone. He had been introduced to the SMC by J. W. T. H. Fleming, who took him as guest to the New Year Meet at Loch Awe in 1919. (*SMCJ*, No. 15, p272). His strongest contacts were with his original club, however, and it was with G. R. Speaker and C. F. Holland, eminent members of that club, that he visited the Alps in August 1922. They climbed together in the Dolomites, but he ended up being involved in a guided climb on the Matterhorn. His climbing diary describes how he had lost a boot descending a rock chimney two days before his intended return to Britain and he was sight-seeing in Zermatt when a young British lady invited him to join her. This necessitated buying a new pair of boots in the morning and setting off in the warm sun. The guides treated Garrick as a novice, which he resented, and he regarded some of the route-finding as bizarre. He later discovered that the guides were not local and did not know the mountain well.

In 1923 and 1924 he was again climbing in the Alps, now including Mont Blanc and the Chamonix Aiguilles in his experience. He retained his membership of the French Alpine Club until 1939. In 1926 he married Isabelle Michell, also a climber, and they often spent two months in the pre-war summers climbing in various places in Scotland, and then turned their attention to Norway, the Lofotens and points north, visiting Lyngen in 1939.

---

[1] Garrick and Biggart had been climbing together in the Lake District before Garrick moved to Glasgow, but how the initial contact was made is not known.

Garrick possessed the SMC 1921 volume which had the revised Munro's Tables, and kept a record of the summits and tops which he and his wife had completed, updating this to 1944. In these days of 'Munro bagging' to find that by the end of his life he had done less than 70 seems incredible, but he never had a car, and had his favourite areas to which he kept returning (Arran, Glencoe, Torridon, Achallader, Kintail). In any case, even the SMC 1921 publication seemed to assume that climbing in Scotland was mainly training for the Alps. His climb on Crowberry Ridge was, in fact, a training outing to build up fitness for a four week spell in the Alps.

A climbing diary in two volumes has survived, covering the period 1915 to 1922, with a gap for war service. This and the two SMC articles reveal an enthusiastic climber, who may have sated himself on long summer holidays, but used days on the mountains to the full. On FRCC meets, he would do several climbs in the morning, then several more with different climbers later on, and then add some solo climbs before the day was done. He seemed to manage to stay on for days after the official meets as well. Short in stature, he often describes himself having to improvise for lack of reach. Technically, he observed how boots or 'rubbers' were appropriate for various conditions or types of rock. In February 1921 he was climbing the NE face of Stobinian alone and had to cut steps for 500 feet (no crampons then!). His article 'Eating Between Meals'' (SMCJ 1925, Vol. 17, p.190ff) gives a sense of the pure enjoyment he found in impromptu exploration of hills and crags in between his longer planned expeditions. During his Alpine holiday in 1922, he was involved in a mountain rescue, and commented that despite the potential seriousness of the situation, he could not help but dwell on the beauties of the sunrise. The outcome was happy, indeed hilarious, and is beautifully described.

Knowledge of Norway, and his photographic record of climbs amongst the fjords, made him useful to Naval Intelligence during the second world war, and he was released from the College to work in Oxford [2] alongside Norwegians, providing detailed topographical information, maps and models for various operations. Later he was interpreting angled air photographs at the time of the V2 rocket discoveries, and working on map formats prior to D Day. He submitted an extensive report on the interpretation of low angled, oblique perspective air photographs, but clearly there was more to investigate, and he returned to the subject post war, using initially his own photographs of the Trossachs to test his hypotheses. Over the years, he extended his study more theoretically to include atmospheric refraction and other factors, but never submitted his Ph.D. thesis. All his calculations had to be done without benefit of computers, and he was never satisfied with the results.

During and after the war, he and his wife had mountain holidays in Scotland, sometimes setting off late in winter and coming down in the

[2] In the Inter Services Topographical Department (ISTD).

moonlight, or just blundering on in the dark. We might not advise this now, but he really knew his mountains, mapping them mentally and adding his own details to OS. tracings. Post war, they once climbed An Teallach twice in as many days, combining routes described by Wilding in The Rucksack Club Journal of 1923, [3] which Garrick had kept in his own library. The journeys made partly explain the huge gaps in the Munro list. For example, their preferred route to the Kintail hills was by train to Mallaig, steamer to Kyle, bus to Dornie, then Totaig ferry to Letterfearn. With long walks, Ben Attow end to end, the Five Sisters and the Saddle were accessible, but the remoter Affric hills and the South Cluanie ridge less so. There seems to have been no inclination to claim Munros anyway, as the Glenfinnan-Ardgour-Ardnamurchan triangle attracted frequent visits. Acharacle was reached by train to Glenfinnan, then boat down Loch Shiel, alongside sheep, horses and other cargo. The same service gave them access to Roisbheinn and the other hills now normally reached by road from the north. On visits in the 1960s they watched the road from Lochailort to Acharacle being built. Glencoe likewise was normally reached by train to Ballachulish. Postwar the hill walks became increasingly of geological or botanical interest. Garrick was a great rock gardener, and made his own composts from stone brought down from the hills.

Pre-war, Garrick had given a lecture in Glasgow which greatly interested Dougie Scott, who subsequently visited the Garricks with Bill Murray. In April 1940 he gave a lecture to 154 SYHA members in Cathcart. He was also invited to give a lecture to the newly formed Glasgow University Mountaineering Club by its first secretary Bill Crombie, and advised Crombie on rope work and on climbing in the Lake District in the summer of 1941. Post war, Garrick gave a lecture to the JMCS in the Saltire Club, Glasgow (January 1946), and to the Grampian Club in Dundee on his Norwegian expeditions (November 1952). There were no further public lectures.

Between 1952 and 1958 the Garricks revisited Lyngen each year except 1954, and he was in touch with members of the Showell Styles expedition of 1952, a Newcastle University expedition, and with Dougie Scott and Tom Weir either side of their Norwegian explorations. The 1952 visit was planned as an expedition, with Eric Maxwell, a climber from Dundee, also involved. This was the last time Garrick described himself as being roped up for climbs. The main purpose of these visits was topographical survey, using his photographs and sextant observations to fill in gaps or correct details in existing maps. In this he was helped by Kare Landmark, keeper of the geological collections at Tromsö museum, who provided him with German air photographs from 1941, poor as they were with cloud cover, and a lack of contrast in the snow-covered landscape. He sent reports and

---

[3] John Wilding *Misty Days on An Teallach.*
[4] W. H. Murray, *Undiscovered Scotland* p109.

rock samples to Tromso after his visits. In the late 1930s, Garrick had climbed with Bill Murray, [4] and Bill regularly visited the Garricks prior to his call-up and posting overseas. They shared the same tastes in music as well as mountains. The friendship was renewed at the end of the war when Bill was released from POW camp, and they met up in Oxford and later in Milngavie. Garrick was a much older man than Murray, and declined invitations to go climbing again. In a more general way, Garrick was a very private man, and this outline of his life would have been impossible to reconstruct without the early climbing diaries, various photograph albums, and pocket diaries which he kept from 1940 to 1982.

References:

SMCJ articles and other references as noted in the text.

Tarn Crag Buttress in *FRCC Journal* No. 15, Vol. V, 1921.

Short note claiming first ascent, Garrick's authorship identified only by initials.

Some notes on the Flora of the Lyngen Peninsula, North Norway in the *Scottish Rock Garden Club Journal,* April, 1958 pp 16-21.

A beautifully written article identified only the initials A. G.

Thanks are due to Douglas Scott, Bill Crombie and Anne Murray for information and help, and to Jim Ingram for giving me access to personal papers.

J. A. Garrick's Climbing Diaries 1915-1922, photograph albums of 1935 and 1936, annotated copy of second edition of *Munro's Tables* published as part of the *SMC General Guide* Vol. 1, Section A 1921, pp 109-144 with the revised *Munro's Tables* and other papers are now deposited together in the SMC Archive in the National Library of Scotland.

Alan Garrick died in 1996 just short of his 102nd birthday.

INHERITANCE

The aging patina of iron,
darkened into years.
He rubbed oil on the shaft
and put it away in cloths.
When I unwrapped it
the slow aroma of activity,
the walk in and wonder,
coired the attic.
I grasped the haft,
wielded its cleaving edge,
turned and parried
its preserved length.
I twirl you in mind again.
Your timeless smile,
your polished strength,
rope burnished, reliable.

Donald Orr.

EXPEDITION TO THE DARK ISLAND – GREENLAND 1997

By I. H. M. Smart

John Hay organised, at very short notice, a two-man boat journey into the inner recesses of Scoresby Sound (East Greenland about latitude 70°N) in the autumn of last year when the Arctic tundras were a-glow with browns, reds and yellows. Our destination was the Dark Island which lies towards the western end of this mighty fjord system. We picked this distant isle as our destination partly because of its scenic position in the middle of a confluence of terminal fjords but mostly because of the romantic connotations of its name.

Neither of us had been there. It just looked good topographically. We knew not whether it was darkly sinister or darkly romantic. We had no specific plans, except to get there and reach its 500m summit. The whole trip was romantic and none the worse for that. We seized an opportunity to make a bold journey and the Goddess of Fortune favoured us. The Dark Island lay about 300km (a ba' hair off 200 miles) from the airstrip at Constable Point where we landed. The round trip with diversions for ice and accessing a fuel dump was roughly the same distance as circumnavigating Harris and Lewis from Oban - with Oban as the last inhabited place. No mean journey even in the less windy seas of Scoresby Sound.

I had been halfway there in the Seventies as a boy with Douglas Scott, Charles Eccles and his son, Chris. We didn't get farther than the Bear Islands that time because during the air drop the parachute to which our outboard engine was attached didn't open properly. After that experience our antiquated, now slightly bent 'British Seagull' could only push us along at one knot. Like that it took a long time to pass an iceberg. This time we had a good inflatable with a 40hp motor. We were lightly laden and could get up on the plane and travel at 20 knots. We were living in more prosperous time. We even wore survival suits which were impervious to the cold. A subjective account of the trip now follows. It is not to be read as a tale of derring-do but as a lovesong to life and the bittersweet danger of being alive.

Greenland, the Grey. 'Here is your anchor,' said Sigi, handing John and myself one of those folding galvanised iron contraptions. He shook my hand looked me in the eye and said: 'Be careful.' This ceremony happened on August 25, 1997 on the bleak airstrip at Constable Point. Greenland was at its most uninviting. It was overcast and grey and a bitter wind blew from the north. Two Swedes who had had the boat before us looked dour and chastened. 'It was a tough trip,' they said, as they climbed thankfully aboard the returning aircraft. We learned that the 1997 summer had been bad in East Greenland with overcast skies and a lot of rain. The sullen ice had lain against the shore around the Scoresby Sound settlement all summer and had restricted movement even for small boats. The visitor accommodation at the airstrip was full and the chief of the station said: 'You would be better to camp so that you can make sure that all your equipment is in working order.' He gave a knowing look and waved a hand towards a dismal windswept expanse of tundra. This is what I like about Greenland - you are expected to handle problems yourself. After a bleak supper we went to look at the boat we had hired. A 4m zodiac lay on a deserted sandy beach about a mile away beside a grey sea with grey horses galloping southwards on the cold grey wind. Sand had blown inside the hull gritting all the equipment. The propeller had a blade missing. We fitted a new one but clumsily lost the only split pin. Finding a replacement was an exercise in problem solving. We walked back to our tent against a bone-chilling wind. I was depressed at the prospect of two dreich weeks stuck among the grey ice floes; John never gets depressed.

Arctic Riviera. The next day Greenland smiled; the sun shone from a cloudless sky and the sea was calm. Then came the most difficult part of the expedition - getting the unloaded, but still heavy, boat down the soft sand into the water. After reloading the rest was down-hill. We left at two in the afternoon and planed over the mirror-smooth, reflection-filled sea, slalomed through 20 miles of ice floes and, as soon as we could, made straight for the Bear Islands, a direct 40-mile crossing of the inner Sound through a city of shining icebergs. A hundred miles from our starting point at the time of the midnight shadows we entered the narrow cleft between the steep sides of the two most southerly of the Bear Islands. We suddenly lost the photo-multiplying effect of the reflections from the open sea and entered the shadows. In this awesome spot we ran out of petrol. In the gloom and silence that suddenly surrounded us we had to refill our tanks from the reserve drums we carried in the hold.

A Gift From the Past. I had been to the north end of the archipelago a quarter of a century before and was suffering from confused memories. The boat, however, seemed to know where to go and guided us to a dimly remembered beach 10 miles away at the northern tip of the right-hand island. We disembarked in the increasing light of the new day. I was fairly sure this was the place where we had left a food dump 20-odd years ago when I was a boy. I walked to where it might still be and there it was, intact and undisturbed. This was just as well. John had done an impeccable job in organising the expedition, except for the food. Out in the field John does not eat very much unless he can actually shoot it. This time he had forgotten to multiply the slender basic rations by two. The antecedent Swedes had left some dried meat in the boat but even with that we would have been on scant rations. There didn't seem to be much to shoot either. The vintage bully beef, sardines, biscuits and chocolate from the old dump saved us from hardship. There was, of course, plenty of whisky; in this department John is more than competent.

The Bear Islands. The islands lie in the angle between the ramparts of Milne and Ren Land. There are about a dozen, each one different: some are rolling boiler plates of bedrock cradling picturesque lochans, others are sharp fins of vertical strata with serrated edges, some are round, others are long and thin, some are mere skerries; one runs a curious wiggly course for 10 miles or so, a branching thread bearing different types of mountain. The rock varies from good to dreadful. Dougie Scott and I had climbed the highest fin (2100ft, with some Diff. and V. Diff. pitches) 20 years ago on a memorable day of silence and colour. The islands are separated by narrow channels opening into bays and secret places; architecturally interesting icebergs drift around the waterways grounding from time to time and then journeying on. Our arrival coincided with the first flush of autumn colour when the leaves of the six-inch-high birch and willow were beginning to glow in the sunlight.

La dolce vita. We cruised the archipelago for some days on an aesthetic high, exploring each island and climbing to the top of the less precipitous summits. We had time to choose pleasing campsites with memorable views and to revel in extended lunch hours on honey-coloured promontories or ambience-prone isles. I remember with gratitude an afternoon of contemplation spent on an intricate islet of jumbled ice-worn rock patterned with multicoloured lichens and rich autumnal leaves. A further item of aesthetic excellence at this time was the waning yellow moon; as each bright day ended it would lean for a while against the dark blue northern mountains before sinking behind them, leaving us in the brief transparent darkness that at this time of year precedes a new sunrise.

Corridor of Power. We eventually continued our journey westwards into the steep-sided Island Fjord leading to the distant Dark Island. This mighty cleft is 40 miles long and four miles across. The sides are formed by buttresses rising straight from the sea to icecaps 6000ft high. The fjord is a major wind funnel channelling strong katabatic winds from the inland ice and dissipating their energy from its mouth. Biggish glaciers breaking through the ramparts on each side contribute their own katabatic cross-winds which generate periodic stretches of extra turbulence. At its west end the fjord is split by a large eponymous central island with 3000ft cliffs. Here, we reasoned, there must surely be converging orographic winds from each side making a spectacular turbulence where they met. It could be a nasty place. The buttresses that face the fjord, by the way, are formed of igneous rock - excellent stuff - polished by ice and done in light shades of ochre and honey. There are also pinnacles and blades of rock separated from the main escarpment. There is some excellent climbing here but few landing places and fewer harbours.

Alea jacta est. We approached on a smooth sea but were turned back by the white horses galloping from the fjord mouth. We dithered for a day in a calm corner of a nearby island, watching for the moment the horses would return to stable, wondering how the dice (or the icebergs) would roll. The weather turned a bit gloomy. Then John got hold of the tiller and committed us to a counter-gallop against the enemy cavalry. He is not known as the 'Kami Kaze Kid of Loch Mullardoch' for nothing. We crept across the fjord, nipping from the lee of one iceberg to another. When he was sure it was too late to turn back he slowed the engine and said: 'It should be a joint decision whether to go on or not.' We went on, even though the objective signs were that things would surely get worse.

Land of the Great Silence. Anyway, the theoretically violent katabatic cross winds did not amount to much. After entering the north branch of the fjord the wind gradually died and we emerged into an inland sea of flat calm, silence and golden evening light. Willow down floated on the smooth black water filled with the reflections of mountains and sky. The cliffs gave way to milder hills cradling broad valleys of richly autumnal musk ox pastures. We entered Rype Fjord and camped on a platform carpeted with the russet and gold of dwarf birch and willow with a panoramic view towards a wide glacier descending from the inland ice. The next day we climbed the mountain overlooking the entrance to Rype Fjord taking our separate ways through the bronze and yellow of the autumn landscape, meeting musk oxen and, on one occasion, each other. We separated rapidly. The finer aesthetics of a place can only be fully appreciated when alone. That evening John returned with a white hare he had shot. I have a picture of him skinning it. A lawyer splitting a hare is in his element.

The Dark Island. On the morrow we made for the Dark Island through two sets of icebergs: the real ones and their exact reflections in the still waters of the sea. The island was roughly round in shape and a couple of miles in diameter - small enough to be intimate and large enough to be mysterious and have many secret corners. We climbed its highest peak, about 1600ft, through mats of chocolate green cassiope, yellow willow, darkly crimson blaeberry and dwarf birch. The colours of the latter ranged through yellow gold, orange, bronze and various shades of deepening red, a *tour de force* in this part of the electromagnetic spectrum. Let me try to describe the view from the rocky summit. To the east lay the ice-capped cliffs and glaciers of Milne Land, to the north the big island that had bisected our line of approach, to the south and west open water and beyond that the spacious russet valleys and broad glaciers descending from the inland ice itself. All of this rugged grandeur was reflected meticulously in the mirror of the sea. There were, of course, icebergs, the sea was filled with them. Then there was the silence.

The Heart of Lightness. The following day we spent exploring the island's sunny southern coastline wandering slowly from one richly-embroidered bay to the next and finally crossing through the interior. Here on the summit of a pass we encountered a lochan surrounded by autumnal cloth of gold. The reflections in its polished surface were sharp and exact. It was difficult to determine where the shoreline was, where the boundary between reality and reflection lay. The reflections of the mountains of Milne Land were, in fact, crisper, richer in colour and much more convincing than the reality they portrayed. I have photographs to back up this statement. I am sure there is some deep metaphysical point to be made here if I could only think of it.

Stretching a Point. One morning we loaded the boat and were ready to depart. At this point we both wandered off in different directions vanishing into the ambient colour and silence. Subjectively at least, it is possible to stop time and expand the transient present into a long moment of detent when the mind can be undividedly part of everything. We knew that when this moment of departure ended we would be cast out of the garden; we would lose grace and return to the world of good and evil, that is to the world of thermodynamics and the dreaded increase in entropy. In the end we pushed off with decision and seamanly competence. We might be romantics but we were also cautious, practical men; otherwise we would not have got to where we were. It is not easy being romantic; in my experience it has always involved a lot of hard work. Nevertheless, to prolong the moment of grace we stretched space-time a bit more by circumnavigating the island amid the clarity of its confusing reflections.

Leaving the Island. In the end, in spite of our ability for time-stretching, we had to turn westwards through the icebergs of Snow Sound and back through the now glassy calms of the once turbulent Island Fjord. On the way John found a tiny harbour on the north side from where a system of terraces, each richly loaded with autumn colour, led up the steep rock of a beetling buttress. From the top of this narrow zigzag on the frowning cliff we scanned the vastness of the landscape and felt fearful and bold, intimidated and elated, in fact, the full chromatic scale of opposites in this part of the emotional spectrum; then we had a lunch of vintage sardines, obsolete brands of chocolate and biscuits a quarter of a century old, still scented with cinnamon.

Hubris and Humility. By now we were getting used to being intimidated and could apply more and more brain to the aesthetics of our situation while retaining enough parallel processing to anticipate any dangerous configurations that might start to form around us. It was, it must be said, imprudent for only two men and one boat to be wandering around in such unforgiving territory beyond the edge of world. Minor acts of carelessness, failures to foresee, failures to react quickly enough particularly when you are tired, can result in a variety of terminal scenarios or, worse still, one in which you might have to face the humiliation of being rescued. Our main vulnerability was lack of physical strength. We had not the brute force and stamina to unload the boat each evening and pull it up on the shore a safe distance from the sea. If it had been washed up on the rocks by a wave dissipating the energy from a capsizing iceberg or a big berg undergoing catastrophic sundering we would have had trouble man-handling it back in. The problems of a forced landing on a stormy lee shore or changing a failed motor in a rough sea did not bear thinking about. None of this happened but you can't be lucky for ever. If you use up too many of your good statistics, only the dud ones are left and that makes you superstitiously prudent.

Evensong in the Islands. We escaped from the confines of Island Fjord and reached one of our old camps on the Bear Islands. From here we beheld two colourful sunsets: the real one and its immaculate reflection in the mirror of the sea, the one separated from the other by a jagged band of black land. We wandered around reverentially in the stained glass light of the roofless cathedral that surrounded us, aware that this was one of these moments of numinous tranquillity far removed from ordinary experience. There are doubtless boringly prosaic neuro-physiological reasons for these states of mind but for all that they are best regarded as rare gifts from whomsoever She is who actually runs the universe.

An Islet in the Storm. The next day complex cloud layers covered the sky and striped the cliff faces. We crossed the 10 miles of icebergs and open water to the South Cape on an immaculately calm overcast evening specialising in shades of translucent greys and blues, from silver to black. We found a little island with traces of palaeoeskimo stoneworks to camp on. Here we were storm bound for a day or two by a fierce, cold wind. During this period the sunlight returned but it was as hard and cold as the wind.

Brief Encounter. Then, proceeding eastwards in a change to sombre weather we met a German sailing ship, looking for somewhere to get frozen in for the winter; the crew were surprised to see a small boat emerge in a gloomy evening from beyond the greyness marking the edge of the world. The yacht was a rebuilt Esbjerg cutter. They knew about the similar *Ada Frandsen* (one of the boats on our Centennial Yacht Meet). The *Dagmar Aaen* and its picturesquely romantic young skipper had spent the last seven winters in the Arctic. They had been through the NW passage to the Bering Sea and the NE passage as far as Cape Chelyuskin - seven winters locked in ice. We were invited aboard for coffee and a chat about things Arctic in the yellow lamplight of the warm saloon.

Into the Gloom and the Gloaming. We proceeded eastwards into a grim evening and a rising headwind. In the end we got stuck in the pack ice in the first real darkness - the equinox was only a couple of weeks away. We had difficulty getting back to land because of the extreme shallowness of the sea along the flat, featureless Jameson Land coast. The boat kept grounding in a foot of water while still hundreds of yards from shore. The pack ice and grounded bergs at least protected us from the onshore wind. Otherwise we would have had to travel among the waves in deeper water four to five miles off this dangerous lee shore. We eventually found a landing and camped a couple of hundred yards inland on the first firm tundra beyond the shifting sands, sleeping intermittently, checking the boat every hour to make sure it did not get blown ashore or get hit by a piece of moving ice.

A Grey Dawn Breaking. Later, as we set off in the small hours of the morning, an immense land- and seascape, intimidating and austere, emerged from the darkness. On the rising tide we escaped from the trap by dint of luck and resourcefulness and loosening floes by bashing the edges with the heavy anchor. (The Goddess may be implacable but she sometimes rewards you if you act intelligently and do not despair). Our escape, however, was mostly due to a change in the wind direction; it started to blow from the west. The 40 miles of pack ice between us and journey's end began to loosen and move out to sea. We reached the settlement of Scoresby Sound after a final day of surfing on the backs of the waves, following the loosening ice floes as we all galloped eastwards in intermittent sunshine.

Alas, Everything Comes to an End. That evening, after 16 days of higher education in the wilderness we were in a warm house dining off Arctic char, smoked seal, mattuk and fresh bread while watching the sun set in splendour from our dining-room window. We also noted that the ice had returned, closing the route we had come by. We had been lucky to arrive at the beginning of the only long, good weather window of the entire summer. The journey had required no more of us than basic competence. We could easily have been more severely tested. When I showed my snapshots and told our story to my old friend of 50 years, Professor Slesser, doyen of Arctic travel, he observed with experienced accuracy: 'Never try to do that journey again.'

WHAT'S IN A NAME?

By Malcolm Smith

This article first appeared in the 1996 Etchachan Club Journal but deserves a wider audience. (Editor).

OF THE names for climbs, like those for the nags that divest you of your hard-earned cash, there is no end. Imagination has no bounds nowadays and a good thing too. Gone are the days when we were restricted to the purely descriptive, and autocratic guide-book editors would take exception to a name and have the authors change it e.g., the insipid Pioneer Route for the inspiring Grandes Jorasses and (tee-hee) Janus Left Face for Hackingbush's Horror. But flights of imagination can lead to difficulties for the uninitiated numbskulls like myself. We long to know the workings of the authorial mind. We go to the dictionary where, very occasionally, all is revealed. However, the Chebecs, Slartibartfasts, Katsalanas and Wachachas leave us scratching our polls, wondering and conjecturing.

One would like to think we are correct in inferring that Dougie and Brian's Sous Les Toits identifies them as classic French cinema buffs *(Sous Les Toits De Paris)* and that their Iron In The Soul proclaims their interest in the works of Sartre and his philosophy. One would also presume, hopefully, that White Mischief is a play on the title of a favourite author's novel (Waugh). The use of 'hopefully' is important; better by far to have fooled around with *Black Mischief* than have Lochnagar saddled for all time with a 'WM' derived from the steamy, though not so hot TV play of many years back. But conjecture over apparently less convoluted reasons for a name can often lead one astray. For myself, I thought long over The Mousetrap. Surely, I guessed, it was the case that, on the day, the climb seemed to go on and on as did the never-ending run of the play. In the event, according to Derek, an actual mouse was involved - a field mouse accidentally killed on the way to the climb. This is a more prosaic, but more endearing explanation in the end; for it now stands in my mind as a mighty epitaph exhibiting a Burnsian sympathy for a very small fellow creature.

Conjecture, too, can lead to egg on the face, especially when it is cited in print. Adam Watson commenting on Firsoff's *The Cairngorms on Foot and Ski* in his general guide, announced that Egyptian Fantasy was a hit by its authors at Firsoff's use of the term 'Egyptian rocks' for the rock structures in the corrie. Given the fly-high nature of Firsoff's prose Adam may be excused. The name, in fact, was the outcome of the climb being done approaching midnight after a non-stop pad from the Derry Gate. So surreal were the circumstances: a glorious summer night, the hour, the Sphinx obelisk appearing, disappearing and re-appearing again and again through veils of thin mist, the snow at its foot, it was almost inevitable for a jazz buff like myself to call it after the strange title of a favourite 78 by Bechet and Red Allen. None of my companions demurred. They knew a good name when they heard one. Kenny and I did, however, go to Firsoff's use of Corrie of the She-Devil (where did he get that from?) for another climb.

Firsoff's book could not be called a good one, but it was different. It reminds me pleasantly of a lugubrious aside from Kenny in a state of shatteration at the Black Bridge after another long snowy march from Braeriach. 'If a ivver write a book on the hills it's ga'an tae be ca'ad the Cairngorms on Foot and Knee.'

Although unlikely for most of you, jazz also features in the name of one of the best known climbs – Squareface. The face is squarish and this might lead one to think the name was at one and the same time factual and a play on 'Scarface', but the clincher was *Squareface* another well-loved 78 classic on which, with a superb backing including Berigan, a self-disgusted Wingy Manone intones this drunken soliloquy to a gin bottle: 'Old squareface, old double-chin, what you hangin' round for leaving me to sorrow and sighs?', and ends, 'better bring in those pink elephants, squareface you got me again'.

It's a pity I missed out on it after naming it, but I did just arrive in time to record its vanquishing on film.

Davie Duncan and Tom Patey used jazz titles for climbs, but only at the coast. Davie with Groovin' High and Tom, not a jazzer but a Waller fan, Alligator Crawl. Tom once admitted to me that he was a martyr to Raynaud's Syndrome or Disease, an arterial affliction that leaves the extremities blanched and painful in cold weather. Considering his delight in winter climbing this was a surprise to me, but I failed to pursue the topic. He could not have known the whole of Waller's oeuvre else he would surely have called one of his winter climbs, Numb Fumbling. I'll hand that one on for a small fee.

Excepting the feeble Back Bay from Artie Shaw's *Back Bay Shuffle* (an area of Boston) and the more recent Sax Appeal, a title used more than once by high-powered tenorists (though here I jalouse that the main interest of the author(s) lay in the punned word) there is little else influenced by jazz in the Cairngorms terminology. The recent Blue Serge gives pause, however. This is the title of an Ellington piece of the 1940s composed by his son, Mercer. Whether its authors are jazz aficionados, bobbies, or were simply hard-pressed at the time to raise cash for proper climbing gear is not known. Off-hand, I can think of a few classic pieces whose titles could be used - Gillespie's *Dizzy Atmosphere*, Basie's *Doggin'Around*, Ellington's *Echoes of the Jungle* (somewhere near Djibangi if there's still room), Willie the Lion's *Fingerbuster* and Coltrane's *Giant Steps*. Feel free to use them if you wish. It would give me pleasure if you do.

Harking back to Tom; he was fearless in most things, but there was in him a dread of snakes and a revulsion towards the more inimical invertebrates. He refused to bivvie anywhere in the Slugain after being told it was a great place for adders (it still is). His Boa, Python, The Serpent and Scorpion testify to his phobia. If only he had been a Holmesian he would surely have latched on to *The Speckled Band* for one of his traverses. It's an old route name, but, perhaps, too good a one to languish in foreign parts.

Objection, though, might be taken towards a deliberate plagiaristic implantation because of the resulting confusion, but surely not for climbs hundreds of miles apart. Duplication, however, has already happened on our very own doorstep in corries separated by a few miles only. Yes, a second Salamander darted from the flames in 1973 to confound us with the original of 1971 on the hellish crag. It is being merely academic here to say that confusion might have been avoided if Dougie had called his climb Hellbender. By doing so, he would have held to his original conception and shown compliance with the familial names of the cliff. For besides meaning a monumental binge, Hellbender is the common name of an American species of the genus *Salamandra*. But this is waffle. The other beastie is the intruder and is rightly banished to the cold depths of the Flume for its temerity.

One could go on to discuss the generic, follow-on names on cliffs. I won't, for without injections of humour, laxity of thought and, eventually, boredom can take over from what may have been original flashes of wit. Coire Etchachan exemplifies this. From a dagger piercing a virgin bit of rock, its surrounding cliff ends up as a mere vehicle for a catalogue of cutting blades. Hell's Lum crag, however, is redeemed by touches of playful fancy and its scope for devilry.

But even here, how long will you be able to stomach an increase in the Auld Mahouns, Auld Clooties, the Devil's Disciples and the Devil-May-Cares?

Humour, unless hidden and only to be appreciated by those in the authors' immediate circle, is strangely absent from our cliffs. For me the palm must go to Big De'il, succinct and no need for pondering. I'm sure the climb itself is much better than the disparagement implicit in the slang phrase would suggest. The Clean Sweep runs it close, but here I sense the tiny prick of the Smith needle. In The Pink and Tickled Pink have their merit for routes on ruddy rocks. And don't forget dour Lochnagar with its fine Pateyian sally of Shylock's Chimney. Nothing hidden here if you've brushed up your Shakespeare, just a patent warning that the climb will go all out for its pound of flesh. I also like Sinclair's Last Stand, but how to treat it? With its play on Custer, is it humorous? With its use of a name of one who is no longer with us it must have a serious content. I would prefer to think of it as a lasting memorial to the folly of a flawed ideal. Beware the enthusiasms of the powerful.

So there is no accounting for tastes, especially in humour. Remember a fearful Des O'Connor going on stage at the Glasgow Empire with his best gags and fainting at the first signs of restiveness in that theatre's notorious audience. That to me is funny in itself. It calls for an illustrative yarn. At one time there was no name for a forlorn moderate on Beinn a' Bhuird, so I took the chance of calling it M and B Buttress for the guide. This was outwardly eponymous avoiding anything that might arouse the wrath of the authors.

But Gordon Mathieson and Ian Brooker were about to qualify as doctors and would henceforth spend much of their working days doling out M and B tablets which contained a series of sulphonamides – at that time before the general use of true antibiotics the universal cure for 'coughs, colds and scabbit holes'. I thought this invention cute, perhaps, nothing more. But Tom Patey when he heard it almost 'filed' himself in his glee. Perhaps the thought of his own eventual entry into that field was the reason. As his pianistic hero had it: 'One never knows, do one.'

And so to one that unfortunately/fortunately failed to materialise. Just before I departed the field in 1960, Freddy and Sticker told me that they had been eyeing-up what is probably now Vulcan near Tiara for a winter climb. And what do you think they were going to call it?. Yes, all together now – Tiara **Boom de ay.** Perhaps not in accord with such an austere place, but a corker, nevertheless.

Eponymity in naming has been ostracised and has now, apparently, disappeared altogether. The last I find in our area is Jewell-Kammer Route on Beinn a' Bhuird done in 1974. Perhaps it was an un-named climb and others used the personal names for convenience. No fear, no favour will be shown in this piece. I'll brave the fire and go over the top with what follows. Before Jewell-Kammer there was the Sand-Pyper of 1961, a good name gone awry. Why was the eponym used so prominently so destroying the subtlety, even grace of the Sandpiper? It puzzles me. OK Derek – Victoria Park at dawn with seconds and peashooters.

It was inevitable in the wacky times we live in that sex should pop its head up in the corries. So far, with one exception, in its milder forms – Cruising, Topless, The Hoarmaster, Hooker's Corner (no castigations, please, over Hooker's Joy named after Joseph Hooker, botanist) The Deviant, Deep Throat, Hot Lips, all but one from that hotbed, Glenmore. We await The Groper. But the nadir, Streakers Root, chided even by a modern team of guide-book editors, is home-grown.

Fie, fie Rob. Why forsake the palatable pun of Route for the blatant crudity, thus offending a majority?

Which leads to the best and worst, the worst first: Nig and Nog, inevitably, Yakaboo, so bad it's almost good, Puke and Boke in that too, too Sic-making corner. Boke is a southern regurgitation, the equivalent of our 'cowk' and quite unknown to me until the perusal of the ghastly Morag The Toerag in the *Weekend Scotsman* (good though for the dog, Hairy Hector, viewing the 'ongans' with a perpetual puzzled air, the while 'sookin' on his tin of mince cola). One that may be thought humorous is Nocando Crack. By running the words together to have us pronounce it as the Speyside hamlet is clever, not funny. I see it as a rather inglorious way of saving the author from an outright showing-up of a hapless second man's failure to follow him. And the man can be readily identified. Why choose such a name in the first place? There may be no precedent. I can't think of one.

Now for what you might have been waiting for - Hackingbush's Horror. Terrible for many reasons. I can't remember being singled out for the name.

Every man in a very close coterie received the moniker. It was sprayed around in times of mild frustration or annoyance: 'Hey, Hackenbush, fit are ye deein' up there?'. 'C'mon Hackenbush get oot o' that scratcher o' yours.' It stemmed from a collective enthusiasm for things Marxian, in particular, Dr. 'Either he's dead or my watch has stopped' Hackenbush. No, no, no, for God's sake, not Hackingbush. Just ponder the decorum shown before it and since in the corrie's names. Spootin' Dootin' was besmirched, and Groucho keeps birling in his grave. So there, 'Approx 4 pegs for aid' indeed.

One must remember then that the climbs you make on a glorious mountain are, in effect, permanent reminders of you as individuals and their names, in many instances, of your personalities. So beware the likes of the Verbal Diarrhoeas. Best to leave their kind to the coast and quarries where few of the squeamish will be upset.

But good, exemplary names abound in the Cairngorms. I'll parade the best, my best from a very personal viewpoint. You will, of course, disagree with me entirely.

Shadow Couloir, not a climb but a great name from the past, held me long before I even thought of climbing. For five years, sandwiched between tin plates for protection at the bottom of a much-travelled kitbag, lay Henry Alexander's *Cairngorms* providing solace and dreams.

How could I fail to appreciate that name of Symmers and Ewen. It introduced an alpine term for gully that fell sweetly on the ears. I used it in the guide as often as was thought decent, most importantly for The Great Couloir on Braeriach without any thought of belittling The Couloir on Cairngorm. The authors of the coldly atmospheric Moonshadow must like it also. Savage Slit, an oldie, is yet modern in its forthrightness. Scorpion with its sting-in-the-tail is perfect for its ascent in winter (False Scorpion may puzzle as it was climbed before the real thing. The answer is that it was unnamed at the time of its ascent and was only dubbed so, much, much later),

Hellfire Corner is a child of mine. I missed out on it though while working 12-hour days on the Lubreoch Dam at Loch Lyon trying to recover some respect from penury induced by too heavy a commitment to that guide - reward, one copy, all of 18 bob's worth, and nary a review from its publishers. The past is, indeed, a strange country - but I'll let that flee stick tae the wa'. The name is a fine one for the cliff, I'm sure, but a terrible one in history, commemorating as it does a small area of an infamous battle-ground of the 1914-18 war.

The French Connection is a good film, the connotation is apt and so the name is a fitting memorial to two fine climbers. Falkenhorst, an ultra tough-sounding name, I like because of a once keen interest in the collective psyche of the German general staff in the last war. Senility has progressed so much I can't remember now whether he was a goodie or baddie. A fine climb too.

Desolation Crack, with the noun used in preference to the adjective, is evocative and steers me to Kerouac's *Desolation Angels*. This, for a mountaineer, contains some of his most sympathetic writing. It stems from a long, solitary spell he did as a forest fire-watcher in a look-out hut high in the mountains of Washington State. You can overlook the faults in a man who can be so overcome by the grandeur of his surroundings that he shouts in exultation to the trees an impromptu: 'Hozomeen, Hozomeen, finest mountain I ever seen.'

The cuneiform buttress of the Mitre Ridge is an imposing rock feature. In 1983 its face was truly The Empty Quarter, that is until Dougie and Greg forged a way through it like a couple of agile Doughtys. The climb is a great one, and for the first exploratory occasion Arabia Deserta provided an apt, dignified name. This aptness will sadly diminish, however, if or when others are tempted to follow new ways.

Getting on to my top flight now. Darwin, father of the evolutionary theory of natural selection, and his supporters, Wallace, Bates and Huxley, T. H. are among my all-time heroes, so I cannot but appreciate the Ascent of Man, the Naked Ape, on his Perilous Journey upwards and onwards accompanied by all the animals, his fellow strivers, in the great struggle.

It might have come out of the *Rover* or *Wizard,* but does anyone really know? Has anyone ever asked? Pax, John, Djibangi is one of the great names. About 40 years ago I wrote: 'For besides being euphonious it conjures up for me the apple and orange matinees of my childhood to see such films as *Trader Horn* and *Africa Speaks."* Good God - 40 years ago and reminiscing of childhood. It's enough to put years on a body.

I'm sure that the use of the definite article in a name gives that climb a certain cachet, whether deserved or not. There are many examples for and against in the Cairngorms. The Blue Max, a decoration, requires it. Without it the name would be meaningless or, at best, would indicate that Maxie had been very cold, indeed, at worst been garrotted by the rope. For me, brought up as a schoolboy to relish the tales in *Air Stories* of the Boelcks and Guynemers, of Spads and Halberstadts, Max Immelmann, he of the eponymous 'turn', was the early German ace to capture the imagination. So this is my second favourite.

And so to the *Pour Le Merite.* This has to be Diedre Of The Sorrows. Here with the pass of a magician a classic Irish play has been turned into a superb name for an epic. Sing its praises. There's real naming for you.

As an annex and antidote to those black sheep of Hell's Lum Crag left-hand corner I must bring back to life The White Ewe by B. Robertson and party sacrificed in that place 35 years ago through a bad editorial oversight. I trust this route will come to the notice of the present editors (see an SMCJ of the very late 1950s). I can't tell now if this was B. W. R. on a very early foray. If it was, he should treat this acknowledgment as my apology and also a thank you for The Blue Max.

N.B. Excluding points of the compass and other positional names three more doubles have turned up to keep the reptilian critters company – Solstice, Trunk Line and Vortex.

THE INACCESSIBLE PINNACLE

JOHN MITCHELL

NEW CLIMBS SECTION

OUTER ISLES

LEWIS, Creag Dubh Dibadale:

Rob Archbold and Geof Cohen note the following two items.

Note 1: We write this in an attempt to clarify the relation between Panting Dog Climb and the earlier Joplin's Wall. A full description of Joplin's Wall was submitted to SMCJ in 1974 but, in accordance with the post-moratorium policy operating at that time, only an abbreviated version was published. The routes are essentially common, up to, and including the 'excellent rock niche' and the 'black corner above' in the description of Panting Dog Climb. Thereafter the first difference seems to be in the vicinity of the 'sloping overhang'. For Joplin's Wall: Move right and up beneath the middle of an overhang. Traverse left on underclings to a small perched block, above which a short wall leads to easier climbing into a prominent depression. Continue diagonally right to a belay in a chimney/crack system at a point level with a horizontal fault on the right (5b). (This belay is probably in the 'line of weakness' at the start of pitch 3 of Panting Dog Climb.) Make an exposed traverse right along the horizontal fault (with bulging rock above) for about 25ft, then climb steeply up to gain easier ground (5a). Climb up and right to gain the big ramp which runs diagonally right towards the top (about three pitches, 110m, 4c).

Note 2: With regard to the History section of the guidebook, while it is indeed the case that we made a free ascent of Via Valtos in July 1974, we feel impelled to point out that we have neither climbed nor claimed to have climbed Solitude.

HARRIS, Glen Scaladale, Creag Mo:

Wee Gommie is 100m and modern grade HVS 5a 5a 5a -. The last two pitches (5a, -) are the same as Herbivore pitches 4 and 5. An independent finish would be much harder and was unlikely to have been done. The route is good despite vegetation and worth a star.

Lost Gandulf – 20m MVS. C. Stupart, M. Moss. 27th July, 1997.
Situated on the smaller crag at the right edge of the main cliff. Two obvious diagonal cracks run rightwards for the full height of the crag from a terrace. Climb the crack, with two deviations out right on to a slab.

Shelob - 15m Severe. M. Allan, S. Marvell. 27th July, 1997.
The right-trending crack 15m to the right of Lost Gandulf, most interesting at the top.

Sgurr Scaladale: A. Nisbet notes that from a distance (Creag Mo), it seemed obvious that the huge central gully is Central Gully, not West Gully as marked in the New Guide diagram. Therefore Central Rib (the original rock climb) is the rib on its left, a very obvious line and dry when everything else was wet, and West Buttress is on its right before West Gully.

LEWIS SEA CLIFFS, Painted Geo:

On the south side of the Geo left of Black Foot, the following three routes start from the right end of a spacious ledge gained by a scramble down a chossy bay towards the back of the Geo. From right to left.

Stripper - 25m Severe*. R. Henderson, E. Pirie. 27th April, 1995.
After climbing the chimney crack of Rub Down for 5m, take the obvious right-trending crackline.

Rub Down - 25m V.Diff. E. Pirie, R. Henderson. 27th April, 1995.
Climb the chimney crack at the right end of the ledge.

Bristles Arête – 25m Diff. R. Henderson, E. Pirie. 27th April, 1995.
The arête left of Rub Down.

Veinous Trap - 20m HVS 5a*. A. Cunningham, K. Geddes. 27th April, 1995.
About 500m to the NE of Painted Geo (MR 010 334) and well seen from the top of the climbs around Mick's Corner is a small cliff with a distinctive diagonal pink quartz vein. This route hand traverses the top of the vein starting from the lowest point.

The Hooded Wall and the Channel Walls (MR 004 333):

These Walls lie just west of the Painted Wall Geo, on the tip of the headland 100m beyond the Radio Mast. From the car park go north-west in the same line as the road and descend slabby rock a short way to the start of a shelf slanting down northwards. Near the top of this shelf there is a notch which looks out over a recessed area. An abseil through the notch deposits one at the foot of the Hooded Wall at the start of a thin crack (Black is Black) running up the left (facing in) retaining wall. An easy scramble around this retaining wall, in fact a fin of rock, leads to a deep channel going right through to the north side of the headland; the Channel Walls lie either side. Both areas appear largely non-tidal with waves tending to be broken up by the seaward wall on the other side of the channel, although spray does fly about a bit in heavier seas.

The Hooded Wall:

Black is Black - 30m E1 5b**. R. and C. Anderson. 28th June, 1997.
The thin crack running up the black wall just left of the abseil ropes.

Paint it Black - 30m E2 5b*. R. and C. Anderson. 3rd July, 1997.
The groove just to the left forces one out right onto a good ledge near its top. Climb the wall above onto the edge and climb up left to the top of the 'fin'.

Buoys in the Hood - 30m E1 5b*. R. and C. Anderson. 28th June, 1997.
Takes a line up the right side of the hooded section starting from the centre of the wall. Climb stepped grooves up and then rightwards to the base of a groove with a thin crack in it at the right side of the hooded section. Climb this and continue to the top.

Buoyancy Aid – 30m HVS 4c*. R. and C. Anderson. 3rd July, 1997.
Follow Buoys in the Hood (the two lower shelfs are blind and often greasy) to just below its groove/thin crack leading to the edge and traverse around right onto the edge where a crack leads to the top.

Buoys From the Black Stuff – 30m VS 4c**. R. and C. Anderson. 3rd July, 1997.
The obvious crack leading out onto the lower right side of the hooded section. Climb the crack to the edge (a line links up with the previous route from here), step right and climb a crack which leads to fine slabby ground and the top.

The Channel Walls:

Blind Alley – 25m E3 5c. R. and C. Anderson. 28th June, 1997. This climbs the centre of the right hand section of wall on the other side of the 'fin' from Black is

Black. From the channel climb to a spacious ledge, then awkwardly up a short corner in the centre of the wall. Continue directly above to the base of a quartz vein, then go up and around left passing the base of a blind groove to climb a pink quartzy flake to the top.

Eileen Geo (MR 013 335):

A lovely little Geo just before the small island of Glas Eileen where the Ard More Mangersta cliffs dip into the sea at Uig Bay. From any of the parking areas along the final stretch of road to the transmission aerial walk north eastwards following the high ground (avoiding the drop down and climb back up from Toras Geo) out to the end before the island. The Geo is a long tidal inlet with a south west facing wall of rock dissected by quartz seams. The rock at the eastern end (right) is not as good as that farther left moving seaward. Routes at the eastern side of the inlet are accessible from the boulders for a while, however, at other times and for other climbs on the wall abseil directly to ledges above the waterline. An abseil down the north eastern corner of the Geo gains the first routes.

Flakeout – 20m E1 5b. R. and C. Anderson. 3rd July, 1997.
Climb the obvious left to right slanting flake on the back (seaward facing) wall of the Geo, just right of the abseil. From the ledge at two-thirds height, step left and climb to the top.

Breakout – 20m E1 5a. R. and C. Anderson. 3rd July, 1997.
The first section of the main wall is a slab of grey rock. Some 5m left of the abseil corner, climb a quartz streak to an accommodating ledge from whose right side a quartz streak leads through a notch to a quartz ledge. Finish up the right side of the groove above.

The next routes are gained by abseiling down an obvious corner further along the Geo, to good ledges. The first route starts from a ledge in the corner.

Sea Pink – 20m E3 6a**. R. and C. Anderson. 3rd July, 1997.
The crack up the quartzy pink wall right of the abseil is excellent, but unfortunately, near the top the holds force moves away from the centre up onto the right edge.

Just to the left of the corner is another ledge.

Deep Blue – 20m HVS 4c. R. and C. Anderson. 3rd July, 1997.
Climb the quartz streak springing from the right side of the ledge.

Aqua Marine – 20m VS 4c*. R. and C. Anderson. 3rd July, 1997.
From the left side of the ledge, gain the crack up on the left and follow this to the top.

The Seal Walls (MR 012 335):

This wall extends north-eastwards from a narrow entranced, deep sea cliff on the other side of Toras Geo where there is another Geo split by a ridge of rock with an arch under it. The wall is severely undercut where it overlooks the tidal trench entering the sea cave, then it turns the corner to a tar black vertical section before turning into another cave before decreasing in height by slabby rocks running into Eileen Geo. The tar black section has a number of cracks running up it with non-tidal ledges just above the sea, gained by abseil from directly above.

Flapping About – 30m E4 6a*. R. and C. Anderson. 4th July, 1997.
The crackline just to the right of the main central crackline

Signed Sealed and Delivered – 30m E2 5c/6a**. R. and C. Anderson. 4th July, 1997.

The main central crackline is only slightly flawed by some suspect rock near the top.

Slippery Customer – 30m E2 5b. R. and C. Anderson. 5th July, 1997.
The crackline up the left side of the wall. Start as for Signed Sealed and Delivered and go left to another crack. On the initial section the climbing is perhaps slightly easier on the left but the gear is better just on the right. Move up left into the easier upper section. Some suspect rock.

Painted Geo (guide p69):
The next five routes are on the small friendly 20m wall down and left as you face Painted Wall. Approached by scrambling or abseiling down a broken gully in the centre of the wall. The first three are right of the descent (facing in).

Callum's Grasp – 20m HVS 5a. K. Pyke, G. Huxter. 9th July, 1997.
Start at the centre of the crag at a shattered left crack line. Follow this, then straight up the final flake with great jugs and gear.

Named by Proxy – 20m HVS 5b. G. Huxter, K. Pyke. 9th July, 1997.
Start 2m right of Callum's Grasp directly below a small overhang. Pull through this, then continue more easily to the top.

Crimp Cocktail – 20m E2 5c. G. Kirk, D. Howard. 10th July, 1997.
Start midway between Callum's Grasp and the descent. Climb a small flake and pull on to a tiny ledge at 6m. Climb the crack and wall above, then move rightwards to beneath an overhang. Follow the crack leftwards through the overhang to the top.

The next two are left of the descent.

Isle be Back – 20m E1 5b. A. Leary, G. Kirk. 9th July, 1997.
Start at the left end of the sloping ledges. Climb a short corner for 2m and step left on to a small ledge. Climb up and leftwards to reach the base of a groove/crack. Pull out leftwards and climb the wall to the top.

Swell Time – 20m E1 5b. G. Kirk, A. Leary. 9th July, 1997.
Start just left of the descent under a hanging arête. Pull over the overhang on to the wall above, then move leftwards and follow the left side of the arête to a fine steep finish.

Moving northwards from Painted Geo across the next zawn, this route has the same start as Ladies Who Lunch (p73).

Out All Night – 35m E3 5c. G. Huxter, K. Pyke. 9th July, 1997.
Start as for Ladies Who Lunch. Climb 6m above the belay to gain a right-facing corner system. Follow the corner for 14m until it steepens, then step right into a hanging groove (suspect rock) to finish.

The Flannan Area – Aurora Geo, The Cioch Wall (p75):
Grease a' Break! – 20m E2 5b. R. and C. Anderson. 1st July, 1997.
A line just left of the slimy wide crack, left of The Chicken Run, was followed for a short way until the rock (or grease) forced moves into the wide crack which was finished up. Probably easier to climb the wide crack, in any case much of the climbing is on the edge of the crack away from the slime.

Landlubber Geo:
Note from R.Anderson: Guidebook page 78 – Landlubber Geo is correctly stated as being just north of the Flannan Area but is in the wrong place in the guide between

Magic Geo and Aurora Geo. It should be described on page 74 after the access notes where it states 'the northern edge of this ridge has a distinct black tail dipping into the sea'. This slabby black tail forms the west side of Landlubber Geo and is used to access it down the west side not the east as metioned in the guide. MR 003 330 – Dry Dock is obvious and looks fine but the rock to its right is certainly very brittle and deterred an ascent.

The following is also on Landlubber Geo and received from K. Pyke (MR 002 330, the same wall? She prefers the name Geodh' an tamana). It is 10 minutes south of Mangersta headland parking lot. A SW wall in a sheltered mini-Geo above large boulders.

Birdsong – 25m E3 5c**. G. Huxter, K. Pyke. 11th July, 1997.
Start on a large flat-topped boulder beneath a prominent orange corner. Follow the grooved crack to gain the orange corner and climb this on good holds to a ledge. Step right and go up 5m, then move right on to another sloping ledge to gain the base of an overhanging corner. Move left along the ledge and pull on to an easy ramp to finish. (Alternatively, finish direct up the corner at 6a – done as second).

The next two routes are hidden away to the seaward side north of Aurora Zawn. Here lies a hidden wall banded on its south side by a deep chimney (abseil).

Sidewalk – 25m E1 5b*. K. Pyke, G. Huxter, A. Leary. 11th July, 1997.
Start at the base of the large crack/cleft. Follow the crack to thinner moves diagonally right. Continue on a rising rightward line following the length of the wall on good holds and ledges.

Mutineer's Return – 25m VS 4c*. G. Huxter, G. Kirk. 11th July, 1997.
The aesthetic arête in an exposed position. Start at its seaward base.

Screaming Geo:

Descriptions have been received that fit Pinky and Perky (p87). Pinky at E1 5b**; Perky at HVS 5a***.

The following routes lie approx. 15m to the right, just left of the descent route.

Screaming Sandhoppers – 10m Severe**. M. Sullivan, J. Garbutt. 22nd July, 1997.
Starts at a prominent 2m monolith with a shallow cave to the left and a deeper one to the right. Climb the crack direct, sustained.

Screaming Miss Molly – 10m VS 4b **. M. Sullivan, J. Garbutt. 22nd July, 1997.
Start from the right-hand side of the deeper cave. Bridge up between the monolith and the right-hand wall of the cave to reacch a crack which is climbed direct. Easier for the tall.

Katrin's Cream – 10m V.Diff **. M. Sullivan, J. Garbutt. 22nd July, 1997.
Start 2m further right. Climb a left-slanting crack into a right-facing groove.

The Screaming Wall (p92):

Necromancer – 60m E3**. K. Pyke, G. Huxter (alt). 10th July, 1997.
This route links the prominent black crystalline bands and crackline on the left side of Screaming Wall Geo. Best viewed from the hut lookout. To reach the start: abseil 60m to black ledges (non-tidal) which are 8m diagonally down and left from the start of Dark Crystal.
1. 30m 5c Follow black crystalline rock always trending up and left steeply at times on a faint prow. For the final 5m, move right up a corner to gain an airy square-cut perch.

2. 30m 5b Move left to gain the crack system and jam securely until stepping left into an obvious corner line. Finish directly as for Dark Crystal.

Rubh'an Taroin (North Bay): Guidebook page 93-94:

This is the small bay which lies just to the north of the Rubh an Taroin promentory, the south side of the bay forms the dark north wall of the promontory which is clearly visible from further up the coast. The route described below is on the same south facing wall as Moac Wall and Twelve Years On and lies just to their right. The shelf at the base of the routes appears to be free from the tide for a long time and although it can be approached by scrambling down the headland and traversing in right, it is probably better approached by abseiling down slabs at the top of the cliff and over a short, steep, grey coloured seaward facing wall at the western end. Traverse right. On turning the corner the cliff gains height, changing colour and appearance to that of quartzy lines, steep grooves and roofs. The first obvious breach in the lower wall, just on turning the corner, is thought to be the start of the two original routes but due to poor descriptions it is hard to match these up.

Achevalier – 30m E3 5c *. R. and C. Anderson. 4th July, 1997.
This lies a short way along the shelf from the earlier routes, nearer the middle of the cliff, just before the going becomes more awkward as the shelf reduces in size. There is an obvious 5m high open book corner at the base of the cliff, thread belay on the shelf below this. Climb the groove/right rib of this open-book corner to a ledge and continue awkwardly up the narrow capped groove into the prominent deep V-groove above and on up a left slanting line to finish.

AIRD UIG AREA, Geodh' a' Bheannaich (Map Ref 037 377):

On the north side of the Geo that the burn from Loch a' Bheannaich drains into, is a fin of rock with a cave halfway along on the slabby south side and a scrambly descent in the middle of the steeper north side which leads onto a large platformed bay. The best climbing on the south side of the fin is to the west/seaward side of the cave and access is by abseil to ledges at the base of the slab. Moving left/west from the cave.

Ride a Wild Starfish – 25m Diff. E. Pirie, R. Henderson. 28th April, 1995.
Climb the arête on the left of the cave.

Nightmare of Prickly Starfish – 25m Severe*. R. Henderson, E. Pirie. 28th April, 1995.
Start up twin cracks to the left of the arête and finish via the left one. **Note:** Juggy Crack, 25m Severe** (1993) climbs the fine wide crack just left of the above route.

Echinoderm – 25m VS 4c*. A. Cunningham, K. Geddes. 28th April, 1995.
A few metres left again climb into a hanging left-facing corner moving right round the bulge and finish up the top crack.

Feather Star – 25m Diff*. K. Geddes, A. Cunningham. 28th April, 1995.
Start 3m right of the left edge, taking wide cracks and avoid the bulge on the left finishing via the final moves of Small Fry.
On the end of the fin accessed from the platform on the north side is a pink vein on the right and a dark vein on the left split by a deep fault (a line of descent).

Small Fry – 20m H. Severe. T. Walker, I. Sherrington. 28th April, 1995.
Climb by ramps on the right side of the pink vein.

Langustine – 15m Severe*. A. Cunningham, K. Geddes. 28th April, 1995.
Climb via a narrow pink quartz vein on the right of the dark area.

Squat Lobster – 15m Diff*. K. Geddes, A. Cunningham. 28th April, 1995.
Cracks up the middle of the dark area.

Rock Goby – 15m V.Diff*. K. Geddes, A. Cunningham. 28th April, 1995.
Cracks up the left side of the dark area.
The next routes are on the steep north side of the fin and at the back of the platform bay where various dark and light 'liquorice allsort' veins are obvious.

Baltic Tellin – 25m E1 5b*. A. Cunningham, K. Geddes. 28th April, 1995.
A few metres to the left of the descent is a steep deep crack. Take to the wall on the right of the crack moving leftwards onto easier ground. Finish by the steep crack through the top bulge.

Saltire Right – 25m Severe 4b**. K. Geddes, A. Cunningham. 28th April, 1995.

At the back of the bay is a white quartz cross high up, with wide quartz veins running up either side. Climb by the stepped quartz rib through the right side of the cross with hard moves over the first step.

Saltire Left – 25m M. Severe**. T. Walker, I. Sherrington. 28th April, 1995.
Takes the stepped rib through the left side of the quartz cross.

Farther left of the Saltire (30m) are a number of corners and grooves.
Seal Dive – 35m VS . E. Pirie, R. Henderson. 28th April, 1995.
Takes the big right-facing corner high up with a black ramp below.
1. 20m 4b From sea-facing ledges climb a clean crack to a ledge below the corner.
2. 15m 4c/5a Climb the corner.

The Abyss – 35m HVS*. R. Henderson, E. Pirie. 28th April, 1995.
To the left of Seal Dive is a deep narrow slot dropping to the sea.
1. 20m 4b Bridge the slot and climb the left-hand corner to a ledge.
2. 15m 5a Continue up the steep fault line to easier ground.
The rock becomes more broken past this area until it heightens again into an impressive Geo, May Day Geo (MR 037 379). The south side consists of a steep, cracked black wall followed by a series of corners and arêtes running into the back wall of the Geo. Above is a diagonal fault/ledge line with shorter routes starting from this higher ledge. The first routes are described right to left descending the fault.

Shortie – 5m Diff. R. Henderson. 1st May, 1995.
A broken right-facing corner where the crag starts to heighten.

Gale Force 8 – 8m VS 5a*. A. Cunningham, F. Fotheringham. 1st May, 1995.
A few metres left of Shortie, pull over an undercut nose into thin cracks.

May Day, May Day – 10m E1 5a/b**. F. Fotheringham, A. Cunningham. 1st May, 1995.
Round the edge from Gale Force 8 is an overhanging corner crack. Strenuous.

Stickybeak – 20m Mod. R. Henderson. 1st May, 1995.
From the end of the ledge below May Day, step left into slabby left-facing corner. Climb this to the top.

Scramble down the fault a few metres to gain access to the next two routes.
Classic Overtrousers – 25m VS 4c**. I. Sherrington, R. Henderson. 1st May, 1995.
The stepped series of ramps and corners 6m left of Stickybeak, trending slightly left.

Australian Snowballs – 25m E1 5b*. R. Henderson, I. Sherrington. 1st May, 1995.

Start 3m left again and climb yet another corner system with the crux at 5m at a short overhanging corner.

Access to the bigger lower wall is via a scramble off the end of the promontory cutting back right under the climbs. The ledges here will be awash at high tide with the usual Atlantic swell.

Rites of Spring – 25m E1 5b**. I. Sherrington, R. Henderson, 1st May, 1995.
This route takes the right-hand groove on the first major steep black wall. Finish via the fine thin crack in the headwall.

Whitewater Groove – 25m E1 5b**. R. Henderson, I. Sherrington. 1st May, 1995.
On the left of the wall is another groove which curves rightwards to the same finish as Rites of Spring.

Snakes and Ladders – 30m HVS 5a**. A. Cunningham, F. Fotheringham. 1st May, 1995.

About 20m left of the first wall is a series of steep short corners and arêtes with a short black wall barring access. Climb the wall moving left into the corners in a fine position.

The End of the World is Knee High – 25m E1 5b***. I. Sherrington, T. Walker. 1st May, 1995.
Traverse left along the platforms to corners before it narrows at a patch of seaweed. Climb a layback crack system until forced to step right. Continue up the top system.

Hard On Yer Heels – 20m H. Severe. A. Cunningham, F. Fotheringham. 1st May, 1995.
On the opposite side of the Geo towards the seaward end is an inviting set of vertical cracks. Abseil down to a tidal ledge below the cracks and take the more obvious right-hand crack.

From the top of the previous route a ramp leads down under a short wall north to the last area of climbing where the cliff gains in height.

CAMUS UIG AREA, Torcaso, The Pool Wall (MR 030 354):

This is the lovely tidal pool which is mentioned on page 100 of the guide. Just north of the cairn at the top of Torcaso is the large Geo mentioned in the guide (MR 029 353). Some 50m north of this Geo is a shallow bay above a tidal pool. The base of the wall above the pool appears to remain unaffected by the tide for quite a number of hours and there is a good high ledge at the base of the three routes described. Approach by abseil down the north corner of the bay, past a platform and down a wide, deep crack to the edge of the pool. A fine wall forms the back of the bay and the three following routes start from the same place after a scramble up to a good ledge on a huge 'boulder' forming the base of the wall. All three routes are very close together.

Pond Life – 30m E2 5c**. R. and C. Anderson. 29th June, 1997.
Step left, climb an awkward leaning section and continue steeply up the thin crackline.

Pool Shark – 30m E1 5b**. R. and C. Anderson. 29th June, 1997.
A few feet right of the previous route climb onto the very top of the 'boulder' and follow another crackline straight to the top with a steeper middle section, always just right of the previous route.

Puddle Duck – 30m E1 5c. R. and C. Anderson. 29th June, 1997. Eliminate climbing immediately right of Pool Shark. Step up right into a steep groove and make an awkward move to holds, then continue directly up a groove with an awkward exit onto a small slab. Continue to the top.

Fiavaig Bagh (MR 031 354, p100), Deep Zawn:
Consequences – 30m E4 6a. K. Pyke, G. Huxter. 12th July, 1997.
The route lies on the west-facing wall and follows a hanging corner-crack system. Best viewed from the opposite side of the zawn. Approach by abseil to a hanging stance down the large corner some 30m from the south end of the zawn. Make tricky moves up a blank wall and corner (RP protection) to a semi-rest under an overhang. Turn the overhang on its right to gain the arête and step back left to follow the final groove line in an excellent position.

Fright of the Cormorant – 25m E1 5b*. G. Kirk, D. Howard, A. Leary. 12th July, 1997.
Climbs the crack in the left wall of the descent corner. Approach as per Consequences and start from sloping ledges. Climb the corner for 4m, then follow the crack in its steep left wall to the top.

Geodha Gunna (p102):
Brutal Reality is wrongly described as in this Geo; it is in the next Geo northwards. The following two routes are on the impressive south-facing wall. Approach by abseil to ledges at sea level.
Rabid Wanderings – 45m E3 5c. G. Huxter, K. Pyke. 14th July, 1997.
Climb the central crack/groove for 20m before moving out rightwards and taking a diagonal line up to the right end of an overhang. Pull through this (crux) and continue straight to the top.

Lucid Visions – 45m E4***. G. Huxter, K. Pyke (alt.). 14th July, 1997.
A brilliant 'out there' route on a rising and exposed traverse leftwards through hanging grooves and finishing up a steep headwall.
1. 25m 5c. Climb Rabid Wanderings for 3m before weaving up and leftwards into hanging grooves to gain a good and exposed stance.
2. 20m 5c. Move left and on to the headwall. Follow a thin crack leftwards on steep ground to finish.

DALBEG, Small West Wall:
Left of Original Route are a number of short routes.
Zosta Slab – Diff.*. I. Sherrington, T. Walker. 26th April, 1995.
From the start of Original Route traverse left along the base of the undercut slab and up cracks in the left edge.

No Choice – MVS 4c. A. Cunningham, K. Geddes. 26th April, 1995.
The first corner crack left of the slab. Pull through the initial bulge and turn the next on the right to finish up Zosta Slab.

Pringles – Severe*. K. Geddes, A. Cunningham 26th April, 1995.
The third corner crack left of the slab - good.
On the seaward face right of Mongrel are a number of short cracks.
Good Crack – HVS 5a*. R. Henderson, E. Pirie. 26th April, 1995.
The obvious vertical crack in the centre of the face.

Just for the Crack – VS 4c*. E. Pirie, R. Henderson. 26th April, 1995.
To the right of Good Crack, pull over the nose to climb the right-trending crack.

Ian's Easy Time – M. Severe. I. Sherrington, T. Walker. 26th April, 1995.
Climb the right edge of the slab of Henry's Hard Times.

Hard to Swallow – E2 5b*. A. Cunningham, K. Geddes. 26th April, 1995.
The crackline just right of Endurance, steep and strenuous.

Note: Ruth's Lazy Day was thought to be H. Severe 4b and Outlaw E1 5b.

NORTH UIST, Eaval:

Waters of Illusion – 50m Severe. D. Rubens. 20th July, 1997.
Although difficulties are short, the climb enlivens an expedition to this fine
viewpoint. There appeared to be minimal protection. Approaching by kayak across
Loch Obisary, a small, but prominent, white scar is seen towards the right-hand end
of the summit cliffs. Start below and right of the steep buttress which has the scar
on its lower left. Climb an easy ridge for about 30m. Near the top of the ridge,
traverse left and on to the steep buttress. Climb the buttress (12m) by the line of least
resistance (trending left, then right). Scramble up to finish.

PABBAY, Allanish Peninsula (MR 592 881):

Hypnotize – 35m HVS 5a*. L. Hughes, G. Nicoll. 28th May, 1997.
Start four metres left of Squeeze Job. Climb a blunt arête and the easier ground
above.

Vitrified Cinders – 40m HVS 5b**. G. Nicoll, L. Hughes. 28th May, 1997.
Romp up the ramp below Sugar Cane Country and climb the fine corner bounding
the right side of the smooth wall.

The Poop Deck (MR 589 871):

The Notorious B.I.G. – 30m E3 6a**. L. Hughes, G. Nicoll. 24th May, 1997.
A fierce route tackling the overhang on the left side of this part of the wall. Start just
to the right of The Immigrant and climb a crack line to the roof. Make hard moves
to surmount this then step right and climb a blunt arête to the top.

The Raven – 30m E5 6a***. P. Thorburn, R. Campbell. 25th May, 1997.
Three cracks lie to the left of Bogus Asylum Seekers. From the left of a pool, gain
and climb the left hand crack to a roof. Pull through this at a hairline crack, then
move up to the large break. Follow this down and left then move up and follow
pockets to the top.

Corncrakes for Breakfast – 30m E3 5c**. R. Campbell, P. Thorburn. 25th May,
1997.
Start between Bogus Asylum Seekers and the left facing corner. Follow a flake to
head for a small overlap in the leaning headwall, passing it on the right.

The Stowaway – 30m Severe*. G. Nicoll, L. Hughes. 24th May, 1997.
This is the deep corner forming the left hand side of the projecting buttress. Wide
bridging leads to easier ground then a steep finish up another short corner.

Poop – 20m Diff.*. G. Nicoll. 24th May, 1997.
The left end of the Poop Deck is formed by a strange projecting nose. Climb easily
up the crest of the nose, move left and finish up a short V-chimney.

The Galley (MR 590 872):

Unnamed – 30m E2 5b. P. Thorburn, R. Campbell. 28th May, 1997.
Takes the middle of the wall between The Abridged Version and Wiggly Wall. A
bold eliminate with good climbing.

Wu-Tang Will Survive – 30m HVS 5a*. L. Hughes, G. Nicoll. 25th May, 1997.
Start as for Winos in a Barren Land and take a diagonal line rightwards across the wall to finish at the right hand end of the big roof.

Conch Corner – 25m VS 4c*. G. Nicoll, L. Hughes. 25th May, 1997.
To the left of Winos in a Barren Land are two parallel, disjointed corners. This route climbs the right hand of these. Start by climbing rightwards to gain and climb the steep flaky corner.

Wu-Tang Forever – E1 5b*. L. Hughes, G. Nicoll. 25th May, 1997.
Follow Conch Corner for a few metres then pull left through a bulge (crux) to gain and climb the left hand corner line.

The Great Arch:
Sturm und Drang – 115m E5**. R. Campbell, P. Thorburn (alt). 25th May, 1997.
This serious route climbs an impressive line on the south flank of the pillar forming the left side of the big corner. Abseil down the corner to the lowest foothold, below the lowest black biotite band. Belay on nuts and the abseil rope.
1. 25m 6a. Taking a high side runner, traverse left just above the level of the belay to gain the top of a large slot. Follow cracks up the wall then move left past a loose block to belay on a ramp on the left.
2. 45m 6b. Climb up to a prominent spike and then ascend the twin grooves above, moving left onto jugs below the roof. Move right into a bottomless corner with care (loose block and crux!) and gain the groove above. Follow this to belay on a vegetated ramp.
3. 15m 4b. Traverse right to belay on the left-hand side of a large ledge. 4. 30m 5b. Climb to a large flake on the right, step left, then follow the cleanest crack to the top.

Banded Geo (MR 592 870):
The Swabber – 25m HVS 5a**. G. Nicoll, L. Hughes. 26th May, 1997.
Start at the left edge of the back wall of Banded Geo, close to where the grass meets the slabs. Climb a richly pocketed groove to below the leaning headwall. Trend leftwards up the obvious ramp to pull over a bulge.

The 36th Chamber – 20m E4 6a**. L. Hughes, G. Nicoll. 26th May, 1997.
Start up The Swabber then launch up the leaning headwall. Climb to an obvious flake, then rightwards, then straight up to finish.

Endolphin Rush – 60m E4***. K. Howett, G. E. Little (alt.). 27th May, 1997.
A magnificent and strenuous route on excellent rock. Start on the long low ledge (below and to the left of the start of Spring Squill). Abseil access.
1. 25m 6a. Climb up to and follow the right-trending wide band of pegmatite across the wall until moves can be made up into a crackline. Follow this, with increasing difficulty, to belay on a small ledge directly under big roofs. A very pumpy pitch!
2. 35m 5c. Move up to the big roof then step down and left onto the lip of another roof. Climb a short overhanging wall, using a fat, black spike, to gain a ledge below another (worryingly detached) roof. Move left to bypass this and then climb straight up on big holds to the top.
To the right of Spooky Pillar is an unclimbed flakey corner then two long smooth walls separated by an obvious left facing corner. A horizontal grassy ledge runs across the top of these walls.

Hyper Ballad – 55m E2**. L. Hughes, G. Nicoll (alt.). 27th May, 1997.
This route takes a line up the wall just right of the left-facing corner. Abseil to a foot ledge four metres to the right of the base of the corner, calm seas preferred.
1. 30m 5b. From the footledge climb directly up to an overhang, traverse 6m left and pull spectacularly through the overhang at a crack. Continue to the grass ledge.
2. 25m. Climb easy cracks and slabs to the top.

Mollyhawk – 55m HVS**. G. Nicoll, L. Hughes (alt.). 27th May, 1997.
Abseil to the foot ledge as for the previous route.
1. 30m 5a. Move up and right and climb a right-facing groove. Move left to an obvious break in the overlap, pull through and continue to the grass ledge.
2. 25m Climb easy cracks and slabs to the top.

Pink Wall (MR 596 869):

The Tomorrow People – 110m E4*. G. E. Little, K. Howett (alt.). 26th May, 1997.
At the top of Pink Wall there are two short rock steps with grass ledges in-between them. The higher ledge holds a small pool, the lower holds a flat block that abuts the wall. Abseil from this block into space.
Note: This route is effectively on the westerly flank of Pink Wall where the cliff is most continuous. It has a serious feel and some very strange rock. Start at a cluster of big spikes above a black glacis about 10m in from the left side of the crag.
1. 25m 5b. Trend up and left on weird rock to a large spike. Climb a shallow chimney then hand traverse right to gain another chimney. Climb this then traverse right across a ledge to belay on a strange pillar (thread) in the far corner.
2. 25m 5c. Step up and make a hard move left. Pull up a steep wall to a jug then step right to gain a big flake edge. Climb this and then a short corner to below a big roof. Traverse hard left below the roof to take a hanging belay on 'fired' rock just after blind downwards moves.
3. 20m 5c. Move left then climb a strenuous shallow chimney line to a capping overhang. Pull over this then move up into a recess. Trend left to belay by a big semi-detached block.
4. 40m 5b. Step right and climb the obvious crack up the edge (seen as a black streak when viewing the cliff from afar). Ascend easier but enjoyable slabs to the top.

The Guga – 90m E6***. P. Thorburn, R. Campbell. 27th May, 1997.
Climbs the large open corner (the only weakness) to the left of the junction between the overhanging pink front face and the overhanging grey sidewall on the right. On the first ascent the wide terrace at the base of this feature was gained in a circuitous manner. However, a direct abseil should just about reach the outer edge of the terrace. Some fulmar dodging is then required to gain the base of a black overhanging corner, 10m to the left of the arête.
1. 20m 6a. Climb the corner with a difficult exit left onto a ledge. Move up the overhanging wall on the right to belay on a ramp.
2. 25m 6b. Climb the corner system on the right, then make hard moves through a bulge to gain the left-arching pegmatite bulge. Follow this to a crack, move up then rightwards to gain a ledge. Belay on the ledge above on the left.
3. 45m 4c. Climb up left from the belay then follow a direct line to the top.

Shag's Geo (MR 597 869):

This Geo lies between Pink Wall and the deep inlet of Sloc Glamari Geo. Its west-facing flank forms an overhanging wall in the back of the Geo which becomes a wall, of diminishing height and seamed with corners and grooves, towards its outer end. A sloping grass ledge, about 10m down, runs across the top of the wall and all abseil descents start from it and all routes finish on it. This ledge can be easily accessed by descending towards the tip of headland on its east side and then traversing around to the foot of the ledge on the west side. A scramble descent directly to the ledge is also possible. The routes are described from left to right – from the back of the Geo out.

Up Before the Beak – 70m E3**. G. E. Little, K. Howett (alt). 24th May, 1997.
Set up an abseil just down from the grass bay near the upper end of the grass ledge. Belay at a small cave a couple of metres above the sea.
1. 35m 5b. Climb a left-slanting ramp to a wide ledge. Move left along the ledge for a few metres to below another ramp. Climb this, crossing an overlap and the juggy wall above to belay at a rounded spike at a band of pink rock.
2. 30m 5c. Climb up into a short corner below a deep horizontal fault. Step right and up onto the break. Pull up on big jugs then move 2m left to an incipient crack. Climb straight up this line into a small bomb bay corner under the big roof. Exit left.

Shags with Attitude – 60m E3*. K. Howett, G. E. Little (alt.). 28th May, 1997.
To the left of an obvious long corner (Cracking Corner) is a huge black roof. Left again is a short, steep, narrow ramp just above sea level. Abseil to take a hanging belay at high watermark at the base of this ramp.
1. 25m 5c. Move up the ramp and then pull up onto an overhanging wall. Continue up to a short left-facing slot formed by a large flange. Pull right then climb straight up to belay on a ledge.
2. 35m 4c. Climb an open corner to a roof. Traverse left below it then climb up on slightly messy ground to reach the grass ledge.

Cracking Corner – 50m Severe**. G. E. Little, K. Howett. 24th May, 1997.
Mid way up the grass ledge is a triangular block a short distance beyond a semi-detached pinnacle. Abseil from the block to just above sea level at the foot of an obvious long corner. Climb the corner on excellent holds to its capping roof. Move right, then continue on the same general line to the top and belay on the abseil block.

Big Block Sloc (MR 600 869):
This small Geo lies to the east of Sloc Glamari Geo and holds a very distinctive west-facing wedge of clean rock. A huge jammed block defies gravity on the upper seaward side of this wedge. The landward side of the wedge is defined by a deep sea cave. Both the recorded routes are on the clean, vertical, outer face of the wedge and are of excellent quality and situation.
Lifeline – 25m E3 5c***. K. Howett, G. E. Little. 26th May, 1997.
Abseil to a half-foot ledge (at barnacle level) at the foot of the striking arête forming the landward edge of the wedge. Pull right and climb the crack. Step right and climb the continuation crack to a ledge just below the top of the wedge. Superb!

Immaculate Conception – 25m E2 5b***. G. . Little, K. Howett. 25th May, 1997.
Abseil to a small ledge on the outer (southerly) edge of the wedge just above high water line. Move left onto the face to gain a thin ledge. From this ascend 3m to reach a layaway hold in a small hole (from where critical protection can be placed). Traverse hard left to reach good holds. Climb up into a slim right-facing corner then pull out left, just below its capping roof, to reach good pockets (in common with Lifeline) and then a break in a second roof. Step right into the final corner and climb it to the top. Brilliant!

Rubha Charnain – Small Bouys Geo (MR 604 868):

This little Geo lies on the west side of Rubha Charnain. A slabby shelf runs down the east side of the Geo below a low wall. Initially, this wall is broken, then seamed with grooves and corners, finally becoming slabby as it bends round to face south. Access to the first few routes is down the shelf (low tide) but most are accessed by abseil. The rock is excellent and the climbing friendly. In marked contrast, the west side of the Geo holds a seriously undercut wall promising sterner action.

Spare Rib – 15m Severe*. G. E. Little. 28th May, 1997.
This is the left bounding rib of the obvious recess holding three grooves.

First Groove – 15m Severe*. G. E. Little, K. Howett. 28th May, 1997.
This is the leftmost of the three grooves in the obvious recess.

Third Groove – 20m VS 4b*. G. E. Little, K. Howett. 28th May, 1997.
This is the rightmost of the three grooves in the obvious recess.

Designer Rib – 20m HVS 5a***. K. Howett, G. E. Little. 28th May, 1997.
This superb little route climbs the right bounding rib of the obvious recess holding three grooves.

Deceptive Corner 20m Severe*. G. E. Little, K. Howett. 28th May, 1997.
This is the corner immediately right of Designer Rib and bounding the slabby south facing section of the wall. Easier than it looks.

What Doing? – 20m E1 5b**. K. Howett, G. E. Little. 28th May, 1997.
Climbs the excellent left-hand side of the slabby south face.

Friends in Tibet – 15m VS 5a*. G. E. Little, K. Howett. 28th May, 1997.
Climbs the right-hand side of the slabby south face.

MINGULAY, Guarsay Mor (MR 548 842):

Lost Souls Direct Finish – 20m E4 6b***. P. Thorburn, R. Campbell. 29th May, 1997.
Follow the top pitch of the parent route to the roof, pull left onto the break, then climb directly out to reach gargoyles on the lip and over to finish. Named Swimming to America.

Longships – 25m E5 6b*. P. Thorburn, R. Campbell. 29th May, 1997.
An eliminate line between Crystal Daze and Ossian Boulevard – the best one-star pitch on the cliff. Start at a small ramp below a small roof at 5m. Climb to the roof and make hard moves up right to gain better holds at the base of a short, flared crack. Move up then right to a deep slot below a bulge. Pull over the bulge and climb the wall above to belay on Ossian Boulevard.

Dun Mingulay (MR 534 820):

Perfectly Normal Paranoia – 105m E6***. P. Thorburn, R. Campbell (alt.). 30th May, 1997.
This worrying route takes an impressive diagonal line across the great wall between The Silkie and Rory Rum the Story Man. From the plinth at the foot of The Silkie cross ledges to the right for 10m to belay below a left-facing blocky groove.
1. 25m 6b. Climb the groove through the square recess in the left-hand side of the lower roof, then make increasingly difficult moves right under the final overlap until a shallow groove can be followed to reach a projecting block ledge. Belay under the roof above.

2. 15m 5c. Traverse right under the roof, rising slightly, to a semi-hanging stance at the start of a left to right diagonal line of undercuts.

3. 25m 6a. Follow the undercuts to the obvious fault in the roof, pull through this and continue to a 'shake-out'. Climb rightwards up the wall then left under the roof to an uncomfortable belay in slanting breaks under the main weakness.

4. 40m 5b. Pull through the weakness then climb directly to the top (sustained).

BERNERAY, Sotan Head, Puffin Buttress (MR 555 795):

This is the big cliff girt headland to the west of Barra Head. Its most southerly tip presents a buttress of excellent rock in its upper half (surrounded by darker, shattered rock). At the top of this buttress is a wide vegetated ledge riddled with puffin burrows which can be easily accessed from above. The abseil descent starts from this ledge.

Huffin and Puffin – 65m E2**. G. E. Little, K. Howett (alt.). 29th May, 1997.
Start below a big triangular roof on the edge of the buttress at the top of the shattered rock that comprises the lower half of the cliff.

1. 25m 5b. Move left from the belay and climb strenuous and gritty twin cracks (crux). Step left onto the front face then hand traverse farther left to gain a short corner/groove. Ascend this then climb diagonally left to belay on a good ledge.

2. 40m 5a. Traverse horizontally right along a break then move up into a short right-facing corner. Climb this over a small roof then move right across the lip. Ascend a slabby section to a bulge then climb it to gain a horizontal break. Step left then climb to a roof. Pull round this to reach a ledge. Move out left and take the line of least resistance to the top. An excellent and sustained pitch.

Sotan Head, Creag nan Clamhan (MR 556 796):

This distinctive, heavily-roofed crag lies on the east flank of the headland close to its termination and is more akin to an inland crag than a seacliff (give or take the odd resident auk!). It base can be easily accessed by descending a wide ramp. The most obvious feature at the foot of the crag is a detached pillar 'supporting' a low roof. The routes are described from left to right – as they are approached.

The Frotteur – 30m E5 6a**. L. Hughes, G. Nicoll. 31st May, 1997.
A strenuous, but well-protected route, with the crux coming just when you think it's all over. Start 4m left of the detached pillar. Climb a crack to the overhang. Traverse the break rightwards to the lip, pull round and make hard moves up onto the slab above (crux). Climb up to the left of the roof then escape rightwards to finish.

The Mauking Bird – 30m E1 5b**. G. Nicoll, L. Hughes. 30th May, 1997.
Climb the left side of the detached pillar then a crack 2m left of the big corner. Make a long reach over a bulge onto the slab below the big roof. Traverse the fine slab leftwards until past the roof then climb up and away rightwards to finish.

Auksiliary Force – 30m HVS 5a***. G. Nicoll, L. Hughes. 30th May, 1997.
This superb route tackles the big corner below the biggest roof on the crag. Start by climbing the right side of the detached pillar then up the corner, moving out onto the right wall to pass the roof. Step right above onto an arête and climb a small overhang at an obvious break. Traverse left then right to finish.

Exit Stage Right – 30m HVS 5b**. G. E. Little, K. Howett. 30th May, 1997.
This is the slim, heavily-roofed corner about 6m down from the detached pillar 'supporting' the low roof. Climb the corner to twin stepped roofs high up. The first is turned on the right. More improbably, the second is also turned on the right by stepping onto a vertical edge then climbing the short wall above (crux).

Millenium Man – 35m E1 5b***. G. E. Little, K. Howett. 30th May, 1997.
Start about 9m up from the lowest corner at a slim, right-facing corner. Climb this and straight up the wall above to a big ledge. Move left onto a clean rusty wall and climb a direct line to the top on good holds (finishing at the same point as Exit Stage Right).

Not So Aukward – 35m VS 4c**. G. E. Little, K. Howett. 30th May, 1997.
This is the lowest corner. Climb it directly to exit right below the capping roof.
The following notes were sent by M. Tighe. The New Routes Editor cannot tell what, if any, coincides with the above, and leaves it to future visitors and guidebook writers.
28th April: Bernerey: C. Fowler, K. Harding, M. Tighe went to Barrahead – Air Cholla – and did four or five routes on the immaculate rock on the extreme south end of the island. They called it Ocean Wall. Routes followed prominent crack and groove lines, one pitch and in the VS/HVS range.
29th April: Bernarey: A 10-15m crag at Keromada produced six excellent little routes, including a sea-level traverse. Also a short, but fine, crack on the east wall of Tresivick Bay, by traversing in from the south at very low tide.
30th April: Pabbay: Allanish Peninsula: Could not follow the guidebook description but did some good routes.
1st May: Bernaray: C. Fowler, K. Harding, S. McNeil: Climbed near a big arch at Rubha Ghralish, and one more route on Ocean Wall.
2nd May: Mingulay, Guarsey Mor: At MR 549 841 is a big arch with a V. Diff descent leading to a sloping ledge running down into the sea from the north (perhaps to the south of Grey Rib). C. Fowler, S. McNeil climbed just south of the Grey Rib; K. Harding and M. Tighe climbed the following two routes.
McCall of the Wild – VS 4c**. Abseil to a sloping ledge just above the high-tide line and to the left of a huge arch. Step across a small inlet and climb a short wall to a big 'dance floor', which is a big open cave. Exit left on to a tricky wall and climb straight to the top of the crag in two more pitches.

The Arch Deacon – 140m HVS 5a***. Describes a wonderful arc across the roof of the arch, initially above the serried ranks of guilliemots, and then above space! Abseil partway as for the previous route and belay. Traverse right towards a brown-coloured perch below overhangs – belay. Go right again on a grey band of immaculate rock on the very lip of the arch with an overhang above and a yawning abyss below. Take a hanging belay at the end of the band and praise the lord. Climb straight up to the top.
3rd May: Climbing at Rubha Liath (MR 552 814), immediately opposite the eastern tip of Geirum Beag. There is a 10m crag on which C. Fowler and K. Harding did several routes up to E2. S. McNeil and M. Tighe also did two routes.

ST KILDA:
The following routes were climbed in 1987 on an expedition organised and led by Pete Whillance (not Chris Bonington, as described in the Hebrides guide, p7). There were 18 routes on the main island of Hirta (map included) and one on the neighbouring island of Soay.

Ruaival, South-West Face:
This is a gabbro crag of excellent rock, usually running to many good holds and protection. It lies immediately above the sea but has convenient ledge systems just above high-tide level.

Approach: Walk round the bay from the village to the col to the west of Ruaival and follow the ridge to the Mistress Stone. Go through the arch and drop down the dyke to a grassy bay. There is a good block anchor on the arête to the right (west) to make a long abseil of around 80m to the bottom of the crag. The routes are described from right ot left.

Brief Encounter – 110m HVS. M. Mortimer, M. Allen. 31st August, 1987.
A rising leftwards traverse to the arête overlooking the zawn which bounds the left-hand side of the cliff.
1. 20m 5a. From the foot of the abseil, move left on to slabs which go straight to the sea and take a rising leftward diagonal line under a roof to belay under a corner.
2. 20m 4c. Continue leftwards in more or less the same line to reach a fine ledge overlooking the zawn on the left.
3. 20m 4c. Move left and climb the arête to a ledge.
4. 20m 4c. Continue up the arête to a large grass ledge below the final headwall.
5. 20m. Move right and climb up to and through a small roof to another ledge.
6. 10m. Climb a short crack and either continue up another crack or traverse easily right to reach the top of the abseil.

Sideline – 90m E2. P. Whillance, I. McMullen (alt.). 1st September, 1987.
Start below the second groove to the left of Maiden's Corner.
1. 35m 5b. Up steeply to enter the groove above the overhang. Climb the groove to a junction with Maiden's Corner. Move up a few feet and take the crackline leftwards (loose) to a ledge.
2. 30m 5b/c. Move up into a groove on the slab above, then go rightwards to a ledge (junction with the top of Maiden's Corner). Up a short wall above, then over an awkward roof and step out left to a grass ledge.
3. 25m. Climb rightwards to the final crack of The First Route. Up this and continue leftwards to the top.

Maiden's Corner – 95m E1. C. Bonington, B. Hall (alt.). 31st August, 1987.
Follows the conspicuous corner that bounds the left-hand side of the steep main crag.
1. 35m 4c. Climb the hanging chimney to reach the base of the corner and follow it more easily to a ledge on the slabby glacis in the middle of the crag.
2. 20m 5b. Climb the steep corner, trending right then left to a ledge.
3. 40m 5a. Move right along the ledge into the back of a corner. Move right again, pull over the overhangs, and keep trending right along the overhanging wall on huge holds to an right-facing corner. Ascend this and the corners and grooves above.

The First Route – 95m E3. I. McMullen, P. Whillance (alt.). 18th August, 1998.
Start in the groove line of Maiden's Corner.
1. 35m 5b. Climb the chimney's initial overhanging section for 8m and move right to a ledge below an overhanging crackline. Start this on the right and follow it to a bulge. Climb the flake-crack on the left to a ledge and continue up to a large glacis.
2. 20m 6a. The obvious groove/corner above. Climb up into the groove and pass an awkward bulge to a resting place. Bridge up the corner above to better holds and a large ledge.
3. 40m 5a. Move up right to a slab below overhangs. Pull over and move rightwards on good holds to a ledge. Climb the obvious grooved crackline above until possible to step up rightwards to the top.

Easy Virtue – 90m E1. C. Bonington, B. Hall (alt.). 31st August, 1987. Direct Finish – M. Mortimer, M. Allen. 1st September, 1987.

Start at the foot of the corner of Maiden's Corner. The route weaves up the face on the right, heading towards the conspicuous flake-crack in the upper wall.

1. 5m. Pull up right on to the ledge system crossing the face. Belay about 3m along this.

2. 35m 5a. Move a farther 5m right to the foot of an obvious crack. Climb this steeply to another ledge. Traverse right, then back left (to a point above the crackline) and climb upwards to the leftward-facing corner on the smooth slab. Belay on a small ledge on the glacis below the obvious flake-crack.

3. 20m 5a. Trend left towards undercut holds and then go back right towards the foot of the flake-crack. Climb this until possible to exit right ot a ledge.

4. 35m 5b. Step right to the obvious roof crack, where the roof is at its smallest. Pull over it into a right-facing corner. Exit left on to the arête, climb directly to a loose dyke, then break slightly right over the dyke (5b) to the top.

A Bit on the Side – 75m E2. S. Boyden, H. Lancashire (alt.). 31st August, 1987. Start at the foot of Maiden's Corner.

1. 30m 4b. Climb up rightwards a few feet and traverse the obvious ledge 25m to the foot of a prominent V-groove.

2. 20m 5c. Climb the groove and crack on the left to gain slabs. Trend slightly right up a shallow groove.

3. 25m 5b. Move left 2m, then up and diagonally right into the base of a corner. Climb this on to easy slabs. Go up and slightly left to a block belay.

Continental Drift – 90m E2. P. Whillance, I. McMullen (alt.). 1st September, 1987. Start as for A Bit on the Side.

1. 30m 4b. Same.

2. 10m 5c. As for A Bit on the Side but exit left at 10m to a small ledge.

3. 30m 5b. Move right on to a ledge system and follow this to where it ends. Step down and continue along a horizontal crack to a good ledge. Move down, across and up into the huge corner.

4. 20m 4c. Follow the corner-crack to the top.

The Dun Face:

Blackface – 35m HVS 5a. P. Whillance. 10th August, 1987.

Round to the right of the main south-west face opposite Dun is a large sea cave with a clean-cut black slab on its right-hand side. From the abseil point go down to the foot of the large grass terrace. Scramble or abseil down from its right-hand edge to sea-washed platforms. Start 6m right of the huge roof. Climb the slab to a ledge at the right-hand end of the overlap. Pull over leftwards and up the slab via a thin crack to reach a break. Move left and up bubbly rock to where the angle eases. Traverse left below an overhang to regain the terrace. Farther right in the Dun passage is a large, grey slab which tapers to become a prominent ridge higher up. The base is best reached by an easy traverse from the right at low tide.

Soay – 45m H. Severe. P. Whillance. 10th August, 1987.

Start below the narrowest point in the overlap. Move up and pull over the overlap on large jugs to gain the slab proper. Follow thin cracks in the slab to join the ridge at the top (several variations possible at Severe to VS).

Upper Tier:

Above Blackface and the large area of grass slope is a black gritstone-like buttress seamed with deep cracks.

Old Men's Dreams – 40m Severe. J. Curran, P. Frost, D. Miller. 5th September, 1987.

Start at the toe of the buttress.

1. 20m 4a. Climb the cracks trending left to an obvious stance below overhangs.
2. 20m. Exit easily right and climb the upper slab direct to finish.

Two other routes of a similar standard were climbed on this buttress by the same party (6th September, 1987). A number of short cracklines on the left-hand side of the Upper Tier were also climbed but do not warrant detailed description.

Oiseval, South Face:

This is a granite cliff of excellent rock, with well-defined groove lines and good protection. It is set about 150m above the sea and is easily approached by contouring around the hillside. Routes are described from left to right.

The Amazon – 40m E2 5b. M. Mortimer, M. Allen. 14th September, 1987.

This strenuous route takes the groove system on the left-hand side of the crag. Left of the central steep section of the crag, the grass slope steepens to join a gully. Start at the foot of the gully. Climb the gully until possible to step right on to the wall to reach a steep groove with a jammed flake. Climb the groove until the angle eases. Step right again to climb the hanging groove strenuously to easy ground. Scrambling remains.

The Harp – 40m E3. C. Bonington, B. Hall (alt.). 5th September, 1987.

To the immediate left of Central Route is another groove line that peters out about halfway up the crag. The Harp climbs the groove and then breaks out to the left up the line of the arête. Start part way up the grassy gully on the left, below the groove itself.

1. 25m 5c. Climb a steep 5m wall to a grass ledge at the foot of the groove. Then climb the left groove which steepens into a bulge near the top. Step right below a small overhang into the continuation of the overhanging crack just to the right of this pitch. Stance on large foothold in the crack.
2. 20m 6a. Step back left below the bulge and pull awkwardly round the arête, up for 2m to a line of good holds leading 3m to the left. Move back right with a long reach for a spike to the crest of the arête. Step round to the right, then up and back left pulling back round the arête and up delicately until possible to move left to better finishing holds.

Lady Grange – 45m E2. M. Mortimer, M. Allen. 14th September, 1987.

Interesting and varied with an exciting finish. Start as for The Harp.

1. 30m 5b. Go up the steep wall to the foot of the groove. Climb the overhanging crack on the right and the groove above to reach the stance on Central Route.
2. 15m 5c. Climb up to the roof, traverse left and climb through the roof on big holds when a few feet of more delicate climbing leads left to join the finish of The Amazon.

Note: The prominent arête in the centre of the crag was climbed except for the final 3m by M. Mortimer – should give an excellent route.

Central Route – 45m E2. I. McMullen, P. Whillance (alt.). 24th August, 1987.

Takes the left-hand of two prominent corner lines in the centre of the crag.

1. 15m 5c. Climb the steep corner past a small overlap and continue to a stance.

2. 30m 5c. Continue up the corner-crack to the roof and climb the widening crack with difficulty to reach easier ground. Scramble up to a belay.

Right-Hand Corner – 45m E1. P. Whillance, I. McMullen (alt.). 31st August, 1987.
Takes the obvious right-hand corner line.

1. 25m 5a. Bridge up the groove to the start of the crack and climb this to a ledge on the right.

2. 20m 5b. Climb the corner-crack to the roof and jam leftwards around this to a sloping ledge. Traverse right and up to a ledge and belay on easy ground.

Botany Bay – 45m E1. B. Hall, C. Bonington. 8th September, 1987.
Takes a groove line starting from the right-hand side of the bay in the lower part of the face.

1. 30m 5a. Climb the groove and two obvious cracked corners until possible to pull out left on to a sloping ledge.

2. 15m 5b. Step back right into the groove, up to the small triangular overhang and step left, treating a semi-detached flake with great respect. Climb the wall above diagonally right to the bottom of the groove. Up this to the top.

Mullach Bi, Summit Cliff, South-West Face:

This is the cliff facing westwards from near the summit. It is reached by traversing grass slopes above the sea from the col near the Lover's Stone.

Rainbow Warrior – 90m E1/2. S. Boyden, H. Lancashire (alt.). 6th September, 1987.
A steep diagonal crack starts just right of centre of the cliff. Start by scrambling right across grass ledges to the crack.

1. 25m 5b. Reach the crack by dubious grass tufts and follow it – awkward in its middle section – to a ledge.

2. 10m 5b. Climb the groove on the left to a crevassed stance.

3. 25m 5b. Above on the right is a black-streaked wall. Attain a ledge up on the right, pull into a bottomless right-leaning groove, then go direct up the blank wall, moving left at the top. Easier climbing leads to the large ledge below the final headwall.

4. 30m 5a. A crackline crosses the headwall diagonally up leftwards from the right side of the large ledge. Follow the crack, strenuously at first, to some prominent grass tufts. Pass these carefully and follow the crack more easily to the top.

Nuclear Arms – 35m E5 (Two rest points). H. Lancashire, S. Boyden. 7th September, 1987.
An extremely strenuous route, continuously overhanging on its first pitch. Start by abseiling to the big ledge system below the final headwall. Traverse left to the end of the ledge and belay below the shorter left-hand crack splitting the overhanging headwall.

1. 15m 6a. Jam the crack, good Friend protection, past the niche and over jammed blocks to a small ledge (one rest below the niche and one above).

2. 20m 5c. Step out on to the right arête. Pull up with difficulty on to the slab, then out left on to a ledge amd climb an easier slab to finish.

The North-East Face of Conachair:

From The Edge of the World cleit, descend the obvious long ridge on the right-hand side of the main face for about 300m, keeping to its grassy northern flank (hand line recommended). From a prominent col in the ridge, an 80m abseil leads to the slopes at the foot of the face. Alternatively, an inflatable boat is needed.

The Edge of the World – 330m E6. P. Whillance, I. McMullen (var.). 15th September, 1987.

Start from shelving slabs about 15m right of the large sea cave.

1. 45m 5b. Follow a groove/crack line in the slab for 20m to a triangular ledge. Traverse left to another groove, then up this past a loose flake to a narrow ledge on the right (three peg runners, removed).

2. 30m 5c. Step back down to the flake and traverse left into a V-groove. Up this and the prominent dyke system above to reach a small ledge in a corner (bolt belay, three peg runners, removed).

3. 55m 6b. Climb the slab diagonally leftwards for 20m to a rib. Move left for 3m and up a short wall to a peg runner. Step down and go left below a small overhang, then up into a niche below a roof. Move right and climb a short groove, then go steeply leftwards to gain a rib and easier-angled rock. Climb the slab to a good ledge and bolt belay (seven peg runners, left in place).

4. 40m 5b. Traverse left into the big corner line and climb this to a large grassy ledge on the right. (Bolt belay, three peg runners in place).

5. 30m 6a. Climb flakes on the left wall to where they end. Move up the steep wall to a bolt runner and make a long traverse left to reach a big ledge below a prominent groove in the centre of the pink wall. Bolt belay.

6. 40m 5c. Climb the slim groove to a break and traverse the ledge leftwards to a good stance and bolt belay (three peg runners in place).

7. 45m 5b. Move up the groove above for a few feet, then swing left and climb a crack in the left wall to a grass terrace. Go left for 5m, then follow cracks and broken rock to a corner. Up this and exit left to a large ledge.

8. 45m 5c. Climb the short overhanging crack above and move up to the corner systam which leads to the top.

The North-West Face of Soay:
This is defined as the stretch of coast between Creagan and Gob a' Ghaill. Midway between the two is a smooth 150m wall which drops directly into the sea. The rock is superb and immaculately clean. The large grass platform at the top of this wall is still only halfway up the face but the upper section is of little interest to climbers.
Approach: A landing is made on the shelving slabs on the southern side of the Gob a' Ghaill promontary. Scramble up rocks to reach grass slopes, then ascend right and up to a prominent col on the ridge. Climb down the opposite side or abseil for 45m to gain a wide ledge system. Follow this for about 200m to the grass platform above the wall. Abseil close to the left arête to ensure finding belays.

Shipwrecked – 105m E2. I. McMullen, P. Whillance (var.). 25th August, 1987.
This route takes the left-hand of two obvious cracklines on the wall, although it was started at a good ledge system some 60m above the sea.

1. 45m 5c. Follow the crack to where it meets the left arête.

2. 15m 5c. Step back down and cross the wall on the right, then up leftwards to sloping ledges. Follow the ledges leftwards to below a corner.

3. 45m 5a. Take a diagonal line of weakness rightwards until a crack leads to the top.

Note: The missing bottom pitches and the escape line taken on the top pitch were the result of a storm breaking and a desperate need to evacuate!

EIGG, Ocean Wall:

Taking the Minke – 35m E4 6a**. K. Howett, G. E. Little. 20th September, 1997.
A large cone of rock ruptures Le Jardin separating its upper and lower levels. Start on the right side of this cone. Climb a pale knobbly wall to near the right end of the fading overlap. Pull over to grasp a good right-facing flat-topped flake. Stand on it, then make increasingly difficult and improbable moves up and left on the blank wall to reach two elongated slots (Rock 3 and 4). Pull up on small flakes, then climb more easily to reach a heather ramp. Continue straight up the face.

East of Eden – 40m E3 5c*. G. E. Little, K. Howett. 21st September, 1997.
Start right of the lower section of Le Jardin, just left of the cairn marking the start of Paradise Lost. Climb straight up by slight cracks to make an interesting pull over on to a sloping ledge. Move up and left via a vague scoop, then climb straight up a broad rib with a difficult exit on to the rock stairway of Paradise Lost. Finish by the rock rib on the right of the stairway.

ISLAND OF MUCK, Camas Mor:

Introduction: The sea cliffs forming the east side of Camas Mor bay are composed of gabbro, approximately one kilometre in length and on average about 30m high. Most of the climbing to date has been towards the southern end of this line of cliffs. The climbs are generally of a friendly nature being on excellent rough rock, south-west facing, free of vegetation and fairly easy of access. The first known rock climbs to be completed on these cliffs were ascended by Ross Greenwood and islander Simon Graves in May 1996. Several productive visits since by Ross Greenwood, Pete Whillance and friends has resulted in most of the 45 routes recorded here. A lot of potential for new routes remains. The cliffs are best approached from the harbour at Port Mor by following a footpath which leads up behind the small cemetery and over the headland – about 20 minutes pleasant walk.
Access: The small headland at the southern end of the cliffs terminates in a long narrow gully inlet. The gully is overshadowed throughout its length by an impressive overhanging wall of jet black rock, aptly named The Dungeon. This gully provides an easy descent route to reach a sea-level traverse and access to all routes as far as Hurricane Cove. A quicker means of descent is via a grassy bowl and easy rocks in the headland 30m west of The Dungeon. Most of the sea level traverse is on big ledges, well above the high-tide mark, with only two tricky moves.
1. A jump down to a small ledge (covered at high tide), or an awkward traverse move (4b) to gain access to ledges in Plunder Bay.
2. A bold move (4b) across a high corner to reach a big ledge leading into Hurricane Cove. In many cases the quickest and best approach to routes is to use a spare rope and to abseil from the nearest belay stake.
First Ascentionists: Ross Greenwood (RG), Pete Whillance (PW), Simon Graves (SG), Pete Swanson (PS), Tony Wright (TW)
Cliffs and climbs are described from right to left, as viewed from the sea (south to north).

The Dungeon:

The Dungeon is the name given to the black overhanging wall of the gully inlet at the southern end of Camus Mor. The wall is seamed with prominent crack lines and provides some of the steepest climbing of the island. It has the advantages of being sheltered from prevailing winds, non-tidal and often remains dry in showery weather. However, some lines suffer from seepage after prolonged periods of rain. After descending steep grass to reach the top of the gully, the first route begins about 2m down from where the grass gives out to boulder scree.

Chain Reaction – E2 5c**. PW, RG. 29th September, 1997.
Start at a small square recess below a steep left-slanting crack. Follow the crack for about 5m to where the angle eases. Ascend directly up the obvious cracks above to the top.

Iron Maiden – E1 5b. PW, RG. 29th September, 1997.
The next reasonable line of weakness lies some 20m lower down the gully and is marked by two large spikes, one above the other, in the middle of the wall. Start just left of these and climb the steep wall to a sloping ledge. Traverse delicately right and up to reach good holds and the first spike. Pull up to reach the second large spike then continue directly up the twin cracks to easy ground.

Sentenced – E1 5b**. PW, RG. 29th September, 1997.
The next route begins at the very bottom of the gully, behind a large detached ridge of rock. Start below a prominent square roofed overhang at 7m. Climb up and slightly rightwards to below the roof then swing up right into the hanging crack and follow this on good jams to the top.

The Keeper – HVS 5a. RG, PW. 29th September, 1997.
Start 3m left of the prominent square-roofed overhang at a small cave. Ascend the steep wall following two diagonal left-slanting cracks to beneath a small roof. Move left around the arête and finish up the easy gully.

Castle Walls Area:
This area encompasses the headland from the Dungeon to the Yellow Walls. It consists of mainly broken, easy-angled cliffs which offer none-too-serious routes on good-quality rock. Climbs are possible almost anywhere and descriptions have been confined to the best and most obvious lines. The first two climbs lie on the square-shaped buttress, just left of the Dungeon inlet and between the two described descent routes.

Gargoyle Grooves – M. Severe. RG, SG. 25th May, 1996.
Takes a line up the front of the square buttress. Follow an easy-angled groove to a line of overhangs. Pull up through an inset corner in the roof and continue up a steep cracked wall above.

Castle Corner – V. Diff. RG. 11th July, 1997.
On the left side of the square buttress, 5m left of Gargoyle Grooves, is a prominent corner system. Easy climbing leads to a large ledge. Follow the short steep corner to the top. The next obvious feature is an apron of slabby rock hemmed in by short overhanging walls. It lies 30m left of the square buttress where the cliff regains its full height.

The Drawbridge – M. Severe. RG, SG. 25th May, 1996.
Follow a stepped groove line up the right side of the apron to reach a short, leaning corner at its top. Steeply up this then easy scrambling to finish.

Bastille – VS 5a. PW. 25th September, 1997.
Takes the short overhanging groove in the wall immediately left of the finishing corner of The Drawbridge. Easy climbing up the left side of the apron to below the

groove. Pull in from the right and up steeply on surprisingly good holds to reach easy ground.

About 15m farther around to the left, a large grey slab leads up to a steeper wall containing three protruding noses of rock.

Ramp Art – Diff. RG. 25th September, 1997.

Start up the right side of the grey slab and climb diagonally rightwards below the rightmost of the steep noses of rock until an escape can be made by pulling out left to a ledge and up to easier ground.

The next two routes take the gaps between the noses.

The Barbican – Severe. RG. 11th July, 1996.

Ascend a crack up the centre of the grey slab to where is steepens. Climb the wall via a groove line just left of the rightmost nose.

The Turret – Severe. RG. 11th July, 1996.

Go up a crack in the left side of the slab and continue up a steep groove formed between the central and left hand noses.

An area of more broken rock now extends leftwards for 30m. Many easier grade routes are possible.

Yellow Walls Area:
The next main feature is a distinctive yellow wall in the upper part of the cliff, split by a series of prominent cracklines.

Yellow Wall:
Route 1 – Severe. RG, PW. 30th September, 1997.

Start from some broken bird-limed ledges below the rightmost crackline. Climb the crack in the slab then step right and up a steeper crack in the headwall to finish.

Route 2 – Severe*. PW. 25th September, 1997.

Starting from the same ledges as Route 1, follow a diagonal break leftwards and continue up the obvious crack in the middle of the wall.

Route 3 – Severe. RG, PW. 30th September, 1997.

Start 6m down to the left at a prominent right-slanting crack. Follow the crack/ groove line to reach a short chimney at the halfway break. Climb the chimney groove and a short steep corner to finish.

The Catalyst – H. Severe 4b. TW, PS. 25th September, 1997.

Start at the same point as the previous route and climb the crack on the left to the halfway ledge. Move across left to the next crack line and up via a small corner crack to the top.

Hard Luck Cafe – E1 5c. PS, TW. 26th September, 1997.

Climb the steep thin crack in the wall just left of The Catalyst to reach the break. Step right and follow the crack to beneath an overhang. Move right and up a short corner to finish.

About 5m farther left, the Yellow Wall ends at the prominent right-facing corner system of The Promise.

Simon's Slip – H. Severe 4b. PW, RG. 30th September, 1997.

Takes the broken groove and crackline 2m right of The Promise.

The Promise - Severe*. TW, RG, PW. 27th June, 1997.

The obvious right-facing corner system at the left hand end of the Yellow Wall.

Climb the steep initial groove on the left or the rib on it's right. Continue up the main corner to the top.

Plunder Bay:

An awkward sea level traverse move on the buttress left of Yellow Walls gives access to ledges in Plunder Bay (see Introduction). The steep dark walls of this bay contain a fine array of superb cracks and corners.

Pieces of Eight – Diff. RG, SW. 25th May, 1996.

On the right-hand side of the bay is a broken left-facing corner. It forms the opposite side of the buttress to The Promise. A series of ledges leads up into the corner and so to the top.

Trophy Crack – E2 5c*. PW, RG. 27th June, 1997.

In the back of the bay, a few metres left of Pieces of Eight, is a black bulging crack in a convex wall. Climb this to easier ground.

The next two routes take the obvious right-facing corner lines in the upper part of the wall left of Trophy Crack.

Treasure Trove Corner – HVS 5a**. PW, TW, RG. 26th June, 1997.

A fine climb. From the foot of Trophy Crack trend leftwards up ledges to the base of the prominent corner. Climb this, awkward to start, and past a small overhang to gain a good ledge. The leaning corner above to the top.

Rich Pickings – E3 6a**. PW, RG. 27th June, 1997.

Takes the next corner system starting a few metres left of Trophy Crack. Climb a steep crack and step up left to below a hanging corner. Difficult moves past a peg runner lead to a small overhung ledge. Continue more easily up the corner above.

Plunder Crack – HVS 5a*. PW, TW, RG. 27th June, 1997.

The striking crack and chimney line starting 5m around to the left of the previous routes, on the front face of the buttress. Follow the crack passing a steep bulge on good holds to enter a chimney. Finish up this.

Ill Gotten Gains – VS 4c*. RG, TW, PW. 27th June, 1997.

Start from a big ledge 5m left of Plunder Crack. Move up left into a corner and follow this up into a square-cut recess capped by an overhang. An awkward pull over the small roof leads to easier ground.

Hurricane Cove:

Continuing the sea-level traverse left from Ill Gotten Gains requires a bold move across a high corner to reach a large ledge (see Introduction). Easy scrambling for 10m leads around the front of a tapering yellow tower to a big platform in Hurricane Cove.

The first three climbs are on the front face of the yellow tower.

Mellow Yellow – H. Severe 4b. PW, RG. 25th September, 1997.

Start below the right-hand side of the face and climb a short awkward crack to reach a good ledge. Follow the stepped groove line leftwards to the top of the tower and finish up the arête.

Yellow Peril – HVS 5a. PW, RG. 25th September, 1997.

Climb directly up the thin cracks in the centre of the face to the top of the tower. Step right and up a wall to finish.

Yellow Fever – HS 4b. PW, RG. 25th September, 1997.

Follow the crackline close to the left edge of the face. Finish up the arête.

Thunderpants Corner – Severe**. RG, PW. 12th July, 1997.
The obvious left-facing corner forming the right side of the cove. Climb a short steep chimney to a ledge. Follow the stepped corner above to the top. An excellent route.

Greased Lightning – E2 5c**. PW, RG. 28th June, 1997.
The steep right-slanting crack in the back wall of the bay provides a fine, sustained climb. Start from the left hand end of the platform 3m left of Thunderpants Corner. Climb the crack throughout.
This last route marks the end of the sea-level traverse. Access to climbs beyond this point requires an abseil approach.

Gale Warning – VS 4c*. RG, PW. 29th June, 1997.
Takes the easiest line up the front face of the buttress some 5m left of the previous route. It follows a crackline which leads into a broken right-facing corner in the upper part of the cliff. Abseil to small, bird-limed ledges about 7m above high tide mark. Climb a crack-seamed wall to reach better holds then the easier corner above to finish.

Atlantic Fury – HVS 5a*. RG, PW. 28th June, 1997.
The prominent crack and chimney system 7m left of Gale Warning. Abseil down the line of the route to a large ledge just above high tide. Follow the steep right-slanting crack for 10m to good ledges. Continue more easily up an open chimney to the top.

Shark's Tooth Cove:
This cove can be recognised by a square-cut recess of black rock about 4m across and running the full height of the cliff. On it's left is a 15m high pillar ending in a flat-topped ledge and to it's right are slabby yellow walls.

Barracuda – E1 5b*. PW, RG. 28th June, 1997.
Start 5m right of the black recess where a thin crackline in the slabby wall leads up to some short steep corners. Abseil down the line of the route to a sloping ledge about 6m above the sea. Delicate climbing up thin cracks for 8m leads to better holds. Follow the crack to where it steepens, make an awkward move past a flake and go up a short corner to a large ledge. Step right to finish up an open corner containing a few doubtful blocks.

Predator – E2 5c*. PW, RG. 29th June, 1997.
Abseil straight down the back of the overhanging black recess to a sloping ledge just above some overhangs, about 10m above high tide mark (in calm seas it will be possible to start from lower down). Traverse right for 2m to the base of a slabby corner forming the right hand side of the recess. Climb the corner for 3m to a small overhang and pull over rightwards to gain an exposed ledge on the arête. Make delicate moves up the arête to a peg runner, then traverse right across the wall to a ledge on Barracuda, just below it's crux. As for Barracuda to the top.

Jaws – HVS 4c. RG, PW. 26th September, 1997.
The next prominent line, 15m left of the flat-topped pillar, is a chimney and crack system leading into a left-facing corner near the top. Abseil down the line to a stance and belay below a cave and V-chimney. Climb the chimney and the steep crack above to gain a corner. Easier climbing up this to the top.

Conger – E2 5c**. PW, RG. 26th September, 1997.
The impressive face to the left of Jaws features a superb right-slanting crackline

which cuts through a horizontal band of overhangs at half height. A free abseil down left edge of the face leads to a belay on good platforms just above high tide mark. Move down and right to a barnacle ledge and gain the start of the thin diagonal crack. Follow this to the band of overhangs and climb strenuously through three stepped roofs to where the angle eases. Continue more easily in the same crackline to the top.

The Witches Slab Area:
One of the most prominent features of these cliffs is the impressive sweep of Witches Slab. The slab is a clean sheet of rock set at right angles to the main line of cliffs. Below and to it's left, a narrow zawn and sea cave separates the slab from North Atlantic Wall, while to the right lies the big corner system of Pendle Hill.
Pendle Hill – E1 5b***. PW, RG. 7th July, 1997.
A superb route. Approach by abseiling down the corner to a ledge at sea level (not accessible at high tide). Good stance, but poor belays, perhaps worth belaying to a spare abseil rope. Start 1m left of the corner at a thin crack. Climb the crack for 5m to a peg runner then move up and rightwards to gain a niche in the corner (crux). Follow the main corner throughout until 4m from the top where a crack in the right wall provides a steep exit.

Alderley Edge – E1 5b*. PW, RG. 26th September, 1997.
A good variation to Pendle Hill which takes the elegant, slim corner in the wall 3m to its left. Accessible at any state of the tide. Abseil down to the bottom of Witches Slab and swing around right to a good ledge and belay at the base of the slim corner. (This ledge is above and to the left of the start of Pendle Hill). Climb the corner and continue up twin cracks above until about 3m below a barrier of overhangs. Traverse right across a break to join the big corner of Pendle Hill at about half-height. Continue as for that route to the top.

The next three routes are on the Witches Slab itself. Abseil down the slab to a large ledge 7m above sea level. All the climbs start from here.
Alice Nutter – HVS 5a**. RG, PW. 7th July, 1997.
A bold route up the right edge of the slab. Start in the middle of the slab and go over a small bulge to a sloping ledge. Move immediately right to the arête and climb the slab close to it's edge with a delicate move past a peg runner at 25m. Continue to the top.

Witches Slide – Severe**. RG, PW. 9th July, 1997.
Start up the middle of the slab, as for Alice Nutter, over a steep bulge to a sloping ledge. Climb more or less directly up the centre of the slab to the top.

Newchurch Corner – Severe*. RG, SG, PW. 7th July, 1997.
Start as for the previous routes to reach the sloping ledge. Move left into the corner and follow this to the top.

Sorcery – VS 4c. PS, TW. 26th September, 1997.
Takes a line of weakness in the wall left of Witches Slab. Start as for Newchurch Corner. Follow that route up the slab and into the main corner itself. After a few metres take a slight groove leading leftwards to gain a more prominent right-trending ramp line. Up this and a short steep crack above to finish.

North Atlantic Wall:
This is the name given to the line of steep walls which stretch from the zawn and sea cave left of Witches Slab around to the big non-tidal bay containing Fragile

Wall. From the loose descent gully left of Fragile Wall, the whole of this area can be traversed just above sea level at most states of the tide. It is often quicker and simpler to abseil direct to good ledges below the climbs. The first two routes start 20m left of the sea cave at the foot of an obvious left-curving corner.

Dreadnought – E1 5b*. PW, RG. 12th July, 1997.

Takes the lowest of several diagonal crack lines in the wall right of the curving corner. From the base of the corner move right onto the wall and delicately follow the most obvious right-trending crack for 15m to reach an exposed ledge on the lip of a prominent arch overlooking the zawn. Step up and make an airy traverse right between overhangs to gain better holds and the continuation of the diagonal crack. Carry on for 3m then go straight up via a small corner and good holds to a big ledge system. Scramble left and up to the top.

Crimson Tide – HVS 5a*. RG, PW. 11th July, 1997.

Start at the foot of the curving corner, as for Dreadnought. Climb the right arête of the corner for 18m with increasing difficulty to the start of a prominent right-slanting crack. Follow this for 10m then up a slight groove to reach large ledges. Easily up leftwards to finish.

Trident – E2 5c*. PW, RG. 11th July, 1997.

An intricate and technical route. Start 20m left of the curving corner, where a thin crack in the wall leads up to the right-hand end of a band of overlaps at 25m. Climb the thin crack for 10m until forced to move right, with difficulty past a peg runner, to gain a sloping foot ledge. Step up to another peg runner and move back left to regain the original crack line. Continue more easily to where the wall steepens then foot traverse a ledge right for 3m and go up steeply to gain some big hollow flakes. From a peg runner on the wall above, climb up first leftwards and then trend right and up to the top.

Red October – E2 5c**. PW, RG. 12th September, 1997.

A good route with some impressive situations. Start 35m left of the curving corner, below distinctive twin cracks leading up to the left side of a square-cut roof. Climb the cracks for 20m and step right to a corner below the roof. Move up then swing out boldly right and pull up steeply on good holds to regain a standing position. Follow twin diagonal cracks rightwards across the headwall to where the angle eases and so to the top.

RUM, Trallval, Harris Buttress:

Ancient Mariner – 175m E1 5b. J. S. Peden, C. R. Ravey. 25th May, 1997.

Right of Central Rib there is a shallow bay leading to a steep wall capped by roofs, bounded on the right by a rib overlooking an obvious right-facing corner. Climb the lowest rocks below the rib and cross a grassy rake to the foot of an overhung groove just left of the rib. Climb the groove to below the overhang (35m). Gain the platform on the left, then step right into the groove and follow it to a large thin flake. Climb the wall above to a recess (crux). Make an awkward move right and follow the groove above to the crest of the rib (40m). Two pitches of pleasant slabs lead to the top of the crag (100m).

MULL, BALMEANACH:

Are You A Man Or A Danny – E1 5a. T. Charles-Edwards, D. Brooks 18th September, 1997.

Climbs the pillar left of the main face. Climb up to gain the flake/crack at the left side of the face, this leads to the ledge. Start up a corner on the left move past a large loose block and continue leftwards more easily to the top.

Yellow Snail – 25m E4 6a**. C. Moody, L. Gordon-Canning, T. Charles-Edwards, D. Brooks 18th September, 1997.
Start at the left side of the main overhang at some boulders. Climb up to the overlap, using a horizontal break above for the hands move right to a good pocket. Continue up slightly leftwards to reach a break in the next overhang, move right through this to a good ledge. Traverse right along the ledge and follow the fault to the top.

ARDCHRISHNISH:
Grade IV – 15m E2 5c**. C. Moody, L. Gordon-Canning. 22nd June, 1997.
The crack and overhang right of Wisdom.

SCOOR, The Slab:
Bonxie – 15m E3 6a*. G. Latter, L. Gordon-Canning. 7th August, 1997.
The prominent thin twin cracks in the wall left of Tystie. Make a hard bouldery start past good Friend slot at the start to better holds, finishing directly by good flakes in the upper wall.

Dune Wall:
Flick-flake – 10m HVS 5a. R. and C. Anderson. 19th April, 1997.
The groove and sharp layback crack immediately right of The Arête, pull out right at the top.

Tippidy Doodah – 10m E4/5 6b**. R. Anderson. 19th April, 1997.
The thin crack up the slab between Flick-flake and Red Shafted Flicker, unfortunately, devoid of gear. Place a Friend and a wire in Red Shafted Flicker from a standing position at its base. Place two wires in Flick-flake just above the level of an obvious hold on the slab to the right and descend back to the ramp at the base of the slab. Gain the base of the crack, climb to the hold and attain a standing position on it from where a Rock 5 can be stretched into place in Red Shafted Flicker to protect an awkward move up the slab. Step up right, then back up left to finish.

Marooned – 12m E1/2 5b*. C. Moody, L. Gordon-Canning. 9th March, 1997.
Climbs the right wall of Stranded Arête. Climb the crack which slants slightly right to an overhang. Swing out left and climb the open groove.

Photo Finish – 8m E3 5c*. C. Moody, L. Gordon-Canning. 28th June, 1997.
Left of Wild Swans is a small slanting overlap. Climb up right to the right end of the overlap, step left and climb the crack. A bold start and a poor landing.

Run-around – 15m VS 4b. C. Moody, L. Gordon-Canning, M. Tweedly. 31st August, 1997.
Climb the crack right of Milk Tray, which runs parallel to it, to a heather finish.

The Cave Monster – 12m E3 6a*. C. Moody, L. Gordon-Canning. 9th August, 1997.
At the left end of the face (left of One Foot In The Grave) is a fin of rock with a letter box high up in the centre. Climb up slightly right to reach the letter box, continue direct.

Fall Factor – 8m VS 5a. C. Moody, L. Gordon-Canning. 1997.
Start right of Doonagear at a dry stane construction. Climb the left side of the huge block.

ARDTUN, Creag Eilean an Duilisg:

Duck Of Death – 16m E2 5c*. C. Moody, L. Gordon-Canning. 20th May, 1997.
The crack running up past the right side of the nose high up, right of Bloody Louse-Bird (SMCJ, 1997).

Declining Moral Standards – 16m E2 5b**. C. Moody, L. Gordon-Canning. 22nd June, 1997.
Twin cracks left of Teb.

Crispi – 20m E1 5a*. C. Moody, L. Gordon-Canning. 13th July, 1997.
Right of Poorwill climb the recessed crack to the overhang, move out left and climb the crack in the arête.

Waterfall Wall:

Sheryl Crow – 20m E3 5c**. C. Moody, L. Gordon-Canning. 9th July, 1997.
Climbs the curving groove at the left end of the overhangs. Start up the crack in the arête left of the groove, after a few moves step right and continue up the groove until level with the first block overhang. Move left across the bulging wall and continue up easier ground to the top.

Little Red Rooster – 20m E3 5c**. C. Moody, L. Gordon-Canning. 20th April, 1997.
Left of the waterfall are three shallow corner cracks. Climb the left hand one then step right and climb a bulging corner crack.

Punk Flamingos – 20m E2 5b**. C. Moody, L. Gordon-Canning. 28th September,1997.
Climb twin cracks up the right side of the short pillar right of Feathers McGraw. Follow the right crack which continues over an overhang.

Snorting Quack – 20m E4 6a***. C. Moody, L. Gordon-Canning, M. Tweedly. 3rd August, 1997.
The pillar left of Doo Stew, the lower section is protected by RPs. The bulge up high was climbed on the left, climbing it on the right would be slightly harder, taken direct harder still, but the grade would not change.

The Pelican Brief – 16m E1 5b. C. Moody, L. Gordon-Canning. 15th April, 1997.
Right of Scrambled is a grassy bay halfway up the cliff, this route climbs the arête left of it. Climb a corner crack below the arête till it finishes and step left. Pull out right to the right side of the arête, step up then finish up a crack in the arête. The crux is at the start but the rest of the route is intimidating with some suspect holds.

Yellow Block:

This is a crag just east of the Blow Hole. There is a willow bush at the top of the cliff which is easily seen from the moor.
Everything He Hates About Climbing – 12m E1 5a.

At the right side of the crag are two wide cracks. Climb the left-hand crack.

Unnamed – 12m VS 4c*.
The corner crack right of the wide cracks.

Ardtun East (MR 383 247):

Twin cracks left of Ascent Route. (Severe).
Bunty's Ducks – 12m E2 5b**.

A finger crack just right of Four Legged Friend.

Tarmac Frogs – 14m HVS 5a*.
The hand crack between Slept In A Bog and the easy corner.

The Green Hill Peace – 12m E1 5b*.
The crack left of Pancakes At Lochdar up the front of the pillar.

Chocks Away – 12m VS 4c.
Well left of Kinloch Bound is a pillar half the height of the crag. Start four metres right of it and climb twin cracks.

Wide And Midgie – 12m HVS 5a*.
The wide crack left of Kinloch Bound has a flake around half height.

Splatter – 12m E1 5b*.
The crack left of Rally Fever.

Erraid Flood Warning – 9m E2 5c*. C. Moody, W. Gordon-Canning. 29th June, 1997.
Right of Weeping Corner, climb an awkward bulge, then twin cracks.

Upper Tier, West Face:
Routes climbed by Louise Gordon-Canning, Gary Latter, Karen Martin, Colin Moody, Derek Stuart and Michael Tweedly in August, 1997. On the left is a boulder.

Left-Hand Route – 9m Severe. Climb corner/chimney at the left side of the boulder; continue up the crack above.

The Gopher Hole – 11m VS 4c**. Gain shelf right of Left-Hand Route, step up, then follow break right and climb the scoop.

One Dead Puffin – 9m VS 4c**. Climb the corner on the right side of the boulder to the break, move left and climb the arête.

Ledge Route – 12m Severe*. Climb a jam crack and go directly up the slab above which faces the boulder.

Smelly Mussels – 9m HVS 5a*. Climbs the left side of the block left of The Dead Pool. Traverse into the centre of the block and finish up a crack (awkward finish).

The Dead Pool – 9m VS 4b. Right again are two huge blocks. Climb the V notch between them and finish up the ramp on the right.

Bacteria Soup – 12m Severe. Right of the Dead Pool is a heather ramp with a short face on the right. Climb the flakes and jam crack in the middle of the short face. Step right and climb the corner.

Blood Orange – 12m Severe*. The corner on the right to the shelf; move right and climb another corner.

Tyke's Lead – 15m Severe 4a*. The chimney near the left side of the highest section of the crag, finishing out left past a small spike.

Misunderstanding – 11m VS 4c*. Start right of the chimney. Move up then left towards the chimney, follow the steep ramp out right.

Covenant – 12m E4 6a**. The prominent steep crack up the highest section of the left side of the crag. Sustained and well protected.

Skerryvore – 12m E3 6b*. The steep crack leading to the left side of the ledge at two thirds height. A difficult bouldery start leads to better holds in the niche at half height. Continue with interest to gain the ledge. Finish easily above.

A Helping Hand – 10m E2 5b**. The deep wide central crack. Large cams useful.

Minor – 8m HVS 5a*. The obvious line below the ramp, moving out right then back left to finish (or finish out right).

IONA, Phort Bhan, Tolkein Crag:
Snip-Snap – 20m E4 6a. R. and C. Anderson. 20th April, 1997.
The short overhanging wall at the left side of the crag. Climb to the ledge below the centre of the wall. A small wire protects the move to an obvious hand slot where good wires protect the stretch placement of a Rock 3 high on the right. Pull past the wire and move up to gain the crack on Yans Route. Step across left and using a flange move up left into the centre of the wall over a small roof and continue to the top.

Allah Be Praised – 25m E3 5c*. C. Moody, M. Tweedly, L. Gordon-Canning. 24th August, 1997.
Climbs the recess left of Yabadabadoo. Follow the left-slanting crack which gets better with height; step right when it ends. Go over a bulge, then follow the easy groove to the top.

Raven's Crag, Main Wall:
God Is Dead – 20m E4 6a**. G. Latter, C. Moody. 8th August, 1997.
The crack up the black seam in the arête. Start as for Jehad and climb the crack up the rib on the left. After the angle eases trend left to finish past a hollow flake.

Solar Temple – 20m E2 5b*. G.Latter, C.Moody. 8th August, 1997.
The crack up the right side of the pinnacle right of Crusade, then the wall above.

Blood Eagle – E5 6a***. R. Waterton (unsec). September, 1997.
Start just left of Smoke Yourself Thin. Climb up leftwards to finish at an obvious slot. The lower section is protected by a rock 1 on the right. The upper half is well protected, crux at half-height.

Il Uomo Da Roma – 20m E2 5b*. C. Moody, L. Gordon-Canning. 12th July, 1997.
Start round right of L'homme d'Iona and climb the easy left-slanting ramp to a ledge and huge flake. Climb up right through an overhang right of the flake to a jug. Pull left into a crack, then climb straight up to finish up a bulge.

Pontificating – 20m E3 5c*. C. Moody, L. Gordon-Canning. 20th September, 1997.
Climb the easy left-slanting ramp, shared with the previous route. Step right above an overhang and traverse right below the overlap. Follow the fault line to the top.

Pope On A Rope – 25m E2 5b**. C. Moody, L. Gordon-Canning. 12th July, 1997.
Start up the easy left-slanting ramp; move right to gain the line of corners which lead to the top.

Aoineidh nan Struth, Labrador Wall:
Infidels – 12m E4 6a*. G. Latter. 9th August, 1997.
Well protected climbing up the left side of the orange arête left of the square-cut corner of Quack. Climb the front face on to a ledge, then a line just left of the arête to a good diagonal crack. Step right on to the arête, finishing on a good jug.

SKYE

AM BASTEIR, North Face:

The Squeeze Box – 110m E3. M. Moran, A. Nisbet. 17th June, 1997.
Climbs the soaring chimney in the centre of the steep North Face. Start at a break left of the chimney where there is a short wide crack at head height.
1. 30m 5b. Climb the crack and groove above. Move on to the slabby wall on the right and up rightwards to the base of the chimney. A serious pitch.
2. 30m 5b. Climb the back of the chimney in two sections. Vertical caving, probably always wet.
3. 30m 5a. Pass a huge chockstone by moving out of the chimney on to a slab on the right, climbed to a ledge system. Continue up the deep narrow chimney with a through route.
4. 20m. Finish easily up the continuation fault.

SGURR AN FHEADAIN:

N. Williams notes that Drainpipe Gully claimed by C. Rowland in 1980 is the same as Spur Gully climbed by A. P. Abraham *et. al.* in 1907. (See Abraham's classic book *Rock-climbing in Skye.*)

SRON NA CICHE, Eastern Buttress:

I. Taylor notes that he considers Pocks to be E3 5b 5c.

CORUISG HUT CRAG:

The Minke – 20m E2 5b*. G. Nicoll, M. Nicoll, L. Kass. 19th May, 1997.
Start left of Beached Whale, directly behind the hut door. Climb the basalt dyke which slants rightwards up the wall. Possibly climbed before but not recorded.

SGURR NA STRI, Mizzen Buttress:

This is the area of rock above and to the left of the Scavaig Slabs, steep in its lower part with slabs higher up. The following route takes the obvious crack-and-corner system up the middle of the buttress and was reached from the top of the Scavaig Buttress by traversing the steep and heavily-vegetated terrace capped by roofs which crosses the right-hand side of the buttress. A better approach would be to climb the broken rib directly below the corner.
Outhaul – 120m HVS 5a. C. R. Ravey, J. S. Peden. 26th May, 1997.
From the left-hand end of the terrace climb a steep slab left of the main roof to the foot of a series of cracks in the wall above. Follow these to a steep corner (crux, 45m). Follow the line of cracks in the slab above (50m). Further slabs lead to the top of the buttress (25m).

BLA BHEINN, East Face:

Finger in the Dyke – 120m E5**. P. Thorburn, G. Farquhar, G. Latter. 4th June, 1997.
A serious and atmospheric route up the arête of The Great Prow. Start at a left-slanting dyke at the left-hand side of the cave below the arête. The dyke climbed by Jib is 10m down to the left.
1. 30m 6a. Follow the dyke to a small right-facing corner (serious) and gain the shelf above. Move a short way up this ramp, swing right into an undercut groove and climb it until the line fades. Make a slightly descending traverse right across the lip of a roof to a curious hole, continue to the right-hand side of a slabby niche and climb the crack above. Take a hanging belay below a loose niche.

2. 30m 5c. Follow the crack through the niche to climb a wall on hollow holds, moving right round the arête below a bulge. Gain the ramp above, move back left round the arête and step down to belay in a scoop.

3. 45m 5b (or 5c). Continue directly above the belay crossing a dyke, then follow good holds leading rightwards on to the arête. Continue more easily up a wide left-slanting crack and its continuation to belay on a broken terrace.

4. 15m. Scramble up left to the top.

CLACH GLAS:
Slighe a' Bhodaich – 115m IV,4. D. Ritchie, N. Marshall. 8th March, 1998.
Situated immediately south of the Clach Glas – Sgurr nan Each bealach is a prominent east-facing buttress holding two parallel left-slanting fault lines The route climbs the right-hand fault, up the chimney in two pitches over several interesting chockstones. Finish left on easier ground to the summit ridge.

ELGOL, Schoolhouse Buttress:
Right of 'Orrible Crack is a very steep clean wall. The following two routes climb it, both starting directly behind the spring.
Overdrive – 18m E4 6a. A. Tibbs, A. Matthewson. 23rd July, 1997.
Start below a big, pointed hold at 5m. Climb to this, then keep going until moves leftward gain a sloping ledge (poor rest). Continue up the centre of the wall above via a thin crack. (the ascent described used preplaced runners; the route awaits a proper lead).
Afterburn – 16m E3 5c. A. Tibbs, A. Matthewson. 24th July, 1997.
Follow Overdrive to the pointed hold, then move right into a shallow slot, and straight up the crackline above. Another sustained route with excellent protection.

Farther right, a shorter section of crag offers a couple of routes.
Pew with a View – 6m HVS 5b. A. Matthewson. 28th June, 1997.

Start 1m left of the recess. A long reach gains a crack and easier climbing.

The Sting – 7m E1 5c. A. Matthewson, A. Tibbs. 25th July, 1997.
The wall left of Pew with a View, starting 3m left. Climb up and left to a hold just right of a heather tuft. The wrinkled wall above is easier.

STRATHAIRD, Suidhe Biorach:
Stretcher Case – 25m E3/4 6a. P. Donnithorne, E. Alsford. 9th June, 1997.
Climbs the wall between Veritas Splendour and Crack of Zawn and contains a very long reach at two-thirds height (6b for the short).

The following routes seem quite close, but different.
Blasphemosaurus – 25m E3 5c. R. McAllister, C. French, D. McGimpsey. 22nd March, 1998.
Start below the right end of the roof and about 20m right of Mothers Pride. Climb steep rock to a small roof under the roof. Traverse left under the roof until under a flake-crack going through the roof. Pull through this and climb up leftwards to a slight easing in angle. Move right and up to finish.

Ogmorian – 25m E1 5b*. E. Alsford, P. Donnithorne. 9th June, 1997.
Climbs the centre of the wall round to the right of Mother's Pride and cannot be approached until mid tide. Low in the grade. Start 20m right of Mother's Pride below an obvious ledge 2m up (and just past the right-hand end of the main roof

at half height). Take a direct line through steep rock and a bulge to gain the final headwall. Climb this just left of an obvious grassy ledge.

Legover – 15m E2 5b. C. French, D. McGimpsey, R. McAllister. 22nd March, 1998.

Another buttress, east-facing, described in the guide (p260) lies 200m right (facing the cliff). The route climbs a steep grooved corner-line to the left of the V. Diff corner. Climb the overhanging corner-line to a rest on a protruding block. Climb diagonally rightwards along the right wall of the corner to finish up through a squeeze chimney.

NEIST, The Upper Crag:

Bad Dream – 60m E3 5c***. C. Moody, L. Gordon-Canning. 17th June, 1997 (first pitch). N. Smith, R. Lupton, C. Moody. 19th July, 1997 (complete).

The big corner at the bottom of Tower Gully. A fine line with considerable exposure, possibly a good route for a wet day.

1. 35m 5b. Climb the corner to the overhang, move right climb a crack and move on to the ledge on the right. An excellent pitch.

2. 25m 5c. Step back left and follow the obvious fault, finish by jamming the left side of the summit block.

Financial Sector:

Fat Cats – 20m E2 5c**. W. Jeffrey, D. N. Williams. 14th September, 1996.

Climbs the obvious crack in the north-facing wall at the southern end of the Financial Sector. Climb a short slab and move left to enter a chimney. Climb this and the crack above with increasing difficulty. Hug a curious column before making committing moves up the crucial headwall.

Hurricane Hideaway – 25m E1 5b***. E. Alsford, P. Donnithorne. 8th June, 1997.

A route very reminiscent of Sunny Corner Lane, Cam Barra. Climbs the main corner feature just left of Wall Street, finishing through the roofs left of the corner. Climb the corner until possible to traverse left along an obvious break to gain a hanging corner above. Climb this to the roof and undercut rightwards to gain a short finishing corner above – a meaty finish!

The following two routes lie to the right (south) of Sonamara.

Transitive Nightfall of Diamonds – 25m H. Severe 4b*. A. Holden, R. Holden. 17th July, 1997.

Start at the first rib right of Sonamara just to the left of the crest. Climb a series of slabs pleasantly to the top, keeping to the left of the crest.

Keeping The Bofs Happy – 22m Diff. C. Moody, L. Gordon-Canning. 29th March, 1997.

Right of Sonamara there are three ribs; the rib right of these has a wide crack on its left-hand side. Climb the crest of the rib; there are a couple of hollow blocks.

The Fin:

The following route is located well east of The Fin, close to the eastmost end of the wall just before the wall fades into easy angled slabs.

Wilfull Neglect – 30m E2 5b. S. Kennedy, C. Grindley. June, 1997.

At the east end of the wall are two obvious corners. This route climbs the left-hand corner. A third corner is located just left again but is usually bird infested. Climb the corner throughout with the crux at half-height. Sustained and not overly protected.

NEIST, The Lower Crag: Poverty Point:
This is the sea cliff below Seagulls. A prominent prow juts out south. The west face of the prow is steep, finishing at a corner-crack.
At The Whelks – 30m HVS 5a*. C. Moody, L. Gordon-Canning. 1st June, 1997.
Climb a chimney left of the corner-crack which runs into another corner crack.
Recovery Day – 25m El 5b*. C. Moody, L. Gordon-Calming. 1st June, 1997.
A corner-crack to the left.
Superlager For Breakfast – 25m VS 4c*. C. Moody, L. Gordon-Calming. 1st June, 1997.
The chimney to the left with a bulge towards the top.
Giro Day – 25m E2 5c**. C. Moody, M. McLeod. 20th July, 1997.
Start next to Superlager and climb the crack on the left.

Homer – 20m HVS 5a*. C. Moody, M. McLeod. 20th July, 1997.
The wide crack.
Broken Wing – 20m Diff. M. McLeod, C. Moody. 20th July, 1997.
The line round the corner.

The following lines are to be found immediately left of Bernard's Dilemma. Approach down the gully as for that route.
Liquidator – 20m VS 4c. A. Holden, P. Arden, M. Hudson. 11th July, 1997.
Start at a chimney 4m left of Bernard's Dilemma. Climb the chimney past a challenging constriction to a wider chimney. Follow this to a terrace and finish up a short crack. Belay on blocks next to the alternative descent corner.

Clockface – 25m El 5a**. M. Hudson, A. Holden, P. Arden. 12th July, 1997.
The hanging slab 5m left of Liquidator. Climb the blocky arête to an airy shelf (unprotected). Leave the right-hand end of the shelf and climb the slab at five-past-three. Finish by a sharp pull up the wall above.
Best Before End – 20m Severe 4b*. M. Hudson, A. Holden, P. Arden. 11th July, 1997.
The clean-cut corner 3m left of Clockface. Follow the crack stepping left at the top to climb a short block. Step left onto the exposed arête, and make some poorly protected steps up to finish.
Mixed Fruit – 10m Severe 4b. M. Hudson, A. Holden, P. Arden. 11th July, 1997.
A short jamming crack high on the wall 5m left of Best Before End.
This Way Up – 20m HVS 4c*. R. Brown, J. Walters, Matti, M. Hudson. 25th August, 1997.
The clean chimney-crackline 20m farther north. Belay well back from the edge.

The next lines are farther north beyond Sore Phalanges. Belay well back on blocks on the coast path, and allow plenty of rope.
The Slammer – 30m Hard Severe**. M. Hudson, A. Holden, P. Arden. 12th July, 1997.
Start below a cracked wall 3m left of Sore Phalanges.
1. 15m 4b. Climb diagonally across the wall to a balcony.
2. 15m 4b. Follow the steep left-facing corner above.

Zia – 30m Severe 4a*. P. Arden, A. Holden. 12th July, 1997.
Start 2m left of The Slammer. Move up to the overlap, step left and climb the right-slanting corner crack to the balcony. Finish up broken blocks on the left.
Curving Crack – 30m El 5b*. A. Holden, M. Hudson. 11th July, 1997.
Start at the arête 10m left of Sore Phalanges. Step up the arête and swing right onto

the front face. Follow the curving crack in the wall past awkward moves to reach better holds. Move up to ledges then continue up broken ground to block belays.

STAFFIN SLIP NORTH, East Face:

The following lines are to be found on the lichenous east face of Staffin Slip North. Some routes need stake belays which seem to go missing – bring your own. The routes are described from right to left. The first line gains and follows the straight crack 3m left of Staffin Classic. *Jean and Jim* – 50m E1**. M. Hudson, J. Walters, R. Brown. 22nd August, 1997.

Start 5m left of Staffin Classic just left of a small chimney.

1. 20m 4c. Climb the edge of the large subsidiary flake to gain the crack just left of the arête. Sustained jamming leads to a good ledge and belays.

2. 30m 5b. (1pt) Follow the vertical crack above (hard to start – rest on FA) past a peapod, and finish up the memorable wall above.

Walk left or south for 30m, passing an ivy-covered wall to an area of four distinctive semi-detached columns. (The positions of the following routes relative to two routes reported in SMCJ 1997 – Loose Woman and Persistent Vegetated State – are uncertain.)

Return of the Stone – 50m Severe**. M. Hudson, R. Holden. 30th November, 1996.
Gains the base of and climbs the second column along on the east face, taking in some impressive ground at a surprisingly amenable grade. Consistent and well-protected. Start below a chimney in front of the third column, which holds an ominously-poised flake at 15m.

1. 15m 4b. Bridge up the chimney taking care with the poised flake. Belay shortly in an ivy dell to the right, below the second (right-hand) column.

2. 35m 4a. A spectacular pitch. Gain the rear of the second (right-hand) column using some steps to cross the giant flake that forms the back wall of the dell. Bridge up behind the column passing a jammed block 10m up. Keep bridging up, pausing to pose on top of the column, before transferring back to the cliff face to gain the top. Stake (possibly missing) and Rock 9 belay 5m back from the edge.

Big Farm Weekly – 35m HVS 5a. M. Hudson, A. Holden, R. Brown. 5th June, 1997.
A bottom-to-top line in the bay 10m left of Return of The Stone. Some good sections marred by excessive gardening and doubtful rock. Start up a tough crack 2m left of the chimney marking the right-hand end of the bay (crux). A rightward rising traverse can be made to avoid this direct start (VS overall). Follow the steep corner above to ledges – the pleasant climbing has now ended. Maintain a more-or-less direct course above past a rather worrying block, moving slightly right to finish up a pillar. Stake belay as for Return of The Stone.

Fourth Column – 20m VS 4b. M. Hudson, D. Brown. 27th October, 1996.
Climbs the smaller detached column some 15m left of Big Farm, which is split from top to bottom by a hand-width crack. Back-and-foot up behind the column, transferring onto the column itself about 5m below the top. Descend by simultaneous abseil from a groove in the very top of the column.

Skyscraper – 40m E3 5c*. D. Brown, R. Brown. 18th July, 1997.
Climbs an impressive crack 10m left of Fourth Column. Follow the crack past a small overhang at 5m and continue more easily until a difficult move (right of a bramble) leads to sloping ledge. Continue up the crack without respite until easier broken ground is reached. Teeter right to a break in the wall and a sloping heathery

finish. Stake belay needed in the dyke 5m back. The southern end of the cliff is dominated by a clean-cut overhang. The next route lies in the groove on its right-hand side.

Dogs and Wolves – 15m H.Severe 4b. R. Brown, D. Brown. 30th November, 1996. Climb the broken crack and groove above.

A White Tail of Hogmanay – 15m VS 4c. R. Brown, D. Pattullo. 31st December, 1996.
Starting 15m left of Dogs and Wolves, take the crack and corner on the left side of the big overhang. From the groove, bridge left onto a spike on the adjacent undercut headwall, which gives enjoyable climbing before the vegetated landing.

Bopp Til You Dropp – 12m HVS 4c. R. Brown, M. Hudson. 4th April, 1997.
Start 5m left of White Tail, and 3m left of a crack which twists into a triangulated groove capped at mid height. Follow a series of steep, unremitting cracks to a grassy finish.

Once Bitten – 12m Severe. D. Brown, M. Lee. 18th July, 1997.
An open chimney 3m left again gives fleetingly pleasant climbing before a loose top.

STAFFIN BAY, Flodigarry Island:
The east coast of Flodigarry Island holds spectacular cliffs which from afar promise columnar-type lines similar to Kilt Rock. Closer acquaintance reveals crumbly buttresses and bountiful birdlife best left alone. The following solitary line deserves no further attention.

Corrugated Chimney – 50m Severe. M. Hudson, R. Brown, J. Walters. 23rd August, 1997.
A grassy diagonal ramp descending rightwards splits the cliff in two and serves as a descent path. Start 100m north of this ramp, roughly beneath the highest point of the island at a huge semi-detached pinnacle. A shaft behind the pinnacle allows unpleasant and mildly-dangerous chimneying on large corrugations. Finish rue-fully up grass to belay three fence posts south of the stake marking the very summit of the island.

FLODIGARRY:
Another Man's Rhubarb – 40m Severe. P. Yardley, S. Halford. 21st August, 1997.
Climb a continuous vague groove to the right of Newspaper Taxis, finishing to the right of a short nose.
South Tunnel Buttress:
Captain Mainwaring – 50m VS 4c,4c. P. Yardley, S. Halford. 21st August, 1997.
Start as for Lucy in the Sky. Traverse right and climb up ledges as for that route. Break right from here past a good spike and climb a crack and wall up rightwards. Traverse right below grass ledges to belay on blocks on the arête. Climb the upper arête to the top. (Climbed by W. Jeffrey in 1990 and not thought worthy of reporting!)

RUBHA HUNISH, Meall Tuath:

A line has been climbed to the left of Northern Lights at E8 6a,6c. Autumn 1996.
Meall Deas:

The Scoop – 65m VS*. M. Hudson, A. Holden. 5th October, 1996.
Takes the easiest line up the left-hand arête of the Minch and Tatties buttress,
through a large scooped out roof. Start from steep grass slopes at the foot of the
arête.
1. 15m 4a. Climb a shattered pillar and the rib above to belay in the recess beneath
the scoop.
2. 20m 4c. Follow the overhanging crack above and step left at the roof to gain an
airy position on the arête. Easier ground leads to belays below the big corner left
of the upper arête.
3. 30m 4b. Tackle the corner and pull over the lip at 15m. Easier scrambling leads
to the stake belay of Minch and Tatties.

The Knowledge – 75m HVS*. M. Hudson, A. Holden. 6th June, 1997.
A delightful and varied line taking in some impressive ground right of The Scoop,
but slightly spoiled by the escapability of the top pitch. Pitch one combined with
the top pitch of The Scoop gives a good VS 5a** combination. Start 10m down and
right of The Scoop start, directly below a gap in the band of overhangs.
1. 40m 5a. Climb a crack, then columns and ribs direct to the gap. Chimney through
the overhangs (crux) and belay beneath the overhanging cracks above.
2. 35m 5a. Move left and up round the corner, following the S crack 2m right of
the Scoop corner. Hand traverse out right across the face ASAP to a shelf on the
arête. Continue directly up the arête (crux) to the stake belay of Minch and Tatties.
Note: The guidebook description for Minch and Tatties should read: 'A prominent
right-facing corner'.

Master of Morgana – 70m HVS***. A. Holden, M. Hudson. 31st August, 1996.
A superb well-protected line following the right-hand side of the face and finishing
up the obvious cleft on the skyline. Start 20m right of the start of Minch and Tatties
below the right-hand of two deep chimneys.
1. 30m 4c. Gain the chimney and climb it on improving rock to a ledge on the left.
Climb a series of grooves trending left to reach a blocky ledge and nut belays.
2. 40m 5b. Climb the crack above the stance to reach a higher ledge. Traverse left
to gain a leftward rising ramp leading to a horizontal break. Hand traverse back
right to gain the bottom of the final crack. Climb this (crux) to a spectacular
grovelling finish.

Rightwards of the Whispering Crack wall a row of five buttresses, composed of a
strangely-sculpted picrodolerite, rise up from sea level. Some of this rock,
especially the bottom 20m, requires careful treatment.
Mercury Mouth – 70m VS*. R. Brown, A. Holden, M. Hudson. 5th October, 1996.
The leftmost buttress is dominated by a pinnacle at mid-height. This climb gains
the pinnacle, starting up the groove to the right of the adenoidal feature.
1. 40m 4c. Climb the groove until a line of flakes allows a traverse left above the
overhang. Pull through steep ground to gain the upper groove and follow this direct
to belays behind the pinnacle.
2. 30m 4b Climb the stepped wall to the right of the pinnacle, trending rightwards
to avoid a tottering finger.

Aegis – 75m HVS**. R. Brown, M. Hudson. 10th May, 1997.
This climb takes a logical line up the centre of the fourth buttress, which is
distinguished by a large 'ear' at 12m on its left-hand arête. Very worthwhile after
the fudgy start. Start slightly right of the central arête.

1. 40m 4c. Head for a prehistoric perch at 10m then move up, taking care with the rock, to a big spike and welcome sound placements at 20m. Gain the spike and step onto the wall above, continuing up a shallow groove to the large sloping ramp.

2. 35m 4b. Follow the ramp to a notch in the left-hand arête. Follow the arête over several bulges to the heather slopes above.

A Piece of Cake – 45m H. Severe. R. Brown, D. Pattullo (alt.). 3rd January, 1997. The fifth buttress is capped by a triangulated top wall, and split by a prominent crack on its right-hand side.

1. 35m 4b. Start in a bay and climb the crack to step right at the arête. Follow the crack to the headwall. Move left to a ledge and a short chimney, and thence the rooftop belay.

2. 10m 4a Follow the grassy ramp diagonally rightwards to choked cracks with an awkward exit.

RAASAY:

M. Tighe provided the following mini-guide, somewhat summarised here.

The various areas are described in a rough north-south progression, though there isn't a great deal of rock in the south, and what there is can be a bit scary (some routes described).

Oskaig Crag (MR 552 377):

Situated parallel to and below the road close to the Youth Hostel (one minute walk), the granophyre crag consists of a series of loose and broken buttresses up to 15m in height. Numerous possibilities, the best being the crackline on the highest part of the cliff at the south end, Jeff's 45-minute Haircut (H. Severe 4b). Climb the crack direct, the crux being just below the small tree. Continue up the open corner with care. Other routes include Swimming with the Sharks (E1 5b), a steep groove opposite the corner of the wood, and The End of the Line (VS 4b), a groove-line on the wall just right of the previous route.

Inverburn Crag:

Situated off Burma Road Trail near the waterfall. Project: Arnold's Jumper (approx. E5 6b). Direct line on an overhanging wall at the right end (south) of the crag – start to the right of small trees in a break and ascend via a dyno and good breaks with the crux at the top.

Honeycomb Wall (MR 567 365):

Situated next to the Fearns road just past the mine buildings at the top of the forest. Small overhanging wall of excellent pocketed sandstone.

Dun Caan:

On Dun Caan's summit crags there are recorded climbs ranging from Flying Flakes (22m, Mild VS) to Fear of Flying (23m, E1 5b) which are reached by roping down from the summit trig point. Fear of Flying takes an arête to the left (north) of the main buttress and then a finger crack to the top. Flying Flakes takes a cleaved crack to the right of the former. A buttress farther to the right gives Warden's Slab (22m, H. Severe 4a) which follows a slabby ramp and corner past an obvious overhang. There are more short routes to be explored.

Creag na Bruaich:

This large escarpment of Triassic sandstone cliffs lies just to the south of the ruined township of north and south Screapadal. The scene is dominated by a huge free-standing tower 65m high and well seen from the road south of Brochel. The tower is known locally as An Coinneal (The Candle). The top was reached by abseil and pendulum by M. Tighe and party in May, 1991. Details of a number of other climbs provided, particularly on boulders down by the shore (Screapadal Boulders).

Arnish:

This north end of the island is composed of Lewisian gneiss and the area abound with tantalising little crags, some have been worked on, some not. The first crag of note which can be seen from the road at Arnish is Callum's Crag (MR 599 485), 15 min. walk from the road end at Arnish. A small compact crag (8m) situated above the trees at the back of Arnish. South-facing with obvious cracklines and narrow face climbs – 10 routes described. Also a route on a small crag farther up the hill with an obvious triangular overhang. And 200m farther up the hillside is a lovely little crag with a fierce overhanging crack in the right wall (E1 5b). Several easier routes on this crag.

Torran, Meall Dearg (MR 595 495):

A large broken crag on the path from Arnish to the north end of the island. Turn right (uphill) from the old schoolhouse at Arnish – the crag is at the highest point of the path (20 min. walk).

Scampi Didley Doo – 30m E1 5b**. S. Younie, P. Johnstone, D. McAulay. 28th April, 1995.

Takes the groove line up the centre of the highest section at the left end of the crag. Start at the lowest point of the buttress and climb through a loose red band to gain a solid crack. Follow the line trending right at first, and then more direct to finish through an awkward bulge.

Windmill in Old Amsterdam – 30m VS 4c*. P. Johnstone, D. McAulay, J. Hendry. 25th April, 1996.

On the solid rectangular buttress to the left of a short stone dyke. It takes the left-hand crack, with a hard move through a bulge. Continue up the widening crack (belay) and finish up a short steep corner.

A Little Mouse with Clogs On – 20m HVS 5a. P. Johnstone, G. Grant, D.? 13th May, 1996.

To the right of the stone dyke is an obvious wide chimney. Start up a faint groove 2m right of the chimney for 5m and step right on to a ledge. Climb a crack and blocky bulge with a hard move to reach a shelf. Gain a slab and belay at the short wall above.

A broken orange buttress with a large scoop at half height lies 50m right of the dyke.

Cinders – 30m VS 4b. D. McAulay, P. Johnstone, J. Hendry. 25th April, 1996.

Climb a short crack to gain the large scoop. Climb up into a small niche before making an awkward step left on to a hanging slab. Finish up a corner (some loose rock).

Right again is a prominent solid rib which forms the lowest point of the crag.

Where on the Stair – 35m H.Severe**. J. Hendry, P. Johnstone, D. McAulay. 25th April, 1996.

Start on the left side of the rib and climb diagonally right on good holds past two large blocks. Continue directly with interest on good rock. There is a direct start at 5a.

Well I Declare – 15m MVS 4c. P. Johnstone, G. Grant, A. Jamesom, D.? 13th May, 1996.

Up and right of Where . . . is a short rib with two obvious V-grooves above. Climb the left side of the rib to below a rightward-slanting shelf to the right of the V-grooves. Climb a wall to finish.

Sgurr na Gall (MR 605 521):

Perhaps should be Sgeir nan Gall, the skerry of the stranger. The cliff is a wonderful sweep of clean compact pink Lewisian gneiss with the sea lapping at its foot at the western end. Most of the routes are around 30m and take prominent groove and crack lines. There is much scope for variation but this is Hebridean climbing *par excellence*. 100m or so along the shore eastwards from the main cliff are 10m walls, another superb little area with a multitude of cracks, overhangs and corners, some of which were climbed by M. Tighe, M. Lake and J. Gould on 21st March, 1996.

Approach: Follow the Coal Rona path as far as an old red roofed shepherd's hut at MR 612 519, then bushwhack westwards along the shore of the bay to the extreme western tip of the Sgurr. The cliff is not visible until you turn the corner right on the headland.

The Tobacco Run – 85m HVS 5a***. M. Tighe, K. Harding, D. McAulay, J. Hendry. 4th September, 1995.

A fine expedition on perfect rock and crossing nearly every other route on the crag. So in effect a girdle traverse at about one-third height, finishing up a shallow groove. Start in the small inlet just to the north of the main crag. Follow a wee track on to the headland and traverse with increasing difficulty about 6m above sea level back south towards the main crag to a wonderful airy belay beside the bottomless groove of Clais Mor (Big Groove). Cross the groove (hard) and hand traverse around the corner to attain the ledge on the main cliff (belay). Go along the ledge almost to the end and take the fine shallow groove to the top.

Clais Mor – 25m HVS 5a***. M. Tighe, D. West. 4th April, 1996.

The fine bottomless groove at the extreme western end of the cliff has a made-to-measure roof at the top. Start at half-tide or less with some gymnastic moves on to the jutting prow. Climb up the excellent groove and turn the roof on the right. Easier climbing to the top.

Fladda – 25m E2 5b***. M. Tighe (unsec.). 21st March, 1996.

This excellent route attains the obvious right-trending ramp at the top left side of the cliff. Make an intricate series of moves up the wall just around the corner from Clais Mor to gain the crack that comes down from the rightward-sloping ramp. Climb the crack and, more easily, the ramp.

Blood Test – 25m VS 4c*. M. Tighe, D. West. 4th April, 1996.

A shallow groove in the middle of the face leads to the ledge at one-third height. Directly above is the shallow groove of Tobacco Run. A couple of metres to the left and almost in the centre of the cliff is another fault line with a flake on the right. Climb the groove.

Oisinn McAulay – 25m VS 4c*. D. McAulay, K. Harding, J. Hendry. 4th September, 1995.

At the right-hand side of the main cliff a wide shallow bay leads to a more pronounced corner higher up. This gives an interesting route.

Am Fasarinen – 25m E3 5c**. D. McAulay, P. Johnstone. 23rd April, 1996.

A prominent flake on the arête to the right of Oisinn McAulay. Start in the back of a small bay and climb to a large sloping shelf. Ascend the flake direct to a horizontal break. Steeply to the top. Sustained and airy!

Oisinn Olga – 20m V. Diff*. M. Tighe, D. West, O. West. 4th April, 1996.

To the right of Oisinn McAulay there are two fierce-looking short hanging flakes which have yet to be climbed. Right again is the extreme back (east) corner of the inlet. Climb this, better than it looks.

NORTHERN HIGHLANDS

SOUTH AND WEST (VOLUME ONE)

CREAG COIRE AN t-SLUGAIN:
The Furrow, climbed direct through the overhung recess by A. Mullin, A. Nisbet, J. Preston at IV,6 on 3rd December, 1997.

SGURR NAN CONBHAIREAN, North Face:
Sunny Side Up – 100m IV,4. A. Powell, S. Elworthy. 29th December, 1995.
Climbs the icefall in the centre of the next wall 100m up and right of Fog Monster/ Misty Byway (and Crystal Couloir presumably – Ed).
1. 45m. Climb the icefall and groove above to below a steep wall.
2. 50m. Step right and climb a recess in the wall. Head up to belay just below the ridge.

Lochan Uaine Buttress:
The Green Man – 90m III. R. Hester, G. Jones, A. Nisbet. 29th January, 1998.
Climbs the face right of Anne Frank's Chimney, starting about 5m to its right. Climb turf to a block, then traverse right to reach a line leading diagonally right to end at a steep headwall (40m). Travese back left to enter and climb a steep groove, gradually easing.

CREAG AN DUILISG (Plockton), Main Crag area:
To the right of the Main Crag and Brigadier's Redoubt is a diagonal stone shoot, which gives access to the cliff containing the 1971 route, Trundle (VS). The shoot is very loose and not recommended for descent. A new section of cliff begins 60m farther right at an impressive overhanging arête. The routes here are single pitch and lack the convenience of tree belays at their tops, but give a variety of grades on quick-drying rock.
Roseroot Ramp – 40m Severe. R. Chapman, A. Jago, M. E. Moran. 29th May, 1997.
The obvious left-slanting ramp in the centre of the crag. Climb the centre, enjoying the clean shield of rock in the middle. Exit left on thick heather to birch belays. Abseil from large rowans 15m left of the top.
Plockton Plonkers – 40m Severe. R. Chapman, A. Jago, M. E. Moran. 29th May, 1997.
Start 15m right of Roseroot Ramp at the right end of the sector. Climb a clean, curving crack into a corner system. Exit left and climb a short corner to the top. Peg belay and abseil point *in situ* 5m higher.

Miracle of the May Midge – 30m E1 5b. M.E.Moran (unsec). 29th May, 1997.
A clean wall with cracked blocks at its foot lies 8m left of Plockton Plonkers. Climb up to the right of the blocks and go delicately up the wall to a ledge. Take the centre of the impending wall of brown rock above, following a vague crackline, to finish at a higher terrace (the peg abseil of Plockton Plonkers is 10m higher).

Western Cliff:
500m west of the Main Crag, well beyond the prominent gully which cuts the centre of the crags, is a prow of beetling green overhangs. Some 80m high, well coated by the sea lichen or dulse which gives these crags their name, and defended by vertiginous vegetation – this crag looks as impressive as it is repulsive. This sector is best approached from a good layby at MR 832 335 from which a 15-20 minute

struggle through birchwood leads to the base. Peregrine falcons were seen preparing to nest here, so the crag is best avoided during the May to August nesting season. The following route climbs directly up the prow.

King Prawn Deathwish – 115m E3 5c. I. Dring, M. E. Moran (on sight). 1st May, 1997.

A route of unusual character and considerable excitement, a real Plockton special! Start just left of the prow at a blunt rib with a tree at 6m.

1. 20m 4c. Climb the rib past two trees to a long vegetated ledge.

2. 25m 5a Go 3m up a wide crack on the right, then move awkwardly left and up to a cleaned ramp. Follow this for 15m up under roofs, where it peters out at a vegetated break. Pull round right and go straight up a wall to a tiny ledge directly below a groove cutting the main roofs of the prow (peg belay *in situ*).

3. 20m 5c. The route now bears its teeth. Climb the groove above the stance through bulges for 15m. Committing moves right gain a ledge with precarious stacked blocks. Climb through the bulging wall above to a fine stance beneath the capping roof (peg and Friend belay).

4. 15m 5b. Hand traverse left 3m and pull on to a ramp. Go back right and swing across the lip of the roofs on good holds to ledges. Belay 4m right on another ledge with a view.

5. 35m 4c. Go slightly left, then up heathery grooves and flake cracks to the top. Descend to the west of the crag via a stony gully and steep heather slopes.

SGURR NA FEARTAIG:

The Topper – 210m V,5. A. Gorman, D. Williamson, H. Wyllie. 4th January, 1997.
The icefall which forms on the left wall of The Stonker recess, gained by climbing the first pitch of The Stonker. Steeper and more sustained than The Stonker, with the fourth of five pitches the crux. The amount of ice is variable but a continuous icefall on this occasion; ice screw belays.

Wee Dribble – 70m IV,5. A. Cunningham, F. Fotheringham. 6th January, 1997.
Start a few metres to the right of Running on Empty. Climb via a series of icicles draining down a vague groove to blocky ledges to the left of a huge recess (30m). Climb over the blocks and short corners to easy ground, with one further short step to the top (40m).

FUAR THOLL, Lower South-East Nose:

The Ramp – 150m II. J. Gibbs, A. Nisbet, A. Petts. 1st March, 1998.
The turfy ramp mentioned in the guide is really a left-slanting groove. Climb the groove for three pitches. Either finish up the groove or traverse right for an extra pitch.

Irish Grooves – 140m III. I. Lee-Bapty, A. Nisbet, A. Wildsmith. 8th March, 1998.
Start 10m left of Olfactory and climb a left-slanting line of turfy grooves in three long pitches to the top.

Mainreachan Buttress:

Snoopy – 180m VII,7. C. Dale, A. Nisbet. 7th March, 1998.
Based on Snoopy, although the relationship in the finish is unsure. Very spectacular, with bold pitches on thin ice leading to a strenuous, but well protected, section through roofs. The more ice, the easier it would become.

1,2. 35m, 30m. Follow Reach for the Sky (Snoopy) for two pitches.

3. 15m. Continue a short way up the ramp-corner, then traverse right along a foot ledge to climb the right side of the ramp to its top.

4. 25m. Climb steep rock trending right to gain the iced 'brown groove' and follow it, probably on increasingly thick ice to a ledge below a prominent ice column.

5. 15m. Climb the ice column into a recess. Make unlikely moves round the arête on the left to easier ground leading back right above the recess.

6. 30m. Climb the chimney above and continue to a terrace.

7. 30m. Move right and finish easily up grooves.

SGORR RUADH:

Gravesend – 200m IV,4. I. Lee-Bapty, A. Nisbet, A. Wildsmith. 11th March, 1998.
At the base of the steep section of the Central Couloir left wall is a prominent left-slanting gully, almost a ramp under a smooth steep wall. Climb the gully to a cave (50m). Exit the cave by ice on the left and cross a big terrace (50m). Enter a big scoop in the upper buttress and finish up a chimney from its top right corner. Perhaps III with the first pitch well frozen.

Raeburn's Buttress:

The Jigsaw – 200m III. H. Davies, G. Bardsley, A. Nisbet. 6th January, 1998.
The easiest mixed start to Raeburn's Buttress, low in the grade, not sustained, and in keeping with the upper part. Start at the ramp which is the first big feature right of the crest of Raeburn's Buttress (the same ramp as mentioned in the guide for Raeburn's original ascent). Climb the ramp to its top (60m), traverse right along a ledge (50m) and reach a fault line leading diagonally back left to the crest (70m). A short pitch on the crest leads to the upper section (20m).

Tritium Chimney – 130m IV,6. M. E. Moran, A. Nisbet. 4th December, 1997.
Based on the narrow chimney line between Raeburn's Original and Direct routes and which cuts directly through The Jigsaw. Start from a big shelf which slopes up right to the base of the line. The initial slabs were not iced so the blocky rib on the left was climbed leading into the top of a ramp (the same ramp as climbed by The Jigsaw), followed rightwards back to the chimney line (40m). Two steep steps in the chimney (30m) and the easier continuation of the line (40m) led to the crest and the short pitch as above to the top of the steep section of the buttress (20m).

MEALL GORM:

Bypass Buttress – 350m II. G. Lewis-Evans, A. Nisbet, D. Winterbone. 20th January, 1998.
Climb the central of the three lowest gullies to its blocking cave, traverse out right for 60m along a ledge to the buttress crest, climb a steep pitch on the crest to an easy finish up the buttress.

Spiral Terrace, Direct Finish – 100m III,4. G. Lewis-Evans, A. Nisbet, D. Winterbone. 18th January, 1998.
Finish up the buttress right of the 'deep gully', the crux being a short vertical wall low down.

SGURR A' CHAORACHAIN, A' Chioch:

Impulse – 70m HVS. G. Reilly, F. Templeton. 1st June, 1997.
Follows a line up the east-facing buttress left of Cioch South Gully and near the left end of Middle Ledge. Start directly below an obvious narrow left-facing corner near the right end of the wall.

1. 40m 5a. Climb directly to the base of the corner and up it until possible to swing rightwards on to the rib using a flaky handhold on the wall. Climb up, then rejoin the corner at the opening of a crack. Move up and right to the top of a pinnacle and continue directly upwards to the left end of a grass ledge.

2. 30m. Continue above trending rightwards towards grassy ledges leading into South Gully left fork. Abseil down the gully or continue traversing to abseil down South Gully itself.

Northern Buttresses:
Independence Day – 50m H. Severe. M. Arkley, D. Counsell. 14th September, 1996.

Climbs arête at the left-hand side of the wall which also contains Chopper Chimney (MR 787 432).

1. 20m. Climb the obvious chimney which is left of the foot of the arête to gain the arête after 5m. Follow the left side of the arête and move right to gain large holds and a steep move to a belay ledge.

2. 25m 4b. Climb a steep crack for 5m and move out right on to a broad sloping shelf. Make an awkward exposed move right round a corner, then climb up and across a broken gully to gain a large ledge finishing left.

Summit Buttress:
Airwaves – 50m E3 5c. M. Moran, A. Nisbet. 31st May, 1997.

An exciting route; the middle section is space walking. Led on sight. The route is two-thirds along the right-hand section of cliff – near the approach path. Immediately below the cliff is a narrow terrace. Walk along this past two pillars to a point where there is a rocky spur on the slope underneath. Above the far end of the spur is the widest section of terrace with a cubic block lying on it. The wall above is beetling with overhangs but the key feature is a big roof with a downward-pointing lip about 10m up. Start at a black right-facing corner which leads up to the left end of the roof. Climb the corner, move left and up a shallow groove to a break below overhangs. Go diagonally right by sensational moves round overhangs to a hidden grass ledge. Finish up the final corner passing a roof.

South Face:
Astrocyte – 40m HVS 5b. A. Nisbet, G. Nisbet. 16th June, 1997.

Climbs the bulging buttress left of Ganglion. Start as for Ganglion.

1. 25m 4b. Start up the groove as for Ganglion but soon move left and climb a left-slanting ramp to the halfway ledge. Traverse left to blocks where the ledge turns the corner towards the left-bounding gully.

2. 15m 5b. Pull through the roof at a wedged block (just left of a central groove). Finish trending left under overhangs.

BEINN BHAN, Coire Toll a' Bhein:
Illegal Grass – 250m IV,5. G. Lewis-Evans, A. Nisbet, D. Winterbone. 19th January, 1998.

Climbs the buttress right of Breach of the Peace, with one disproportionately hard pitch. Start from the toe up a zig-zag pitch leading to a steep band (60m). This was tackled right of the crest (crux) leading to easier ground, continuing up a line generally on the right.

BEINN DAMH, Little Coire (MR 881 516, see SMCJ 1995, p646):

All the chimneys/gullies in this coire have now been climbed, including The Thin White Line, 140m, II, M. C. Jacob, P. J. Biggar, 11th February, 1997, and The Slanter, 135m, II, P. J. Biggar, 15th February, 1997. Both routes are located on the buttress right of the obvious central gully, Neerday Gully, P. J. Biggar, I, 1st January, 1987. P. J. Biggar also notes that an ascent of Stirrup Gully (SMCJ 1996) was described in SMCJ 1992, pp1-5.

Creagan Dubh Toll nam Biast:

Erica's Ridge – 450m III. J. Gibbs, A. Nisbet, A. Petts, C. Platten. 4th March, 1998.
The ridge left of Stag Gully. Start 60m left of Stag Gully and climb a turfy pitch (the easiest line on the lower buttress) to a terrace (45m). Traverse easily right to overlook Stag Gully (45m). Climb the crest thereafter, becoming easier after two long pitches.

LIATHACH, Coire Dubh Mor:

Georgina – 80m II. H. Davies, G. Bardsley. 4th January, 1998.
A line going out diagonally right from the base of George on to the North ridge of Spidean.

BEINN EIGHE, Coire Mhic Fhearchair, Central Buttress:

Flying Finish (to Central Buttress) – 75m H. Severe. A. Nisbet, A. Goring, P. Patterson, I. Sneddon. 10th June, 1997.
Start 10m along the Upper Girdle, traversing from the base of Central Buttress final tier, just before a dangerous-looking column of rock.
1. 35m 4b. Climb a chimney to a ledge, then trend left up flake-cracks past an awkward block to the arête right of a big left-facing corner, an obvious feature on the face when seen from the left. Climb the chimney just right of the arête to an airy ledge.
2. 40m. Climb an easy chimney on the left, then finish left and right by a big pinnacle (as for Flight of the Condor, also the easiest finish to Piggott's Route).

DIABAIG, The Domes:

Apprentices Route – 50m M. Severe. N. Kenworthy, D. W. M. Whalley, K. Holland. 26th July, 1997.
This route lies right of the Condome and starts by traversing rightwards 50m from the recess (as described on p195 of Northern Highlands Vol. 1), beyond Charlie's Tower and Boab's Corner. Climb a short, steep wall for 3m. Go straight up the groove above and follow a crack to easier ground.

Oor Wullie – 60m E1. J. Lyall, A. Nisbet. 1st April, 1998.
Climbs a line just right of Boab's Corner. Start 2m right of the stepped corner.
1. 30m 5c. After a boulder problem start, go diagonally right up scoops overlooking a steep wall to reach a roofed recess. Leave it out of its left corner and make thin moves to heather.
2. 30m 5c. Go up to a black-streaked section of wall. Climb this with difficulty to reach a short corner right of Boab's crux corner. Climb this and continue up a dwindling ramp rightwards to reach easy ground.

BEINN A' MHUINIDH, The Bonnaid Dhonn:

North by North-West – 45m E7***. P. Thorburn, R. Campbell, A. D. Robertson. 19-20th July, 1997.

Climbs the right wall of the crest taken by A Walk on the Wild Side. Start on a ledge below a striking vertical crack.

1. 20m 5c. Climb the crack past a hollow flake until near a huge roof. Follow a thin break out left to belay on a small ledge on the arête.

2. 25m 6b. From just above the belay, follow a break dipping rightwards to a low traverse line in the roof. Follow this to a spike, then climb the sustained right-slanting crack and continue in the same line to gain a good hold at the top of a faint left-facing groove. Move up left to a break and follow this, pulling over a bulge on to the arête to belay.

GAIRLOCH CRAGS, Meall Lochan a' Chlerich, Stone Valley Crags, Red Wall Crag:

The Wallace – 25m E4 5c. G. Ettle, D. S. B. Wright. 16th June, 1997.
Start 2m left of the obvious groove of Lucky Strike and climb a crack to a ledge at 4m – layback boldly left round a giant flake on treacherous holds. These moves lead to a vital Rock 1 runner, which may eliminate deck-out potential. Continue to the nest of hollow spikes on Lucky Strike, then step left to finish more easily up good cracks. Only Bravehearts need apply.

The Bruce – 25m HVS 5a. G. Ettle, D. S B. Wright. 16th June, 1997.
Follow the initial groove of Lucky Strike for about 5m. Take the groove on the right, laybacking regally on flakes, to a good finish right of Lucky Strike. Beware of spiders!

Strike Two – 40m HVS 5a. D. S. B. Wright, J. R. Mackenzie. 30th May, 1997.
To the right of Lucky Strike is a less-pronounced groove above a spike in the heather ramp. A tricky bulge gains access to the groove which gives enjoyable climbing. Care is needed with some hollow flakes. Continue up to the left on good rock.
Note: Short Sharp Shock regraded as HVS 5b.

Behind Red Wall Crag is a long line of 10m high wall of perfect rock above a grass ledge. The obvious and most tempting line is the centrally placed groove above a narrow ledge.

Playtime Wall – 10m 6b*. J. R. Mackenzie, D. S. B. Wright. 30th May, 1997.
The narrow ledge is not reached easily and the climbing is not over when it is.
Note: Stone Valley Crag: Open Secret regraded as H. Severe 4b***.

Blood Feud – 40m E2 5b**. J. R. Mackenzie, D. S. B. Wright. 30th May, 1997.
Another excellent route and a worthy companion for Bald Eagle. Start to the right of Open Secret's initial crack at a cleaned ledge with a small tree.

1. 20m 5b. Climb the short wall left of the tree to a recess. Climb the bald wall behind the tree via a crack but reach straight up where the crack veers right. Step left and continue up the fine slab to a grass stance.

2. 20m 5a. Above are a pair of black streaks. Start left of them and traverse right and up into them to holds on their left. Finish up the crack above as for Stone Diary.
Note: Pitch 2 done before in mistake for Stone Diary, by the Editor and no doubt others. Melting Pot regraded as E3 4c 6a.

Golden Eagle – 30m E3 6a**. G. Ettle, I. Taylor. 14th June, 1997.
Scramble up the gully or climb to the base of Melting Pot. Climb the excellent left-hand crack of Melting Pot on improving holds. A superb pitch on excellent rock gives the best of the cracks on this wall.

The Time Warp – 30m E3 6a*. G. Ettle, D. S. B. Wright. June, 1997.
To the right of Beer Bottle is a crack. Predictably strenuous, it gives good sustained climbing to easier rock above.

Rum Doodle Crag, Red Barn Crag:
Directly below Rum Doodle Crag lies a lower tier, Red Barn Crag.
Curse you Red Barn! – 25m Mild VS 4b. D. S. B. Wright, G. Ettle. 10th June, 1997.
Red Barn Crag sports a narrow rib of rough rock with a smooth side wall on the right. Climb the short wall to gain the central crackline immediately to the right of the rib, then climb the fine flake crack on the right.

Flying Circus – 30m VS 5a. J. R. Mackenzie, R. Brown. 10th June, 1997.
Start below and left of Curse you Red Barn! and climb a rough slab to the base of the rib immediately to the left of Curse you! Awkward moves to a small overhang which is climbed on hidden holds, then follow the rib direct to the top.

A Load of Old Bosche – 20m VS 4c. R. Brown, J. R. Mackenzie. 10th June, 1997.
To the right of the narrow rib is a smooth wall with a two-step V-groove. The upper groove is a bit messy and restricted.

Hun in the Sun – 20m HVS 5a. G. Ettle, D. S. B. Wright. 10th June, 1997.
The smooth wall to the right has a wide crack which is climbed on marginally hollow holds but good gear. Quite pleasant and open.

Flowerdale Wall:
Lies 250m behind Rum Doodle Crag. It provides a pleasantly steep middle-grade crag composed of juggy but blocky rock or rougher but less hold-ridden red rock. Described from left to right.
Rock Around the Block – 25m HVS 5a. J. R. Mackenzie, R. Brown. 10th June, 1997.
To the right of a small buttress is a narrow crack leading to a wider one. Climb the crack on sharp holds. Step across the wide crack and move right to climb the rib direct taking care of some unsound flakes.

Blyth Spirit – 25m VS 4c*. R. Brown, J. R. Mackenzie. 10th June, 1997.
Good rock. Stand on top of a rock finger right of the last route and climb direct to a small overhang. Climb over this and up a thin, but helpful, crack to the top.

Tormentil Grooves – 25m VS 4b. R. Brown, J. R. Mackenzie. 10th June, 1997.
A pair of wider cracks lies to the immediate right of Blyth Spirit. Climb the right one and move up right to a wide corner-crack, climbed to the top.
Lily of the West – 25m E1 5a*. G. Ettle, D. S. B. Wright. 10th June, 1997.
To the right is a narrow buttress with a snaking crack providing well protected steep climbing in an excellent position. Follow the crack over the crux bulge and finish directly up the edge.

Veinous Fly Trap – 25m HVS 5a. G. Ettle, D. S. B. Wright. 10th June, 1997.
A red slab lies to the right of the buttress of Lily of the West. A shallow corner bounds its left-hand side. Climb this corner somewhat tenuously to the top.

Blood Red Roses – 25m VS 4b*. D. S. B. Wright, G. Ettle. 10th June, 1997.
Just right of the shallow corner, up superb dark red rock. Climb the slab to runners at 13m and exit near some heather.

Mountain Everlasting – 25m HVS 5a. J. R. Mackenzie, R. Brown. 10th June, 1997.
Climb the increasingly thin and bold red slab to the right of Blood Red Roses directly up its crest where the crux awaits near the top.

Note: The Domes: Demon Razor regraded as E3 5c. The Thin Red Line regraded as HVS 4c. The Thug regraded as E2 5b***.

The Flashing Blade – 20m E3 6a*. G. Ettle, I. Taylor. 14th June, 1997.
To the left of The Thug is a left-slanting thin crack. Start up The Thug and climb the blocky groove to the base of the crack. The thin crack gets steadily harder with the crux at the top. Well protected by small Friends.

Cat Burglar – 30m E4 6a***. I. Taylor, G. Ettle, R. Brown. 24th June, 1997.
The formidable-looking wall between Flashing Blade and The Thug. Superb sustained climbing, easier and better protected than it looks. Start up The Thug and then step on to the wall, following a thin overhanging crack all the way.

The Domino Effect – 25m E3 6a. I. Taylor, G. Ettle. 14th June, 1997.
Climbs the left arête of Dome Corner. Climb over a steep bulge to cracks in the wall below the arête (crux), swinging right to gain cracks in the right side of the arête. Finish up easier ground to the top.

Percussion Wall:
There are two clean walls behind and slightly lower down towards the glen than the Domes, the upper pink and quite short, the lower grey and of excellent rough rock. This is Percussion Wall. The wall has a pronounced crack system towards its right end.

Percussion Crack – 25m V. Diff. R. Brown, J. R. Mackenzie. 11th March, 1997.
Climb the crack direct past a ledge at one-third height.

Syncopation Wall – 25m VS 5a. J. R. Mackenzie, R. Brown. 11th March, 1997.
To the left of the crack is a slabby wall; climb this to a ledge, then climb the excellent crack which leads up right to a ramp which is followed by a short wall and the top. Fine climbing.

The Slabs:
Lower down the hillside are a spread of slabby walls, The Slabs, which appear from below as a lower continuation of the right-hand dome.

Wander at Will – 30m Diff. R. Brown, C. White. March, 1997.
The centre of the slabs provide pleasant sport picking the lines of choice.

Stratospheric Pachyderms – 25m VS 5a. R. Brown, J. R. Mackenzie. 11th March, 1997.
The right of the slabs steepens into a pair of cleft bulges.
1. 10m 4b/c. Climb the lower overhang to a cosy niche below the next bulge.
2. 15m 5a. Climb the top bulge more energetically.

Atlantic Wall:
Well to the left of Rum Doodle Crag is a shallow amphitheatre with a vertical back wall as seen from the track. The west-facing right-hand wall of this back wall is Atlantic Wall. Though relatively short, it is vertical and varied, with reasonable protection.

Cannonade – 10m Severe. L. Cannon, D. S. B. Wright, J. R. Mackenzie. 25th August, 1997.
To the left of the right-hand wall is a nice slab which is quite thin and climbed centrally.

The Compleat Angler – 13m Diff. J. R. Mackenzie. 25th August, 1997.
Start up the lichenous slab to the right and take a rightwards line to the top near the next route.

Casting a Line – 12m Diff. J. R. Mackenzie. 25th August, 1997.
Climb the crest of the rib left of the main crag to and over a niche at the top.

The crag now runs rightwards in a continuous wall.

Mutineers – 12m HVS 5a*. D. S. B. Wright, L. Cannon, J. R. Mackenzie. 25th August, 1997.
Start to the right of the left edge of the crag and climb a steepening wall direct to a short crack at the top. This is best turned by a move to the left but can be climbed direct at a higher standard.

The Cruel Sea – 12m E2 5c**. J. R. Mackenzie, L. Cannon, D. S. B. Wright. 25th August, 1997.
By far the best route here. Start in a shallow scoop near the centre of the crag and climb up to a horizontal crack. The top wall overhangs and is climbed direct. Protection is good but awkward to place.

The Ancient Mariner – 12m HVS 5a*. J. R. Mackenzie, L. Cannon, D. S. B. Wright. 25th August, 1997.
Climb directly up the wall to the left of a flake. Step right to a square perch and continue up and slightly left to the top – a strenuous top section.

The Cat – 12m Severe*. D. S. B. Wright. 20th August, 1997.
A tricky route for its grade. Climb over a bulge right of The Ancient Mariner and continue up an exposed wall, moving left near the top to reach hidden holds.

Fruity Crag (MR 794 714):
A small crag north-west of and seen in profile from the left end of Raven Crag. Routes by N. Hodgson and B. Williamson, 15th June, 1996.

Lime – 8m V. Diff. Near the right end of the crag is a bush-filled crack. Climb the corner just to its right.

Mango – 8m Severe. The left-slanting crack line about 3m left of the bush-filled crack.

Orange – 8m Severe. The next full-height crack line about 5m to the left.

Lemon – 8m Severe. At the left end of the crag is a pillar forming a chimney on its right and a crack on its left. Climb the crack and finish right over the top of the pillar.

GRUINARD CRAGS:
Not every route has been recorded here. Several easier ones have been left until next year to coordinate with routes done by local climbers.

Gruinard Crag, Upper Tier:
Quick on the Draw – 40m E5 6a/b**. R. Anderson. 25th May, 1997.
The shallow corner/grooveline immediately right of Paradise Regained. Start right of the holly at a left facing corner. Climb the corner and its shallow continuation to where it blanks out, small wires (good wire out on right also). Move up and place a Friend 0.5 with an RP 2 a wires length above (both poor). Step up and either place a wire in the horizontal crack above, or go for it out left to the ledge of Paradise Regained. Move up and right and continue to a heathery ledge. Either belay here (Friend 2.5) or continue up the crozzly slab on the left.

Pistolero – 40m E3 5c**. R. and C. Anderson. 25th May, 1997.
The crackline immediately right of Quick on the Draw. Start up the short corner, swing out right and climb to the left end of the roof. Pull into a recess and continue up the cracks above to a heather ledge, possible belay (Friend 2.5), then find a line to the top, out left is on more continuous rock.

How The West Was Won – 25m E5 6a***. R. and C. Anderson. 27th July, 1997.
The thin crackline in the front of the buttress between Overlord and Stand and Deliver. Gain the start of the crack from the groove, pull out left onto a ledge, then step right and climb the crack to where it stops. Move left, gain a ledge, then step right to climb the wall and short slab.

Stand and Deliver – 25m E5 6a/b*. R. Anderson. 24th May, 1997.
The thin crackline up the right side of the wall right of Overlord, just left of the fissure at the right end of the crag. Climb the crackline to a ledge. Pull out up right (Stopper 1s) then back up left, good Stopper 2 or RP2 high above, and continue up the crackline, Friend 1.5 up left, to the top.

Dome Crag:
Flawed by Design – 35m E3**. P. Thorburn, R. Campbell. 12th May, 1996.
Climbs the hanging flake right of The Silk Road. Left of Call of the Wild a diagonal crack splits a red wall. Start just to the right.
1. 15m 5b. Gain and climb the crack, then go right up easy ground to belay below a groove.
2. 20m 6a. Follow the groove in the slab and climb the hanging flake.

Call of the Wild, Variation Start – G. Latter, P. Thorburn. 12th May, 1996.
Provides a very sustained route, same grade. Start up Dead Calm, then trend left above the low roof and up the wall to the rest ledge.

Sunk Without Trace – 30m E3 5c*. P. Thorburn, N. Craig. 11th May, 1996.
Somewhat eliminate but pleasant climbing on excellent rock, following the faint groove on the right edge of the wall. Start 3m left of a large block (Grand Recess). The start is probably the same as The Missing Link. Climb a cracked bulge to a ledge (runner in diagonal crack). Pull left into the initially difficult slim groove and follow it to belay in a scoop. Scramble to the top.

Gruinard Jetty Buttress:
At the far right end of the Back West Wall, the crag turns a corner to run up and disappear into the hill side. This arête has a groove and crack in it, and is slightly undercut. There is a clump of trees about 10m up where two routes finish.
Shallow End of the Gene Pool –12m VS 4b. T. Archer (unsec.). 4th August, 1997.
Takes a groove/ramp line just down and to the left of the arête. Many loose flakes.

'I wish I was a little bit taller...' – 10m H. Severe 5a. T. Archer (unsec.). 4th August, 1997.
Climbs the arête. Start with a hard pull over the undercut into the groove in the arête, go slightly to the right to a fine crack and follow this to the ledge and trees. Probably only 4c or 4b if you are taller or get a bunk up from your second!

CREAG BEINN NAM BAN:
Balancing Act – 40m E1 5b*. J. R. Mackenzie, R. Brown. 13th August, 1997.
To the right of Blockbuster is a slab and to the right again a shorter corner. Start at a flange belay to the right of this and climb a steepening rib parallel to it over a bulge

on excellent holds. Climb a thin slab beyond and then step left to a small ledge. Continue up the centre of the slab to the roof at the top and turn this by a crack on the right. Good varied climbing with spaced protection.

Far Cry – 45m HVS 5a**. R. Brown, J. R. Mackenzie. 13th August, 1997.
To the right of Long Distance Runner is a steepening corner that starts above a narrow grass band. Climb a short wall (cairn) to the grass and the corner above. The corner is sustained, strenuous and well protected. Continue in the same line up open slabs on clean rock to the top. Probably the best route here.

To the right of the main crag is a gully. On the gully's right wall is a prominent pinnacle, separated from the sidewall by a chimney. To its right is another slender buttress with another bounding chimney to its right and then a broader buttress. The rock is not so good as on the main face and all the routes are serious for their grade.

Hound-dog Pinnacle – 15m Severe. J. R. Mackenzie, R. Brown. 13th August, 1997.
Climb the frontal (south) face of the pinnacle direct without using the chimney. Rather bold and airy.

Shepherds Warning – 18m HVS 5a. R. Brown, J. R. Mackenzie. 13th August, 1997.
Climb the frontal face of the slender buttress direct to the right of Hound-dog Pinnacle which gives a bold but good climb.

CARNMORE CRAG:
Carnmore Corner Direct – 50m E3 5c***. G. Latter, L. Arnott. 22nd July, 1997.
A brilliant varied pitch, though one of the last routes to dry on the cliff. Belay at some horizontal pockets high on the slab, about 8m above the start of Wilderness. Climb the corner and hand traverse right on a large block at its top to gain the normal route. Continue up this, then direct up an awkward hand crack (wet) to finish up the easier final corner.
Note: The same party also made the second ascent of Wilderness, thinking E4 6a and three stars – a brilliant route on immaculate rock, and one of the hardest on-sight in Scotland for its day (1980). The top pitch does not finish up the original finish of Gob, but another short corner much farther right.

The Grey Wall:
The Proprieter – 35m E2 5c*. G. Latter, L. Arnott. 22nd July, 1997.
A well protected direct finish to The Trampoline. Follow that route to beneath the steep twin cracks in the headwall. Climb the left crack, moving into the deeper right crack with difficulty. Up this past a dubious looking block near its top, then more easily up slabs above to large block belay at top.

NORTHERN HIGHLANDS NORTH AND EAST (VOLUME TWO)

STRATHCONON, Geologist's Slabs (Sheet 26, MR 363 556):
A small but not inconsequential crag composed of the same perfect rough schist as the nearby gabbro slab on Meig Crag. Quartz lenses, unexpected holds and superlative friction up rippled slabs characterises the climbing here, not to mention holds composed entirely of massive brown garnets. Approach from the minor road as for Meig Crag but 250m farther west. The routes are described from left to right.
Pure Gold – 20m E1 5b*. J. R. Mackenzie, R. Brown. 20th April, 1997.
The best route here giving varied climbing on excellent rock. Start near the left of the crag close to an open corner and jam up the overhanging wall to a tricky landing above. Step left and climb an undercut wall and slab via the twin cracks to a tree. Step left and follow the curving thin crack above the overlap to the top.

Garnet Wall – 20m H. evere 4b. R. Brown, J. R. Mackenzie. 20th April, 1997.
The central slab has an overhang at three-quarters height. Start at a tree roughly in the centre and climb the slab via quartz lenses to a garnet-encrusted flake. Climb this to the overhang and surmount on good holds to a tree belay.

SGURR NA LAPAICH, Sgurr nan Clachan Geala (MR 162 343):
The north flank of its east ridge presents a series of striking grooves and ribs. (Lapland Buttress is on the SE side of the ridge, Northern Highlands vol. 2, p32.) The most obvious feature is a slim corner line with a roof part way up and an impressive wide crack high on its left wall. As this crag faces north and its foot lies at an altitude of 950m, a sustained period of dry weather is required.
Lap of the Gods – 75m E1*. G. E. Little, J. Finlay. 12th July, 1997.
This route climbs a near parallel line up the wide rib to the left of the obvious slim corner. Start at the very foot of the rib a few metres down and left of two distinctive leaning flakes.
1. 30m 5a. Gain and climb a slim groove on the left side of the rib to reach a short messy diagonal fault. Move left up this to stand on a spike at the very edge. Step across left to blocks on a turf ledge.
2. 15m 5b. Ascend the surprisingly awkward groove above the belay, then move left on to a tiny rock ledge. Pull up into an open corner and climb this to a rock ledge under a roof on the right.
3. 30m 4c. Move back left into the corner, then pull up on to a turf cap. Climb a short strenuous wall, then move up into a chimney/corner. Climb this and broken ground above to the top. Traverse off right along a wide grassy shelf.

AN RIABHACHAN:
Redcoats Weep – 75m III. R. Bale, K. McKintosh. 1st February, 1998.
The obvious icefall on the right of the coire – Sheet 25, MR 142 352. Climb the three-tiered icefall (steeper on the left) for 50m. Belay on a large spike in a corner. Climb the easier iced corner above (25m). (Also climbed by N. Kenworthy and C. Wright next day.)
Note: The route may have been done before, possibly in the early 80's by T McDonald and party.

SGURR NA MUICE, North-East Face:
Suckling for Suckers – 120m IV,4. J. R. Mackenzie, P. Whitfield. 10th March, 1998.
The left-bounding rib of Pearls Before Swine. The climb was started from the Snow Apron but could include any of the more direct routes from below to extend the line considerably. Start just left of the gully of Pearls at the lowest rocks and climb steepening ground to an overhanging wall. Surmount the left wall of this groove to follow the arête to a bay (45m). Continue up the groove on thin ice to turf, then climb another thin cracked and unhelpful groove to overlook the left fork of Pearls (25m). Climb the rib parallel to the left fork to a big bay and climb either the central ice runnel or move right and up to the same place; the top is just beyond (50m). Climbed under heavy snow and marginal turf; thinner but icier conditions should transform it into a very pleasant excursion at Grade III.

Pork Scratchings – 160m III,4. P. Whitfield, J. R. Mackenzie (alt.). 24th January, 1998.
Follow the right-hand couloir and turn the lower tier of crags on the right, to gain

the snow rake on the left. Pork Scratchings takes the overhang-blocked groove to the left of a deeper overlapped V-groove. Climb the groove to the overhang (18m). Step right and climb to a narrow slot which provides an entertaining crux, then continue straight up (42m). The angle now lessens but the climb takes the central groove direct which gives the most interest (50m). Continue in the same line to the summit (50m).

Totally Hamless – 160m II/III. J. R. Mackenzie, D. Broadhead. 31st January, 1998. This is the next groove to the left of Pork Scratchings, unfortunately lessening in angle after 50m or so. Climb a narrow groove (which is to the right of the deeper chimney of Three Little Pigs) and step left into a turfier one. Continue over a steepening to thread belays above (40m). Continue straight up (40m). Continue up the best line above which takes in a thin slab (50m). Continue easily to the summit (30m). Not very inspiring but the easiest route on the face.

Pigsty Gully, Central Finish – II. J. R. Mackenzie, D. Broadhead. 31st January, 1998.
This direct finish is the central narrow exit to the left of the usual bay. It gave very steep snow and a cornice. Good.

FANNICHS, Sgurr Mor, East Face:
Transfiguration – 300m IV,5. B. Davison, A. Nisbet. 5th February, 1998.
Climbs the left side of the Resurrection face. Start on the right side of the buttress between Easter Gully and the dead-end gully at the start of Resurrection. Climb a groove, then easier ground to a recess on the right which leads to easy ground (100m). Continue up a vague rib on the right of Easter Gully to a final steepening. This could be climbed direct to make a Grade III, perhaps even II if the left side of the initial buttress was climbed, but a more interesting finish was to go diagonally right on ramps into the hanging groove in the steep ground above the final snowfield of Resurrection. Finish up this.

Note: Sgurr nan Clach Geala: Rob Archbold and John Higham note that the description of the original winter line on Skyscraper Buttress in *Scottish Winter Climbs* is incorrect (as is the line diagram in *Cold Climbs*). The original route moved left onto the crest of the buttress after one pitch above the summer crux. Thereafter the narrow frontal face, which forms the 'crest ' or 'headwall' of the steep upper buttress, was followed in its entirety (c.120m). It would appear that Empire State Variation lies nearby on this steep frontal face, touching the left edge in part.

BEINN DEARG, Coire Ghranda:
Campbell's Corner – 100m III. J. Currie, G. Robertson. 8th March, 1998.
The icy line on the right of the broken crag below and right of the Upper Cliff.

Cona Mheall, West Face:
Twisted Rib – 300m III,4. J. Currie, G. Robertson, P. Robertson. 24th January, 1998.
The longest defined ridge on the face (immediately left of Tower of Enchantment), almost reaching the loch. Entertaining; the final step is hard.

Spindryer Buttress – 200m V,7. G. Robertson, P. Robertson. 1st March, 1998.
The steep buttress immediately right of Spaghetti Gully gives excellent icy climbing in its lower half. Start just right of the gully mouth and left of an obvious smooth diedre.

1. 25m. Climb a short difficult crack to a ledge. Move up into the obvious groove and climb this past two overhangs to large blocks.
2. 15m. Make an exposed traverse right and step down round the edge. Move up.
3. 50m. Work back up left immediately to gain and climb a series of excellent icy grooves in the crest.
4. 100m. The upper half is easier, climbed just right of the crest.

SEANA BHRAIGH, Luchd Coire:

A Girl's Best Friend – 245m IV,5. M. Bass, S. Yearsley. 24th January, 1998.
A fine mixed route taking the steep ground on the right flank of Diamond Buttress, before crossing Diamond Edge to an independent finish. Start in Diamond Diedre, 20m up from the foot of the buttress at an obvious ramp.
1. 45m. Climb the left-slanting ramp. Just before reaching the buttress crest, climb a steep wall above the ramp. Move right, crossing an awkward step, and continue straight up to a large stance.
2. 25m. Continue up and right by short chimneys, staying below the crest of the buttress, to the top of a snowfield.
3. 25m. Move left round the obvious rib. Continue straight up, then make a short traverse right to below an obvious chimney with a large flat chockstone. Climb steeply up to the foot of the chimney.
4. 25m. Traverse delicately right, then pull steeply upwards through a series of short corners to the buttress crest. Continue up to belay on the ramp of Diamond Edge.
5. 45m. Cross the ramp of Diamond Edge and climb an obvious corner to gain the top of the rib on the left of Diamond Edge. Continue up the rib, easily at first and then on steeper rock. Step left round a nose, then up.
6. 40m. Gain an open corner line leading to easy ground.
7. 40m. Climb the easy ground via a short wall to the plateau.

BODACH BEAG (p112):

Light Entertainment – 220m II. R. Webb. February, 1998.
The buttress right of Freevater Gully. Finishes on the summit, 'similar to Dorsal Arête but far better views'.

RHUE SEA CLIFFS:

Hold Steady – 12m VS 4c*. A. Cunningham, J. Cunningham. May, 1996.
Climb straight up just to the right of Halcyon Days.

Nil Desperandum – 15m E1 5b**. A. Cunningham, J. Cunningham. June, 1996.
Pull over the undercut to the left of Ruder Games and right into the hanging left-facing corner. Climb the corner to the roof and move right on to the slab to finish up the left edge.

Firing Line – 25m E1 5b*. A. Cunningham, C. Downer. August 1997.
Between Cat's Whiskers and The Barchan. Climb a right-facing curving corner line, move right at its top into a crack (often wet) and up to the break. Swing left into the large left-facing corner above and up this and crack on the slab, moving left at the top capping bulge.

Sun Trap – 8m Severe. B. Chislett, I. Brandt. July, 1996.
Start 3m left of Picnic Slab. Climb the steep wall and the left-slanting crack in the slab to a ledge. Step right and up to finish on the descent rib.

RHUE:

Low sandstone walls at MR 097 977, west-facing. Short and scope limited, but good climbing.

Southern Outcrop:

A steep bank below the southern outcrop means a nasty landing. Routes 6m-9m long, by J. Oberhauser and R. Pringle (Headless Chicken only) on 3rd May, 1997.

Slow Strain – HVS 5a. The obvious crack-line. Short but sharp.

Headless Chicken – VS 5a. The undercut scoop 4m right of Slow Strain.

Left Edge – H. Severe. The left arête of the detached block.

Right Edge – HVS 4c. The overhanging right arête.

Back Wall – VS 4c. Up the middle of the back wall of the detached block.

Back Wall, Right-Hand – H. Severe. Right of Back Wall.

Right Wall – Severe. Up the flake on the right-hand side of the rightmost wall, and wall above.

Northern Outcrop:

Same day, routes 7m-13m long, by R. Pringle.
Serious Slab – Mod. The obvious slab provides an easy ascent/descent.

Ocean Arête – Diff.

Avoiding the Cleft – Severe. Between Ocean Arête and The Cleft.

The Cleft – V. Diff. Up the wall to the cleft, then up the cleft.

Caileag Bhoidheach – Severe. The wall right of the cleft.

Fruitcake Wall – Severe. Up the obvious blind crack in the largest unbroken part of the wall.

North-Facing Buttress:

This lies on the north side of the 102m hill north of Rhue, about 200m round from the previous buttresses. Thickly lichened, might become with more traffic, a worthwhile inland option.
Sand Martin – 30m VS 4c. R. Pringle, J. Oberhauser. 3rd May, 1997.
Start at the lowest point of the buttress. Move up a whitish slab and up the left-hand side of an overhanging block, then walk right to an overhanging block abutting the red wall on the right. Interesting moves over the block, then traverse rightwards across the gently overhanging red wall by a continuous handrail to reach an easy arête, followed to the top.

Gwirx – 30m VS 4c. J. Oberhauser, R. Pringle. 3rd May, 1997.
Start as for Sand Martin, then continue up leftwards from above the overhanging block, initially along a block-filled crack before moving slightly rightwards up a rounded wall to avoid a large overhang. Finish up an easy lichenous groove.

ARDMAIR, Fish Farm Walls:

The following two routes are on the broken three-tiered buttress first encountered on the path and bordered on the left by a wide heathery gully – a line of descent.
Peace at Last – 50m E1*. K. Geddes, A. Cunningham. June, 1996.
1. 20m 5a. Start by a 4m detached pillar by the high path at the base of the first tier. Climb on to the pillar and step into the right-facing corner above. Move up to the bulge and left on to the slab. Go easily up the slab to belay below the steep wall.

2. 12m 5b. Climb the steep 'red and green' crack in the wall to the right of the overhung corner. Belay well back on the next terrace.

3. 18m 4b. Move rightwards up the slab into an overhung recess. Pull up into the wide crack and out left. Move up and right into the corner to finish.

Family Life – 40m E3*. C. Lesenger, A. Cunningham. July, 1996.

1. 20m 5b. Scramble up and left of the detached block of Peace at Last and start below the undercut slab. Move up to and climb a short overhanging straight crack and make a difficult move left and up on to the slab. Go easily up to a heathery pull onto the first terrace below the steep wall.

2. 10m 5c/6a. Awkward starting moves up the right diagonal crack lead to a steep finish up the vertical crack half way up the wall. Belay behind the block.

3. 10m 4a. Move right and step up on to the cracked slab to finish.

Brent Spar – 35m E3*. A. Cunningham, J. Cunningham. August, 1996.

To the left of Loan Shark is another vague crack in the slab.

1. 20m 6a. Scramble up to the heathery terrace below the vague crack. Make steep tenuous moves rightwards across the overhanging base into the crackline. Move up on to the slab and follow the crack on to the terrace.

2. 15m 5b. Climb a right diagonal groove at the left end of the top wall.

Rainbow Warrior – 30m E2 5b**. A. Cunningham, J. Pickering. May, 1994.

To the left of Hammerhead the crag has a steep lower wall, a mid-height horizontal break and a bulging upper wall cut by a few groove lines. To the left of centre is a right trending ramp in the lower wall. Climb the ramp to the break and pull directly over the bulge to finish up the right-trending groove above.

Monster Buttress:

The following two routes are on the slabby wall round on the left side of the little 'Laggavoulin' buttress.

Bowmore – 10m V. Diff. A. Cunningham, J. Pickering. 1st December, 1994.

Cracks up the left side of the slabby wall.

Clyneleish – 10m M. Severe. A. Cunningham, J. Pickering. 1st December, 1994.

Cracks and heathery breaks near the right side of the wall.

La Petamine – 30m HVS 5a**. A. Cunningham, K. Geddes. 16th June, 1996.

The left hand of the three 'ramplines', left of Les Rosbif. Start up Raven in the big bay and climb out rightwards onto the line. Move awkwardly round the big block and finish up the top corner in a gripping position.

Arapiles Wall:

Dounreay Exposé – 20m E2 5c. A. Cunningham, K. Geddes, J. Cunningham. June,1996.

A line to the right of Antipodean Cruise. Move left along the low ledge and climb up through the bulging wall to the big break. Finish by twin wide cracks in the top wall.

Beast Buttress:

Beast in the Undergrowth – 25m Severe. K. Geddes, J. Cunningham, A.Cunningham. June,1996.

Start to the left of Market Day and climb up into a heather topped corner. Climb this and the big slabby right facing corner and wide crack above.

On the Western Skyline, Alternative Start – E5 6a/b overall. D. Cuthbertson, B. Hall. May, 1994.

Takes the thin diagonal crack in the lower wall, protected at half-height by a Friend #0 inverted in a little niche. A very good route.
Note: On the Western Skyline is quite bold in its own right.

Big Roof Butttress:

Close to the Bone – 25m HVS 5a*. A. Cunningham, J. Pickering. 1st December, 1994.
Start between Bolshie Ballerina and First Fruits. Climb a right-facing groove and short corner right of B.B. onto the slab. Move up and finish via a crack in the wall on the left (right of Old Dog, New Tricks).

Kidz on the Block – 30m E1 5a. F. Fotheringham, A. Cunningham. August, 1996.
Takes a left-curving line of least resistance up the ground below Town Without Pity. Climb up into a wide flake crack on the right of the bay. Move up on to the slab above and traverse left under the overhangs to finish.

KEANCHULISH CRAG (Sheet 19, MR 128 998):

This SE-facing crag is in a narrow defile that runs up from Keanchulish House. Access is from a parking bay on the A835 at MR 134 997, as for Evening Wall (SMCJ 1995, p663). The crag lies behind and west of the outcrops above. The easiest approach is to walk down the road until past the short outcrops and then head round the hillside to the crag. The crag is of a pronounced horizontally-layered Torridonian sandstone and is mainly lichen free although there are areas of heather. The heavily-eroded rock runs to some bizarre roofs and sculpted flutings which, so far, have proved sounder than appearances would suggest. The left end is undercut by huge roofs and bottomed by a pink slab. The central section is continuous and undercut and runs past a little buttress leaning against the wall. Farther right is a corner and beyond that, more broken ground leads to another huge roof. The best descent is by heather ramps on the right or north side where a short corner leads to easy shelves. The climbs are described from right to left.

Patey's Back Yard – 50m Mild VS*. R. J. Brown, D. Ogden. 5th May, 1996.
Start at the inset corner near the right end of the central section.
1. 30m 4a. Climb the corner or the arête to the right and climb another corner above. Trend right to climb flakes and belay in a large square-cut niche.
2. 20m 4b. Leave the niche by a crack up its right corner and continue up this fine crack to the top.

The Limboist – 40m E2*. J. R. Mackenzie, R. J. Brown. 9th September, 1997.
Climbs the wall left of Patey's Back Yard over the twin roofs.
1. 15m 5c. Climb a short wall and surmount the roof via a thin crack; continue to the next roof which is as awkward and has a thin landing on a shelf.
2. 25m 5a. Continue up a slabby wall, then take the short steepening wall just right of the arête to step right to a slab. Climb this to a ledge and finish up the wide corner-crack.

Zig-Zag – 60m Severe. R. J. Brown, D. Ogden. 5th May, 1996.
This starts at the small buttress left of Patey's Back Yard.
1. 25m. Climb up to a good ledge and move leftwards into a large open bay and climb this to another ledge. Traverse along this to the left to a square notch in the floor.
2. 35m. Move slightly right and climb the bulge and zig-zag up the wall briefly looping beyond Fancy Free to avoid difficulties en route and reach a crack which is climbed to a square block.

Fancy Free – 30m Mild VS 4c*. R. J. Brown, J. R. Mackenzie. 9th September, 1997.

A line of roofs runs above the lower wall; where these end just right of a jutting roof with a loose block, climb slabby rock trending left to a break through an overhang higher. Above this, continue up delightful slabs, surmounting the crux bulge and climbing the fine wall just right of a straight crack to the top.

Aeolian Wall – 30m VS 4c*. J. R. Mackenzie. 4th March, 1997.

A good route, easier than it looks. To the left of the crag are large overhangs and right of these a corner runs up bordering the main face. Start in the corner and climb this for a few metres until possible to climb the right wall before stepping right below a short corner. Climb this and continue to the overhung corner above (crux) which is climbed before trending left up shelves to finish up a nicely-rounded wall.

MORNING WALL (Sheet 15, MR 137 000):

A few hundred metres to the left of Evening Wall (SMCJ 1995, p663) and at a slightly higher level is Morning Wall, 20m high, composed of sound Torridonian sandstone, steep and protectable mainly by Friends. Park at the same layby as for Evening Wall and an approach of less than 10 minutes takes one to the crag which has a continuous overhanging lower section that ends in shorter corners and walls towards the left-hand end. It is reasonably quick drying and provides some strenuous climbing in the central area and more relaxed climbs to the left. Routes described from left to right.

Morning Wall – 20m E2 5c*. J. R. Mackenzie, R. Brown. 9th September, 1997.

The right end of the crag is marked by a steep groove with an oak tree. Start to the left of the groove beneath a break in the overhanging wall and climb it on excellent holds. Climb the sustained and thin slabby wall parallel and left of the groove, past a weirdly technical crux and then up, to move left and exit rather thinly.

Steel Spider – 25m E2 5c/6a**. R. Brown, J. R. Mackenzie. 28th October, 1997.

A superb route, much easier than it looks, and takes the centre of the overhanging wall, small Friends essential to prevent deck-out. Start at a shallow overhanging bay and climb the steeply overhanging edge to a long reach up right, vital FR#0 up left under a small roof. Continue up on good hidden holds to overcome the lower crux section. Continue straight up on steep rock to the capping overhang and jam left underneath this to exit.

Grumbling Grooves – 15m Severe 4b. R. Brown, J. R. Mackenzie. 28th October, 1997.

To the left of Steep Spider the overhanging wall ends in a corner. To the left again past a flakey chimney is a deeper inset corner. Climb this corner to the capping roof, traverse left under this to another corner. Climb this which widens to a narrow chimney, to the top. The bald buttress to the right of the second corner has been top-roped at a tenuous 6a.

CAMUS MOR SEA CLIFFS (Sheet 15; MR 103 009):

Near the coastal path from just north of Ullapool to Achiltibuie. Best approached either by the boggy track from Blughasary or infinitely better by boat. The Torridonian sandstone crags take the form of a curved edge with a steep west-facing side wall above heather rakes and which swings round to a south-facing sea wall that can only be approached from the west unless at low tide. The rock is basically sound but the yellow areas and those which are honeycomed require caution. Much of the climbing on the crag is more like gritstone than Torridonian and has deep cracks, flanges and surprisingly good holds in unlikely places, particularly the areas to the right of the Concave Slab.

The rock is largely clean and has excellent friction. Friends provide the bulk of the protection, as do an armoury of large nuts, although wires are useful. The climbing is by and large quite serious. The left end of the side wall has a shorter series of groove lines before displaying an impressive concave slab that epitomises the best of the negative features of this rock. To the right the crag steepens and forms walls and corners including a most impressive gully. To the right the wall contains a splendid corner before rounding to the south. The maximum height of the cliffs is in excess of 100m. The left end of the crag is the shortest but on good rock, with the crag rapidly gaining height to the right of the Concave Slab in a series of grooves, corners, slabs and walls, sometimes with areas of loose rock flakes.

The best descent is to follow the left edge of the crags up left and to follow a ledge that reaches the base adjacent to an easy-angled buttress that marks the extreme left end of the cliff. To approach from the track above, follow a small burn that runs down to the sea with the crag on its left. From a sea approach the best landing is a small rock inlet with a little waterfall to the left of the crags. The climbs are described from left to right, starting to the left of the Concave Slab at the easy-angled buttress.

Flotsam – 30m M. Severe 4b. R. Brown, J. R. Mackenzie. 28th May, 1997.
The easy-angled buttress has a steep base which rises up the hillside. A short distance up rightwards is a prominent undercut nose which gives the technical crux. Move up left, then follow much easier but clean rock up right.

Concave Slab:
The central section is bottomed by a roof with a nose of rock split by a crack. The climbing is on rounded holds with spaced protection and gets progressively steeper.
Carpe Diem – 30m VS 4b/c*. R. Brown, J. R. Mackenzie. 17th April, 1997.
Start at a wide crack in the nose centrally under the roofs and gain a shallow crack up left. Follow this pleasantly to a marginally wobbly pinnacle and climb over this to the top. Technically quite easy for the grade but a bit bold in places.

Midges Ate My Friend – 30m E1 5b**. K. Howett, G. E. Little. 19th September, 1994.
Takes a good line up the middle of the Concave Slab. Start as for Carpe Diem and move right above the roof to a central crack. Climb the grass-tufted crack to the top in an elegant position.

Good Intentions – 35m H. Severe 4a. J. R. Mackenzie, R. Brown. 17th April, 1997.
Start to the right of the roof and follow the narrow slab up left to a delicate section on the front face which leads quite boldly up before traversing right to a niche below a corner. Climb the corner and then step left to climb the final slab.

To the right of the Concave Slab is one of the best areas on the crag, a steep buttress of rough rock with a pair of opposing-angled corners to the left and right.
Corsair – 40m E2 5b**. J. R. Mackenzie, R. Brown. 28th May, 1997.
This excellent climb takes the wide groove to the left of the central buttress. Climb a slab and a wide crack left of a chimney to a corner which is awkward and leads to a little ledge. Climb the crux corner above which is particularly unhelpful and then climb the easier buttress above to the right of some broken ledges.

Pieces of Eight – 40m E2**. J. R. Mackenzie, R. Brown. 20th September, 1997.
Takes the cleft rib between Corsair and Buccaneer. Superb climbing with a serious second pitch.
1. 25m 5b. Climb the cleft and step left under a bulging crack; jam up this to a hidden ledge and move up right to the edge in a superb position. Climb this edge to awkward belays below a roof.
2. 15m 5a. Climb the roof above the belay and gain the unprotected slab; traverse this delicately up left to the exposed edge (vital Fr 1 runner on left). Climb directly up the edge and continue straight up over a footless bulge on the right to finish above.

Buccaneer – 40m HVS 5a**. G. E. Little, K. Howett. 19th September, 1994.
Takes the corner to the right of the crest of the buttress. This is a really good route, much easier than its appearance would suggest, with the crux the very last move. The protection is good. Climb the steepening slabby left wall to a small ledge, then surmount bulges up and right in an exposed position to finish up a short hanging corner which is seen from below as a straight leaning crack to the left of a more contorted one.

Grapeshot – 50m VS. R. Brown, J. R. Mackenzie. 20th September, 1997.
To the right of Buccaneer is an inset groove with a poised flake and rose bush.
1. 30m 4b. Climb up the wall to the groove and a narrow chimney past the flakes and enter a narrow corner. Climb level with the rose bush and make a step right to a shelf. Climb directly up the slabby wall to the big roof above. Step left on to the lip of the roof and traverse left to its far edge in an exposed position, continue up mossy rock to a ledge below the top wall.
2. 20m 4c. Climb through the cracked roof above via a fragile jug handle and easier rock to the top.

Right of the last route and past a chimney are some heather rakes bottomed by a fine short wall of cracks. Just beyond and above some heather ledges, a superb clean wall of top-quality sandstone extends right to end at more dirty rock to the right. This immaculate wall is topped by a heather ledge and a shorter top tier of rock.

Pure Gold – 45m E1***. R. Brown, J. R. Mackenzie. 20th September, 1997.
The daunting-looking wall is climbed right up the centre and is far easier than it looks. Start left of a square-cut overhang.
1. 25m 5b. Climb steep flake holds to a narrow ledge. Now climb the wall up and slightly left to near the top where a move left leads to a final wall. A brilliant pitch.
2. 20m. Climb up the top wall right of a crack, following the best line to the crest.

Fools Gold – 35m E3 5c**. J. R. Mackenzie, R. Brown. 24th September, 1997.
An excellent, bold route with delicate climbing; the crux section is sustained and unprotected. Start to the right of Pure Gold, following the black streak. Climb up to and across the square-cut overhang on its left side and follow an increasingly rounded crack up the black streaked wall. The rock is friendlier above, following the black streak to near the top where the route traverses out right and takes the centre of the wall, climbing between two boulders and so to the top.

Hidden Treasure – 40m VS 4c*. R. Brown, J. R. Mackenzie. 24th September, 1997.
This interesting climb takes the flanged crack to the right of the square-cut overhang. Climb a nice, brown slab to the first bulge and climb the crack to the wide flange. The crux is quite bold and negotiates this curiosity to a thinner crack above.

Bob Brown on the first ascent of 'Hit and Run', Camus Mor. Photo: John Mackenzie.

Step right on to a pleasant slab where the crack becomes mossy and continue straight up to finish.

The steep and less attractive crag to the immediate right of the 'immaculate wall' soon improves and is composed of two tiers of cracked sandstone separated by a heather shelf. The next route takes a line up these tiers.

Freebooter – 65m E1*. J. R. Mackenzie, R. Brown. 19th August, 1997.
Start on a ramp that runs below the lower cracked wall which lies to the right of a dirty short corner.
1. 25m 5a. Climb the left-hand crack, initially overhanging, and continue up to a large heather terrace.
2. 20m 4a. Climb the shorter wall behind, overcoming an initial bulge to belay below a fine pink cracked wall.
3. 20m 4c. Climb the crack to the right of a cracked roof to step right and move up right to a short finishing crack roughly centrally in the wall, an excellent pitch.

Up and right of Freebooter's second pitch is a steep orange wall that ends in a vertical arête. To the left of this arête and wall is a hidden corner running up to a conspicuous overhang. To reach this area, gain a heather ledge to the right of Hidden Treasure and traverse right to reach the terrace. Continue going right to the base of the corner in an exposed position.

Hit and Run – 40m E1*. J. R. Mackenzie, R. Brown. 24th September, 1997.
Good protection, variety and fine positions.
1. 15m 5b. Climb the impending corner more easily than it would appear from below, exit left below the roof to a ledge above.
2. 25m. Traverse the crack on the lip of the roof rightwards to a wide groove and climb this very pleasantly to the top.

To the right the cliff rapidly gains in height as heather shelves drop towards the sea. The next major feature is an impressive pale corner that runs the height of the cliff, bounding the vertical wall and arête mentioned above.

Keelhaul – 70m E2**. R. Brown, J. R. Mackenzie. 28th May, 1996.
A fine 'butch' route, which takes the corner, definitely not for lycra or shorts. Take huge Friends and nuts, the larger the better. Scramble up heather to below a short hanging chimney, usually wet.
1. 20m 4b. Climb the chimney to heather and follow this to below a fine lower continuation of the main corner.
2. 10m 5a. Bridge the corner on rather powdery rock to continue up the groove to a slab stance in the main corner.
3. 20m 5c. The overhanging and off-width crack is best climbed by deep jams to emerge like a cork from a bottle on to a Billiard Table stance.
4. 20m 4b. Easily at first up the deep chimney behind, then an exposed rib is gained which leads to a step left and a delicate finish.

To the right of the corner is a deep and overhanging gully, often wet with some cavernous chockstones near the top. The crag is at its most continuous to the right of the gully and presents a vertical wall that swings south facing the sea.

Hearts of Oak – 45m VS 4c**. J. R. Mackenzie, R. Brown. 28th May, 1996.
To the right of the overhanging gully is a bulging buttress, then a vertical shallow chimney/groove. Easier than it looks. Scramble up a short wet chimney to the right of the lower one on Keelhaul and follow heather below the gully to a crack directly beneath bare oak tree.

Lynn Hill and Dave Cuthbertson on the televised first ascent of the Great Arch, Pabbay. Photo: Richard Else.

1. 15m 4c. Climb the crack which has an awkward landing.

2. 30m 4c. Work right below an overhang, then step left before stepping back right. Follow the flakes in an impressive situation to surmount loose chockstones (crux) before easier rock leads to the top.

Hang Dog Cracks – 60m E4 *. J. R. Mackenzie, R. Brown. 19th August, 1997.
Midway between Hearts of Oak and Dreadnaught a crackline snakes up the wall. Start to the right and lower than Hearts of Oak at a slab.

1. 25m 5b. Climb the overhanging wall on huge jugs to a rounded landing on a ledge, move right to below a thin crack and follow this with interest to a heather ledge. Move left to belay below the left-hand of the overhanging cracks.

2. 25m 6a. The left-hand and straight crack is rounded, sustained and provides neither holds nor rests and is difficult to protect, though the protection (mostly Friends) is good when placed. Continue up merely vertical rock above, trending right on good holds, to finish in a tremendous position near the edge by a crack.

3. 10m. Continue easily up the arête to finish by scrambling.

Dreadnaught – 80m E3 5c**. J. R. Mackenzie, R. Brown. 17th April, 1997.
Takes the prominent hanging corner and steep headwall well right of the gully and left of the edge of the crag where it swings south. Possibly the best line on the crags, sustained and well protected. The heather rakes end about 30m or so above the sea.

1. 20m 4b. Contour into the crag at a slightly higher level to gain a short corner to the left of a flanged corner up right. Climb three short walls left of this flange and move right to a stance at the base of the main corner which is of a pale yellow rock.

2. 20m 5b. Climb the fine corner over various bulges, often wet, to a stance below a cracked bulge.

3. 25m 5c. The bulge above is the crux. Move up left to gain a vertical crack which leads to a cave (probably more logical to belay here). Traverse out right and climb the pleasant groove to a stance.

4. 15m. Continue up the easier blunt rib on the left to the top.

Albatross – 120m VS 4c*. J. R. Mackenzie, R. Brown. 15th May, 1997.
The longest possible route on the crag; the top pitches make up for what is rather broken lower down. The first pitch is only accessible at low tide, otherwise it is possible to contour round precariously on heather shelves to the right to gain the second pitch. To gain access at low tide, descend to the small inlet and climb a flake-chimney on the right. Traverse a ledge past a small tree and descend to sea level. Enter a hole and follow a narrow squeeze passage to a bay on the other side. Cross this and traverse an overhung ledge a short distance above the water to a low platform with a honeycombed cave above.

1. 35m 4c. Climb to the cave and step up right. Continue up and right to an exposed step right, then climb up to gain the edge of the crag where three mantleshelves on rounded rock lead to a narrow chimney.

2. 40m. Climb the chimney and step right to gain a corner which is climbed to further short walls and slabs which end in a little buttress below a big rock ledge. Gain the ledge.

3. 25m 4c. Walk left along the ledge to below the recessed central corner. Climb the shelves, then the vertical corner and its continuation, a fine pitch.

4. 20m 4c. Climb the short steep corner above to a ledge, then the next corner which has a difficult exit.

Top Crag:

A short but well-defined line of crags running along the top of the main wall.
Rectangular Recess – 10m Severe 4a. J. R. Mackenzie, R. Brown. 17th April, 1997.
Above the exit of Dreadnaught is a well defined square recess in the crag left of an overhang. Climb the recess with some interest.

STAC POLLAIDH, West Buttress (No.1):

Party Direct – 70m VS*. A. Cunningham and Party. September, 1996.
2. 15m 4c. Climb the chockstone corner above the belay of pitch 1 to belay at the top of pitch 3.
Note: The awkward bulge on pitch 3 was also climbed without a nut for aid at 5a.
Note: H. Lancashire and M. Waters note that they repeated Walking on Air considering it E5 6a 6c and failed on Mid Flight Crisis, possibly E5 also because of a bold and a not-obvious start to pitch 2. A number of other routes in the area at E4 and E5 were climbed and the grades thought OK.

Upper No.2 Buttress:

Cold Shoulder – 25m E2 5c**. C. Lesenger, A. Cunningham. July, 1996.
At the right end of the buttress is a large recess. Climb the very steep crackline out of the right side of the recess. Move left at the final bulge and back right to finish.

No. 3 Buttress:

Summer Isles Crack – 15m E1 5b. A. Cunningham, C. Downer. 20th August, 1997.
This is the widening finger crack in the final tier of Summer Isles Arête which is avoided by that route. A bit loose at the top bulge! Access may be made by a traverse in from Pinnacle Basin on the left.

REIFF: Pinnacle Area:

Becalmed – 15m E1 5c*. A. Cunningham, J. Pickering, B. Chislet. July, 1995.
The arête below and left of Atlantic Swell. Start down in the tidal slot right of Tangle of the Isles, with the crux being the initial overhanging wall.

Underworld – 20m VS 4c. A. Cunningham, J. Pickering. July, 1995.
The wall below Edge of the Sea, starting in the tidal boulders. Climb the corner and move right to the edge. Up this via the horizontal breaks.

Velvet Scooter – 10m M. Severe. A. Cunningham and party. May, 1996.
Climb the wall right of Midreiff

Reiff Case – E3 6c. P. Higginson. 23rd June, 1997.
Climb the wall just right of Earth Shaker via a small vertical layaway in the centre of the wall.

Booby – 8m V. Diff. A. Cunningham and party. May, 1996.
Up steep blocky ground at the end of the wall left of Diagonal Crack.
Chimney Corner – 8m Diff. A. Cunningham and party May, 1996.
Opposite Booby on the right of the descent.
Unnamed – 5m 5b. A. Cunningham. 1993.
A boulder problem via horizontal breaks up the leaning wall round the corner from the Wedding Wall.

Bouldering Cliff:

Razorback – 10m E3 6c. A. Powell. 30th August, 1997.
The arête right of Romancing the Stone, taken direct via a very dynamic start.

Undertow – 24m E7/8 6b/c***. D. Cuthbertson. July, 1995.

The magnificent wall left of Wyatt Earp. Start at a little stepped overlap. Stand on a block to reach the undercuts and gain the podded crack. Climb this to the upper and smaller of three beaks (large Friends useful in the middle break). Step right and climb the next podded crack with a long reach to the central break. Move right into the cave. Exit the cave by means of a horizontal crack on the right and ascend to a pocket. Gain the base of a short right-facing hanging groove (wires) which leads strenuously to the top.

Black Rocks:

Dalriada – 20m E1 5b**. A. Cunningham, J. Pickering. October, 1994.

The blunt arête left of Pot Black. Start up Poll Dubh and climb across the leaning wall onto the arête.

Robin – 25m E2 5c*. A. Cunningham, J. Pickering. June, 1994.

The headwall between Tystie Slab and Batman. Up the easy slab (possible belay) and up the headwall via long reaches between thin breaks.

Enlightenment – 20m VS 4c*. A. Cunningham, J. Pickering. October, 1994.

Escape from the crux at the top of Dark Truths via a hand traverse along the break on the right and up to finish. A great position!

Seal Song Area:

Final Fling –15m E1 5b. S. Richardson, J. Wilkinson. 22nd June, 1997.

A counter-diagonal to Moody Blues. Start just right of Overhanging Crack. Climb up and right crossing Moody Blues to finish up the short hanging right-angled corner in the centre of the wall left of Diamond Back.

Slab Inlet:

School's Out – 20m VS 4c. C. Lesenger, A. Cunningham. June, 1996.

Climbs the wall right of Ali Shuffle near the right edge, via amenable horizontal breaks. Access by abseil to a ledge round the corner on the right and start by a swing down on to the wall.

Mellow Water Melon – 12m HVS 5b. L. Johnston, M. Collins, S. Thompson. July, 1997.

Takes the prominent central crack in the rectangular wall 5m right of Ali Shuffle and 10m left of Finger Bowl. The start requires low tide.

Turbulent Indigo – 12m E2 5c**. A. Cunningham, C. Lesenger, J.Cunningham. June, 1996.

Take the right diagonal crack up the overhanging wall above the tunnel entrance. Start off the big block.

Platform Walls:

The Irish Agreement – 12m E2 5c*. A. Cunningham, I. Rae, M. Rae. October, 1994.

To the right of Submarine Badlands is a vertical wall. Climb close to the left arête of the wall, moving slightly right with a long reach at mid-height.

Thumper – 12m E2 5c**. C. Lesenger, A. Cunningham, J. Cunningham. June, 1996.

To the right of The Irish Agreement, climb the 'fierce crack rising out of the roof of a small recess'. Committing.

Under Pressure – 12m E2 5c*. C. Lesenger, J. Cunningham. June, 1996.
The steep narrow wall to the right of Reap the Wild Wind. Climb to the roof, move right and pull back left over the overlap to finish up a short right-facing corner.

Pink Bay:
Good Grief – 15m M. Severe. A. Cunningham, C. Downer. 18th August, 1997.
The left edge of the slab of B.F.B.

Stinking Geo:
This is the narrow inlet cutting away from the Spaced out Rockers Cliff towards the Leaning Block Cliff. It sports a slabby left side and an overhanging right wall.
Pooh Pong McPlop – 12m E1 5b*. A. Cunningham, J. Pickering. May, 1995.
The middle? of three overhanging corners on the right wall.

Leaning Block Cliff:
Goldeneye – 20m HVS 5a*. A. Cunningham, F. Fotheringham. May, 1997.
The first corner right of Memphis Belle, finishing up the leaning crack on the left.

Rubha Coigeach, Amphitheatre Bay:
The Roaring Forties – 30m E4 5c. S. Clegg, H. Lancashire. 2nd June, 1994.
The route takes a fairly central line up a very obvious series of overhanging grooves in the back wall. An exhilarating pitch, reasonably well protected, with Friends 0 to 4 doubled up useful.

CLACH TOLL (MR 037 267):
The climbs lie on the seaward side of the obvious vice-like rock feature which is well seen when looking SW from Stoer village. Scramble over the landward formation to reach a short channel. Cross to the main rock at low tide or wade (a simple tyrolean is also possible). The first five routes were sent by a Creag Dubh team but had been climbed previously by A. Cunningham and party in 1995.

South Face:
Climbs start from a platform above sea level – described right to left.
1. The bold SE arête – 10m HVS 4c.
2. The diagonal crack which rises rightwards to finish at the top of the SE arête – 10m VS 4b.
3. The central crackline on perfect rock and good holds – 10m V.Diff.
4. The faint crack 3m to the left – 10m VS 4c.
5. A left traverse from the platform is also an access route to the north face – 4b.

Landward (East) Face:
Abseil approach recommended. The obvious crack on the left side of the wall is Slip Sliding Away (SMCJ 1996, p81).
Miss Auchinstarry – 12m E2 5b**. C. Struthers, A. Finch, D. Sanderson. 29th May, 1997.
Climb the corner right of the crack by its right wall, making moves out right, then back left to finish up an overhanging layback.

North Face:
A Few Inches Short of a Reach Around – 12m E3 5b/c**. A. Finch. 29th May, 1997.
Climb the obvious overhanging corner on the NE arête which is gained by traverse ledges on the north face.

THE POINT OF STOER (MR 018 353):

The following routes are easily visible from the stack and can be reached by wandering SW for about 200m along the rock platforms at the base of the main cliff.

Crack and Scoop – 30m VS 4b. B. Ottewell, F. Stoddart. 26th July, 1997.
Climb a left-slanting crack at the left-hand side of a slab, then trend slightly right up a scoop and short wall. Follow a crack through an overhang on the left to finish.
Centre Slab – 25m VS 4c. M. Robson, T. Ward. 26th July, 1997.
Climb the centre of the slab direct.

Black Guillemot – 25m HVS 5a. M. Robson, B. Ottewell. 26th July, 1997.
Start right of Centre Slab. Take the corner groove direct to a niche, follow the crack through an overhang and continue direct up the slabby wall to the top.

No Fish – 25m M. Severe. T. Ward, M. Robson. 26th July, 1997.
Follow the obvious wide crack on the right-hand side of the slab, passing through a small overhanging niche at half-height.

The following routes are 50m south of the tyrolean belay where there is a slabby wall defined by a corner on the right.
Check-out – 20m H. Severe**. J. Burns, C. Struthers, G. Harrison. 20th July, 1996.
On the wall 8m left of the corner is an obvious left-trending crack/cleft. Good rock and protection.

Slightly left again is a black slabby wall.
Look-out – 20m E1 5b*. G. Harrison, J. Burns, C. Struthers. 20th July, 1997.
Climb the slab right of a thin crack to a break. Take the wall above via an L-shaped overlap.

OLD MAN OF STOER:

A Clean Old Man – 60m E1***. C. Struthers, G. Harrison, J. Burns. 20th July, 1997.
Start from the belay at the end of the Original Route traverse.
1. 30m 5a. Climb a chimney and crack directly above. In the same line, enter a pod and then a wide continuation crack. Avoid the roof on the left and climb up to belay as for Original Route pitch 2.
2. 30m 5b. Surmount the roof above to gain a groove leading up and right to a large ledge. Stand on top of the block on the left and stretch up to the next break. Trend up and left to an obvious corner. At its top a short traverse right gains the belay.

BRAEBAG, Glas Choire Mor (Sheet 15, MR 294 173):

Approach: Take the path following the Allt nan Uamh to the lochans south of the 718m north top of Braebag. Contour north above the cliffs, passing a narrow slot until the next slot north is reached. This is an extraordinary defile over 30m high, vertical and very narrow. Descend the grassy bed of this to reach scree. The crags described below lie immediately to the left (in descent) or north of this slot in Glas Choire Mor. There are three buttresses. The one closest to the slot is the most impressive, the second is essentially a right-hand section to it, joined by a broken rib, the third separated by another deep, though less extensive slot. The rock is quartzite, with many areas of looseness although the upper sections are much firmer. Protection is mainly small wires in the better rock with a much wider variation in the often expanding cracks of the lower. All the routes have been led on sight. However, it is probably wiser to pre-clean the areas of looseness from above as this may save the second's head. The routes are described from left to right facing the crag.

Wall of Mists – 40m E1*. J. R. Mackenzie, R. Brown. 18th July, 1997.
The best of the routes so far – clean, sound but quite bold. A broken and very loose scree rake rises up to the right from the foot of the wall. Halfway along this and to the right of a square-cut overhang and just right of a ledge is a cairn.
1. 20m 5a. Climb the unprotected wall on sound rock to runners in a thin crack at 8m. Continue up to wider cracks, then traverse left to a ledge at the base of a corner.
2. 20m 5b. Instead of continuing up the corner, go up, then traverse left out on to the middle of the pink wall (clearly seen from below). Climb up past a tiny crack and finish direct, an excellent pitch with some exposed moves.

Angels Delight – 35m VS 5a. R. Brown, J. R. Mackenzie. 18th July, 1997.
This route climbs the right edge of the buttress overlooking the next slot to the north.
1. 20m 5a. Climb up the edge of a pinnacle, balance on its top and surmount the crux bulge above. Better rock leads up to a ledge at the foot of a corner.
2. 15m 4b. Climb the pleasant and more-or-less solid corner to the top.

Isolation Buttress – 35m Severe. R. Brown, J. R. Mackenzie. 18th July, 1997.
To the right of the slot is a narrower buttress with a prominent crack splitting its top pitch.
1. 18m. Climb up to a narrow groove via some loose steps, move right into the groove and much better rock which is climbed to a ledge below the crack.
2. 17m. Climb the crack direct to the top, a fine pitch.

KINLOCHBERVIE, Creag Mhor (MR 218 553):
This is the NW-facing red pillar on the south shore of Loch Inchard. Three routes were climbed by R. Campbell and P. Thorburn. The central one is thought to have been climbed before by P. Swainson and P. Nunn but they found an engineering nut in the top crack! The pillar is about 40m high and has a traverse ledge at about half-height.
1. HVS/E1 5a. A diagonal line on grey rock in the lower left part of the pillar.
2. A central 4c pitch leads to a belay on the traverse line, followed by two alternatives above, either side of a pink pegmatite band. HVS 5a*** on the left, heading for finishing cracks. E1 5b** – the line on the right of the pink band.

SHEIGRA, Polin Crag:
Turn left just before Sheigra and continue to the end of the road at Polin (near Oldshore Beg). A path leads down to the beach but instead, continue on the coast round to the left until a small Geo is reached. The crag lies below, facing south and overlooking Eilean na h-Aiteag. The crag is characterised by a horizontal band of crumbly black schist at two-thirds height. Described right to left; the first two reached by abseil descent.
Prester Didwick's Congener – 16m V. Diff. A. F. Thomas, A. M. Dela Hoyde. 7th August, 1997.
Start on the pedestal at the right end of the crag, which is about 2m above the water line. Climb straight up to and climb a flake-crack to its top. Traverse left into another flake and up this to finish.

Alice in Wonderland – 18m H. Severe 4b. A. F. Thomas, A. M. Dela Hoyde. 7th August, 1997.
Start on the sloping ledge in the middle of the crag (just above the waterline). Go straight up over an overlap to the right-hand end of an overhung flake, climbed rightwards to the top.

Triple Ripple – 18m VS 4c. A. F. Thomas, A. M. Dela Hoyde. 7th August, 1997.
Approached by scrambling down the big slab on the left of the crag. Start at the foot of the slab. Climb up to and inside an inverted V-notch and pull out to the right. Step up and left over an overlap and go left past pockets to the next overlap at a huge flake in the black schist. Surmount this to the left and continue straight up to the top.

Treasure Island Wall:
The route Long John Silver (SMCJ 1997) is on the dark wall to the south-west of the descent gully. It was gained by an abseil from an outcrop on the grass slope above. Starting farther right on the same ledge are the following two routes.
Brace Yourself Sheigra – 40m E2. R. Campbell, P. Thorburn. 15th June, 1996.
1. 20m 5c. Climb a flake line, step right and make a harder move past a distinct overlap to an easier finish.
2. 20m 4c. Finish as for Long John Silver.
Ben Gunn – 40m E2 5b. R. Campbell, P. Thorburn. 15th June, 1996.
Climb the pocketed line about 5m to the right and finish as for Long John Silver.

Left of the above routes is a left-slanting black ramp, well seen from the descent gully promontary. An abseil was made to the right end of a narrow ledge 5m above the sea. It would be possible to climb to this at low tide.
Designed to be Flawed – 40m E4 6a**. P. Thorburn, R. Campbell. 15th June, 1996.
From the left end of the narrow ledge, follow the ramp with awkward moves across a blank section. Finish up a stepped left-facing corner.

CAPE WRATH:
Opposite Am Bodach is an area of dark rock cut by several vertical quartz veins.
White Lining – 35m Severe*. A. Cunningham, M. Blyth, J. Pickering, D. Horsburgh. July, 1994.
Climb via the widest left-hand quartz vein of the two widest on the face.

Stac Clo Kearvaig, The Landward Stack:
Stac Clo Kearvaig has three tops, the so-called landward and seaward stacks are connected at the base with huge wedged boulders between, the highest block being visible from the lighthouse road. The third top is in front of the seaward stack as seen from the road and again connected at the base to the other two.
In Season – 50m E1. A. Cunningham, K. Geddes. June, 1996.
1. 30m 5a. Start by the gap between the third top and the other two, opposite Clo Mor Crack on the mainland. Traverse right onto the 'landward' stack and climb by a corner crack to the first ledge. Move up via short walls, ledges and ramps to a large ledge below a big left-facing corner leading to the narrow summit.
2. 20m 5b. Climb the corner and wide crack to finish.

FOINAVEN, Lord Reay's Seat:
Fishmonger – VI,6. R. Webb, N. Wilson. January, 1998.
An excellent route. Follows the summer line except where the summer crux takes a corner to the right of the natural line, the winter line continues straight up a right-facing corner/crack. Large gear an advantage.

FARAID HEAD (MR 715 378):
The seaward end of this large peninsula is reached by pleasant walking across the dunes. There is a lot of rock here but much of it is uninspiring. There are several

clean areas of rock at the western extremity of the headland. The routes lie on the attractive square-cut buttress which is visible from a distance.

Yet Another McAulayism – 25m VS 5a*. A. Finch, D. Sanderson, G. Harrison, C. Struthers. 28th May, 1997.

Abseil down a black corner to belay on a ledge 5m above the sea. Climb through overlaps and continue up the corner.

In Denial – 35m E3***. C. Struthers, D. Sanderson. 28th May, 1997.

The photogenic arête provides serious but technically easy climbing on reasonable rock.

1. 10m 5a. Follow 'Yet Another' to belay in the corner.
2. 25m 5a. Climb left and up to gain a depression and thence a ledge leading to the arête. Follow the arête past two peg runners of doubtful holding power (hence the name).

Note: Many more routes were received from Ceannabeinne beach crag from two different parties but were assumed to have been climbed before (see SMCJ 1995, p669). The crag is very popular, particularly for bouldering and soloing.

ORKNEY, Yesnaby, Qui Ayre Point (Sheet 6 MR 218 154).

A mini-guide from Mick Tighe. Routes were also climbed here by D. Turnbull in 1994 (he is the Orkney author for the next guide), so the following may not all be first ascents:

If you don't have a car there's a fairly long, but wonderfully scenic, approach along the clifftops from Stromness – 8km approx – otherwise vehicles can be left by the old military buildings at the road end, about 800m north of the crags. Qui Ayre Point forms a beautiful compact cliff facing south, with various other inlets and walls running south again towards the Castle of Yesnaby itself. The lovely compact sandstone here has been quarried for centuries to make millstones and stone troughs for Orkadians, and a myriad of little climbs and boulder problems can be found in and about the old workings.

The main, south-facing crags have been called the 'quarry walls' and are best viewed across the bay from the south. At the extreme western end of Qui Ayre Point the cliff runs down into the sea making an almost perfect wedge shape. The routes are described from this most westerly point working back inland (eastwards). Except at this westerly end, where they are a little shorter, the routes are all around 30m long. A ledge runs below the wedged-shape cliff, partially covered at high tide – reached by abseil or a wonderful little traverse from the west. Three of the routes have appeared in SMCJ 1996.

The Half Bouy – 10m Severe. M. Tighe, J. Armour, C. Duncan, H. Clarke. 18th June, 1997.

The first line in from the point is a wonderful little honey-combed fault with huge jugs and superb protection.

Route 91 – E1 5b. (toproped). So called because it overhangs by 1°. It takes the first vertical crackline in from the west up the otherwise blank wall. Brilliant climbing on perfect rock with excellent protection.

Tuttie's Wall – E2 5b. M. Tighe. 17th June, 1997.

This first, wedge-shaped part of the quarry walls runs into an almost perfect vertical corner (Tuttie's Neuk). A couple of metres back left, a vague black crack heads off up the wall. Follow the crack first and then a series of fabulous horizontal faults. Strenuous.

Tuttie's Neuk – HVS 5a. M. Tighe, K. Proudlock, K. Harding, J. Cargill, S. Fraser. 3rd June, 1995.

The fine open-book corner, not easily seen except from immediately above or below. An acrobatic start with a slightly easier finish.

The cliff juts out a little now to form a sort of 'tower face' with an excellent groove line at either side - neither of which have been climbed. Right again the cliff falls back to create a groove/corner line on which the following two routes are based.

Definitely Maybe – E2 5b. A. Park, N. Gilman, N. Kekus. 6th May, 1995.

Takes the groove for 5m before moving left on to a rib, then left again to climb a crack to the top.

The Creel – E2 5b. M. Tighe, J. Cargill, I. Lee. 12th May, 1997.

Follows the previous route for 5m and then continues up the gently overhanging groove to the top.

Ebb and Flo – MVS. J. Cargill, K Harding. 3rd June, 1995.

A short wall to the right of The Creel has a wee groove in the middle which is easy to get into, and hard to get out of.

Right again (eastwards) is the Crevasse, a 5m chimney-groove which is the best access/escape for this part of the cliff. It's a tricky little down-climb and a short abseil might be a better prospect. Around the corner again (going east or inland) is a lovely wall of almost perfect rock with a small curving arch midway along which gives its name, Arch Wall. A fault line runs right across this wall 6-8m above the tidal ledge.

Crab Crawl – 40m HVS 5a. M. Tighe, I. Lee, J. Cargill. 13th May, 1997.

Follow the traverse line in either direction on immaculate rock. Sometimes delicate, sometimes strenuous, and with a convenient ledge for a rest and/or belay half way along.

Velvets – VS 4c. M. Tighe, J. Armour, C. Duncan. 17th June, 1997.

A shallow groove line starts at the extreme left of the wall, just a few metres below the start (or finish) of Crab Crawl. Follow the groove to a ledge on the left 3m from the top. Either, make much harder moves up the wall to the top, or descend to a ledge and belay, leaving a high runner. Escape left into the crevasse.

Handbags and Gladrags – E2 5b. N. Gilman, N. Kekus, A. Park. May, 1995.

The crescent overhang, or arch, that gives this wall its name has a thin crack coming from its right-hand end. The route climbs the steep wall and open groove directly below the right-hand end of the overhang and takes the crack above to the top.

Nyook Waa – M. Severe. S. Fraser, K. Sherstone. 3rd June, 1995.

Arch Wall ends in a chimney/cleft at the eastern end. Climb up the chimney for about 10m before transferring on to the right-hand wall to finish.

The Lang Hudauf – V. Diff. K. Proudlock, J. Finnan. 3rd June, 1995.

Around the corner from Nyook Waa is another chimney/groove line with some slightly loose brownish rock near the top.

Wee Lum – HVS 5a. M. Tighe, K. Proudlock, K. Sherstone. 3rd June, 1995.

Around the corner again from the Lang Hadauf, the beautiful clean rock sweeps into the back of the bay. The first feature encountered is a fierce little bottomless chimney reached by a short sea level traverse from the bottom of the Lang Hadauf. Wide bridging saves the day.

The vertical sweep of cliff that now issues eastwards has been named Gardyloo (Gardez L'eau) on account of the old quarryman's rubbish tip that is evident part way along. Thirty metres or so along from the top of Nyook Waa and the Lang Hadauf, there's a wee depression on the cliff top, and a diagonal fault line in the cliff below. The fault line has been toproped – The Hinge, E3 5c. The following route has a common start.

Freeloader – E1 5b. N. Kekus, A. Park. 7th May, 1995.
Abseil from the depression to a fine little black triangular ledge just above the high water mark. Climb The Hinge (left-facing corner) for 10m before pulling steeply up and right on to the wall with small pockets. A shallow left-facing groove leads to the top.

Wander Wall – HVS 5a. M. Tighe, I. Lee, K. Sherstone, J. Cargill. 13th May, 1997.
Start from the same triangular ledge as the previous route. Move up and right a couple of metres to another ledge. Climb a crack/fault line in the wall above for a few metres, then go right again along another fault lie (scary) to head for the top as soon as possible.

Ebb Tide – E1 5b. M. Tighe, S. Fraser, K. Harding, J. Cargill. 3rd June, 1995.
About 10m below and right of the triangular ledge, another bigger ledge appears at half-tide. From the ledge climb up the wall passing a wee overhang on the right at 6m, then follow the wall to the top.

With a couple of spectacular lines still to be done, Gardyloo Wall now runs into the back of the Geo terminating in some brown stepped overhangs. The cliffs now turn through 90° and run generally south, though punctuated by numerous inlets and promontaries, several of which have produced excellent routes of about 20m length. There are three good landmarks along this section of cliffs, the first to be seen when approaching from the north will be False Stack, the pseudo stack with a little slab, or drawbridge, propping it up. Back north a bit a little stream runs into the sea midst a welter of bright green moss - The Moss Ghyll.

Finally, there's the fine-looking stack of Yesnaby Castle. Routes are now described heading south, starting at Moss Ghyll. Belays are hard to find at the top of the cliff here, and a spare rope, preferably pre-stretched, could be handy for an anchor around the two square piles of stones by the fence.

Moss Ghyll Groove – Severe. M. Tighe, C. Duncan. 18th June, 1997.
Immediately north of the green mossy stream outlet a little arête springs up with a nice crackline above half-height. Start right, left or centre and climb to a wee platform below the crack/groove which is followed to the top.

There are two small Geos between here and the False Stack, the promontary between the two having a fine, sightly slanting fault line which gives an excellent little climb.

Video Show – Severe. M. Tighe, C. Duncan, J. Armour. 17th June, 1997.
Follow the fault line, passing a tricky little overhang about a third of the way up.

False Stack:
The Crow's Nest – VS. M. Tighe, J. Armour, C. Duncan. 17th June, 1997.
Abseil down to the seaward side somehow! Take the south-west arête for a few metres by a groove line or some big steps on the right. Go right at the top of the groove (tricky) on to the beak. Don't go straight up the obvious arête above which is a bit loose; instead follow the lovely little slabby wall diagonally rightwards to

the top. The south side of the stack is overhanging and has been climbed on a top rope at E3-ish.

Variety Show – HVS 5a. M. Tighe, J. Cargill. 14th May, 1997.
A little Geo that can only be reached by abseil lies 30m-40m south of the False Stack. At the south end of the geodh is a rib split by a perfect crackline. Climb through the initial overhang on immaculate holds and with perfect protection. Follow the crack until it becomes a brown-coloured slabby depression near the top. Keep going or go right under a rock beak and finish up a little groove.

The next group of climbs are based on the west-facing walls immediately opposite the Castle of Yesnaby and are accessed by abseiling down to sea level right opposite the eastern arête of the stack. This is the same place to start the swim to the stack. From this sea level ledge a wee crevasse gives access to a vast sea cave that runs under the whole cliff and is a wonderful aquamarine world to explore on a calm day. From the ledge opposite the stack, a wonderful traverse line goes around the corner to the north, steps across a chasm (the entrance to the sea cave), and carries on for 30m-40m before ending in the next Geo.

Late Night Special – E1 5b. M. Tighe, R. Veitch, R. Robertson, K. Harding. May, 1995.
Follow the traverse line to its end and belay. Great place for photos. Take the groove line at the extreme left (north) end of the wall. There are two grooves very close to each other. See which one you can get into!

The Master Class – HVS 5a. M. Tighe, S. Fraser. May, 1994.
Take the same traverse as for the previous route but only go halfway along. A crack and fault line almost in the middle of the wall leads to the top.

On the Edge – HVS 5a. M. Tighe, J. Cargill, K. Sherstone, I. Lee. 13th May, 1997.
Same as before, but immediately after the step across the chasm, climb a stiff little crack and make a difficult move right on to a ledge. Zig-zag to the top.

The cliff now turns through 90° to face south and right on the corner is a diagonal crack, Diagonal, E1 5b, which was toproped by M. Tighe in May, 1995, although there was evidence of chalk on the holds. This and other routes hereabouts may well have been done by teams returning/escaping from Yesnaby Stack.

Howard's End – VS 4c. M. Tighe, S. Fraser, H. Clarke. May, 1994.
Going along the south-facing walls and just by the start of Diagonal, there's a little hoodie groove that can be climbed to an escape on the right. The steep little wall can then be followed to the top.

Howard's Way - VS 4c. M.Tighe, K.Sherstone, J.Cargill. 13th May, 1997. Take the same hoodie groove as the previous route but continue rightwards along a fabulous traverse line in a spectacular position. Head for the top as soon as you can.

The big bay to the south has some steep walls at the back which are yet to be explored, but there's another headland with some steep but more broken rock. Some routes were done here in the early 1970s by M. Tighe, B. Newton, J. Barry and D. Kirtley, and by M. Tighe and S Fraser in 1994.

Around the corner again is a fine diagonal crack that has yet to be climbed. Unfortunately, access without a swim is difficult as it overhangs two ways.

Yesnaby Castle:
The route up the south face of this fine stack is described in the Northern Highlands Guide. There is also a similarly graded route up the eastern arête past a bunch of

rotting pitons. Also an E3 addition up the western arête by M. Fowler and party in 1996.

HOY, St John's Head:

Note: Big John: A. Donson and K. Pyke on the second ascent on 15th July, 1996, freed the aid point on pitch 12 at a poorly protected 6a. E4/5 for that pitch – the rest of the route is about E3.

Rora Head, Orange Wall:

This is the west-facing wall roughly at right-angles to Mucklehouse Wall. The corner between the two is the descent, two abseils to tidal ledges. The routes follow obvious lines; take some large hexes and/or #4 Friend for both these routes.

Spoots – 80m E4 5c 6a 5b. A. Donson, K. Pyke. 22nd May, 1995.

The right-most crackline above the tidal ledge. Start about 20m right of the abseil on a grassy mound. The crackline gave pitch lengths approx. 25m, 35m, 20m, finishing up an awkward off-width in a hanging position.

Orange Wall – 90m E4 5b 6a 5c. A. Donson, K. Pyke. 20th May, 1995.

The central line in the orange wall, gained by a rising traverse from the left.

1. 30m 5b. Reach the crack system by traversing right above an obvious square-cut cave at the back of the tidal ledges.

2. 35m 6a. Climb the left-hand of two crack systems until they merge.

3. 25m 5c. Finish up the crack.

East Wall of Gully 1:

Walk down the gully to start. Routes described left to right.

Ben Doone – 20m HVS 5a. A. Evans, C. Rolfe. August, 1997.

Climbs the centre of the obvious grey buttress at the head of the gully, finishing by the right arête.

Fulmar Cavity – 30m VS 4b. A. Evans, C. Rolfe, R. Carter, D. Moss. 23rd July, 1997.

Takes the centre of three prominent cracks on the left-hand side of the wall. Easier than it looks.

Craa'nest – 30m E1 5b. K. Pyke, A. Donson. 17th July, 1996.

The right-hand of the three prominent cracklines, 3m right of Fulmar Cavity.

Mater – 35m E2 5b. A. Donson, K. Pyke. 17th July, 1996.

The obvious bottomless left-facing corner in the centre of the face. Approached via an indefinite finger crack.

Note: Repeated by D. Wood, D. Jones in August, 1997, but reaching the corner by going right to a flake, then left along a ledge. Thought excellent.

Paneer – 38m E2 5b. A. Donson, K. Pyke. 17th July, 1996.

The wall right of Mater. Attain a jutting ledge at 10m and follow a flake line above to a break. Step right and climb up trending left to a niche beneath the left end of the roof. Pull over to fine finishing cracks.

Paternoster – 50m HVS. A. Evans, C. Rolfe, R. Carter, D. Moss. 23rd July, 1997.

The huge crack and corner system on the right of the wall.

1. 25m 4c. Climb the obvious crackline with some slightly worrying rock to ledges and an *in situ* peg.

2. 25m 4b Climb the crack and corner line on superb rock exiting left at the capping roof.

Gully 4:

Avoiding the Issue – 18m E1 5b. D. Jones, D. Wood. August, 1997.
The obvious pillar with a capping overlap at the upper end of No. 4 gully. Start in the middle of the wall, head straight up and avoid the overlap by stepping left at the top.

Pocket full of Fulmar Shite – 60m E1 5b. D. Jones, D. Wood. August, 1997.
Start in a square-cut cave to the right of an obvious red overhang in the wall 50m left of the waterfall.
1. 25m 5a. Head up and left to the foot of an obvious corner crack through red ledges.
2. 8m 5a. Classic hand jamming crack up the corner.
3. 25m 5b. Finish straight up the headwall.

Puffins for lunch – 30m E1 5c. D. Jones, D. Wood. August, 1997.
The obvious red corner to the left of Fillets of Sole.

A Piss in the Ocean – 15m H. Severe 4b. D. Wood, D. Jones. August, 1997.
A crackline in the first buttress on the descent of No. 4 gully.

Learning to Fly – 25m E1 5b. D. Jones, D. Wood. August, 1997.
The left-hand arête of Fillet of Sole Buttress.

Scare of the Century – 50m MXS 5a. D. Jones, D. Wood. August, 1997.
An incredibly loose trip up the right-hand skyline of No. 4 gully. Not likely to be there after the next big storm!
1. Start at the foot of the buttress below a groove in the arête. Head up decomposing ledges to the groove avoiding the obligatory fulmar crux, climb the groove without pulling on anything (lots of loose blocks), and avoid the washing machine-sized loose block roof at the top on the left and belay in the vibrating crack in the front of the large block.
2. Run away in to the gully on the left, climb the off-width crack in the wall (this goes through the block your mate is belayed to, so don't fall off!) to the foot of the final corner.
3. Climb the corner, avoiding knocking the block on your second, and belay to some flakes in the top of the crag.

Waterfall Wall:

A new area. Approach via Gully 4 descent and walk west.
The Last Yole – 95m E5. K. Pyke, A. Donson. 18th July, 1996.
Midway between the waterfall and the sea arch is an overhanging yellow grooved arête (stunning!). Yole is the name of the Hoy fishing boat. Start on a clean ledge at the left side of the arête.
1. 25m 4c. Climb a rounded stepped flake line to reach a blocky terrace. Trend right to belay beneath the groove.
2. 40m 6a. Climb the initial groove to a pie-shaped roof. Layback steeply around this until the crack runs out and reach left to another crack. Move up to a bottomless groove (crux) and then climb the short wall above to a ledge and belay on the left end.
3. 30m 5b. Climb steeply up broken grooves on the left to the top.

SHETLAND, Sandness, Pobie Skeo:

The following sea cliff climbs can be found in Pobie Skeo, a beautifully wild and private inlet on the Sandness peninsular of Shetland, beyond the community of Huxter.

Much of the coast here is composed of spectacularly crumbly sandstone. However, this particular Skeo is firm and trustworthy with very good frictional qualities offering a charismatic array of whorls, pockets and ripples. The promontory provides a platform raised above most seas and tides, and the climbs do not appear to disturb birdlife. Sheet 3 (Shetland North), MR 167 566.

Approach: Take the A971 to Sandness and follow signs to Huxter. Park at the end of the road and follow the signed footpath past Huxter Water Mills. From there follow the cliff edge over a stone wall, past the Loch of Huxter, over a gated fence, stopping 200m short of a second stone wall. A 50m-long tilted promontory is easily visible jutting out below the cliff top. Time from car – 5-6 minutes. Scramble down easy slabs to the promontory and make a tiptoe *mauvais pas* westwards to arrive below a long wall of black sandstone. This holds the following easy routes of up to 15m, running from left to right:

Charlie Crumb – 12m V. Diff. M. Hudson, R. Brown. 4th September, 1997.
The right-facing corner at the extreme left end of the wall.

Tabloid – 12m V. Diff. M. Hudson, R. Brown. 4th September, 1997.
Start 5m to the right of Charlie Crumb at a slight nose in the wall. Climb this and the slabs above.

A Concise History – 15m VS 4b. M. Hudson, R. Brown. 5th September, 1997.
Start 15m farther right, 5m left of the arête. A direct line taking the left-hand side of the top slab. Pull over initial bulges and move up to the overlap, 2m right of the rotten-looking corner. Last gear here. Pull onto the slab above and finish direct up the right side of a protruding block. Poor protection.

Twenty Golden Greats – 15m Severe 4c*. M. Hudson, R. Brown. 4th September, 1997.
An absorbing and unlikely way up the slab – the best of this wall. Start 3m right of Concise History and 2m left of the arête, at an overhanging crack that splits the jutting ledges. Climb this (crux) and move up to the overlap. Take the middle of the slab above via small twin scoops.

Stars On 45 – 15m Severe 4c. M. Hudson, R. Brown. 5th September, 1997.
Start as for Twenty but take the exposed arête above the overlap. Good positions but rather contrived.

Now turn the corner to find a taller and steeper west-facing wall of creamier-coloured sandstone. It has a large cave at its foot above the sloping apron of slab.

Silent Street – 25m HVS 4c***. M. Hudson, R. Brown. 5th September, 1997.
This line takes the centre of the wall through some impressive territory. From the right-hand side of the cave mouth, make a steep pull up onto rising ledges leading rightwards into a small overhung bay. Pull over via a small pocket onto the wall above. Traverse back left above the cave mouth to a ledge, in an exhilarating position. Climb directly up flakes above to finish over a jutting block on the highest point of the cliff.

Unst, Skaw Point (Sheet 1, MR 669 153):

Skaw Point has vast potential for new routes, the routes described below are the cleanest area of rock and are easily accessible. You can drive to the top of the cliffs for belaying as there are no natural belays. The only restriction is associated with nesting birds, April to August. Permission to climb on the cliffs was easily obtained from Bill Spence, who is clerk of the land. He can be contacted on 01957 711439. The routes are all contained within a small area of sound rock called the Buss, although there is some loose rock at the top of the routes.

Back Seat – 20m Severe 4a. J. McGlade, C. Tidswell. 6th June, 1996.
The main feature on the land side of a triangular pinnacle. Start right of a detached block and ascend by an obvious corner. Abseil or rightwards descent.

Top Deck – 18m Severe 4a. J. McGlade, C. Tidswell. 6th June, 1996.
Start 2m right of Back Seat. Climb twin rightward diagonal cracks until a vertical crack and small corner leads to the top.

Half Fare – 15m Severe 4b. J. McGlade, C. Tidswell. 8th June, 1996.
On the sea side of the pinnacle, take the main crack which starts from the left corner of the pinnacle. Start from the top of the lower slab and traverse in.

Opposite the pinnacle and across the rock pools on the main cliff are two diagonal cracks either side of a damp recess.

Double Decker – 20m VS 4c. J. McGlade, C. Tidswell. 6th June, 1996.
The left-hand crack. Ascend a large block to gain the steep crack, which bears right to the top.

Last Stop – 20m VS 4b. J. McGlade, C. Tidswell. 6th June, 1996.
Take the wide crack to the right of the damp recess. It goes up right and on to the main face. The crack slowly thins out towards the top.

Mr Bounce – 22m Severe 4a. J. McGlade, C. Tidswell. 8th June, 1996.
Climb the slab away to the left by laybacking the corner and several overhangs.

Park and Ride – 16m HVS 5a. J. McGlade, C. Tidswell. 8th June, 1996.
Climb the acute corner (one wall overhanging) opposite the pinnacle area by bridging and overcoming a small seat half way up (crux, only runner).

CAIRNGORMS

LOCHNAGAR:

Mantichore – VII,7. W. Moir, N. Ritchie. 7th February, 1998.
By the summer line. The route is well protected, sustained, with nothing desperate on it. The twin cracks of pitch 1 have good tufts and torques; similarly pitch 2 has tufts.

The Amphitheatre:
Amphitheatre Buttress – 200m V,5. S. Richardson, J. Ashbridge. 30th January, 1998.
The prominent buttress between Amphitheatre Route and Pinnacle Gully 1.
1 and 2. 80m. Climb Pinnacle Gully 1 to the crevasse stance.
3. 40m. Follow the fault of Amphitheatre Route for 5m then climb a steep groove on the right (crux) to easier ground. Move up to belay on the right side of the toe of the buttress (well left of PG Corner).
4. 40m. Follow the prominent turfy fault on the right flank of the buttress to a good stance.
5. 40m. Continue straight up the crest of the buttress to the plateau.

The Pinnacle:
Tiptoe Edge – 200m IV,5. R. Allen, S. Richardson. 2nd January, 1998.

Graeme Ettle on 'The Millennium Line', Coire an Lochain, Cairngorm. Photo: Rob Milne.

Above: Dougie Dinwoodie on the first ascent of 'The Empty Quarter', Garbh Choire, Beinn a' Bhuird. *Photo: Greg Strange.*

Below: Greg Strange on the first ascent of 'Tickled Pink', The Palette, Carn a' Mhaim. *Photo: Dougie Dinwoodie.*

An independent line up the left edge of The Pinnacle based on the well-defined rib between the upper section of Pinnacle Gully 1 and Grovel Wall. Follow Pinnacle Gully 1 for two pitches to the cave. Climb the steep right wall of the cave via a stepped crack (crux) and exit on to moderate ground above. Continue parallel to Pinnacle Gully 1 to gain a discontinuous chimney-line which splits the rib. Two pitches lead to the summit of The Pinnacle. The upper rib has been climbed several times before as a variation finish to Pinnacle Gully 1 or Grovel Wall.

The Complete French Connection – 215m VI,6. S. Richardson, C. Cartwright. 25th January, 1998.

A sustained mixed climb up the left side of the front face of the Pinnacle taking in The French Connection *en route*. Above this, the route follows a stepped ramp system parallel to, and right of, Grovel Wall. Climbed under powder using frozen turf with limited ice (verglas only). Start 10m left of Katsalana below a line of vegetated cracks.

1. 20m. Climb the cracks over bulges to an easing below a steep left-facing corner. Junction with Winter Face.

2. 40m. (The French Connection). Climb the corner using a crack on the left wall to a ledge. Continue up the shallow corner system above (thin) to below overhanging cracks. Junction with Grovel Wall.

3. 35m. Traverse right for 10m and climb a slab to the right of Grovel Wall to reach a steep left-facing corner. Climb this and follow a shelf rightwards underneath a steep wall.

4. 40m. Pull over a steep corner at the end of the shelf and continue more easily to join the upper fault-line taken by Route 1.

5 to 6. 80m. Continue up Route 1 to the summit of the Pinnacle.

Fools Rib - VII,7. A. Benson, P. Benson. 1st February, 1998.

By the summer route, with one rest point on pitch 2.

The Link Direct – 180m VIII,7. S. Richardson, C. Cartwright. 1st February, 1998.

An outstanding climb.

1. 30m. As for the Direct Start to The Link.

2. 20m. As for pitch 2 of The Link Face.

3. 25m. Follow The Link Face over the roof to reach the 'vegetated groove'. Climb this for 15m to a good stance on the left.

4. 15m. Continue up the groove for 5m to the junction with Route 2. Reverse the crux of Route 2, and move up to the groove running through the headwall.

5. 20m. Climb the groove, past the 'rotating block', to a good stance. (The Link Summer).

6. 10m. Pull over the roof (crux) directly above the stance. (The Link, Direct Finish).

7 and 8. 60m. Move up to join Route 2, and follow this to the summit of the Pinnacle.

West Buttress:

A full description of the following route has never been published.

Quasimodo – 290m VII,8. S. Richardson, A. D. Robertson. 25th February, 1995.

A fine and varied mountaineering route with a technical crux and difficult final pitch. It follows a direct line up the tapering pillar to the left of West Gully, and takes in sections of the summer lines of Gargoyle Direct and Dod's Diversion. Start 20m left of West Gully below an open gully line which cuts through the lower tier.

1 to 3. 120m. Climb the gully and mixed ground above to the first terrace. Belay by a large split block (old peg) about 5m right of the shallow gully of Gargoyle Direct.

4. 45m. Step right and climb a left-slanting ramp to reach a second terrace. Move right and belay near the right side of the rib below the twin cracks of Dod's Diversion.

5. 30m. Climb the cracks with conviction (crux) and the continuation groove until it is possible to gain an easy left-slanting ramp which leads to a large block on the crest.

6. 45m. Take the narrow chimney which splits the crest of the buttress and continue up several steep steps to an awkward exit onto the summit of the pillar (as for the summer line of Gargoyle Direct).

7. 20m. Make a difficult step down and follow the ridge easily left to below the final triangular headwall topped by the Gargoyle.

8. 30m. Gain a stepped crack-line from the left, and continue up a series of short corners and cracks to exit just right of the Gargoyle (as for the Direct Finish to Gargoyle Direct).

West Rib Direct – 275m V,6. S. Richardson, R. Allen. 4th January, 1998.
A direct ascent of the left edge of West Rib overlooking West Gully. A long and sustained mixed climb with the crux near the top. Pitches 1 to 4 are common with the original winter route of West Rib which took a line farther right on the upper section. No detailed account of the original winter route was published, so here is a full description.
Start 20m right of West Gully below the left-slanting slash which cuts through the left side of the lower buttress.

1 to 3. 140m. Follow the line of the slash to the terrace at the top of the first tier. Move easily up and slightly right to belay in the *cul-de-sac* below the slabby central tier.

4. 40m. Climb the huge right-facing chimney-flake to a good ledge below the headwall.

5. 20m. The direct route now follows the Patey-Coutts summer Direct Finish. Climb overlapping slabs (awkward) up then left to reach a groove which leads up to the foot of the vertical right-angled corner overlooking West Gully.

6. 20m. Climb the impending right wall of the corner via good cracks to a ledge (crux). A superbly positioned pitch.

7. 15m. Take the continuation corner-chimney to below the Organ-Pipe Pinnacles.

8. Traverse right and finish up a choice of groove-lines to the plateau.

CREAG AN DUBH LOCH, South-East Buttress:
Dogleg, Legless Variation - 150m VI,8. B. Davison, A. Nisbet. 2nd February, 1998.
A direct version of Dogleg. Climb Dogleg until 5m below the roof (60m). Step left on to the Rock Island Line rib and climb cracks directly to easier ground (30m). Continue more easily directly to the top of the buttress.

Central Gully Wall:
The Origin of the Species – 70m E6***. P. Thorburn, G. Latter. September, 1997.
The compelling blunt arête of The Naked Ape. Take all the microwires you can muster and start below the groove 2m right of The Naked Ape.

1. 15m 5b. Climb the shallow groove parallel to the larger groove of The Naked Ape to the first small ledge.

2. 40m 6b. Climb the groove past a PR at a rock scar to a wide flake-crack (Fr#4), follow it to a thin crack, then move to the right side of the arête (skyhooks on a good flake on the right). Climb up, then make committing moves on to a sloping shelf. Follow the thin right-hand crack with difficulty to a good hold, move up left to The Naked Ape and follow it right, then up, to the PR on the arête. Climb the hanging groove above, exit on to a slab and belay under the right-hand end of the roof.

3. 15m 6a. Climb the final section of pitch 3 of The Naked Ape and link it with the overhanging crack of pitch 4 to gain an abseil spike (50m abseil reches the ground on the stretch).

Note: G. Latter thought E7.

False Gully Wall:

An Spearag – 30m E6 6c***. G. Latter (unsec.). 23rd September, 1997.
Varied climbing with a short, well-protected technical crux. Midway between Slartibartfast and Sans Fer is a thin crack leading to a prominent orange streak high on the wall. Start below this. Climb the crack with a tricky move to clip a PR in the horizontal break. Make hard moves to become established in the break level with the PR. Step right and continue past some underclings to a prominent undercut flange. Pull on to the sloping shelf above (at the end of the traverse on Sans Fer) and follow the groove of Sans Fer, then break out left for 4m to the base of the prominent right-slanting ramp/groove. Belay on the small shelf (P) down on the left, 3m right of the belay on Slartibartfast.

GLEN CLOVA: Lower Doonie:

Alcopops – 40m E1. S. Richardson, J. Ashbridge. 25th May, 1997.
Takes the fault between Four Corners Route and Summer's Over. A good sustained climb on excellent rock. Start by scrambling up to the tree at the base of Summer's Over.

1. 20m 5b. Step up then make an awkward move left to reach the fault. Climb the fault to its top, step right and continue up the wall above to the stance at the end of Guinness pitch 2.

2. 20m 5a. Move up past the old peg on Four Corners Route, continue up the short smooth corner above, and finish by a crack.

Upper North-West Crag:

Fool's Edge – 15m HVS 5a. S. Richardson, J. Ashbridge. 15th September, 1996.
A poor route up the arête defining the right edge of the crag. Scramble up W and S Chimney to the foot of the arête. Climb cracks to a ledge (loose blocks) and continue up the arête using holds on the left wall to the top.

BEN TIRRAN, Coire Brandy:

The Brandy Pad – 90m III,4. S. Richardson, C. Cartwright. 18th January, 1998.
To the right of the stream line at the head of the coire are two buttresses. This climb takes a line up the front face of the rightmost buttress which is characterised by two towers low down in its right flank, and by a prominent hanging slab cutting through the left side of the headwall. Start below and left of the two towers below a gully cutting through the right side of the front face.

1. 40m. Climb the gully to a cave. Step left and continue up a vegetated groove to the terrace below the headwall.

2. 50m. Move left, and climb the groove-line and hanging slab to easier ground and the top.

BEINN A' BHUIRD, Coire na Ciche:

Hot Toddy – VI,7. J. Currie, G. Robertson. 31st January, 1998.

1, 2. As for summer. There was a trickle of ice in the summer crux crack.

3. 20m. Climb straight through the bulge above the belay, then traverse hard left along a giant flake to step down and belay below a short icy corner.

4. Climb the icy corner and continue up the obvious icy line to the top.

Coire an Dubh Lochain:

Alpha Gully – 70m I. S. Richardson. 13th April, 1997.

The gully to the left of Central Rib.

Note: The current guide confuses the whereabouts of routes on the left side of the coire. According to Mac Smith's 1961 guide, the rib between A Gully and B Gully is called Winter Rib. Central Rib lies farther left.

Beta Gully – 80m II. J. Ashbridge, S. Richardson. 11th January, 1998.

The gully between Central Rib and Smooth Buttress. In early or late season, this sports a thinly-iced section at one-quarter height.

Smooth Buttress – 110m III,4. J. Ashbridge, S. Richardson. 16th January, 1998.

The short but prominent buttress on the left flank of the upper section of A Gully as mentioned in Mac Smith's 1961 guide.

1. 35m. Climb turfy grooves and cracks just left of the crest to a belay in a triangular alcove.

2. 25m. Pull straight out of the alcove (crux) and continue up to a slot on the left. Ascend a short chimney to the top of the buttress.

3. 40m Finish along the snow arête to the cornice.

Garbh Choire:

Laminated Crag – IV,4. B. Findlay, G. S. Strange. 24th January, 1998.

The original summer route was followed for three pitches with no real difficulties after the initial flake which was climbed *à chêval* to belay in a rock crevasse. A short wall into a niche led to a stepped groove and easier ground. A handy snow arête led through the large cornice.

GLEN SHEE, Creag Leacach (Sheet 43, MR 157 748):

Singapore Blues – 15m H. Severe. J. Lines. 14th June, 1997.

A small, slabby buttress lies just down from the main summit ridge. The route climbs direct up the slab on good rock.

COIRE SPUTAN DEARG:

The Smooth Groove – 100m IV,6. R. Webb, N. Stevenson. 13th December, 1997.

The smooth groove on the right-hand side of Pinnacle Buttress. Harder than it looks. Finish up the Buttress.

Anchor Route Direct – 120m III,4. C. Cartwright, S. Richardson. 14th December, 1997.

A good direct route up the front face of the buttress. Start at the foot of the rib, just right of Anchor Gully.

1 and 2. 60m. Climb the left side of the rib for two pitches to a terrace. Belay below the centre of the upper tier directly in line with the groove between the 'twin arêtes' at the top of the buttress.

3. 30m. Continue up the stepped shallow corner to the foot of the twin arêtes.

4. 30m. Climb the groove between the arêtes to the top.

Spider Buttress:

Flying Saucers – 55m E5. W. Moir, T. Rankin. 27th July, 1997.

1. 35m 6a. Start up the initial crack of The Fly to gain the left arête of the wall. Climb the arête to its top. Continue up the bold scooped slab-rib rightwards to a horizontal break. Step right to reach a short crack which leads to a belay.

2. 20m 4c. Go directly up from the belay to climb flakes up the slab above.

Bolero – 50m E5. W. Moir, T. Rankin. 27th July, 1997.

1. 30m 6b. Start up the initial corner of 'the big low-angled corner', then pull into the small left-facing corner on the right which leads to the PR on The Skater (the peg is worthless, but other gear, including a $1^1/_2$ Flexi Friend can be arranged). Step up, then reach left to climb the arête (crux) to a ledge. Continue up the easier arête above to a belay.

2. 20m 5c. Traverse 5m right and pull over the overhang via a flake layaway. Climb the hanging slab to the top.

BRAERIACH, Garbh Choire Mor:

Liaisons Dangereuses – 80m V,6. S. Richardson, C. Cartwright. 30th November, 1997.

The groove system on the left flank of She-Devil's Buttress. Start in Great Gully opposite Cherokee Chimney.

1. 40m. Climb a slab and shallow groove to 5m below a roof. (Much of this section banks up in late season). Step left on to small triangular ledge, move up, then cross back right to enter second groove above the roof (crux). Climb easily up to a ledge and belay.

2. 40m. Climb the steep wall up and right then continue straight up to join the final groove of She-Devil's Buttress, Original Route.

Fantasy Rib – 80m IV,5. S. Richardson, C. Cartwright. 23rd November, 1997.

The prominent right edge of the Tiara buttress. Start 10m up Bunting's Gully on the right side of the rib.

1. 50m. Climb a short wall to enter a turfy corner system. Follow this just left of the crest (well right of Tiara) to a good platform overlooking Bunting's Gully.

2. 30m. Turn the steep final tower by an awkward wall on the right, move back left, and continue up the short final arête to the top.

Daddy's Gone A-Hunting – 60m III,4. C. Cartwright, S. Richardson. 22nd March, 1998.

A short, mixed climb up the inverted triangular headwall between the Left and Right Branches of Bunting's Gully. Start 40m up the main gully at the foot of the Left Branch.

1. 25m. Trend diagonally right up an open groove to a ledge.

2. 35m. Move right along the ledge for 3m and climb a steep right-facing groove to the cornice.

Coire Bhrochain, Braeriach Pinnacle:

Left Face Route – 140m IV,4. A. Nisbet, G. Nisbet. 6th April, 1998.

A route up the left side of the front face of the buttress, finishing up Original Route (summer). The face has a big slabby area capped by steep ground. Start at the base of the diagonal line of South Face original (some 30m left of South Face Direct, see below). Go diagonally rightwards to enter the slabby area, then back left until below a cave. Travese left to pass the steep ground and climb a steep corner about 5m right of The Lampie. Original Route, which comes in from the left, has now been joined. Finish by it, rightwards then up a shallow gully.

Note: The most likely line of the 1970 winter route (in which case South Face is a misnomer) was from Slab Terrace up The Lampie but finishing as for this route – Original Route (summer).

South Face Crest Route – 140m IV,4. A. Nisbet, G. Nisbet. 13th December, 1997. Keeping as near as possible to the vague crest of the buttress. The 1970 route followed the original summer route. Start about 20m left of the base of East Gully. Climb the first and largest groove (left-facing corner) left of the crest for two pitches to regain the crest. Now cross the 1970 route to follow grooves just right of the crest to the headwall which was climbed at its left side (although the first step was passed by the 1970 route on the left).

South Face Direct – 140m IV,5. B. Davison, A. Nisbet. 7th February, 1998. Probably the route followed by the direct summer version. Start about 10m left of Crest Route and climb a shallow chimney to the diagonal line of the South Face original route. Cross this and climb a groove which leads into a big left-facing corner which lies just left of the crest. Climb the corner with two loops out left to finish up the final chimney of Original Route.

Titania – 110m IV,5. B. Davison, A. Nisbet. 31st January, 1998. A groove system on the right side of the Ninus buttress. Start in a bay right of the toe of the buttress. The groove starts from the top of the bay, then angles left (with one short difficult section) to reach the plateau at the same point as Ninus.

CARN ETCHACHAN, Upper Cliff:

Jumping Jupiter – 50m E2 5c. J. Lyall, A. Nisbet. 22nd August, 1997. Climbs cracks in the left side of the Time Traveller slab. Start about 5m up the overhung ramp of Poison Dwarf at a small grass ledge and block close under the right-bounding wall, gained by climbing fairly easily up Equinox and Poison Dwarf or by a 50m abseil from the top of the wall.

1. 20m 5c. Step up the ramp, then traverse right through the leaning right wall to a crack, climbed to an easing in angle. Go up right to a corner, then traverse back left to the crack. Climb the crack to belay below where the corner curves over to become a roof.

2. 30m 5c. Climb the crack through the roof and continue up it to flaky ground leading to the top.

Bedsnake – 90m VI,7. A. Powell, A. Benson. 25th January, 1998. The following seems only to be new for the short groove on pitch 1 and the last 25m. Start 7m left of Guillotine at the foot of the parallel fault (Nathrach Dubh).

1. 40m. Take a 5m left-slanting groove (Nathrach Dubh), but continuing past blocks to the left-hand of two grooves in the rock rib on the left (Pythagoras takes the right-hand one). Climb the left groove stepping right just below the crest.

2. 15m. Move up corners under the headwall to belay at the far end of the large platform.

3. 35m. Take the prominent right-slanting crackline heading up to the blunt nose on the skyline (started up by Snake Charmer). At 20m an easier line leads left towards Snake Charmer. Instead step right and follow the crack to its end under the top block and make a hard exit left to finish.

Guillotine Direct – 100m VII,7. A. Mullin, A. Nisbet. 29th December, 1997.
An exciting direct finish up the headwall. The lower chimney was climbed direct to the amphitheatre, probably the normal route these days (30m, 25m). The direct continuation is blocked by an overhanging wall, passed on the left. Left of the wall is a sharp V-trough. Having failed to enter it direct (would be better), a turfy line 1m left was climbed curving back right to the headwall just above the trough, followed by a descent into the trough (peg *in situ* for second). An inset slab led up right to reach the crackline above the overhanging wall. This was climbed steeply to a chimney with a chokestone, which was threaded from behind (with a 16ft sling, used for aid) and leading to an easier finish.

SHELTER STONE CRAG:

Andy Cave's partner in the free ascent of winter Citadel was J. Jeglic. Sadly, he died at the top of Nuptse, having completed the first ascent of its West Ridge, the route twice tried by Mal Duff and mentioned in Mal's obituary (SMCJ 1997).

STAG ROCKS:

Gable End Buttress – 180m IV,6. G. Ettle, K. Grindrod, J. Lyall. 8th January, 1998.
Climbs the centre of the buttress which contains The Tenements. Start on the right.
1. 30m. Trend left on easy but slabby ground to a vegetated fault in the middle of the second tier. Another similar fault to the left is Tenements.
2. 35m. Climb the fault to a step right at a large block. Easier ground leads to the next steepening.
3. 40m. Move right to gain a slabby fault on to the big leftwards ramp above. Climb a bulge, then move hard right to small ledges.
4. 35m. Climb up and right over steep blocks to gain a small chimney-corner. Climb this exiting rightwards.
5. 40m. Ascend the final tier by cracks on the right.

COIRE AN T-SNEACHDA, Mess of Pottage:

Note: E.Brunskill and A.Clarke made a 20m direct start to Melting Pot – more logical and V,7 in December, 1997. Go straight up from the start of No Blue Skies taking the right-hand of two parallel cracks directly into a small corner/chimney which then leads into the high left-hand sided corner of the normal route. A line leading left into the first corner has probably been climbed before.

Pot Doodles – 45m VS 4c. I. Taylor, J. Lyall. 18th August, 1997.
Right of Yukon Jack is a thin crack leading to a corner line. Climb this and the continuation above the Haston Line to finish on The Slant.

Bethel – 45m E1 5a. J. Lyall, I. Taylor. 18th August, 1997.
Start right of Pot Doodles. Climb the right-hand of two cracks to an overlap. Go right, then climb another crack to The Haston Line. The climbing is now very good, but bold. Gain a wide V-scoop, traverse left to the left end of an overlap, then up on pockets before a thin move right gains a crack. Follow this to finish on The Slant.

Aladdin's Buttress:

Snowy Owl – 20m E4 6a. I. Taylor, H. Burrows-Smith. 21st July, 1997.
Start left of Babes in the Wood at an A-notch in the roof. Bold climbing gains a jug at the apex of the roof (RP3 at back of jug). Pull on to a slab and follow a thin crack left of a pink streak (Fr2). Move up and right past the top of the pink streak to gain Babes in the Wood and finish up this. Easier for the tall.

Ali Baba – 30m VII,7. G. Ettle, J. Lyall. 4th February, 1998.

Follow the summer line generally with good protection to start, then the rock quality and protection decrease but the interest does not (skyhooks helpful).

Note: Edgewood – J. Lyall notes that the last pitch is more than 50m and should be split (5b 4c).

Fiacaill Buttress:

Men in Black – 50m VI,8. G. Ettle, M. Garthwaite. 31st January, 1998.

This route climbs the wide corner-crack between Straight to Jail and Houdini.

1. 15m. Start up Escapologist for 10m, then move right to a left-facing corner-crack.

2. 15m. Ascend the wide crack past two essential chokestones to an easier finish and good ledge.

3. 20m. Move right into Houdini. A wide crack splits the wall on the right (Fiacaill Buttress Direct). Climb the thinner crack on its left to the Terrace.

Men in Red – 70m III,6. G. Ettle, M. Garthwaite. 31st January, 1998.

This route ascends the ramp line above the start of Polar Crossing.

1. 20m. Climb the easy initial ramp to a recess.

2. 50m. Move a few metres above the belay to cross the overlap left via slanting cracks (crux). Climb the obvious continuation groove line direct.

Note: Smokestack Lightnin': A. Mullin and A. Nisbet made a free ascent on 23rd December, 1997 at an unchanged grade. The original route was followed except for a first pitch independent of Fiacaill Buttress, which also climbs the bay and groove as for Smokestack original ascent. Start at the same place but go immediately left about 5m to climb a long right-facing corner to the main ledge system. The route is now independent of Fiacaill Buttress until the final chimney and was thought to be worth one star at least.

Invernookie, Georgian Variation - IV,5. S. Elisashvili, L. Griffin. February, 1997.

Not very independent but climbed when all other routes were busy. After the first step of Invernookie, move up right and take a narrow ramp above Invernookie leading to the Short Circuit belay below the corner. Go left as if for its arête variation but step left again and up to join Invernookie 5m below its top.

COIRE AN LOCHAIN, No.1 Buttress:

Coronary Bypass, Direct Start – 20m VI,7. A. Mullin, M. Macdonald. 8th March, 1998.

Start 7m left of the chimney-crack start and climb a slabby corner and overhung wall with a crack on its left.

Inventive – Diff. A. Mullin, S. Paget. March, 1998.

By the winter route.

No. 2 Buttress:

Nivalis – 80m III,5. A. Fyffe, B. Barton. January, 1998.

Lies between Snow Bunting and Crows Nest Crack. Start about 10m below the dead-end left-hand branch of The Couloir. Move left and climb a fault in the edge of the buttress and continue up and left into a big snow bay, common with Snow Bunting. Exit the bay on the right and go back left with the crux gaining ledges leading to easier ground and the top. It is possible to go right before the hard move and join Crows Nest Crack making the grade an easy III.

No. 3 Buttress:
Migrant – VS 4b. A. Mullin, J. Maybee. 27th September, 1997.
A summer ascent by the original winter line.

Stagefright – 40m VI,7. G. Ettle, R. Milne. 25th January, 1998.
Climbs a fault line on the extreme left of the pillar between the Y-gullies, facing the left branch. Start up and left of Grumbling Grooves in the gully bed.
1. 20m. Climb the fine crack on the right wall to a point where it widens (big gear). Step left into a steep leftwards crack to reach a ledge (Hex 10).
2. 20m. Ascend the wide crack-fault above to reach good ice leading direct to the top.

No. 4 Buttress:
The Millennium Line – 120m VII,7. G. Ettle, M. Garthwaite. 7th February, 1998.
This line climbs between the starts of Western Route and Sidewinder, up the left side of the steep wall to gain the obvious flying groove. Start at a short wall.
1. 20m. Ascend moderate ground rightwards to a ledge. Gain a short tricky groove above (poor peg) to a long stretch right and an even steeper groove (good peg). An awkward bulge leads to a flake belay.
2. 20m. Move rightwards to arrange protection near a large plaque. Swing left into a flying groove and ascend to belay on Sidewinder.
3. 20m. Climb the corner above direct to easy ground.
4. 60m. Finish up Sidewinder.

NORTH EAST OUTCROPS

With page reference to the guide.

THE LONG SLOUGH, The Inlets of the Red Rocks (p38):
Self Abuse – 20m E3 5c. T. Rankin, A. Cow. Summer, 1997. Belay on the ledge of Vibrator. Climb the obvious corner right of Vibrator to the top.

SOUTER HEAD (p52):
Karma Souter – 10m E2 5c. W. Moir, G. S. Strange. 21st March, 1998.
Climb the thin crack just left of Overhang Crack and its continuation. Go diagonally leftwards across the impending headwall to reach the top.

BUNSTANE WALL (p55):
Abseil to a south-facing ledge on the mass of rock joining the cliff to the Bunstane itself.
Bun-Puncher – 20m E4 6a. W. Moir, P. Allen. 2nd November, 1997.
Go up into the central black corner, pull left into a subsidiary corner, then move up and back right to the top of the black corner. Continue up to a PR under a roof. Climb the roof and follow left-slanting grooves to the top.

Bun-Fight – 20m E3 5c. W. Moir, P. Allen. 2nd November, 1997.
Start as for Bun-Puncher and gain the big shelf on the left. Climb the obvious black corner line, step right and finish by grooves.

FINDON NESS (p104):
Down seawards from Gronk is a recessed area of rock characterised by a central alcove capped by a big double roof.

Guru – 18m E3 5c. W. Moir, G. Elrick. 24th April, 1997.
Start up the corner line running up the left side of the alcove, then traverse a horizontal break leftwards to gain a crackline which is climbed to the top.

Brahma – 20m E3 5c. W. Moir, G. Elrick. 15th May, 1997.
Start beside Guru. Climb up and left to gain the obvious handrail. Go left on this, then climb up to gain the start of the diagonal crack which leads to a junction with Guru. Follow Guru to the top.

Halo – 22m E5 6a. W. Moir, G. Elrick. 24th April, 1997.
Start in a small cave and zig-zag up the streaked wall to gain the arête running up the right side of the alcove. Move round right on a horizontal break and continue up via a black streak to finish up the gold-coloured bulges above.

DOWNIES STACK (p109):
Laa-Laa – 10m E2 5b. W. Moir, M. Levack. 15th October, 1997.
Climb the overhang just left of Black Napkins, then go leftwards to a perch on the arête. Finish up the hanging groove above.

FLOORS CRAIG (p119):
The Louisville Lip – 16m E6 6b. W. Moir, R. Buchanan. September, 1997.
Climb The Manassa Mauler to its final peg (nuts in crack to right). Move right to a big jug and forge up the overhanging wall to finish by a juggy prow.

JOHNS HEUGH (p136):
Arrhythmia – 25m E6 6b. W. Moir, P. Allen. 11th October, 1997.
The thin crackline between Jaded Ledge Lizard and Veinspotting (which is E5 6b, not E4 as in SMCJ 1997). One PR *in situ*, 00 Quadcam required.

COLLIESTON, Smugglers Cliff (p141):
Man Friday – 15m HVS 5a. T. Rankin and partner. Summer, 1997.
Start right of Robinson Crusoe. Climb the left of two shallow corners and the groove above.

HARPERS WALL (p158):
Rock Mushroom: A direct finish at marginally harder E2 5c by M. Reed.

THE OUTPOST (p160):
All the routes here suffer from slightly crumbly rock, especially lower down, but gear is generally good.
Ultra – 20m E5 6b. M. Reed, A. Crofton. 10th June, 1997.
Left of Parallax Crack are twin cracks. Start left of Parallax. Climb broken steep cracks up to a sloping ledge on the right (Rock 1,3 on right), slap left to a crack, then move left and up a yellow crack above on the right of the headwall.

Interstate – 25m E4 6a. M. Reed, G. Robertson. 10th June, 1997.
Climb Parallax to the break. Traverse right to the soaring overhanging arête, climb cracks up to a sloping ledge just left of the arête, swing around the arête and finish up the east-facing wall. Perhaps E3 5c.

Freestate – 25m E4 6a. M. Reed, M. Bruce. 9th June, 1997.
Climb cracks up to the roof as for Outrider, move left over the roof and climb up to the arête and finish as for Interstate.

M and M's – 15m H. Severe. M. Reed, M. Bruce. 9th June, 1997.
This climbs cracks on the left, curving up and around the main headwall, up a corner on the left. Some loose rock remains.

ALLIGATOR RIDGE (p188):

Simon Goes East – 25m HVS 5b**. M. Reed, S. Christie. 9th August, 1997.

Climb Black Wall to the break, traverse right across Slim Jim and Seapod (above the pod) to join Encore above the ledge and finish up this (may be E1).

RED WALL QUARRY, Bridal Cave (p192):

Family Life – 45m E3 5c**. M. Reed, G. Robertson. 29th August, 1997.

Climbed on sight. Start right of the Bridal Cave.

1. Climb into and up an obvious groove to attain a standing position. Place good, well extended gear, then move left on to the face above the cave at the very obvious flake-line. Climb the flake across the centre of the wall to a large fist-sized pocket. Climb up the left of two grooves to a ledge and belay. A brilliant pitch.

2. Climb the line of least resistance above (about 4a), then up grassy grooves to the top (no belay).

The Heightist – 15m E2/3 6a/b. G. Robertson, M. Reed. 31st August, 1997.

This route is on the north-facing, south wall of the old quarried area, below a huge boulder in the SW corner. Climb cleaned cracks to a small slab below an obvious small horizontal roof. Reach over the roof to gain the crack in the corner above (crux), climbed to the huge boulder. The split grade is due to the crux being desperate for vertically-challenged people.

MUNICH BUTTRESS (p199):

United Germany – 20m E5 6b. W. Moir, P. Allen. 12th October, 1997.

Nazi-swine linked with Munich Buttress Direct Finish.

MEAKIE POINT (p221):

Tax Collector, The Rebate Finish – E1 5c. M. Reed.

Go straight up the short overhanging crack where Tax Collector goes right.

HERRING COVE (p228):

Tom the Cabin Boy – 25m HVS 5a. T. Rankin, M. Reed. 2nd July, 1997.

Left of Captain Pugwash is a short wall and slab. Climb the left end of the wall on to the slab, go up this to easy ground (possible belay), then up the left of two chimneys.

HIGHLAND OUTCROPS

Future policy is to include routes in the New Routes Section even if they will appear in a new guide that year (or have appeared). But this guide is the last under the old policy, so the following are not in Highland Outcrops:

GLEN NEVIS, Secretaries Buttress:

Colours Blue and Grey – 30m E3 5c**. G. Latter, C. Prowse. 11th July, 1997.

A bold pitch up the right edge of the Upper Tier. From the belay at the end of the second pitch of Vincent, start up the initial crack of that route, then make hard moves up right to gain a standing position on a good ledge. Continue up the wall to gain a diagonal crack beneath the top, and follow this leftwards to pull out right on to a flake on the slab. Easily up the edge of the slab to finish.

MALLAIG CRAGS, Druim Fiaclach:

Approach: Take the A830 to Mallaig. Pass under a viaduct a few km after the Lochailort pub. About 200m after this viaduct (at MR 726 844) turn right and park near to the road opposite a wrecked boat. The three peaks of Druim Fiaclach are now visible and the face is the farthest peak of the three. Walk up a ridge on the left of the small glen with the electricity poles. Continue up the hill to a face with a distinctive chockstone-blocked crack (not the same as Charlies Crag, despite the chockstone). Both climbs take you to the summit of the mountain. Descent is made by the steep gully to the left of the face.

Big Boots and Denims - 90m VS. B. Wilkinson, R. Boakes. 17th October, 1997. The crest of the buttress.

Back to Work – 90m HVS. R. Boakes, B. Wilkinson. 17th October, 1997.
The wall on its right.

Gleann Mama Slabs (MR 737 846):

This sprawling, slabby schist crag is well seen from the A830 Fort William-Mallaig road, approximately three miles west of Lochailort. Park just before the railway viaduct near the end of the private access road leading to Glen Mama Farm. Walk past the farm for a few hundred metres, before heading diagonally right up the hillside to reach the crag in about 20 minutes. The crag is south-facing, reasonably quick-drying and divided into two sections by a shallow gully. The following routes are located on the large left-hand section which is characterised by a series of small arch-like overlaps. About 30m up and left of the lowest rocks is a steep undercut wall containing a quartz band. The first route starts at the left end of the wall below a small ramp.

Scooby Dubh - 55m HVS. S. Kennedy, C. Grindley. 12thApril, 1997.
1. 30m 5a. Climb the small ramp for 2m, then pull out right onto a steep slab below a deep crackline splitting the wall above. Climb the crack (crux) and mantelshelf onto a ledge. Traverse hard right across a large slab to belay.
2. 25m 4c. Pull out right, then climb straight up to a short corner high on the right. Climb the corner to finish up a quartz-studded slab.

Above and right of the undercut wall is a steep, black wall. Right again is a small heather terrace running rightwards. The following route starts just below the terrace, at the left end of a narrow ledge.

Underneath the Arches – 55m VS. S. Kennedy, C. Grindley. 12th April, 1997.
1 35m 4c. Traverse right along the narrow ledge to reach a prominent clean slab. Climb the slab direct by some shallow grooves to belay below a small nose.
2 20m 4b. Climb the nose, then slabs to finish. Belay on the left.

Black Cliff:

Approach: Take the A830 to Mallaig. Turn left three miles from Arisaig at the Druimdarroch signpost opposite two cottages (Quality Cottages, MR 687 849). Follow the single track road for 1km approx to a dead-end and park by the shore. Follow the coast westwards for 1km to the cliff (MR 677 837). For a stay, there is a bothy another 750m round the coast with a superb location perched on the edge of a cliff. The routes are located to the left of a corner which separates the two main faces of the cliff and which has a big tree at two-thirds height.

Dragons Blood – 20m E2. B. Wilkinson, R. Boakes. 12th July, 1997.
Start about 5m left of the corner. Climb through a low roof and a stepped one above to finish direct.

Boakes Route – 20m E2. B. Wilkinson, R. Boakes. 12th July, 1997.
Start about 8m further left to climb through a roof above and left of the low roof, then past the left end of the stepped roof to finish slightly rightwards.

Soiled Denims – 20m E1. N. Foster, B. Williamson. 31st January, 1998.
Start just left of Boakes Route and take a fairly direct line passing left of all the roofs.

DUNTELCHAIG:
Note. R. Webb and A. Keith made an ascent of Drum, possibly Scotland's only I,6, I,4 if trees are allowed.

STRATHNAIRN, Skyline Slabs:
These are seen in profile above the Tynrich Slabs.
Quaker Slab – 18m VS 4b. C. and S. Steer, J. and K. Bolger. 18th June, 1996.

In the centre of the slabs are two large flakes. Climb on to the left flake and up a short crack to a ledge. Step left on to a cleaned slab and go up to a ledge. Finish up the slab above.
Sans Grimp – 10m HVS 5a. C. and S. Steer, J. and K. Bolger. 18th June, 1996.

At the right-hand side of the crag is an area of short slabs. This route climbs directly to the cleaned slab and up this, via a short bulge.

BEN VRACKIE (MR NN 974 646):
A small SE-facing schist crag, about 40 minutes from the A924 Pitlochry to Braemar road. There is scope for numerous other lines.
The Inveterate Liar – 15m HVS 5a*. G. Latter, P. Thorburn. 2nd May, 1996.
The prominent steep crack up the right edge of the steep isolated buttress on the left side.

Dr. Luthers' Assistant – 20m E3 5c*. P. Thorburn, G. Latter. 2nd May, 1996.
The square-cut arête on the highest section of the crag, gained from the right.

WEEM CRAGS, Weem Rock:
This route, the most obvious line on the crag, was accidently left out of the new guide.
Back to Basics – 25m H. Severe**. G. Nicoll, M. Nicoll, W. Wright. 26th August, 1997.
Start 2m right of the arête and climb the prominent crack and groove line. At the overhang, move right and climb another groove to the top.

Every Last Drop – 15m 7b. R. Anderson. 26th October, 1997.
Climb to the fourth bolt on One Peg One and pull up left to climb the leftmost line of bolts

Aerial Buttress:
Saving up for a Rainy Day – 20m E5 6a***. G. Latter, R. Campbell. 31st August, 1997.
Excellent sustained well-protected climbing, taking the obvious challenge up the centre of the very steep left wall. Climb the immaculate steep finger crack to a break at its top. Move out left along the break and up to good holds, then climb the flange to a good nut placement in quartz near the top of the flange. Climb the wall above slightly rightwards on thin slots to gain good flat holds at a small ledge. Stand on this to finish more easily.
Note: Direct and independent start – E3 6a. A. D. Robertson, P. Thorburn, R. Campbell. 31st August, 1997.
The thin hanging crack-line on the left side of the front face. The crack was gained boldly from the left by stepping off the boulder.

BEN NEVIS, AONACHS, CREAG MEAGHAIDH

BEN NEVIS, Number Three Gully Buttress:

Gargoyle Wall, Summer Route – 120m VI,6. S. Richardson, C. Cartwright. 22nd February, 1998.

A complete ascent of the summer line provided five excellent and sustained mixed pitches. Previous ascents avoided the first two pitches by traversing right from the top of the icy groove of Thompson's Route.

El Niño – 80m III,4. C. Cartwright, S. Richardson. 14th March, 1998.

The short buttress right of Winter Chimney. Start below the right side of the buttress and climb a wide stepped crack for 20m until a ramp leads back left to the crest. Follow this easily to the cornice.

AONACH MOR:

Saints Slip – 150m II/III. D. W. M. Whalley, S. Coleby and party. 22nd December, 1996.

This is the first icefall 15m left of Smoking The White Owl. Start by taking the left fork at the base of Smoking The White Owl. Follow leftwards, then right taking the line of least resistance. Never steep, but tricky brittle bulges are encountered.

Coire an Lochain, North-East Face:

Homo Sapiens – 60m IV,4. S. Kennedy, A. Nelson, D. Hood. 25th January, 1998.

Climbs the left side of the barrel-shaped buttress containing Homo Robusticus. Start just left of the toe of the buttress and climb into a large recess. Pull steeply out left to gain a groove splitting the left side of the upper buttress. Climb the groove (50m). Easier mixed ground leads to the cornice, sometimes large (10m).

Sideline – 90m III. S. Kennedy, A. Nelson, D. Hood. 25th January, 1998.

The wide fault-line between Riptide (and the unnamed Grade III groove just to the left) and the slabby buttress defining the southern edge of the corrie. Forms almost a gully in its upper section. Climb a narrow groove on ice to reach the upper gully (45m). Climb a groove on the right side of the gully to below a large cornice. The cornice was outflanked by a long leftwards traverse (45m). Climbed in thin conditions; the lower section may bank out.

Twins Area:

Siamese Twin – 120m IV,5. M. Pescod, T. Barton. 10th January, 1997.

Start at the foot of Left Twin.

1. 30m. Climb the narrow groove on the right side of the main gully of Left Twin, hard up against the right wall of the gully, to a snow bay.

2. 30m. Continue up the groove to a steep bulge on the right; pull round this on the left and belay 5m higher at rocks on the right.

3. 60m. Easily to the top.

AONACH BEAG, North Face:

Sellout Direct – IV,4. R. Webb, N. Wilson. February, 1998.

The original Sellout starts from the left-hand end of the large ledge from which Stand and Deliver starts (hence the name). The direct line climbs directly to the left end of the ledge via a chimney which cuts through the steep wall below it. This is right of Camilla and changes the route from mediocre to good.

MOIDART, Sidhean Mor (Sheet 40, MR 729 866):

South Ridge – 300m II/III. B. Wilkinson, N. Foster. 14th January, 1998.
Following the A830 to Mallaig, park at the sharp corner just before Beasdale station. Walk up Glen Beasdale for just under 2km where the obvious south ridge sweeps down off Sidhean Mor into the glen. Follow the broad ridge crest to the summit.

An Stac, North-West Face (Sheet 40, MR 763 793):

From Inverailort, climb over Seann Cruach to the col between it and An Stac. This is the obvious deep-cut gully which runs to the summit of An Stac.

CARN LIATH (near Creag Meagaidh), Coire nan Gall:

Winter routes have also been climbed here by S. Jenkins, A. Cain, C. Dale and parties. Descriptions have yet to be received but may coincide with the following. This is a relatively low-lying crag barely breaching the 900m contour. The crags line the east face of the corrie (similar avalanche risk and cornices to Creag Meaghaidh). Wait for a good freeze and if blessed with snow down to the road, a ski approach, but more importantly a ski return, has much to commend it. Later in the season the crag is largely banked up. The undeveloped nature of the crag means there is ample turf on most of the routes and take a wire brush to clear the lichen when rock climbing. The rock is largely slabby and appears good.
Access: Park in the roadside carpark (MR NN 525 894) on the A86 Laggan Road, half-a-mile west of the closed Kinlochlaggan filling station. Take the forestry track on the north side of the road, follow the right fork under the telegraph wires, past a Larch plantation to a second more youthful Sitka plantation. At its north-east corner, a magnetic bearing of 300° takes you across rough country into the corrie. A six-foot deer fence leads into the corrie and terminates at the bottom of Room to Roam slab, the southerly point of Ann's buttress, amid a boulder field – two hours if under soft snow. Alternatively, from a sharp bend on the A86 at MR NN 513 887 at the road stream junction. Follow the west bank of the stream to a deer fence and follow to the foot of the crag (SMCJ 1993).

There are four buttresses. As there did not appear to be any names associated with them, the first has been christened No.1 Buttress, the next Jolly Buttress. The large intervening gully between these two gives an easy descent before the cornice builds up. The third and largest buttress is Ann's Buttress which merges into Waterfall Buttress farther right and contains all of the recorded climbs. The last buttress is No.4 Buttress. The South Face, which starts at the large slab high on the left at the back of the corrie, is shorter and more broken with no routes apart from The Boulevard, the shattered ridge two-thirds of the way round the Corrie, used for descent.

Ann's Buttress:

Room to Roam – 100m E1. (see SMCJ 1993). Takes a wandering line up the middle of the cleanest slab of rock.
Turfinator – 200m II/III. C. Jones, A. MacDonald. 2nd January, 1995.
Start 4m left of the gully of Crampoff Corner. Ample turf. The slabs were covered with powder snow on the first ascent.
1. 40m. Move 10m up over broken rock to a gully then over a bulge and up.
2. 25m. Continue up slabs trending gently right.
3. 25m. Move out left on to slabs, then straight up.

4. 30m. Continue over the steepening slab to a shallow corner, climbed to 12m up.

5. 30m. Using the edge of the corner, move up bare slabs then a corner to broken rocks above. Easier ground leads to a good spike and the belay block of pitch 4 Crampoff Corner.

6. 35m. Easy steep ground leads to a block belay (under snow later in season).

7. 35m. Continue over the cornice.

Edge of Emotion – 165m HVS 5a (two points of aid). C. Jones, A. MacDonald. 28th September, 1997.
Start at foot of Ann's Buttress immediately left of the large intermediate slab and the corner line of the winter route Crampoff Corner and right of the line of Turfinator. This is about 100m right of Room to Roam slab.

1. 25m 5a. From talus, climb the buttress directly moving up awkward grooves to a wall. Move up and trend right to sloping holds and pull strenuously over a bulge on to the arête (two points of aid). Continue to a thread belay. Alternatively, go left at the foot of the wall, move awkwardly on to an easy slab and follow a deep crack directly to the arête (30m 4a).

2. 25m 4c. Follow the obvious exposed edge (nice pitch).

3. 15m. Continue up the edge, move left on to the slab then on to vegetated easy ground.

4. 30m. Move together up easy ground to foot of the next slab.

5. 30m. Climb on to the slab and move left to climb a corner. The top half of the slab can be turned on the left.

6. 45m 4c. Scramble 40m left over easy ground to the obvious upper slab. From the middle of the foot of the slab move left up a thin groove, then go boldly straight up a shallow crack to a comforting right trending ramp. From the top of the ramp move left on small holds to finally teeter onto the summit plateau. (See article, this issue.)

Crampoff Corner – 200m II/III. C. Jones, A. MacDonald. 12th December, 1993.
Start at the toe of Ann's Buttress immediately left of the large intermediate slab but right of the buttress, 100m right of the start of Room to Roam. The first pitch could be avoided by traversing in from a shallow gully on the right.

1. 45m. Climb the excellent corner to a cave belay in the left wall.

2. 40m. Move up the corner for 4m, then move out right on to a right-trending slab and continue to a small bay on the left wall.

3. 40m. Continue up the easing ramp for 6m then into an easier gully.

4. 45m. Finish up the gully and on to easier ground at the top of the buttress. Easier ground leads to the cornice (70m).

Direct Variation – 220m III. C. Jones, A. MacDonald. 12th December, 1993.

1. Climb Crampoff Corner to the cave.

2. Move up the corner for 4m, then continue directly up the steep corner (crux).

3. From the belay move up over broken rock and slabs.

4. Join the gully of pitch 4 Crampoff Corner.

Waterfall Buttress – 120m II. (see SMCJ 1993). Approx 300m beyond Room to Roam slab is a large gully/recess containing a waterfall high up on the left. The route climbs the buttress left of the waterfall.

Jambo – 120m II. A. MacDonald, C. Jones. 8th March, 1997.
On the extreme right flank of Ann's Buttress a steep, shallow gully or groove soars straight up to the plateau. The gully is right of the line of Waterfall Buttress. Just right of the last main area of rocks of the Buttress start up steepening snow.

Continue with a deviation to the left to avoid rocks and over bulge to rocks. Continue up the easing slope to the plateau.

BEN ALDER, Garbh Choire:

Bloody Noise – II. J. Davis, N. Johnstone. No date. A left-slanting line from the lowest point of cliff. Follows a groove for a pitch, then two more pitches to a snow bay. Finish by the second groove from the right out of five.

Thick Lip – 70m III/IV. N. Johnstone, J. Davis. No date. On a small cliff right of the South Buttress. A deep-cut icy gully about midway along the cliff.

MONADHLIATH, Geal Charn:

The following were climbed by C. Dale and E.Todd in February, 1996. A Grade I on the crag above Lochan a' Choire and below Beinn Sgiath. An open groove in the centre of the crag below Geal Charn (MR approx. 566 986) which leads into an amphitheatre and two subsequent branches, both Grade III. The left-hand has a cave pitch and the right an icicle. On the right corner of the crag (MR 567 988) is a twisting gully with several short pitches, Valentines Gully, Grade II. These were combined with a good one pitch icefall (Grade III) situated just under the plateau to the north beyond a snow gully (MR 565 989).

GLEN COE

BUACHAILLE ETIVE MOR, Slime Wall:

The New Testament – 135m E4***. D. Cuthbertson, J. George. 6th August, 1995. A superb route, one of the best in Glen Coe, taking a direct line up the entire cliff.
1. 25m 4a. As for Shibboleth to belay below the Apocalypse corner.
2. 27m 6a. Climb the corner above for 6m (initially as Apocalypse), then follow a little stepped overlap going left to enter an obvious groove (the slim, hanging groove immediately right of the Shibboleth groove). Negotiate the 'slime factory' and enter the groove. At its top move right into a wet corner. Climb the corner and its right edge (there is another slim corner to the right again which you enter towards its top). Climb the mossy thin cracks (probably the Apocalypse crux) to belay on the left.
3. 27m 5c. Climb up and left from two fingers of rock (forming a V) and climb a slim groove to a 3m tapering crack cum groove (also taken by Nightmare Traverse and Apocalypse). Climb the crack and instead of following the obvious line of stepped holds going up and rightwards (Nightmare Traverse and Apocalypse), trend left and follow a shallow groove-cum rib which becomes parallel and close to Shibboleth's 4th pitch. This leads to the right side of Shibboleth's isolated overhang. From a juggy handrail, climb the wall above and enter a small left-facing corner to reach a ledge and belay on Apparition.
4. 27m 5c. Step right and climb two thin tapering cracks to a ledge. Go up and right to a sloping shelf leading to the right edge of this steep section of cliff. Climb up and left to a square-cut hold, then continue to a good side-pull beneath the bulge. Move left and join Shibboleth True Finish at the traverse into the hanging groove. Belay on the edge above.
5. 27m 5c. Halfway along the belay ledge, climb a brown streak to gain an obvious stepped right-trending crack. Climb this in a fine position to easier ground.

Note: D. Cuthbertson notes that the FWA of Guerdon Grooves did not involve any leader falls (The note in SMCJ 1997, p347 being wrong) and that other than an ascent of the summer line 10 years' previously, the climb was not inspected.

Cuneiform Buttress, West Face:

The Mighty Atom – 90m E2/3**. D. Cuthbertson, J. George. 7th August, 1995.

A satisfactory dry solution to the unclimbed corner between Ba's and Lift Off. Start immediately left of the corner.

1. 25m 5c. Move up and left quite boldly to beneath a small overlap to reach good holds and protection in a vague horizontal break. Continue left into a groove. Climb this (hollow) and boldly move left to easier ground before going back up and right on excellent rock. Follow a crack rightwards into an overhung corner and protection. Cross the silver/grey wall (crux), then move back right to the base of an obvious bottomless corner. Climb this in a fine position to a good ledge and belay.
2. 50m 5a. Step left from the ledge and ascend a protectionless wall going leftwards to easier ground. Climb the open corner of Lift Off to a belay on the left.
3. 15m 4b. Step right and climb the steep ribbed wall to the top.

Coire na Tulaich, Blotch Buttress (SMCJ, 1997):

Dodgy – 35m E2 5b. R. and C. Anderson. 19th July, 1997.

The arête right of The Shield. Climb up and right to a ledge on the right side of the arête. Move left around the edge and up into a recess. Step right and climb the edge to the top. To descend, traverse left and locate the top of the corner with the *in situ* abseil gear.

Crack Cocaine – Possibly E2.

A Friend in Need – 30m E3 5c*. R. and C. Anderson. 19th July, 1997.

The wall between Crack Cocaine and Slack Alan looks mossy but the main holds were brushed on abseil. Bridge up the pinnacle onto the wall and follow holds which lead up right towards Crack Cocaine where it seems sensible to step right and place a wire before moving left to a small recess, poor gear. Awkwardly move up using a suspect hold to better holds, (Friend 2 in small slot) and stretch up out left to a large pocket (good gear), then continue to the top just right of Slack Alan. Abseil descent from the *in situ* gear.

Note: A new description of Symbiosis (Creag a' Bhancair) provided by D. Cuthbertson at E8.

GEARR AONACH, West Face, The Hamlets:

These terraced walls of excellent rock are situated opposite and at a slightly higher level than the East Face of Aonach Dubh. They are clearly seen from the approach path to Stob Coire nan Lochain and easily reached from the path in about 10-15 minutes. They receive the late afternoon and evening sun which makes them an ideal venue for an evening's cragging. The best approach is to continue a short distance from the stream crossing to the East Face of Aonach Dubh and then strike obliquely left to the foot of the wall. To descend from Yosemite Wall, either traverse a long way right, cross a shallow gully and scramble down to a boulder field before cutting back left under a long mossy wall or, abseil from one of the birch trees overhanging the top of the square recess.

Yosemite Wall (see also SMCJ 1996, p100):

This is the obvious overlapping wall at the lower left-hand end. Bounding this wall on the right is a square recess which contains two obvious cracks on its back wall (unclimbed as yet and often wet). To the right of the recess the crag continues as a long mossy wall which with a bit of gardening should yield some pleasant routes. The first described route climbs the relatively steep slabby south-facing wall to the left of the aforementioned cracks. The wall is characterised by overlaps at one third and two-thirds height, the second overlap being considerably larger.

Magnitude – 40m E5 6a**. D. Cuthbertson, C .and R.Anderson. 25th June, 1995.
Easy climbing for 6m leads to the base of a shallow left-facing groove, usually wet at the start. There is a more prominent corner to the left. Climb the groove (spike runner on the left wall), which is only adequately protected, to a rest beneath the right side of the overlap. Pull leftwards round this to attain a more comfortable position and good protection. Follow the thin crack with increasing difficulty culminating in a bold move going left beneath the top overhang. Finish up an easy groove.

Rock Lord – 25m E7 6b***. D. Cuthbertson, R. Anderson. 26th June, 1995.
In the centre of the overlapping wall, an obvious short, right-facing corner provides the only weakness through the lower overhanging barrier, the line of A Sweet Disregard for the Truth. Start 4m to the left of the corner at an undercut cave, usually wet for the feet (mat useful). Difficult initial moves reminiscent of limestone lead to an *in situ* peg runner (can be stick clipped). Continue up and rightwards on good holds to a break level with the top of the aforementioned corner. Move left and go up to another break where some protection can be arranged. Protected by an assortment of cams and small wires, continue up the impending wall on undercuts to the final bulge (cams). Pull over the bulge (crux) and bend slightly left to a break. Now go up and right on mossy rock to a hollow flake. Step left and up to a tree belay.

Avon Walls (SMCJ 1996, p101):

The following climbs lie on the upper right-hand wall of excellent rock situated above the descent to Yosemite Wall. It is best approached by either climbing a route on Yosemite Wall, followed by a scramble from the left to reach a tree-lined ledge or by climbing a route on the cliff directly below the wall or by reversing the descent route to Yosemite Wall. The best descent is to abseil from a sling which was left on a spike at the top of Multitude (please leave).

Multitude – 24m E3/4 5c**. D. Cuthbertson, J. George, R. Anderson. 1st July, 1995.
In the centre of the steepest part of the wall, an obvious slim right-facing groove peters out 6m up and bends right as a curving overlap. A fine pitch, bold and quite sustained. Climb the groove to the overlap. Pull out left via a pinch hold and continue left to the base of a shallow groove. Go up and right to the base of a thin crackline (it is now possible to step right to a foot ledge and protection). Continue directly to a ledge and belay.

Avon Calling – 27m E3/4 5c/6a*. D. Cuthbertson, B. MacMillan. VJ day, 1995.
Start to the right of a shallow groove at a prominent finger crack opposite a stunted rowan tree. This is to the right of Multitude. Slightly contrived but worthwhile. Climb the crack to a junction with VJ Day. Step left and climb the right-leaning overhanging crack (protection is awkward) until possible to step right on to a block. Climb the undercut groove above to join VJ Day and continue up the pleasant wall above.

VJ Day - 27m E1 5a*. D. Cuthbertson, B. MacMillan. VJ day, 1995.
Start 5m to the right of Avon Calling at a shallow groove leading to a small overlap at 5m. Climb the groove which is unprotected, then trend left and up to an undercut block. Continue into the left side of a large scooped area and exit by a steep cracked

groove. Now trend leftwards to a ledge and belay (the initial crack of Avon Calling would be a better protected start).

AONACH DUBH, Lower North-East Nose:
Supernova – 48m E6***. D. Cuthbertson, J. George. August, 1994.
Excellent climbing between Freakout and Spacewalk. Start as for Freakout.
1. 18m 5b. Pull out rightwards from the base of Freakout's initial groove and climb the centre of the wall going rightwards to join the last couple of moves on Spacewalk.
2. 30m 6b. Climb the thin crack leading to the right side of the Freakout alcove. Undercut the flake rightwards and pull up into a scoop. Clip an old peg runner above and slightly to the left of the Spacewalk groove, step back down to the scoop, then ascend going leftwards (bold) to a good hold at the foot of a thin crack. Climb the fine crack to the top overhangs which are turned via a rib on the right. Continue diagonally rightwards to a ledge and tree belay at the top of Crocodile.

East Face:
Bivvy Wall – 45m E3**. D. Cuthbertson, P. Moores. August, 1994.
A more attractive route than The Fly but equally serious. Start to the right of Anonymouse, just right of an obvious crack. Climb the wall (without using the crack). Now make an awkward move up the arête, then trend slightly right to a scoop (poor wires and spike). Climb the wall above to gain a line of holds trending slightly right. Easier climbing leads to a ledge.

West Face, B Buttress:
Bumblebee – 140m V,7. P. Moores, A. Nelson. 6th March, 1998.
Climb the summer line in three pitches.

STOB COIRE NAN LOCHAIN:
Innuendo, Direct Finish – 50m V,6. N. Wilson, S. Campbell. 9th March, 1997.
Possibly done before, this direct finish climbs the line of stepped grooves/chimneys above the awkward chimney of the second pitch.
2a. 25m. At the top of the awkward chimney, climb straight up to the base of the leftmost groove/chimney system.
3. 10m. Climb straight up until it is possible to step left into an overhung bay.
4. 25m. The overhanging chimney above, exiting over the capstone onto easy snow slopes leading to the narrow gully above the crux pitch of Scabbard Chimney. Short but strenuous. Pitches 3 and 4 were split in order to reduce rope drag.

BIDEAN NAM BIAN, West Top, Bishops Buttress:
The Gallery – 80m IV,5. R. Hamilton, S. Kennedy, A. Nelson, M. Thomson. 1st February, 1998.
Takes an exposed diagonal line leftwards across the buttress immediately left of the deep gully of The Fang. Start just below the narrows of The Fang. Climb out left along narrow ledges to a wide snow shelf below the steep upper wall (45m). Continue up leftwards to below a steep wall near the edge. Climb the wall for 3m, then traverse left along a narrow ledge in an exposed position to finish (35m).

Parthian Shot – 90m V,7. S. Kennedy, A. Nelson. 8th March, 1998.
The first obvious open groove-line 25m left of The Gash. Sustained in the lower part. Make a rising leftwards traverse from the foot of The Gash to reach the wide ledge which girdles the face. Climb directly up the steep open groove to reach the

easier upper groove-line (45m). Ignore a ledge system leading out left and continue up the steep groove on the right, over an obvious bulge, to reach easier ground. Finish just left of the top of The Gash.

STOB COIRE NAM BEITH, West Buttress:
Grand Mal – 55m HVS 4c. S. Kennedy, C. Grindley. 20th July, 1997.
Climbs the steep clean slab between the winter routes Team Machine and The Gathering. Reasonable climbing but sparsely protected. Start at the lowest rocks and climb a clean slab to a grass ledge at the foot of the main slab (10m). Move leftwards to the edge of the slab overlooking the chimney of Team Machine. Climb close to the edge a short distance, then move diagonally up rightwards across the slab, then directly to reach easier ground. Belay by the large block belay on the ledge above (The Junction). Abseil descent from the block.

The Sphinx:
Direct Route – 205m IV,7*. R. Anderson, R. Milne. 28th December, 1997.
A winter ascent of the Direct Route for which a more accurate description follows. Sphinx Buttress has a stepped appearance with its upper section being set back to the right. The lower section is formed by a steep wall overlooking the gully (Cleftweave) and Pyramid Buttress to the right. Just to the left is a blunt crest, then an area of easier ground beneath the most distinguishing feature forming the left side of the buttress, a steep wall cut by a number of wide faults/chimneys. The Ordinary Route climbs the easy ground, slanting up right beneath the steep wall. Direct Route takes the blunt crest to the right. Climb NW Gully to a short leaning wall just below Sphinx Butress proper.
1. 45m. Traverse out left around the edge to climb a chimney groove, crack and steps, then trend up right to belay beneath a groove in the blunt crest of Sphinx Buttress.
2. 40m.Climb the groove for 5m, step left and climb an open groove to a large ledge. Above is an obvious clean-cut groove, the right wall of which the summer route climbs – the groove will go in winter but the turf will have to be frozen. Instead, step left and climb grooves running up the left side of the steeper rocks, then go up right to a large ledge on the crest.
3. 50m. Above is a prow of rock, to the left of which is the recessed area beneath the steep faulted wall marking the left side of the crag. To the right of the prow is a wide fault. Part of the next pitch is common to the Sphinx Buttress Ordinary Route. Climb short steps to enter the fault from the left, then climb a short chimney and move right to a shallow recess at the right side of the fault. Pull out of the fault using a pinnacle flake, then climb diagonally up right to belay beneath an obvious corner.
4. 20m. Climb the corner, the crux of the summer route, to a belay at its top.
5. 50m. The buttress above is split by a fault, enter this from the left and climb it to easy ground. A couple of easier pitches lead to the top of the buttress. A choice of lines can be followed to the top. On the first ascent, having crossed the neck behind the buttess, an obvious ramp cutting up left, just left of a steep narrowing in the gully, then a groove, led onto the upper buttress where easy ground eventually leads to the top of Stob Coire nam Beith. The Ordinary Route is likely to be IV,5.

AN T-SRON, East Face:
The following routes are located on the excellent slabby wall described in SMCJ 1996, p104.

Halcion Daze – 55m HVS. S. Kennedy, C. Grindley. 29th May, 1997.
Takes a direct line up a vague flake line on the upper wall, just right of the black groove of Coco Leaf.
1. 40m 4c. Climb the initial hanging corner followed by Poppy Straw. From the top of the corner climb up and diagonally left to the grass ledge directly below the black groove.
2. 25m 5a. Move horizontally right to a deep pocket. Climb the wall directly above by way of a flake on the right (always right of the black groove). Finish in the large recess at the top of the slab.

Angel Dust – 60m HVS. S. Kennedy, C. Grindley, D. Hood. 20th July, 1997.
A direct line up the right portion of the wall. More direct and better than Poppy Straw, which it joins near the top.
1. 35m 4c. Climb the slab directly between the hanging corner of Poppy Straw and the corner of Coco Leaf to reach a prominent flake at 6m. Climb the flake, then directly up the slab above. Belay on the right below the upper wall (as per Poppy Straw).
2. 25m 5a. Move back left for 2m and climb a crackline to reach a prominent roof near the top. Surmount the roof (joins Poppy Straw) at the right end by a deep crack which is followed to the top.

A prominent hanging slab is situated high up, left of the black groove of Coco Leaf. The following routes congregate on the slab and follow three obvious crack systems. All are worthwhile and on excellent rock. It is possible to climb the routes in one long pitch but probably better to split as described.
Great Expectations – 46m HVS. S. Kennedy, C. Grindley. 28th June, 1997.
Start 2m left of the initial hanging corner of Poppy Straw at the left end of a small overlap.
1. 30m 5a. Climb a thin crackline to easier ground. Move up leftwards, close to the edge of the slab, then move straight up to the grassy ledge below the black groove (shared with Coco Leaf).
2. 16m 5a. Climb the obvious cleaned crackline up leftwards for 6m to a narrow ledge. Continue above in the same line following the incipient crackline to the top.

El Fatso Finish – 10m HVS 5a. S. Kennedy, C. Grindley. 28th June, 1997.
A good alternative finish to Great Expectations. Follow Great Expectations to the narrow ledge on the second pitch. Instead of climbing the crack above, traverse right for 2m to reach a left-slanting parallel crack system. Climb the cracks to the top.

The Chic Finish – 10m E2 5c. S. Kennedy, C. Grindley. 9th July, 1997.
Another good alternative finish to Great Expectations. From the narrow ledge on the second pitch, traverse left for a short distance until below a prominent thin crackline. Place gear low down on the left near the edge, then move back right into the crack. Follow the crack throughout, avoiding the temptation to move left to the edge near the top.

Note: The description for Coco Leaf (SMCJ 1996, p104) is misleading. On the first pitch, a long leftwards traverse is made to the left edge of the slab after the initial corner is climbed. Also, the top pitch of Poppy Straw is 25m - mistake in SMCJ description.

Codeine – 30m VS 4b. S. Kennedy, C. Grindley. 29th May, 1997.
The following route climbs the area of clean rock a few metres right of the initial

corner of Coco Leaf. Take a fairly direct line up the centre of the slabby wall. Poorly protected. To descend, traverse up and right by grass ledges to join the normal descent.

ALLT DOIRE BEITH:

On the South side below the HVS crack (which is a very good wee route done by the Squirrels) and Mouldering and Smouldering is another crag.

Sin Nombre – 25m HVS 5b. D. Gunn, P. Mills. April, 1997.

Climb the central diagonal crack after a difficult start, to a small dead tree. Continue past this using the crack and a parallel groove to the top. A wee gem.

Sertire – 20m E2 5b. D. Gunn, M. Tennant. May, 1997.

Just left of the groove of Sin Nombre on a white piece of rock are two thin cracks. Climb to the thin crack just left of Sin Nombre to a small overlap and horizontal crack with a runner at 10m. Move up and right past the dead tree and finish up the groove.

Ascoltare – 20m E2 5c. D. Gunn, M. Tennant. May, 1997.

Left of Sertire is an obvious deep groove and crack with two down pointing spikes. After a difficult start climb the crack past the two spikes (5c) to a block with a good hand jam behind. Finish strenuously up the deep groove to the tree.

Slightly farther up the Allt doire Beith from the crag with Ascoltare etc. but on the same side is a bulging crag on the south side. The crag is split by a deep crack which is hidden by trees. This good little route follows the crack.

Inertia – 15m HVS 5a. D. Gunn, M. Tennant. May, 1997.

After a difficult start, climb the steep crack on good holds to a birch tree and top. Well protected.

Above the Allt doire Beith facing west is an extensive area of crags low on Beinn Fhada.The left side of the left crag forms an arête before easier and more broken ground. The following route has been done. The rock is good and clean the holds accommodating and the situation superb.

Alan's Arête – 55m H. Severe. D. Gunn, M. Tennant. May, 1997.

Left of a thin crack is a booming flake with a ledge and flange going up the wall on the left. Mantelshelf on to the ledge and make a long reach to good holds. Continue to a belay at 20m. Continue up the crest on good holds to a block belay at 30m.

AONACH EAGACH, Gleann a' Chaolais (Loch Leven):

On the north side of Stob Coire Leith (Aonach Eagach) is a hanging corrie called Coire na Steill. The water draining from this corrie spills down quartzite slabs reminiscent of An Steall in Glen Nevis, though on a smaller scale. In cold conditions this waterslide offers one of the most accessible winter climbing venues in the area. Park just east of Caolasnacon and follow a path on the north-east side of the Allt Gleann a' Chaolais. (J.Grieve is known to have climbed here some years ago, so the line described is probably not original.)

Morning Glory – 90m IV. A. Wielochowski, D. N. Williams. 3rd January, 1995.

Climb easily up introductory slabs right of centre and head for a wall on the right to find a belay. Make an awkward move to gain a higher slabby ramp, and traverse hard left across the main water channel. Make some steep moves just left of this channel to reach an easier section of streamway. Traverse hard left and find a way down some distance east of the waterslide.

Meall Dearg:

D. N. Williams notes that a very striking gully cuts into the north-west flank of Meall Dearg (Aonach Eagach). Several fierce pitches discourage investigation in summer, but in lean winter conditions the gully is sure to offer good sport. Although it is known to bank out in a good winter (Grade I), it is strange that such a major feature has not been described previously. It is approached from Gleann a' Chaolais.

BEINN A' CHRULAISTE (Glen Coe guide, p273):

In cold thin conditions the various watercourses on the south flanks of the hill give pleasant ice climbing – MR 246 561. Both routes are clearly visible as watercourses from the Glen Coe road. Some harder icefalls to the left (west) of the following have been climbed by A. Spink and parties.

Highest Gully – 350m II/III. P. W. F. Gribbon, P. J. Biggar. 30th January, 1995. The gully which finishes nearest the summit. Continuous water ice and one (avoidable) blocky buttress pitch at the top.

Candlemas Gully – 300m II. P. J. Biggar, P. W. F. Gribbon. 2nd February, 1995. The next gully to the right.

BEINN BHEITHIR:

Dog Leg Gully – 120m II/III. D. Gunn, A. Nelson. December, 1995. Left of the large central gully on Beinn Bheithir on the face overlooking Ballachulish is an ice fall which after 90m enters a chimmney. Exit near the top of the south east ridge.

Ramp Line – 60m II. D. Gunn, J. Greive. November, 1996. From the coire under the summit of Sgorr Dhonuill an obvious ramp line runs up to a steep exit near the summit. Contains a short steep ice step early in the season and has a steep corniced exit late on. An attractive easy route to the summit from Glenachullish.

Sunset Fall – 60m III. D. Gunn. November, 1996. At the foot of the western descent gully into Glenachullish on the east side is a prominent ice fall coming off the edge of the buttress. Climb the fall direct to the ridge.

GLEN ETIVE, Creag Charnan:

This crag lies some 3km up Gleann Charnan from Invercharnan. It can be seen from the Glen Etive road in the vicinity of MR 478 143. It consists of baked mica schist very like the Polldubh crags in Glen Nevis. Although much of the crag is rather vegetated the line described is on relatively clean, sound rock. The crag is south facing and hence catches the sun. (The party set off with the intention of winter climbing, but couldn't find a parking space in Glen Coe!) Follow a track through the forest on the east side of the Allt Charnan. Exit from the forest and continue northwards. Cross the Allt Charnan and head up the hillside to the centre of the crag.

Foxtrot – 105m VS 4c. S. Abbott, D. N. Williams. 21st February, 1993. Follow a central line in three pitches. Protection is sparse. The second stance is taken by traversing left to a corner. The third pitch starts with an awkward overlap and finishes up a short steep wall by a fence post.

Trilleachan Slabs:

Paddington Bare – 105m E2. M. Pescod, A. L. Wielochowski. 27th May, 1997.

This route climbs the cleanest line on the left of the start of Claw. Start at the lowest slabs left of the coffin stone, 20m left of the start of Claw, 2m below an overlap and right-facing groove above.

1. 25m 4b. Climb the overlap and right-facing corner-groove for 10m, move up and left to a spike on a horizontal break.

2. 45m 5b. Go straight up the middle of the slab with a blank section at 20m providing a purely friction crux. Go slightly right to runners, back left to the top left of the slab and a small tree above.

3. 35m 4a. Go left for 4m to heather, climb up and left around a bulge to belay on a large heather ramp. To descend, scramble down the heather ramp.

Bitten by the Bug – 110m HVS. A. L. Wielochowski, M. Pescod. 27th May, 1997. Finds a way through the steep walls left of the main slabs. From the foot of the lowest slabs, down and left of the coffin stone, a prominent red corner can be seen in the steep walls and containing a large holly tree. Start by scrambling over steep heather to the corner and belay at the tree.

1. 30m 5a. Climb a groove in the rib on the right of the corner (behind the holly) until possible to traverse left to ledges. Go up to an overlap and left to the base of the upper slabs.

2. 40m 4a. Climb the slabs above, following the cleanest line to a heather break. Belay 5m above, right of a steep wall.

3. 40m 5a. Climb a quartz band in a steep clean slab to easy slabs above, not well protected.

Penguin's Paradise – 180m H. Severe. A. L. Wielochowski, I. Munro. 26th May, 1997.

This route finds a way up the steep walls half way between Bitten by the Bug and the main gully to reach the pleasant slabs above. Start at the left end of a very steep section of wall about 40m right of the descent gully and at a spike below an overhang.

1. 30m 4b. Move up and left, then climb walls trending left to avoid difficulties to just below an obvious oblong overhang and the easy slabs.

2. 30m 4a. Step right under a roof to clean rock leading to a fine sweep of slab. Go straight up via a faint groove to a diagonal slot.

3. 30m. Regain the groove, then traverse right just below a heather terrace to gain a big tree at the left end of the walls above.

4. 20m. Move 3m right of the tree, then straight up the steep walls to ledges. Move right.

5. Go up slabs to the next heather terrace and a niche on a comfortable rock ledge below a roof.

6. 30m 4c. Go awkwardly up through a break in the overhang and up a steep unpleasant wall (this pitch is optional and best avoided). Walk off left to the descent gully.

The Right-Hand Slab (p303):

Situated about 300m right of the main slabs. The following route starts just right of Comatose (described as Nausea in the guide) and takes a direct route up the slab, left of centre.

Confusio – 75m E1. S. Kennedy, C. Grindley. 27th September, 1997.

Start near the right edge of the base of the slab, just right of Comatose.

1. 25m 4b. Climb the slab to the left end of a small overlap at 5m. Continue up and slightly right to a larger overlap.

2. 50m 5b. Surmount the left side of the overlap, then climb cracks to reach prominent veins running across the slab at 30m. Follow the veins rightwards, then go straight up by a crack and slabs to a tree. Abseil descent from the tree.

Note: (from S. Kennedy). Comatose does not correspond in any way with the vague description originally given for Nausea. Comatose is a diagonal line for the most part and is almost certainly an independent route.

Note: Beinn Trilleachan: (note by D. N. Williams): There is a note in SMCJ No.165 (by I. Rowe and G. Tiso) concerning The Chasm of Beinn Trilleachan. It states: 'This remarkable rift is the right-hand branch of a gully system some two miles beyond the Etive Slabs. There are no unavoidable difficulties...' The chasm is identified in the current Central Highlands District Guide as 'the right-hand fork of a gully divided by an obvious dark tongue of rock (Teanga Dubh)'. Although this feature (Teanga Dhubh on O.S. maps) is exactly two miles beyond the Etive Slabs, the right-hand fork of the gully does not seem to match the original description. It is a moderately interesting streamway (which I ascended a few years ago with Willie Jeffrey), but it is neither a remarkable rift nor a chasm. Having examined a number of gullies on this hillside, I think the most likely candidate for The Chasm is the Eas Doire Dhonncha, which lies a little over one mile beyond the Etive Slabs (2km). The right-hand gully is certainly a remarkable rift. However, Ken Crocket and I failed in an attempt to climb it with full rock climbing paraphernalia in unprecedented drought conditions in September 1996. It would seem that either we have reached a worrying level of decrepitude (certainly possible), or The Chasm has changed in character over recent years, or it is somewhere else. I would be interested to hear of any other opinions regarding The Chasm's whereabouts.

ARDGOUR, Garbh Bheinn, Bealach Gully Buttress:

Eye of the Beholder – 55m E1. R. Pringle, M. Reynard. 24th May, 1997.
Opinions of the first ascensionists were divided as to its merit, hence the name. Vast quantities of loose rock cleaned on ascent. Start a long way right of Garnet at wet niche between short white wall split by obvious left-slanting crack and pinkish wall.

1. 35m 5b. Start below the groove, and go up the sharp, left-slanting crack (like a handrail) to easier ground. Traverse leftwards following the weakness of a quartz-dyke (some loose rock), then up slightly awkwardly into unexpectedly steep corner, then up wall left of green streak to good belay in a superb position at horizontal flake.
2. 20m 5b. Traverse left along line of hollow flakes to wall on left of roof. Enjoy fine moves up this passing overhang in splendid position (avoid loose rock in chimney), then up arête to top.

Garnet Groove – 55m HVS. R. Pringle, O. Metherell. 10th July, 1997.
Slightly loose in places, but considered as good as Garnet.

1. 30m 5b. Follow Garnet to an overhang, then move left and up around the overhang (strenuous) to reach shattered belay stance.
2. 25m 5a. Pull up left around edge into a vile-looking groove. Move blindly left onto the wall, and pleasurably up (good nut) on flake holds, then back into the groove. 3. Climb groove without much difficulty to top (beware loose block).

Bealach Buttress:

Nice 'n Easy – 50m V. Diff. R. Pringle, O. Metherell. 10th July, 1997.
A lovely little route which looks VS. Climb the middle of the pink slab then climb

an overhang by a weakness on the right. Trend left to below a second overhang, and pass it to the right. Pad up a slab above and either surmount a third overhang direct, or pass to right – continuing to scrambly ground.

Sun Fun – 50m Severe. R. Pringle, O. Metherell. 10th July, 1997.
Go up a corner at the left of the slab, then easily up the wall below an overhang to the left edge. Traverse right below a bulge to the bottom of a triangular second overhang, then up the overhung lichen-streaked wall on the left (wet – one awkward move) to gain the slab above. Go through a second overhang to easier ground and the top. Another enjoyable route. Some loose rock.

South Wall of The Great Ridge:
Leviathan – 20m E3 6a*. P. Thorburn, R. Campbell, N. Craig. June, 1997.
The wide overhanging crack right of Golden Lance.

ARDNAMURCHAN, Beinn Na Seilg:
The guidebook mentions three crags, however, there are effectively five; four facing west and one facing south. Some new names are therefore proposed, Eigg Buttress for the first and unclimbed crag, and Rhum Buttress for the section of crag just right of Cuillin Buttress which now has seven routes.

Eigg Buttress:
The northern-most of the crags is slabby and fairly small, there is a short north-facing slab on the left, from where a wide ledge cuts through the crag to give it a stepped appearance.

Cuillin Buttress:
A short way to the right and much bigger than Eigg Buttress. At the left side of the crag there are some short slabs. The main crag is formed in two sections with the left-hand portion tapering off to easier ground fairly quickly. A heathery break separates the buttress from the next buttress a short distance to the right. The first few routes lie on the right-hand portion of the cliff.

Rum Punch – 50m E2 5b. R. and C. Anderson. 5th August, 1997.
Start beneath a roof at the left end of this section of the crag. Climb to the roof and cross this in its centre by the obvious break. Stand on the block on the ledge above and climb directly up the bold mossy wall and continuation slab – easy but with little gear. Good climbing but could do with a brush/traffic.

Moving right the crag steps up a little at its base.

Coll of the Wild – 50m E3 5c**. R. and C. Anderson. 5th August, 1997.
An excellent route right up the middle of the crag. Start at a pointed ledge beneath a large block some 5m up. Climb directly to the block and on up the short crack above. Step right and climb a thin crack to the base of a right slanting faultline which is followed to the top.

Cuillin Down – 50m E1/2 5b*. R. and C. Anderson. 5th August, 1997.
Start beside Coll of the Wild and climb to the left end of a grassy ledge. Move up, then step right and climb the slanting crack almost to a large V-shaped recess (Grigadale Groove, Severe, SMCJ 187 appears to climb into this groove from the right). Step up left and climb an inclined groove just above the recess to finish up a corner.

Rum Buttress:
A short way to the right just beyond a grassy break. Formerly described as part of

Hebrides Wall but in reality a separate entity. The lowest part of the crag is narrow with the rocks slanting up rightwards over a grassy spur as the crag decreases in height towards Gabbro Slab. There is a short chimney rock step on the path to gain the top of the grassy spur, beyond which is Hebrides Wall. Just above the lowest rocks is a small roof with a green streak down it. The first two routes climb either side of the roof/green streak.

Muck Up – 50m E2 5b/c**. R. and C. Anderson. 6th August, 1997.
Move up left from the lowest rocks and climb the thin crackline into the middle of the slab and take a line slightly up left to reach easier ground. Belays well back on the right.

Mull Over – 50m E3 5c*. R. and C. Anderson. 6th August, 1997.
Start at the lowest rocks, climb to the roof and move up right to a ledge. Climb the crackline above to the slab, then go up right onto the slabby rib which leads to easier ground and a finish as for Muck Up.

Skye High – 50m E3/4 6a*. R. Anderson. 16th August, 1997.
The blunt buttress edge and the big groove. Climb the edge (small wires) to holds (Rock 4 on right) and continue to the groove which then leads to the top.

Eigger Sanction – 50m E3 5c**. R. and C. Anderson. 6th August, 1997.
Start just around the buttress crest on top of a boulder above the lowest rocks and climb a thin crack (small wires including an RP2) up a grey streak to better holds. A line slants right to Cannaloni, instead step up left and go up the wall above to climb slabbier ground just right of the prominent groove. Finish up a slabby rib.

Barra's Irn Bru – 50m HVS 4c*. R. and C. Anderson. 16th August, 1997.
A line immediately right of Eigge'r Sanction. Move up a slabby ramp, pull into a shallow groove and take a direct line to the top.

Sanday Shore – 50m VS 4c . R. and C. Anderson. 16th August, 1997.
The thin slanting crackline immediately right of Eigge'r Sanction. Make an extra move up to the top of the blocky ramp and move up to the crack. Follow this and easier ground just left of a wide crack to the top.

Cannaloni – 30m HVS 4c. R. and C. Anderson. 16th August, 1997.
Start from the top of the grassy spur above the short chimney-rock step in the path left of the heathery crack of Geologists Groove where there is a clean pillar with a crack up its left side (there is another crack to the left). A thin crack springs from this crack some 5m up. Climb a shallow runnel and step left to the thin crack which leads to easier ground and the top.

ARDNAMURCHAN, Rubha Carrach (MR NM 461 707):
A long band of cliff extending leftwards to an impressively overhanging promontary. The rock is a strange pocketed basalt, very reminiscent of limestone in places. A big extensive cliff with much scope for future exploration, definitely 'terrain exploration'. Aspect SW.
Approach: From the car park at the end of the road at Sanna, head north towards a ruined cottage, then follow the coast round to the cliff – 35 minutes. Descent: Down the scree-filled gully near the right end of the cliff. The crag generally becomes more impressive from right to left, culminating in a steeply overhanging wall on the point, before degenerating into poorer scruffy ground just beyond a prominent grooved arête. Near the right end is an amazing diagonal fault/gully.

There is a superb cave at the base of this, extending back for about 100m to a small chamber with some fine stalactite formations – take a head torch.

Nostromo – 35m E5 6a**. R. Campbell, N. Craig. 29th June, 1997.
Start 100m left of the deep huge cave towards the right end of the crag, beneath a prominent left-trending snaking black dyke. The route follows a direct line cutting through the centre of the dyke, aiming for a shallow left-facing groove above the dyke.

THE ARDNAMURCHAN RING CRAGS:
These descriptions have been organised by R. Anderson, who will write up Ardnamurchan for the next Glen Coe guide, following reports from four different parties. There are rumours of others!
The following crags lie within the volcanic ring-dyke complex known as the Ardnamurchan Ring. The crags are composed of excellent rough gabbro and can all be reached from various parking places within the Ring in the vicinity of Achnaha on the way to the road end at Sanna. Stalking takes place in September and it is best to check the access situation with Mingary House (Tel: 0197 251 0208).

Meall Sanna (MR NM 453 686):
The lies on the southern side of the road. Approach from the parking place where the road crosses the Allt Sanna at MR NM 458 687. Walk over the bridge and climb westwards up the hillside. The crag, a small clean face, lies south of the summit and is split by a central crack.

Seaview – 10m Diff. M. Riley, J. Stevenson. 15th June, 1997.
Follow the right-trending flakes, then finish left or right.

Preview – 10m VS 4c. J. Stevenson, M. Riley. 15th June, 1997.
Takes the obvious central crack. Go over a small bulge and follow the shallow crack to the top.

Dimview – 10m V. Diff. M. Riley, J. Stevenson. 15th June, 1997.
Follows the broken groove on the right of the crag.

Achnaha Buttress (MR NM 461 697):
On the north side of the road the ring-dyke continues. The rocky ridge running away eastwards (right) leads over at least three smaller knolls to Meall Clach an Daraich. The first sizeable torr/knoll has a steep south facing wall, Achnaha Buttress. Approach from the parking place at MR NM 458 687, or one a short distance further north.

Plocaig Rock – 25m VS 5a*. J. Stevenson, M. Riley. 21st July, 1997.
On the sea-facing end of the crag, start just left of the arête. Climb an obvious crack over a bulge (crux) and continue up a right-slanting crack. Keep left of the arête and finish up a slabby wall. Friends useful.

Plocaig Walk – 22m V. Diff. M. Riley, J. Stevenson. 21st July, 1997.
Near the right end of the main face is a dark slab below a roof. Go up the slab, then over easier ground to a terrace with a small wall. Go up this via a leaning block to the top.

Button Slab (MR NM 464 694):
South-west of and situated in front of the 93m high knoll, on which Achnaha Buttress is located, just west of Meall Clach an Daraich is a smaller south-facing buttress with a protruding block (or button) on its face. Routes go from left to right.

Pash – 18m Severe 4b. J. Stevenson, M. Riley. 22nd July, 1997.
Climb a steep wall 2m left of Mickey (4b, no gear). Trend left to a slanting crack and finish through a bulge.

Mickey – 18m Severe. M. Riley, J. Stevenson. 22nd July, 1997.
Just left of a grass-filled corner. Go up a steep wall to better holds and continue up a slab (gear on left) through dark broken rocks to the top.

Ludo – 18m V. Diff. J. Stevenson, M. Riley. 22nd July, 1997.
Start left of Felix and go straight up to a bulge. Move left to a crack and finish up this.

Felix – 18m V. Diff. M. Riley, J. Stevenson. 22nd July, 1997.
Start 1m left of the base of a diagonal crack. Climb up to a right-trending fault to the 'button', then straight up over a bulge to the top.

Meall Clach an Daraich (MR NM 465 697):
This crag is situated on the south-west flank of Meall Clach an Daraich not far from Button Slab. A fence which runs northwards across the flat, boggy floor of the Ring passes beneath the crag.

Sanna Ferry Ann - 15m V.Diff*. M. Riley, J. Stevenson. 20th July, 1997.
On the left side of the crag climb an obvious crack to the top.

Rum 'n Bata – 12m VS 4b. J. Stevenson. 20th July, 1997.
Climb the slabby wall towards the right end of the crag on small holds with no gear.

Noah's Oak – 12m H. Severe 4b. J. Stevenson, M. Riley. 20th July, 1997.
Right again is a Y-shaped crack. Gain the crack and climb it through a slight bulge keeping right.

Sgurr nan Gabhar (MR NM 470 698):
Immediately east of the summit of Meall Clach an Daraich is a knoll of the same height, Sgurr nan Gabhar. A south-westerly-facing crag is situated here, just before the Bealach Mor and the crags on the knolls of Meall an Fhir-eoin.

Thor – 50m Severe 4a**. C. Prowse, R. Kerr, G. Latter. 8th July, 1997.
Near the left side of a genearally broken crag is a narrow whale-back slab with a prominent left-facing groove and crack up the centre. Scramble in from the left to belay beneath a steep short groove. Climb the groove and pull steeply out left on to the groove above. Up this and continue in the same line to finish more easily up the slabby ridge above.

Meall an Fhir-eoin Beag (MR NM 482 699):
There are two main masses of south-westerly-facing rock on the knoll of Meall an Fhir-eoin, clearly visible on the rim north-east of the farm at Achnaha. The right-hand mass comprises of a series of ribs lying beneath the summit of Meall an Fhir-eoin itself. The second is more obvious and lies a short way to the left on a subsidiary knoll - not named on any map but for convenience called Meall an Fhir-eoin Beag. Approach from the parking place described for the previous crags, or from that for Meall Mheadhoin described later, just under an hour from either. The left-hand section of the cliff presents a flattish frontal face with a smooth wall, set above a slab, as its centrepiece. The smooth wall is cut by some thin cracks, while to the left the upper sidewall is cut by obvious left-slanting diagonal cracks. A thin grassy gully runs up the left side of the main part of the crag. To the right, separated from the lower slab forming the left-hand portion of the crag by a sloping grassy

recess, is a protruding, blunt, leaning buttress. This buttress is cut by a horizontal break to produce a feature resembling Darth Vader. The right-hand portion of the crag is made up of three slabby ribs, topped by a short headwall.

Crater Comforts – 60m VS**. R. and C. Anderson. 3rd August, 1997.
This takes the crackline running up the left side of the crag, immediately to the right of a thin grassy gully, to finish up the obvious diagonal crack in the upper side wall. Start at the lowest rocks beneath the crackline, beside a pointed flake, just left of the edge which turns into a slab.
1. 25m 4c. Climb the crack and its continuation up a whaleback to where it thins to form a hollow flange. Step down and around the flange, then step up right to belay just left of the thin crack in the left side of the smooth central wall.
2. 35m 4c. Step down into the grassy gully and after a few moves pull back onto the rock and climb the side wall to reach, then finish up the obvious left-slanting diagonal crack.

Volcane – 45m E2**. J. George, D. Cuthbertson. 3rd August, 1997.
This fine route climbs the obvious crack between Crater Comforts and the smooth central wall. Start just right of the toe of the buttress beneath a crack on the slabby left wall of the grassy sloping recess.
1. 15m 5a. Climb the obvious crack to a ledge beneath the left side of the smooth wall, and continue to the shoulder to the left.
2. 30m 5b. Climb a short steep ramp to a thin break above. Make a delicate step up and go right to a crack leading to a ledge. Continue up the crack and shallow corner to a large ledge below the top.

Trauma Crack – 45m E3**. D. Cuthbertson, J. George. 3rd August, 1997.
The obvious curving crack on the right side of the smooth central wall. Slightly contrived but good climbing. Start as for Volcane and belay down to the left of the crack.
1. 20m 6a. Climb the tapering groove and crack to a point very close to Magma Force (runner). Avoid possible escape on to that route and follow the crack which now bends back to the left (crux) to a ledge.
2. 25m 5a. Climb the continuation cracks and corners (with a tricky move above a ledge) to the large ledge below the top.

Magma Force – 50m E2/3 5c**. R. and C. Anderson. 3rd August, 1997.
Start up the sloping grassy recess just right of Trauma Crack at the base of a heathery crack. Step up, then move out left to climb the centre of the slab. Climb the short left-facing corner and continue up the left side of the rib to below a wide crack. An awkward move up a groove gains the crack directly. Climb the crack to a ledge, step up right and climb via short steps and slabs to a short corner leading onto the flat ledge at the top of the crag.

Vulcanised – 50m E2 5c**. R. and C. Anderson. 4th August, 1997.
A parallel line just right of Magma Force. Scramble to the top of the grassy recess, then go up left to climb the crack and short right-facing corner. Continue up the slabby rib to a heathery ledge and climb a thin crack to beneath a steepening with a thin crack. Climb the steepening, continue above, then step right to finish up the right edge of the crag.

Night Falls – 50m E3**. G. Latter, C. Prowse. 8th July, 1997.
Towards the left side of the face is a prominent right-slanting diagonal crack cutting through the steepest section of the crag. Start beneath the centre of the buttress.

1. 25m 6a. Move up and step left past a small juniper bush to a short crack leading up into a niche. Pull out right and over the roof on a superb jug. Continue more easily up the flake-crack, then by a fine thin crack up the slab to belay on a large ledge.
2. 25m 5a. Climb the blunt rib which soon eases.

The next two routes were climbed after the previous route, not knowing of that ascent, and take more direct lines up the buttress, effectively providing an alternative finish and start. All the routes are very good and full descriptions are given to be sorted out at a later date.

Star Wars – 55m E3**. R. Anderson, D. Cuthbertson. 4th August, 1997.
Takes the crack up the right side of the Darth Vader feature. Start at the base of the crag well below the crack.
1. 30m 6a. Scramble up grass and rock to climb a short crack leading to the leaning cracked wall. Climb this past a niche into a diagonal break running up right, then step up left and climb a steep crack to a ledge and a belay just above.
2. 25m 5b. Cross the heathery garden above, then climb the centre of the wall to gain and follow a slanting flakeline-cum-crack up right. Finish up a slabby rib.

Return of The Jedi – 50m E3 5c**. R. and C. Anderson. 3rd August, 1997.
Climbs the right side of the Darth Vader-like buttress. From the right side scramble up a heathery slab to a steep, stepped groove/crack. Climb this up towards the crack of Star Wars, then go up right along a horizontal break to the edge of the buttress. Step right around the edge and make some bold moves to gain the diagonal break coming up from Star Wars. Climb the crack just right of the edge and continue to the top.

To the right are three slabby ribs.

Yir – 55m VS 4c***. C. Prowse, R. Kerr, G. Latter. 8th July, 1997.
Just right of the central grass-filled fault on the first slabby rib is a prominent crack leading up into a slabby groove.
1. 45m. Follow these to a grass ledge at the top of the groove. Move right to the crest, and continue up this past a further break to belay on a large ledge just below the top.
2. 10m. Climb the crack above the belay.

Minky – 60m E2**. D. Cuthbertson, J. George. 3rd August, 1997.
A direct line up the first slabby rib just right of Yir.
1. 45m. Pull over a small overlap and follow a break slanting up to the left to a junction of cracks with Yir. Go up a few feet, step right and take a direct line up the whaleback by some thin and poorly protected climbing. Belay where the angle eases.
2. 15m 4b. Either climb the gully above or move left and climb the surprisingly straightforward crack to the top.

Up-Pompeii – 60m E3 5b/c**. R. and C. Anderson. 4th August, 1997.
A direct line up the front of the second slabby rib. Start at the lowest rocks. Gain and climb a crack up the crest of the initial short buttress. Climb a short crack in the left side of the rib and continue up into the centre. Step up left and climb the left side of the rib to easier ground. Continue to the headwall (possible belay), swing left and climb the short crack to a spacious ledge (55m). Climb the short wall above via the obvious step (5m).

Unnamed – 55m Severe 4b**. The wide crack up the right side of the second slabby rib, start from a ledge at the base of the crack.

1. 55m 4b. Gain and climb the crack to the headwall (possible belay and escape right at a lower overall grade). Climb the crack in the headwall (crux) and continue to a capacious ledge from where a 5m VS 4c finish (An Deireadh – M. Riley and J. Stevenson, 22nd July, 1997) can be made up the continuation crack.

An Toiseach – 50m V. Diff***. M. Riley, J. Stevenson. 22nd July, 1997.
The crack up the third slabby rib, just left of the arête and right of the heathery grooveline between the ribs, large gear.
1. 30m. Go up the corner to the crack and follow this to a very large ledge.
2. 20m. Continue up the slab behind and left of the belay to the large crack which comes up from the heathery groove-line between the ribs, then climb delicately up the slabs.

Oswald – 55m H. Severe 4b. C. Prowse, A. Simpson, T. Harper. 17th July, 1997.
Start just right of the blunt rib of the third slabby rib at the right end of the crag. Follow the left-hand of twin cracks for 5m, then move out left to follow another crack and easier ground to finish.

Tremor Crack – 50m E3**. D. Cuthbertson, J. George. 4th August, 1997.
1. 40m 4b. Climb the first pitch of Oswald to a belay beneath a short overhanging crack in the steep headwall.
2. 10m 6a. Climb the steep and strenuous crack to an awkward exit.

Cuil Iolaire – 60m VS 4c. C. Stead, J. Newsome. August, 1972.
Follows the longest groove right of a prominent nose in two pitches of 45m and 15m. This is probably the groove left of Yir.

Around the edge, right of the third slabby rib and some 25 up the slope is a short slabby wall with two right-slanting cracks.
Oisean Bheag – 20m Severe***. J. Stevenson, M. Riley. 24th July, 1997.
Pleasant climbing up the corner left of the two right-slanting cracks.

An Rathad Ard – 15m H. Severe*. J. Stevenson, M. Riley. 22nd July, 1997.
The left-hand crack starting below a traingular niche leads to a belay below an overhanging wall. Well protected pleasant climbing.

An Rathad Losal – 15m Severe*. M. Riley, J. Stevenson. 24th July, 1997.
The lower (right-hand) of the two slanting cracks leads to below the heather ledge and a step left to finish as for the previous route.

Creag an Fhir-eoin, or Dome Buttress (MR NM 485 698):
This smaller buttress with a slabby right face lies 100m right of the main crag. Routes from left to right.
Claude – 25m VS 5a*. T. Harper, C. Prowse. 17th July, 1997.
Start at a large detached flake. Climb rightwards up the flake for 3m to gain the crack and up this to an overlap. Traverse left below the overlap to a steep groove, pulling through this on a 'mega-jug' to finish.

Greta Gabbro – 25m HVS 5a***. J. Stevenson, M. Riley. 24th July, 1997.
Start at the toe of the slab and head up right to a flake, then go up a left-facing corner to the top. The difficulties increase with height, well protected.

Canna Do It – 25m Diff. M. Riley. 24th July, 1997.
The main fault up the middle of the slab. Climb up the grassy crack to a block, then up and right to the arête and straight up a crack to the top.

Rum Do – 25m Severe 4b. M. Riley, J. Stevenson. 24th July, 1997.
Climb the narrow crack (crux) just right of Canna Do It. Head up to the overhangs left of the arête and straight up a crack to the top.

Meall Meadhoin, Coire na Raineach: The Apron Slabs (MR NM 496 687):
Meall Meadhoin is the highest point visible from the road within the Ring, and when viewed from here a large slabby crag can be seen down and to the left of the summit. The slab is some 90m high with its most obvious feature being an overlap/roof part way up, at the left side of the frontal face before the crag turns a blunt edge to form a north facing side wall. The main frontal face presents an apron of slabs facing west into the coire. Descent is best down the left side but can also be made down the right side. The best approach is to follow the footpath which starts from the road at MR NM 469 677 just beyond where the road crosses the Allt Uamha na Muice shortly after entering The Ring south of Achnaha. The path leads to the old settlement at Glendrian. Leave the track and head gradually up east to the slabs which are visible high on the right.

Dance on a Volcano – 70m E1**. R. and C. Anderson. 17th August, 1997.
The blunt edge formed between the frontal face and the side wall on the left.
1. 45m 5b. Climb directly up the edge just left of Dance on a Volcano and continue up easier ground to a belay.
2. 25m 4a. Scramble up slabs to the top.

Ne'er Day Corner – 75m VS**. C. Stead, J. Newsome. August, 1972.
The first half was climbed on New Years Day 1961. The obvious corner and slanting crack leading up and around the left side of the roof, originally graded Severe.
1. 45m 4c. Move up the corner and follow the crack which slants up left towards the edge of the buttress. At the level of the roof, step right and climb a wide crack, then follow the slabby rib to a small stance.
2. 30m 4c. Continue up slabby ribs rightwards to finish on the summit block. Climbed in 1997 by L. Curtis, F. Sadiq and D. Virdee, then R. and C. Anderson all thinking they were first!

Gift of the Gabbro – 75m E3**. R. and C. Anderson. 17th August, 1997.
The centre of the slab between the corner of Dance on a Volcano and a corner on the right.
1. 45m 5b. Climb the initial wall by a flange and climb the slab to a small ledge occupied by a small boulder. Move up right to a thin crack in a shallow scoop and place the last wire for some distance. Pull out left at the top of the scoop, then go up left to the base of a blind flange. Move right to a thin, blind crack and follow this to a flat-topped spike (sling). Go left, then up to the overlap and pull through this by the obvious flange. Continue for some way up and left to belay on the slabby rib as for Dance on a Volcano.
2. 4c. Step back right into the groove and climb up right to follow a parallel line to Dance on a Volcano, up short walls and slabs. The final short wall is climbed centrally by an obvious ear.

Dragster – 50m VS. D. Virdee, L. Curtis, F. Sadiq. 19th July, 1997.
Start below the obvious left-facing corner leading to the roof.
1. 30m 4b. Follow a big crevasse up to the corner made by the overhang and the right slab. Pull up right and over onto the upper slab (hard). Continue up steeper rocks to a dubious block-belay.
2. 20m. Continue up slabs and steeper sections to a terrace.

Glendrian Corner – 90m VS. C. Stead, J. Newsome. August, 1972.
Start a few metres left of the diagonal grassy groove in the centre of the crag. Climb a right-facing corner, go left and climb the more prominent second corner. Cross the diagonal groove and gain a slabby faultline which is followed to the top.

Slanting Groove – 90m V. Diff. J. Newsome. August, 1972.
Climb the diagonal grassy groove up left to the skyline and climb slabs to the top.

Leac Glas – 90m V. Diff. J. Newsome, C. Stead. August, 1972.
Climb the grey rib and slab starting just right of the diagonal, grassy groove. A variation follows the curving fault on the left in the upper section (C. Stead, 1980s).

Solas – 90m V. Diff. C. Stead. 1970s. Climb the slabs a few metres right of Leac Glas, keeping right of a curving crack. A variation climbs the two curving cracks on the left (C. Stead, 1980s).

Gall – 90m V. Diff. C. Stead. 1970s. At the right side, start at the foot of a short crack which leads to easier slabs.

Glendrian's Express – 80m Severe***. M. Riley, J. Stevenson. 20th June, 1997.
Although probably the same as Solas or Gall this appears a more precise description and is left for someone to check in the future.
1. 25m 4b. Start at the foot of black seepage marks (small flake). Follow the right-slanting crack for 8m (crux, good gear). Trend right and go up to a narrow ledge, then straight up to belay, bold after the initial crack.
2. 38m. Continue up good rock on the right side of the fault to belay on a large terrace.
3. 17m. Finish up the same line on easier ground to the top.
Note: On 19th July, 1997 after pitch 1, D. Virdee, F. Sadiq and L. Curtis climbed the loose gully then stepped left onto easier slabs.

SOUTHERN HIGHLANDS

MULL OF KINTYRE, The Jester:
Bopp Till You Drop – 60m E2*. K. Howett, G. E. Little (alt.). 29th March, 1997.
Climbs the left-hand section of the wall. Start at the middle of this section at a slight rib to the right of a short corner.
1. 40m 5b. Climb the left side of the rib up to steep rock and a small overlap. Step left and up, past a horizontal crack, on to the clean wall above to be forced to pull right on to a small ledge. Follow the ramp above the ledge until moves left into a short groove lead to easier rock. Climb directly up the centre of the wall to steeper rock and a diagonal break. Pull out right and move up to a heather ledge.
2. 20m 5a. Step on to the clean slabby wall on the right, then climb diagonally up and right, with interest, until an exit can be made up a slight groove.

Creag na Lice:
Heaven's Gate – 30m E3 5c***. G. E. Little, K. Howett. 29th March, 1997.
This excellent route lies on the pale left-hand section of the crag. It contains some serious sections but has improving protection (small Friends) as height is gained. Start right of centre below an obvious left-facing hanging flake (the right-hand of two similar features). Climb up to the base of the hanging flake, then move right to ascend a diagonal, rounded fault to step up on to a narrow ledge below a short blank wall (joining Honeysuckle Wall). Move left, pull up the wall, then move left again to a good rest below another short, blank wall. Step up and right until holds

at the top of the wall can (surprisingly) be grasped. Gain an undercut rounded flake above, then using an obvious pocket, make a strenuous blind move to gain a rest. Move up to a horizontal crack, then follow it leftwards to reach the top.

Signal Stack:

Splish, Splish, Splash – 30m VS 4b*. A. Todd, G .E. Little. 30th March, 1997.
Tackling the seaward face of Signal Stack, this route ascends a broken wall to reach then climb the wide rusty rib immediately left of the central chimney-fault. At times it is possible to traverse in to the base of the route at sea level from the north. However, with seas running or a high tide, a short difficult wall below the north face of the stack must be scaled (5c) before a ledge leads round to the seaward face from where a descent to the start of the route can be made.

THE COBBLER, South Peak, North-East Face:

Lovehandle – 45m IV,5. S. Burns, D. Crawford. 28th February, 1998.
A short but good route that takes the parallel crackline 10m to the left of Jughandle. The route is north-facing and slabby in nature which means it is often in condition when many of the south-facing routes have been stripped by the sun.
1. 30m. Climb the off-width crack direct up the slab to reach a belay in a steep corner.
2. 15m. Climb the corner direct over a bulge.

BEINN NARNAIN, Crag at MR 275 066:

The following routes lie on a crag below and to the right of Spearhead Ridge when approaching from Beinn Narnain's SE ridge and at the same altitude as the bealach between Cruach nam Miseag and Narnain's summit slopes. It is east-facing and overlooks Coire Sugach from where it appears to form the east face of the Spearhead Ridge. This is not the case as the path to the summit of Beinn Narnain passes above the crag and between it and the Spearhead Ridge proper. It may, however, be considered part of the Spearhead massif, there being a lot of rock hereabouts. The crag as described consists of three buttresses although further broken buttresses extend to the right. The left-hand buttress is clean, about 25m high and sports a number of thin vertical cracks. To its right is a recess where a steep crack above a cave opens into a deep gully. The next buttress is slightly taller and a little dirtier. It is partially detached from the mountain, being bound on its right by an easy gully which runs up and left into a chock-filled chimney behind it. Right of this gully is a mossy slab with turfy ledges, the location of the winter route 'The Twilight Zone'. Descent from the first two buttresses is best made to the left of the crag.

Equinox – 25m E1 5b. J. Love, N. J. Smith. 25th September, 1997.
A very good route of sustained interest on sound rock up the crack system on the right-hand side of the left-hand buttress. Start at the right-hand end of the buttress just before the recess and cave. An awkward start gains a right-trending crack system leading to a small ledge at about 10m. Up and left is another thin crack which leads to the left end of a jutting block. The obvious wider crack above and to the right leads to the top.

September Song – 35m VS. N. J. Smith, J. Love. 25th September, 1997.
Start below the centre of the second buttress at the foot of a left-slanting rake. Would benefit from cleaning.

1. 25m 4c. Climb the rake to the foot of a vertical crack which is climbed to an exit right on to a ledge. Above the ledge is an undercut groove which can be climbed direct at 5b or another groove farther right can be climbed until moves left past a shelf lead to an exit on to a large ledge. Belay at a boulder on the left.
2. 10m Climb the blocky arête to the top.

THE BRACK:
I. and G. Griffiths note that they climbed the direct start to Plunge (SMCJ 1997, p361) on 30th March, 1996 and it appears in the new guide.

BINNEIN AN FHIDLEIR, Aquila Buttress:
Thoughtluss Crack – 18m E1 5b. N. Warnes, N. J. Smith. 11th April, 1997.
The short steep crack in the left side of the buttress is climbed on sharp jugs and jams. Start 5m left of Aquila directly below the crack.

Central Wall:
Between Witch Doctor and Abyssinia Chimney a smooth wall is capped by an impressive band of overhangs. These are breached in two places, a V-groove capped by a roof shaped peculiarly like giant beetle mandibles on the left and an impending left-facing corner above a deep crack on the right. The following two routes take these features directly. Near the foot of Abyssinia Chimney a grass ledge leads off to the left below a mossy slab. At its left end is a sapling.
Gorillas in the Mist – 45m E1 5b***. N. Warnes, N. J. Smith. 20th April, 1997.
Start 3m right of the sapling. Climb the mossy slab by the cleanest rock trending right to a grassy break. Climb awkwardly over a bulge to gain the upper wall and climb this delicately (and delectably) by a clean strip between two mossy streaks. Step left to gain a shallow recess and bridge up this to the foot of the deep V-groove. Climb through the overhang using the left wall of the groove and finish at the left of 'the beetle'.

Born Free – 45m E1/2 5b**. N. Warnes, N. J. Smith. 20th April, 1997.
Start at the right end of the grassy ledge where it joins the foot of Abyssinia Chimney. Ascend the slab trending left to a deep crack leading to the foot of the impending corner (possible belay at top of crack). Bridge widely up the corner until thin moves can be made left to a good foothold on the undercut arete. Continue up the headwall on improving holds to the top.

BEINN AN DOTHAIDH, North-East Coire:
Pillager – 165m V,6. A. Powell, R. Cross. 27th January, 1996.
Climbs the ramp on the severely overhung wall right of Haar and Valhalla.
1. 25m. Climb the icefall to where it steepens. Belay on the left.
2. 20m. Step back down, gain and follow the ramp to a steep corner. Cross this to a large ledge 2m up right.
3. 40m. Traverse 5m right and pull steeply up the barrel wall (crux). Head up and slightly right to climb the 4m corner just right of the crest. 4, 5. 80m. Climb easy ground to the top.

BEN CRUACHAN, Drochaid Ghlas:
Super Trouper – 110m V,5. C. Cartwright, S. Richardson. 28th February 1998.
A direct line up the right edge of the buttress taken by Gaoth Mhor. Low in the grade. Start 20m right of Gaoth Mhor.

1. 50m. Move up to the prominent corner. Climb this and the wall above to a stance on a horizontal ledge cutting across the buttress.

2. 30m. Move up and right to gain a shallow fault line cutting up the right edge of the buttress. Climb this to a stance on a good ledge as for Gaoth Mhor.

3. 30m. Continue directly up the fault line to the top (to the right of the diagonal line taken by Gaoth Mhor).

MEALL NAN TARMACHAN, Cam Chreag, Fan Buttress:

Floating Rib – 90m III. K. V. Crocket, R. T. Richardson. 9th March, 1998.

Just left of Turf Going is an easy gully, starting some way up the buttress. Left again is a blunt rib, providing the line of this route. Climb easily to the foot of the rib (the gully starts on the right). Climb up the left flank of the rib to easy ground, then finish up the terminal buttress above.

Carlin's Buttress:

Oochahoarye – 60m V,7. A. Clark, E. W. Brunskill. 17th December, 1997.

A fine direct climb taking the parallel groove line left of Witches Brew.

1. 40m. Climb the groove directly through a roof and hanging chimney crack to a large recess below an off-width.

2. 20m. Climb the off-width and continuation corner above.

Caledonian Cruise – 90m III,4. S. Burns, D. Crawford. 17th December, 1997.

1. 45m. Start about 10m right of Clark's Gully and climb up steepening mixed ground to the base of an obvious chimney. Good thread belay.

2. 45m. Climb the chimney direct to a squeeze exit (crux). Follow the rib above via a small corner to the top.

One For The Road – 50m II/III. S. Burns, D. Crawford. 17th December, 1997.

To the right of Beldame Buttress there is recess of easy ground. Follow this up to the start of a striking chimney/corner line. The line cannot be seen from the corrie base.

1. 30m. Climb the chimney to its end.

2. 20m. Continue right to the top of the buttress.

BEN LAWERS, Coire nan Cat, Creag nan Fitheach:

Catabridged – 65m III,4*. G. E. Little, K. Howett. 11th January, 1997.

This route takes the general line of the icefall that lies close to the left-hand side of the crag and runs up past the left-hand end of prominent roofs. Start at an open groove to the right of a rib, below the line of the icefall.

1. 35m. Climb the open groove for about 10m until a step left on to the rib can be made. Climb the rib to a ledge below the left end of the line of prominent roofs.

2. 30m. Climb two short vertical ice steps (or mixed ground to their left), then progressively easier ground to the top.

ARRAN

A' CHIR:

The Cave of Adullam – 175m VS. A. Fraser, D. McGimpsey. 26th September, 1997.

A traditional mountaineering route up the thin buttress between The Minaret and Intruder buttress. Start at the right toe of the buttress, at the start of Imposter Crack.

1. 20m 4a. Climb left, upwards, then slightly right to belay at the foot of a sweep of slabs.

2. 25m 4b. Follow a ledge left across the slabs, then climb the left edge of the slab to a grassy terrace.

3. 30m 4c. Move right for 2m, then up a thin crack to slabs beneath the main overlap. Traverse slabs right for 3m to a spike, then up into a corner above. Climb this for 5m, then follow a crack out left. Belay at the top of the corner. A good pitch.

4. 30m 4a. Move up and left to a bulge, which is surmounted directly to a grassy ledge. Move right and up to belay.

5. 35m. Climb up and right, maximising rock or turf to taste.

6. 35m. Scramble to the top.

CIR MHOR, Lower East Face:

The following two routes were intended for the Arran guide but were sent to the wrong address, so appear belatedly. From the finish of either, an easy traverse leads to the belay above the Y-cracks on South Ridge Direct. From here an abseil down South Ridge Original is possible. Both routes are excellent and Ariel's Arête sounds very similar and predates Squids and Elephants, climbed in 1996.

Ariel's Arête – 40m HVS 5b. M. Reynard, D. Musgrove. 6th May, 1995.

To the right of The Crack is an arête split by a prominent flake-crack. Start below this on a grassy ledge. Climb up to the left end of an overhang, pull over and follow the rightwards-slanting flake-crack leading to the arête. Continue up the arête and an easy slab.

Fox Amongst the Chickens – 40m E2 5c. M. Reynard, P. Benson, D. Musgrove. 6th May, 1995.

To the right of the previous route is a prominent wall with an obvious pocket high up and three short flake-cracks lower down. Start below the centre of the wall. Climb an undercut corner, then move left and up to gain the lowest of the cracks; climb these to their top. Make a move right, then climb the wall directly, finishing up a short groove.

Note: For the sake of historical accuracy in the new guide, Labyrinth, Pinnacle Gully Buttress and Shelf Gully were climbed on 5th February, 1983 (not 7th) and Bypass Route, Stoneshoot Buttress on 6th February, 1983 (not 8th), noting that George Harper was Scottish 3000m champion at the time and was not far off the required distance with his four routes on 5th Feb. C. MacLeod and not MacLean was on the first ascent of Labyrinth.

LOWLAND OUTCROPS

GALLOWAY HILLS, Craignelder, Craig an Eilte:

About 8m right of the prominent tower with the existing guidebook routes is a paler, moss-flecked wall which rises steeply for about 40m. Routes on perfect granite with excellent protection.

City Bumpkin – 30m Severe. A. Faulk, M. Harvey. April, 1997.

Start about 8m right of Elite Pinnacle Rib at an open corner. Climb the corner to a ledge. Step left and climb a second corner to another ledge. Move left and climb steep cracks to finish via ledges and large granite blocks.

Diagonal Route – 40m VS 4c. M. Harvey, A. Faulk. April, 1997.

The obvious diagonal route rising from left to right. Start about 10m left of an obvious overhang at the base of the crag where there is a stalactite hold. Climb the ramp line rising to the right and where it runs out move directly up via a short crack (crux). Continue straight up to finish via ledges.

GALLOWAY SEA CLIFFS, Finnarts Point, Main Cliff (SMCJ 1997, p364):

Last Night at the Prawns – 25m E3 5c**. A. Fraser, R. McAllister, D. McGimpsey. 14th August, 1997.

An excellent and varied route, no brain thuggery, leading to a delicate and cunning crux. This is the line of mildly overhanging corners 5m right of Edge of the Abyss. The crux is the pale blank corner just above half height, climbed by blindly moving left to easier ground.

Full Speed Ahead – 25m E3 6a**. R. McAllister, A. Fraser, D. McGimpsey. 14th August, 1997.

Technical and strenuous, but delicate, with increasing difficulty. Representative of some of the best climbing on the face. To the right of Last Night at the Prawns is an uncompromisingly steep wall with a right-trending stepped ledge on its right. The route takes the initial step in the ledge via a wide crack in its corner, then climbs directly, then right to a slim and difficult groove on the immediate right of the uncompromising wall.

Camp Boss, Can't Cook, Won't Cook – 25m E2 5c*. D. McGimpsey, S. Mearns, R. McAllister. 28th September, 1997.

Another good route, protection increasing with height. High in the grade. Start just right of Red, Hot and Blue. Climb up and rightwards with poor gear to gain the obvious crack above (up and left of the big corner of I Should Coco).

MEIKLE ROSS: Note: M. Reed made the second ascent of Spectacular Bid with different gear (particularly without the skyhook) and thought it a superb route, perhaps E6.

PORTOBELLO, Slab Bay: Changeling:

The two pegs have been removed, and R. McAllister with D. McGimpsey has led the route at E5 6a. Although the upper crack is the technical crux, it is well protected and the lower unprotected arête now becomes the overall crux.

Screamadelica – 15m E5 6a*. R. McAllister. June, 1997.

Intimidating (with good cause!) and difficult to read. This is the arête to the right of The Changeling, starting up Changeling and climbing its crux before moving out left on to the arête.

Main Cliff:

The Lowland Outcrops guide erroneously describes Floating Voter as being to the right of The Crayfish Twins, when it appears to lie to the left.

Monsieur Dubois – 22m E1 5b. R. McAllister, S. Mearns. June, 1997.

To the right of The Crayfish Twins is a leftward-curving overlap, which gives enjoyable climbing. Finish up the top of The Crayfish Twins.

Shark Fin Bay:

Buckets of Doom – 25m E1 5b. D. McGimpsey, R. McAllister. June, 1997.

A good route which will improve with traffic. To the right of Silence of the Clams is a corner, on the right side of which is a pocketed wall. Climb the pockets to a large nest ledge, then climb the narrow wall above with difficulty.

The U-Boat Pen:

Paranoid Android – 6m E5 6b. M. Reed. 7th July, 1997.

At the seaward end of the south wall of the inlet (opposite the main crag) is a short leaning wall. Climbs the right-hand overhanging crack and groove line above a sloping ledges.

LAGGANTULLACH HEAD, Hoodlum Bay:
The following two routes are situated to the right of The Oyster Thief.
Sam I Am – 25m E4 6a***. D. McGimpsey, S. Mearns, R. McAllister. 17th August, 1997.
A tremendous route on flawless granite, one of the best in Galloway! To the right of The Oyster Thief is an overhanging wall. This route takes the corner immediately to the right of the wall. Climb the initial corner (crux) to a ledge. Move right for 1m, then climb directly up the wall above until possible to move back left into the corner. Climb up to a roof until possible to swing out left to finish. Climb an easy slab to the top.

Green Eggs and Ham – 25m E1 5b**. S. Mearns, R. McAllister. August, 1997.
This fine route takes the tapering steep slab corner, which is the only break in the overhangs. Start 6m right of Sam I Am. Climb the slab corner. At the top move on to the slab on the right to finish.

Foam Zawn:
Toxygene – 25m E5 6a*. R. McAllister, D. McGimpsey. 11th August, 1997.
The arête right of Refusnik, a last great problem. The climbing is good but difficult to read, while the gear is spaced and the upper section somewhat loose. Start to the right of the arête and climb up to a niche, then move left with difficulty on to the arête. Climb up into a shallow corner on the right side of the arête, climb this, exiting left back to the arête. Climb to a wide ledge beneath the final arête, which is loose and 5a, but one can scramble off left.

The Auld Ship:
This cliff is situated about 500m north of the Dragons Cove. From Dragons Cove, continue north along the coast until it is necessary to climb steeply up to avoid a high cove. Descend on the far side of this to the cliff, a narrow arête with a north-facing 25m slab of excellent greywhacke falling sheer to the sea. Access is by abseil. At low tide there are ledges at the foot of the cliff which can be traversed between routes, otherwise abseil directly. Routes described left to right.
Read the Small Print – 20m E5 6b**. R. McAllister, S. Mearns. August, 1997.
Technical bridging and udging, gear being good but spaced. The left corner of the cliff, above the cave, divides into two main corners at mid height. Between these is a slab split by a thin blank corner, the line of the route. Due to high seas on the first ascent, the route was started at a niche about 6m below the corner. From here climb the roof into the corner, then proceed with increasing difficulty, using small edges on the right wall of the corner.

Optical Illusions – 25m HVS 4c*. A. Fraser, R. McAllister, S. Mearns. 9th July, 1997.
Fairly steady wall climbing, gear and holds both improving after a bold start. The route climbs the wall between the left corners of the cliff and the obvious central groove line. Start on a ledge up and just left of the central groove line. Move out left, then directly up the wall.

The Auld Ship – 25m Severe*. A. Fraser, R. McAllister. 29th June, 1997.
A sheep among wolves (albeit a rather attractive young sheep). This is the central groove line on the cliff, the obvious bulge being climbed on the right.

Higher than the Sun – 25m E2 5b**. R. McAllister, A. Fraser. 29th June, 1997.
A sustained and delicate route with spaced protection. High in the grade. Between The Auld Ship and the right arête of the cliff are two thin cracks. The left, more obvious crack leads leftwards, while this climbs the clean strip around the right-trending right-hand crack. Climb the crack for 5m, then move out slightly right. Continue directly above with difficulty and follow the cleaned strip to the top.

Zero Tolerance – 25m E5 6b**. R. McAllister, D. McGimpsey. 10th August, 1997.
A very thin route, with just adequate (albeit well tested) RPs for the crux. The route climbs the wall just left of the right arête of the cliff, starting as for Higher than the Sun. Follow a right-trending diagonal crack out to nearly the arête. Place a good nut at 8m, climb straight up from this to a good hold and small wire placement on the right. Move slightly left, then up on small holds past a small horizontal break with a long reach to better holds (crux). An easier (6a) but less satisfying variant is to stand on the good hold and make a hard move up to better holds. The climbing above is easier but not well protected until just before the finish.

MULL OF GALLOWAY (Sheet 82, MR 146 303):
The Mull is Scotland's southern-most point, the last redoubt of the Picts, where the secret of the legendary ale finally vanished. These are the highest and most extensive cliffs in Galloway, high in atmosphere and with some remarkable caves and coastal scenery. It has long been assumed that the cliffs were hopelessly loose but closer acquaintance has revealed areas of impeccable quality rock and climbing (interspersed with total structural instability). Some areas are relatively free of seabirds, while others should definitely be avoided in the nesting season. Development is under way but the following unique experience is included as a taster for the future.

The Traverse – 2.5km E1 5b. S. Lampard, D. McGimpsey. April, June and July, 1997.
One of the truly great voyages of sea-cliff climbing, taking in some remarkable scenery and situations. The climbing is surprisingly fine and continuous. The traverse starts at West Tarbet, the bay on the right where the peninsula narrows to an isthmus about a mile from the lighthouse. It finishes at Seals Cave, under the foghorn just past the lighthouse. The route was climbed over four days and divides into sections which can be climbed individually according to taste, sea conditions and the state of the tide. Time will largely depend on the amount of soloing.

1. The first main section is from West Tarbet to Gallie Craig (this is the high cliff with a prominent corner line, well seen by looking back north from the lighthouse car park. This was climbed over two days. About midway through the first day was a cave, which requires low tide to cross without swimming (start from West Tarbet about 3-4 hours before low tide). It is possible to scramble in or out immediately to the south of Gallie Craig. Technically 5b.

2. The next section from Gallie Craig onwards contains the finest climbing and the most impressive rock architecture. Low tide is essential to start this section. Farther on there are two sea caves which require swimming. Calm seas are essential and it should be noted that the Mull is both exposed and prone to difficult undercurrents. It is possible to scramble out in the vicinity of the car park next to a steep yellow wall. Technically 4c/5a; one abseil.

3. The final section, while worthwhile and interesting, is not as sustained and can hold much guano. Technically 5a; four-five abseils.

MISCELLANEOUS NOTES

The W. H. Murray Literary Prize.

As a tribute to the late Bill Murray, whose mountain and environment writings have been an inspiration to many a budding mountaineer, the SMC have started a modest writing prize, to be run through the pages of the Journal. The basic rules are set out below, and will be re-printed each year. The first year open to contributions will be 1998, with a deadline, as is normal, of the end of January that same year. So assuming you are reading this in early July, you have, for each year of the competition, six months in which to set the pencil, pen or word processor on fire.

The Rules:

1. There shall be a competition for the best entry on Scottish Mountaineering published in the *Scottish Mountaineering Club Journal.* The competition shall be called the 'W. H. Murray Literary Prize', hereafter called the 'Prize.'

2. The judging panel shall consist of, in the first instance, the following: The current Editor of the *SMC Journal;* The current President of the SMC; and two or three lay members, who may be drawn from the membership of the SMC. The lay members of the panel will sit for three years after which they will be replaced.

3. If, in the view of the panel, there is in any year no entries suitable for the Prize, then there shall be no award that year.

4. Entries shall be writing on the general theme of 'Scottish Mountaineering', and may be prose articles of up to approximately 5000 words in length, or shorter verse. Entries may be fictional.

5. Panel members may not enter for the competition during the period of their membership.

6. Entries must be of original, previously unpublished material. Entries should be submitted to the Editor of the *SMC Journal* before the end of January for consideration that year. Lengthy contributions are preferably word-processed and submitted either on 3.5" PC disk or sent via e-mail. (See Office Bearers page at end of this Journal for address etc.) Any contributor to the SMC Journal is entitled to exclude their material from consideration of the Prize and should so notify the Editor of this wish in advance.

7. The prize will be a cheque for the amount £250.

8. Contributors may make different submissions in different years.

9. The decision of the panel is final.

10. Any winning entry will be announced in the *SMC Journal* and will be published in the *SMC Journal* and on the SMC Web site. Thereafter, authors retain copyright.

The W. H. Murray Literary Prize (1998).

The four jurors: Bob Richardson – Hon. President; Ken Crocket – Hon. Editor; Simon Richardson – SMC member, and Dave Hewitt – columnist and editor of the *Angry Corrie,* deliberated long and hard over the articles submitted for the 1998 SMC Journal. In the end, the clear winner was duly noted as *Failure,* written by Donald Orr, and of course, printed in full in this issue and on the Club web site. Mr Orr has been a contributor to this Journal several times, though only the Editor was aware of the identity of authors during judging. Some of the judges' comments on *Failure* are reproduced below.

'Top of my list is *Failure.* Well written and thoughtful, dealing with areas that are usually at the back of the climbing mind and rarely expressed.'

'Very good, certainly trying to convey something both in language and in form. Good on dislocation – again with the here-and -there structure supporting this, but with interesting (and perhaps unintended) connections between the far-flung and diverse places. Understated "incident" has enough weight to carry the story. Very human and non-judgemental.'

'I have experienced the sort of tragedy described in this story, and I am aware of how it can affect one. Most of us manage to get on with life, but others may be affected more deeply.'

Self-Written Obituaries

This repeats a request first made in the 1989 issue, that members send in self-written, short biographies. There was an encouraging response to this, and several have appeared in due course, as none of us, not even SMC members, avoid the grim reaper for ever.

But some SMC members do seem to have extraordinarily long and active lives – witness some of the *In Memoriam* notices in this issue – so that when the final ascent is contemplated, or even made, there are few witnesses left to re-tell the life round the tribal fires. 'The song is finished but the melody continues.' (I. Berlin). But only so long as someone is left to pass it on.

Such biographies will be filed in confidence with the Editor. There is no set format, though reference to notable mountaineering exploits would obviously be in order. (Only thus, for example, will we ever learn just which hooligan it was inserted a rock in President Wallace's rucksack, on the day of the Centenary Dinner.) Other trivia, such as education, employment, birthday honours etc., may be briefly alluded to. A photograph of the soloist, preferably in relative youth, would be of immense values to the archives. (Editor).

Mantelshelf. I am becoming increasingly testy over the mis-spelling of this word. One climbs on to a mantelshelf, a mantel being 'a structure of wood, marble etc., above and around fireplace', hence a mantelshelf climbing move. A mantle, on the other hand, may commonly be a 'loose, sleeveless cloak', or a 'fragile, lace-like tube fixed around a gas-jet to give incandescent light' etc. (Editor).

THE PAST PRESIDENTS SOCIETY

Charlie Orr theorises . . .

YOU'VE heard of the 'Dead Poet's Society' in which actor, Robin Williams, made famous the role of the eccentric Professor whose self-appointed role in life was to pass on archaic literary lore to up-and-coming generations? Yes, well, it is my contention that a similar society is to be found not too far under the surface within our own organisation.

Let us for convenience sake refer to this as 'The Past Presidents Society'. However, in doing so, I would stress at the outset that this loose grouping does not include all past holders of that esteemed position as will immediately become clear when I tell you that the avowed purpose of the group in question, rather than passing on literary traditions, is to ensure continued fascination in up-and-coming generations with a rather large and barren island situated completely within the Arctic Circle.

On joining the Club in 1992, I had some vague notion of unlimited access to the CIC and of climbing with people who would ensure that my grades would go shooting up. I also thought, naively as I look back on it, that I made all the running in my efforts to be accepted into membership. I have no idea to this day why or on whose information I was targeted by the PPS but be assured, targeted I was.

One winter's evening as the wind rattled the, at that time, not too well secured shutters of the Raeburn Hut and I was glad to be sitting close by that wonderful gas stove, the door opened and I had my first sight of a man, tall and lean of shank with a mane of silver white hair, who was to be instrumental in changing my life. A kindly man who, after partaking of a few Glenlivets which he, not I, carried with him, asked me if I had ever considered joining the SMC. To say that I was flattered would be to understate my feelings and I questioned whether or not my mountaineering qualifications would be sufficient unto the day. To my surprise he told me that a friend of his, in fact the incumbent President of the Club, was in the process of introducing a motion to reduce the qualifications for older members. How fortuitous I thought then. I now know different, this was the PPS at work. Little did I know then that my well-read companion of that evening who retired to bed three or four healthy drams to the good and quoting *Horace* was none other than arguably the most zealous of the PPS – the good Dr. Sm***.

Within six months I was a fully-fledged member of Scotland's premier climbing club and, almost by accident as it then seemed, fell into company with two other staunch members of the PPS; firstly the proselytizing Professor Sl***** and his less militant, but equally committed companion, William Wa*****. Now, you may well say that I should have smelled a rat or perhaps a lemming would be more appropriate in the circumstances. Here was I, a novice member, suddenly surrounded by professional men, doctors, academics you name it, all old enough to be my father and all current or past presidents of the club – and I thought that they just wanted to be friends. Come on! But believe me, at that time conspiracy was the farthest thing from my mind.

What of my apprenticeship or, some might say, indoctrination then. Well ski-touring became compulsory, of course, and conversations were often peppered with references to strange sounding people like Knud Rasmunsson and Eric The Red. It was amazing really the seguways that were employed by these erudite gentlemen to introduce these topics. I was frequently, by accident, coming into contact with maps of Greenland carelessly left on the back seats of cars and the like. This came to a head when a certain Mr Ben***, a man I strongly suspect to be an elder statesman of the PPS, but who took no active part in my case, spoke to me about Greenland, actually addressing me by my first name! I was in short subjected to this slow drip, drip of suggestion bordering on coercion over a period of three years until finally I could hold out no longer, the PPS had won and in December, 1995 I signed on for *The Liverpool Coast.*

There remained one further test, winter camping in the Gorms to, as the Professor put it, familiarise me with the arcane mysteries of camping on snow prior to our departure. This went well apart from one shaky moment when, after the tent was pitched on snow in Coire-ant-Sneachda, the Professor turned to me, produced his John Thomas and bade me do the same. The years of indoctrination had taken their toll and I was powerless to resist, but boy, was I glad when he instructed me in the art of peeing round the base of the tent poles to freeze them in!

About a month before we left I was instructed to attend at the Professor's home in Edinburgh where I would meet other members of the expedition and assist with the packing of food which was to be flown out ahead of us. On arrival I was met by his delightful wife, Ja**, who I learned was to accompany us on the trip. The Professor was not present having been called away on urgent business and anyone who has tried to pack two weeks' food for eight into 10 small cardboard boxes will realise just how urgent that business was! I must stress at this juncture that I was sure on that first meeting, and nothing happened in Greenland to change my opinion, that Ja** is blissfully unaware of the existence of, and her husband's participation in, the PPS.

The other two members of the expedition that I met that night were Alan Petit and Gerry Rooney neither of whom were club members but who had nevertheless I feel, been carefully selected by the PPS ostensibly because they were both members of the Starav Mountaineering Club, the effect of that being that the joint trip could still be referred to as an SMC expedition. The darker side of the selection process became clearer during the expedition when I learned that Alan, a dentist, (always handy) had, in fact, been indoctrinated some 20 years previously having visited Greenland with the Professor when the leading lights of the group were still only free radicals so to speak, none of them having attained the status of President never mind Past President. Unlike me however, 20 years on Alan was still blissfully unaware of the powers of the PPS and was happily taking the cardboard centres out of toilet rolls so he could get the box lids closed, secure in the knowledge that he was doing so of his own free will.

Gerry, of whom more later, is a psychologist who specialises in dealing with the criminal mind and is somewhat of an expert in hypnosis, quite obviously selected (apart from the SMC solution) to keep me under control should rebellion surface. You see although they have to be pretty sure that they've got you hooked before the invitations are sent out so to speak, they can never be 100% sure until they get you up there.

Club member, John Hay, was to join us with plans for a solo sledge-hauling trip round the coast with the intention of living and hunting with the Inuit at the Scoresbysund settlement. John, to use an analogy from the drug world, is mainlining on the Arctic at the moment, having fallen under the spell of the PPS only four years ago; this was to be his fifth trip, sometimes twice in a year. Even the Scientology guru, Ron Hubbard, would be impressed with his response to PPS techniques! I tried briefly to share my ideas with John while building an igloo at our base camp on the Heks Glacier but he reacted badly to my initial approach and as he is a big man and with the additional problem of his wielding the snow-saw at the time, I let it rest.

The eminent glaciologist Scots/Canadian, Stan Paterson, made up the team. I'm somewhat unsure of Stan's role in the conspiracy but as he has known the main players for more than 50 years it would be naive in the extreme to imagine that he is unaware of the existence of the PPS. One thing that did occur to me was that this expedition might be being used as some sort of training exercise for prospective members of the PPS as Stan was very keen on taking what I would term – covert photographs. When I say that he was keen, he sometimes took these photographs at much expense to his personal comfort, secreting himself in freezing temperatures until what he deemed the appropriate moment before capturing me, yes more often than not it was me, the new boy, or so it seemed, who was the object of his attentions and I couldn't help wondering if, given his apparent tenacity in this matter, he was acting under orders.

As we flew out of Glasgow bound for Reykjavik the white-haired one, whom I counted as instrumental in me being bound for the icy wastes, was regrettably not with us, I did, however, contact him by telephone prior to leaving at his lair in Glensh**. We had a very pleasant conversation during which I gave no hint of my suspicions regarding the existence of the PPS and neither did he give me any information intentionally or otherwise which would tend to harden these suspicions. Having said that, he did make a parting comment which was to exercise my mind for sometime. He said, and these chilling words will remain with me always: 'Given the nature and constitution of your part take very good care of your spoon'.*

I immediately tried to clarify what he was obviously trying to tell me other than the far too obvious 'Take care of your spoon' but the line went dead and further attempts to contact him were met with the engaged tone. This was still very much in my mind as we flew later that day from Reykjavik on another scheduled flight to Akeureyri in the far north of Iceland.

After overnighting in Akeureyri under the good care of Sigi, boss of the travel outfit Arcturus, we were loaded, squeezed might be a better word, with our gear into a Twin Otter aircraft which had been chartered for the flight to the airstrip at Constable Point in East Greenland. It was while loading that any doubts I might hitherto have entertained about my theories were well and truly banished.

---

* I have, since the time of writing, learned that this fascinating remark has its genesis in an incident which occurred during an expedition to Greenland in 1958. It did not make headlines in the national or indeed even in the climbing Press at the time however, 40 years on it is still very much a subject shrouded in mystery and one which, like the grail quest, might never be solved. It is this new-found knowledge imparted to me by 'A well-wisher' that has led me to make every possible attempt to disguise the identities of those involved in this tale of intrigue and I would strongly advise anyone who thinks they might know of whom I speak against broaching this subject with them.

I had sight of a letter on Zigi's clipboard and there along the bottom of a letter headed:

SMC EAST GREENLAND EXPEDITION 1996
were the letters PPS.
with some smaller writing underneath which I couldn't make out, this and another small section came after the main body of the letter which was signed
Yours sincerely
(Professor) M. Sl*****.

There was no longer any doubt, this clinched it and I further clinched it by adroitly removing the letter from the clipboard and stuffing it inside my duvet. It did cross my mind that committing himself to paper like this was rather sloppy for a mind as sharp as the Professor's but I suppose he's not getting any younger and after all Zigi is a Dane and PPS would mean nothing to him would it.

It was thus confirmed in my own 'conspiracy theory' that I was deep in thought as we flew towards the airstrip at Constable Point in East Greenland. Unknown to me the Professor had spoken to the pilot at Akeureyri prior to our departure and this, as well as crossing Zigi's palm with a bottle of Highland Park (future expeditions would do well to remember this worthwhile and relatively inexpensive tip), resulted in him agreeing to fly us from the coast inland up the Pedersson Glacier and over the proposed site of our base camp on the Heks Glacier. Being oblivious to this, I was somewhat alarmed when I looked up from reading a book to see a rock face filling the whole window, same on the other side and, most alarmingly of all, the same through the pilot's screen, but before my brain could order this somewhat anomalous situation we breasted the top of a col and in the distance I could see the tiny airstrip that is Constable Point.

This austere grouping of huts and outbuildings which prides itself in the sobriquet The Arsehole of The Arctic was originally built by the Americans (perhaps it should be asshole!) to aid oil exploration in the area, now serves as the jumping-off point for expeditions to this part of East Greenland. There is not a lot going on here in what is reminiscent of a set from *Ice Station Zebra* and the highlight for me was the not unpleasant experience of using a toilet which relied for its efficacy on a rather strong vacuum effect! (please do not try this at home!). What they did with the resulting neatly sealed plastic bags is anybody's guess.

The next stage of the trip was a short hop by helicopter 15 miles or so inland where we set up base on the Grete Glacier at around 800m. During my months of indoctrination I had been told of the beautiful calm and sunny weather awaiting me in Greenland but, of course, I realised that this was simply a sales tool designed to get me there for whatever reason. Until that is, I woke up next day to just such weather which continued the next day and the next, in fact, for every day of the two-week trip barring two when snow and high winds kept us confined to our tents.

During that first idyllic week we made many ski ascents of the easily-accessible peaks all around the 5000ft mark, many of which can be skied to their summits. What with the peerless skiing and the grandeur of being surrounded by 1000ft walls of unclimbed rock, I pushed any thoughts of the machinations of the PPS to the back of my mind and simply enjoyed the moment. This naive and elemental joy was often accompanied by the thought that I could be the first human being to ski through a given hollow or climb a given slope, an experience which induces a feeling of connection with the past and with the future. I even went as far as to have my first doubts, the first inklings of the possibility of paranoia on my part until, that is, I recalled something that I was once told by a friend who clearly did not grasp, on one level at least, the implication of that state: 'Just because you're paranoid doesn't meant that bastards aren't watching you,' was his maxim.

On our first day of storm the Professor, the most experienced Greenlander among us, decided that we should construct an igloo which seemed like a good idea at the time. What he didn't tell us and what we didn't find out until after two hours of hard manual labour by us, he was the non-labouring architect, was that said igloo was to be used, no was being/had been used, is more appropriate, as a toilet! It was in the aftermath of this discovery and the attendant grumblings that I had my conspiratorial chat with John Hay which I alluded to earlier. It did not go down well and the next day, which dawned fine, he left alone intending to journey round the coast to Scorsbeysund.

After a week at Grete base, we decided to move over a col about three miles distant and set up camp on the Age Nilssons Glacier. This was my first experience of sledge hauling and I would have to say that I was pleasantly surprised. Uphill or on the flat was a pleasure as it was easy to get lost in the rhythm of skinning along on fresh unmarked snow, however, the downhill runs took a bit more guile. Partly, in the cause of frugality and partly as a weight-saving exercise, we had eschewed the use of the rigid poled pulkas normally used on such expeditions in favour of common or garden kid's sledges purchased from such diverse sources as 'Toys R Us', 'Jenners' and the petrol station down the road (in Scotland, not Greenland!) These worked remarkably well being pulled by varying lengths of cord clipped into climbing harnesses, downhill running being controlled after much trial and error, by a steadying influence from the rear. The only alteration made to these sledges was the gouging out of some additional holes on either side (heated screwdriver recommended) to facilitate the use of criss-cross cord to secure the payload.

From this second camp we were within a mile or so of the pack ice and therefore very much in polar bear country. John Hay had been the firearms expert of the party but, as I said, he had taken off on his own leaving us in charge of a big and very heavy rifle. I think it would be fair to say that by a process of not speaking about the, 'you know what', or indeed the 'what's its name' themselves, we convinced ourselves that all would be well. My choices in all this were somewhat limited by the fact that my teenage daughters had told me that were I to shoot a 'what's its name', they would never talk to me again. Luckily, the choice of whether to die gloriously at the claws of such a noble beast or be denied the delight of my daughters' company was not forced upon me. I suppose that had things turned out differently, requests for money and the like would have been made through an intermediary!

It was on a long day-trip from this camp made with Gerry and Alan that I tested my theory on them and it was Alan, the one who had been in Greenland with the Professor 20 years earlier, who immediately went on the attack. His argument being along the lines of, if what I was suggesting was true then why hadn't similar attempts been made to indoctrinate him. On further questioning, however, he did accept that he had been repeatedly asked over the intervening years to join the premier club and when I pressed him for the names of his would-be sponsors . . . well need I say more! Gerry professed to have a more Marxist-based resistance to joining apparently perceiving divisions of status and class, not within the membership he was quick to add, but between the membership and the rest of the human race. (Whatever can he mean?) However, in a moment of weakness while resting on what might well have been a virgin summit and viewing the rugged grandeur of Rathbone Island rising sheer out of the pack ice, he did confess that some years back he was caught by our current president, Bob Richardson, as an uninvited guest in Lagangarabh having entered via a window. And I feel sure that given the enormity of his crime and the identity of his tormentor this youthful aberration had more to do with his not coming into or indeed being brought into the fold than any Marxist-based notions he might hold.

Two days before striking camp for the long haul out to Constable Point, an ascent was made of Twillengerne which at 1475m is the highest peak in the area. This was made on a day of high winds on which, with the exception of Stan, all members of the party climbed fairly steep mixed ground to a shoulder from where it was obvious that the final rock tower of 200ft or so was going to require some technical climbing. I was somewhat surprised to witness the angst it caused the Professor to decline the summit given that he had made the first ascent in 1971 but, given my misgivings regarding the role of the PPS I became immediately suspicious when he took Alan to one side and on the pretext of sorting out some gear, indulged in some furtive conversation most of which was carried off on the wind which was buffeting our rather exposed position. The only word I managed to grab out of the maelstrom was 'Beans' and as I was trying to make sense out of this latest development Alan was off up the first pitch like a a scalded cat.

As I belayed him from a rather precarious stance my thoughts were divided between the wonderful views out over the pack ice broken now into long blue leads by the onshore wind, and the meaning of the word 'Beans'. Wind and Beans, quite a combination. BEANS could it be yet another acronym British Expedition . . . no, there was nothing British about the Professor, I knew that. B . . . E . . . Arctic N . . . Society. Half an hour passed and I was still on belay. I tried shouting but it was hopeless, the words were just ripped away on the wind. This was less than 200ft of V. Diff. climbing, what was he doing up there?

I had my back to the others but perhaps I had caught some movement out of the side of my eye, I'm not sure and, as I turned round, I saw the Professor looking towards the summit through a pair of binoculars and directing with his right arm. I made up my mind there and then that there was something up there that I was not meant to see. Now the other explanation is that Alan was having difficulty and the Professor, having climbed the route before, albeit 25 years before, was giving him directions but I was in no mind to look for the obvious.

Right away I gave the shout 'climbing', which I knew would be immediately snatched away on the wind, and was at the top of a wonderful pitch of superb rock inside 10 minutes. Finding Alan on the slightly higher of twin summits about 10 yards away grubbing about on his hands and knees, I soloed across to him carrying coils of rope and when I tapped him on the shoulder from behind he got such a fright that I thought the good people of Bridge of Allan might well be looking for a new dentist.

When he recovered his composure, we carried on a shouted conversation during which the only two words I could decipher were 'Professor' and 'Beans' and, given that Alan had failed to find whatever it was he was looking for in half-an-hour, it was unlikely that I was going to find it now. At least he knew what *it* was! We were soon joined by Gerry and after a brief photograph session, we rejoined the rest at the shoulder. Given the circumstances surrounding this ascent, I was stupid enough to descend last, the result being that I did not see the post-summit meeting between Alan and the Professor which might have given some clue as to what was going on.

Later that night, after a supper of semolina pancakes and marmite, one of the Professor's specialities, (not recommended for those of a delicate constitution), I ensured that his customary two Glenlivets were somewhat larger than usual which, coupled with the warm post prandial fug of a leaky primus, I thought might make him more receptive to subtle interrogation. No so. Beans . . . a tin of beans which he left on the summit after the first ascent. He was interested to see if they were still there and, if so, what condition the tin was in given it's degree of exposure to the elements over the intervening 25 years. A simple experiment was how he put it, nothing more.

I left early next morning leaving a note saying that I was going to try and find one of my ski-crampons which had become detached on a trip earlier in the week and, by carefully retracing our route of the previous day, three hours of hard work put me once again on the summit of Twillingerene, this time with a somewhat rusty tin of Heinz beans in my hand. It had been concealed beneath a large loose boulder on the first of the twin summits which accounted for Alan's failure to find it. On first examining the tin it seemed as if the Professor's account was standing up but, on closer examination, I saw that the bottom of the tin sported a neat weld around its circumference. It had been opened and resealed! Could the answer be here? I laid it on a flat rock and gave it a hefty blow with my axe but, to my horror, the blade glanced off the weld and I watched helplessly as the tin bounced and rattled down the mountain disappearing into the early-morning fog.

Over the next two days as we sledge-hauled down the glacier, camping for the first time in two weeks on the sparse vegetation of areas of Tundra coming through the retreating spring snows, I committed most of what I write here to a diary and as I read and re-read the happenings many of which, it has to be said, belonged solely to my own internal landscape, I again began to question the whole PPS theory. Perhaps it *was* the product of a fevered imagination, perhaps the letter, remember the letter? *had* simply dropped out of my duvet pocket before I could read it, perhaps Heinz *did* weld their tins in these far-off days. It was while sitting once again on that wonderful vacuum contraption at Constable Point that I felt a calm acceptance come over me and, as I listened to the bag being sealed, I determined to seal away my theories . . . at least for the time being.

PS. As we waited for the plane at Constable Point one of the Inuit workers there handed me a spoon with the letter 'S' scratched thereon which he said his brother had found on a hunting trip many years ago during the summer thaw. I could not understand too much of what he said but I gathered that one of their people's Shaman had told him that this spoon had its origins in the land of the Scots and that the 'S' stood for – now was it Sm*** or was it Sl*****? I don't suppose it's very important really!

PPS. The bean tin fell down the NNE face from the top of a prominent flat-topped red-coloured boulder on to fairly steep but not impossible ground. A team of two working roped should have a good chance of success. One word of caution however. Should this tale be told in the pages of the Journal, those involved might see any further attempts to 'out' this powerful group as subversive and retribution could well be swift – and severe.

LETTER TO THE EDITOR

Sad Tales from the East
By John Steele

It occurred to me that as I travel round the mountains of the world, some areas are just at the beginning of the tourist boom involving such activities as trekking, eco-touring, river-rafting, bungy jumping and the rest, while others have been at it for decades. However, it appears to matter not at which stage this development is when man's appetite to pollute and destroy nature is considered.

Trekking is still at a fairly rudimentary stage in some of the more remote parts of equatorial Indonesia. It is sad to see that even here can be found the same signs of outdoor decay and destruction, familiar to us all in the old world. With more than one million hectares of primary and secondary jungle lost to burning in several months during 1997, Indonesia and its immediate neighbours will have to pay a heavy price. Witness the blanketing by smoke haze of an area from 10° north of the equator to 10° south and 50° along it. Millions of people did not even see the sun for several month last summer. The El Niño effect, of course, made matters worse.

Turning to a more established area, to mountains in particular and to even the balance a bit. It is a real pleasure to see the steps taken by the authorities in New Zealand to ensure the care and maintenance of huts, paths, plants and wildlife. It is just a pity that nature herself is so actively destructive in the South Island. Again, the right sort of moves can be seen elsewhere. For instance, local guides are paid a bonus for bringing litter off Mount Kinabalu in Borneo, an idea, we as mountaineers, could export around the globe perhaps. I still remain astonished at not having been poisoned when visiting Mount Kenya some years ago, given the huge rotting tips of garbage outside the huts and the polluted catchment pools.

It also occurred to me that we in the West should perhaps be measured in our criticism. Even in New Zealand, where there have recently been floods on the west coast and drought in the east. Again, made worse by the El Niño effect and, of course, the vast tracts of land stripped of vegetation during the last century. The drive from Nelson down to Christchurch was not a pretty sight. The sheep are even being taken off the land. Closer to home, take a glance westwards from the pulpit of little Carreg Alltrem, the watchtower of Pillar Rock or the fleeceback of our own Ben Wyvis and you will see the results for yourself of the latest round of generational destruction.

What follows is a short rueful tale of a recent journey into the wilderness.

The tale is of a short break in sultry Sumatra just an hour's flight across the equator from Singapore.

After arrival and much bargaining, transport is eventually organised to take us into the mountains. Next morning, we arrive at our drop off point, which proves to be the most extensive of tea plantations – Bodmin Moor under bushes. This is the country of *minang kerbau,* which loosely translates as stinking cow. A matriarchal society where women inherit and men are gypsies – never been conquered and I suspect never likely to be – except perhaps for the damned HAZE. 'Dari mana?' – no not an inquiring Aberdonian climber – 'We are from Britain.' – (room, bunk, meal have you?) - we all know how it goes. This *is* mana – though warm hostess, clean mattress, food and drink a plenty.

Buff bop barp – we join the rush hour of tea plantation workers as they cart fart to their particular part. Then out of the HAZE zooms a *gnomie* (boyish grin, leather jacket and all). 'Antar ke Gunung?' Yes, here we go again. An hour saved on the back of a 125 – but at a price. Still no mountain in sight though. Is he having us on? After all, the peak we had come to climb is nearly 4000m high and rises some 2500m straight up from where we were standing. After much finger pointing and reassurance from the lad, we continue on our way and soon pass under the rotten wooden portals which act as the entrance to Sumatra's largest national park. Broken beams, broken glass, up your **** – bahasa style.

The memory of such a pleasant greeting had just about dimmed as we reach base camp – Bynack Lodge, Sixties fashion. All the floor boards have gone but the crap is dry. There are tigers and elephants roaming wild here, however, it is the dry season in an El Niño year – and there is the HAZE. We soon quit the hovel.

Stout roots, slimy shoots and filthy flats are our companions on the way to set up camp in a small square of volcanic ash which appears just as the vegetation disappears, having given up on its upward montane struggle. An ascent of the highest volcano in mainland Indonesia, Gunung Kerinci at 12,500ft, soon follows. We are met on the summit by sun and light to the south and the darkness of night to the north – and BELOW, billowing balls of deep red magma pulse, convulse and vapourise into clouds of poisonous gas some 100m high.

For the first time we are above the smog and can see our mountain, but not for long, as nightfall comes quickly on the equator.

A restless night under the stars,
then
Back to cows, haze and habitation.
'Outside please – with stars ***'

Swim, beer, leer, warm bath,
massage fingers path,
then
Ships smash, Airbus crash.

Trip's end had come,
but
The haze remains
Mankind must burn!

Avalanches

Following the note in SMCJ, 1997, 188, p.370 by Bob Aitken, on what was possibly the first recorded account of an avalanche in Scotland, Peter Drummond adds: While staying in Tibbie Shiels Inn by St. Mary's Loch in Yarrow, and on engaging the hostess in historical discourse, she produced an 1886 volume entitled *Reminiscences of Yarrow,* by the Rev. J. Russell M.D. Not exactly a riveting read, but one bit caught my eye. It related the experience of one Alexander Laidlaw, shepherd of Bowerhope, a farm on the southern shore of the loch, tucked under steep north and west-facing slopes.

'Passing over some treacherous snow on the hillside, his weight had the effect of detaching the large mass: and down came the avalanche, bearing him in its fall, and burying him under it. His dog marked the spot where he lay. He was found alive with some measure of consciousness. He was carried home and having been put in a warm bed, he was soon himself again. Humanly speaking, his preservation, after being 14 hours under the snow, was due to his own presence of mind, making a desperate effort with his hands to clear a breathing space round his head.'

Unfortunately, no date is given to allow the good man to make posthumous claim to fame, but we are told he died (implicitly of old age) in 1842, so it seems probable that the mishap took place early in the 19th century. He may not be the earliest victim (the Atholl dog and the Gaick bothiers probably share these honours), but he is perhaps the first recorded survivor.

SAILING WITH JOHN PEDEN

SMC Afloat

Iain Smart sends in this account of three sailing/mountaineering adventures with the Commodore of the 1997 Centennial Yacht Meet. We were all quite safe in his hands on this historic cruise; he is not only a master organiser but has the knack of getting a quart into a pint pot. The weather on the Yacht Meet was admirable. This was not due to high influence but to John Peden's other attribute, namely, 'luck'. As you will find out, if you read on, he is not always associated with good weather, but seems to have the luck the Gods bestow on those competent enough to receive it.

A failed ascent of Dun Da Gaoithe.

New Year is not a popular time for sailing. Nevertheless, responding to an invitation from John Peden (not something to be done lightly, as you will know) I found myself one New Year's Day scudding south down the Sound of Mull in wild Wagnerian weather under gloomy clouds with occasional shafts of sunshine illuminating our white sail against the wine-dark sea. My fellow crewman was a friend of John's who had never sailed before, a strangely introverted character who smoked curiously aromatic hand-rolled cigarettes and seemed bewildered by what was going on, as well he might. In real life there is no background music except on rare occasions. This was one of the exceptions; the ride of the Valkyries was being played by a full orchestra discretely hidden somewhere off stage. We zig-zagged south in the gathering storm, and at dusk escaped from the white-horsed sea into Salen Bay for the night. We had a nebulous plan for climbing Dun Da Gaoithe on the morrow. There was a lot of weather about. Sheet lightning backlit the mountains and phosphorescence glowed along the anchor chain. Down in the cabin the whisky glowed in the lamp-light and we fell asleep to the sough of the sea-dark wind in the rigging.

Next day the weather was again gurly, the cloud low with battering rain in the passing squalls; not a day for a summit. To fill in time we sailed south to Seill Island and in the gloaming entered the Poll Dobhrein, a bomb-proof anchorage, over-crowded in the summer but now lonely and forlorn with the winter sea growling outside its gates. In due course we made our way through the trackless bogs to the pub at Seill Bridge. We were offered a lift to a dance at Easdale by two nice, but inevitable, Englishmen. This was a West Highland Dance in the old style. There were still enough locals around for it to be authentic. It had started an hour late as is the custom. The band played fast and well, the bar flowed fast as well. Every now and then someone would get up and sing. The dances were danced with enthusiasm and with small regard to the perjinkitiness of the RSCDA rules. I danced with a girl who said she remembered me well, that my name was Spike Maxwell and when was I coming to see her again. I remember doing a schottische with a wee smasher who wore a luminous blue bangle on her ankle. All in all, aged, unshaven and wellie-booted though we were we seemed to be doing well. We had, I suppose, a sense of mystery. We were off a yacht in a stormy January night. 'A likely story,' said the luminous blue bangle. Anyway the time passed, as it does. As the dance ended at god-knows-what hour I confided in her that we were indeed the Flying Dutchman and his crew and that this was the one night in seven years we were allowed ashore, hoping that some damsel would take pity on us and save us from our doom of sailing the seven seas for ever. I got the impression that blue bangle and her friends would willingly oblige.

We got a lift back to the bridge with the two obliging, but culturally disorientated, Englishmen, staggered across the bogs in the wind-tossed darkness, found the dinghy and got back on board. We were all very drunk. I collapsed in my bunk. I was drifting off to sleep when I heard the rattle of the anchor chain and then, the sound of the sails going up, followed by wind in the rigging, the surge of the sea and the feeling of being tipped from the bunk. I eventually understood from all this carry-on that we were out in a very rough sea. I staggered on deck to find the Flying Dutchman at the helm of his craft, obviously bent on starting another cycle of seven sea sailing, doomed to live his own legend. It was an appropriately theatrical night for it. The Firth of Lorne shimmered in the light of the full moon with silver horses galloping across undulating fields of heaving pewter. The dark tooth of Gylen Castle stood out on the skyline of Kerera. Although bats were not actually flying about it at this time of year the ambience was such that their absence zenly, as it were, echoed their presence. Clouds scudded across the sky and when they covered the moon the scene became dark and ominous and the tone of the hidden orchestra as it played the Dutchman motif became more menacing. Had the scene been recreated like this in a theatre I am sure it would have seemed grossly overdone and would have been slammed by the critics as an inappropriately Gothic intrusion into an essentially Gaelic ambience. However, here it was for real and underlined once again how essential it is to tone down real life if you want to make believable fiction.

There is a time and a place for everything, even a mutiny. The crew now mutinied. The Flying Peden tried to compromise by offering to run for the 'shelter' of Duart Bay. This was disallowed. We returned to the Poll Dobhrein and very firmly put down the anchor. The next day we rose late and decided to postpone the ascent of Dun Da Gaoithe till another time. It was in any case a piece of hubris to approach a hill with a name like that in a yacht.

Looking back on all this I now realise that everyone has got the Flying Dutchman story the wrong way round. The Dutchman epitomises the gallus, carefree bachelor sailing the seven seas of adventure. The symbolic night ashore is the perennial risk of meeting a heroine and his doom is landing up with a wife, a family, a pram, a mortgage, and a suburban bungalow with a lawn needing to be cut while his heroine turns into a matriarch. From time to time the erstwhile hero sees the ship of adventure sail for some far horizon without him and is duly perturbed. As the years go by his inner eye grows dim and eventually he sees such things no more. Such an ending although biologically satisfactory is without romantic interest. And so for the purposes of making decent drama it is necessary to introduce a role reversal by inferring (oh, irony of ironies) that freedom is the doom from which we must be rescued by some heroine with a luminous blue bangle round her ankle.

A successful ascent of a new route on Druim nan Ramh.

We left Arisaig on a fine Friday morning in September, close bosom friend of the equinoctial gales. Naturally, with John as skipper, we did not follow the normal exit from this complex harbour but went to the north through the lacework of submerged rocks which in good weather provides a more direct, though more dicey route to Loch Scavaig. This we reached before darkness fell. Loch Scavaig as we all know is a place where Rugged Grandeur is spelled out in Duttonian Capital Letters. It is an impressive place even in good weather but in a storm it is a bit like anchoring in a washing machine. We dined that night to the music of a rising breeze in the rigging. What cared we for wind and weather when every inch was nearer to our Mingulay – a supper of moules marinières. This is what it must have been like on Kismul's Galley when 'they'd brought her to 'gainst wind and tide 'neath Kismul's walls. Here was red wine and feast for heroes, aeolian harping too, o hee o hoo'. (It's easy to get carried away in these dramatic circumstances.) During the night the storm got going in earnest. The wind birled the rain-lashed boat round and round its anchor rope like the galley, galley ship in the song. A leak started over my bunk. I complained to the owner. 'I know,' he said: 'That's why you are in that bunk and not me. There's nothing we can do about it anyway.' He then lost interest.

In the morning, wind and water roared around us and the rain shafted down in grey javelins. Some tents that had been pitched on the shore the night before were now no longer there probably blown away with their inmates to Scandinavia. At that very moment they were probably walking into some Norwegian town in their jock-straps dragging their ruined tents behind them trying to explain to the sceptical local police how they got there. Sometime in the mid-morning we jaloused things were getting a bit better. Bryan and Pat set off to bag Sgurr Dubh na Da Bhein, a Munro lacking from their collection, while John and I went to Bidein Druim nan Ramh to see if we could do a route. Loch Coruisg was in what the cookery books would describe as a rolling boil. Large parts of it were being scooped up by the wind and blown all over the western hillsides. (We have photos to prove it). We did, in fact, do a V. Diff. climb on the flank of Druim nan Ramh – not a very good one. I don't suppose we could ever find it again. We returned along the Druim which in Gaelic is a masculine noun signifying 'back' or "spine" as in: 'Ach tha slat airson druim an ti a tha as eugmhais tuigse.' 'A rod is for the back of him that is void of understanding.' *(Proverbs Chapter 10, verse 13).*

It seemed to have some present relevance. A druim can also be viewed from underneath and be used to signify "roof" as in: 'Gu druim Sheallamha shin mi mo lamh, Tha'n fhardach gun druim ach adhar,' which translates literally as: 'To the roof of Sealma I stretched my hand; The abode is without a roof but sky,' which is from the 44th poem of the Sean Dana collection.

Druim is probably cognate with "drum" in Chaldean which signifies "high". "nan Ramh" expresses the genitive plural of "Ramh" which as you know, means "oar" as in: 'De dharagaibh Bhasain rinn iad do ramhan' – 'Of the oaks of Bashan have they made thine oars.' *(Eziekel, Chapter 27, verse, 6).*

Ramh is also a word of respectable antiquity being cognate with the Latin "remus" as in "Quinquireme of Nineveh from distant Ophir". In the Cuillinic use of the word the "oars" are the buttresses which descend in pairs from the druim.

Knowing all this we returned along the ridge pussyfooting gingerly like cats on a cold, stone roof as we followed it back from distant Ophir to Nineveh.

The gale meanwhile, being constrained by the equinox, was unable to abate and continued to blow with vigour. Back on board I was impressed by the state of the anchor cable, a pleated rope affair, stretched to such a tightness that it twanged at middle C. John Peden affected to be unperturbed, said there was nothing we could do about it anyway and lost interest. During the night the wind got worse. One squall knocked the boat over on its side. My bunk lay to windward and I got pitched out onto the floor half asleep. I expressed alarm shouting: 'What the hell is happening?' The phrase I was searching for was: 'Sauve qui peut,' but it wouldn't come out, perhaps because it was too intellectual for the occasion. In spite of real concern I could not arouse much in the way of response from the others. John, on the lee side, was cradled in his bunk more deeply by the tilt and returned to his original position as the boat righted itself, thus solving his problem, but he did mutter that there was nothing we could do about our situation and again lost any small interest he may have had which, as you must be beginning to realise by now, is an ingrained defensive mechanism of his, a psychological quirk that, over time, has become hard-wired and which he has developed to the point of being, for those subjected to it, an irritating behavioural cliché, but which, if it has done nothing else, has generated, almost spontaneously, the labyrinthine complexity of the present sentence, one which Proust, were he alive and by chance reading this copy of the Journal, might well have approved of as indicating the homage of a pedestrian apprentice, acknowledging that imitation, however clumsy is, nevertheless, provided it eschews parody, a sincere form of flattery, perhaps the only one the mediocre can render to the original and the great. There was also some sharp, non-Proustian muttering from the pair in the fo'c'sle but I think they were telling me to shut up and stop keeping everyone awake.

I had a similar experience in Spitzbergen with other SMC members as recently as 1994. We had taken great care to surround our tents with trip wires which set off a noisy rocket to alert us to polar bears approaching our camp as we slept. The defensive ring was constructed with considerable care and seriously checked by all the group (Messrs. Bott, Hay, McKerrow and two Slessers, in case you are interested). We went to bed with rifles and pistols loaded and at the ready. The rocket did go off with a rather penetrating shriek during the night. I was the only one who leaped a foot in the air (quite difficult lying supine in a sleeping bag), grabbed a pistol and stuck my head out the tent door to defend the camp. It was, in fact, a false alarm but the only response from the afore-named individuals to all this cufuffle was to turn in their sleep and grumble at the noise. They would probably have done no more if one of the party had actually been crunched up outside the tent door by a noisily breakfasting bear. I would like to warn all these people here and now that you can cry *sang froid* once too often for your own good.

Anyway the boat survived the night. The day dawned no better. In rain and wind we explored the watery glooms and manifold dooms of the great hanging corries high on the unfrequented west side of Coruisg. This was stern and wild country, strong meat only to be relished by the brave and the sane. Kodachrome blues and balmy winds are for intellectual vegetarians and emotional cissies, for the 'pallid pimps of the deadline and the enervates of the pen', as Robert Service described them so well. On the Monday the equinox slackened its grip, the gale eased off, things got better and we returned to Arisaig on a calm sea. Actually, it was still very rough but seemed calm in comparison. As a final triumph we prevented John from circumnavigating the Isle of Soay on the way back which he wanted to do in order 'to fill in time'.

A failed ascent of Ben Hiant.

This attempt to climb Ben Hiant fell once again about the September equinox, the season of gales and mellow fruitfulness. As the story once again involves John Peden and his good ship, *Hecla*, what I am about to relate will be hair-raising and complex. This particular episode is recounted chiefly as an example of time dilatation not by relative speed but by number of contrasting events occurring per unit of elapsed time. The plan was to leave Arisaig on the Saturday, round Ardnamurchan, anchor off the ruined castle at Mingarry Bay near the foot of Ben Hiant, do a quick traverse of this small but well-proportioned mountain from an unusual approach and then seek shelter for the night in Lochan Droma Buidhe, a safe haven on the opposite Morvern shore. The next day we would sail down the Sound of Mull, having our gin and tonics on deck, to Oban where the co-owner of the yacht would be waiting to take over for a week's holiday. It was a neat plan for collecting a little gem of a mountain by a connoisseur's route.

We met on the Friday evening at Crianlarich, parked our cars and caught the evening train to Arisaig. During the 15-minute stop at the Fort, we were able to make a quick nail-biting sortie for fish suppers. I shared mine with a famished wee refugee lassie who had managed to escape from England who was sitting opposite me. She had a boyfriend at Loch Ailort. I gathered she had plans for his future. At Arisaig we rowed around in the inky darkness of the capacious harbour until we found the good ship *Hecla*.

The next morning we left in sunshine and a light breeze. I seem to remember we motored a long way in mellow sunshine amid the splendour of the inner Hebrides at their magic best. We stopped for lunch at Sanna Bay where time stood still and the jade-green sea creamed gently against the silver sands. We would get to Ben Hiant for an ascent on a fine evening; from its summit the peaks of Tir nan Og itself might be visible.

As we all know one of the most certain signs of imminent bad weather in Scotland is sunshine, blue skies and a light, balmy wind. By the time we had rounded Ardnamurchan, therefore, we were beating slowly along an inhospitable lee shore against a cold, grey wind. Ben Hiant had retired into a boudoir of gloomy cloud and was obviously not available for a frolic on this particular evening. We headed for Loch an Droma Buidhe finding the entrance well after nightfall and instead of lowering sails and motoring in through the 100m-wide, half-mile long channel we appeared to be bent on tacking in against wind and tide with searchlights ablaze and much shouting of 'ready about' and 'lee-oh' (terms sailors use to commence pulling in or letting go ropes attached to the sail at the front, an essential procedure as you change direction when going into the wind; it is noisy with ropes racing through shackles and the crew getting in each others way). After a few splendid tacks we started to hit the sides of the channel, particularly the port side where we grounded for a bit among the rocks until the wind blew us off. In the end we got in by cheating – that is by using the engine.

The next morning we lay in our sheltered harbour watching the clouds scud across the sky. A large ocean racer sharing the anchorage set off and returned 15 minutes later, put down the anchor again and securely retied its sails. We could see the crew disappearing rapidly down the hatchways, probably for intravenous hot rum. We too set out and headed for the Sound of Mull in a wild sea. So fierce was the wind that it blew the skipper's cap off. We had to do some pretty complex sailing to recover it. The rest of the morning we zig-zagged against the wind making about a 100 yards of southing on each tack while Ben Hiant stifled an amused yawn. By lunchtime we were about level with Tobermory having avoided the Red Rocks and the Big and Little Stirks with their resident Loreleis, mermaids, seamews and other mythical seductresses whom I'm sure I remember waving and beckoning and blowing kisses as we passed. The equinox obviously had its teeth sunk deep into the throat of the weather and wasn't going to let go. Even John, eventually, accepted that Oban was unreachable that day, so we went in to Tobermory, phoned the relief crew who, fortunately, had not left Glasgow and asked them to meet us that night at the head of Loch Sunart.

This is a magnificent loch of narrows and expansions set about with considerable scenic grandeur verging on the need for Duttonian Capital Letters. We entered with the wind behind, gybing from time to time, a much more difficult manoeuvre than tacking as it involves bringing the mighty mainsail across the mid-line. Badly done it can tear certain important attachments out by the roots and knock the crew's heads off. Within the loch the wind lessened and the rain increased. It got very dark as well. No friendly star appeared to guide us with its light. The searchlight was fired up and from time to time and sometimes just in time indicated where the shore was. About midnight we ran out of the loch and saw a car flashing its headlights to stop us going any farther. We anchored and exchanged vehicles with the Ducharts. Five of us crammed into their car. Since Corran Ferry was closed at this small hour we drove round the head of Loch Eil, down to Oban to collect another car which for some reason had been left there, then to Crianlarich and finally home to the twin hubs of Scotland, namely, Bridge of Cally and Bearsden. Everyone apparently got to work on time the next morning.

Recollecting this trip it seems to occupy a greater portion of mindspace than my whole working life which is the point I think I'm trying to make. Life begins as an extended concertina on which you are allowed one squeeze; you can either play it in jig time, that is, with lots of notes per unit time or more slowly with grace and with fewer notes as in a Strathspey. What you must not do is to waste the wheezy concertina of a briefly squeezed life-span by not trying to pick out any tune at all. My excuse for ending so portentously and pompously is that I have taken so long to write this account that I'm now on my fourth (possibly fifth) dram and beginning to lose my grip.

By the way, even more importantly, you must also avoid mixing duff metaphors and losing literary style. Most importantly of all you must never lose the thread of what you're trying to say or should I say play. I had better stop now and refrain from telling you about how we sailed to St. Kilda and didn't climb Stac an Armin but how from the top of Hirta saw what some believed to have been the torch of the Statue of Liberty appearing just above the western horizon, while others thought it was the top of Beinn an t-Soluis, the highest peak of Tir nan Og itself and one crippled soul plumbed the bathos by suggesting it was a tanker hull-down on the horizon. Maybe I will tell you about that trip. It's an interesting story. I can't remember now which year it was but . . . [That's enough – Hon. Ed.]

How to land running

I HAVE been lucky enough to work in the outdoor hillwalking and climbing industry for about 15 years. I consider it particularly fortunate that I could climb to about El, went on three or four overseas climbing trips a year but was always able to pay off a massive mortgage and keep a couple of cars on the road and two daughters off the streets while better men could climb to E6 and lived in a bedsit.

Those balmy days came to an end when I fell from grace on a mere VS. The landing was nasty. The list of injuries appropriate to all the occupants of all the cars in a M25 pile up. Bad bounce, as they say, and I was encouraged no end when my youngest daughter fainted in the intensive care unit at Raigmore. The long spell in hospital allowed time to reflect while I considered religion. Five weeks looking at a ceiling in the Queen Elizabeth Spinal Injuries Unit clears the mind no end and puts your money-grabbing capitalist ideas into true perspective. I came to a decision – making money is fun. As captivating as climbing and the penalties for a mistake far worse. As D. H. Lawrence said: 'Life is ours to be spent, not saved.' Or as Jess Stock said: 'How many people on their death bed have wished they spent more time in the office?'

The problem was I was on my death bed and even if I did survive I was definitely going to be spending a lot of time at a desk with the proud scars of experience to tell me I still had a lot to learn. But learning is what it is all about. When you stop learning you stop living. So I decided I would start designing waterproof clothing. I would again run my own business and support my controversial belief that a man is not a man if he works for himself. 'Better to own your own brush and sweep the road than drive a rolls owned by the shareholders.' Which is a fine sentiment until you discover the shareholders also own the road and your contract is subject to competitive tendering.

I put the idea of letting me loose on the manufacturing side of the climbing industry to a few of my contacts and got an immediate yes, a second-hand state-of-the-art computer system and a contract. From now on I would only climb in one design of waterproof. My own! Problem, I can't yet climb or could I ever? So I'll settle for being seen with a rope and a few crabs and leave the rest to the imagination. In a short while for competitive interest, I skulked around the Alps, Highlands and the Arctic in just about every brand of waterproof in every fabric north of the South Pole. What a learning curve! The so-called best if you blindfolded yourself to the hype, the gloss and the advertising were frankly **** (Editor's deletion).

In reality, we seem to have gone backwards and substituted 'breathability' for 'waterproofness' and walk round in a perpetual sauna with a perpetually-leaking credit card hidden in a poorly-designed storm pocket. I soon perceived that the art of designing waterproofs has more to do with Public Relations than the quality of the fabric. Strangely enough, I also discovered that many of the top climbers going on the hardest and most difficult climbs in the remotest corners of the world take a similar view and their sponsors provide 'specialist' clothing for those rare occasions when they are actually climbing.

The quickest way to learn to swim is to jump in at the deep end. Out of the blue I got involved with a high-profile expedition and was given the job of designing 24 sets of waterproofs for 24 unknowns. I say high profile in that this expedition had CASH (how I love that word) sponsorship of £240,000 and not one of the participants had even done Curved Ridge. Can you imagine that. To be honest, they were the most motivated set of housewives, secretaries and saleswomen you could expect to meet but had yet to do a single Munro and actually giggled when I explained that the connection was male not female. This was an opportunity not to be missed. So many innocents as yet untainted by professionalism so perfectly were safe with me.

The expedition became known as the McVitie's Penguin Polar Relay and it achieved national and international coverage on a lavish scale. A lot more than the sponsors could ever have hoped for and several times greater than they could have bought for the same money as advertising TV airtime or advertising space in magazines and newspapers. There is a lesson to be learned here. How come unknowns with a relatively safe objective are given more cash than hard-nosed nutters with a one-way ticket to the North Face of something or other in the back of beyond? But that is another story for which I have received professional fees of several thousand guineas so therefore outwith the scope of writing as a vocation.

I digress but hope it was worthwhile. Back to the story. These highly-motivated people went into an overtime training schedule led by SAS trainers that would have left most climbers dead in their tracks so it quickly became apparent they were unlikely to need much help from me. However, I resolved I would give them the most energy-efficient clothing possible and make absolutely sure if they failed – and many said they would – I would not be blamed. The first problem was blindness. Professional advisers from the US swore they would all die if they didn't wear what they wore which was the most famous of all fabrics. They said the fabric had to be the most 'breathable'. Which is absolutely right, but incredibly wrong, if it is also treated to be waterproof. Set up a sweat in -40° and you are soon walking around in an ice straight-jacket if there is even a hint of condensation. The reality of the situation is breathable waterproof fabrics are all as bad and actually shift very little condensation but are good at crunching numbers. So sharp exit professional advisors who by now have wasted lots of time and money.

Enter uncoated micro-fibre fabric with filament-hollow fibre bonded to it with pin prick drops of laminate. Exit micro-fibre fabric bonded to laminate because it didn't actually wick away moisture along the filaments to the outside air at the rate I predicted. So almost exit yours truly! I was saved by the sheer brilliance of the design. I have always been an advocate of only taking off your clothes at infrequent occasions and that even includes going to bed. The basic design that went into production featured layered micro-fibres. These were uncoated so had a very soft handle and were therefore extremely comfortable and could quite literally be worn to excess. As such there was no need for it to be a conventional two-piece. A suit was born with in-built snow gaiters to go over ski boots, with thermal legs to the knees to heat the blood before it got to the extremities, articulated knees and tight but not restrictive waist so that a harness would not create pressure zones, a full blouson chest for upper body freedom, two huge slanted cargo pockets across the chest to rest the arms and big enough for full-sized mitts, GPS, Penguin chocolate bars, compact mirror and make up and that most sought after of all technical features for image conscious climbers – a crap flap. A huge hood with two volume adjusters was incorporated into the one-piece suit and it was bulked up for halts between sledge hauling with a hoodless Eskimo smock. This smock used the combination of hollow-fibres, micro-fibres and pin-prick laminates that having failed to shift all condensation in the one-piece suit was working up to spec on the smock. While the hood was on the suit and not the smock it offered greater versatility of protection for the head.

Four of the 24 reached the North Pole with none of the mental or physical scars that seem to go hand-in-hand with most polar expeditions and were soon back enjoying breakfast TV fulfilling their promise of being on it rather than watching it. I haven't yet seen a photo from the expedition that did not feature anyone not wearing their suits at any time of the day. There is no doubt the initial teething troubles while the team were testing the suits on Baffin Island during February caused some concern. But I can now hang up my laurels and look for some other way to earn an honest crust because one of the suits was featured full page in the most prestigious of climbing magazines – *Hello!* If anyone is looking for a suitable suit for an Arctic, Antarctic or high-altitude expedition send me a cheque for £1 500 plus £2 post and packing. The smock is PV.

Tim Pettifer.

The Scottish Mountaineering Trust – 1997/98

As was noted in last year's report, the Trust now deals directly only with applications for grants. Decisions regarding publications are taken by the Company whose Directors during the period were T. B. Fleming (Chairman), D. J. Bennet, K. V. Crocket, D. F. Lang and N. M. Suess.

Trustees met on February 20, May 21, October 2, 1997 and February 12, 1998. In the course of these meetings support was given to three expeditions: Scottish Torssuqatoq Spires 1997, EUMC Apolobamba 1997 and BSES Himalaya 1997.

Three current NTS footpath projects (Goatfell, Ben Lomond and Coire Dubh – Horns of Alligin) were supported. Support in principle was given to two large and long-range NTS footpath projects on Ben Lawers/Morenish; Glen Coe (subject to EC funding), and to a further project on Ben Lomond. Three footpath projects from the Ross and Cromarty Footpath Trust (Kernsary-Carnmor and Loch Gainemach) and one from the John Muir Trust (Bla Bheinn) were also supported.

Small grants were given to Jim Maison's Clachnaben path project and to a joint initiative in the Inverness area (Meall Fuar Monaidh). Support in principle was granted to the Arran Access Initiative for mountain-path projects. This is a complex initiative involving several organisations but the pathworks will be supervised by the NTS.

Footpath projects consume the bulk of the Trust's available income and this state of affairs has obliged Trustees to fund them selectively. To assist this process, advice is now taken regularly from Robert Aitken and Trustees have made the occasional site visit. Feedback from Club members regarding any SMT funded pathwork would be most welcome.

A small amount of grant is allocated annually to projects other than expeditions and footpaths. In the current year, such grants have been awarded to the MRCS (new computer), the Jonathan Colville Trust (winter training courses), the MCofS (hypothermia conference) and the Edinburgh JMCS (Smiddy repairs).

Standing grants are made over to the MCofS toward administration costs including the Access Officer, and of course, the SMC benefits through annual royalty payments for the use of the Club's name in publications and a substantial portion of the production costs of small-print Journal pages is met by the Publications Co.

Trustees at the February meeting also agreed to support the Publications Co. in its proposal for a CD version of *The Munros*. This is a major project which will undoubtedly impinge on the ability of the Trust to make financial awards until probably the summer of 1999. Trustees took note that a considerable number of awards made recently have not been taken up and some of these have now been withdrawn.

The present Trustees are R. N. Campbell (chair), D. C. Anderson, G. Cohen, C. D. Grant, A. Kassyk, W. A. McNicol, S. Murdoch, D. C. Page, R. T. Richardson and A. Sommerville.

The bulk of the work of the Trust is however carried out by its long-suffering officers – Treasurer Bryan Fleming and Secretary John Fowler – to whom we should all record our thanks. John Fowler has since stepped down and the new Secretary to the Trust is James D. Hotchkis, 39 Harbour Street, Nairn, IV12 8DS to whom all correspondence including applications for grants should now be directed.

The following grants have been paid or committed by the Trustees.

General Grant Fund

Grants paid	Scottish Torsuqatoq Spires Expedition	£800
	Jonathan Conville Memorial Trust	£840
	British Schools Exploring Society	£100
	Edinburgh University Apolobamba Expedition	£600
	Hypothermia Seminar	£400
	Library shelving	£478
	Scottish Mountain Safety Group	£900
Grants committed	MCofS Conference Expenses	£100
	Stirling University Photo Exhibition	£100
	Mountain Rescue Committee	£600
	Edinburgh JMCS	£1500
	Jonathan Conville Memorial Trust	£1015

Footpath Fund

Grants paid	Ross & Cromarty Footpath Trust	£6765
	John Muir Trust	£2000
Grants committed	SNH - Glen Rosa	£10000
	National Trust for Scotland	£16675
	Inverness Area Community Project	£100
	Clachnaben	£500
	Ross & Cromarty Footpath Trust	£4025
	National Trust for Scotland	£25,000
	Arran Access Initiative	£10,000

R. N. Campbell, J. R. R. Fowler.

MUNRO MATTERS

By C. M. Huntley (Clerk of the List)

This year has been the busiest for the Clerk of the List with 208 new names to be added to the list, more than 40 amendments and 30 requests for certificates from those already on the list. These requests usually start with 'my wife/husband/children have suggested I should ask for a certificate'.

The additions to the List and the amendments follow. The columns used are Munroist's number, name, year of Munros, Tops and Furths. * SMC member.

No.	Name	Munros	Tops	Furths
1706	John H. Scholtens	1997	1997	
1707	Keith Grant	1997		
1708	Albert C. McAdam	1995		
1709	Matthew Clarke	1997		
1710	Malcolm Clarke	1997		
1711	Stewart Newman	1997		
1712	Richard Davison	1997		
1713	Derek Thomas	1997		
1714	Richard Glover	1997		
1715	Sue Hunter	1997		
1716	J. Gordon Cameron	1997		
1717	Gordon J. Dykes	1997		
1718	Paul N. Craven	1997		
1719	Lesley Hickton	1997		
1720	Alec Hickton	1997		
1721	Jim Young	1997		
1722	John Newman	1997		
1723	Karin Marshall	1997		
1724	Raymond Marshall	1997		
1725	Craig Weldon	1997		
1726	Peter Gillman	1997		
1727	John Arkell	1997		
1728	John S. Spencer	1997	1997	
1729	Dennis R. Pickett	1997		
1730	Keith Anderson	1997	1997	
1731	Ian Munro	1997		
1732	Ian Barnett	1997		
1733	Jean Hunter	1997		
1734	Andrew Reston	1997		
1735	Joseph Small	1997		
1736	Lesley Leiper	1997		
1737	Malcolm Leiper	1997		
1738	John Pulford	1996	1990	
1739	John Maundrell	1997		
1740	John Kerry	1997		
1741	Lorna Macgregor	1997		
1742	Mark Swinden	1997	1997	
1743	William S. McKerrow*	1997		
1744	Alex. Cuthbertson	1997		
1745	Mark T. Wight	1997		
1746	James King	1997		
1747	Anthony Halhead	1997		
1748	Helmar P. Hurrell	1997		
1749	David A. Hurrell	1997		
1750	Mark N. Aiken	1997	1997	
1751	John Baddeley	1997		
1752	John Benthan	1997		
1753	Simon J. Wright	1997		
1754	Moira Burks	1997	1997	
1755	Alver Burks	1997	1997	
1756	Morag MacLean	1997		
1757	Tony Baker	1997		
1758	Steve Hinde	1997	1997	
1759	Doug Bain	1997		
1760	David May	1997		
1761	Dorothy Adam	1997		
1762	Keith Nightingale	1997		
1763	Alda Russell	1997		
1764	Robert W. Templeton	1997		
1765	Frank S. Cummings	1997		
1766	Peter J. Williamson	1997		
1767	H.E. Jennings	1997		
1768	Anne M. Jenkins	1997		
1769	Andrew Vickery	1997		
1770	Tom Sharpe	1997		
1771	Paul V. Kennedy	1997		
1772	Sylvia Morrow	1997		
1773	Matt Morrow	1997		
1774	Kris Howard	1997		
1775	Stuart France	1996		
1776	Maureen F. Johnson	1996	1996	
1777	Peter Johnson	1996	1996	
1778	C.R. Fishwick	1997		
1779	David Judd	1997		
1780	Marion O'Connor	1997		
1781	John Goodman	1997		
1782	R.J. Cross	1996		
1783	Bryce Reynard	1997		
1784	Jackie Jackson	1997	1997	
1785	David Scott	1997		
1786	Norman A. Todd*	1997		
1787	Mary Robinson	1997		
1788	Bill Robinson	1997		
1789	Paul V. A. Kilvert	1997		
1790	Robert Hopkin	1997		
1791	Jamie McLeod	1997		
1792	Dave A. Redding	1997	1997	
1793	Davie Hamill	1997		
1794	Henry Sutcliffe	1997		
1795	Lucy Nisbet	1997		
1796	John L. Robinson	1997		
1797	Elaine Stewart	1997		

No.	Name	Years
1798	Colin P. Watts	1997
1799	Gillian Ferry	1995
1800	Gordon Brown	1997
1801	Lindsay Boyd	1997
1802	Carl J. Schaschke*	1997
1803	Adrian N. Wylie	1997
1804	Val Meredith	1997
1805	David Westall	1997
1806	Ross Jervis	1997
1807	Alan J. Black	1997
1808	David D. Taylor	1993 1993
1809	Roger Smithies	1995
1810	Bill Robertson	1993
1811	Ray Morgan	1997
1812	Robin Wilson	1997
1813	Peter E. Odell	1997
1814	Roy Marlow	1997
1815	Lesley Protheroe	1997
1816	Alastair Protheroe	1997
1817	Geoff Cumming	1997
1818	Olga West	1997
1819	David West	1997
1820	Pam C. Volwerk	1997
1821	Phil Eccles	1997
1822	Alex Horsburgh	1997
1823	Alan Blair	1997
1824	Margo Webster	1997
1825	Greta Fraser	1997
1826	Jonathan M. Chapman	1997
1827	Geoffrey N. Chapman	1997
1828	Corina Cramer	1996
1829	Andy Cairns	1997
1830	Forbes Craig	1997
1831	Melinda J. Walker	1997
1832	John R. Cobb	1997
1833	Fred Nind	1996
1834	Hugh Skivington	1997
1835	David Jones	1997
1836	Wendy Dodds	1997
1837	Carol McNeill	1996
1838	Bill M. Mason	1996
1839	Sue Dunbar	1997
1840	Shirley A. Mitchinson	1996
1841	Pamela Bridge	1997
1942	Iain Milne	1997
1843	Patricia Notman	1997
1844	Irving Notman	1993
1845	Allan Hughes	1997 1997
1846	J.E. Kelsall	1997
1847	P.Hollingsworth	1997
1848	Kerr Elliot	1997
1849	Jim Elliot	1997
1850	Colin Mathieson	1995
1851	Iain Paton	1995
1852	David Henry	1995
1853	Anne J. Fletcher	1997
1854	Graham R. Bunn	1997
1855	Iain Price	1997
1856	Alan Bertram	1997
1857	Andrew Henderson	1997
1858	Graham Laird	1996
1859	George R. R. Rusk	1997
1860	Rob Milne*	1997 1997
1861	John J. O'Keefe	1997 1997
1862	Charles W. Simmonds	1997
1863	Alan D. Grant	1992
1864	Neil E. G. Coltart	1997
1865	David Wolf	1997
1866	Malcolm Fleming	1997
1867	John Mackie	1997
1868	Hamish D. Clark	1997
1869	Ian Fraser	1997 1997
1870	Ed Montgomery	1997
1871	Edward A. Rigby	1997
1872	Ian McLeod	1997
1873	Spence McLeod	1997
1874	Bryan Rynne	1997 1997 1997
1875	Graham R. Pearson	1997 1997
1876	Colin D. Grant*	1994
1877	George F. Erskine	1997
1878	Bill Walker	1997
1879	Peter Stewart*	1997
1880	Ian Pascoe	1997
1881	Anne Wylie	1997
1882	Colin Wylie	1997
1883	Allan Downs	1997
1884	James Lamb	1997
1885	Brian Tuck	1997
1886	Alex Macmillan	1997
1887	Alan Shand*	1997
1888	Richard J. Plumb	1997
1889	Gordon S. Paterson	1997
1890	Stan da Prato	1997
1891	Dave Marshall	1993
1892	Charles Campbell	1997
1893	Roy Baird	1996 1996 1996
1894	Bob Fowler	1997
1895	Bob Robertson	1996
1896	C. J. Gough	1997
1897	Alan M. Ure	1996
1898	Karami A. Ure	1996
1899	Steve Honeyman	1995
1900	Hugh O'Kane	1997
1901	Susan D. Littlewood	1998
1902	Trevor J. Littlewood	1998
1903	Colin J. Green	1998
1904	John A. Dunn*	1997
1905	Gordon Greig	1997
1906	Douglas Trail	1997
1907	Ian MacPherson	1997
1908	Philip McAra*	1997
1909	Thomas G.F. Rankin	1994
1910	Iain Barr	1997
1911	M. J. Almond	1997
1912	S. A. Hodges	1998
1913	Ron F. Bowie	1997

AMENDMENTS AND CORRECTIONS

I have included all notifications of changes to the List and the errors that were identified from the publication of the Tables. Many may have noticed one duplication which has been resolved by John Owen (soon to compleat), with H. H. Mills* posthumously reclaiming 971 and Brian Gardiner now only occupying 990. Only number of rounds and the year of the latest round are given. The columns given are Munros, Tops and Furths.

No.	Name	Munros	Tops	Furths
73	Andrew Fraser	1996	1980	1977
		x4		
230	John Howorth	1996	1996	1996
		x2 x2	x2	
258	Iain R.W. Park	1997		
		x2		
299	Laurie Skuodas	1983		1997
317	Grahame Nicoll*	1997	1993	
		x2		
320	John A. Wild	1997		
		x2		
327	Stewart Logan	1997		
		x9		
354	George J. Borland	1993	1984	1997
		x3		
376	Simon Stewart	1984	1984	1995
384	J. M. Gear	1996		
		x2		
455	A. Laurence Rudkin	1996		
		x2		
534	Peter Warburton	1987	1997	1996
652	Leslie B. Aird	1989		1995
653	Irene D. Aird	1989		1995
675	Geoff Skeaping	1997	1993	
		x2		
743	Ian Turner	1990	1997	1997
783	Frances A Wilson	1990		1993
784	Peter Wilson	1990		1993
927	Dorothy Spencer	1991		1997
1023	Alan Fortune	1992	1994	
1045	Steve Fallon	1997		
		x5		
1052	David C. Seivewright	1997		
		x2		
1054	David Hoyle	1992	1992	
1143	Steve Evans	1993	1997	
1256	Keith Yates	1993	1997	
1271	Tony M. Deall	1994	1997	
1298	Graham T. Illing	1994	1997	
1299	Michael McLaggan	1994		1997
1313	Michael Smyth	1994		1997
1329	Gillian Green	1994	1994	1997
1330	John Green	1994	1994	1997
1331	John Mackay	1994		1997
1397	Douglas MacLeod	1995	1997	
1437	George Kincaid	1995		1997
1511	Fred Siddaway	1995		1997
1527	A. Blandy	1997		
		x2		
1557	Andrew Moignard	1996	1996	
1559	Graham Hemsley	1996		1997
1613	James M. Thomson	1996	1996	
1630	Gill Nisbet	1996		1997
1640	Geoff Scott	1994		1997
1654	Ken Coote	1996		1997
1675	Paul Caban	1996		1997
1694	Sam Johnston	1996	1997	1997

The notes which follow are a summary of the wealth of experiences and comments I have received in letters over the last year. As I was collating the List this year I certainly noticed that there was a considerable number of those who had compleated a few years ago, and have only now decided to get their names in print. Perhaps the news that the new edition of the Tables was about to List eight Tops that were now deemed worthy of Munro status, spurred many to write in promptly. J. E. Kelsall (1846) was the most delayed compleation, waiting 11 years, followed by David Taylor (1808), Bill Robertson (1810), Irving Notman (1844), and Alan Grant (1863), all from 1993. Irving appears to have waited until his wife Patricia compleated (1843), and Alan's wife says that his reason for getting his Munroists number is that he would like to have the chance of wearing the tie (see below).

The planned change to the Munro List had been rumoured for a while, mainly because the Editor of the Tables had been canvassing opinion from around the Scottish hillwalking fraternity. Once the final decision had been made by the Editor and the SMC committee, the relevant information was sent to the climbing Press for expected publication a few weeks' later. However, the national Press took much more interest than expected, with the result that the changes were in such journalistic heavies as the *Scotsman,* the *Herald* and the *Telegraph.* This obviously took many by surprise, which was unintended.

C. J. Gough (1896) says that although he had just completed, he was feeling slightly flat. However, the new eight gave him his next goal which has now rolled into searching out the Corbetts. Bill Walker (1878), thought he had compleated on Beinn Sgritheall and duly held his celebration that night only to read the next morning that the goal posts had been moved. Craig Forbes (1830) comments that when he thought he had three to go, the List was changed, so that he now had seven to go. However, this meant he had a 'wonderful tramp over Braeriach to Angel's Peak and back along the Larig Ghru'. Similarly, Anne Fletcher (1853) and Graham Bunn (1853) thought they were nearly there and only needed a trip to Skye to clean up. Then their copy of the *Angry Corrie* arrived to inform them that Beinn Sgreamach was needed. I felt that no one should be expected to include the 'new eight' until the date of publication of the Tables. This left about four months between the Press news and the Tables reaching the shops, which seemed to be a reasonable time for most compleation plans to be amended as necessary, and for those who had, or were very close, to compleation, to get their letter in promptly. I can understand some of the frustration the changes may have caused (although hopefully, short lived when the new Munros were explored), but I did hear the opposite interpretation when a former university club colleague told me he was pleased to find, as he read his morning paper, that he had just done eight new Munros, and all before breakfast.

A great many compleations are husband-and-wife teams and readers can quickly identify the pairs of surnames in the List above. Other family permutations are the brothers, Matthew and Malcolm Clarke (1709, 1710), and Ian and Spence McLeod (1872, 1873), the father-and-son teams of Kerr and Jim Elliot (1848, 1849), and Jonathan and Geoffrey Chapman (1826, 1827). The Chapmans compleated in the same week but on different hills and were very nearly a family trio but for the fact that Geoffrey's wife had decided to stop at 283 and miss out the Inn Pinn. She asks if there is another List for the Inn Pinn-less. Another family connection this year is that of Alda Russell (1763) and her sister, Anne Jenkins (1768), who have kept each other company over much of their respective rounds. Peter Odell (1813) reported that he hoped his letter found the correct Clerk as his most recent SMCJ is a 1927 copy which belonged to his grandfather – Noel Odell. Peter correctly perceived that the Editor had also changed. Lesley and Alastair Protheroe (1815, 1816), tell me that as a couple they now join Lesley's father, Ian Spence (137), on the list. Couples who have walked every hill together include the Robinsons (1787, 1788), and the Wests (1818, 1819). Even more hills were ascended together by the Johnsons (1776, 1777), who have included the Tops, and the Burks (1754,

1755), who have the Munros, Tops and Corbetts ticked. Once the Hurrells (1748, 1749) started counting they found their tally had begun to diverge, such that a few solo trips were needed to ensure they could share a joint compleation.

The routes to the hills vary greatly. Some manage a few long periods in the Highlands each year, particularly for those living hundreds of miles away. In contrast, Charles Campbell (1892) recorded that almost every hill was done as a day trip from Glasgow, as one of his party rarely seemed to be able to be spared from the house for more than 24 hours. This meant some long drives for very little time on the hill and one car written off. Other Munroists who fared poorly with cars are David May (1760) who wrote off two cars (neither his fault), and John Baddeley (1751) who left his car at Loch Arkaig and spent a very wet day ascending Sgurr na Ciche before returning for a night in a bothy. The next day they found the road out blocked by massive extensions to the loch. Sportingly, he says they floated the car through some sections but were finally barred by a stretch which had almost covered the passing place sign. As a result the car had to stay put for some weeks until they could return to collect it. Roger Smithies (1809), who compleated one day after his 70th birthday, had used a full range of transport, which has included regularly hitch-hiking from Harrow, London. His favourite hitch was the night sleeper from Corrour which dropped him off at Fersit.

As usual the most popular Last Munros have remained Ben More (Mull) and Beinn na Lap. However, this year these two have been closely followed by Ben Sgreamach and An Stuc which seemed to be hills often omitted until they received their elevation and as such, have become the unintended scene of a number of champagne celebrations. James Lamb (1884) needed to be quite selective on which Munro to compleat on as he also wished to compleat his Corbetts on the same day. In the end he selected Beinn Sgritheall and Beinn na h-Eaglaise. John Pulford (1738) found himself rather pressurised into compleating when his Leeds club organised a meet around his planned dates. With only a week to go he was still 10 short and so had to set off early to ensure his club really did have a compleation to celebrate. In the end he reached Mull with a few hours to spare. On Norman Todd's (1786) last Munro, after a round of 52 years, one bottle of champagne that safely arrived the carry to the top, exploded as it was placed on a rock. Fortunately, Norman found it was one of a number and the celebrations were able to continue unhindered.

As usual there are a few comments on lucky escapes. Allan Hughes (1845) was unlucky enough to be avalanched at 2000ft on An Gearanach and only returned to the hill once all the others had been visited. Kris Howard (1774) has been in the SMCJ before as a result of a fall. The accident statistic mentions a fall of 20ft but Kris says that the 20ft was just his last bounce. Fortunately, no lasting damage. I always tend to note the address a letter comes from, and although Edinburgh and Glasgow predominate, there is a growing Munrosis cluster on East Kilbride and its environs. For example, Allan Hughes (1845), Marion O'Connor (1780), Bill Robertson (1895), the Wylies (1881, 1882), Richard Plumb (1888) and Gordon Paterson (1889) are all residents of the town. There is also an active core from near the town including Davie Hamill

(1793) who is this year's oldest starter and compleater, having been introduced to the Munros at the age of 71 and compleated at 76. Another quirk of the addresses is that the nearer you live to the hills the less likely you are to climb them (or at least admit to it), and the exceptions to this are almost all women! For example, Greta Fraser (1825), Pam Volwerk (1820) and Morag Mclean (1756) are some of a few Highland residents.

This year a number of groups have told me of their multi-compleations. John Robinson wrote to say that he, Elaine Stewart and Colin Watts (1796-1798) compleated together on Sgurr Eilde Mor, and asked that I 'allocate consecutive numbers as I see fit'. My convention in this case, is that the writer comes first followed by ladies, then men. Another trio were the Littlewoods and Colin Green (1901-1903) who found their complement was further increased by three uninvited farm dogs on Ben Lomond. Two dogs kept them company all the way to the top and back, but one was last seen at 700m on the descent; obviously the pace or supply of sandwiches was not to its liking.

I've enjoyed the enormous variety in the letters, but I also get to recognise the surprising overlap of tales. For example, the navigational errors that abounded in the Glens Pean and Dessary this year. Gordon Brown (1800) managed to walk for many hours in the wrong direction, and Alex Horsburgh (1822) made a similar error in the Cairngorms. Although lost or 'slightly mistaken' crop up in many descriptions of Munroists' rounds, Val Meredith (1804) managed to expand the experiences to include bivvied, camped, botanised, and geologised.

During the last two years the SMC has maintained a Web site (www.smc.org.uk). This has proved of interest and many have commented on getting my address from the site. This is clearly not the only site that Munroists may use and now Paul Kennedy (1771) informs me that he has set up his own site with articles on his hillwalking days which include pictures (www.gillcon.demon.co.uk).

Finally, I was passed a cutting from a running magazine entitled *Munro Shuffling*. It described that the effect of the new Munro in Kintail, and the loss of one in the Mamores, has meant that attempts on the record number of Munros in 24 hours may move from the Mamores-Loch Treig area to Kintail, and has meant that Jon Broxap, who previously thought he had done 28 Munros in 24 hours, finds himself now with 29.

For those who wish to be registered on the List of Compleat Munroists, they should write to the Clerk at the address below. I am always pleased to hear of your experiences, time taken on the round, age, etc., etc., and I prefer to hear direct from the Munroist. If an A4 sae is enclosed I will return a colour A4 certificate to mark their Compleation. Also if those already on the List would like to avail themselves of the certificate, they should write to me with a reference to their Munroist number (and enclose sae please). All Notification should be sent to Dr. C. M. Huntley, Old Medwyn, Spittal, Carnwath, Lanarkshire. ML11 8LY. Once registered, Munroists can claim, and purchase, a tie and/or Brooch.

Authorised Misinformation?

Readers of the latest *Munro's Tables* will have been interested in the comment contained in the introduction, that the SMC was aware of a publication predating the Tables in which, county by county, hills are listed in descending order. The initial correspondence which brought this to our attention is given below, followed by our reply.

Peter Warburton writes: Before Sir Hugh Munro brought out his *Tables of Heights over 3000ft,* in the first (1891) volume of the SMCJ, it was generally believed that only some 30 hills were of that altitude; the authoritative Baddeley's Guide, for instance, listed 31.

Munro's Tables, 1980, 1984 and 1990 editions.

A similar statement, rather more cautiously worded, appeared in the foreword to the 1974 edition of the Tables. It is surprising that such an unlikely assertion seems to have gone unchallenged, except for the qualification in the following sentence that perhaps a few early Club members thought they knew rather better. In the way of these things, the qualification has gone largely unnoticed and the 30/31 figure has been so widely quoted that the myth has come to be regarded as a fact, backed by the authority of the Tables.

Baddeley's 31 did not claim to be a complete listing and any reader glancing casually at the many half-inch to the mile maps included in the guides would have noticed dozens more mountains with spot heights above 3000ft. The rival firm of Black were more prudent; their list of 23 3000-footers was headed *Some of the Principal Mountains in Scotland according to the Ordnance Survey.* It is a pity that, in trumping Black's 23, Baddeley chose the single line title *Heights of Scotch Mountains.*

The source for all serious guide book writers was the OS who had completed their large scale (six-inches to the mile) field survey of Scotland by 1877. This survey, with some later revision, became the basis for the one-inch series, publication of which Baddeley noted, in June 1883, was 'all but complete' for the Highlands. Those who found that a smaller scale commercial map met their needs had a choice. One of the best was published by Johnsons of Edinburgh. Even at the scale of 10 miles to the inch their editions in the 1850s named and gave heights for 46 hills of more than 3000ft. or 42 if hindsight is used to exclude four mistakes (Ben Ledi, Ben Vrackie, Foinaven and Beinn a' Bha'ach Ard).

Before Sir Hugh's Tables appeared, the full listing of Scottish hills in order of height may well have been considered an eccentric and pointless pursuit, but it had been undertaken. Robert Hall's *The Highland Sportsman and Tourist* (Third Edition, 1884) lists 236 heights of 3000ft. or more plus 1867, yes 1867 lower hills, each with county and district. Mr Hall was in business in London and Inverness as a shooting and estate agent and the 313 page *Highland Sportsman,* priced at 2/6d, was probably circulated, gratis, to clients. The extent to which he cast his bread upon the waters is indicated by the inclusion, among the end papers, of three pages of Press Opinions of an earlier edition – 40 quotations in all and all favourable. My copy is stamped 'With the Author's Compliments' and it is probable that many Highland proprietors received copies on that basis – perhaps one even reached the library at Lindertis?'

Chris Huntley replies: Peter Warburton's text arrived at what could be considered an inopportune time. The Scottish Mountaineering Trust and the Editor of *Munro's Tables* were putting together a new edition and the possibility that the Tables were pre-dated needed to be investigated.

My first attempts to acquire a copy of the book came to nothing, although most antiquarian booksellers I spoke to seemed to be familiar with this publication and others of a similar vogue by Mr Hall. One bookseller told me he knew the book well, and had a copy which he would send. It duly arrived but was actually by a Herbert Hall, published in the 1850s, and was entitled *The Highland Tourist.* This was also a tourist's compendium, very much aimed at the sporting tourist. However ,no lists of hills. Fortunately, a call to the National Library of Scotland confirmed that they had a number of editions and so I finally managed to see a copy. Sure enough, there, chapter by chapter, were lists of hills although these were largely swamped by the salient information directed at the Victorian tourist who was far more interested in the shooting and fishing opportunities than the hills. I found that the hills warranted almost no comment, and when I did come across a mention of Ben Lomond in the text I found that it wasn't on the list! The publication seems to have been annual from 1882-1885, and looking at each one I could not actually see any changes. Perhaps some of the detail on prices and estate owners necessitated new editions.

Having seen the Hall publication, I then went back to check the first publication of the Tables and found that the claim of there only being 31 summits exceeding 3000ft did not originate from that time, and seems to have only appeared in the more recent editions. Therefore this observation did not come from Sir Hugh. Once this was clarified the element of doubt that Sir Hugh Munro had either not read up on the subject (i.e. searching out guides such as Hall's), or that he was not making good use of the existing maps, is removed. Instead what we have is Sir Hugh producing a publication which was using available information from the existing maps, enhancing it by setting a cut-off point of 3000ft, and then thoroughly exploring each area to search out the Mountains from the Tops.

In making a direct comparison of the lists there is much variation in the spelling of hills and even heights, making a straight copy very unlikely. In addition, Sir Hugh created his own areas (The Sections) grouping together logical clusters of hills rather than using county boundaries. One issue that Hall had to resolve, and Sir Hugh avoided, was in which county should a top be listed when it falls on the county border (as many do)? For this reason we find Stob an t-Sluichd on Ben Avon being the only hill above 3000ft listed in Banffshire, with all the other tops on Ben Avon found in the chapter for Aberdeenshire. Sir Hugh's reasons for selecting the 3000ft limit is interesting, and never given as far as I know, although he was defining a sufficiently demanding, but feasible List to occupy a lifetime of hillwalking, given the conditions at that time.

In conclusion we have two very different publications, both of which have their origins in the maps of the 1880s. The first from Mr Hall, a fascinating guide to the 'Sporting' opportunities of the Highlands, which, no doubt, was useful to the tourists of its day but with little or no comment on the quality of routes on the hills, and secondly *Munro's Tables,* which was directed to all those interested in the hills and which is still generating much discussion and pleasure! And readers of the new Tables will find no mention of the '31 hills' in the *Introduction.*

SCOTTISH MOUNTAIN ACCIDENTS 1996
REGIONAL DISTRIBUTION

(Geographical Divisions are those used in SMC District Guidebooks)

| REGION | CASUALTIES (of which fatalities are bracketed) | | | | INCIDENTS | | | | | | | Animal Rescues | Non-Mountaineering Incidents |
| | | | | | Actual Rescues | | Other Callouts | | | | | | |
	Injuries	Exhaustion/Exposure Hypothermia, Hyperthermia	Illness	Total Casualties	Incidents with Casualties	Cragfast or weatherbound	Separated	Lost	Overdue or Benighted	False Alarms	Total Incidents		
All Regions 1995	180 (37)	35 (2)	20 (12)	235 (49)	198	32	17	12	72	12	339	2	27
Northern Highlands	16 (2)	2 –	2 –	20 (5)	18	–	–	1	5	3	27	–	4 (2)
Western Highlands	7 –	– –	5 –	8 –	7	–	–	–	3	3	13	–	–
Ben Nevis	25 (2)	1 –	5 –	31 (2)	25	2	–	–	4	–	31	–	–
Glen Coe (Inc Buachaille)	18 (2)	– –	2 (1)	20 (3)	19	5	–	–	9	2	35	–	–
Other Central Highlands	19 (3)	1 –	2 –	22 (3)	17	5	1	–	6	3	32	–	5 (1)
Cairngorms	23 –	4 –	4 (1)	31 (1)	28	1	1	9	8	4	51	–	2
Southern Highlands	24 (5)	2 –	3 (3)	29 (8)	29	2	1	2	2	6	43	–	3 (1)
Skye	15 (5)	– –	1 –	16 (5)	15	4	–	–	2	1	22	–	–
Islands (other than Skye	6 (1)	1 –	–	7 (1)	7	1	–	1	3	–	12	–	–
Southern Uplands	4 –	3 –	1 –	8 –	8	–	4	3	5	2	22	–	6 (1)
All Regions 1996	157 (20)	14 –	21 (4)	192 (25)	173	20	7	16	47	24	288	–	20 (5)

SCOTTISH MOUNTAIN ACCIDENTS 1997
REGIONAL DISTRIBUTION

(Geographical Divisions are those used in SMC District Guidebooks)

| REGION | CASUALTIES (of which fatalities are bracketed) | | | | INCIDENTS | | | | | | | | Animal Rescues | Non-Mountaineering Incidents |
| | | | | | Actual Rescues | | Other Callouts | | | | | | | |
	Injuries	Exhaustion/Exposure Hypothermia, Hyperthermia	Illness	Total Casualties	Incidents with Casualties	Cragfast or weatherbound	Separated	Lost	Overdue or Benighted	False Alarms	Total Incidents			
All Regions 1996	157 (3)	1 –	1 –	192 (25)	173 –	20 –	8 –	18	39	18	237 –		–	20 (5)
Northern Highlands	22 (3)	1 –	1 –	24 (3)	22 –	–	3	2	8	4	39		1	–
Western Highlands	11 (1)	1 –	1 –	13 (1)	7	12	–	1	4	–	17		–	–
Ben Nevis	20 (3)	8 –	6 (3)	34 (6)	29	0	–	1	2	2	34		–	–
Glen Coe (Inc Buachaille)	17 (1)	–	2 (1)	19 (2)	18	6	1	–	1	1	27		–	–
Other Central Highlands	35 (5)	–	5 (2)	40 (7)	33	2	2	1	2	–	41		1	–
Cairngorms	36 (1)	1 –	2 (1)	39 (2)	35 –	1	2	3	9	1	51		5	–
Southern Highlands	24 (1)	4 –	6 (3)	34 (4)	32	–	1	2	7	1	44		4	2
Skye	14 (2)	3 –	–	16 (5)	17 (2)	15	1	–	5	3	24		1	–
Islands (other than Skye)	2 –	3 (1)	2 (1)	7 (2)	7 –	1	1	1	1	–	11		1	–
Southern Uplands	3 –	2 –	–	5 –	4	–	1	1	4	–	10		21	1
All Regions 1997	184 (17)	23 (1)	25 (4)	192 (11)	232 (29)	207	11	12	43	12	298		34	3

SCOTTISH MOUNTAIN ACCIDENTS

STATISTICS FOR ALL SCOTLAND FROM 1987

ALL REGIONS	CASUALTIES (of which fatalities are bracketed)				INCIDENTS							Animal Rescues	Non-Mountaineering Incidents
					Actual Rescues		Other Callouts						
	Injuries	Exhaustion/Exposure Hypothermia, Hyperthermia	Illness	Total Casualties	Incidents with Casualties	Cragfast or weatherbound	Separated	Lost	Overdue or Benighted	False Alarms	Total Incidents		
1987	122 (21)	11 (–)	16 (7)	149 (28)	136 (–)	18 (–)	8 (–)	18 (–)	39 (–)	18 (–)	237 (–)	–	16 (–)
1988	121 (21)	34 (2)	10 (2)	165 (25)	131 (–)	18 (–)	7 (–)	13 (–)	34 (–)	16 (–)	21 (–)	–	14 (–)
1989	130 (20)	15 (1)	13 (4)	158 (25)	141 (–)	8 (–)	15 (–)	12 (–)	25 (–)	14 (–)	215 (–)	–	11 (–)
1990	132 (23)	36 (1)	13 (6)	181 (30)	161 (–)	20 (–)	15 (–)	16 (–)	56 (–)	23 (–)	291 (–)	–	20 (–)
1991	217 (34)	23 (2)	20 (9)	260 (44)	235 (–)	22 (–)	13 (–)	28 (–)	46 (–)	10 (–)	254 (–)	1 (–)	10 (–)
1992	164 (31)	26 (1)	16 (11)	206 (43)	194 (–)	20 (–)	11 (–)	13 (–)	46 (–)	14 (–)	298 (–)	4 (–)	7 (–)
1993	173 (34)	16 (3)	25 (10)	214 (47)	221 (–)	20 (–)	16 (–)	13 (–)	47 (–)	7 (–)	324 (–)	5 (–)	41 (–)
1994	183 (35)	29 (1)	23 (8)	235 (44)	218 (–)	25 (–)	19 (–)	12 (–)	42 (–)	10 (–)	326 (–)	3 (–)	10 (–)
1995	182 (35)	35 (2)	20 (12)	237 (49)	200 (–)	32 (–)	17 (–)	9 (–)	72 (–)	12 (–)	342 (–)	2 (–)	27 (–)
1996	182 (27)	30 (–)	24 (7)	236 (34)	215 (–)	17 (–)	9 (–)	12 (–)	60 (–)	11 (–)	324 (–)	–	25 (–)
1997	184 (17)	23 (1)	25 (11)	232 (29)	207 (–)	11 (–)	11 (–)	12 (–)	43 (–)	12 (–)	298 (–)	3 (–)	34 (–)

SCOTTISH MOUNTAIN ACCIDENTS 1997

Compiled by John Hinde

Police have not been mentioned in every incident as they are involved in all.

NORTHERN HIGHLANDS

JANUARY 2 – Torridon MRT, airlifted by RAF Sea King, vainly ground searched Coire Dubh, Liathach after a report of a white flare. It could have been a meteorite. 22.

JANUARY 3 – A party of Scouts, some with crampons, some without, turned back on a path to Beinn Dearg because of icy conditions. One of the leaders (m31) slipped descending when wearing crampons, fracturing an ankle. Airlift by RAF Sea King, Dundonnell MRT. 12.

JANUARY 21 – Keeper (35) deer counting for 11km in extended line with five others from Gualin Lodge to Oldshoremore, near Kinlochbervie. He soon lost radio contact with his colleagues and was thereby overdue, but turned up at rendezvous in failing light. Coast search by HMCG helicopter. RAF Sea King scrambled, then cancelled. 10.

FEBRUARY 9-May 3 Body of a woman (32) found by walker on May 3, half in and half out of a burn, below extreme NW tip of Baosbheinn Ridge, 7km SE of head of Loch Gairloch. She had been reported missing from home on February 9, but no route plan had been left. Evacuated by CID officers in PLM helicopter on May 4. No suspicious circumstances. 115.

MARCH 4 – Walker (29) sufferd head cut and unconsciousness from 240m fall on Glas Mheall Liath of An Teallach.

MARCH 4 – HMCG Scrabster rescued injured girl (13) who had fallen from a cliff path at Thurso. 1.

MARCH 29 – Father and son (45,18) overdue on Seanna Bhraig. Turned up safe after Assynt and Dundonnell MRTs had been contacted. 26.

APRIL 13-14 – Man (23) had to get back to work so he left his companions at 8.30am on Sunday. They were fishing at Poca Buidhe Bothy, near Beinn an Eoin, Loch Maree, as they had all been overnight. He did not know the area and got lost walking out in mist, so his car was still there when his companions later walked 11km to the road. He was found safe by a dog on an overnight search by SARDA, Torridon MRT and RAF SEA King. 272.

MAY 4 – Woman (53) in a party of 31 walking from Coire Mhic Nobuill to Coire Dubh Mor, slipped on wet rock breaking an ankle. Torridon MRT and RAF Sea King. 18.

MAY 6 – Coast walker with broken leg near Lochinver. HMCG helicopter. 1

MAY 11 – Assynt MRT and RAF Sea King alerted for two boys (7, 5) missing at Backies, Golspie. Turned up safe. 6.

JUNE 3 – Assynt MRT alerted for one of three anglers missing returning to car at Inchkinloch from Loch Halium. For some reason he had gone over a shoulder of Ben Loyal and reached road at Lettermore, Loch Loyal.

JUNE 4 – South-east of Horns of Alligin a man (45) suffered heat exhaustion. Companion went for help and two passing climbers gave him water, so he recovered enough to get down. Torridon MRT. 6.

JUNE 4 – Climbers reported to Assynt MRT as overdue on Old Man of Stoer but they had just been enjoying good weather.

JUNE 24 – Man (71) slipped on grass on Ben Klibreck injuring his leg. Airlift by RAF Sea King. Assynt MRT standby. 8.

JUNE 28 – A woman (44) descending west from Ben Tongue (300m) down steep heather, slipped, fracturing a leg. Splinted by Police and carried to vehicle. 4.

JULY 9 – Casualty (54) was walking rocky ridge east of Sail Liath, An Teallach, below Loch Toll an Lochain, when he slipped on dry scree breaking an ankle. Winched by HMCG helicopter. Dundonnell MRT. 18.

JULY 28 – Assynt MRT and HMCG helicopter searched around Suileag Bothy in Upper Glen Canisp after a red flare had been set off inadvertently. 24.

JULY 29-AUGUST 13 – Last phoned parents on July 29, solo walker (35) was reported missing on August 11. His body was found by HMCG helicopter on August 13. He had fallen 60m from NE Face of Horns of Alligin. Torridon and Dundonnell MRTs and SARDA searched for two days. 179.

AUGUST 2-3 – Kinlochbervie and Lochinver Coastguards, Lochinver lifeboat and HMCG helicopter searched overnight for two male rock climbers (47, 45). They had been cut off by the tide when on Am Buachaille (sea stack, Sandwood Bay) and got back ashore before being found. 133.

AUGUST 8-9 - Walker (49) on Ben More Assynt got off route chasing his dog which had run off. When found by RAF Sea King and Assynt MRT he was heading for correct descent route having bivvied overnight in bad weather. 124.

AUGUST 11 – Descending dry scree of Allt Sugach, Mullach an Rathain, Liathach, a man (38) slipped, bruising his upper thigh. Winched by RAF Sea King, Torridon MRT. 27.

AUGUST 19 – Boy (11) fishing in remote hill loch somewhere about 5km NE of Ben More Assynt got separated from his group. Reported missing after five hours. After seven hours he was handed over safe in Glen Cassley by German tourists who found him. Assynt MRT, HMCG helicopter. 42.

AUGUST 24 – HMCG rescued two men (45, 22) with minor injuries after having fallen on rocks at Kyle of Durness.

AUGUST 24 – Lead climber (36) on West Buttress, Stac Pollaidh, dislodged a large rock slab which fell on top of him. He fell 9m sustaining a compound leg fracture and arm injury. Slab also caused a slight head injury to the second (m26). Both wore helmets. Second had been winched by HMCG helicopter, and a helicopter crew member was on ground preparing leader for lift, when rotor of helicopter scraped rock. It then crash-landed at base of mountain causing no further injuries. RAF R137 Sea King was then called and winched off the more seriously injured leader. Dundonnell and Kinloss MRTs. 110.

AUGUST 24 – Walking on SW Ridge Spidean a'Choire Leith, Liathach in good weather, accompanied man (34) injured a knee. Torridon and Leuchars MRTs went up to carry him down due to non-availability of a helicopter (above incident) but RAF Sea King did the task. 129.

AUGUST 24-25 – Male (59) overdue on Ben More Assynt walked off at 01.00 and was sent to hospital. Assynt MRT had been called out for 05.00 search.

AUGUST 29 – One of two climbers (23) soloing a crag at Loch Dubh (2.7km NE of Lochinver) fell among boulders injuring his back and cutting forehead. Police and ambulance. 2.

AUGUST 30 – Woman (56) stayed put after getting separated from her companion in mist on Sgurr Fiona summit, An Teallach. She was led off the mountain by eight passers-by uninjured, meeting up with Dundonnell MRT. HMCG helicopter. 41.

SEPTEMBER 15 – Loch Toll nam Biast, N of Sgurr Mhor of Beinn Alligin. Casualty (55) slipped into a runnel jarring his knee. RAF Sea King landed and took him aboard. Torridon MRT. 34.

SEPTEMBER 21-22 – Three walkers (m50, f34, m33) benighted near Central Buttress of Coire Mhic Fhearchair, Beinn Eighe. Walked out next morning as Torridon team assembled. 9.

SEPTEMBER 23 – Descending the Bad Step on SE Ridge Corrag Bhuidhe, An Teallach, walker (42) slipped and fell 9m stopping on a small ledge with chest injuries. Companions descending a different line helped him down a little way. Mobile phone brought HMCG helicopter and Dundonnell MRT. 54.

SEPTEMBER 26-27 – Subject (32) became separated from companion (who was carrying map and compass) west of South Top of Ben More Assynt, on steep and difficult ground in mist. He walked down as far as he could in gathering dark without a torch, then reported next morning as RAF Sea King landed and Assynt MRT mustered. 16.

SEPTEMBER 26-29 – Car found on September 29 up a forestry track below Strone Nea at the head of Loch Broom. Owner (49) had been missing since September 26. Dundonnell and Kinloss MRTs searched. His body was found below a climb, The Shaft, from which he appears to have slipped when soloing. Stretchered to road as area was not suitable for RAF Sea King involved. 137.

SEPTEMBER 27 – Party of eight ascending east end of Liathach by recognised path to Stuc a'Choire Dhuibh Bhig, casualty (19) slipped on terraced rock at about 800m. He fell 10m slightly injuring head, arms and legs. Torridon MRT airlifted and casualty winched by RAF Sea King. 72.

SEPTEMBER 28 – Bouldering on West Buttress, Stac Pollaidh, climber (35) stumbled and dislocated his shoulder. Stretcher lowered to foot of buttress, then down to road by Dundonnell MRT. 198.

OCTOBER 18 – Man (29) and woman (22) climbing on Old Man of Stoer reported overdue, needing more time for climb. Found by RAF Sea King and Lochinver lifeboat and coatguard. 48.

OCTOBER 26-27 – Man (56) in a party of four was descending very steep, broken ground on Ben More Assynt near Dubh Loch Mor, following a route (only 500m south of subject of benightment of September 26-27). He slipped in mist on wet rock and scree with concussion and chest injuries, cuts and bruises. Assynt MRT, RAF Sea King. 380.

NOVEMBER 27-28 – Starting at 04.00 from Corriehallie and crossing three Munros in the ridge due S of Shenavall Bothy, walker (m23) got benighted and bivouacked descending towards Shenavall. Dundonnell MRT searched two lines. Found near Achnegie and evacuated by 4WD vehicle. 102.

WESTERN HIGHLANDS

JANUARY 10 – Postponing Meall na Teanga, one of the two Munros he attempted near Loch Lochy, an experienced walker (59) tried to get down Gleann Cia-aig but ran out of daylight and torch batteries, taking refuge in forest and walking out at first light. Full search by Lochaber MRT, SARDA and RAF Sea King. 504.

FEBRUARY 22 – A woman (44) in a party of eight attempting Ben Tee from Invergarry became ill lapsing in and out of comas. She was walked off by companions before Lochaber MRT searched. 2.

APRIL 4 – One of six walkers doing Glenfinnan Horseshoe, a woman (59) slipped on Sgurr nan Coireachan causing two fractures to her left ankle. Lochaber MRT tracked vehicle. 48.

APRIL 6 – Leading climber (30) an outdoor instructor in a party of three, slipped at Mussel Ropes Crags, situated at Bromisaig on Knoydart shore of Loch Nevis. He fell 10m suffering head injuries, despite wearing a helmet. Lowered to shore then taken by boat to Mallaig. Police. 1.

MAY 8 – Wife (52) stumbled on East Ridge, Beinn a'Chairein, Glen Cannich, breaking her ankle. Although above the forest, forestry workers rescued her using an Argo. Dundonnell MRT. 10.

MAY 9 – Allt a' Ghleannain (pass south of Sgurr Mhic Bharraich, Shiel Bridge). Pair doing circular walk as part of coast-to-coast challenge, but carrying no gear. Man (62) suffering heat exhaustion/diabetes collapsed and was unconscious for a short time. Other walkers gave him food and drink and escorted him to rescuers. Glenelg and Kintail MRTs. 30.

MAY 11 – Wife (32) slipped descending wet, rocky East Ridge Druim Comhnardaig (near bealach from Glen Moidart to Glen Alladale). She fell 8m wearing rucksack, fracturing a lumber vertebra and sustaining rib injuries. Well equipped, her husband left her in a tent with food, water and aspirins. Airlift by RN Sea King. 14.

MAY 26-27 – Two men (50, 30) and a woman (30) walked through Glen Arnisdale to Kinlochhourn but got benighted trying to return to Arnisdale by the coast of Loch Hourn. This route is treacherous in darkness and they had no lights. Recovered by Glenelg MRT boat. Team also did an outward route search. 12.

JUNE 23 – Quad bike on steep ground on E. slopes Beinn Raimh (2km. SSW of Stromeferry) went over when it hit a rock. Badly bruised passenger went for help. Driver with shock and smashed clavicle was walked to a vehicle and driven off by Kintail MRT. 21.

JULY 24 – Walker ran out of prescribed medication on coast path near Glenelg. HMCG helicopter. 1

JULY 29-31 – The body of a solo woman hillwalker (48) was recovered from River Elchaig, 7 km downstream from Falls of Glomach from which she had slipped on wet rock when wearing sandals. Searches carried out by Kintail and Kinloss MRTs, SARDA, RAF Sea King, HM Coastguard and Lifeboat. 600.

AUGUST 23 – Descending Sgurr Fhuaran by Allt a'Bhuilg, a man (42) stopped for a drink from the burn, slipped on mossy rock, slid 12m, then fell 6m from a rock ledge and was knocked unconscious for five minutes, also with bad scalp cuts, pelvis and arm injuries. Assisted down by Kintail MRT and SARDA. 19.

AUGUST 26 – Party of five stopped to rest by path on north bank Loch Beoraid. Schoolboy (14) sat on a drystane dyke and overbalanced. Part of wall fell on him, spraining an ankle. Winched by RAF Sea King and Lochaber MRT. 41.

SEPTEMBER 21 – Woman (63) in a guided party of seven descending The Saddle injured her ankle when a stone slipped under her foot going down the stalker's path from Meallan Odhar in good weather. Stretcher carried down by Kintail MRT. 36.

SEPTEMBER 21-22 – Four men (53, 50, 49, 44) benighted in good weather on Sgurr na Lapaich (Affric) waited for daylight and walked out. Kintail MRT and RAF Sea King. 17.

NOVEMBER 1-2 – Local walker (67) with dog lost path in forest east of Strathglass. He did not carry a map or compass but knew the forest well. He decided to stay put rather than risk injury in the dark. Found next morning by RAF Sea King 10km NE of Cannich, well off intended route. Kintail MRT and six SARDA dogs. 50.

DECEMBER 14 – Pair staying at Corryhully Bothy reported unequipped, solo, novice walker (38) overdue from Glenfinnan Horseshoe. He got hopelessly lost in good weather and descended at head of Loch Arkaig. By lift and train he travelled 93km to get back to Corryhully to collect his rucksack at 23.00 as Lochaber MRT started a search. 5.

BEN NEVIS

MARCH 1 – In a party of eight going up to Steall Hut by Nevis Gorge in rain, wind and darkness, a man (54) slipped, despite using a headtorch, and fell 20m stopping against a tree. He sustained broken cheekbone, multiple cuts, abrasions and bruises. Stretcher carry by Lochaber MRT. 30.

MARCH 6 – Two men started climbing Orion Direct unroped on good ice. After some time they roped up when ice deteriorated. Ice then improved so they unroped. At 300m witness was 3m above and to the right of his companion (27) traversing right when he heard an expletive. He saw the now deceased falling to the bottom, hitting the face on a number of occasions. In Observatory Gully he slid a farther 180m down a snow slope. Five other people witnessed the fall, three of whom were members of Oldham MRT. A doctor reached the casualty, still conscious 45 minutes after the fall, but he died during rescue. Lochaber MRT, RAF Sea King. 2.

MARCH 6-7 – Leader (46) was 12m above his second (33) climbing Point Five Gully when he had to stop due to poor visibility in heavy spindrift. He got tired and slipped, falling 15m on to his third man (32). Leader got chest injury and was left on the climb, tied off. Second man and third, who had got a back injury when leader fell on to him, climbed down and raised alarm. Lochaber MRT could not go on hill due to adverse weather. Rescue resumed at 0600 including Kinloss MRT and RAF Sea King. Rescue of leader, now with some cold trauma, was undertaken from top of gully. He was lowered to base, then stretchered down for helicopter winch. 250.

MARCH 8 – Solo climber (35) slipped when 6m from top of No. 4 Gully falling to its base sustaining serious facial and spine injuries. Helped by other climbers, and Lochaber MRT stretchered him to CIC Hut from where he could be winched by RAF Sea King. 60.

MARCH 8 – When 5m from top of Tower Gully, solo climber (31) stopped to assess condition and how he would negotiate small cornice. As he moved off, the windslab below him (0.6m in depth) gave way and he fell 100m. He blacked out as he fell and got a fractured rib and facial cut. Helped by other climbers to walk to CIC Hut, then winched by RAF Sea King. Lochaber MRT already called for No. 4 Gully incident 30 minutes previous. 38.

MARCH 23-24 – Woman (26) and man (23) started Point Five Gully at 14.30 hours, completing it at 01.00. They stayed night in summit refuge and walked off to Halfway Lochan and were airlifted by RAF Sea King. Kinloss and Lochaber MRTs involved. 109.

APRIL 2 – While descending, poor navigation in mist led pair off track on to steep screes of W. Face Carn Dearg NW. Woman (38) got cramp so they stayed where they were and alerted police by mobile phone. Sweep search by Lochaber MRT found them. Assisted down. Uninjured. 120.

APRIL 4 – Roped pair successfully abseiled back down its first pitch to the base of Point Five Gully. Unroped and retrieving the abseil rope, instructor (34) pulled one end and found it had jammed. He tugged the other end which freed suddenly, causing him to stumble back and slide 210m down snow. During the slide he was seen to strike a number of rock outcrops and received fatal injuries. Client (m24) got cuts and bruises. Recovered by Lochaber MRT and RAF Sea King. 76.

APRIL 12 – Male (23) in a guided party of 11 climbing hill for charity got a locked knee when 120m from summit. Later both knees seized up and casualty was exhausted. RAF Sea king airlift from Halfway Lochan (see incident below). Lochaber MRT. 79.

APRIL 12 – Male (22) in a party of 17 trainee adventure sports instructors slipped descending dry scree at seconded zig-zag above Red Burn. He aggravated an injury to a knee for which he was already taking pain-killers. Mobile phone alerted rescuers engaged in above incident. Both casualties were airlifted and both received treatment for ligament strains.

APRIL 15 – Woman (55) descending solo from the summit, wearing tennis shoes, slipped on dry scree at third zig-zag above Red Burn, causing dislocated ankle and spiral fracture of lower leg. Passing group used mobile phone. Lochaber MRT and RAF Sea King. 19.

MAY 1 – Going up track and 15 minutes from summit, a man (54) suffered a heart attack. Evacuated to hopital for treatment by RAF Lossiemouth helicopter R 137. 10.

MAY 3 – Body of Bristol man (53) who went missing Christmas Day 1996 was found by a hillwalker in burn in Coire Giubhsachan, below SE aspect of Ben Nevis. He possibly died from drowning. Evacuation by Police, Lochaber MRT and RAF Sea King. 32.

MAY 4 – Near Halfway Lochan, a walker (56) bent down and injured his back. Airlift by RAF Sea King. Lochaber MRT. 52.

MAY 8 – Descending track from summit with her husband, a woman (54) had got down just below Halfway Lochan when her legs gave in due to exhaustion and dehydration. Carried down on a stretcher by Lochaber MRT for overnight hospital observation. 54.

MAY 31 – Lochaber MRT and RAF helicopter searched track for man (19) suffering exhaustion and sunstroke one hour's walk above the glen. He had got down unaided. 16.

MAY 31 – Man with his daughter (10) descending track from the summit had already treated her at 900m for dehydration with water given by passers-by. She was recovering, but his wife at the bottom got concerned, alerting police. Girl and father airlifted from path junction at 150m by helicopter from RAF Valley. 4.

JUNE 16 – Soldier (26) tried to get up track with colleagues but felt unwell and descended a short distance alone to 500m above youth hostel. Police were alerted and treated him for mild hyperthermia and dehydration (rest and lots of water) then he walked down with help. 3.

JUNE 17 – Woman (54) descending Nevis Gorge path with her husband from Steall to car park slipped/stumbled on dry rock and fell about 90m into gorge. Fatal. Lochaber MRT. 48.

JUNE 21 – Descending track, a man's (58) knees seized up at Halfway Lochan. Stretchered to hospital by Lochaber MRT where he was treated for muscular injuries. 27.

JUNE 22 – SOS lights reported on track at 01.35 hours turned out to be a false alarm with good intent. Mountain bikers were in the area. Lochaber MRT. 18.

JUNE 28 – Being guided by Lochaber MRT on a charity walk, a man (60) died of coronary artery disease despite immediate cardio-pulmonary rescusitation. Airlift by RAF Sea King. 22.

JULY 10 – Starting very early from the youth hostel to walk/run to the summit, a student (42) died and was found at 06.55 hours on the track 500m from the top. Lochaber MRT, RAF Sea King. 21.

JULY 19 – Two hours into an ascent of Tower Ridge, leader pulled up on a handhold which crumbled and gave way. He fell, suffering minor abrasions. His wife was also dislodged with leg injury, but both were held by the rope and belay. Winched by RAF Sea King, Lochaber MRT. 34.

JULY 19-20 – Lochaber MRT called out at 23.00 by woman, concerned that a poorly-equipped man (70) who had fallen near the summit and could not complete descent of path. Not found. 8.

AUGUST 10-11 – Collapsing with exhaustion at 20.30 hours at 700m altitude on track, walker (58) got down to glen by 00.35 hrs with the help of others. Lochaber MRT, RAF Sea King. 90.

AUGUST 14 – Descending on the path from the summit, poorly-equipped solo walker (63) wearing training shoes, was nudged by two younger walkers overtaking. He stumbled and sustained a small fracture to an ankle (medial malleolus of tibia). He walked from 800m to 610m then he was lifted by RAF Sea King and Lochaber MRT. 39.

SEPTEMBER 6 – Competitor (39) in Nevis Race fell at third zig-zag and got severe cramps and mild hypothermia. Stretchered to Halfway Lochan by Lochaber MRT then lifted by RAF Sea King. 29.

SEPTEMBER 6-7 – Man (55) descending with two male clients (46, 33) got disoriented in heavy rain and mist at 19.30 hours. He believed one client was getting hypothermic so decided to radio for help, but left both to transmit a clear signal. At 00.40 Lochaber MRT found older man at '4000ft. Cairn'. At 00.57 Kinloss MRT found two clients at head of Coire Eoghainn. All three airlifted from Halfway Lochan by RAF Sea King, all suffering mild hypothermia. 236.

SEPTEMBER 18-19 – Son (35) delayed by slower father (67) descending track. Slowed again by darkness as they had no torch. Escorted down by Lochaber MRT. 5.

SEPTEMBER 22 – Man (72) died from stroke or heart attack at summit. RAF Sea King airlift. 12.

SEPTEMBER 24 – Man (25) strained knee on ascent and got to summit with help. After 30 minutes' rest knee painful going down. Aid was summoned by mobile phone. RAF Sea King lifted him with two companions from 1300m on track in extremely clear, calm weather. At hospital no swelling was found – normally evident in such a case. 11.

OCTOBER 6 – Student (24) complained of nausea descending path. His companion went to call RAF Sea King, but he felt better and got down helped by four passers-by. 8.

OCTOBER 21 – Instructor (30) suffered permanent spinal damage from a fall of 10m when unroped. He was working near the big ledge on Pinnacle Ridge, Polldubh Crags, fixing belays for instuctional climbs. Stretchered down. Paramedics and Lochaber MRT. 24.

OCTOBER 29-30 – Poorly-equipped, intoxicated man (34) airlifted from summit shelter by RN Sea King at night in good weather. Lochaber MRT. 125.

GLEN COE

NOVEMBER 5 – Climbing Clachaig Gully took two men (21, 18) longer than they thought. After dark they flashed torches for help. Glencoe MRT hauled them up out of the gully by ropes. 77.

NOVEMBER 14-15 – Trying to get down off Sgor nam Fiannaidh after traverse of Aonach Eagach, man (25) and woman got lost and bivvied near the top of Clachaig Gully West in good weather. Soon, the bivvy bag slid 5m and the man's knee got slightly injured. They flashed torches and were winched by RAF Sea King and Glencoe MRT. 65.

NOVEMBER 15-16 – Doing an unspecified route on Bidean nam Bian three male students (24, 24, 23) were benighted in bad weather, bivvied and came down at 09.15. Night search by Glencoe MRT. 48.

DECEMBER 27-28 – After E-W traverse of Aonach Eagach movements of two men (30, 28) were monitored by police. Though moving they were making little headway. Loudhailer and headtorch communication established they needed help. They were escorted down from Clachaig Gully West by Glencoe MRT. 57.

DECEMBER 28 – Roped climber (27) injured back and leg by fall of 30m into soft snow, from a slip when descending Big Step of Am Bodach to Chancellor Ridge. Glencoe MRT, RAF Sea King. 50.

JANUARY 5 – Unroped ice climber (M36) attempting Curved Ridge, Buachaille Etive Mor, with six friends, slipped and fell 180m sustaining serious skull, spine, chest and abdominal injuries. Winched by RAF Sea King with Glencoe MRT. 69.

JANUARY 7-8 – Two men (56, 55) and two women (39,19) overdue from climbing Curved Ridge, Buachaille Etive Mor. Exhausted headtorch batteries caused them to be cragfast in Crowberry Basin. Guided down by Glencoe MRT. 35.

FEBRUARY 9 – Glencoe MRT member climbing on Stob Coire nan Lochan witnessed a hillwalker (21) fall 135m down Broad Gully. Not carrying ice-axe, crampons or helmet, he only suffered cuts and bruises. Rescued by team and airlifted by RN Sea King. 50.

FEBRUARY 14 – Man (45) descending Coire na Tulaich of Buachaille Etive Mor suffered illness, later diagnosed as angina. Escorted down by Glencoe MRT. 4.

FEBRUARY 14 – Two men descending north slopes Stob Coire nan Lochan were separated when one man's crampon struck a rock below surface snow. He tumbled, unhurt, out of his companion's sight, then made his own way off the hill, but the incident was reported. Glencoe MRT. RN Sea King flight cancelled. 8.

MARCH 1 – Three climbers walked up Aonach Eagach East Path in gales gusting to storm force. About 100m above road man (32) in front slipped on wet rock and scree, fell into a gully and sustained two broken vertebra, facial fractures and hip laceration. Stretchered by Glencoe MRT. 36.

MARCH 29 – Using crampons and ice-axe, walking the ridge from Stob Coire nan Lochan to Bidean nam Bian, man (23) slipped somewhere near Diamond Buttress and fell into Coire nam Beith, sustaining pelvic injuries. Glencoe MRT stretchered him to below cloud whence he was winched by RAF Sea King. 47.

MAY 28 – Policeman (46) with two colleagues had climbed to the top of Curved Ridge, Buachaille Mor. When descending unroped he jumped down to a ledge, but slipped and fell 90m to the base of Easy Gully. Fatal. Recovery by Glencoe MRT, RAF Sea King. 32.

MARCH 31 – Practising rope and climbing techniques on a 25m climb/scramble on Lagangarbh Buttress, Buachaille Etive Mor, a student (18) unroped to descend the side of the buttress to start again. He slipped on wet rock, fell 20m with spine injuries and broken arm. Winched by RAF Sea King Glencoe MRT. 30.

MAY 27 – Poorly equipped and shod, a solo walker crossed Stob Coire nan Lochan and Stob Coire nam Beith in good weather. Descending Arch Gully, Stob Coire nam Beith she got cragfast. Her cries for help were heard by other walkers and she was airlifted by RN Sea King from HMS Gannet. Glencoe MRT. 40.

MAY 28 – Descending from Buachaille Etive Mor by steep scree in Coire na Tulaich a walker (18) slipped on loose scree. Then he began to run down to preserve balance, but fell head over heels for 18m. He sustained wrist and femur fractures, with cuts and bruises to face, head, arms and legs. RAF Sea King, Glencoe MRT. 24.

JUNE 2 – Man (46) slipped, with deep thigh laceration when descending path from Pap of Glencoe. Conveyed to ambulance by Glencoe MRT. 6.

JUNE 12 – One of a group of seven on an organised walking holiday, a man (58) collapsed and died of a heart attack at the bealach SE of Sron Garbh. Stretchered to below cloud by Glencoe MRT, then airlifted by RN Sea King from HMS Gannet. 51.

JUNE 21 – Attempting to traverse Aonach Eagach E to W, two men (35, 33) decided to descend south before completing the ridge because they were tired and it was getting dark. They got cragfast at "The Ramp" of Stob Coire Leith. They alerted motorists by flashing torches. Rescued by Glencoe MRT and RAF Sea King. 75.

JULY 25 – Walker (36) dislocated his shoulder when he slipped on scree descending path from Stob Coire nan Lochan. Unable to descend, his companion called out Glencoe MRT who reduced the dislocation so that he was able to complete the descent. 19.

AUGUST 3-4 – Two women (45, 40) descending, went into An t-Sron Chasm. Both slipped on scree, with minor cuts and bruises, ending up cragfast. They signalled with torches and were winched by RAF Sea King, but declined medical help. Glencoe MRT. 57.

AUGUST 9 – One of seven climbing Sgorr Dhonuill (Beinn a'Bheithir) a man (61) collapsed near the summit and died of a heart attack. Glencoe MRT stretchered him to the roadside. 34.

AUGUST 16 – With eight others descending Stob Coire Raineach, of Buachaille Etive Beag, into Lairig Gartain, walker (26) got his foot into a hole causing ankle injury. Stretcher carry by Glencoe MRT. 20.

AUGUST 19 – When descending Sgor nam Fiannaidh with a companion, a woman (34) got her leg struck by a large boulder which dislodged itself, causing a fall/stumble of 6m. Evacuated with a severely gashed leg by Glencoe MRT and HMS Gannet Sea King. 29.

AUGUST 24 – Abseiling from a pitch 30m below Ossian's Cave, casualty's abseil anchorage (1.9cm chock) broke free, causing a fall of 20m. He (36) sustained skull, spine, chest and arm injuries. He was winched by RN Sea King which returned for Glencoe MR Team. 53.

SEPTEMBER 12-13 – Two of a party of three men intending to climb Curved Ridge, Buachaille Etive Mor, stopped at foot to wait for better weather. The other (33) continued. Those who had waited eventually climbed Curved Ridge. They saw their companion to their right on Crowberry Ridge. He signalled that he would complete the route and they would meet on the summit. They waited for an hour on top then went down Coire na Tulaich. Glencoe MRT ascertained by loudhailer that he was cragfast on Crowberry Ridge but uninjured. They him down by 02.30 on 13th. 85.

SEPTEMBER 27-28 – Motorist on A82 reported lights flashing but stationary near top of Buachaille Etive Mor. Glencoe MRT established by loudhailer that two men (benighted on January Jigsaw, but descending slowly with one head torch) did not need help.

NOVEMBER 1 – Walker (68) descending Buachaille Etive Beag with two companions by the usual path, slipped on mud near the bealach fractured his leg. Stretchered below cloud by Glencoe MRT then winched aboard R137 RAF Sea King. 29.

OTHER CENTRAL HIGHLANDS

JANUARY 1 – Sledging at Meall a'Chuit, above Melgarve, Corrieyairack Pass, a schoolgirl (15) slipped on heather dislocating a kneecap. There was a history of two similar injuries. Airlifted by RAF Sea King for hospital treatment. Cairngorm MRT. 19.

JANUARY 2 – Army officer (29) leading an ice climb on a waterfall on NE Crags of Sgurr Finnisg-aig, Aonach Mor, and fell 10m on to a small ledge. His crampons stuck in, but he continued falling back, breaking both ankles. Airlift by RAF Sea King, Lochaber MRT. 17.

JANUARY 3 – When an unroped man (37) was climbing out of the soft snow fan at the top of Upper Couloir, Stob Ghabhar, the snow would not hold his weight. He fell back down the gully sustaining head and arm injuries. Glencoe MRT stretcher lower to RN Sea King airlift. 55.

JANUARY 11 – Descending NE Ridge, Am Bodach, Mamores in a party of three, a hillwalker (43) tripped when her crampon snagged in a gaiter. She fell/slid 70m with head, leg and arm injuries. Glencoe MRT stretchered her to the roadside. 73.

JANUARY 27 – Climbing a snow gully between Creise and Sron na Creise with two companions, a man (36) was killed in a 150m fall from the top of the gully. Glencoe MRT, RN Sea King. 47.

FEBRUARY 2 – Two men (55, 32) were roped climbing Cinderella on Creag Meagaidh when they were swept out of the gully by a cornice collapsing. Older climber had facial cuts with possible hip and femur fractures, while other had ankle injury. Stretchered to airlift by RN Sea King. Lochaber MRT. 56.

FEBRUARY 9 – Six from a party of eight decided to climb Cinderella, Creag Meagaidh because it had already avalanched. Roping in three pairs they had almost reached the top when the cornice gave way and avalanched them all. Five were seriously injured (f29, m27, m26, m25, f24) and one slightly (m31). They were tended by the pair waiting at the bottom. All six winched into RAF and RN Sea Kings. Kinloss, Leuchars and Lochaber MRTs. 196.

MARCH 2 – Rescuer (28) on exercise on Puist Coire Ardair, Creag Meagaidh, walked through a cornice in a white-out. He fell a considerable distance towards the loch at the head of Coire Choille-rais, causing bruising and abrasions. It was snowing, with gale and low cloud. Separated from companions he walked down to A86 unaided. Kinloss MRT and RAF Sea King diverted to following incident on nearby Beinn a'Chaorainn. 13.

MARCH 2 – Attempting to lead a party of eight down from the Centre Top, Beinn a'Chaorainn, in a white-out, two men (64, 54) walked through a cornice to the north of the Centre Top. The safest direction down would have been SW. They were both killed by a fall of 300m. Found half buried in snow by RAF Sea King and winched aboard. Kinloss and Lochaber MRTs, SARDA. 103.

MARCH 6 – Skiing Nid Run on Aonach Mor, man (33) caught by spindrift in a gale fell and slid 20m into rocks, suffering hip dislocation and pelvis fracture. Airlift RAF Sea King, Lochaber MRT. 44.

MARCH 30 – Woman (67) wearing shoes, descending forest track on lower slopes of Carn Dearg (516m), Farr, Strathnairn, slipped on wet grass, causing an ankle fracture dislocation. Her husband went for help. Ambulance paramedic and RAF Sea King evacuation. 20.

MARCH 30 – Descending steep slopes to SE of Stob Coire a'Chairn, Mamores with three companions, woman (43) slipped on wet mud, breaking a lower leg. Glencoe MRT, RN Sea King. 42.

MARCH 30-31 – Inexperienced walker (47) parted from her experienced partner when she got tired between two summits of Beinn Bhreac 840m (Carn an Fhreiceadain) Kingussie. Lost, she survived reasonable weather overnight in heather, not calling out and moving only 3.5 km N into remote Monadhliath rather than S towards Kingussie. She had seen lights and flares of rescuers, but thought flares were comets or shooting stars. She had flashed her camera through a whole spool, but only one flash had been spotted and not fixed. She was found by RAF Sea King at 08.10 hours. Cairngorm, Kinloss, Leeming MRTs, SARDA, estate workers, five 4WD vehicles, Police, estate quad bike with searchlight. 412.

MARCH 30 – Descending west in mist from Sgurr a' Mhaim, Mamores, with companions, woman (40) slipped on snow, sliding about 130m over snow and rocks, stopping at a rock and gashing her leg. Lochaber MRT moved casualty to accessible point for RAF Sea King winch. 83.

APRIL 4-5 –1 Descending N from bealach Stob Coire Easain/Stob a'Choire Mheadhoin, Loch Treig Hills, man (32) carrying but not wearing crampons, slipped on ice, fell 75m, causing pelvic injuries, cuts and bruises. Compound incident (see below). 46.

APRIL 4-5 – Descending to assist his companion in the above incident, rescuer (48) wearing crampons, tripped over them and fell a similar distance injuring a leg. Both men were found next day by RAF Sea King and winched aboard. Lochaber MRT. 46.

APRIL 26 – Traversing the two Corrour Forest Munros with nine others from Loch Ossian Youth Hostel, walker (60) stumbled on boggy ground when descending W from Bealach nan Sgor. She pulled ligaments on both sides of an ankle. Manual transfer to RAF Sea King. Lochaber MRT. 31.

MAY 5 – Searching woods for a sheep-worrying dog on shore of Loch Treig, shepherd (60) slipped. After 20 minutes he went unconscious. Acquaintance went for help. Lochaber MRT found him walking back to his vehicle uninjured. 44.

MAY 9 – West Highland Way walker (29) slipped on forest track above Glen Nevis Youth Hostel fracturing his ankle. Rescued by Lochaber MRT in vehicle. 2.

MAY 25 – Walker (48) slipped on rock beside Uisge Labhair 2.5km NE of Corrour Lodge, Loch Ossian, breaking his ankle. Rescue by RAF Sea King. 13.

JUNE 8 – Having solo walked Carn Mor Dearg, Aonach Mor and Aonach Beag, a man (50) was descending into Coire Giubhsachan (about 15.45 hours) when he slipped down wet rock slabs for an unknown distance and was knocked unconscious. He came to at 17.25. Despite serious injuries (including dislocations of C4 and C5 vertebrae, right skull fracture with subdural and extradural haematomae) he walked 3km to Steall Ruin, where campers raised the alarm. Lochaber MRT stretcher carry down Nevis Gorge. Air Ambulance transfer from Belford to Glasgow. 42.

JUNE 17-22 – Searches had been made and media details issued for a missing Japanese woman (30) last seen in Fort William on June 17. On June 22 her remains were discovered on the east side of Steall Waterfall at a height of 115m above the base. Although steep it is climbable without gear to about 150m where vegetation stops. To go higher would mean moving west into rock and water. It is most likely she climbed to there, wearing light fashion shoes; finding herself only 16m from top she may have tried to climb the rocks and fell 35m. Stretcher recovery by Police and Lochaber MRT. 27.

JUNE 25 – About 300m from top of Devil's Staircase, descending West Highland Way towards Kinlochleven, deceased (m57) slipped, sat down and slumped over. Witness called other hikers for help and CPR was given, but victim died from a heart attack. Airlift by RAF Sea King. Glencoe MRT. 29.

JULY 8 – Supervised students on an outdoor education course were jumping from the triple wire-rope bridge into River Nevis at Steall Cottage. On his seventh jump a 16-year-old struck a submerged rock with a knee tearing ligaments. Stretchered down gorge by Lochaber MRT. 40.

JULY 10 – In good weather at 13.45 hours three hillwalkers found the body of a walker (55) in Coire Giubhsachan (between Carn Mor Dearg and Aonach Beag). It appeared he may have slipped on rock slabs falling some 100m. Lochaber MRT, RAF Sea King. 31.

JULY 14 – Man (28) leading 23 French Scouts with four other instructors from Corrour to Kinlochleven via Steall over two days, slipped on rocky path in Upper Glen Nevis, spraining his ankle. Airlift by RN Sea King for treatment. 14.

JULY 15-16 – Twelve French teenagers attempted to walk from Steall Car Park to Kinlochleven. They had three maps and three compasses, but made a navigational error. On Stob Coire a'Chairn a girl (17) became ill, apparently hypothermic. Five went down with two (of three) walkers they met. Three went on to Kinlochleven having been shown the way. Three plus the other walker were escorted down by Lochaber MRT with the ill girl on a stretcher. She was later hospital treated for shock. RAF Sea King had ferried rescuers, who had reached the group about midnight. 221.

JULY 15-16 – Three French Scouts (all female aged 18) took a wrong track from Stob Coire a'Chairn. Heading for Kinlochleven they got to Loch Eilde Mor. Found by Glencoe MRT. 9.

JULY 29 – Man (42) reported missing after separation at Tigh-na-Sleubhaich, Lochaber, on West Highland Way. He had not met a friend at Nevis Bridge as arranged and returned to Glasgow without telling police. Lochaber MRT did a route search. 8.

AUGUST 7 – Walking Land-Rover track to Blackwater Dam, Kinlochleven, student (18) camped at Loch a'Coire Mhorair. On waking he could not continue due to an old back injury. Companion went for help and Glencoe MRT evacuated him by 4WD vehicle. 9.

AUGUST 7-8 – Attempting six Munros in Ben Alder and Geal Charn ranges, walker (63) got lost in mist between Bealach Dubh and Geal Charn (1132m). Tried to walk out after dark but there was no moon. He bivvied in Glen Cam, 10 minutes up from Lubvan Ruin. Walked out next day to notify police because he had left a note on his car. Search by Cairngorm MRT and RAF Sea King called off. 9.

AUGUST 8 – Hillwalker (57) winched by RN Sea King from moors 1km N of River Tummel between Loch Tummel and Dunalastair Water. He had a leg injury from a slip. Taypol SRU.

AUGUST 9 – One of seven climbing Sgorr Dhonuill (Beinn a'Bheithir) a man (61) collapsed near the summit and died of a heart attack. Glencoe MRT stretchered him to the roadside. 34.

SEPTEMBER 28-29 – Leuchars MRT recalled en route to join Lochaber MRT and RN Sea King search for three hillwalkers (m47, m46, f38) overdue on Ring of Steall.

One had slipped on wet ground, and they bivouacked when it got dark. Found uninjured walking out next day by helicopter, they walked out unaided. 114.

OCTOBER 20 – Leading Inbred at Creag Dhubh, Newtonmore, climber (19) fell when a loose rock hold gave way. Runners came out and he fell 12m to the foot of the route, breaking an ankle and suspected shoulder fracture. Stretchered by Cairngorm MRT. 18.

OCTOBER 28 – Attempting Ring of Steall, walker (49) missed out An Garbhanach and tried to descend Coire a'Mhail. He got cragfast near Steall Waterfall on steep, wet ground above Steall Cottage and flashed an emergency signal. Winched by R137 RAF Sea King. Lochaber MRT. 43.

NOVEMBER 29 – Benighted and lost in good weather descending Mamores to Glen Nevis, two walkers (m27, f24) got cragfast on North Ridge of An Gearanach. Occupant of Steall Cottage saw their flashing torch signal. Winched by Rescue 137. Lochaber MRT. 40.

DECEMBER 6 – Hillwalker (49) slipped on wet scree on lower slopes of Creag Beag (486m) immediately above Kingussie, breaking a lower leg. Cairngorm MRT got a Land-Rover right up to her. 6.

DECEMBER 6 – Extensive searches, now reduced to sporadic searches, have been carried out for Samuel Sinclair (37) overdue from walking Aonach Mor and Aonach Beag to Glen Nevis, by Glencoe, Kinloss, Leuchars and Lochaber MRTs and Sea King helicopters from HMS Gannet and RAF Lossiemouth. Not yet found. 2081.

CAIRNGORMS

JUNE 29-30, 1996 – Correction to last year's report. Bird watcher (50) moving on crag east of Loch Loch to get a better view of nest, slipped on dry scree, causing chest injuries from which he died a few days' later. Local stalker knew all nest sites and was able to direct rescuers. Tayside MRTs stretcher carry.

JANUARY 1-2, 1997 – Two men reported themselves lost in mist on Dreish by mobile phone. Through the night they made occasional calls to Police reporting movements. Tayside teams decided to guide them down but they walked in at first light. 14.

JANUARY 11 – After their companion retreated because of wet weather, two men (45, 41) carried on. They climbed up Twin Burns (NH978028) west of the lochan of Cairn Lochan: the exact location of the spectacular fatal avalanche of March 4, 1995. At 11.30 hours as they almost topped out at the "meadow area" the snow 2m above them cracked. They were carried 130m down to the lochan, trapped by large blocks which provided some air spaces. They were stuck together in a head to tail situation – same as the two 22-year-olds from Cumbria who had not been so lucky. One was buried. The other had head and a hand above the surface. By moving his chin he managed to free some space round his head and then got his hand free. Somehow, he extracted a compass from a pocket and used it as a mini shovel to dig himself out. It was serious as he did not manage to free his companion till 18.00. One had a frostbitten hand, the other a nasty cut chin. They then walked out. Some of Cairngorm MRT opined that, since the avalanche force cracked the surface of the loch, the bending of the ice reduced the impact of the snout debris, also creating air spaces which saved the climbers' lives.

JANUARY 17 – Hillwalker (36) slipped on vegetation on Kinpurnie Hill (345m) near Newtyle, Sidlaw Hills. She injured a leg and was rescued by Taypol SRU using 4WD vehicle. 10.

JANUARY 19 – Man (62) missing in woodland and lower Spey river bank found safe. Coastguard mustered.

JANUARY 22 – Man (30s) killed by fall over sea cliffs at Clashach Cove 1.5km east of Hopeman. HM Coastguard, RAF Sea King.

JANUARY 23 Practising ice-axe braking with five others at about 1000m in Coire Bogha-cloiche of Braeriach, a man (46) lost grip and fell 60m into a boulder-field, with severe facial injuries. Cairngorm MRT and RAF Sea King. 50.

FEBRUARY 8 – Rope of three men (30, 25, 25) climbing Crotched Gully (135m II) in Coire an t-Sneachda, Cairngorm. Lead climber started up route. Climber at belay slipped off down hard névé slope pulling second off belay, who in turn pulled off the leader. They suffered cuts and bruises. Winched by RAF Sea King training in area, Dundonnell MRT (training) and Cairngorm MRT (working in area). 34.

FEBRUARY 9 – At noon two parents with four children set out to climb Mither Tap of Bennachie from Rowantree Car Park. Halfway up an exhausted son (9) was left on the path to await the others' return. However, they did not find him so alerted rescuers. Step-father found him at 16.20 hours lying in deep heather 150m south of path. He had walked less than 1km since separation. Braemar and Grampian Police MRTs, RAF Sea King. 26.

FEBRUARY 14 – Accompanied walker (26), carrying but not using helmet or crampons, reached Meikle Pap col on Lochnagar path. Crossing an icy patch he was blown over by a wind gust, striking his eyebrow on the ice, receiving a laceration which needed six stitches.

FEBRUARY 22 – Two men (30, 27) from a party of 10 under instruction in winter skills near Fiacaill a'Choire Chais, Cairngorm, were blown up in the air and transported 60m, falling about 3m. One had fractured tibia and fibula, the other a badly injured ankle. Carried by Cairngorm and Leuchars MRTs to airlift by RAF Sea King. 41.

FEBRUARY 23 – Male (54) walking with 28 companions had a suspected angina attack when 5km WSW of the head of Loch Lee, Angus. Mobile phone used to get RAF Sea King airlift. 8.

FEBRUARY 25 – Ski-touring in a party of four near the foot of the North Ridge of Fiacaill Coire an t-Sneachda, a woman (24) fell and injured a knee. Winched by RAF Sea King. 11.

FEBRUARY 26 – Three men (31, 30, 27) set out at 10.00 to climb Parallel Gully A, Lochnagar, despite the avalanche warning being Cat. 4. Snow up to waist deep on the climb slowed them. They had to abseil after completing 75% of the route, reaching the foot at 22.30. Police had been told they were overdue and found them walking back to Loch Muick Car Park. 3.

MARCH 9-10 – Two men (60, 55) hoping to traverse Right-of-Way from Dunkeld to Kirkmichael via Meall Reamhar (53/033568) got lost and returned to Dunkeld six hours' late. Taypol and Tayside teams, SARDA. 60.

MARCH 21 – Unroped with 11 others, cramponing down snow in Coire na Ciste, Cairngorm, a man (37) slipped and slid 30m into boulders. His patella was fractured. Airlift by RAF Sea King. 10.

MARCH 23 – Roped climber (31) slipped on The Milky Way, Cairn Lochan in winter condition, falling 30m with injuries to his spine, pelvis and thigh. Cairngorm MRT were training nearby. Hospitalisation by RAF Sea King. 12.

APRIL 20 – Schoolgirl (15) on award hike practice in Glen Dee injured her lower leg by stepping in a small hole. Braemar MRT. 6.

APRIL 22-25 – Car parked at Cairn o' Mount, summit of Banchory to Fettercairn road, with suicide notes left on April 22. Searches were carried out by Grampian Police dog handlers, Braemar and Kinloss MRTs, RAF Sea Kings. Man (35) was known to have sheltered in a remote bothy 2.6km east of the car, but hid in Drumtochty Forest when building was searched. He was found by SARDA on 3rd day of search, fit and well, on moorland halfway between bothy and car. 613.

MAY 3-4 – Route searches by Taypol and Tayside teams found two men (both 36) lost in mist in Glen Doll area. RAF Sea King. 50.

MAY 19 – Man (33) tried to rescue a dog which had fallen into water in the gorges above Bruar Falls and also slipped into the water. Suffering cold trauma he was rescued by Taypol SRU and taken to hospital in Pitlochry. 7.

MAY 25-26 – Four people got disoriented near Macdui summit in mist. Two men (47, 30) went on to try and find trig. point leaving the others to await their return. Those waiting got cold and returned to Derry Lodge by their ascent route, reporting the seekers missing at 22.50. The seekers said they had returned to the rendezvous to find those who waited were missing and then descended via Lairig Ghru, boulder-field and Pools of Dee. Police found them on Luibeg Path at 01.30 hours. Braemar MRT. 9.

JUNE 4 – Soldier (30) slipped walking on rock and grass in Coire an Lochain, Cairngorm, spraining his ankle. Companions tried to evacuate him on a make-shift stretcher, but he was winched by RAF Sea King. 9.

JUNE 4 – HM Coastguard recovered a fallen rock-climber (m21) with minor injuries from the foot of sea cliffs at Burnbanks Haven, Aberdeen.

JUNE 10 – Abseiler on double rope at Pass of Ballater got stuck when 8m down from the crag top, hanging free under an overhang. His doubled rope had "larks-footed" around the descendeur, locking it. It was his first abseil. There was no safety rope, as only one rope had been used, doubled and looped over a boulder above the cliff. No safety (Prusik loop) was used and there were no precautions to prevent larks-footing. Two Braemar MRT members, climbing nearby, used their single rope to set up an assisted hoist and recovered the man to the crag top with little difficulty. 2.

JUNE 10 – RAF Sea King airlifted sea cliff climber (27) who injured his back and pelvis at Cummingstown, near Hopeman. HM Coastguard.

JUNE 17 – Accompanied walker (66) wearing trainers slipped crossing Capel Burn on Capel Mounth Track in Glen Clova. He sustained arm and leg injuries. Taypol SRU. 14.

JUNE 21 – HM Coastguard, RAF helicopter, and two lifeboats were involved rescuing a woman (65) with minor injuries cragfast on a ledge of a sea cliff at Victoria Park, Arbroath.

JUNE 24 – Retired man (69) in a party of seven at Pools of Dee, Lairig Ghru, slipped and suffered skull and collar bone injuries. Evacuated by RAF Sea King exercising in area. Cairngorm MRT. 9.

JUNE 24 – Schoolgirl (18), one of six on an award scheme near Fords of Avon, slipped with slight leg ligament injuries. Three girls lifted to Lossiemouth by RAF Sea King. Cairngorm MRT. 9.

JUNE 28 – On a sponsored walk through the Lairig Ghru starting at Linn of Dee a man (78) died of a heart attack near old Sinclair Hut site. He had recently completed all the Munros. Stretchered to Rothiemurchus path, then out by Argo. Cairngorm and Kinloss MRTs. 19.

JUNE 29 – Male runner (40) in the Lairig Ghru Hill Race slipped and tore knee ligaments at Pools of Dee. Lifted by RAF Sea King. Cairngorm MRT. 13.

JULY 4 – Schoolboy (13) slipped from a path on the west slopes of Coire an Lochain, Cairngorm, sliding 10m down snow and fracturing a wrist. No ice axe. Winched by RAF Sea King. 18.

JULY 9 – Cairngorm MRT and RAF Sea King searched vainly after cries for help had been reported from Pinnacle Gully, Shelter Stone Crag. Other witnesses had reported two people cragfast. 31.

JULY 16 – Man (65) slipped on Jock's Road 1km SE of Crow Craigies. He injured a leg. Taypol SRU. RAF Sea King. 8.

JULY 28 – HM Coastguard and RAF Sea King rescued man (43) with back injuries fallen down cliff at Fraserborough.

AUGUST 8 – RAF Sea King rescued woman (36) sustaining leg injury from a slip on Ben Vrackie when she was above the dam on the SW slopes.

AUGUST 10 – Loch Brandy Path at 400m, Glen Clova. Hillwalker (39) with leg injury. Air Ambulance took him to Glasgow, due to fog at Dundee. Taupol SRU. 12.

AUGUST 10-11 – Male walker (61) bivvied in mist when attempting five Munros in Ben Alder area during calm weather. Cairngorm MRT did an early search but he turned up OK. 59.

AUGUST 12-13 – Paddling barefoot at Pools of Dee, a schoolgirl (13) cut a foot, but walked on down to Corrour Bothy with party after bandaging. Next morning, unable to walk, she was rescued by Braemar MRT Argo-Cat. 23.

AUGUST 23 – Turning to talk to another member of his group, a walker (56) tripped when 200m NE of Derry Lodge. Due to rucksack weight and entanglement of hands in straps, he was unable to stop the fall and sustained facial cuts and gravel rash. Grampian Police. 1.

AUGUST 24 – Fund-raising walker (26) got bad blisters crossing Devil's Point, Cairn Toul and Braeriach. Other members of her party helped her to Rothiemurchus Lodge. Cairngorm MRT. 6.

SEPTEMBER 6 – Walker (38) slipped on wet tree roots at Luibeg Bridge breaking his ankle. Braemar MRT. 5.

SEPTEMBER 15-16 – Cairngorm MRT and SARDA searched forests around Loch Morlich for missing woman (67). She was found asleep in a locked shower block at the campsite. 132.

SEPTEMBER 28 – Descending Beinn Bhrotain, walker (43) slipped, spraining a foot, delaying his party. Braemar MRT. 12.

OCTOBER 19-NOVEMBER 8 – Aberdeen, Braemar, and Kinloss MRTs, SARDA and RAF Sea King searched Glen Muick on November 26 for an unemployed woman (30). Her car had been left without petrol, but with some clothing at Spital of Glenmuick about November 19. There was no proper hill clothing, but some clothing had been found on the hill. There had been a reported sighting in Glen Clova on November 20. Aberdeen MRT again searched extensively on November 2. Subject not found. 269. On November 8 she was found quite well, asleep in a cave near a waterfall in Coire Fee, above Glen Doll by two firemen on one of their regular off-duty hillwalks.

OCTOBER 21 – Upper Tier, Cave Crag, Craig a' Barns, Dunkeld. Climber (m32) in a roped pair, got a leg injury from a rock dislodged by other person. Taypol and Tayside teams. 27.

OCTOBER 25-26 – When found 1.7km NE of Jock's Road (N of Craig of Cowal), person (24) who had separated from companion and got lost, had a slight cut to the hand. Tayside teams, RAF Sea King. 60.

DECEMBER 9 – Creag an Righ (481m) 2km east of Carrbridge to Forres road. Man (18) in a party of four crossing wet heather at night, stumbled and slid 15m on to rocks, suffering concussion, strained ligaments and bruising. Winched by RAF Sea King. Leeming and Leuchars MRTs. 47.

DECEMBER 27 – Youth (17) reported he had left his parents near Strath Nethy Saddle. Mum was exhausted but mobile. Subjects found safe by Cairngorm MRT between Glenmore and Ryvoan. 5.

SOUTHERN HIGHLANDS

JANUARY 3 – Ochils MRT callout cancelled when overdue walker (48) turned up. He had been engaged on W to E traverse of the Ochils.

JANUARY 4 – Walker in party of two slipped on ice under snow when near summit of Beinn Tharsuinn, Glen Luss, injuring her leg. Police helicopter in attendance, but lifted by Air Ambulance. Arrochar MRT. 10.

JANUARY 5 – On Stob Garbh, north slopes of Ben Lui, man (52) died of a heart attack when accompanied by his daughter. Oban Police MRT. RN Sea King airlift. 13.

JANUARY 5 – Glissading South Ridge of Ben More, casualty (32) fractured a tibia and fibula when one of his crampons caught in snow/ice. Called out Killin MRT with mobile phone. RN Sea King. 37.

JANUARY 11 – Climbing West Gully, Beinn an Dothaidh roped to a companion, man (27) slipped on ice and suffered leg injury. Strathclyde Police and RAF Sea King. 24.

JANUARY 21 – Student (18) fractured his pelvis, with head and arm injuries, on the east slopes of Meall Monachyle (647m) Balquhidder. Walking with six others, he saw dog chasing a sheep which appeared to run over a vertical cliff. Running to investigate he slipped and fell 15m vertically, then rolled another 15m. Winched by RN Sea King. Killin MRT. 46.

JANUARY 25 – Descending Creag Mhor with his partner, to Glen Lochay, man (45) with no ice-axe slipped on névé falling 45m on snow then grass. He lost a lot of blood from a big gash in rear thigh, also back injury, multiple cuts and hypothermia. RN Sea King winch. Crew had difficulty spotting him in a dark sleeping bag among heather. Killin MRT. 60.

FEBRUARY 1 – Descending east from summit Beinn an Lochain walker (45) slipped on grass and fell 150m. When his friend got to him, he was unconscious with cuts, bruises, chest and head injuries, but no bone damage. Winched by RN Sea King. Arrochar, Strathclyde Pol. MRTs. 26.

FEBRUARY 11 – Descending snow with two others on NE Ridge, Beinn Dubhcraig, man (53) tripped over his crampons and fractured a fibula. Just below cloud, he managed to slide down to better site for spotting and evacuation. Stretchered to manual transfer by RN Sea King. Killin MRT. 22.

FEBRUARY 17-22 – Searches of Glen Luss area by lifeboat, police helicopter, Arrochar MRT and SARDA carried out for German airline pilot who had left three suicide notes in his car. Traced to Germany. 50.

MARCH 8 – Two women (both 25) in slight mist, with no map, compass or torch got lost trying to follow fence posts on Ben Ledi as described in their guide book.

Mobile phone call home alerted police. Found on Ben Vane about midnight. Killin and Lomond MRTs. RN Sea King. 68.

MARCH 10-11 – Solo walker (45) reported overdue at Ardvorlich. Killin MRT found his body at the foot of the 150m crag on Stuc a'Chroin on *The Munros* route to Ben Vorlich. He had slipped on snow and rock in freezing conditions. Airlift RAF Sea King. 131.

MARCH 16 – Japanese girl (27) with two friends visiting waterfall a few hundred metres NE of Rowardennan Youth Hostel, slipped about 45m into burn, with spine injuries and abrasions. Spanish friend went to phone for help. Language problems caused police and rescue boat to think casualty was in the loch. Lomond MRT and SARDA called out. Winched by RN Sea King after paramedics carried out first aid. 66.

MARCH 18 – Retired male (62) descending wet grass of path to Loch Katrine sluices slipped and broke a tibia and fibula. Stretchered by Killin MRT to loch for boat to ambulance. 28.

MARCH 23 – With a companion on steepish slopes 500m to NW of Beinn Ghlas (Lawers Range) walker (34) slipped, injuring his head, arm and leg. Good weather. Taypol SRU and RN Sea King. 10

APRIL 6 – One of two poorly equipped novices descending Ben Ledi in rain and mist (m23) got faint and passed out. Companion (f24) got mild hypothermia waiting for him. Stretchered by Killin MRT. 30.

APRIL 13 – Walking Kinlochearnhead to Killin via Glen Beich, man (46) drifted off route in good weather, got directions from a passer-by and arrived overdue. Killin MRT standby. 2.

APRIL 20 – Climbing up steep grassed path on Wester Kirk Craig at Tillicoultry, man (39) had a heart attack and was airlifted by RN Sea King to hospital. 12.

MAY 5 – Ochils MRT requested to help police carry a drunk youth out of Tillicoultry Glen at night. They did so on a stretcher. Two friends of his were in a slightly better condition. 6.

MAY 6 – Descending steeper section of Ben A'n path woman (61) slipped on dry scree, causing leg injury. Stetcher carry by Killin MRT summoned by mobile phone. 20.

JUNE 1 – Two men (both 65) scrambled up parallel gullies of Craig Leith, Alva, intending to meet at top, but one stopped to eat halfway up! Ochils MRT called out and soon recalled. 1.

JUNE 1 – Male (76) on Beinn Dubhcraig had been separated from party. A bit over ambitious on a hot day, he was behind schedule. Traced by Police walking from hill. 6.

JUNE 7 – Walking with friends in good weather in Alva Glen, man (71) tripped, fracturing a lower leg. Ochils MRT treated and stretcher carried him. 30.

JUNE 21-22 – Two girls (both 14) injured in a compound accident in Campsie Glen at 21.40 hours. One slipped into the gorge, was held by the other who fractured her wrist and let go her friend who then fell 18m with head, spine, chest, arm injuries and hypothermia. Evacuation by RN Sea King winch very difficult because of gorge terrain and heavy foliage. Ambulance, Police, Lomond MRT. 48.

JUNE 24 – Walker (36) broke her ankle on remote beach SW of Machriahanish, Mull of Kintyre. Rescued by RNLI inshore boat, HMCG. 19.

JUNE 29 – Male (21) hillwalker injured a leg on the Saddle, 5km SSE of Lochgoilhead. Picked up by RN Sea King. Arrochar and Strathclyde MRTs. 15.

JULY 12 – Walker (m66) suffered a heart attack near the summit of Ben Lomond. No helicopter used because doctor confirmed death on the hill. Stretchered by Killin and Lomond MRTs. 95.

AUGUST 8 – Schoolgirl (13) tripped from viewing platform at base of Wallace Monument, Abbey Craig, fell 9m to a ledge sustaining fractured humerus and bruising. Ochils MRT helped firemen by setting up belay for a stretcher lower down 60m steep slope. 44.

AUGUST 11 – Woman (40) slipped on a dry grassy path on the Cobbler sustaining a leg injury. Stretchered by Arrochar and Strathclyde Police MRTs. 50.

AUGUST 14 – Male overdue on Beinn Narnain found by Arrochar MRT on Glen Loin slopes. 15.

AUGUST 18 – At 11.15 stalker found the body of a hillwalker (69) lying in bracken on Meall Ghaordie footpath 1.6km from Glen Lochay road. The stalker had spoken to him an hour before. Police in Land-Rover attempted resuscitation unsuccessfully using a defibrillator. 4

AUGUST 18 – Woodcutter (m36) timber harvesting got severe arm, leg and spine injuries when struck by a steel rope after hi-line winch failure. Ambulance service could not evacuate due to steep ground and trees. Killin MRT used vacumat and McInnes stretcher after workmates cut 50m evacuation route through thick trees. 12.

SEPTEMBER 6 – Cow giving birth to stillborn calf slid down banking. After vet did prolapse repair, Killin MRT helped fix ropes and pulley to tow cow out by tractor. 10.

SEPTEMBER 21 – Retired woman (61) slipped just south of bealach Beinn Ghlas/ Meall Corranaich, suffering head and abdominal injuries. Taypol SRU. Helicopter from RAF Boulmer, Northumberland.

SEPTEMBER 23 – North Ridge Ben Vorlich (Loch Earn) about 1.5km N of summit. Woman (57) descending, tripped on scree and broke an ankle. Winch by RN Sea King. Killin MRT, Taypol SRU. 36.

SEPTEMBER 27 – Male (42) in a party of three suffered a medical illness near Narnain Boulder on Cobbler Path. Winched by RN Sea King. Strathclyde Police. 8.

OCTOBER 4 – Red flare fired by adult in party of five camping near climbing cliffs of Ben A'an to 'show the children'. Killin MRT. 31.

OCTOBER 4-5 – Three boys (16, 15, 14) and two girls (14, 13) on an award scheme starting at Dollar carried an unauthorised heavy canvas tent which slowed them down. Reported overdue they were found next day on Elistoun Hill, Tillicoultry, but they thought they were above Alva, 4km farther west. Ochils MRT and RN Sea King (training with MRT). 72.

OCTOBER 12 – Party of four overdue in Glen Lednock. Check by Killin Police. 2.

OCTOBER 14 – Casualty (47) and his wife got lost on steep ground 200m above Loch Dochart. He slipped on wet, loose rock fracturing a tibia and fibula. Stretchered down by Killin MRT. 30.

OCTOBER 21 – Man (60) in rain and mist on Creag an Fhithich (between Lawers and An Stuc) slipped descending a snowy path, causing a head injury. Airlift by RN Sea King. Taypol and Tayside teams stood down en route. 18.

DECEMBER 9-10 – Solo walker (50) caught out by mist and darkness on Ben Vorlich (Loch Earn) by path from Ardvorlich in snow. He sat out the night then descended unharmed. No ice-axe, crampons, compass, bivvy bag. No route plan left. Tayside MRT. 19.

SKYE

MARCH 31-April 1 – Two men (33, 25) descending Sgurr Sgumain in mist and rain were benighted and overdue due to poor navigation, but walked in at 11.20. Skye MRT, RAF Sea King. 77.

MAY 7-8 – Six Germans left two cars to walk from Luib to Sconser in downpour with flash flooding. Reported missing next day. Found in Portree Hotel. Skye MRT. 12.

MAY 8 – Off route due to a deep covering of late snow, roped, about 3m below summit Sgurr a'Mhadaidh, casualty (25) who was leading, pulled up on a large rock which dislodged on to his own leg, breaking tibia and fibula. Rock would have been obviously loose in summer. Fellow club member in a nearby group gave him painkillers. In good weather he was airlifted by RAF Sea King. Skye MRT. 44.

MAY 18 – Climbing a HVS gully on dry rock on the lower tier at Neist Point, west of the car park, leader (33) climbed 3m and placed a nut. A metre above he slipped and fell back and the running belay pulled out. He fell head first down a large hole on the shore surrounded by boulders, unconscious and also with shoulder injuries. His second, with mobile phone, alerted two coastguard sectors, ambulance, police and doctor. Winched by HMCG helicopter. 61.

MAY 22 – Casualty (77) and his son were walking path from Elgol to Loch Coruisk. When 1.3km N of Elgol he tried to make a step up on the dry path, but lost balance and fell backwards over a cliff. Fatal injuries. Winched by RAF Sea King. Skye MRT. 38.

MAY 31 – Party of five climbed Pinnacle Ridge, Sgurr nan Gillean. Descending Tourist Route in training shoes, last of party (29) slipped when 30m down, fracturing her ankle. Winched by RAF Sea King, Leuchars and Skye MRTs. 38.

JUNE 6 – With tour guide and two friends, casualty (29) was crossing a waterfall in Lealt Gorge, 17km N of Portree when he slipped on wet rock and broke a femur. Eight coastguards attended with doctor and police. Airlift by HMCG helicopter. 45.

JUNE 8 – Reports of mirror flashes from Cioch, Sron na Ciche. Skye MRT found nothing, suspecting persons with racks of new climbing gear. 8.

JUNE 15-16 – Man (76) separated from a group walking off a charter vessel berthed in Loch na Cuilce. Searchers located him, mildly hypothermic, at the head of Loch Coruisk HMCG helicopter, Mallaig lifeboat, two passing N. Ireland Rescue Team, Police, Coastguard. 37.

JULY 14 – Walker cragfast on east-facing cliffs of Ben Dearg, 3km SW of Old Man of Storr. HMCG helicopter lowered winchman with strop, recovering him and subject to aircraft because person appeared very frightened and was inadequately clad. Skye MRT. 20.

JULY 22 – Belgian walker got stuck on a ledge near the Prison, Quiraing. He got himself off as police and Skye MRT investigated. 6.

JULY 31 - August 1 – Male made a hoax mobile phone call to a local hotel requesting hotel callout emergency services to Staffin Ridge. HMCG helicopter, Kinloss and Skye MRTs. 337.

AUGUST 18-19 – Two adults with three children set off late on Ben Staic (481m),

Glen Brittle. Skye MRT searched forest tracks at midnight. Lights would not penetrate mist. Turned up at 03.00. 10.

AUGUST 20-21 – Party of 14. Two males (20, 16) got soaked spending night in a leaky tent on the west side of Trotternish Ridge getting mild hypothermia. Winched by HMCG helicopter. 33.

AUGUST 25 – Leader (m42) fell 15m climbing out of long side of Thearlaich Dubh Gap, using insufficient runners. Leg injury. Stretcher lower and carry by Skye MRT. RAF Sea King winch. 72.

AUGUST 28 – Hillwalker (34) descending into Coir' a' Ghrunnda near Caistell a' Gharbh-choire was hit by a rock dislodged by his father, receiving skull, spine and abdomen injuries. Winched by RAF Sea King (night vision goggles). Skye MRT. 47.

AUGUST ? – Party trying to get from Coire an Lochain to Glen Brittle shouted to people on Sgurr Mhic Choinnich because they did not know the way. Someone dialled 999.

AUGUST ? – Five exhausted teenagers unable to get over Cuillin Ridge to Glen Brittle alerted rescue by mobile phone. Mallaig lifeboat from Coruisk to Elgol. HMCG. 5.

SEPTEMBER 4 – Pony trekking in strong wind and heavy showers near the head of Loch Snizort Beag, a woman (23) was thrown from a Shetland pony and sustained spinal injuries. As riders turned their mounts the pony bolted when startled by wind in its face. Stretchered by Skye MRT. 10.

SEPTEMBER 14-15 – Five students (f23, 20, 19, m22, 20) were stopped by a spate burn in Strath Mor between Torrin and Luib. They camped overnight and were traced by Skye MRT. 67.

SEPTEMBER 19 – Man (45) slipped at Nead na h-Iolaire, 2km south of Sligachan, causing leg injury. Skye MRT, HMCG helicopter. 20.

SEPTEMBER 22 – Walker (51) wearing trainers in Fionn Choire, under Sgurr a'Bhasteir, got an injured leg from a rock dislodged by her companion. Skye MRT. Winch by RAF Sea King. 31.

OCTOBER 22 – Accompanied walker (38) slipped on rock descending Upper Coire Banachdich, suffering head, arm and leg injuries. He also suffered hypothermia. He had no torch to use as marker till found by Skye MRT. RAF Sea King crew, praised by MRT for brilliant flying, used night vision goggles for long cable winch evacuations of casualty and team members. 52.

NOVEMBER 5 – Small hill S of Fairy Glen, 2km E of Uig. Australian student (m21) climbed to top then tried to return to companion (f21) who was only halfway up. He reached up to grab a large rock which came away in his hand. He fell on to the woman, then both fell to the bottom. He got a serious leg injury. she had head, back, chest and leg injuries, cuts and bruises. Coastguard and ambulance. Airlift by HMCG helicopter. 29.

NOVEMBER 27-DECEMBER 4 – Hillwalker (34) suffering from diabetes camped alone near Loch Scavaig. A note attached to his car left in Elgol revealed he was due to return on November 27. He was reported overdue on December 3. Search by Skye MRT and HMCG helicopter on December 4 found him dead near Coruisk Hut. His diary revealed he had fallen on November 27 and felt unwell. 45.

ISLANDS OTHER THAN SKYE

JANUARY 18 – HMCG search for missing person at Marwick Head, Orkney. Turned up OK.

JANUARY 24 – CG helicopter en route to search for missing hillwalker, Leverburgh, Harris, informed person found well. 2.

FEBRUARY 21-22 – Taking a short-cut across a 100m hill, Billia Field, Shetland, after a party, a man (32) died of hypothermia in sleet squalls. HM Coastguard teams and helicopter.

APRIL 22-24 – Retired woman (72) solo hillwalking spent two nights out on the hill in poor weather. Rescuers thought she would not have survived another. She was found, hypothermic, on East Ridge Meall Breac, Goat Fell. Searches by Arran MRT, SARDA, RN and Police helicopters. 158.

APRIL 24-25 – Man (50) was found, chilled at 03.09 on 25th by CG helicopter. Wearing jumper, jeans and shoes, with no food and no equipment, he was lost on the shore of Loch Eynort. Temperature was +4°C. with 10-knot wind. He had planned to climb Ben Corodale, South Uist, probably via Beinn Mhor, took a short-cut and got lost, missing his car by 1km. He walked in same area in 1996 with same total deficiency of equipment. Police, Lochboisdale CG. 32.

MAY 17 – Photographer (49) who had filmed Dundonnell Team near Clisham, North Harris, taking no part except low-level walking, winched by CG helicopter to Western Isles Hospital suffering a mild heart attack. Dundonnell MRT, Stornoway and Tarbert CG Units. 32.

MAY 30 – Man broke arm while walking on Rum. HMCG helicopter lift from Kinloch. 1.

MAY 31 – Woman (40s) broke her leg on Lunga, west of Mull. RN and RAF helicopters.

JUNE 4 – Walking with her husband at an isolated place on NE Arran coast near 'Fallen Rocks', wife (20+) fell, fracturing kneecap. Airlift by RN Sea King. Arran HMCG stood down *en route*. 11.

JUNE 5 – Walker (36) slipped while trying to rescue a dog at Glenashdale Falls, near Whiting Bay. Uninjured, he was rescued from a crumbling ledge by RN helicopter. Arran MRT. 12.

JUNE 8 – In cloud, just east below the Hallival/Askival Bealach, Rum, a Scottish Natural Heritage worker (32) slipped, dislocated his shoulder and got head lacerations. Stretchered, due to severe turbulence, by Kinloss MRT to suitable position for airlift by CG helicopter. 144.

JULY 3 – CG helicopter search of Beinn Mhor, South Uist after a woman with a heart condition became separated from her husband on the hill and was three hours' overdue. She walked off by a different route. 8.

JULY 15-16 – Father (38) and son (15) loch fishing on Lewis were lost overnight on the moors in fog. Found near Cuisashader by CG helicopter using FLIR detector.

JULY ? – RAF helicopter airlifted fallen walker from Dervaig Hill, Mull. 1.

OCTOBER 11 – Man (56) with five neighbours gathering sheep 4km NNE of Tarbert, Harris on Sgaoth Aird (559m) died from a heart attack. CG helicopter and Coastguard Auxiliary. 51.

Willie Speirs. Photo: Douglas Scott.

SOUTHERN UPLANDS

JANUARY 1-2 – Couple (in 40s) overdue snow walking in Glentress Forest from Peebles Hydro. Found, very cold, after midnight, by SARDA dog with Tweed Valley MRT. Helicopter standby. 30.

JANUARY 19-20 – Overdue boy (14) cycling in Glentress Forest (3km NE of Peebles) had run away from home. He spotted rescuers, avoided them, and abandoned bike, tent and survival gear. In freezing weather he made his own way home in darkness. Borders SARU, Tweed Valley MRT, SARDA. 284.

MARCH 22-23 – SARDA called out to assist Galloway MRT at Forrest Lodge, St. John's Town of Dalry search for man separated from friends when trying to ford a river. Stood down when he was found by main road 10km distant.

APRIL 16 – Crag at Upper Clifton, NX 84/909572. Leader (29) slipped on dry rock, ripping out two runners, falling 8m on to grass with chest and coccyx injuries. Three Galloway MRT climbers were at top of crag and helped him down scree to ambulance. HMCG unit arrived. 4.

APRIL 20 – Man cragfast 15m up a sea stack near Culzean Castle. Rescued by Fire Brigade ladder as Coastguards arrived. 14.

JULY 17-18 – Experienced diabetic cyclist (41) got lost on remote forest roads and spent night out near Castle Douglas. He turned up at Minigaff YH at 17.00 on 18th. Galloway MRT and SARDA. 6.

AUGUST 27 – Moffat MRT called out for four teenage girls overdue on award hike (Polskeoch on Southern Upland Way). They turned up but one had Achilles tendon injury. 12.

AUGUST 30 – Moffat MRT searched a wooded lochside near Lochmaben for an elderly lady overdue. She turned up OK as team deployed. 10.

SEPTEMBER 9 – Moffat MRT helped fell runner in Breweries Race to get off the hill with an ankle injury. 3.

SEPTEMBER 23 – RN Sea King rescued a Clydesdale horse from a ravine at Kirkmichael, South Ayrshire.

OCTOBER 18-19 – Moffat and Tweed Valley MRTs found five Scouts (m15-13) lost in forest in darkness and rain on Southern Upland Way near Selkirk. RAF Sea King en route. 154.

NOVEMBER 28 – Male teenager killed by falling from a cliff at Dunskey Castle, Portpatrick. HMCG and RN helicopter. Recovery by RNLI lifeboat as stretcher recovery up slopes would have been too hazardous. 18.

NON MOUNTAINEERING 1997

FEBRUARY 8-9 – HMCG searched Wick Harbour area for male (24). Body recovered by divers. 1.

FEBRUARY 10 – SARDA, Police underwater unit and RN Sea King called out for woman (31) missing near River Forth and fields near Stirling. She turned up OK.

FEBRUARY 17 – Borders SARU called out for flood alert at Newcastleton. Tweed Valley called out at Hawick for severe flooding. Did vehicle recoveries, sandbagging, evacuations. 175.

FEBRUARY 19 – Borders SARU flood callout at Hawick. Tweed Valley MRT call out at Selkirk. 16.

FEBRUARY 19 – Cairngorm MRT called out because of danger of people in cars

Iain Ogilvie on Mount Kenya. Photo: Dick Allen.

being trapped in snow on A9. On this occasion weather improved and road was cleared. 40.

FEBRUARY 21 – SARDA dogs searched east shore Loch Lomond for man (32) missing from car containing a suicide note. Search in strong SW winds from Balmaha to Ross Point. Not found. 12.

FEBRUARY 27 – Tweed Valley MRT mobilised in Galashiels for missing person who turned up safe.

MARCH 10 – SARDA dog found man (77) missing from nursing home at Ayton, Berwickshire. He was found in dense undergrowth, weak, cold and barely coherent. Borders SARU.

MARCH 10-23 – Searches by Strathclyde Police MRT, HMCG ground teams and RN Sea King for sea canoeist (34) missing off Iona. Her body was found off Elgol, Skye on 23 March. 86.

MARCH 15 – Young man committed suicide in forest remote from road near Portree. HMCG helicopter. 1.

MARCH 15 – Skye MRT helped police search for missing youth (19), armed with a rifle, believed to be a possible suicide victim. His body was found by HMCG helicopter in a forest on the road from Portree to Bracadale.

APRIL 13 – SARDA South searched Sheriffmuir Forest after a suicide note was found in a car. Subject returned to carpark brandishing a knife. 20.

JUNE 3-4 – RAF and RN Sea Kings used after RAF Harrier crashed at Gelston, Castle Douglas. Possible bird strike. Pilot had suspected post-ejection back injuries. Leuchars MRT crash guard. 552.

JUNE 23-24 – Search of flat coast near Alness Point in Cromarty Firth carried out by HMCG, Lifeboat, Police, RAF Sea King and SARDA for a woman (46) thought to be suicidal. Her body was found in the firth by Fishery Board employees. 468.

JUNE 23-24 – Aberdeen MRT helped police search River Dee banks at Aboyne for a retired man (73). His body was found on 24th by police divers. He appeared to have fallen in. 43.

JUNE 29 – Lowland search by Galloway MRT and SARDA for a man (36) with a history of collapsing, missing near River Dee. He turned up in London. 30.

JUNE 30 - JULY 1 – Vain search of woods and coast by SARDA South on first day for a woman (24) who left suicide notes. Her body was found in dense undergrowth near her home in Bo'ness by SARDA dog next day. 26.

JUNE 30-July 1 – Woman (unconnected with above incident) found dead in a pond near Bo'ness, outside SARDA search area.

JULY 17-21 – Aberdeen MRT helped police search in an inquiry into the murder of a boy (9). 193.

JULY 20 – Montrose Coastguard called out to search for man (26) missing near St. Cyrus. OK.

AUGUST 6 – Coastguard team and helicopter called out when two men were killed, trapped under a concrete slab while building a sea wall at North Ronaldsay. 2.

AUGUST 31 – Moffat MRT searched quarry, river and woods for a missing teenage male who was found in Dumfries. 100.

SEPTEMBER 2 – HMCG rescued a woman (37) suffering from an overdose on a rocky hilltop, Easter Heog (81m), East Burra, Shetland. 1.

SEPTEMBER 4 – Coastguard helped ambulance crew recover woman trapped in car which had left road and gone into the sea at Kyle of Durness.

SEPTEMBER 15-18 – Aberdeen MRT and SARDA searched at Keith, Banffshire for a missing man (40). His body was found by a search dog. 10.

SEPTEMBER 29 – Last vehicle in Leuchars MRT convoy, returning to base after recall from an incident in Glen Nevis, was flagged down by a hysterical mother whose child (5) was choking. The girl had swallowed an ice lolly, complete with stick! Team member successfully did a Heimlich abdominal thrust restoring normal breathing and also recovering a 2p coin from her throat in the process. She went to hospital by ambulance.

OCTOBER 9 – SARDA searched for a man missing from work on a farm at Bridge of Allan. OK.

OCTOBER 12 – Tweed Valley MRT and SARDA searched for person missing from psychiatric hospital. 56.

OCTOBER 24 – Successful search by Tweed Valley MRT and SARDA for woman (26) missing from hospital. 9.

OCTOBER 28 – Tweed Valley MRT and SARDA searched hospital grounds for confused lady (80). OK. 18.

NOVEMBER 21-24 – SARDA and Tweed Valley MRT searched Galashiels parkland and river banks for missing male (47) suffering depression. Found dead close to his home in a disused mill three days later. 33.

DECEMBER 12 – HMCG Montrose searched for man missing near harbour. He was OK.

DECEMBER 18 – Aberfoyle residents, Roderick Aitken (39) and Anne Marie Aitken (39) missing since December 18. Strathclyde MRT and Police helicopter searched fruitlessly on January 7-8, 1998 including abseil into Finnich Glen, Garabhan and Loch Ard Forests. On March 26, 1998 two bodies were found in a shallow grave in Ayrshire and positively identified as the missing couple. 208.

DECEMBER 21 – Cesna 152 missing *en route* Carlisle-Prestwick. Dead pilot (m44) found next day in wreckage on south top of Barrholm Hill between Creetown and Gatehouse of Fleet by rescue team. Galloway, Leeming and Leuchars MRTA, SARDA, RAF and RN helicopters, four lifeboats. 300+.

DECEMBER 23 – Tweed Valley MRT located missing lorry driver, in another lorry several miles farther into a forest (engaged in timber haulage) after his lorry had been found empty. 14.

DECEMBER 23-24. – Search by SARDA (South and Highland), Ochils MRT and Central Scotland Police of area around Coalsnaughton for a man (25) missing for more than a week. Search widened to include electricity sub-station near Fishcross where police found him dead by hanging. 212.

DECEMBER 25 – Borders SARU, Tweed Valley MRT, SARDA searched banks of swollen Tweed for man seen in difficulties by people on opposite bank. Body found at Kelso several days later by police divers.

DECEMBER 26 – Tweed Valley MRT aided police in search for runaway boy (8) missing at night on Tweed banks at Galashiels. He turned up OK. 2.

DECEMBER 26 – Moffat and Tweed Valley MRTs and SARDA sweep-searched a forest near an abandoned car at Newcastleton and found the body of a woman (60) suicide victim. 132.

DECEMBER 28-29 SARDA standby for missing man in Stenhousemuir who turned up safe.

IN MEMORIAM

WILLIAM B. SPEIRS j. 1927

Willie Speirs started climbing in Scotland in 1922 at the age of 15, and in the course of family holidays at Spean Bridge that year and again in 1923 he climbed all the peaks from Ben Nevis to the Grey Corries. So began a lifelong passion for mountaineering which took him far beyond Scotland in the following 50 years. By 1923 he was going north from Helensburgh regularly, at first by train and bicycle, then a year later on his Excelsior two-stroke motor cycle. Those were years when climbing in Scotland was at a low ebb after the First World War, and Willie and his brother, George, must have been among the most active and enthusiastic of young climbers going to the hills regularly, not only to climb but also on fishing expeditions to remote mountain lochs where their presence would not be noticed by local keepers.

The summer holiday of 1925 saw Willie and friends in Skye for two weeks, climbing on Sron na Ciche and fishing the lochs. His financial records of that holiday show his early talent for keeping the accounts in good order. The total cost for the four of them for 14 days, including transport , was £21.17s.$^1/_2$d. A month after returning from Skye, Willie and several friends had a meeting under the Narnain Boulder (described in his diary as a pow-wow) which resulted in the formation of the Junior Mountaineering Club of Scotland. Two years later a little route-finding problem on Crowberry Ridge with brother George and Bob Elton resulted in the first ascent of Speirs' Variation, described by subsequent guidebook authors as being as direct as Abraham's Route and equally sensational. At the end of that year he joined the Club.

Willie also had a passion for skiing and was one of the pioneers of cross-country touring in Scotland. At a time when everyone in Scotland was still using plain wooden skis, he imported a set of metal edges from Switzerland and laboriously fitted them to his skis, thereby improving his performance considerably on the icy slopes of Meall a'Bhuiridh.

In 1932, three years after the CIC Hut was built, Willie in his capacity as secretary of the Scottish Ski Club was responsible for the building of another hut even higher than the CIC. Hearing that the stalkers' bothy at Luib Shooting Lodge was for sale, he bought it for £15 and arranged for the Killin joiner to dismantle it and have it transported and re-erected high up in Coire Odhar on Ben Lawers, where it still stands.

In the Alps, Willie's spiritual home must have been Zermatt, for he returned time and time again, and climbed many of the major peaks there in the course of two decades, starting with the Matterhorn in 1936 and climaxing in his 1957 season. At that time he was President of the Club and had gone to Zermatt to represent the SMC at the Alpine Club's Centenary Meet. Arriving off the night flight from London to Geneva, he was promptly marched by his three companions, Graham Macphee, Ian Ogilvy and Charles Warren, up to the Schoenbiel Hut with a view to climbing the Dent d'Herens. At the hut several AC members, including their President Sir John Hunt, were heard to make some disparaging remarks when they were told of the SMC party's intentions. 'One thing is certain, those four old men will never climb the Dent d'Herens', were the words reported by George Roger. However, next day the peak was climbed and that evening in the Monte Rosa Hotel the AC President had to eat his words. Meanwhile, Willie and his three companions had enough puff left to climb Nordend and Lyskamm in the following three days. In 1966 he went to Mount Kenya with Douglas Scott and Charles Warren and the three had a fine expedition, only just failing to reach Batian in falling darkness and deteriorating weather. They went on the following week to climb Kilimanjaro, Willie's high point.

Five years later he made his last sorties on rock. With Charles Warren and Ivan Waller he climbed Observatory Buttress, and next day the Crowberry Ridge. Forty-four years after the first ascent of his eponymous variation, he traversed left at Abraham's Ledge and led his companions up the Direct Route. It turned out to be his last route of that standard as doctor's orders restricted his activities thereafter, but it was a fitting swansong to a long and varied climbing career.

By profession Willie was a chartered accountant and company secretary. These skills he used also in the service of the Club, as Committee Member, Treasurer, Editor, Vice-President and President. His membership of the committee was apparently not even interrupted by a wartime posting to the Faroes. However, above all Willie was a great gentleman whose modest manners and sense of humour concealed the quiet determination of which mountaineers are made.

D. Bennet.

IAIN HAMISH OGILVIE j. 1934

HAVING just returned to the hut from his guided ascent of the Aiguille d'Argentière, Iain decided to have a rest before descending to the valley where he had to catch a train. He overheard the anxious guardian talking to his guide,

'Votre client ne marche pas aussi vite que vous.' 'Marche? Dieu, comme il marche, c'est formidable!' the guide replied.

For those who climbed with Iain this is a fitting epitaph.

Iain's father, who retired to Perthshire in 1911, after prospering as a tin miner and rubber planter in Malaya, died in 1924, when Iain was 11 years old. His godmother was Mrs Grant of the whisky family. Iain, the oldest of seven children, took on his father's role and developed the strong and determined personality that was to characterise his life.

He climbed his first Munro (Ben More – Mull) with the butler, at the age of 14, and collected alpine plants for the garden. This is the third entry in Iain's complete climbing diaries in which he recorded in his all routes, summits, companions and walks more than 20 miles long, and the birds he had seen on his Alpine holidays.

After school at Ampleforth he went to Edinburgh University and started climbing with two fellow students who were to become friends and climbing companions for the rest of his life – Jimmy Marjoribanks and Charlie Gorrie. At the age of 20 he walked alone for five days from Glenfinnan to Ardnamurchan Point carrying his food and tent. He often chose to walk unaccompanied. The weather was mixed and the midges were fierce, but nevertheless, he recorded in his diary that it was a 'most enjoyable little tour'.

Graduating from university with a degree in Civil Engineering, he joined Scottish Consulting Engineers, Blythe and Blythe and continued to climb at every opportunity. He volunteered for the Army and was evacuated from Dunkirk. Iain married Bernardine Greenshields in 1942. He later instructed at the mountain warfare school in the Lebanon with Wilfred Noyce, going on to Italy and returning home in 1945 to see his daughter, Sonia, aged 15 months, for the first time. His son, Alasdair, was born after the war. On several occasions during the war Iain met up with Charlie Gorrie and they would share a dram or two and let their hair down. On one of these occasions they climbed to the top of a tall tree in the middle of the night, sang bawdy songs and refused to come down until ordered to do so by a senior officer.

After the war he returned to civil engineering, working in England, Iraq, Turkey and India as well as on an early Channel Tunnel proposal. He was an excellent engineer, enjoying solving problems and taking great pleasure in training young people. He thrived on the independence of overseas work. At the time of the Kassim revolution in Iraq when he was general manager of Holloway Brothers, his family was on leave and Iain was able to avoid the troubles by leaving his home and going on what he described as a '10-day cocktail party'.

However, his single-minded focus was directed to his climbing. He climbed The Chasm with Jimmy in 1933 and made an early summer ascent of Observatory Ridge with Charlie in 1934. Later, his frequent companions were Charles Warren, Ivan Waller, Graham MacPhee and many others; enjoying an Alpine holiday every second year and trips to the Himalayas, Kenya, Crete, Corsica, Greece, and Ireland as well as climbing in all the countries where he worked, Turkey, Iraq, and India.

Iain was awarded an OBE for his remarkable efforts in trying to save the lives of two friends who had fallen while traversing An Teallach in winter conditions. After lowering one friend, Iain fell 500ft while trying to lower the other, was badly injured and then struggled five miles to get help. The epic is recorded in *The Black Cloud* by I. D. S. Thomson and in Hamish MacInnes's book, *High Drama.*

Iain suffered a stroke in 1977 which left him with a lame leg. With more than 60 Munros still to climb, this was a huge setback but Iain's ambition was not diminished. Having been informed by his doctor that he would not be able to take long walks again, Iain was determined to prove him wrong and as a result, his health and stamina improved for several years.

Bernardine was a great support encouraging Iain to climb whenever he could. He completed 50 walks more than 20 miles long and 60 walks more than 15 miles long in the following years! Iain attended Easter meets and continued to climb alone and with old friends and younger friends including Oliver Turnbull and myself. In 1989 we sailed up Loch Quoich to climb Sgurr Mor. Iain was blown over several times but went on to complete his final Munro. Sixty two years had elapsed since the ascent of his first Munro, for which he probably holds the record. The only disappointment was that his life-long friend Charlie didn't make it to the top to celebrate.

Iain died in September 1997. He will be remembered for his sense of humour, and wonderful stories. Many of those who climbed with him still tell his jokes. His other interests were watercolour painting, sailing and model-boat building, at which he was very accomplished. Iain was a tall, well-built and distinguished man of immense determination with a great sense of fun, who set the pace and whose excellent company will be missed by all.

Dick Allen.

JAMES NORMAN LEDINGHAM j. 1945

As a neighbour in Kilmalcolm of both the late Harry MacRobert and the late Allan Arthur, I was well informed of the SMC and its activities and frequently joined Harry in his then revolutionary Ski Sundays on Ben Lawers in the Thirties.

As a student at Glasgow University reaching rather than climbing hills was my principal concern. Using an old push bike and the facilities offered by the Erskine Ferry and Loch Lomond steamer service, I climbed all the Arrochar and Falloch peaks. Later by motor-cycle I extended my activities as far as Glen Coe, the Lawers range, the Strathyre peaks and the Cruachan area.

I attended all the JMCS Glasgow section meets from 1934 to 1939 including autumn holidays in Arran, and summer meets in the Cuillin and Torridon hills. During the war I was commissioned in the 2nd Glasgow Highlanders having joined the Territorial Army in 1938. After serving as a Company Commander I was posted to 12 Commando in North Wales as an instructor to the commandos and latterly to the Lovat Scouts who were being converted to Alpine training. With Bill MacKenzie and Theo Nicholson and the late Sandy Wedderburn I joined the Lovat Scouts and in 1943 did six months Alpine training at Jasper in the Canadian Rockies.

Several mountains of 11,000ft.-12,000ft. were climbed in severe winter conditions with snowhole and bush bivouacs. Having been appointed Signals Officer of the Scouts I then proceeded to Italy where I served until I was wounded and mentioned in despatch near the end of the war. Thereafter I served as a Staff Officer to 9 Brigade HQ in Carinthia and Vienna. Having formed a Brigade Mountaineering Club our activities ranged from Monte Cristallo in the Dolomites to the Gross Glockner.

After demobilisation in January 1946 I joined the SMC and served on the committee in 1951-53 before leaving Glasgow to farm in Sutherland in 1953. I attended all but one meet until 1985 and again served on the committee in 1978 thereafter being appointed vice-president in 1979-81. Climbing was largely restricted to Club meets and summer holidays due to my remote location and the demands of hill farming, but an annual attendance at Sligachan with SMC friends was always faithfully kept in June for many years.

Having rejoined the Territorials I was awarded the Territorial Decoration in 1955 and as chairman of Sutherland Territorial Association was made a Deputy Lieutenant of the county in 1964.

With Myles Morrison and the late Fred Wylie we made use of the Ramblers Association during the Sixties and Seventies to annually visit less known but rewarding mountain ranges in the Tyrol, Dolomites and North Italian Alps.

I completed the Welsh 3000ft. mountains during my war appointment to the Commandos, and the English and Scottish Munros in 1963.

With Fred Wylie I hired a Ford Fiesta and spent a week completing the Irish 3000ft. peaks. And in our mid-70s, and latterly, we climbed about 50% of the Corbetts. Arthritis and worn knee joints finally finished all hillwalking activities in 1987 after nearly 50 active and memorable years and invaluable friendships.

Norman Ledingham.

R. R. S. Higgins continues: Norrie Ledingham joined the Club in 1947, immediately on his return from what had been a distinguished war career; first, in the Glasgow Highlanders, then, after as a spell as a climbing instructor to 12 Commando, with the Lovat Scouts for action with whom, on the approach to Florence, he was mentioned in despatches.

After the war, he returned to his first occupation as a geography teacher, when he was one of the first to take his students out on the ground, until, on the death of his father-in-law in 1953, he moved to Brora to take over the running of the family sheep farm

Typical of the man, he soon became an expert and was the Sutherland representative for the Scottish National Farmers' Union. He also renewed his connection with the Territorial Army, becoming the local chairman. He was also appointed a Deputy Lieutenant to the County. Such are the facts, but they only dimly describe the man. The love of the hills was, second only to that for his wife and daughter, paramount to him. As a companion he was a constant delight and his ability to illuminate a map rather than just read it, was unequalled, through his knowledge of our landscape in all its aspects and seasons.

Both pre-war, in the JMCS, and thereafter, he was an avid supporter of the Club Meets and those he could not attend were the poorer for his absence. He, and a bunch of cronies, continued to attend even when the natural infirmities of age began to take their toll. He served on the Committee from 1951 to 1953 and was Vice-President from 1979 to 1981. By the extent of my own sorrow at his passing one can, to a small degree, know what Helen and Joan must feel.

JAMES R. HEWIT j. 1947

JIMMY HEWIT loved rock-climbing and followed the sport all his life. He joined the JMCS in 1931 at the age of 22, and would have joined the SMC in 1934 but for a misunderstanding over the deadline for applications. In the event he did not join the senior club until 1947, and had completed 50 years' membership at the time of his death in February, aged 88.

His wife, Elsie, was also a good climber, and Jimmy took her to the CIC Hut for part of their honeymoon in 1940. (How many members can equal that?) While there, Jimmy climbed the Comb with R. F. Rolland and Ian Ogilvie – with Elsie's permission of course!

In the 1930s money was short, cars were few, and holidays limited, yet Jimmy managed to reach and climb in Glen Coe, Ben Nevis and the Cuillin, and other places besides, not to mention Blackford Hill and the Salisbury Crags nearer home. He wrote a guide to climbs on the Crags, which might have been published but for the War. He was also a cyclist and hillwalker, and was familiar with every part of the Pentlands – hills he loved to the end of his life.

Jimmy was a great story-teller, walks with him were never dull. He had a clear memory going back over 60 years of climbing, and of the 'characters' in the Club. He knew A. E. Robertson, Bob Grieve, Tom Weir, Graham Brown, J. K. Annand, Freddie Mantz, L. St. C. Bartholomew, Benny Horsburgh, Dick Brown, Jimmy Marshall and John Donaldson. On Jimmy's first night in the CIC Hut J. H. B. Bell arrived late and cooked bacon and eggs when everyone else was in their bunks. Older readers may also recall David Sandeman, Gordon Lindsey, George Henry, George Elliot, Graham McPhee, George Chisholm, Charlie Bruce, Adam Stewart, Tom Drysdale, Alan Horne and Dave Gordon, all of whom had shared climbing days with Jimmy. He claimed to have invented the first headtorch, putting it together from an old felt hat by making a dent in the middle with lace holes alongside to hold the torch. He said it worked. The Army claimed Jimmy for more than five years, and he ended the War in the Burma campaign as a combat cameraman, being present at the re-taking of Mandalay and other actions in that theatre. In 1945 he had accumulated a month's leave, and what better than to make the acquaintance of the Himalayas? It took not a little ingenuity in Calcutta, but he was able to borrow a tent, boots, rucksacks, ice-axes, sleeping bags, snow goggles and 100ft of rope for himself and a friend. They made a trek to Nanda Kot, a neighbour to Nanda Devi, and climbed to more than 17,000ft – a remarkable achievement for the two servicemen, which was written up in the newspaper of the SE Asia Command.

Jimmy spent all his life in Edinburgh, and after the War worked for DCL as a photographer. He had a fine mind and was very well read. He could sketch and write comic and serious verse, and though a good companion he remained essentially his own man. He was a rugby enthusiast over many years and deplored the influence of money in sport. He despaired for the future of rock-climbing, feeling it was becoming more and more artificial. Jimmy felt the SMC had too little of the club atmosphere of his early days; that it had become too elitist, and it always mystified him that despite the explosion of mountain activity over the last quarter of a century Club membership had increased very little.

But, however decided Jimmy might have been in his views, he was generous in all he did and said, and there was nothing he liked better than a crack with a fellow wayfarer met on the hill. Whether it be a shepherd, a dyker, or a cottager out walking his dogs, Jimmy was always ready to stop for a word about life and work and changing times. He put one in mind of Leigh Hunt's *Abou Ben Adhem,* and the line: 'Write him as one that loves his fellow men' could fittingly serve as Jimmy's epitaph.

Jimmy and Elsie became increasingly frail in the last 12 months, and their son, Jim, a professor in Dundee, and his wife, Lena, moved his parents to a nursing home near to their home in north Fife, where the old couple were happy and well looked after. Elsie died last August, and Jimmy has survived her by only a few months. Knowing them has enriched my life, and it has been an honour to be their friend.

Bill Shipway.

LITTLE has been written about Jim Hewit, but he achieved a mention in the *NZAC Journal* of 1936 as a red-haired youth. With Jim Donaldson, he made a variation on the right of Raeburn's Arête on North-east Buttress, Ben Nevis. While on honeymoon he made a new route on the Tower with Charles Holland. Life was hard before the Second World War.

Working at Grey's of George Street in Edinburgh Jim only had his Sunday's free. Salisbury Crags provided an outlet for his energies and he became the local expert. Local mythology has it that an eponymous route, 'Hewit's Groove', required the insertion of an old halfpenny in a crack in order to provide the crucial foothold.

His guide with names and grades was an instant success. Anyone who climbed in Edinburgh knew of Hewit's Guide and it was a prized possession. Military service brought a visit to India and the Himalayas. Return to civilian life brought a job in photography and much more leisure. He was a regular attender on bus meets; he once kept the bus waiting as he returned late from a winter's night on Carn Dearg. As he grew older he made long, solitary walks in the Border Hills. Eventually, his conversation was grudging but he was still happy to talk about his beloved Crags. Somewhere there is a film made by Viking Ropes. It shows Jim in Skye and the Crags. I would like to see it again.

A. H. Hendry.

IAN BLAIR MOWAT j. 1927

I AM indebted to Miss Helen Mowat for providing notes on the life of her father who died on June 3, 1997 having been a member of the Club since 1927. In that respect he shared the same length of membership as Willie Speirs who sadly also left us this year.

Ian was born at Bridge of Weir in 1902 and moved to Canada with his family in 1912, returning to study organic chemistry at Glasgow University. He was clearly fit and strong having boxed and played rugby in the University teams before briefly working as a fireman on a shunter at Carlisle during the General Strike! Following a short period as an academic, he eventually specialised in armaments research, initially with ICI in Ayrshire and finally in Government establishments at Girvan, Woolwich, New Longton and the Royal Aircraft Establishment, Farnborough where he remained until retiring in 1967.

His climbing experiences started as a young man in 1921. He climbed regularly during holidays and at weekends until back problems forced a premature retiral while in his early Forties. He joined the Club in 1925 and climbed with Kenneth Steven, Macphee, Baxter, Corbett and T. R. Paterson on the popular routes of the day in Arrochar and Glen Coe. In Skye he traversed the Cuillin Ridge. He was an excellent photographer and kept a photographic record of his trips including the Easter Meet at Tomdoun in 1931 where the Journal records his party being forced off Sgurr na Ciche by a lightning storm. The following day there was greater success on Aonach Air Chrith, Druim Shionnach and Creag a'Mhaim at the eastern end of the Cluanie Ridge.

He was proud of his membership of the Club which helped sustain his old age as visits to Scotland became less frequent and he passed on his great fondness for the hills to his family, to whom we extend our sympathies.

John R. R. Fowler.

EDWARD S. CHAPMAN j. 1954

IN E. S. Benson's autobiography he describes an old Don who walked on the grass in the college quadrangle every morning, prodded the worms with his stick and muttered: 'You've not got me yet.' In similar vein my generation reads the obituaries in the *Scotsman*. In this column I read of Chapman's death. It brought back happy memories of meets at Crianlarich when winters had snow and ice.

Chappy had an open Bentley. One operated the door with a spanner and wore a balaclava. He also had a small motor-cycle. Tall, bulky, bearded Eddie Chapman could talk on any subject at length and with humour. The said humour led to him putting a rock in my sack. He enjoyed my surprise when he discovered it on the top of the Buachaille. Latterly, he often visited the ski hut on Beinn Ghlas. He was a safe skier who sought adventure by himself. An engineer with Babcock and Wilcox he left there in his 50s. Working at a crammers in Edinburgh was his last job.

A. H. Hendry.

Notice has also reached us of the deaths of David Easson and Sandy Cousins.

PROCEEDINGS OF THE CLUB

New members

The following nine new members were admitted and welcomed to the Club in 1997-1998.

Jonathan A. Baird, (29), Retailer, Fort William.

David John Cuthbertson, (50), Mountain Guide, Dores, Inverness-shire.

David Alexander Kirk, (29), Chartered Mechanical Engineer, Glasgow.

Scott Fraser Moir, (21), Physical Education Teacher, Prestwick.

Michael John Reed, (35), Air Traffic Assistant, Ellon, Aberdeenshire.

James Scott Thin, (29), Bookseller, Edinburgh.

Nicholas Francis Turner, (26), Window Cleaner, Oban.

E. Anthony M. Walker, (48), Farmer, Alness, Ross-shire.

David Wilkinson, (52), University Lecturer, Birmingham.

EASTER MEET – LOCH MAREE HOTEL

The Easter meet attracted a large gathering and we were not disappointed. Despite forecasts of severe winter weather sweeping Scotland during the holiday, and consequent warnings to keep off the hills, clear skies and a mild frost welcomed those arriving on Thursday. There were, however, reports of rain in the Midlands. Generally, the weather was very good, with spells of sunshine between sleet and snow squalls giving spectacular views of this wonderful area. The highlight of the meet was the opportunity to cross Loch Maree to Letterewe – kindly arranged by Bill Wallace. Nineteen made the crossing and it was reported 20 came back; this confusion arising perhaps from the need for an almost Alpine start and the scramble to get aboard.

The return was carefully planned: two crossings, at 4pm and 6pm. Unfortunately one member, underestimating the length and hard going, or so he claimed, of his route rather than his age, as the boatman averred, delayed the last boat by 45 minutes. The Meet Secretary (for it was he) tendered his resignation. This was refused and he was sentenced to a further unspecified term of office. More praiseworthy was the presidential ascent of a gully on Beinn Lair, and a probable first ascent of a neighbouring gully by Macdonald and Slesser still pointing the into the record books. This had been a significant day in the history of recent Easter Meets and will be a hard act to follow. Any ideas?

Hills ascended included: Beinn an Eoin, Baosbhein, Beinn a' Chearcaill, Meall a' Ghiubhas, Beinn Dearg, Beinn Lair, Meal Mheinnidh, Beinn Airigh Charr, Beinn a' Chaisgein Mor, A' Mhaighdean, Ruadh Stac Mor, Meall nan Meallan.

Those present included the President Bob Richardson, Robin Campbell, Malcolm Slesser, Iain Smart, Bill Wallace, Tom Weir, Dick Allen, Rick Allen, Bryan Fleming, Mike Fleming, John Fowler, John Hay, Scott Johnstone, Peter Macdonald, Bill Myles, Douglas Niven, Douglas Scott, Alan Smith, Nigel Suess, Oliver Turnbull. Guests: Alison Allen, Iain Cumming, Mike Dean, Mike Esten, Audrey Scott, Ronald Turnbull. John Mackenzie and Bob Brown came for dinner.

Oliver Turnbull.

The One-Hundreth-and-Eighth AGM, Reception and Dinner

You get a feel for these things after a few years in the job and the signs were not good. The word was out that something ominous was afoot at the CIC; the first choice after dinner speaker had cancelled, and the night before the 'do' we had no presenter for the Club song. But, the members and their guests were oblivious to the majority of these problems as we pursued the well-worn path to the Alexandra once again. We commenced in that dreich barn to the rear of the hotel where John Peden reminded us of the superb sailing event in May, and Graham Little continued the parochial theme showing the range of technical climbing which the Scottish islands have to offer.

The President then called his first AGM to order. Picture boards describing intentions on the Ben and in the North West had attracted much earlier interest. Are there any comments on the Minutes he asked? Silence. Has anyone any comments on the Secretary's report he inquired? Nothing. Has anyone any questions for the Treasurer? No response. We proceeded in this way carving up the agenda lickety-spit until we came to the real business – hut matters. There was no lack of enthusiasm here. The North West hut, or rather the Naismith Hut, provided the *hors d'ouvres* as the huts team got some close questioning on the tenders, or the apparent lack of them, before the members cautiously gave approval for the conversion to go ahead. Some deserved praise was accorded by the President to the members who had found the property and secured the purchase. And then on to the main course – what was happening at the CIC.

The President explained the Hut Committee's concerns about increasing faecal contamination of the hut environs in winter and their feeling of obligation to do something about it. That part went well. The proposed solution was a complicated twin-level extension with a waste disposal system wholly dependant on an electricity supply to be provided by a wind generator mounted on a 6m steel mast close to the hut. The costs were massive.

The ensuing debate was remarkably well ordered as objectors voiced a wide range of concerns. The Huts team defended their corner, but perhaps were a little unprepared for the size of the mutiny and an eventual vote turned down the proposals by a ratio of 2-1. The members had spoken and the team were philosophic. The Club was, however, undoubtedly spared the pressures of such a controversial course of action and it is back to the CAD systems for the huts men to come up with a more acceptable idea.

The tensions over, we were all now in a mood to dine and we repaired to the Hotel for manly helpings of haggis, broth, guinea fowl and trifle. The Club song was rescued by Bill Wallace who gave a fine performance and the musical theme continued as Bob Richardson produced a recording of the master entertainer, Tom Patey, delivering *The Last of the Grand Old Masters* and other numbers.

The President welcomed the new members as well as listing the successes of the year and Bob Reid gave an eloquent and flamboyant welcome to our guests from the Grampian Club, Lochaber JMCS, the LSCC, the Ochils MC, and for the first time the Wayfarers' Club and the Eagle Ski Club. Alan Blackshaw had been discovered living in Newtonmore and was asked to reply for the guests. A long and complicated ramble was duly provided on the subject of access rights – a worthwhile topic, of course, but of limited value as after-dinner entertainment. One item remained – the President's Sunday walk. In true Fort William tradition, the rain was bouncing off the pavements as they set off up Glen Nevis. However, the Steall bridge was confirmed as still being there and they were rapidly back at the cars. That then was it for 1997. Members generally seemed to think that it was one of the best Dinners for a while which, given the problems of the preceding few days, just goes to show that you never can tell.

J. R. R. Fowler.

Ski-mountaineering Meet 1998.

The customary SMC ski-mountaineering meet took place on February 6-7, 1998 at the An Teallach mountaineering hut called Strawberry Cottage in Glen Affric. In theory, it is far enough north to be a splendid centre providing access to some big hills and with wide snow cover in north-facing corries and reasonable weather it would be a ski touring paradise.

Fifteen seasoned SMC members and guests eventually assembled at the Cannich Hotel later than planned on Friday night. The hut is 5km from the Glen Affric car park up a private forestry track and hut users are permitted to use only two cars for access. Despite written invitations no-one – especially the three ex-presidents – went in early either by ski, bike, snowshoe, horse, parapent or on foot. Despite the late arrival, the hut was soon nice and warm and we retired in anticipation of a fine day skiing. The hut is fully equipped with wood-burning stove and wood, gas cookers, gas lights (but no mantles) and electric lights plus generator.

Saturday was cold and sunny with snow visible on all the high summits. The skiing contingent gamely went skiing and had a fine day on the north corrie of Mullach Fraoch-choire, later reporting that they skied to within 150m of the hut. The walkers, eschewing the delights of humping skis up to the receding snowline, stalked off up An Socach and Sgurr na Ceathreamhnan, where in contrast to the skiers, the first snow was not found until at least 400m above the hut. A second cohort climbed Mam Sodhail.

Saturday night saw culinary and victual extremes outdone only by the increasingly exaggerated claims of what daring exploits had been done that day. It was also noted that, excepting one guest, all those present had visited the Staunings Alps in North East Greenland.

Sunday was warm, wet and windy consistent with recent Scottish winters and the majority enjoyed a chat and a walk along the North shore of Loch Affric to the public road with a following wind. On the drive home the Glasgow contingent was in fine voice and respectfully rewrote two verses of the club song:

With a bent shaft axe in a holster on your harness
and hard copy of a forecast off the Internet to warn us
the bolts we're carefully clipping, vibram soles on wet rock slipping
as we go up to the mountains with no snow.

There's no ice or snow or névé, and wet ropes make rucksacks heavy
after torquing now we're walking on a path paid for by levy
rocks and nuts and friends are camming and with arms and legs we're jamming
then we come down from the mountains with no snow

Oh my old hobnailers, oh my old etc

A most enjoyable weekend for all despite the marginal conditions. Apologies to those members who attempted to book but could not be accommodated.

Members present: Colwyn Jones, Ann MacDonald (guest), John Bickerdike, Tim Pettifer, Brian Shackleton, Charlie Orr, Ian Angell, Bob Barton, Bill Wallace, Gordon MacKenzie, Susan MacKenzie (guest), Iain Smart, Malcolm Slesser, John Peden, Mandy Peden (guest).

C. M. Jones.

THE CENTENNIAL YACHT MEET (1997)

Report by Charlie Orr – with support from John Peden.

History involves not only a perception of the pastness of the past, but of its presence. T. S. Eliot.

On the afternoon of Thursday, April 15, the steam yacht *Erne,* under the dual but harmonious control of Captain Turner (the owner) and Captain Smith, steamed into Oban Bay, having on board the president of the SMC and two or three other hardy passengers who had braved the squally showers round the Mull of Kintyre. Late in the evening the remaining members and their guests – making 29 in all – who had been delayed by holiday traffic, arrived by rail and after the usual turmoil of hunting for berths and sorting luggage we all sat down to supper and to discuss the gloomy subject of the waves and the weather. (SMC Journal Vol. 4, 1897)

So wrote Professor R. Lodge, one of the less-than-happy band, at that time at least, at the start of The SMC Yacht Meet in April, 1897. Little more is known of the Professor, who recorded the events of the Meet in the Journal of that year. The same fate has, however, not befallen one of the other participants, and the name of Sir Hugh T. Munro is now known throughout the land by those who have even the most casual acquaintance with the Scottish Mountains.

Yachts and mountains may have appeared to be rather strange bedfellows in 1897 but, given the relative inaccessibility of many of the mountainous regions on the western seaboard, and the unparalleled rock climbing to be had on Skye and many of the other inner islands, one can see the attraction. Mountaineering and sailing are also remarkably compatible activities. Both place similar demands on participants (including a perverse ability to enjoy discomfort), and both offer similar intense, if

intangible, rewards. All coastlines possess an innate tension by virtue of being the interface between two worlds, but the intricacies of our coastline make these two worlds inseparable.

The seed of an idea to celebrate the centenary of the voyage of the *Erne* was sown on the customary after-dinner President's Meet in December,

1995, when the newly-elected President, Robin Campbell, was conducting his newly-acquired charges around the Western Mamores. The man who was to become ultimately responsible for the organisation of The Centennial Meet, 'Commodore' John Peden, recalls its genesis.

'Robin took the opportunity of soliciting for interesting events to mark his Presidency. I carelessly let slip the idea of commemorating the yachting

meet of 1897. Others I know had harboured similar thoughts but wisely kept their own counsel. As I have now discovered, any display of enthusiasm in this Club is mercilessly exploited and notwithstanding the minor detail that Campbell would no longer be in office by the time it took place, I was promptly press-ganged into organising something.'

Serious planning started about a year before the event, which the Commodore moved from Easter to the end of May, in the hope of securing better weather than the original meet experienced. The first thoughts were to charter one moderately large yacht, to serve as a 'mother ship' for several satellite boats. Events had other plans however, and as the numbers swelled so did the size of the flotilla.

In August 1996 the Commodore came across the steam yacht, *Carola.* Perhaps the most interesting boat on the trip and certainly the one closest in use and design to the *Erne,* the *Carola* was built by the apprentices at Scott's of Bowling in 1898, the year after the original Meet.

It was designed as the Scott family's personal pleasure yacht, being used mainly on the Clyde and around the inner islands, although it was later

pressed into service as a general purpose boat about the yard, picking up debris after new launches and the like. In the 1960s, after passing through the hands of several owners, it lay rotting at its moorings on the River Leven at Dumbarton, when it was 'rescued' and taken to the Scottish Maritime Museum at Irvine and lovingly restored to its present condition. With the exception of the skipper, Ian Smith, the boat is crewed entirely by volunteers of the Royal Naval Auxiliary Service – a registered charity, and is used for charter trips. Some 70ft long and with a 13ft beam, her elegant lines emoted a resonance with the past.

The next classic boat to be signed up was the *Eda Frandsen*. Based at Doune in Knoydart, the *Eda Frandsen* is a gaff cutter, built in Denmark in 1938 for lobster fishing in the Baltic. The Robinson family, who have built up the community in Doune from scratch, bought her in 1990 and brought her back to Doune, where she was converted for charters. Shortly before launch in 1993 the boatshed caught fire and she was reduced to a charred hulk. With commendable good will and astounding energy, she was lovingly built up again, and at 73ft LOA became the largest boat in our fleet.

Skipper Michael Humphries confirmed that *Alpha* would join the fleet. She was built in 1904 as a Bristol Channel Pilot Cutter, and there is an interesting link to mountaineering history in that this type of boat was used (and sunk!) by Bill Tilman. Designed for sea-keeping qualities in all weathers, and for speed in order to win their pilotage work, the *Alpha* was immediately reserved as the Flagship.

Members and guests were now booking for the Meet in increasing numbers, and the *Rosa and Ada* was taken on. She was an East Coast oyster smack, built at Whitstable in 1908.

Anna Stratton brought her boat, *Mary Bryant,* all the way from Falmouth. Though only 16 years old, she was built on the lines of a traditional New England gaff schooner, and she became the smallest of our classic yachts at 48ft LOA.

So it became that on the evening of Friday, May 23, 1997, as the advance group of members and guests, about 40, foregathered at the clubrooms of the Oban Sailing Club, there was no talk of 'the gloomy subject of waves and weather'. On the contrary the five charter yachts and 11 privateers which made up the flotilla were anchored in Oban Bay on a millpond sea bathed in the red of the setting sun and all looked set fair for the morrow.

At two o'clock the following day, on a fresh sunny afternoon, the *Carola* led the flotilla out into Oban Bay, to a skirl of pipes from the pier, bound for Tobermory. Saltires were flying from the mastheads and the music was continued out into the Sound of Mull from the pipes of one of the club members; Iain Macleod, standing stoically, if somewhat precariously, on the foredeck of his own yacht *Seol-na - Mara:* 'Ach it could have been

NORMAN LEDINGHAM

JIMMY HEWIT

IAIN MOWAT

IAIN OGILVIE

worse,' said Ian. 'Judging by the weather last week, I was thinking maybe I would have to lash myself to the masthead.'

After a fine sail out of Oban into the Sound of Mull, the breeze fell light, and engines were started, to maintain progress. In view of the favourable conditions and general enthusiasm to reach the hills, a decision was made to press on round Ardnamurchan. Most of the classic yachts anchored in Gallanach Bay on Muck, and watched the sun setting on the hills of Rum. However, gremlins in the communication system resulted in most of the private yachts being spread out between Tobermory and Loch Scresort on Rum, those at the latter not arriving until the early hours of Sunday morning.

The crew from the *Eda Frandsen,* and others who had overnighted on Muck, spent Sunday morning on a leisurely ascent of Beinn Airein followed by the short sail to Rum with most parties being taken ashore at Dibidil at the east end of the island. The more adventurous then traversed to Scresort via the summits of Askival and Hallival with others choosing the more leisurely coastal path.

Most of the crews opted to climb Askival and Hallival on the Sunday with the notable exception of 'Commodore' Peden and his guest and aspirant member Chris Ravey from the flagship *Alpha.* This intrepid pair put up a new rock route on the Harris buttress of Travall (175m E1 5b) which now rejoices in the name Ancient Mariner. The name was chosen by the Commodore, who by this stage was presumably feeling the responsibilities of his office and the weight of planning over the previous year.

One other notable 'alleged' incident, was reported by skipper Derek Fabian and his crew and their guests aboard the *Mistress Malin.* On their arrival at the Scresort anchorage on Sunday afternoon while everyone else was on the hill they, and here I quote the skipper:

'Observed a derelict GRP sloop on its beam ends on the rocky shore near the pier – closer examination found her to be flying (in sad disgrace) the new SMC pennant. She was the *Souple Jade.* Her crew, ashore in the hills, reboarded at high tide, apparently unaware of her near demise.'

This sad interlude has been denied of course, and here, as cabin boy on the *Souple Jade,* under the dual captaincy of Professor Malcolm Slesser and Robin Shaw, I am instructed by these gentlemen to inform you that 'photographic evidence', (a slide was produced at the 1997 Club Dinner at the Alexandra Hotel, Fort William, which appeared to show quite clearly the *Souple Jade,* lying on her side, high and dry on a rocky shoreline, a slide, I must report, produced with not a little touch of Schadenfreude) is clearly a photo-montage of the type so beloved of the tabloid Press. The owners of the *Souple Jade* do not wish to comment further on this scurrilous allegation, and trust that the matter is now laid to rest.

The crew of the small private boat *Dubbel Dutch,* club members Richard Bott and Gavin Swinton, had undoubtedly the most adventurous course to Rum. Having overnighted in Tobermory they rose late on the Sunday morning (courtesy of the bar of the Mishnish!) and sailed to Muck, accompanied much of the way by a school of dolphins, and after making a quick ascent of Beinn Airein made for Loch Scresort in a Force 8! This resulted in a rudder bent through 30° and torn through half its width. A visit to the estate workshops of Kinloch Castle, a blow torch and some gate hinges, made all the difference, and *Dubbel Dutch* lived to fight another day.

Monday morning saw a freshening wind provide ideal sailing conditions, and after a private and fascinating tour of Kinloch Castle, the crossing from Rum to a calm and sheltered anchorage in Loch Scavaig on Skye was made in brilliant sunshine under a cloudless sky. Nestling in through the narrows under Gars Bheinn one couldn't help but compare our visit with that attempted by our predecessors 100 years earlier;

'It was at last decided that a resolute attempt to return to Loch Scavaig should be made in the morning and that the President should be roused at an abnormal hour and that he should be authorised to change the vessel's course only in a case of an absolute decision of the captains that landing in Scavaig was impracticable. So we woke once more to find ourselves tossing about after the peace of the last two nights, and with the prospect of a very transitory breakfast. But at the last minute, prudent council prevailed and we ultimately breakfasted at anchor in Loch Nevis instead of off the churlish coast of Skye.'

How different it was for us who spent a glorious two days in Scavaig with a colony of seals for company and I think it unlikely that such a wonderful sight as these classic yachts rafted together in such majestic surroundings will be seen for many a long year (another 100 perhaps!). No sooner were the boats at anchor than Ravey and the Commodore were at it again, puffing up another new route (Outhaul 120m HVS 5a). This was on the crag above Scavaig Slabs on Sgurr na Stri.

The next day the pattern of fine weather continued, and I would imagine that rarely, if ever, have 'The Dubhs' been so well and truly 'Done' on that one day, with the majority of crews opting for that classic route. There was a fairly insistent mist early on which cleared spectacularly around lunchtime to give those parties lucky enough to be on top superb views of the whole Cuillin Ridge. One such party, Messrs Fabian, Chalmers and Bennet, on confirming that they were indeed part of the 'Centennial Meet', were asked, unthinkingly, by a young couple encountered on the ridge if they had been on the original expedition!

There were more adventurous things done that day, just in case anyone is reading a shift of emphasis into this dalliance with the sea. Robin Campbell and Peter MacDonald attempted a route to the right of The Chasm on Sgurr nan Eag, while Richard Bott and Gavin Swinton climbed King Cobra (E1), Bott in bendy boots, the old 'forgotten PA's' ploy failing to cut any ice with his partner.

There was a 'very social' party held on the 'Classic Raft' that night which was ably summed up by Richard Bott in his diary: 'Great party, time and method of return to *Dubbel Dutch* unknown!'

Knoydart was our next port of call, but before finally departing Loch Scavaig on Wednesday morning activists were at work on Mad Burn Buttress above the anchorage. One climb of note done here was a 'first ascentionist's second ascent', with former President and septuagenarian Malcolm Slesser repeating Warsle, a 300ft Severe, a route he had pioneered 35 years earlier! He was ably assisted on this occasion by Bill Wallace and Charlie Orr. 'Slightly more difficult than I remember it,' he said with a wry smile. This impressive performance was witnessed by two ropes from *Alpha,* namely Ken Crocket/Brian Dullea and John Peden/Chris Ravey, who climbed the unfortunately named Mayday (300ft Severe).

The fleet then made its way round the Point of Sleat, in light winds, giving a gentle cruise to Loch Hourn. The main fleet anchored in the shelter of Eileann Rarsaidh, below Beinn Sgritheall, but some eschewed conviviality in favour of late evening sunshine at Barrisdale. Those intrepid Dubbel Dutchers (again!), last to leave Loch Scavaig (and the smallest yacht in the fleet), were involved in the rescue of five people and three dogs from Soay, adrift in an ancient open fishing boat, whose engine had coughed its last. Their just reward, in addition to an ascent of Beinn Bhreac

(464m) on Soay, was to round the Point of Sleat as the sun set dramatically behind the Cuillin.

The weather was clear, bright and calm on Thursday morning, and most who could leave their boats opted for an ascent of Ladhar Bheinn, shooting straight from the shore to its full 1020m. (One of the disadvantages of a boat approach is that you've got to climb it all!) I would be surprised if Ladhar

Bheinn has seen so many on its summit at once for many a long day, if ever. One poor couple, having made the ascent from the landward side, were clearly surprised and doubtless disappointed at what they found when they breasted the summit. And their chagrin was doubtless not helped one bit when our phlegmatic President Bob Richardson offered his consolation,

'Ach shoor enough, we're all here for the solitude now,' he said in his best West Highland accent.

Many made the traverse over Aonach Sgolite and Sgurr Coire Chonnichean to Inverie on Loch Nevis, and it was during this traverse that the crew of the *Mary Bryant* came on an interesting natural phenomena on the slopes of Aonach Sgolite. A huge lightning strike had shattered rocks over a large area and formed scorched tracks radiating out up to 50m in all directions. At least, this is the explanation that Bob Duncan records in his diary! (The answer is out there!) It was a drouthy multitude that regrouped at Inverie in the afternoon, and the stocks at The Old Forge were seriously depleted by the time the party rejoined its transport for the short trip round the coast to Doune, at the western tip of Knoydart.

Doune comprises a small scattering of rebuilt houses and newly-constructed outbuildings from where the Robinson family charter the refurbished Danish sailing cutter *Eda Frandsen,* and cater for those in pursuit of that '– bit of solitude'. Here on the Thursday evening followed an undoubted highlight of the week, as 66 of us sat down at one sitting to a marvellous meal of local crayfish followed by local venison and all the trimmings and, wonder of wonders, free beer, courtesy of club member Russell Sharpe and Caledonian Brewery. Mary Robinson did us proud.

Speaking with Mary after the meal she admitted that: 'We have only

Centennial Yacht Meet: The Sound of Sleat and Skye from Doune. Photo: Derek Pyper.

Photograph by Chris Striker

CENTENNIAL YACHT MEET – members and guests

1. Ian Philip (G); 2. Barrie Philip (G); 3. Derek Fabian (M); 4. David Grieve (M); 5. Bill McKerrow (M); 6. Mike Fleming (M); 7. Richard Bott (M); 8. Peter MacDonald (M); 9. Morton Shaw (M); 10. Paddy Buckley (M); 11. Evelyn McNicol (G); 12. John Havard (G); 13. Allan McNicol (M); 14. Derek Pyper (M); 15. Anne Bennet (G); 16. Brian Duchart (G); 17. Bill Greaves (M); 18. Dave Simpson (G); 19. Matthew Jack (G); 20. Gavin Swinton (M); 21. Donald McCalman (M); 22. Helen Thomson (G); 23. Robin Shaw (M); 24. Jim Thomson (M); 25. John Wood (M); 26. Bryan Fleming (M); 27. Andy Wightman (M); 28. Robin Chalmers (M); 29. Paul Bryan (M); 30. Chris Ravey (M); 31. Mike Taylor (M); 32. Phil Gribbon (M); 33. Keith Williams (G); 34. David Stone (G); 35. Margot Gribbon (G); 36. Bob Duncan (M); 37. Dick Allen (M); 38. Robin Campbell (M); 39. Bill Young (M); 40. John Wells (G); 41. Ken Crocket (M); 42. Bill Brooker (M); 43. Malcolm Slesser (M); 44. Brian Dullea (M); 45. Bob Richardson (M); 46. John Hay (M); 47. Bill Wallace (M); 48. Mandy Peden (G); 49. John Peden (M); 50. Iain Smart (M); 51. Oliver Turnbull (M); 52. Mike Jacob (M); 53. Bill Myles (M); 54. Charlie Orr (M); 55. Lyndsey Kinnes (G).

Members and guests on Meet, absent from the photograph.

Graeme Nicol (M); Donald Bennet (M); Ewa Maydell (M); Iain MacLeod (M); Barbara MacLeod (G); Seonachan McLeod (G); John Offord (G); Stephen Offord (G); Brian Robertson (G); David Hamilton (G); Dan Convery (G); Roger Parry (G); Graham Parry (G); Tom Butterworth (G); Bruce Barclay (M); Maggie Barclay (G); ANO (G).

ever catered for families or small parties before, so you can imagine I was having nightmares about this.' Nightmares she may have had but the meal was superb and as Bob Richardson said afterwards: 'If the SMC wasn't enjoying itself, what more could be done?'

In his speech which followed, the President was clearly delighted at the success of the venture, which boasted the largest attendance at a Meet in the Club's 108-year history, and, as we watched the great orange orb of the sun throw the assembled yachts into silhouette, as it dropped behind the jagged peaks of the distant Cuillin, the toast was 'The Mountains and The Sea'. As if blessed from on high, the skippers who had remained on their boats that evening saw the elusive 'green flash' as the sun set over the Cuillin.

The following day, in most un-West Highland like manner, the weather again continued fine (and midgeless!) and some parties took the opportunity to sail up the remote Loch Nevis with ascents being made of Luinne Bheinn and Meall Buidhe. The classic yachts set sail (metaphorically speaking – the sea was like a mirror) for Tobermory, the final port of call before a return down the glassy Sound of Mull to Oban on Saturday.

It was said 100 years ago that: 'Those of us who were not on the committee and who were therefore free from the chilling impression that they had planned something which proved impossible, would have no hesitation in asserting that the expedition was an unqualified success.'

And, if that was the case then, ours was doubly so, and our thanks should go to 'Commodore' Peden for having been good enough to allow himself to be press-ganged into undertaking the mammoth task of organising what I feel sure will be the first of a long tradition of 'centenary yacht meets'.

PS. Some members have reported spotting what has been described as a 'Hugh Munro-like figure' disappearing into the mists on the col between Askival and Hallival – not only the pastness of the past but of its presence – I hope he was pleased.

CREW LISTS
Classic Yachts

Skippers' names and number of additional professional crew in parentheses.

ALPHA – Bristol Channel Pilot Cutter Rig. Gaff Cutter Built: 1904 LOA: 60ft LOD: 51ft Beam: 14ft 6ins Draft: 9ft.
(Mike Humphries +1). Bob Richardson, John Peden, Iain Smart, Chris Ravey, Ken Crocket and Brian Dullea.

CAROLA – Steam Yacht Built: 1898, by Scott's of Bowling LOA: 70ft 6ins Beam: 14ft Draft: 7ft 6ins Displ: 59 tons.
(Ian Smith +3). Bill Brooker, Mike Taylor, Derek Pyper, Allan McNicol, Evelyn McNicol and Mike Fleming.

EDA FRANDSEN – Sailing Fishing Cutter Rig. Gaff Cutter Built: 1938, in Grenna, NE Denmark LOA: 73ft LOD: 55ft Beam: 15ft Draft: 6ft Displ: 58 tons.
(Toby Robinson +2). John Hay, Bill McKerrow, Phil Gribbon, Margot Gribbon, Mike Jacob, Paddy Buckley, Bryan Fleming and John Wood.

MARY BRYANT – Sailing Yacht Rig: Gaff Schooner Built: 1981 LOA: 48ft LOD: 41ft Beam: 12ft Draft: 6ft Displ: 16 tons.
(Anna Stratton). Robin Campbell, Bob Duncan,Lyndsey Kinnes, Jim Thomson, Helen Thomson and Peter MacDonald.

ROSA AND ADA – Oyster Smack Rig: Gaff Cutter Built: 1908, by Collar Bros., Whitstable LOA: 70ft LOD: 47ft Beam: 13ft 6ins Draft: 5ft 6ins Displ: 20 tons.
(Don Hind +1) Bill Myles, John Havard, John Wells, Brian Duchart, Oliver Turnbull and Dick Allen.

Private Yachts

CRISTALA – (Macwester Malin 32). Donald McCalman, Bill Greaves, Matthew Jack and Bill Young.

SEOL NA MARA – (Fastnet 34). Iain MacLeod, Barbara MacLeod and Seonachan MacLeod.

SOUPLE JADE – (Nicholson 32). Malcolm Slesser, Robin Shaw, Morton Shaw, Bill Wallace and Charlie Orr.

TWO HOOTS – (Spectrum 35 Cat). John Offord, Stephen Offord, Brian Robertson, Dave Hamilton and Mandy Peden (Thursday)

FREYA – (Gladiateur 33). David Stone, Keith Williams, Paul Brian and Andrew Wightman.

MOLITA – Sailing Yacht Rig: Bermudian Ketch Built: 1898 LOA: 50ft LOD: 44ft. (Dan Convery Thursday)

BESULA MHOR III – (Moody 35). Ian Philip. B.W. Philip, David Grieve and Graeme Nicol.

DUBBEL DUTCH – (Etap 22). Dave Simpson, Richard Bott and Gavin Swinton.

MISTRESS MALIN – (Fantasi 31). Derek Fabian, Ewa Maydell, Donald Bennet, Anne Bennet and Robin Chalmers.

CORUISK – (Contessa 32). Roger Parry, Graham Parry and Tom Butterworth.

MINGULAY (34) – Bruce Barclay, Maggie Barclay, and 'Frantic'.

The 1997 Yacht Meet

A Distillation of Memories from Neil Gunn (1891 – 1973)

'. . . *time may give it its form and the spirit of the age its turn of phrase, perhaps, but the communication itself is timeless . . .*'

Is there anything more pleasant in the world of travel than sailing by islands in distant seas, gazing at sandy bays on wild, uninhabited coasts . . . ?

And the hills! We know their shape; the uplift, the down-sweep, the flow of them; each by name, in that silence of intimacy that comes very near the dark speechless centres.

During the day sunshine and shadows keep up their endless play on these mountains; but with evening the colour changes to a strange, darkened, eerie green, deepening to dark velvet, until the western side becomes like a living hide ever approaching and spreading. The tops are now in mist; purple and withdrawn, the mountains become great in size, are changed from sleeping animals to primordial gods.

Never before had I found this part of the world so full of light, so peaceful, so beautiful . . . heavy clouds massed on the Cuillin, on the peaks of Inverness-shire, on Ben More on Mull; Ardnamurchan, Caliach Point, the Dutchman's Hat and Coll lay in a faint haze. But these Inner Isles were in a ring of light.

The great rock pinnacle high above the breast of the moor is smoking like some gargantuan factory chimney as the clouds divide upon it and sweep round it, the dark of the rock seeming itself to move like an inner black smoke. The wide floor of the sea, green over the sand, purple-brown over the tangle, and deepening blue into the far distance. You feel that this world here is not only immensely old, but that it is living now . . .

The day . . . was one of those perfect days that, falling upon the Hebrides at any odd time, are for ever memorable. Travelling then by sea in a halcyon calm, one – becomes imbued by the fabulous nature of this western world. The islands take upon them the stillness of a dream. Colour softens and holds the eyes like a memory one does not care to define, like a memory one could never define, so that it has a wash of emotion faint as the farthest purple that fades into the haze . . . a whale crosses our wake, shouldering the sea slowly . . . All at once there is the cry of the pipes . . . the piper is a Canadian who many years ago emigrated with his mother and six brothers and sisters from one of the Outer Isles. His fingering is not too sure. Phrases are slurred a little. But after a time he settles down to a tune and plays it with a fine deliberation. I know every note of it but cannot for the moment recall its name. Presently . . . I ask him the name of the tune. 'Mo dhachaidh,' he says. 'My home.' And adds: 'It was looking at those hills . . .'

(Compiled by Mike Jacob from a collection of Neil Gunn essays. Grateful acknowledgment is made to Alastair C. Gunn and Dairmid Gunn for permission to use words from one of Dairmid's 'favourite' books.)

JMCS REPORTS

Lochaber Section:– In 1997 the membership remained around the mid-fifties, that's numbers not ages, with a couple of new faces joining over the year. Most of the membership stay in the Lochaber area and many enjoy an active role in the Lochaber Mountain Rescue Team as well as participating in the Club's activities.

The section meets in the Nevis Bank Hotel, Fort William each Thursday evening. During the winter season these evenings sometimes incorporate a slide show.

In March 1997 the section was saddened by news of the untimely death of a former member – 'Wee Gus' MacLean. Gus was a local lad and had been a long-time active member of both the club and the rescue team, beginning his association with both in the early 1950s. He will be sadly missed by many.

Throughout the year the section held meets to various venues including Braemar, Glen Affric and the Lake District, culminating in the annual dinner, held in the Aultguish Inn near Garve on the last weekend of November, and was a great success being attended by more than 40 members and guests.

The section continues to lease Steall Cottage in Glen Nevis and the money received from renting the cottage is the section's main source of income. The cottage is continually being maintained and improved – utilising the skills within the Club. This year's main task was the replacement of the roof which was completed over two consecutive weekends.

Officials elected were: *Hon. President,* W. Munto; *Hon. Members,* B. Bissell, D. Scott; *President,* I. Walker, *Vice-President,* D. Ford; *Treasurer,* George Bruce, *Secretary,* K. Foggo, 4 Parkan Dubh, Inverlochy, Fort William, PH33 6NH, (01397 706299); *Hut Custodian,* J. Mathieson, 43 Drumfada Terrace, Corpach, Fort William, PH33 7JU, (01397 772599).

K. Foggo.

Perth Mountaineering Club (JMCS, Perth Section):– Club membership stands at 86 with c. six potential new members, and seven Honorary members. This leads to generally well-attended meets and full hut bookings – and all the related joys of extras sleeping on floors; in broom cupboards, and camping outside in winter snow and wind etc. BUT, we gain by having a more relaxed and contented treasurer now confident of a small, but reliable, surplus in the year. Not so relaxed that free wine is in prospect for the next Club dinner, but we are working on this as a realistic possibility for the Millennium event!

Although walkers outnumber climbers by about 2-1, the climbers continue to be very active and well catered for by the co-ordinating activities of Grahame and Mel Nicoll with Alex Runciman in support. A full spring/summer season of 17 Wednesday evening climbing sessions were held – mostly at the Polney Crags at Dunkeld. This is augmented by autumn and winter work on the climbing wall at Dunfermline. At most weekend meets there is an active climbing team who head for some of the local routes.

A total of 21 outdoor meets took place in the April/March 12 months – a weekend two-or-three-day meet each month and nine day-meets. Additional winter evening hotel-based meets are held for President's night, Member Slide nights, First Aid training, Mountain Safety presentations and MC of S presentations. The Mountain Mind Quiz was held in the Isle of Skye hotel last year with a win for the Grampian Club of Dundee, but in the event in March hosted by the Grampian Club the illustrious Perth three won, so we will host the event next year.

Club members' expeditions included climbing in the El Choro Gorge in the Spanish Sierra Nevada, trips to Pabbay and Mingulay (Grahame and Mel Nicoll, Alex Runciman and Lawrence Hughes), trekking in New Zealand's Southern Alps (Richard and Brenda Davison), cross-country skiing in Norway 1997 and 1998 (Ron Payne, Mike Thewlis, Alan Vaughan).

A new Club constitution was introduced at the December 1997 AGM, and together with a slightly more formal approach to prospective members. This is to brings the Club more into line with the MC of S guidelines as well as safeguarding the Club and members in its duty of care. Details of the document involved has been circulated to all JMCS Sections.

Officials elected: *President,* Mike Thewlis; *Vice-President,* Beverley Robertson; *Treasurer,* Tom Rix; *Secretary,* Chris Bond, 2 Mansfield Place, Isla Road, Perth PH2 7HS.

Chris Bond.

Glasgow Section:- The Section remains in good health with seven new members, including four women members, admitted during the year bringing the total to 92 of whom 19 are life members.

Activity during the last year has centred around the tried-and-tested formula of fortnightly weekend meets, together with monthly pub meets. Innovations which have been introduced this year are occasional curry (or other meal) evenings and informal slide shows.

A total of 24 outdoor meets were organised during 1997. The choice of venue for meets closely followed that of previous years. Average attendance at meets increased with a particularly successful meet in Mull for Niel Craig and Davie MacDonald's last Munro, where the weather was brilliant and the 'sand bagging' contingent was well pleased by the beaches visited. In fact, two other Club members finished their Munros the following two weekends, also in Mull, but with much poorer weather.

The 1997 winter season had never really got going. The now familiar cold spell over Christmas, with almost no snow about, was followed by a month of warmer weather with no prospect of true winter conditions. Better conditions returned in February for the CIC meet but the Milehouse meet in early March was a washout with large areas of Strathspey flooded. The early summer meet to Mill Cottage once again provided an opportunity for rock climbing but poor weather during much of May meant that this was not built upon.

Most of the summer and the autumn proved to be remarkably dry, although, as ever, what rain there was seemed to fall at weekends and on top of members out in the hills. One notable summer activity was the JMCS's first 'Yacht Meet': a two-week Hebridean adventure to St. Kilda. The first week of stormy weather and rough seas was replaced for the second by clear blue skies and light winds leading to much swimming, sunbathing and general enjoyment of the Hebrides at their best.

The overseas activities of Members this year included visits to France, Spain, Switzerland, New Zealand, Canada and the US which were visited with varied ambitions but with much success being reported.

The dinner, at the Four Season's Bistro, Inchree, was well attended and our Honorary Member, Alan Thrippleton, provided a very interesting speech in which he entertainingly detailed the events leading to the establishment of the Section hut at Coruisk.

At the AGM in November the following officials were elected: *Hon. Member,* Alan Thrippleton; *Hon. President,* Niel Craig; *Hon. Vice-President,* Ian Thomson; *President,* Alasdair Reid; *Vice-President,* David Lawson; *Secretary,* Donald Ballance, 1/R 11 Airlie Street, Hyndland, Glasgow, G12 8QQ, (Tel: 0141 357 3073, email: D.Ballance@mech.gla.ac.uk); *Treasurer,* Andrew Sommerville; *Coruisk Hut Booking Secretary,* Sandy Donald, 15 Smeaton Avenue, Torrance, Stirlingshire, G64 4BG, (Tel: 01360 622541); *Coruisk Hut Maintenance Organiser,* Alex Haddow; *Committee Members,* Dave Eaton, Mark Evans, Hilary Groom, Stevie Hazlett, Ann MacDonald, Scott Stewart, Benny Swan.

Donald Ballance.

Edinburgh Section:– The highlight of the Club year was undoubtedly the celebration of the 25th anniversary of the Smiddy, one of the club's cherished huts, which was discovered in 1966 and opened in 1972. The event (which was coupled to the AGM, the Dinner and, yes, a ceilidh for the occasion) was a real blast from the past; many of the members who worked so hard to make it what it is today, made their way up to Dundonnell.

Those of you who have been around long enough may remember that the Smiddy won the very first award given by the Association for the Protection of Rural Scotland, against fierce opposition. In 1997, the club was given an award again, this time a generous grant from the Scottish Mountaineering Trust for refurbishment of the Smiddy, which was gratefully accepted. So who knows, we might even get a microwave! Thanks to the continuing dedication of both hut custodians and the enthusiasm of the work parties, the huts continue to be a popular base for members and other parties alike.

The club stuck to its tradition of meeting on Wednesday nights, which seemed to get more popular all the time. The summer evening meets took place on various Lowland outcrops and, light and midge permitting, ranged farther afield from the Northumberland outcrops to Dunkeld. Weekend meets were held approximately every second weekend, at the club's huts in Newtonmore and Dundonnell, as well as other (wild) campsites and huts. A number of members explored the awesome sea cliffs of the Outer Hebrides, the wiser ones took their kit abroad – to those sunny crags in France, Norway, US, Spain and New Zealand.

Membership of the club started the year with 80 members and has been fortified during the year with about five keen and capable new members, while quite a few prospective members are tramping through the door regularly. The Club nearly lost two members, who managed to survived an epic in Coire-an-t-Sneachda, where one of the pair survived a rather rapid descent through a cornice while the other had to make her way down through whiteout conditions.

Officials elected: *President,* Nick Cruden; *Vice-president,* Beryl Leatherland; *Treasurer,* Charles Stupart; *Secretary,* Frederike van Wijck; *Newletter/Website Editor,* Chris Eilbeck; *Meets Secretary,* Euan Scott; *Smiddy Custodian,* Fraser Fotheringham, Tigh Na Sith, Braes, Ullapool. Tel: 01854-612 354; *Jock's Spot Custodian,* Alistair Borthwick, 2 Aytoun Grove, Dunfermline, Fife. Tel: 01383-732 232; *Other Committee Members,* Euan Scott, Beryl Leatherland, Stuart Buchanan, Douglas Hall; *Honorary Committee Members,* John Fowler, Alan Smith.

Information about the club may be obtained from the Secretary: 21 Spottiswoode Road, Edinburgh EH9 1BJ. Tel: 0131 447 8162, also on email: F.vanWijck@shore.qmced.ac.uk, via the Web: http://www.ma.hw.ac.uk/jmcs/

F. van Wijck.

SMC AND JMCS ABROAD

Greenland

COLWYN JONES reports:– The SMC Staunings Alps, East Greenland, Expedition 1996, Colwyn Jones (leader), Ian Angell, John Bickerdike, Gordon and Susan McKenzie, Jonathan Preston, Stephen Reid and Brian Shackleton.

The Majestic Central Staunings Alps of Scoresby Land in North East Greenland, between 72°N to 72°30' N and 24° to 26°W, were the target for our successful three-week climbing expedition.

The expedition members assembled at Glasgow Airport on July 22 and flew by scheduled airline, to Akureyri on the Northern coast of Iceland. After an overnight stop a chartered ski-equipped Twin Otter flew us north across the iceberg-studded Denmark Straits to Greenland. The first stop was the gravel airstrip on the Hurry Fjord serving Scoresbysund, called Constable Point (Nerlerit Inaat). A flight of two and a quarter hours

At Constable Point 250kg of freighted equipment, food and fuel was collected. The Twin Otter then continued north to the Central Staunings Alps where the clear weather and good snow conditions allowed an exciting landing on the Gully Glacier, within a kilometre of the top of Col Major, in the early afternoon. We had left Scotland 26 hours earlier and spent less than seven hours flying. This was the first time an aircraft has been recorded as landing in this area. The aircraft GPS altitude was 6700ft or 2040m.

After establishing camp a nearby peak was ascended by everyone and was named Susan's Peak (PD-, 2238m). The Peak is south of the descent gully called Col Major, which gives access to the upper Bersaerkerbrae glacier and is connected by a short ridge to Shirley's Peak. The first ascent of Shirley's Peak was made by an SMC party in 1994.

On July 24 four members ascended the most north eastern of four rock peaks on the continuation of the South West Ridge of Dansketinde. The Ridge was named Dodornryggen (Dead eagle ridge) as it bore a resemblance to a dead eagle lying on it's back. A party of two made the ascent by forking right in a snow gully named the Jones/Bickerdike couloir which delineated the body and left wing of the deceased raptor. Thereafter rocks were climbed to the awkward summit ridge. The peak was named Aliertinde after Ali(son) and (Rob)ert Bickerdike (AD+, 2580m).

The second party reached a snow col between Dodornryggen and the start of the South West ridge of Dansketinde. This col was ironically christened Col Wyn. A rock peak on the Dansketinde (north east) side of the col was ascended and named after (Ja)ck and (Al)ex Reid; Jaalspids. The second party then climbed directly from the col to the summit of Aliertinde and both parties descended by this route (AD-). The West Ridge of Lambeth was attempted but poor snow conditions forced a retreat.

Two members of the expedition experienced nausea and vomiting on the first day. Both members had recovered sufficiently to climb the next day and the likely diagnosis was mild altitude sickness coupled with dehydration.

Overnight on July 26 there was 5cm of snow. Camp was struck and an attempt was made to descend the Gully Glacier. Despite absolute calm the weather worsened to a whiteout, the move was abandoned and camp was re-established. The ridge from Susan's to Shirley's peak (PD+) was later climbed by Angell and Bickerdike.

Brian Robertson and the Squirrels at work on Birnam Quarry 1970. Photo: Robin Campbell.

Next day a party of four ascended the larger snow gully on the other side (south) of the body of the dead eagle. This more Westerly gully was called the Reid/Preston couloir.

Annsketinde – *North East ridge of Annsketinde (2460m, D) via Reid/Preston Couloir.*

Despite my back-to-front balaclava the early morning sun blazed off the snow and prevented me from returning to the arms of Morpheus. John was snoring again. Cheynes/Stokes breathing apparently – he breathed deeper (and noisier) until he suddenly stopped completely. This was bliss until my medical training took over and I started wondering if I should try and resuscitate him. Then with a groan and a snore he would stumble back to the world of the living. I rather brusquely got up.

It had been the coldest night so far, -7°, but it was a perfect day. Clear and still with an azure sky framing compact granite and glinting ice. The MSR was soon purring and I carved out a chair to sit on and provide snow for melting. Stephen was already about, busy in the middle of his white fitted kitchen, complete with breakfast bar. We passed steaming mugs to our respective tent-fellows with coarse suggestions that they should get up before they, and the snow, got too soft.

The 24-hour daylight favoured a leisurely start and as we readied ourselves Susan, Gordon, Brian and Ian left to attempt the highest peak in the range - Dansketinde. Shortly afterwards we skied off in a more westerly direction, back to the Dodornryggen. Stephen and Jonathan were ahead and we followed them up the Reid/Preston couloir, torn between the choice of breaking trail and getting first choice of the two unclimbed peaks ahead, or conserving energy at the back. In reality we couldn't catch them anyway.

At the breche on the Dodornryggen proper they opted for the northerly peak. The summit was a perfect triangle of rock and I had suggested we call it the Dead Eagle Beak Peak, no one had seemed very keen.

The peak to the south west was a long, complex, uninviting ridge. I led off the snow and climbed some rotten choss, before reaching solid rock on the ridge proper, where a tower blocked progress. I belayed as I couldn't see a way up and had no intention of going back down onto the broken rock to turn it. John came past to the foot of the tower, found a crack line on the left and was soon grinning on the top. Perhaps we would reach the summit after all. From there the ridge unfolded, never too hard, too loose or unprotected. Usually we climbed along the crest with short airy traverses on both faces of the ridge until we came to the summit block.

Abandoning plastic boots, we climbed lovely, warm, golden, granite in rock boots, up a well-protected corner/chimney to a notch, then a not-so-well protected arête, to finally pull onto the billiard table sized summit. The view was breathtaking and we could see the party on Dansketinde and Stephen and Jonathan descending from the Beak Peak. The ice-cap to the west, the shapely forms of Norsketinde and Bolvaerket, the jumble of the Gully glacier tumbling down to Alpe fjord and the smooth Bersaerkerbrae flowing down to Kong Oscars Fjord with its icebergs.

We built a small stoneman over a note left in a film container to mark the first ascent and abseiled back down to our gear using a blue sling. The return along the ridge was slow, as we relished the exposure and took the photos we had been too nervous to stop for on the ascent.

Back at the breche we decided to climb the Beak Peak. Two lovely pinnacles of solid rock, plenty of holds and gear in a beautiful, isolated place. There was a cairn

Mark Garthwaite on 'The Silk Purse', Upper Cave Crag, Craig a' Barns, Dunkeld. Photo: Neil Gresham.

on top which didn't look new and on return to the UK we found it had been climbed by another route and named Tårnet (The Tower) two months' earlier by a Norwegian ski-mountaineering expedition.

We found an abseil sling at the top of the Reid/Preston couloir which explained our companions fast departure. So gratefully clipping in to it, I nearly slipped off the end of the rope. At last I found the next sling about 6m below and remembered Stephen was using 60m ropes. A couple of abseils later we crossed the bergschrund and were soon skiing back to camp.

The peak took some time to name and after Stephen suggested Annsketinde after Ann MacDonald, the partner of one of the first ascensionists, no one could argue. Dansketinde had been climbed by the party of four via the original east col route and included Susan MacKenzie – the first woman to ascend the highest peak in the Staunings Alps.

Next day a party of two ascended the long unclimbed North West ridge of Dansketinde (TD), the highest peak in the Staunings Alps (aneroid height 2870m). After crossing Col Wyn they ascended a steep 500m couloir (Preston/Reid Couloir) to the ridge.

Dansketinde – The North-west Ridge

STEPHEN REID reports:– At 3.30a.m. I poked my nose gingerly out through the rime-covered tent door and surveyed the scene. Crystal clear, Dansketinde stood outlined against a cobalt sky, the golden granite of its South Ridge an open invitation to sticky rubber and a rackful of Friends. The snow of its glaciers looked crisp and firm too, enticing forth the cramponed boot. But, already in a few days, we had learned not to trust the fickle weather. Calm conditions in the morning could turn to blizzards by mid-afternoon, and then just as quickly become still again, leaving rock faces plastered with snow. No-one fancied being stuck high on a long and technically difficult ridge in such conditions, and while we all had prevaricated in the name of common sense, the weather had grown more unsettled.

The South-west Ridge looked more assailable, until, that is, one studied it with binoculars and examined closely a gendarme the size of the Eiffel Tower. Then it too became over-daunting eliciting endless 'will it, won't it' conversations. So, instead, we had climbed three of the peaks that formed the continuation of this ridge and thus gained a view round the corner to the north where Jonathan Preston claimed to have seen an easier option, the North-west Ridge. I was not so sure how much easier it would be but we were unlikely to have another chance to find out. I prodded him into wakefulness and we had a hurried breakfast.

Skis swished swiftly over frozen crust as we descended a few hundred feet from base camp to a snow bowl at the division of two glaciers. If all went well, our descent would be by the right-hand one while our present path lay to the left. We left our skis and crunched onwards to a small col, a nick in the ridge ahead.

Thus far, all was explored ground, and the going simple. We had christened this col, Col Wyn, in honour of our esteemed leader only two days' earlier and also made the first ascents of the peaks on either side of it. Now we were descending into *terra incognita* - in fact we suspected no-one had ever crossed this col or stepped on the glacier beyond before.

The west side of Col Wyn was considerably more impressive than the east. The ground was steeper and comprised of 50° hard ice and shattered rock. One could opt either for an abseil descent from a succession of disintegrating rock pinnacles straight down a nasty looking couloir that steepened rapidly out of view, or for a long traverse on icefields that might, or might not, lead more directly to our distant goal. Jonathan favoured the latter and settled the issue by setting off directly. I followed on, finding it to be the type of mountaineering I most dreaded, rock hard, easy-angled ice. The sort of teetery, awkward climbing that always sets my calves aching, my axes skittering and my nerves jangling. I confessed as much to Jonathan who quite rightly told me to stop being so negative and get on with it. There was really no reply to this except to grit my teeth and run the rope out diagonally downwards for four pitches until a single abseil and a short down climb dropped us over the bergschrund and onto the glacier.

Our route to the start of the ridge lay up a wide couloir with several branches at the top, the left hand of which appeared the best option. It all looked straightforward enough, but one of us had to go first, and I could see no good reason for risking life and limb when I had a newly-qualified Mountain Guide with me. So Jonathan set off up the couloir leaving a token ice screw every 50m or so just to keep me happy. The only hitch occurred at about the halfway point when our strange expedition diet began to do odd things to my stomach. Squares of tissue paper, floating skywards in the updraft, accompanied me for much of the rest of the pitch.

Near the top, hard ice gave way to easier snow and the cornice, though of Kilnsey Overhang proportions above the central section of the couloir, dwindled to nothing on the extreme left. We accordingly exited leftwards and took a well-earned breather to survey our first view of the Vikingbrae, mysterious and dark through gathering clouds. On our left a broken ridge of snowy high ground extended westwards towards Norsketinde. It was peppered with summits and pinnacles, three of which seemed significant and were unlikely to have been climbed. A short jaunt along the ridge and they could have been ours. But our hopes lay in the opposite direction and we turned to the task in hand and the traversing of the cornice. Jonathan stepped cautiously ahead caught between the Scylla of north-facing avalanche prone slopes on the one hand and the Charybdis of a honeycombed cornice on the other. There was a muffled gasp as, poking tentatively at the snow in front of him, his axe thrust through into space and revealed a large hole giving a fine view down the 500m couloir up which we had just ascended. A hurried detour in favour of Scylla brought him quickly to solid rock at the base of the North-west Ridge where I joined him. It had taken us eight hours to reach this point from base camp.

Sensing easy ground, I took over the lead and we moved together for half-a-dozen pitches up mixed terrain and snow slopes that by-passed initial gendarmes on the left but soon forced us towards a very obvious nick in the crest of the ridge at the foot of a huge and seemingly unassailable pinnacle. So daunting was this megalith, that initially we had tried to outflank it to the north but quickly retreated from the rotten rock and bald snowy slabs that confronted us. So I was pleased to discover, on eventually reaching the breche that things now looked easier than they had seemed from below. Crampons were removed and Jonathan led through, up an easy groove and over the most unlikely looking overhang at surprisingly little more than Severe.

Ahead was an even more impressive gendarme. The left flank looked impossible, a direct attack improbable, but rightwards a tricky traverse on dubious flakes and shattered grey blocks led me to a comfortable flake belay on a snow ledge and a fine view to the south-west of the endless grey Gletscher and a tantalising glimpse of the distant Greenland Icecap. A corner looked obvious, but a chimney to its left proved easier and took Jonathan back to the crest and a belay in the bowels of a monstrous gendarme. My pitch took us to its summit and a regaining of the crest which was followed for several more rope lengths.

None of these pitches were easy, all involved bypassing gigantic gendarmes, and yet the view ahead showed yet more gendarmes, each one more impressive than the last, and no end to them in sight. What is more, the bell clear skies of the morning were now half masked by fleeting wraiths of mist that boded snow, wind and other evils and hid from view what lay ahead – though we suspected further gendarmes. Perhaps we had bitten off more than we could chew? Perhaps we should turn back? And yet the climbing so far, on coarse golden granite, had been of no great technical difficulty. Anyway, retreat was unthinkable; carrying on, the lure of the unknown, beyond the next gendarme, was far too exciting!

The 10th pitch, or thereabouts, and Jonathan's turn. He took the obvious shelf on the left of the umpteenth gendarme ahead, but eventually, stuck on a sloping mush covered shelf. After a while he returned, offering to swap places. But from my vantage point some 10m back I had spotted the non-obvious line to the right (as they should say in guidebooks) that he had failed to see through being too close. Now, like an air traffic controller landing a fog-bound plane, I talked him through it. Up a flake the size of that on the Central Buttress of Scafell and then down it's other side. Then hand over hand down a jug ladder on an impending wall, feet feeling blind for hidden holds, until a roof on the right could be undercome by a sudden swing on the rope and a lunge for holds on the rib beyond. Thankfully mine bergen-führer found a stance immediately and protected his faithful second with a top rope on the pendulum – teamwork at its best.

Leading through, I found myself in an area of loose blocks and poised pinnacles and sought sanctuary in a rotten chimney. Common-sense forced me to leave it immediately for a more solid wall on the right and a thin descending traverse ended in an icy corner. A few bridging moves regained the crest and a howling gale that almost pitched us from our holds and tore ragged fingers of mist from the gigantic tower that confronted us, the biggest of any so far. Its right-hand side was perpendicular and smooth, plummeting into swirling nothingness, but up and right a broken cavity stretched to God knows where. Jonathan clambered up to a stance at its entrance. There was no other choice.

My final lead and again the rock was rotten - only two bad pitches on the climb and both of them mine. Great teetering flaky piles and ground granite mush. I distributed my weight like a spider and tried to be careful. If only I wasn't so tired, or so cold, or so hungry . . . Up to the right was a chimney but I could not reach it directly - everything I touched broke off in my hands. Instead I was forced downwards and traversed underneath it, tricky moves on ice coated holds. Runners were placed more for effect than through cause and a decent belay seemed but a forlorn hope. Then at last I reached a snow ledge and a single but solid, welcoming flake: there was no rope left to take in.

From the stance, Jonathan made the chimney in two quick moves and thrutched onward into the murk. On following, I was amazed that he had managed to avoid precipitating any of the huge blocks that formed the only holds. All ended at a wind-swept breche where we could see, from what little we could see, that the difficulties were truly over. We abseiled quickly into the lee and donned crampons. The ridge stretched ahead, firstly mixed and then on rapidly-deepening snow, for by now it was snowing hard. Several isolated looming towers were easily by-passed on the left until a final one seemed more prominent than the rest. Could it be the summit? We ploughed up steep snow and climbed it just in case, but there was no sign that it was – surely there should be a cairn. But if this was not the summit, then what was and where was it? Looking back, the cloud parted for a second and golden shafts of Arctic midnight sun pierced the gloom and warmed our hearts. Then the gap closed and we were enveloped in dusk again.

We took compass bearings and discussed the matter but our befuddled brains could not cope with a magnetic variation of anywhere between 30° and 45°. Ahead I felt that I might have glimpsed a soaring snow arête, but did it go up, or down? East or south? Whatever, it was the only recognisable feature and I duly struck out along it, keeping as near as I dared to its corniced edge as every step to the other side released worrying little avalanches of powder slab. Ahead, in the whiteout, a shadow lay across our path. I approached it tentatively, fearing it was a crevasse or the edge of a broken cornice. At only a few inches distance, it suddenly resolved itself into a footprint, a trace left by Angell, Shackleton and the McKenzies from the day before. Twenty steps or so farther and we were joyfully shaking hands at the true summit. It was 1a.m.

Little needs to be said of our return journey via the Original Route except that it was steeper than we would have liked and that the route-finding would have been a deal harder without the footsteps of the previous day's party to follow. Visibility got progressively worse as we descended, and this coupled with the gradual receding of obvious features as the couloir flattened out into glacier meant that we were more than a little astonished to happen on our skis where we had left them, standing upright in the snow like Narnian lamp posts shining forth a friendly light.

Gratefully, we skinned back the last few hundred yards to camp, arriving at 4 a.m., exactly 24 hours after we had left, and collapsed into our sleeping bags where my restless soul still seemed to hear a bitter snow-laden wind that smarted my face and roared in my ears. I drew my hood up tighter and snuggled in more deeply, a little warmer for the knowledge that we had 'done our bit'. And what a 'bit' it had been.

A snowfall of 150mm overnight led to a day (July 29) of rest and recuperation. An attempt to descend the Gully glacier revealed a badly-crevassed icefall which proved impassable to the lightly equipped party.

On July 30, a party of two ascended the unclimbed South Ridge of Hjornespids (TD+, 2860m). Another two reached the same summit by the col between Hjornespids and Dansketinde (D). During the descent a huge avalanche was triggered on the North Face as the party of four descended the slopes of Hjornespids to the col.

The South Ridge of Hjornespids

COLWYN JONES and JOHN BICKERDIKE report:– The cloud was hanging down in the valley as John and I skinned slowly in the tracks left by Ian and Brian earlier that morning. Hjornespids was the target and we had procrastinated over breakfast again, avoiding the need to break trail. We reached the ski dump, and crossing the big crevasse which splits the glacier basin between Dansketinde and Hjornespids, set off up to the connecting ridge. The early morning sun prompted us to stop and take some photos, and while studying the south side of the peak, I suggested we approach the summit directly. We had taken only one rope but felt we could easily traverse onto the main ridge if we got into difficulty.

The bergschrund was quickly crossed and we started up a steep ice gully (Pearly Gates gully) to the west of the ridge. We stopped to put the rope on as the ice was hard but continued moving together for 1000ft until we reached a snow crest between two obvious towers like gate posts of a stately home. These we christened the 'Pearly Gates'.

From the breche we climbed up a chossy mixed gully to gain the ridge proper and crossed onto the face beyond. A vague groove line was followed for three pitches to a small snow gully then a small overhanging corner was turned on the left. Far below the cloud seemed to be thickening but retreat from here was problematic. A further three steepening pitches lead to below an imposing steep wall. It looked impossible apart from a thin traverse line 10ft up which traversed round the right edge of the wall to a 15ft detached flake with a 'thank God' jammed block. I seconded the pitch on a tight rope with both rucksacks and had to agree with John that a technical grade of 5b was appropriate. From the wide ledge we were belayed on, I moved right again, with only one sack, up a short snow gully and an ice choked chimney to the crest proper.

Above was a steep thin corner to the left and a shorter but overhanging crack line, which we avoided by moving up and traversing rightwards round the corner, into a short V-groove. This was climbed and exited to the left to arrive at a big ledge above the steep alternatives. From there a climb up a pleasant 12ft crack and a move left onto a large platform just below the summit block, led us to the top.

We had imagined a simple walk off the north side of the peak and were dismayed to see a long complex ridge leading to the snow beyond. As we sat wondering how long the descent would take, footprints around the base of one of the gendarmes were seen and a few minutes later Brian appeared and hailed us from the distance.

We spent the time taking photos and looking for the orange nylon scarf allegedly left by the first ascenders to mark their success (ACJ 1961). There was no sign of any gear left on their retreat from the summit down the south ridge where we had ascended. The big disappointment, however, was that another fashion victim must have beaten me to the genuine Slesser orange nylon scarf.

Ian and Brian arrived directly and after congratulations and photos all round we returned, not without incident, following their footsteps. I slipped and fell while traversing across the top of the North-west Face and although slowing courtesy of an ice-axe arrest, was happy when an ashen-faced John held my slide. A few minutes later while now leading, John shouted that cracks had just appeared in the snow. Then, the whole north face avalanched just below his feet. A 1m crown wall was a sobering feature just below the crest as we delicately continued back to camp.

Next day, July 31, Lambeth (2450m) was ascended by the North Ridge. A prominent pinnacle on the ridge was climbed by Stephen Reid and Brian Shackleton and named after Jilly Reid; Point Jilly.

On the same day a party of three, Bickerdike, Jones and Preston, left camp at 1900 hours to ascend Dansketinde by the 'Tourist Route'. The summit was reached after midnight and it was confirmed the sun never dips below the horizon. It was a perfectly still night. All eight expedition members had now reached the summit of Dansketinde. Poor weather prompted a descent to climb lower down the Bersaerkerbrae but agonisingly slow progress was made from August 1-5. The descent of Col Major in soft snow and a large bergschrund took 14 hours. Then roped together we skied as two parties of four in very poor visibility to the main icefall on Bersaerkerbrae where fixed ropes were needed.

It brightened on the 5th and with the better visibility a fine view into the Skel valley and down to the coast of Kong Oscars fjord appeared. We crossed onto the lateral (south) moraine of the glacier and established camp in the Skel valley after ferrying many loads.

Sadly, there was plenty of evidence of previous expeditions. Plastic sleds, tin cans, broken survey poles and tattered lengths of tape measure, heralded our return to 'civilisation.' The sun did come out in the evening and mosquitoes appeared.

August 6 saw an early-morning wade over the Skel River. Ferrying loads over to a camp on the Gefion Pass on our returning for a second load in the afternoon the river was at least a metre higher. Next day, the sun shone and a lone Musk Ox circled the camp before fleeing the paparazzi attention. We continued down to the Washburn Hut above Mestersvig. Some ferried, others carried huge single loads.

Next day, we arrived in Mestersvig to have our papers checked by Danish Military personnel but returned to stay in the Washburn Hut overnight. There was mild excitement as a polar bear had been spotted two days earlier and as it was overcast, and the return flight was cancelled, we went on a bear shoot, with cameras of course. There was a storm overnight with snow down to 200m. A Fairchild Metroliner collected us at 12.30 (midday) but it was a disappointing flight with low cloud all the way to Akureyri, and we returned to Glasgow on August 12.

With thanks to The Scottish Mountaineering Trust, Foundation for Sport and the Arts, The Mount Everest Foundation and the Mountaineering Council of Scotland for their financial support.

Australasia

JOHN STEELE reports:- Last December, John Steele and Barbara Gibbons made a return trip to the Mount Cook region of South Island, New Zealand.

The first week was spent watching the snow fall, but ascents were made of Mount Ollivier (1900m), Mount Kitchener (c 2000m) and Mount Annette (2200m) all from the Mueller Hut, which is sited on an exposed ridge above the Mueller Glacier. The second week was spent watching the snow melt in high summer temperatures, during which ascents were made of Baker Saddle (c 2200m), Mount Sturdee (2700m) and Nazomi (c 2800m) all from the Gardiner Hut, sited on a precarious rock dome under the west ridge of Mount Cook. The third week involved the inevitable long wait for Cook to clear and the wind to drop, however the prospect of soothing tired limbs in natural hot springs, swimming with seals and dolphins in the ocean and going on a whale-watch eventually won the day and caused us to move north and quit the high mountains.

Notes: In Mount Aspiring park, a new hut has reportedly been constructed close to the old Colin Todd Hut at the foot of the mountain's North-west (Shipowner) Ridge. A quick descent can be effected from the low point on this ridge (opposite the top of the Ramp) by two tricky abseils onto the Therma Glacier to the north.

In Mount Cook park, the normal severe conditions are taking their toll. The Beetham Hut, located halfway up the Tasman Glacier, has been destroyed by avalanche and is not being replaced. Access to Malte Brune etc. is now either by camping or bivvy. The path to the Hooker Hut has been destroyed by a massive washout and access is now by climbing a dangerous moraine wall direct from the glacier trench below the hut. The ancient Sefton bivvy has reportedly been condemned by the park authorities and the Copeland shelter has moved location nearer to the col. The daily hut rate is $NZ 18 and to fly into Mount Cook Hut is $NZ 100 plus. (For the good news see *SMCJ* 186 p 692).

Canada

SIMON RICHARDSON reports:– In August, Dave Hesleden and I made a two-week visit to the spectacular Coast Range mountains in British Columbia. A 500-mile drive, followed by a 20-minute helicopter flight saw us on Tiedemann Glacier within 24 hours of arriving in Vancouver.

The weather was unsettled, so we kicked off with a two-day ascent of the South-east Chimneys route on Mount Waddington (4019m). We then turned our attention to the unclimbed South Ridge of Mount Asperity (3716m) on the 1500m high Combatant-Tiedemann-Asperity wall. The South Ridge is made up of a series of towers divided by deep notches. We reached the summit on the morning of the third day after some tricky route-finding and 65 pitches of varied climbing on good granite and mixed ground. The weather was superb, so rather than risk a descent down the dangerous south-east couloir, we decided to traverse the Serra Peaks to reach the Upper Tellot Glacier.

The traverse began with the free-standing tower of Serra V (c.3600m), which is reputed to be the hardest summit in the range. We climbed a new mixed route on the North Face and made the fourth ascent of the peak. Our route then followed the line of the 1985 traverse of the major peaks of the range (Waddington-Combatant-Tiedemann-Asperity-Serras V to I). As expected, the abseils down the overhanging loose diorite on the east face of the Serra V into the IV-V notch were the technical crux of the traverse. We bivouacked that night below the summit block of Serra IV, continued along the complex mixed ridge to Serra III next morning, and descended the icy Serra II-III couloir to reach the Upper Tellot Glacier by mid afternoon. We arrived back at our tent on the Tiedemann Glacier that night, and concerned that the weather was about to break, we flew out next day. We spent the next few days sport climbing near Penticton before rounding off a memorable holiday with an ascent of the classic North-east Buttress on Mount Slesse in the Northern Cascades.

America

NIALL RITCHIE reports:– With Jon Taylor I spent the Easter fortnight in the desert areas of Red Rocks, Nevada and South California's Joshua Tree. With usually assured, warm to hot weather in spring, El Niño's presence meant unseasonal cold temperatures to begin with – giving snow down to tent level and a green desert beneath. Although not entirely welcome it was still possible for Scots to climb in this while locals retreated to warmer spots like Ceasar's Palace in the nearby surreal Las Vegas.

The superb sandstone walls at Red Rocks offer sport and traditional climbs of high quality from single pitch to big multi-pitch mountain routes. It is worth noting that in Vegas accommodation, food and drink are all at ridiculously cheap prices.

From Red Rocks – after a three-and-a-half-hour drive – it gets better and better at the even more surreal Joshua Tree with its Granite Wonderland of rocks which provide superb crack and face climbing in an exquisite setting. Other highlights were the colours of the wild desert flowers in bloom and the weird and fantastic rock formations that abound.

In between these two main climbing areas we squeezed a brief visit to Utah's Zion National Park. In the land where big is beautiful Zion's walls were no exception. Unfortunately, the A4s couldn't be attempted because the snowploughs were still out in the park clearing the roads!

Get across there – and as they say: 'Have a good one.'

TIM PETTIFER reports:– I made three overseas trips during 1997. The first in April, ski-touring in Austria and Italy with Robin Chalmers, my wife, and a close friend from Bavaria.

The second and the most interesting trip was a mountaineering venture to Turkey in June. Very easily and economically arranged, as a package holiday to Cavus, it opened up the Taurus mountains on the Mediterranean. In this area they rise to approximately 8250ft, and apart from the highest, they are largely unpathed. Useful maps of even the most popular mountains are hard to obtain and don't exist for the back country. Guide books cover only a small area of Turkey so you can choose a mountain because you like the look of it; figure out a route as far as you can see with binoculars, and hopefully, find your own way up to wherever the summit may be and then design your own cairn. The way all climbing should be.

Most of our routes involved steep scrambling over weathered limestone and we left the car at about 6am and got down by late afternoon. The rock-climbing potential is immense with all grades of routes from V. Diff. up to E Impossible and close to the road/tracks. There are long ridges there rising from sea level to 3000ft, not dissimilar to Tower Ridge.

You don't achieve as much as when climbing in an area with a comprehensive climbing guide. There are the inevitable *cul-de-sacs* and disappointments and going down if you are planning a circular route is often harder than going up. But above all else you will have truly climbed your 'own' mountain and you can have endless recriminating arguments as to what went wrong or right. The climate and vegetation are very like the Balearics but the mountains are far rougher. As in Majorca the family can enjoy the coast. Cavus and nearby Olympus are quiet, pleasant resorts with turtle beaches, boat trips to archaeological sites, islands and secluded beaches. Adventurous members with young families or non-climbing partners could achieve the impossible – do a new route, perhaps every day and still be on speaking terms in the evening. Valhalla!

The third trip was in October, again with Jan, and was a cycle trip across the Spanish Camino. This is an ancient pilgrim's route that crosses the north of Spain, east to west and traditionally used to finish at Cape Finisterre. Finisterre or Fisterre in Spanish, translate as 'The End of the World' so pilgrims were literally walking just as far as they possibly could as atonement. A most beautiful and historically interesting path, 500 miles long across plains, through delightful countryside and rising to 5500ft and 4400ft through the Galician mountains. Some 3000 to 6000 pilgrims walk this route during July and August and it is a lesson in environmental care that so many walk, cycle and horse ride the route with little impact on the villages, the physical nature of the path, the old refugios, or huts, along the way and maintain the very best of relations with the indigenous population.

Pyrenees

ADAM KASSYK reports:– I visited the Sierra del Cadi in the Spanish Pyrenees while on a family seaside holiday on the Costa Brava. The Sierra lies south east of Andorra and about two-and-a-half hours' drive north of Barcelona. With my brother, Andy, we climbed the North Buttress Diretissime (via Anglada-Guillamon) on the Pedraforca, 2491m. The area, and this climb, are described very briefly in the English language series of guidebooks to the Pyrenees. This 600m route was very fine, with sustained climbing in the lower part. We encountered climbing up to E2 standard, with some aid – despite the guidebook reference to a TD grade. The Pedraforca offers many other routes at a variety of grades, and the area as a whole appears to provide good climbing in a quiet and unspoiled mountain setting.

CASTLE RIDGE

JOHN MITCHELL

REVIEWS

The Duke of the Abruzzi - An Explorer's Life:– Mirella Tenderini and Michael Shandrick (Bâton Wicks, 1997, £17.99, ISBN 1 898573 38 1).

The Duke is best known for the eponymous ridge on K2, and most of us might have some vague recollection of a huge expedition way back in 1909. (Eight Italian 'amateurs', four guides and 150 porters to carry five tons of equipment to be more precise.) We might also have some impression of an aristocratic thrill-seeker being cosseted along by guides and porters. This would be to do Luigi di Savoia a grave injustice, as this book makes clear. He was a more than competent mountaineer who was well used to hardship and who left parts of his fingers north of the 80th parallel.

The House of Savoy provided kings of Italy and, very briefly, Spain. Luigi was not directly in the line of succession (although his father was King of Spain for two years) but lived in a culture in which he was severely constrained by the expectations of his family and public opinion of the time. Part of the interest of this book is that it shows the way in which, even then, the 'media' could help screw up people's lives. The book fails to bring him alive as a person, although, the facts make it clear that he must have been an interesting character to know. This may not be the fault of the authors but more a result of the milieu in which he had to live.

The facts are interesting enough. It is obvious that his membership of the CAI and the Alpine Club were not merely gestures to his position. When Mummery decided to make his second ascent of the Zmutt Ridge, (25 years after the first), he was accompanied by Norman Collie and Luigi de Savoia, who was 21 at the time. By this age he had already made a number of difficult (guided) ascents in the Alps and was intending to attempt the Zmutt when he met Mummery who thought highly enough of him to invite him along.

The Duke is best known for his exploration and mountaineering. The arduous first ascent of Mt. St. Elias in Alaska after five previous expeditions had failed seems to have given him a taste for discomfort for it was followed by an abortive attempt to reach the North Pole (which involved the aforementioned loss of parts of his fingers). A thorough exploration of the Ruwenzori mountains gave him experience of a different set of discomforts. His last big mountain expedition was to K2 in 1909. Thereafter, his naval career and war intervened. The Italian drive for colonies took him to Somaliland where he again managed to do some exploration. He founded a farm settlement for Somalis and eventually lived there until his death.

This book is not primarily a mountaineering book, but as a portrait of a complex and able man it manages to be both interesting and frustrating. The life of the Duke of Abruzzi is there but Luigi di Savoia, the man, is only briefly glimpsed. One is left with the impression of a man who was the victim of his station in life. Being a member of a Royal family could have its drawbacks even then.

Bob Richardson.

Classic Rock - Great British Rock Climbs:– Compiled by Ken Wilson (Bâton Wicks. 1997, 256pp, £19.99. 130+ photographs, crag diagrams. ISBN 1 898573 11 5).

The first edition of this milestone in climbing history was in 1978, and it marked a personal pleasure for this reviewer too, as he wrote, and photographed, one of its 80 routes - The Chasm on Buachaille Etive Mor, Glen Coe (or Glencoe, as the Glen was then called). Looking back at the review of it in the 1979 SMCJ is cause for some angst however, as it was not only written by a friend and climbing partner (who indeed suffered for the art in The Chasm), but it was also given what could only, even with charity, be called a harsh and even heartless review. And don't even think that I'm in Wilson's pocket. I'll fax this review to him tomorrow (he hates e-mail) and he'll phone me up the same night and spoil my herb tea with a breathless and ear-dinning critique of my critique.

So how does it compare with the first edition, and what do I think of both? Remaining dispassionate, and despite my youthful input, I always found in the book much inspiration. It provided a warm glow, in the sense that I felt I could climb any of its routes (unlike *Hard Rock,* with its granny-stoppers). The routes I had climbed could also be re-climbed through another's eyes, often with rosy specs on. The writing, of course, was as widespread in quality as the routes themselves. The Long Climb (not the longest climb in the country, despite the gush) is, I feel, not worth half the praise it receives. Two-and-a-half good pitches out of its 1400ft is hardly an objective rationale for excellence, while Clachaig Gully, despite several fun ascents, still gives me arrhythmia at it's recollection. The vivid memory of a head-sized rock whirring past with my name on it, dislodged by a clumsy soloist above, is a cooling thought. The lush Spring flowers would have made a handy wreath.

One obvious test of the book is to ask whether, after an interval of some 19 years, the routes stand the test of time. Would you still want to climb them? Yes, mostly, The Long Climb excepted. Time has changed some factors of course. On the Cuillin Ridge you may well get run over by other parties, while approaching Ardverikie Wall you will definitely get run over by gleaming mountain bikes. But time has changed other factors, and in these cases the book is partly deficient. I pulled out my first edition (pristine dust-wrapper, nice photo) and set it against the current book (pristine dust-wrapper, even nicer photo).

It is not an exact facsimile, as it has been added to with a *Historical Commentary. The Preface* too, has an appended note, in which Wilson worries over the current trend to upgrade routes. He at least acknowledges that four of the Scottish routes upgraded since 1978 (The Chasm, The Long Climb, Clean Sweep, and Ardgarten Arête - all Severe to VS - corrected bizarre local anomalies), but states that the bulk of the other 26 upgraded routes, out of a total of 80 routes in the book, represents something to be worried about. It may be that many of these route grades are not actually experiencing a natural upward progression, but are instead, showing the cushion effect, whereby pressure from above, squeezing the grades ever closer, work down so as to have an osmotic effect on the easier routes.

Another Wilsonian worry is the death of climbing rock in big boots. He's right that it is a dying art - we did Red Slab on the Rannoch Wall in big boots at the same period as we were posing in The Chasm (also in big boots, see p.50 *et seq.*) But not all rock climbers go on to the Alps, and even there rock boots are much more widespread anyway. But then Red Slab was supposed to be a Severe then and it is now a VS. Ignorance is bliss, if you get away with it.

So differences? Photographs first. The dust-wrapper has a different shot, one which ironically has a climber wearing the old EBs. Many of the old, grisly black-and-whites remain just that – grisly (e.g. John Mackenzie in The Crypt – the photograph that is, not John), while many have been improved. I am unaware as to the techniques used; scanning or reprinting, but the contrast of many in the first edition, often too high, has been reduced, e.g. the big shot of Tower Ridge on pp.30-

31, the traverse on Sou'Wester Slabs on p.91. This allows more details of the cliff or route to filter out. Some of the colour shots are either new, such as the excellent telephoto looking up The South Ridge (p.89), or again have been improved to some extent. The full-page colour shot of the Buachaille for example (p.44), no longer has its awful green cast, redolent of many a Sunday morning under the Glen Coe clouds after too good a Saturday evening. It now sports a reddish cast, closer to the rhyolite I daresay, and definitely an improvement.

At first look I was irritated that all references to guidebooks were as in the first edition. By all means keep these references, but I feel that the current guidebooks, over which the SMC, to name only one club publisher, has sweated long and hard, should also receive a more prominent mention, with each route, and not be tucked away in a tiny note later in the book. As I said before, it is not a true facsimile, so why not make it more functional with this small, but important, point?

It is understandable that Wilson, to keep costs down, does not seem to have gone round the scene asking for new photographs of the routes. Even a score of updated colour shots might have made a huge difference in its visual appeal. I would, as no doubt Wilson was, have been sorely tempted to chuck out the dozen or so shots that were not worth keeping, and commissioning replacements.

It is a better book for the tinkerings however, and one that should still inspire the silent minority who don't climb E-something. I'll keep on taking the vitamins, meanwhile, and stay up late waiting for the phone call. And I know who gave Wilson my number. The lads will be around.

Ken Crocket.

Escape Routes:– Further adventure writings of David Roberts. (Cordee Books, 1997, pp267, £15.95. ISBN 0 89886 509 3).

Nearly 300 pages in hardback written in essay format without illustration may at first glance be a bit off-putting but the cover of this wonderful collection gives us the clue to the quality of writing which lies within. A lone figure, the author? You? Me? Silhouetted in the doorway of a mountain hut looking out onto snow-clad mountains and blue sky. This is the 'escape route'. It is one that all of us with a love of the mountains and adventure know well and the same feelings of escape apply whether the tunnel mouth gives out, as in this case, onto the Coast Range of British Columbia or onto the ice-draped cliffs of Ben Nevis or indeed to any number of places limited only by the power of our imagination.

The mark of a good essayist is that he does not leave his reader as a spectator, sitting on the bus as it were, but carries him along into the action and Roberts does this to perfection. Whether it be a bouldering picnic in 'Bleau' while taking in a brief history of Millet (the painter not the sac!), Rousseau and the Barbizon School: 'Venturing each day into the forest, I began to see Fontainbleau through the painters' eyes and to recover the wild revolutionary fervour with which their landscapes teem.'

Or cave exploration/archaeology in New Mexico: 'At 0815a.m. on the morning of a new day, I emerged from Lechuguilla after a push of 18 hours. As the sun touched my head and shoulders, I breathed in the smell of earth, and saw the green of the grass and the blue of the sky and I could not help whooping out loud wordless cries of self congratulation at my successful rebirth into the world.'

Roberts here lets you experience the mud, the fear, the claustrophobic enclosure of the caving experience and share his relief, buoyed by euphoria, when you complete the journey.

In this particular essay he broaches a theme to which he returns again and again, when he says of the Lechugilla cavers: 'They reminded me of the homey oddball ranks of climbers I had joined in the late 1950s, when I had first taken up mountaineering, an all but vanished breed now that climbing has become a trendy sport whose stars wear Day-Glo lycra and make good money endorsing everything from tents to lipstick.'

Now some may argue that this is just an old fogey's failure to embrace change, but I think in Roberts' writing this amounts to something more than a longing for some far-off youthful idyll. His arguments in *The Moab Treehouse* will doubtless upset some of the conservation lobby. When speaking of Moab, a small, but growing, town in the Canyonlands of Utah, he flags up some of the paradoxes that far too few conservationists are willing to acknowledge, never mind address.

'I observed that the most avid voices for keeping Moab small and pristine belonged to residents who had moved there relatively recently.'

While another long-time resident says: 'Some folks have found our treehouse. Now they want to pull the rope up.'

These are real debates relevant world-wide and Roberts, not known for pulling his punches, senses their climax: 'At it's most extreme, in the strictures of the eco-fanatics who would teach us never to step on a meadow or camp within sight of stream, to drink our own dishwater, to shit into plastic bags and pack them out, a germ of nihilistic misanthropy is at work. Rather than an arena for play, these watchdogs imply, the backcountry is such a deadly serious place that it can only be approached in a spirit of self expunging ascetisim. Only a short logical step leads from these strictures to their *reducito absurdum:* the best way to treat the wilderness is never to go there at all.'

Roberts has an impressive climbing record behind him, having led a total of 13 expeditions in Alaska including many major first ascents, but I get the feeling that now in his 50s he feels the need to diversify, to look for other *Escape Routes* whether it be mountain biking, caving, river-rafting and even, horror of horrors, golf! Although, it has to be said, two crisp three-iron shots off the summit of the Gamshag in the Austrian Tyrol were included in the itinerary which he relates with a wry humour in the essay *Wandergolf in the Tirol.*

There are many exciting, and indeed, dangerous moments included in this book but Roberts' philosophy with regard to danger, and one which is shared by the many and varied companions he will introduce you to, is well summed up in the prelude to the essay *Storming Iceland:*

> ***Who travels widely needs his wits about him,***
> ***The stupid should stay at home.'***

from *The Words of the High One,* a medieval Icelandic poem.

This is a book to read at home and one which will doubtless inspire the reader to find and explore his own escape routes and in the pen of David Roberts, you couldn't ask for a better companion.

Charlie Orr.

Into Thin Air – A personal account of the Everest disaster:– Jon Krakauer.
(Macmillan, 1997. £16.99, ISBN 0 333 69527 5).

I began by wondering if I would like a book which fed on a mountaineering disaster. Reacting to the bad Press our mountaineering scene gets in Britain, I almost hoped I wouldn't like it. Unfortunately, it was the opposite; I couldn't put it down, which shows how well written it is, mixing a dramatic tragedy tale with calculated analysis by an author who was immediately involved. The fact that we already know the outcome (hermits excepted) didn't seem to spoil the drama which, as in a Shakespearean tragedy, built up to an inevitable finale.

They say that knowing when to turn back is the ultimate mountaineering skill. Certainly the author, an experienced mountaineer himself as well as a client, centres his analysis on this point. The non-mountaineer, more interested in the story than the analysis, might just leave it as a simple mistake. But the mountaineer knows that it's not that simple (with just a nagging doubt that perhaps it is that simple), and the nearer you have been to a mountaineering accident, presumably having survived, in contrast to many of the players featured in this book, the more you can relate to the decisions made on Everest despite their grim outcome. And if you've climbed in the Himalayas, you'll know how there are always apparent reasons for turning back, and only by ignoring some of them do you ever achieve anything. And if you've ever guided clients, or perhaps if you've been guided, you'll understand the pressure to achieve a successful result, and that can lead to a slight influence on decisions which can, if you're unlucky, each add to the total picture, which suddenly a small unpredictable event can turn to disaster.

Turning to Scotland for a minute, you might think of a time when you were avalanched, all the clues that you ignored, possibly aware of them or possibly only in retrospect (because we never know what Rob Hall was thinking). And you know that in Scotland if you never leave the road unless the official avalanche risk is classified as 1 (safe), you'll live a long time but achieve almost nothing (except in August). So why didn't you pay attention to soft snow, spindrift and wind direction, or why didn't you dig a snow pit? Was it because the risk didn't occur to you, or was it that you were so keen to climb the route that you decided to chance it, and how deliberately did you decide to chance it? And were you a little bit unlucky?

But if you push your luck often enough, you're bound to be unlucky eventually. Was this the case on Everest? Jon Krakauer strongly argues not, at least for the Rob Hall expedition of which he was one of the few members who survived unscathed. Nor does he claim that the Himalayas, especially Everest, are safe. So he comes down largely on commercial pressure and rivalry, allied to unspoken client pressure, influencing Rob Hall's decision making, which was clearly flawed. And it's hard not to notice how seriously the friendly but still rival teams of Hall and Scott Fischer got in each other's way. Not literally, but the agreed co-operation (the best Sherpa from each group teaming to fix the Hillary Step ropes) failed and delayed the ascent.

It must be said that if the groups had been summiting on separate days, Rob Hall's team on its own would have failed and turned back, forcing the correct decision. But those delayed by slow rope-fixing were not the ones who died. It was those who later in the day used the fixed ropes to continue into a trap who died. Which leads to a crucial question. Does fixing rope for clients, which seems an obvious thing to do, lead to more safety as one would expect, or lead weaker clients into a trap? Obviously, it can do both, and the leader's decision as to their use is crucial. Here the decision was certainly flawed. Agreed you might have to push clients a bit, but how come the stronger clients turned back (with the exception of the author who was strong enough to reach the summit somewhat independently) while the weaker ones continued to be guided to the summit, and subsequently, no return for them and their guides?

The fierce criticism by Jon Krakauer of an incompetent Taiwanese team and a disruptive South African team sounds very justified and is good for the story but seems a minor factor in the accident. And the rather brutal analysis of the survivors' roles suggesting that some of them, particularly himself, failed to help enough seems unduly hard. So any analysis ends at the problem of the two rival teams climbing simultaneously and causing a dangerous competitive atmosphere.

In terms of my personal high altitude guiding, all my clients have returned in good condition, but the success rate is very low. What sort of a guide does that make me, good or bad? Depends on your priorities, and judging by the tunnel-driven attitude of some of the Everest clients, bad would be the answer. Or did they just have too much faith? Wandering farther off the point, whose fault is the high expectation of clients? Not only in the Himalayas, but in the Alps too. My observation of British guides is that they are much more amenable to the clients' wishes than my impression of many Continental guides. Both in terms of the difficulty of the route and the number of clients taken (i.e. price). But is this a compliment, or are safety margins being unwittingly trimmed to fit commercial pressures? Will we learn a painful lesson sometime? Who knows, but the British have done well so far. And will future expeditions to Everest learn the lessons of this ill-fated one? Is it possible to be safer and still have any chance of success?

So it's easy to blame the leader (or the pilot in an air crash, or the driver in a train crash). But no-one is immune to error. So perhaps it is the system that is at fault to put the leader in such an exposed position. In other words, don't relate guiding Everest with any safety. Maybe Rob Hall's high success rate had conned him into thinking he could? I won't be typing in 'Everest Guide' at the Job Centre. But whether you want to get involved in the analysis (like I obviously have) or just read the story, you'll find it as compelling a read as Joe Simpson's story.

Andy Nisbet.

Deep Play:– Paul Pritchard (Bâton Wicks, 1997, 192pp, £16.99, ISBN 1 898573 14 X)

Paul Pritchard is a 'big wall' climber. Most of the world's big walls lie in mountain environments, and over the last 10 years we have seen an explosion of activity as talented climbers have turned their attentions to these great alpine challenges. In the main, it has been those with a rock-climbing background, rather than mountaineers who have been most successful, and reading this book, we can begin to see why.

The book consists largely of re-worked essays that first appeared in *On The Edge* magazine or American journals. The opening chapter, previously unpublished, describes Paul's early life and his beginnings as a climber. This sets the book up on an autobiographical theme as we move into the 1980s North Wales Llanberis rock-climbing scene. I found the descriptions of new routing at Gogarth very exciting, and a real insight into the commitment, motivation and skill required to climb some of the most serious traditional rock climbs in the world today. As the book progresses, we move on to Paul's mountain successes, starting with the first ascent of El Regalo de Mwono on the East Face of the Central Tower of Paine. The story of this awe-inspiring 1200m route climbed with Sean Smith, Noel Craine and Simon Yates makes fascinating reading as the necessary mountaineering skills are painfully learned by a process of trial and error. Paine was a fantastic entree into the world of big wall climbing, and easily one of the most impressive British mountaineering achievements of the 1990s. More successes follow - The West Face of Asgard in Baffin, a new route on El Cap, and a lightning ascent of the Slovene Route on Trango. Interspersed with this are various excursions in Brazil and Columbia and more routes in Patagonia.

The key Scottish content is a chapter about the first free ascent of the Scoop on Sron Ulladale with Johnny Dawes – surely one of the most inspirational rock-climbing achievements in our islands. Pritchard writes well and with a variety of different styles as diverse as his own climbing experiences, and in my view, this book was a worthy winner of the 1997 Boardman-Tasker award. If you want to understand more about the hard end of traditional rock-climbing, or want to know what it is like to be high up on a remote big wall, then read this book.

Simon Richardson.

Hamish's Mountain Walk and Climbing The Corbetts:– Hamish Brown (Bâton Wicks, London, 1997, 704pp, 215mm x 135mm, 17 b/w and 15 colour photos, 36 maps cased/jacketed, £16.99. ISBN 1 898573 08 05. First published separately by Victor Gollancz, London 1978 and 1988 respectively).

Never such innocence again:
Hamish's Mountain Walk, and the Munrobagging Big Bang.

Back in 1978, Hamish Brown reportedly disliked his publisher's insistence on an eponymously-titled book, and rightly so. The intervening years have given us too many Bob's Full Houses and Noel's House Parties, and the trend is still heading that dumbed-down way: how long before we all have to raise our hands and ask nicely for favours from Tony's Government? It would be wrong, however, to judge the book by its cover, to see Brown as just another name-checking self-publicist with froth oozing where the creative juices ought to flow. When read, or re-read, this book (now issued in an omnibus edition with *Climbing the Corbetts)* seems not only a work of great driven energy and considerable linguistic beauty, but also, two decades on, to be wiser by the minute. Whereas many accounts of hills, or climbs, or contorted stravaigs such as this often feel stale and stultified after only a short shelf-life, the story – and, crucially, the perceptions – offered by Brown show no sign of becoming any less rich or refreshing.

Hamish's Mountain Walk is now a period piece, yet this has become its greatest strength. Without at all reading as some kind of pre-cagoule costume drama, it feels very much of its time. Yet the balance with time-less hillscapes provides a sense of the fading of a more easy-going era, an end to what Brown refers to as The Long Tradition. Even as *HMW* was written, older ways were breaking down, the hills were being overtaken by a hustle-bustle attitude, by a more dynamic demography. Positioned so pivotally, and already possessing a canny wisdom, *HMW* now also has an uncanny prescience.

Looking back via books, newsclips, films, music, the late Seventies mark the threshold at which things suddenly seem really dated. It was one of those strainingin-every-direction periods of social reform and cultural turmoil, the iceberg tipped by politics, music, fashion, the media explosion, but with weightier and more profound changes creaking beneath the visible waterline. Society (whether or not such a thing existed) was changing tectonically, undergoing crazy structural mood-swings, with the effects felt not just in the housing schemes and financial markets, but in the quiet places too. Even when acquiring a ski-slope here, a bulldozed track there, the hills have remained largely the same: that is why we love them. But the people who come to walk and climb have changed radically, in type, in number, in how they come. And so the landscape, most subtle and susceptible of backdrops, has changed too. This is why *HMW* is so evocative and so pertinent: it's not just about landscape, it's about us, and what we do in the context of landscape.

Chiefly a day-to-day narrative of a meandering trek across Scotland's highest points, the basic facts will be familiar to most readers. First published in 1978, *HMW* tells of a marathon Munro-bag made in 1974 when its author was chiefly known for the oddity of already having appeared in triplicate in the list of Munroists. That much is weel-kent, as Hamish would have it, as is the localised fame and glossy-magazine ubiquity which has accompanied Brownian Motion through the subsequent decades. Yet the book's broader feeling, of the walking world about to change, comes partly from Brown's adroit casting of his own drives and frustrations on the very stage where 'peripatetic catharsis' could be enacted. To draw a parallel from a far larger theatre, *HMW* shares timing and feeling with the much-discussed 'pause' before the start of the First World War, when a seemingly never-ending idyll stumbled blithely into the rude awakening of the modern era. Compare Hardy's April, 1914 poem, *Channel Firing,* with its eerie foresight (the writer hears the crump of the big guns practising in France, and thinks ahead). Or compare the sublime rural world of Sassoon's *Memories of a Fox-Hunting Man,* doomed by a far less tranquil future. Their context was much weightier than any discussion of hills and those who climb them could ever be, but the same poignant, almost elegiac sense of impending change runs through Brown's hill-tale. Here again is the brief, pivotal silence which immediately precedes the clamour and clatter of a new and not altogether alluring dawn. To understand this, it's necessary to recall the sepia-toned situation in Scottish hillwalking before Brown's appearance. Think back. The walk, and the book, spanned the final few years before the Munrobagging Big Bang, whereupon everything suddenly went exponential and a little haywire: books by the shelfload, eroded paths on every ridge and plateau, a broadening highway of access problems, muddled (and often muddied) thinking on what to climb and where, shiny new equipment racked up as the commercial feeding frenzy blurred distinctions between 'luxury' and 'essential'. And, above all, sheer weight of walkers. At the end of Hamish's mountain year there were only 130 recorded Munroists; indeed, his introduction suggested that the list 'now grows at an annual average rate of five people'. Yet the present Tables Editor, Derek Bearhop, is able to indulge in a little joke by cropping the latest Munroist listing at the emotive figure of 1745. That's 130 names in 73 years (129 in 51 if A. E. Robertson is sacrilegiously omitted), followed by 1615 in 23 years. Hyper-inflation. And that's without considering the sprawl of Corbetteers, Grahamists, etc. (although walkers were perhaps more tick-eclectic before the Munro boom, back when size – or at least height – wasn't everything).

If the late Seventies and early Eighties saw the Big Bang (or Big Bag?), they also produced a generation of Munro babyboomers – this writer is one such – for whom hill activity was suddenly trendy, almost in fashion, seeming to fit like a Dachstein mitt. Overnight, hillwalking became worthy of mention on CVs and in lonely hearts columns; and, if sweaty days on dreich slopes were now viewed as a fast-track to sex, then something must have changed. Gone was the old, stuffy division of Scottish hill-demography, Bentleyed gentry versus hitch-hiking Clydeside fitters. Perhaps this schism never existed half as much as touted, but now both it and the hills themselves were overwhelmed by a middle-class, middle-income muddle of eager outdoors-men and – women, thronging northward of a weekend to collect a windfall of freedom and space. For all that archaic feudalism in landownership remains, there was great democratisation of the Scottish hills during these years, with many old elitisms literally trampled underfoot. It was like watching those folk who rush on to the pitch after the last game at a much-loved football stadium and haul up squares of turf before the contractors move in. And so the reasonably pristine, only slightly charted hills (or at least those of Munro height), were avalanched by solitude-seekers, all trying to spirit away sods of wilderness experience. First come, first served, don't get trampled in the rush. A bagfest. That Brown's book now seems a prelude to the deluge is perhaps because we're nearing the end of this supermarket-sweep era of Munrobagging. More and more pub-discussions and magazine inches are given over to broad-based doubts about activity-ethics. Not doubts about going on the hill *per se*, but about how the hills should be approached, where 'approached' is meant in the abstract, not the turn-left-at-the-sheep-fank of the cheesier guidebooks (and which Brown smoothly avoids with the ease of one who knows his hills and knows he can write).

There is another take on this. Look not just at the hills themselves, but at the accompanying literature. Again, Brown's book is pivotal. And, again, think back: to a time when there was no shelf-wide welter of glossy hillbooks, no pick-and-mix scoop of Munro guides. Before 1985-6, when the SMC's *The Munros* and Butterfield's *High Mountains* appeared, most mid-table Munrobaggers spent their Friday planning sessions poring over maps (these were days when folk still thought for themselves), and over Hamish's book, with its vital – in both senses – account of crafty routes and boobytrap no-noes. That was it really: a smattering of other books, with Poucher's *Scottish Peaks* the pick of a poor crop; and some older, wiser, out-of-print words, hard to find even had anyone the patience for their flora and fauna and thoughtfulness. Thus many were the walkers who skimmed the relevant pages of *HMW* before their day's walk, then cross-checked again once safely home and wet the next night. Brown's pen-portraits, plus the exasperating imperial/metric hotchpotch of the Landranger First Series: speak with anyone who took up Munrobagging in the late Seventies or early Eighties, and these will provide a common thread, almost a folk-memory.

I was one such walker. My cracked-spine copy of *HMW* was a 1982 Christmas present, received just as I was starting to climb hills. I had been up the Mither Tap of Bennachie, on a deep-snow trudge to the Dubh Loch, had inspected the Canberra wreckage on Carn an t-Sagairt, and had, crucially, twice climbed Lochnagar on 20-20 days. The first was in blazing summer: my first Munro, an experience so new, so uncertain, that I took two changes of clothes, a sleeping bag, four cans of Tennent's Special, and 24 (24!) salmon sandwiches. The second ascent came in deep winter, a day so startlingly clear that The Cheviot could be seen 100 miles to the south. Already hooked from the sandwich day, this time I was planning ahead, dreaming, gazing around at other hills with a wanderer's eye, thinking ... And now, post-pressie, I knew what a Munro was. It felt like all I needed to know. The Tables themselves, and Hamish's book: essential reading, and as inseparable as Tolmount and Tom Buidhe.

It might seem strange that *HMW* affected a novice so deeply, being written by someone who, even before his Big Walk, had climbed and explored extensively in Scotland and beyond. Strange perhaps, but a sign of the book's catch-all quality. Reading it again now, 15 years on and with 100s of Munros climbed and re-climbed, with more than half the Corbetts and nearly 100 Grahams visited, with a second round of Donalds almost done, with the watershed walked and with even, heaven help me, a century of Ben Cleuch ascents achieved, it still seems fresh and meaningful and relevant.

What manner of book is it that appeals to an eager, bright-eyed, wet-behind-the-ears proto-bagger, but also to a grizzled, grumpy clag-cynic? A good book, that's what. Brown conveys enthusiasm better than any other Scottish hill-writer, recognising that it's one thing to walk a great walk, quite another to write a great book. He knew this implicitly, and had the physical and intellectual machinery to carry off both parts. There have been Big Walks poorly written – Caldwell's Munros/Corbetts round for instance – while several fine hill-writers have never attempted an epic, restricting themselves to weekend forays. Brown managed both, marvellously.

What makes it so satisfying, so rounded? Many factors, obviously, but, fundamentally, Brown being both a readable writer and a considered walker. Lovely descriptive phrases abound, full of energy and vigour. From the macro: 'the veldt sweep of ocherous miles' for the Grampians; to the micro: bracken fronds unfurling, insects heard ahead of being seen. Individual hills, as would be expected from a writer with 2000 Munros in his bag, are beautifully evoked: Beinn Heasgarnich is 'a gently-sloping chaos'; Beinn Mhanach, encircled by the Achaladair ridge, is 'a ball held in a fist'; Sgurrs a' Ghreadaidh and a' Mhadaidh are 'two jagged hedgehogs meeting nose to nose'; and Beinn a' Ghlo, most clean-limbed of massifs, is penned near-perfectly: 'big brown and grey domes, clean-honed by the wind, runny with screes and seamed with deer tracks'. Shiel, Affric, and Farrar are rightly 'the big glens'; 'a casual weekend ploy' delightfully understates the Cuillin ridge; and 'the whole dome was icy' (Aonach Beag) has come to mind on many subsequent bare summits.

This sense of shared experience, of being part of a scattered but like-minded community, is endlessly tapped. Any well-trod walker will empathise and remi-nisce along the lines of, say, my own grilling on Sgulaird, or peeling pegs from fingers on frost-rimey campsite mornings. And as one with the added angle of having undertaken my own Big Walk, I can identify with Brown's odd disengage-ment at the start, his periods of cocooned focus (what modern sports-speak calls 'the zone'), and the hard-to-convey importance of steadily-upped numbers and day-to-day landmarks.

Stylistically, Brown is a classicist, yet also his own man, lovely rhythms and fine timing interspersed with evocative Scots ('slaistery', 'spreug') and trademark single-sentence paragraphs: 'I did not recognise the col' (Sgor na h-Ulaidh). Being also a cratur of habit, it's a book of tics as much as ticks. He forever stops for 'a brew'; he bellows arias; he seems to wear few if any clothes, and then never new; he has a love/hate relationship with cuckoos; he reads on the hoof (usually Scots Lit. such as Neil Munro or R.L.S.) without once tripping over; he abhors litter but wedges questionnaires into cairns. His basic character wells up too: work-ethicsome, unexpectedly competitive, nervously secretive (second is no use: he dreads 'letting on' too early); his occasional sermonesque homilies; his love of adventuring in the spirit of Shipton and Tilman (who, along with W. K. Holmes, come across as mentors).

He rarely, if ever, slates a hill, utilising previous ascents to balance a 'dull' Munro with a good story. All walkers favour certain hill-types: the cluttered spiry west, or the spacious sweep of the east. Despite openly espousing love of the north and west, Brown keeps his occasional mild reservations not for the easy-target Monadh Liath or Drumochter (he sings the praise of A'Bhuidheaneach Bheag!), but for craggy-tendency hills which 'just fail to fire the imagination': the Crianlarich group, or Beinn a'Chlachair. This holism is as it should be: too many moorland-lovers mouth paeans of crag-praise because that's the macho, glossy-picture, complete-mountaineer accepted admissible thing to do. Brown also deserves a medal for his long, self-analytical recounting of the battlefield bogs of Mount Keen; likewise his lowest ebb (entering Knoydart) is no more flinched at on paper than it was on foot. And he is, perhaps oddly given the context, an unusually fine describer of woodland and lowland; the ornithological thread, never just some twitcher's checklist, always seems to fit (and flit). Bird-life, not just birds, period.

Human wildlife crops up all the while: Hamish's Highlands are well-populated. Dewi Jones, visited in Blair Atholl, wrote in a letter: 'no great kudos in that: I think Hamish crammed in the names of all friends and acquaintances, plus a few more!' It's here that the book feels most dated, although in a quaint, endearing, unavoidable way: talk of Syd Scroggie, of a meeting with A. E. Robertson's widow, of the dreadful time when Crianlarich hostel was little more than a barracks complete with bugle-blowing sergeant-major, of late lamented Nancy's drop-in (although its retention in the 'useful addresses' is needless). This was the era when Tranter (and not Ramsay, Belton, or Broxap) was the name by which mega-Munro-days were judged. Similarly, Brown's own precursors – Cousins, Hinde, the Ripleys – all seem very distant now. Even the hills have moved on: Beinn an Lochain was a Munro, Beinn Teallach and Sgurr nan Ceannaichean weren't; indeed, it's chastening to realise there have now been two major revisions, such that Sgor an Iubhair ('deserves to be a Munro') has been and gone. Even Ballachulish Bridge was only just being built.

What most of all connects the book's text with its 'feel' is Brown's layered experience, which he converts into language with great facility. Hamish knew his hills even then: having climbed all Munros thrice or more, his walk was no passing whimsy, no bag-on-sight impulse. (But note that 18 further months of planning preceded his stepping off the Craignure ferry.) He had strolled, skied, slithered, sneaked, and scurried across these hills since boyhood: a boyhood with which he seems wonderfully at ease. The youthful enthusiasms make it easy to forget that he turned 40 soon after the walk, particularly since his fitness is so understated; only occasionally (the massive Mamores day; up and down Schiehallion in well under two hours) are figures allowed to boast for themselves.

Crucially, Hamish had had a life. Too many modern experts seem to have done nothing but: the blank-faced generation of snooker automatons, the flat-charactered, straight-out-of-Uni politicos. Far more walkers now blitz-bag their hills young; and, while it's in the nature of the game that they'll soon have tales to tell, they often lack a wider context in which to embed them. Not so Brown, since the underlying energy for his walk came from the perfect combination of push and pull: the pull of the hills themselves, the push of disaffection from being 'tied to a desk with no view of sky or hill'. He never pretended to paper over these raw motivations when writing of his walk, thank goodness; it shows, and provides much of what makes the book.

Some readers find the Dollar-pupil and Braehead-teacher tales an irritant, just as the religious quotes and snatches of poetry jut out like barns from the Ben Avon plateau; but any book of this scope needs personal input and idiosyncrasy so as not to seem bland. Brown maybe doesn't go far enough in giving of himself: there's a moment (on Mhanach again) when a mention of 'most erotic imaginings' cries out for more such clues. If the book does have a structural failing, it's the over-use of historical plug-ins (not that Brown doesn't know his stuff), when space could have been cleared for more personal thoughts. This is offset, however, by one of the most relevant threads for a late-Nineties reader: Brown's outspoken radicalism, his unwillingness to leave politics out of the hills. When first read, this stood out less; but now, with so much subsequent change and regression, clear common-sense jumps from every chapter. Few have been more vocal about SYHA upsizing than this hostel-lover who tallies bednights as diligently as he counts Munros. There are heartfelt doubts about the over-certification of youth leaders, fears of burgeoning bureaucracy and the risk of destabilising the qualification/experience balance. And fierce anti-trackism: another situation which has steadily worsened.

Yet, for all the positive aspects, any attempt at two-decades-on assessment of the book's Munro-core inevitably throws up a possible paradox, or at least the worry of a circular argument. Was Brown not merely a prophet of the Munro explosion, but its progenitor, central to the event, integral to the changes, instigator of what followed? While no-one doubts his voice crying in the wilderness, was he not so much John the Baptist as Jesus himself? It's tempting to see such a popular, well-written book proactively rocketing the list of Munroists skyward; and Brown, via his subsequent writings (and his perhaps unfortunate co-editorship of the 1981 *Munro's Tables*), has not been altogether adept and surefooted at debunking this notion. Wise words on eclecticism in walking seem not always to have translated into legwork: a rare case of foot-not-in-mouth disease? His round of Corbetts didn't come until the mid-Eighties, while only now is he beginning to close in on the Grahams. This wouldn't matter so much, if at all, were his a general behavioural antipathy akin to that of unequivocal anti-baggist writers such as Watson or Crumley. Yet while Brown pleads, as he has done many times, that he is 'not a Munro-bagger' (it first crops up on p23: pre-emptive retaliation), a glance at the scoreboard shows five, then six, then seven rounds clocked up. Heads are scratched in puzzlement, phrases about protesting too much drift into mind, wisps of doubt swirl around the high tops of achievement.

The problem is that Brown, deny it though he might, surely is a bagger, by nature. There is nothing wrong with this, it's the way many hillgoers are. What is ironic is that, far from single-handedly instigating the Munro boom, he fell victim to it by failing to delineate his overall motivations as precisely as those for the walk itself. He was – and perhaps still is – fearful of 'Wainwrightism': the inadvertent popularising of hills you love, such that they forever change in consequence. It's a high-ground version of Heisenberg's Uncertainty Principle: the very thing recorded inescapably altered by trying to record it. Wainwright, a populariser on a more thorough and perhaps more wilful scale, responded to flickers of guilt by hedgehogging further into curmudgeonly invisibility. Brown, a lighter, more enlightened character all along, was never likely to do this – for all the occasional old-fashioned sexism, his writings are more egalitarian than elitist – so he now and again half-apologises for enthusiasms in an awkward and ungainly manner. It's the classic hill-writer's bind. Non-scribbling walkers have it easy, not needing to write (or even think) about what they're doing, where they're going.

There should be no need for squirming, yet it has taken until the late Nineties, amid the explosion of hill-lists and increasingly open discussion of tabular revision, for this to be seen. Brown, of all people, has nothing about which to be embarrassed. If baggerish (or precise, log-keeping, orderly) is the way he is, then that's fine. A whole character-type loves the hills in ways every bit as subtle and scarcely definable as the rest, yet needs an exoskeletal structure to coax motivation into action. Hill-bagging provides this, beautifully: far more than 'trainspotter' or 'twitcher' preoccupations, it is inherently healthy, and brings fantastic, otherwise unvisited, places. It might even (although whisper this not near Ridgway's junior executive boot camp) build the character. It's okay. What is less satisfactory is when eyes are narrowed instead of minds broadened, when obsession stands in for enlightenment, when the bagger sees nothing beneath the notional 3000ft cut-off. That is good neither for walker nor for hill, whether the hill is big and over-subscribed, or small and under-frequented; and, admittedly, that situation has arisen, to a degree, through the years of the Big Bang.

Brown should have no fear of this, should have no guilt pangs that being a witness to the explosion makes him somehow culpable in the death of quiet spacious hills he loves (not that this is the reality anyway: the rumours have been greatly exaggerated). He, more than most, has hill-maturity, is able to view summits far more fully than as ticks on lists or names and numbers in logbooks. His dilemma – if indeed he has one – is not resolved by retreat into defensiveness and gawky self-apology, rather by heeding those who offer reassurance that there's nothing to be afraid of, that everyone should go with their natural leanings.

Considered as a whole, enthusiasms and doubts together, it's unsurprising that Brown has written nothing quite as good again. There are many fine passages and heartfelt thoughts elsewhere, but none as meant, none as together as in *HMW*.

The other book bundled in this reissue, *Climbing the Corbetts,* (originally from 1988) provides a good example. It too is a cairn of information, yet the ascents and reascents often seem cluttered, confused, in need of good sub-editing, and lacking the ooomph that gave *HMW* its shape and energy. The second book is more amorphous, although not unpleasantly so: in the absence of Big Walk pressure or worries about Munrobagger-denial, it feels more relaxed. It's more of a dipper-in, a book at bedtime, of daily readings, whereas *HMW* (which was already hinting at the worth of Corbetts) is a big-dipper of weather-changes and mood-swings. So very different in shape and character, they're an odd pair to bind together; but maybe this works, just as Glen Coe works despite having the orthogonal complexi-ties of Bidean and the Buachailles on the page facing the Aonach Eagach's linear unavoidability.

As one whose own Big Walk and book[1] were inspired by Brown, it seems entirely natural that *HMW* offers more direction, since a certain type of walker has a burning need to do One Big Thing. And, when achieved, there follows a more mellow period, possibly happier, healthier, less desperately driven. Just as 'there's a book in every man', so the same may be true of the walk behind the book. It seems less natural that, for all its influence, *HMW* hasn't prompted a completion of Munro's list: I remain nearly 40 short. But look on it another way. A sign of the book's maturity is that, although an account of a ringfenced round of Munros, it can be read on a deeper level: no list can ever be 'completed', only started, restarted, endlessly cycled. Munros, indeed any hills, are never 'done', or 'completed'; only gradually, imperceptibly, known.

Concepts of reprise and return bring back the initial thought: were Hamish to belatedly rename his first book, and stick with the eponymous idea (it would now be difficult, after all, to think of it otherwise), he might do worse than steal a title from American crime writer James Ellroy: *Brown's Requiem.* Ellroy's metier (cops, criminals, urban mayhem) could hardly be farther removed from, say: 'An Teallach and Coigach, vanishing into a haze of apple redness'. But the title is wonderfully apt, since *HMW* is, however inadvertently, a hymn to a bygone age, with thought given to present and future too. On this basis alone, the reprint is timely.

Some say that Bill Murray's first two books were great works, and they surely are – although I have never felt qualified to judge, being neither a climber, nor relishing Murray's style and outlook. *HMW,* however, felt familiar the first time round, and still does. I would argue against all-comers that it was, and remains, the finest of all Scottish hill books.

Dave Hewitt.

[1]*Walking the Watershed,* TACit Press. (Ed.).

Eddie Campbell, An Appreciation. Available from Editor, Leen Volwerk, c/o Lochaber High School, Camaghael, Fort William, PH33 7ND, £3.50 inc. p&p. Cheques to Lochaber Athletic Club. All profits to charity and a commemorative running trophy.

In any year, the hill-going world sees a startling number of new books. Big-format glossies; small hand-drawn guides; joshing, jocular stories; precise, pedantic, number crunching lists; even books which inadvertently provide the hill-equivalent of Anthony Burgess's nicely narky poem, *The book of my enemy has been remaindered, and I am glad.* But, for each reader, there is usually only one Book of the Year, one book which moves you and makes you smile but leaves you sad and makes you think. And this, for me, in 1997, was it.

It's scarcely even a book proper, merely 20-odd pages stapled in A5 form. But who cares? In literature, as in life itself, content is everything. From 1951 until his early death in 1996, Eddie Campbell never missed the Ben Nevis hill-race, winning three times in the early Fifties, becoming so much a fixture in the fixture that it's now named after him. (Quite right: don't name sporting events after corporate sponsors, fag companies, car firms, insurers, booze merchants; that is not only crass, but abusive and exploitative of the memory of great competitors. When last did an insurance company sweat? Name events after people, and sod the lost revenue.)

Despite the 1997 race being just about the only event to resist cancellation in the wake of Di's funeral, it hasn't always gone ahead: bad weather, if not bad etiquette, can put a stop to it. But not to Campbell: in 1980, with conditions so foul as to prevent an official start, he led a happy rebellion, a splinter saunter to the top and back. This type of tale forms the basis of the booklet: hotch-potched memories and tributes from friends and friendly rivals alike.

Campbell emerges as a cross between Old Testament patriarch (that mad mop of white hair! that beard!), anti-materialist minimalist, and kindly bloke. The minimalism appeals hugely. In middle-age, Campbell woke one morning, impulsively decided to run the 95-mile West Highland Way, set off from the Fort in sweltering conditions, and had reached Rannoch Moor before standard notions of sense and logic began to kick in and he turned back to the Coe. Like Harold Wilson's housewife, Campbell had a pound in his pocket (he always had a pound, only a pound), and this would have comprised his survival rations in the urban jungle of Milngavie had he made it that far. As it was, he backed off; but what was crucial was the initial move having been made. Many walkers and runners have 'the legs'; far fewer have this level of psychological motivational ooomph. There are other fine stories, especially of Campbell's near-mystical ability to materialise ahead of rivals having been minutes behind at the summit. There are also great pictures: of middle-aged Campbell loping down a snow slope like a yeti with a number pinned to its chest; of a young Campbell, big-hearted Highland youth personified, stretching out on some quiet backroad.

The hill-running world (as with the running world generally, but more so), seems a loose knit shuffling-striding mobile community, an off-road roadshow. As with any unsung, unhyped mass participation event (a weekend chess congress for example), for all that there are Top Performers, and, occasionally, Stars, the main thing – the thing that makes it happen, the thing that it's All About – is for people just to turn up and take part and love it for what it is: a purposeful gathering. Eddie Campbell knew this, intuitively, down to his gristle.

It may be that Massacre of Glen Coe grievances linger on in Lochaber, that the McDonalds still see themselves as holding the moral high ground, that the sign in the Clachaig – 'No Campbells' – is still there and still meant. But, if so, now's the time to take it down – and to put up a picture instead. A picture of a massive, slightly mad, certainly kind, ramshackle ragbag of a man from just over the hill, who paid more than enough dues for his name and whose messy, indeterminate role model would make the ad-men and image makers cringe and flee. Campbell the athlete was miles from Sky Sports or some Golden Four money-earner in Oslo; Campbell the man was even farther from cushy, cosy shallowness and frippery. As with Nancy Smith before him, he deserves to be remembered for application and attitude, for what we all need to do if we're to make the hills (and life generally) that bit better for everyone. This booklet forms a fine start-line for such hopes: nothing so human or so heartfelt was published last year.

Dave Hewitt.

Arran, Arrochar and the Southern Highlands:– (The Scottish Mountaineering Club, 1997. Graham Little, Tom Prentice and Ken Crocket. 385pp, 22 illus., 46 maps and diagrams. £14.95. ISBN 0 907521 49 5.)

Nine years after the last edition, the latest Arran, Arrochar and the Southern Highlands guide appears with an increase of 50% in route numbers. Where will it all end? Despite the increase the guide remains the same size. This is an excellent guide and it is good to see a large number of people contributed. Photos are the first thing people notice; these are just what are expected, fine and varied, especially the Arran shots. Although I like the cover photograph of Nimlin's Route it has already appeared in Donald Bennet's book and the Journal, couldn't we be treated to something new? Previously unpublished rock climbing areas include the Mull of Kintyre (which will be handy if I miss the ferry to Ballycastle), and the Arran conglomerate – how many KiloNewtons will a tied-off rusty bicycle spanner hold?

The winter grounds around Bridge of Orchy have been expanded, Ben Lawers and the Tarmachans are included for the first time. A collection of snowy routes at Beinn Mhor should keep the Dunoon climbers busy.

There is plenty of history to read in a wet tent – the aid and bolts are written up for people to draw their own conclusions about Arran. The Glen Croe bolt created quite a stir 10 years ago, but didn't get a mention, neither did the fact that Wild Country was originally recorded at E4! The black-and-white pictures are an interesting idea and spice up the historical section.

Many routes gain a grade (a healthy trend that will hopefully catch on at Newtonmore) and a few even go down. I'm told the peg on Lawyer's Leap is past it's best and the route might now be worth E2.

I have found diagrams to be the biggest irritation in recent guides. I couldn't find Bullroar with the diagram from the latest guide, and I now carry the 1969 guide up Ben Nevis. Similarly, the latest Glen Coe guide diagrams lack the detail of the 1980 guide.

The diagrams in this guide are as good as any but are very faint, presumably to make the lines of the routes stand out. Other guides avoid this by marking the routes in red or blue. The drawing of Goatfell South Slabs is a bit cluttered, again the 1980 drawing of the Etive Slabs shows a way out using different symbols. Finally, what criteria is used in deciding whether a crag gets a diagram? Kinglas Crag has several icefalls which can be checked from the road thereby avoiding a wasted day, if there was a diagram.

After seeing this guide I'm keen to get back to the old haunts but I'll still pick on a few more points. Right On and Silo are not fully described, some sad person might want to climb them. Creag Liath still seems a bit confused, Hadrian's Wall (renamed Paranoia) is probably Guides Route. The Abseilers at Glen Croe get a bad Press but not the Pegomaniacs. The rock routes at Kinglas Crag are too steep for any self-respecting seepage.

A couple of years ago a friend in England said the SMC guides were the best in Britain – praise indeed. Keep it up.

Colin Moody.

Munro's Tables and other Tables of lower hills:– (1997 The Scottish Mountaineering Trust, viii + 168pp, ISBN 0 907521 53 3, £15.95. Revised and Edited by Derek A. Bearhop.)

The new edition of Munro's Tables arrived with unprecedented publicity which many an aspiring author must have envied. Even the daily papers latched on to the announcement of eight new mountains in Scotland. The outdoor Press were more circumspect and in some cases critical but certainly none could ignore the deliberations of the SMC in promoting further summits to Munro status.

With this review coming some time after the event it is perhaps best to accept the changes as *fait accomplii* and concentrate on the book itself. Essentially, with the welcome addition of the Graham list, it is very much the mixture as before, albeit in a smart new format.

Tops are now more clearly differentiated from their parent Munros by the use of a lighter typeface. The heights are given only in metres which is perhaps inevitable now that all the figures are based on new surveys but this accentuates the quirkiness of a list which cuts off at 914.4m. It would be convenient to be provided with space for recording the date of ascent but one feels that the SMC rather disapproves of

Munro-bagging and provides this list purely as a scientific record of hills above a certain altitude.

A welcome addition is the list of 34 hills furth of Scotland. It would be pleasing if the next edition of the book incorporated a list of the 53 furth Corbetts and the 134 furth Grahams.

The list of Munroists inevitably occupies more and more space and might seem designed only to boost the egos of those whose names appear therein. There is much of interest to be found in perusing this list. It is pleasing to see the columns for completion of tops and furth reappearing. The drop, over the years, in the percentage of those tackling the tops in addition to the Munros is particularly noticeable. It is a matter of conjecture as to whether the majority of those ascending the Munros are completely ignoring the subsidiary tops or omitting only a few awkward summits. The percentage not completing the tops seems destined to increase with Knight's Peak added to the list.

Of course, the Munros are the heart of the book and come with both an index and a height order list, as do the Donalds. The Corbetts have an index but no list in height order, while the newly-included Grahams have no index and their height order list includes only the top 20 which seems particularly pointless. A major wish for the next edition is a height order list for all the hills. Perhaps there is a fear that people will notice how close the top three Corbetts come to qualifying as Munros and may go and climb these fine hills which are currently the preserve of the connoisseur.

There are excellent clear maps which show both Munros and Corbetts, two extra maps being provided for those Corbetts (in the Southern Uplands and in Morvern, Sunart, Ardgour and Moidart) which are far from any Munros. An obvious wish for the next edition is that the Grahams should be added to these maps. Oddly enough, although the Corbetts lie beyond the Munros to north, south, east and west, the Grahams do not extend the boundaries in all directions. Corbetts Beinn Spionnaidh and Mount Battock are the most northerly and easterly hill more than 2000ft in Scotland, respectively.

Although essentially a triviality, the irritating issue of sections should be mentioned here. After climbing more than a 1000 of the Scottish Marilyns listed in Alan Dawson's addictive book the section numbers still cause confusion, which is further compounded in this book by the use of different but still illogical numbering. There seems no good reason why the Munro section numbers cannot be used throughout, with the introduction of appropriate sub-sections as has been done for the Corbetts. Dawson's region 18 is the same as Corbett Section 10A. Graham region 19 straggles some 20kms beyond Beinn Bheula into the Cowal peninsula and perhaps, to prevent Section 1 becoming too unwieldy, could become 1A which would also contain four Corbetts and possibly the cluster of Grahams immediately west of Loch Lomond and south of Arrochar which are currently left in Section 1 anyway. Graham region 21 is indistinguishable from Section 8, Cook's Cairn and Corryhabbie Hill, Morven and Mona Gowan, being a couple of convenient combinations for the sub-Munro collector. This leaves the two hills in region 23 to be accommodated. Uamh Beag was in Section 1 in the original book and remains close in both distance and character to Ben Vorlich and Meall na Fearna, its removal being based purely on a geological anomaly. The Ochils, with their single Graham, are more clearly distinct and whether they should belong to the Southern Highland Section 1 or the Southern Upland Section 0 (or perhaps some subsection thereof) is open to debate.

This is one book which is unlikely to go out of print so it seems appropriate for this review to incorporate a wish list for the next edition. As usual Donald's tables are included in the book. Their scope is now extended to include a couple of hills, one the aforementioned Graham, Uamh Beag, which previously were assumed to belong in the Highlands.

The appendix has been dropped in this edition. As the editor rightly points out, the existence of a single contour does not, in general, imply a significant top. However, before this addition to the tables disappears for ever into unlamented oblivion it is perhaps worth pointing out here that the 1981 revision of the tables failed to understand its significance. Far from incorporating every bump with an isolated contour of any height the original appendix listed only those with a single 2000ft contour. It was designed to pinpoint areas of land which would become tiny islands were sea level to rise to exactly 2000ft.

A Gaelic Guide is included which translates the hill names into English and gives an indication of the pronunciation, although not entirely eliminating the confusion which many feel over the apparently perverse spelling. Why are there letters which are not sounded at all? The notorious Fhionnlaidh, suggested elsewhere to be Ula, appears here as Yoonly. A lot of visitors from south of the Border will probably continue to speak of 'cheesecake' and 'Ben Agony' but it is to be hoped that many will at least read this section of the book and benefit from an understanding of the meaning of the names.

Along with this goes the wish, expressed in a short coda, that the many walkers and climbers drawn to the Scottish hills by books such as this one, will learn to respect the mountain environment and the people who live and make their living there. In return we can hope that these people will understand that the influx of such tourists, while it may cause some disturbance and erosion, is mainly beneficial to the Scottish economy. For example, a blanket ban on hillwalking from July to February seems quite unreasonable in any area whether it contains Munros or not.

As is customary the introduction gives a brief appreciation of Sir Hugh Munro and of the first Munroist, the Rev A. E. Robertson. It reveals the fact that Munro may have failed to ascend Carn an Fhidhleir as well as the 'In Pinn' and Carn Cloich-mhuillin, now sadly only a 'top', on which he planned to celebrate his compleation.

Although few will mourn the disappearance of the other 14 rather insignificant tops it seems a pity to delete Sgurr Dearg which, as pointed out in the introduction, was once the official Munro. It has subsequently remained as a consolation prize for the many walkers who climb all except the Inaccessible Pinnacle. Here, surely, sentiment should have taken precedence over survey.

And there is room for sentiment, for herein lies part of the fascination of the Munros. As the stunning pictures in this book remind us, this is not just a list of dry statistics. Behind the figures lie real mountains, rock and snow, grass and bog, sunny days with long-ranging views and equally memorable days of mist and storm. The pictures are superb but only the one of Ladhar Bheinn captures any hint of the beauty which still haunts the Highlands on a less-than-perfect day.

These lists inspire fanaticism both among those who become obsessed with climbing the hills and those who despise them for doing so. The addition of the Grahams will perhaps persuade more people to realise that there is life after the Munros and many worthwhile hills lower than 3000ft. That said, even the most single-minded, blinkered fanatic who ascends nothing but Munros can surely not climb these 284 hills and remain unmoved by beauty along the way.

Ann Bowker.

Eiger Dreams – Ventures Among Men and Mountains:– Jon Krakauer. (Pan Books, 1997, 186pp, £6.99, paperback. ISBN 0 330 37000 6).

This is a collection of essays and journal articles by an award-winning author, all but one previously published. The book is subtitled *Ventures among Men and Mountains* and is prefaced by two intriguing quotations on the nature of adventure. One reflects on the relationship between adventure and storytelling, the other on adventure and incompetence. In his introduction the author tells us 'by the end of the book I think the reader will have a better sense not only why climbers climb, but why they tend to be so goddamm obsessive about it'.

So far, so promising. However, there is a sub-text. Both author and publisher tell us that the book is intended for a non-climbing readership, and presumably to attract these readers they trot out a string of hackneyed cliches about: ' . . . the thrill of dicing with death . . . the attraction of high risk sports . . . those who elect to participate in this hazardous pastime do so not in spite of the unforgiving stakes, but precisely because of them.'

Regrettably, many of the essays merely fuel the fires of tabloid-style sensation. Krakauer paints a gory picture of glory-seekers playing Russian Roulette among the peaks and glaciers, lacing his stories with casualty statistics, morbid anecdotes and gung-ho bravado. I rapidly came to the conclusion that the non-climbing reader would merely have had his or her superficial prejudices confirmed, exactly on the lines of the publisher's hype. Equally, Krakauer's attempts to write for a non-climbing audience are unconvincing. He explains all the technical details (an ice screw is 'a threaded eight-inch aluminium or titanium tube with an eye at the end'), but his account of climbing, whether on an unprotected ice pillar or a major peak, gives too little insight into the climber's feelings, fears or motivation.

But it's not all bad. Krakauer is at his best with reportage – recounting (other people's) experiences and profiling personalities. Among several good profiles, there is an excellent piece on John Gill, based on thorough research, which does explore one man's motivation. Another tale of a solo trip to Alaska describes youthful over-ambition and a painful learning experience.

Krakauer writes for a living – and not just about climbing. His journalistic style seems most suited to interviews, anecdote and travelogue. Indeed, much of the book's subject matter is not his own personal experience, but the paraphernalia of climbing conversations – bar-room tales, recycled news, history, assorted trivia. He frequently repackages snippets of all too familiar European climbing lore for a North American audience.

Despite the promise of the book's opening, the author never gets to grips with the intriguing dichotomy about adventure posed by the opening quotations. The collection lacks any common thread, other than that the essays were first published over a short period in the Eighties. Krakauer may be a competent journalist, but the chapters seem to follow a too-obvious formula. I felt his prose (with a few rare exceptions) was mostly superficial and lacking in feeling. Apart from a few brief passages, the writing was devoid of a perceptive response to the mountain environment. For me, at least, the distinctive thing about climbing is the intensity of its experience. That intensity is rarely present in the pages of this book.

Adam Kassyk.

The First Fifty Years of the British Mountaineering Council – A political History. (1997; British Mountaineering Council; 321 pp.; illus.; £16.99; ISBN 0 903908 07 7).

This incestuous book is a potpourried compendium of historical events in the politics of British mountaineering. The Council righteously felt that it had to produce its own curate's egg and cook up something that would be sometimes good, but could often be bland and tedious after each of its numerous contributors had put in their ha'penny worth of literary pabulum.

Its first aim was to record sequentially the tale of events from one decade to another that brought in a recognisable role for a Mountaineering Council. These sections are well done. They show how 'the BMC circulated crucial safety advice in the years [before nut protection and good equipment] when the sport was particularly hazardous...the efforts that were made to secure better equipment and training standards...the tensions that came about between the over-regulating zeal of educationalists and trainers and the mainstream sport keen to keep certification realistic and marginal...' They also chart 'the never ending struggle to maintain access to mountains and cliffs', and describe 'the often turbulent relationship with the Sports Council – an organisation constantly perplexed by the anarchic nature of climbing'. Yes, the interest is maintained through a tortuous saga that led to the successful role that the Council now plays in British mountaineering.

However, the reader's concentration may falter as each of the many business committees starts a mundane litany through an agenda of the over-familiar topics of access, conservation, training, insurance, safety, technique, manuals, books, guides, walls, competitions, marketing, finance, and public relations. Worse follows as each in turn of the nine area committees blows its parochial trumpet about its local issues that can only be of much interest to those in the areas themselves. It goes on slipping downhill into mere data to make a catalogue of its sponsored and backed international expeditions and meets that go here, there, and everywhere; of its affiliated clubs and its phonebook lists of its officers, officials, and professional staff right down to the most junior toiler in the office, until it settles 'for some fascinating'...well, you could have fooled me... 'articles from *Mountain-eering,* its admirable house magazine'....now defunct.

Let's flag up some redeeming national features. There are numerous antique photos: some rare mug shots arranged in gallery style that include a fair complement of Scottish personality pics. Not only Bob Grieve in his stint as a BMC patron, but from the earlier days our series of presidential worthies, like Wordie, Macphee, and Murray. Sometimes, when we filled the minor presidential role consistent with our relative numbers within the British mountaineering scene, in came Ogilvie, Gorrie and Cunningham, and there is delight in a wonderfully jolly pair of photos of two Vice-Presidential alpinists, unshaven, paddy-hatted, draped with a nylon rope halter, posing in turn on what looks like someone's verdant backgarden rockery.

Significant events turn up in long-forgotten snaps. Take the June day of the official opening of the BMC Memorial Hut at Glen Brittle, in which the style and social milieu of the mid-Sixties has been captured beautifully; the honoured guests in costume, suit and kilt ,while there plonked in the front row stands the Unknown Punter broiling in his flatcap duncher and his padded Michelin-man duvet jacket, but with his priorities right as he keeps his glass firmly grasped in his hand.

It tells how the role of the SMC within the BMC was initially uncertain and equivocal. Although at first it was antagonistic towards the existence of such a body it eventually accepted that it could dutifully play its part in this new-fangled piece of bureaucracy.

When the clubs within Scotland withdrew from the distant southern seat of power and brought into existence the Association of Scottish Climbing Clubs the SMC still kept its boots placed within the portals of the BMC. However, the pressure of conservation and other local difficulties, such as 'that farce of lies, intrigue and incompetence by officials, public bodies, etc., that was to become known as the Coruisk Affair,' indicated that a more professional and comprehensive organisation was essential to deal with all the Scottish issues, and so, in 1970 the Mountaineering Council of Scotland came into existence. Sandy Cousins, Hon. Sec., and in reality Mr MCoS, represented the new body to the BMC, BMC Technical Committee, SSC, MRCS, SMLTB, SCAC, SLF, SNSC, MBA, FC, NIMC, NTS, etc. (no prize on offer for the first correct set of translations). His informative account from memory of the first 25 years of MCoS is thankfully brief because both early and current files and minutes appear to have vanished into the mist – and that's naughty, folks.

Politics? Yes, jousting, squabbles, and creative powerplay. Take the birthpangs of the organisation in 1944. It was launched in the name of the Alpine Club, but there was a quick response from an irate cabal of AC and SMC members who wrote objecting to the formation of a Council without the AC Committee having been consulted and, further, that this project had not been brought before the members at a General Meeting for their approval. Among the signatories to this letter were such dignified SMC ex-Presidential members as Ling, Glover, Garden, MacRobert, Harrison, Parker and P. J. H. Unna. This all begins to sound somewhat familiar and topical, doesn't it? Much wind had generated much heat. A revolt had started. Consternation swept through the Club. Progressives were trying to make sweeping changes. There were those who were worried that the new body might steal the thunder and prestige of the Club. Old guard members were ready to fight any action. North of the Border was the fiefdom of the SMC and in no way did they want their authority usurped. The clans were about to rise and with a hearty shout the claymore was quickly brandished.

Like many an historical lost cause, this uprising was squashed with a carefully-orchestrated broadside driving the final nails into its coffin. Quoting from a well-crafted speech later delivered to the Committee by a major protagonist and proponent for the new body... 'over-generous sympathy has been extended for Scottish nationalism...my heart is curiously unwilling to bleed for Scottish woes...the SMC [heavily opinionated in the righteousness to the letter] played a somewhat ignoble part in the negotiations leading up to the formation of the BMC – and one may be forgiven for thinking that a club which is quite unable to keep the younger and more active climbers within the club framework is scarcely the body to have any preponderant voice of shaping the future of climbing in this country'.

Great stuff, the essence of cut and thrust and how to win friends and influence people. Ain't history wonderful!

Yes, this is a 'unique and somewhat unusual publication'. Just right for archivists, club libraries, historians, archeologists, plagiarists, browsers, pedants, politiconerds and mountain trivial pursuitists. If your name is in it, buy it.

Philip Gribbon.

Into The Wild:– John Krakauer. (Macmillan, £14.99, ISBN 0 333 73542 0).

A young man disowns his parents and his affluent background, assumes the name Alexander Supertramp, and proceeds on an odyssey to seek the simple, unfettered, independent and immediate life as extolled by his heroes Leo Tolstoy and Jack London. Two years' later, Chris McCandless's body is found in the wilds of Alaska.

John Krakauer – the author of *Into Thin Air* – first came across the story when asked to write an article on McCandless for *Outside Magazine.* Intrigued and sensing echoes with his own life, he could not let it drop, and this book is the result.

McCandless befriended many people on his travels and made a considerable impact on quite a number of them. It could be said that the majority might be considered somewhat out of the mainstream and perhaps inclined to be affected by someone holding – and living – such earnest, unorthodox and uncompromising views. Still, McCandless clearly had charisma, was well-read and believed in himself completely, and was perhaps not the typical youthful drop-out.

However, what did he learn from his journey? His insights, as revealed in his journal, are those of someone yet to mature, someone still living out a kind of fantasy, and they remain unshaped by any real depth of experience. If his certainties were at all shaken when things started going wrong we do not know, because as time passes so his journal entries become briefer, until finally, they are simple factual entries of game killed or other food collected and his thoughts can only be guessed at. His great self-belief is ultimately not enough, but he doesn't live to learn that.

Many people go through similar phases, although rarely expressed in quite so extreme a manner, and fortunately, usually without fatal results, but McCandless is not alone. Krakauer places him in some sort of context by weaving in stories of others who died on similar adventures, and makes explicit the link with mountaineering in a couple of chapters on an obviously significant personal experience on the Devil's Thumb, when he was a similar age to McCandless.

In some respects any general insights don't ultimately amount to much. The young tend to reject their parents. Some people are drawn to high-risk activities, youth in particular, and arguably few fully comprehend the size of the stakes because they don't really believe they are mortal. Those left behind to worry, or to grieve, suffer the greatest burden.

However, obvious though such insights may arguably be, I found the book moving, thought-provoking and disturbing. Like many others, I suspect, I have done largely what I wanted, believing in myself and what I considered to be a sober assessment of the risks I took. Rarely have the thoughts and feelings of others significantly influenced me. It is no bad thing to be reminded that our actions affect more than ourselves, that we too are subject to the same rules as everyone else and that we may run closer to the line than we realise.

Had he survived, I suspect McCandless would have mellowed and his views become less dogmatic. As it is, he remains forever young, headstrong, selfish and a bit of a pain in the arse. But weren't we all once.

[The extremes of opinion which exist about McCandless and about this book can be explored by reading the reviews at http://www.amazon.com.]

Bob Duncan.

John Muir: His Life and Letters and Other Writings by John Muir:– Terry Gifford, Editor. (Bâton Wicks/The Mountaineers, 1996, £20.00, ISBN 1 898573 07 7) **John Muir: The Eight Wilderness Discovery Books by John Muir:-** (Diadem/The Mountaineers, 1992, £20.00, ISBN 0 906371 34 1).

The rediscovery of John Muir in the UK has accelerated since the 1970s, when the late Frank Tindall initiated the John Muir Country Park (1976) and the restoration of the John Muir House Birthplace Museum (1980). Terry Gifford has made a valuable contribution to the process of repatriating Muir as a Scottish environmental and cultural icon, through two omnibus editions of Muir's writings. *The Eight Wilderness Discovery Books* made Muir's writings much more widely available than before in the UK, and Terry's second compilation *John Muir; His Life and Letters and Other Writings* provides us with an entire library of Muir material. It includes the first, and arguably the finest biography of Muir, by William Frederic Badè; Muir's own *Cruise of the Corwin, Studies in the Sierra, Picturesque California* and the memorable *Stickeen* - which many would rate as the best 'canine adventure' ever told. The inclusion of Samuel Hall Young's *Alaska Days with John Muir* is a rare pleasure, because it gives us one of the finest portraits of Muir the mountaineer.

The Life and Letters of John Muir was published in 1924 by William Frederic Badè, Muir's literary executor and one of his closest confidants. The research for this book laid bare the bedrock from which all other subsequent works were quarried. The broad canvas of Muir's life and the epic scale of his achievements in establishing the American conservation movement are clearly portrayed. And although it is a work of truly massive scholarship, it is a well-told tale, richly embroidered with anecdote, adventure and incident.

Gifford's inclusion of Muir's *Studies in the Sierra* constitutes a self-tutor in geology and glaciation, richly illustrated with 50 of Muir's own field sketches of the rocks and mountain ranges he was exploring. Far more readable than any modern geology textbook, it reveals the workings of an incisive mind and a talented artist. If geology has always puzzled you – read this and you will be inspired to learn more.

Samuel Hall Young's *Alaska Days with John Muir* relates the engaging story of Young's adventures with Muir in the northern wildernesses. Young describes the famous 1879 expedition to the 8000ft. Glenora Peak, on which he dislocated both his shoulders in a fall near the summit. Muir saved Young's life that day by carrying him down the mountain on his back and at times suspended from his teeth! The book provides us with perhaps the best description of Muir's self-taught mountaineering skills and legendary endurance. The following extract gives a flavour of what a great read this book really is.

'Muir began to slide up that mountain. I had been with mountain climbers before, but never one like him. A deer-lope over the smoother slopes, a sure instinct for the easiest way into a rocky fortress, an instant and unerring attack, a serpent glide up the steep; hand and foot all connected dynamically; with no appearance of weight to his body. And such climbing! . . . crawling under an overhanging rock, edging along an inch-wide projection while fingers clasped knobs above the head, pulling up sheer rock faces by sheer strength of arm and chinning over the edge, leaping fissures – always going up, up, – no hesitation, no pause – that was Muir!'

Terry Gifford's compilation deserves a place on the bookshelf of every mountaineer and conservationist.

Graham White.

Scottish Highland Estate, Preserving an Environment. Michael Wigan (Swan Hill Press, 1991, £18.95, ISBN 1 853101 62 1. Also in paperback at £15.95, ISBN 1 840370 03 3).

This is no more than a brief note to draw your attention to a book which was first published in 1991 but only came to the attention of this reviewer last year.

Michael Wigan is a North of Scotland landowner and journalist, and his book is a most readable, and entertaining, account of the various economic activities on which the highland estates and those who live on them depend. Anyone who recognises that the Highlands are more than a public park for mountaineers will find this handsome, well-illustrated volume compulsive reading.

Bryan Fleming.

Trekking in Nepal, A Traveler's Guide. Stephen Bezruchka (7th Edition, Cordee, 1997, £12.95, ISBN 1 871890 93 4, 383pp, paperback, many illus.)

Quite simply, this is a labour of love and it shows. It is much more than a guide, though it excels at that function. It also educates, drawing on almost 30 years' of personal experience of the author. If you buy one guide to Nepal, this is the one.

Ken Crocket.

Also received: Romsdal, **Norway. Walks and Climbs in Romsdal** by Tony Howard. (3rd Edition, 1998, n.o.m.a.d.s., ISBN 1 871890 04 7, £14.99, softback. 128pp.) More than 200 routes in this reprint of a long-out-of-print guide.
Kilimanjaro and Mount Kenya. A Climbing and Trekking Guide. Cameron M. Burns. (Cordee, 174pp, ISBN 1 871890 985, £11.95) A guide to the top 30 routes. How to get there and how to get up.

Journals of Kindred Clubs

The American Alpine Journal, Vol. 39, 1997. Editor Christian Beckwith.

Just like our Journal the American Alpine Journal is a very impressive publication. Enclosed within its 432 pages there are many striking monochrome and colour plates, 19 separate articles, more than 200 pages on expeditions and climbs followed by American Alpine Club activities, reviews, obituaries and three appendices – the most useful to me being an attempt to compare some of the main climbing grading systems in use throughout the world. It shows no deterioration in quality following the death of the former Editor, H. Adams Carter.

The editorial and articles reflect many contradictions and tensions within climbing. One theme that features throughout the many excellent pieces is the influence of sponsorship; the resultant commercialisation of climbing and the recognition that many climbing decisions (both routine and at the elite end of climbing) are increasingly business decisions. Described elsewhere in the journal as 'Raging Consumerism', the Editor's preface asks if this was the real reason why two guides (Rob Hall and Scott Fischer) died while working on Everest in 1995. The labyrinthine influence of money seems present at every level of Himalayan guiding and a later article asks: 'Do commercially guided expeditions attract clients (consumers) with mediocre abilities who pay $65,000 but are not competent for Everest.' This is complemented by a thought provoking article on the use of supplementary oxygen for high-altitude climbing. Does it reduce the ascent of Everest to a drug enhanced experience for those with money to spend. It also introduces extra danger such as an oxygen system malfunctioning close to the summit, plus inadequate acclimatisation by an individual; very likely to be fatal. Empty oxygen cylinders are reported to be an even bigger eyesore on the South Col of the highest mountain in the world than the bodies of dead climbers.

The first main article is an account of a Slovenian Alpine style ascent of the North-west face of Ama Dablam. It captures the danger and seriousness of the climb and on reaching the summit the first activity is 'taking our advertising shots for sponsors'. There is also a very readable and terse account of Catherine Destivelle breaking her leg in Antarctica resulting from her falling through a cornice while posing for summit photos.

In addition to addressing the tensions within climbing, it is occasionally a journal of refreshing honesty. Mount Kennedy is in the St. Elias range in Canada and an epic ascent of the North-west Face in May 1996 ends on the North Ridge, linking nicely with an established route. It begs the question, should the route or the summit be the prime goal of mountaineering? If it is just the route are mountains then reduced to big crags? On page 86, at a low point in the epic when both climbers are exhausted, they are entirely committed and then a crampon is irretrievably dropped. The comment here is: 'We keep moving up. Could be worse . . . we could be in Scotland.' I'm still not sure what was meant! Then in a late addendum to the article the author candidly states: 'But we failed to stand on the highest point of the mountain . . . I know that deep down really, we failed.' Well, they may have failed to reach the summit but at least they got their article published!

The climbs and expeditions sections naturally favour North America, but later Worldwide sections appear well researched and comprehensive, and include the SMC Greenland expedition in 1996. Another SMC member who climbed Kulu Eiger was also included although credited as coming from the UK. The journal is in no sense parochial.

There are short reports of the activities of different sections of the American Alpine Club and of feeder clubs, emulating the way we record JMCS activities.

The AACJ is excellent for general mountaineering reading and earlier volumes provide an excellent resource for research about the history of climbing in remote areas throughout the world. The inclusion of outstanding photos, hand-drawn diagrams and topos evokes in this modern journal a solid, traditional feel. As our former president D. F. Lang once wrote: 'I implore members to borrow this volume if only for armchair excitement.' However, unlike the membership, I have to await the next edition.

C. M. Jones.

OFFICE BEARERS 1997-98

Honorary President: W. D. Brooker

Honorary Vice-Presidents: James C. Donaldson, M.B.E., Douglas Scott

President: Robert T. Richardson

Vice-Presidents: Derek G. Pyper, D. Noel Williams

Honorary Secretary: John R. R. Fowler, 4 Doune Terrace, Edinburgh, EH3 6DY **Honorary Treasurer:** Drew Sommerville, 11 Beechwood Court, Bearsden, Glasgow G61 2RY. **Honorary Editor:** K. V. Crocket, Glenisla, Long Row, Menstrie, Clackmannanshire FK11 7EA. **Assistant Editor:** I. H. M. Smart, Auchenleish, Bridge of Cally, by Blairgowrie, Perthshire. **Convener of the Publications Sub-Committee:** D. C. Anderson, Hillfoot House, Hillfoot, Dollar, FK14 7PL. **Honorary Librarian:** R. D. M. Chalmers, 14 Garrioch Drive, Glasgow G20 8RS. **Honorary Custodian of Slides:** G. N. Hunter, Netheraird, Woodlands Road, Rosemount, Blairgowrie, Perthshire, PH10 6JX. **Convener of the Huts Sub-Committee:** G. S. Peet, 6 Roman Way, Dunblane, Perthshire. **Custodian of the CIC Hut:** Robin Clothier, 35 Broompark Drive, Newton Mearns, Glasgow, G77 5DZ. **Custodian of Lagangarbh Hut:** Bernard M. Swan, Top Flat, 8G Swallow Road, Faifley, Clydebank, Dunbartonshire, G81 5BW. **Custodian of the Ling Hut:** Hamish C. Irvine, Feoran, Craig na Gower Avenue, Aviemore, Inverness-shire, PH22 1RW. **Custodian of the Raeburn Hut:** William H. Duncan, Kirktoun, East End, Lochwinnoch, Renfrewshire, PA12 4ER. **Custodian of the Naismith Hut:** William S. McKerrow, Scotsburn House, Drummond Road, Inverness, IV2 4NA. **Committee:** William S. McKerrow; Simon M. Richardson; Matthew G. D. Shaw; Oliver Turnbull; John S. Peden; James W. Hepburn; Alex Keith; Brian R. Shackleton. SMC Internet Address – http://www.smc.org.uk

Journal Information

Editor:	K. V. Crocket, Glenisla, Long Row, Menstrie, Clacks. FK11 7EA (e-mail: kvc@dial.pipex.com).
New Routes Editor:	A. D. Nisbet, 20 Craigie Ave., Boat of Garten, Inverness-shire PH24 3BL. (e-mail: anisbe@globalnet.co.uk).
Editor of Photographs:	Niall Ritchie, 37 Lawsondale Terrace, Westhill, Skene, Aberdeen AB32 6SE.
Advertisements:	D. G. Pyper, 3 Keir Circle, Westhill, Skene, Aberdeen AB32 6RE. (e-mail: d.pyper@leopardmag.co.uk).
Distribution:	D. F. Lang, Hillfoot Hey, 580 Perth Road, Dundee DD2 1PZ.

INSTRUCTIONS TO CONTRIBUTORS

Articles for the Journal should be submitted before the end of January for consideration for the following issue. Lengthy contributions are preferably typed, double-spaced, on one side only, and with ample margins (minimum 30mm). Articles may be accepted on floppy disk, IBM compatible (contact Editor beforehand), or by e-mail. The Editor welcomes material from both members and non-members, with priority being given to articles of Scottish Mountaineering content. Photographs are also welcome, and should be good quality colour slides. All textual material should be sent to the Editor, address and e-mail as above. Photographic material should be sent direct to the Editor of Photographs, address as above.

Copyright.Textual matter appearing in the Miscellaneous section of the Journal, including New Climbs, is copyright of the publishers. Copyright of articles in the main section of the Journal is retained by individual authors.

David Hesleden on Mount Asperity, Canada. Photo: Simon Richardson.

SCOTTISH MOUNTAINEERING CLUB

SCOTTISH MOUNTAINEERING TRUST

DISTRICT GUIDES

Southern Uplands	£16.95
Southern Highlands	£16.95
Central Highlands	£17.95
The Cairngorms	£17.95
Islands of Scotland (including Skye)	£19.95
North-west Highlands	£17.95

SCRAMBLERS GUIDE

Black Cuillin Ridge	£4.95

CLIMBERS GUIDES (Rock and Ice Guides)

Scottish Winter Climbs	£16.95
Ben Nevis	£14.95
Northern Highlands Vol. 1	£13.95
Northern Highlands Vol. 2	£14.95
Glen Coe (including Glen Etive and Ardgour)	£13.95
The Cairngorms Vol. 1	£11.95
The Cairngorms Vol. 2	£11.95
Skye and the Hebrides Vols. 1 and 2 1997	£19.95
Arran, Arrochar and Southern Highlands 1997	£14.95

Outcrop Guides

North-east Outcrops	£13.95
Lowland Outcrops	£14.95
Highland Outcrops	£14.95

OTHER PUBLICATIONS

The Munros	£16.95
Munro's Tables	£15.95
The Corbetts and Other Scottish Hills	£16.95
A Chance in a Million – Scottish Avalanches (Out of print)	
A Century of Scottish Mountaineering	£15.95
Ski Mountaineering in Scotland	£12.95
Ben Nevis – Britain's Highest Mountain	£14.95
Scotland's Mountains	£17.95
The Cairngorms Scene – And Unseen	£6.95
Heading for the Scottish Hills (1996 Edition)	£6.95
Scottish Hill and Mountain Names	£9.95

MAPS

Black Cuillin of Skye (double-sided)	£3.95
Glen Coe	£2.95

Distributed by:
Cordee, 3a De Montfort Street, Leicester LE1 7HD
Telephone: Leicester 0116 254 3579 Fax: 0116 247 1176

These books and maps are available from many bookshops and mountain equipment suppliers

i

Jon Taylor in 'The Wonderland of Rocks' area, Joshua Tree, Southern California. Photo: Niall Ritchie.

Alastair Matthewson on East Buttress of El Capitan, Yosemite, California. Photo: Jamie Andrew.

DUNMHOR HOUSE

Proprietors:
Graham Christie & Valerie Johnston

BED & BREAKFAST
67 High Street, Kingussie
PH21 1HX
Tel/Fax: 01540 661809

5 letting rooms. CH. TV. Tea & Coffee in all rooms. £15 pp per night. 5-10 mins walk from bus/train station. We take walkers/climbers and drop them off in a 15 mile radius — no need to back-track to collect your vehicle.

NA TIGHEAN BEAGA

Ben Nevis 12 miles — Creag Meagaidh 15 miles

Self-catering chalets and bungalows sleeping 2-8 persons.
Site drying room available (FREE).
Hotel restaurant & bar 250 yards. Colour brochure available.

Contact: Ian Matheson, Na Tighean Beaga, East Park, Roy Bridge, Inverness-shire. Tel: 01397 712370 Fax: 01397 712831

CLUB MEMBERS

are asked to support

the Advertisers

in the Journal

and to mention

the Journal in any

communications with

ADVERTISERS

The Ernest Press
Publisher

BIOGRAPHY AND HISTORY
May the Fire be Always Lit: a biography of Jock Nimlin. By Ian Thomson. ISBN 0-948153-39-3. P/back. £11.95. H/back £16.

The First Munroist: a biography of A.E. Robertson. By Peter Drummond & Ian Mitchell. ISBN 0-948-153-19-9. H/back. £13.95.

Menlove: a biography of John Menlove Edwards. By Jim Perrin – Winner Boardman/Tasker Award 1985. ISBN 0-948153-28-8. P/back £9.95.

Hands of a Climber: a biography of Colin Kirkus. By Steve Dean. H/back £15.95. ISBN 0-948153-21-0.

Gary Hemming: the beatnik of the Alps. By Mirella Tenderini. P/back £11.95. ISBN 0-948153-38-5.

Whensoever: 50 years of the RAF Mountain Rescue Service; 1943-1993. By Frank Card. ISBN 0-948153-23-7. H/back £17.95.

ADVENTURE AND TRAVEL
Mountain Holidays. By Janet Adam Smith. ISBN 0 948153 45 8. P/back £12.50.

The Black Cloud: Mountain Misadventures 1928-1966. By Ian Thomson. ISBN 0-948153-20-2. P/back £9.99; H/back £16.

In Monte Viso's Horizon: climbing all the Alpine 4000m peaks. By Will McLewin – Winner Boardman/Tasker Award 1992. ISBN 0-948153-09-1. H/back £16.95.

The Undiscovered Country: the reason we climb. By Phil Bartlett. H/back £15.95. ISBN 0-948153-24-5.

Arka Tagh; the mysterious mountains. By Wm. Holgate. H/back £15.95. ISBN 0-948153-33-4.

Over the Hills & Far Away; essays by Rob Collister. P/back £11.95. ISBN 0-948153-40-7.

Tight Rope: the fun of climbing. By Dennis Gray. P/back £9.95; H/back £16.00. ISBN 0-948153-25-3.

Breaking Loose: a cycle/climbing journey from the UK to Australia. P/back £9.50; H/back £16.00. ISBN 0-948153-26-1.

MOUNTAINEERING ESSAYS
The Ordinary Route. By Harold Drasdo. ISBN 0 948153 46 6. P/back £12.50.

A View from the Ridge: essays by Dave Brown & Ian Mitchell – Winner Boardmen/Tasker Award 1991. P/back £6.50. ISBN 0-948153-11-3.

A Necklace of Slings: essays by Dave Gregory. H/back £15.00. ISBN 0-948153-37-7.

THE ERNEST PRESS, 8 Rehoboth Est., Llanfaelog, Anglesey, LL63 5TS. Tel/Fax 01407 811098.

viii

ix

xi

xvi

SCOTTISH MOUNTAINEERING CLUB JOURNAL BACK NUMBERS

163 – 1972 – £2
164 – 1973 – £3
166 – 1975 – £1
167 – 1976 – £2
168 – 1977 – £2
169 – 1978 – £3
170 – 1979 – £4
174 – 1983 – £4
176 – 1985 – £5
177 – 1986 – £5
178 – 1987 – £5
180 – 1989 – £3
181 – 1990 – £5
182 – 1991 – £5
183 – 1992 – £5
184 – 1993 – £5
185 – 1994 – £5
186 – 1995 – £6
187 – 1996 – £6

Indices for Volumes 28, 29, 30, 32, 33 are available at £1 each and the cumulated Index for Volumes 21-30 at £2. Postage is extra. They may be obtained from Mr C. Stead, Camas Cottage, Portnellan Road, Gartocharn, Alexandria, G83 8NL.

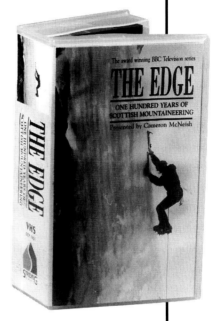